Educating Young Children

Active Learning Practices for Preschool and Child Care Programs

Third Edition

Mary Hohmann, David P. Weikart,
and Ann S. Epstein

HIGHSCOPE
PRESS®

Ypsilanti, Michigan

Published by

HIGH/SCOPE® PRESS

A division of the High/Scope Educational Research Foundation
600 North River Street
Ypsilanti, Michigan 48198-2898
(734) 485-2000, FAX (734) 485-0704

Lynn Taylor, Nancy A. Brickman, and Sally Mitani, Editors
Pattie McDonald, Editorial Assistant
Linda Eckel, Book Design
Kazuko Sacks, Profit Makers LLC, Cover Design and Production

**Ann Arbor photographer Gregory Fox took most of the photos displayed
in this book. We appreciate both his patience and his skill in capturing
young children in action at the High/Scope Demonstration Preschool.**

Library of Congress Cataloging-in-Publication Data
Hohmann, Mary.
  Educating young children : active learning practices for preschool and
child care programs / Mary Hohmann, David P. Weikart, and Ann S.
Epstein. -- 3rd ed.
       p. cm.
  Includes bibliographical references and index.
  ISBN 978-1-57379-354-4 (soft cover : alk. paper) 1. Active learning.
2. Early childhood education. 3. Children and adults. 4. Education,
Preschool. 5. Day care centers. I. Weikart, David P. II. Epstein, Ann
S. III. Title.
  LB1027.23.H64 2008
  372.13'9--dc22

                                     2008004960

The quotation on page 172, from page 162 of *Intellectual Development
Birth to Adulthood* by Robbie Case, appears with permission from
Academic Press. Copyright © 1985 by Academic Press.

Printed in the United States of America
10 9 8 7 6 5 4 3

To all young children in action
and to the thoughtful adults
who support their initiatives

Contents

Acknowledgments

Since the publication in 1971 of High/Scope's first preschool manual, many adults in early childhood centers and child care homes in the United States and around the world have used the High/Scope educational approach to guide their interactions with children. Through their daily practices, these teachers and trainers have shaped and expanded the collective body of knowledge about the High/Scope Preschool Curriculum presented in this third edition of *Educating Young Children—Active Learning Practices for Preschool and Child Care Programs.*

The late David Weikart, who initiated the development of the High/Scope Curriculum, began the Perry Preschool Study, established the High/Scope Educational Research Foundation, and led these efforts for many years, played a central role in the development of previous editions of this volume. His work continues to shape our thinking about how best to encourage young children's learning and development. We are grateful to the other authors of the first two High/Scope preschool manuals—Linda Rogers, Carolyn Adcock, Donna McClelland, and Bernard Banet.

We are indebted to the early childhood specialists based at the High/Scope Foundation in Ypsilanti who have played a major role in the continuing evolution of the High/Scope Preschool Curriculum. They have taught in the High/Scope Demonstration Preschool, conducted and participated in the give and take of training, kept up with new developments in the early childhood field, and read and critiqued drafts of this volume. In particular, we are grateful for the significant contributions of Susan Terdan, Beth Marshall, Shannon Lockhart, Kay Rush, Polly Neill, Suzanne Gainsley, Chris Boisvert, Rosie Lucier, Karen Sawyers, Andee DeBruin-Parecki, Sam Hannibal, Charles Hohmann, Becki Perrett, Mark Tompkins, Jane Maehr, Michelle Graves, Barbara Carmody, Ann Rogers, Ruth Strubank, Bettye McDonald, Julie Ricks, Marilyn Adams Jacobson, Bonnie Freeman, Karl Wheatley, Ed Greene, Warren Buckleitner, Amy Powell, Vincent Harris, Carol Beardmore, Diana Jo Johnston, Linda Weikel Ranweiler, and Ursula Ansbach.

We also thank the many High/Scope certified trainers who have conducted training, worked "on the floor" with children and teaching teams, shared their insights from the field with us, written articles for the *High/Scope Extensions* curriculum newsletter, and read and responded to drafts of this book. In particular, we appreciate the contributions of Betsy Evans, Cathy Calamari, Moya Fewson, Deb Handler, Karen Molinario, Carol Montealegre, Shelley Nemeth, Jackie Post, Sandy Slack, Paul Niemiec, Karen Hammons, Annriette Stolte, Linda Kluge, Joanne Dalton, Joan Sharp, Malek Pirani, Eeva Lius, Carole Dowdy, and Diane Brads. We also appreciate the feedback we received from Hilary Marentette and Robert Egbert, who used drafts of this volume with their postsecondary students.

High/Scope administrators, research staff, marketing and support staff, and special consultants, including Lawrence Schweinhart, Sherri Oden, Pat Olmsted, Philip Hawkins, Cynthia Sewell, Pat Elekonich, Anne Hudon, Clay Shouse, Pattie McDonald, Gavin Haque, Kathy Woodard, Lisa Wasacz, Rita Toderan, Kevin McDonnell, Mary Leinaar, Phyllis Weikart, and Elizabeth Carlton provided ongoing assistance and support. We thank each of them.

For the readability and design of this book we are indebted to the dedicated work of High/Scope editors Lynn Taylor and Nancy Brickman; editorial assistant Diana Knepp; book designer Linda Eckel; and graphic artists Kazuko Sacks and Margaret FitzGerald. Finally, we wish to thank our photographer, Gregory Fox, for the photographs displayed throughout this book of our young children and adults *in action!*

Educating
Young Children

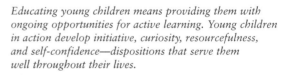

Educating young children means providing them with ongoing opportunities for active learning. Young children in action develop initiative, curiosity, resourcefulness, and self-confidence—dispositions that serve them well throughout their lives.

Introduction

In the High/Scope approach to early childhood education, adults and children share control. We recognize that the power to learn resides in the child, hence the focus on active learning practices. When we accept that learning comes from within, we achieve a critical balance in educating young children. The adult's role is to support and guide young children through their active learning adventures and experiences. I believe this is what makes our program work so well.
—David P. Weikart, 1995

The High/Scope Approach to Preschool Education

Curriculum development is a complex process requiring a commitment to a broad-based educational philosophy; extensive knowledge of human growth and development; practical experience with children and an understanding of their interests; and an ability to consolidate and interpret an ever-expanding body of research about teaching and learning. *Educating Young Children: Active Learning Practices for Preschool and Child Care Programs* represents the High/Scope Foundation's progress to date in the ongoing development of the **High/Scope Preschool Curriculum.** This introduction describes the origin of the High/Scope preschool approach, its basic principles, and its effectiveness for children, families, and society.

Origin of the High/Scope Preschool Curriculum

Although the High/Scope approach is now used in settings serving the full range of preschool-aged children, it was originally developed to serve at-risk children from poor neighborhoods in Ypsilanti, Michigan. In 1962, David P. Weikart, director of special services for the Ypsilanti Public Schools, initiated the Perry Preschool Project (which later became known as the High/Scope Perry Preschool Study). He designed this project in response to the persistent failure of high school students from Ypsilanti's poorest neighborhoods. Over the years, these students consistently scored in the lower ranges on intelligence tests and academic achievement tests. Alarmed by these trends, Weikart searched for causes and cures. He

concluded that the low IQ scores largely reflected the students' limited opportunities for adequate school preparation. He also found that low student achievement in secondary school correlated with attendance at elementary schools in poor neighborhoods.

After much consideration of Weikart's findings, Ypsilanti school officials decided that they would not alter their basic approach to education, since the majority of the students in the district were doing well. Nevertheless, an ad hoc committee of Weikart and three elementary principals—Raymond Kingston, John Salcau, and Eugene Beatty—agreed that something had to be done for the students who were failing. They initiated a series of discussions to examine teaching methods, achievement patterns, referrals to outside agencies, and elementary-school boundaries. The special services department also formed its own action committee. This committee—John Mader, countywide director of special services; Norma Radin, school social worker; Byron Aldrich, school psychologist; and David Weikart—looked for practical programs the special services division might implement to counteract school

3

failure. During their search, the Special Services Committee began to consider early intervention for 3- and 4-year-olds, a prospect that became increasingly attractive as committee members realized they could administer this type of intervention outside the usual public school channels. In doing so, they could avoid the time-consuming complexity of districtwide school reform. Their goal was to prepare preschool-aged children from poor neighborhoods for future success in school. In support of this idea, Weikart obtained permission to operate Michigan's first preschool education program funded through the Michigan Department of Education and hired teachers and support staff. Hiring appropriate staff was especially difficult due to a severe national teacher shortage. In addition, the state required that teachers hired for the project be licensed in both elementary and special education. Nevertheless, four qualified teachers joined the project. Weikart found space in a community center for the preschool project's first school year (1962–63) and then located the preschool classroom for its remaining five years in the Perry Elementary School, where Eugene Beatty was principal.

With teachers hired and classroom space secured, the Special Services Committee faced another hurdle—the selection of a curriculum approach. Typical play schools and cooperative nurseries of the day focused primarily on children's **social and emotional growth** (Sears and Dowley 1963). Considering the particular needs of the children they were serving, however, the committee believed that their program needed to devote more attention to children's **intellectual development.** They wanted a curriculum with a cognitive orientation that would support children's future academic growth. Because such an approach to preschool education did not seem to exist, the Special Services Committee consulted with several outside experts. The experts advised against proceeding with the project, however, because they believed 3- and 4-year-olds lacked the mental and emotional maturity to cope within a school-based setting.

In responding to this advice, Weikart decided to modify the plans rather than abandon the project. He therefore set up a carefully designed research project to compare children's progress in the preschool program setting to children's progress without preschool program experiences. To do so, Weikart and other members of the committee randomly assigned preschool-aged children from the target neighborhoods to a treatment group, whose members were enrolled in the preschool program, and to a control group, whose members remained at home and were not enrolled in the preschool program. In this way, the extent to which children were helped or hindered by such a preschool program experience could be measured. Having dealt with the issue of the efficacy of teaching 3- and 4-year-olds, the committee turned again to the issue of curriculum development. They agreed on three basic criteria for the development of an effective preschool curriculum:

(1) A coherent theory about teaching and learning must guide the curriculum development process.

(2) Curriculum theory and practice must support each child's capacity to develop individual talents and abilities through ongoing opportunities for active learning.

(3) The teachers, researchers, and administrators must work as partners in all aspects of curriculum development, to ensure that theory and practice receive equal consideration.

With these criteria firmly in mind, Weikart, along with the teachers, administrators, and psychologists, turned to the writings of Jean Piaget. They were initially drawn to Piaget's child development research by a summary of his work presented in *Intelligence and Experience* by J. McVicker Hunt (1961). Clearly, Piaget's theory of development supported the curriculum team's philosophical orientation toward active learning. Through a series of seminars and discussions the team began the work of building a classroom program for 3- and 4-year-olds around processes, goals, and content areas derived from Piaget's research. Gradually, however, the team split into two factions—several researchers, who advocated a literal interpretation of Piaget's theories; and the teachers, who pressed for a practical interpretation of theory shaped by their daily observations of children and their desire to include some traditional nursery-school practices. With Weikart's direction, the group of researchers pursued an in-depth study of Piaget's work, while the teachers continued to wrestle with the pragmatics of integrating theory and daily classroom practice (Weikart, Rogers, Adcock, and McClelland 1971; Hohmann, Banet, and Weikart 1979).

As this team worked with children and conducted daily staff meetings, the basic framework of the High/Scope Curriculum emerged with a **plan-do-review process** as its core. Teachers in the Perry Preschool Project provided time for the children to plan their play activities, carry them out, and reflect on what they had done. Another key aspect of the program was a **parent component.** Through home visits, teachers offered ideas about learning and child development to parents and involved children and parents in educational activities. Teachers engaged parents in thinking about the process of schooling, while parents alerted teachers to the interests and needs of children and families.

In 1967, Weikart launched the Preschool Curriculum Demonstration Project (later known as the High/Scope Preschool Curriculum Comparison Study). This study examined the effectiveness of three preschool curriculum models—the Cognitively Oriented Curriculum (the High/Scope model); the Language Training Curriculum (the Direct Instruction model); and the Unit-Based Curriculum (the Nursery School model) (Weikart, Epstein, Schweinhart, and Bond 1978; Schweinhart, Weikart, and Larner 1986; Schweinhart and Weikart 1997). In 1970, at the conclusion of the demonstration phase of this project, the children in all three preschool programs performed well on IQ tests, and later, at age 10, on school achievement tests. (Subsequent results, explained later in this chapter, found differences in social behavior favoring the High/Scope model.)

Also in 1970, David Weikart left the Ypsilanti Public Schools to establish the High/Scope Educational Research Foundation. Weikart focused on the preschool approach (then called the Cognitively Oriented Curriculum) that he and his staff had conceived and initiated during the Perry Preschool Project. High/Scope staff have continued to develop and expand his active learning approach to early childhood education throughout the 1970s, 1980s, 1990s and into the 2000s. This book consolidates their findings and provides guidelines for establishing and operating high-quality active learning programs for young children.

The Central Principles of the High/Scope Preschool Curriculum

The diagram (p. 6), entitled the High/Scope Preschool "Wheel of Learning," illustrates the curriculum principles that guide High/Scope preschool practitioners in their daily work with children. This section introduces each component of the wheel diagram; subsequent chapters discuss each of these principles in greater detail.

Active Participatory Learning

Through *active participatory learning*—having direct and immediate experiences and deriving meaning from them through reflection—young children construct knowledge that helps them make sense of their world. The power of active learning comes from *personal initiative*. Young children act on their innate desire to explore; they ask and search for answers to questions about people, materials, events, and ideas that arouse their curiosity; they solve problems that stand in the way of their goals; and they generate new strategies to try.

As children follow their intentions, they engage with the curriculum's content as identified in the *key developmental indicators (KDIs)*. Formerly called *key experiences*, KDIs are child behaviors that reflect developing mental, emo-

---

Publications That Track the Development of the High/Scope Approach

1971   *The Cognitively Oriented Curriculum: A Framework for Preschool Educators*
by David Weikart, Linda Rogers, Carolyn Adcock, and Donna McClelland

1979   *Young Children in Action: A Manual for Preschool Educators*
by Mary Hohmann, Bernard Banet, and David Weikart

1986–present   *High/Scope Extensions: Newsletter of the High/Scope Curriculum*

1989—present   *The Teacher's Idea Book* Series
by High/Scope staff and field consultants

1991–2005   *Supporting Young Learners: Ideas for Preschool and Day Care Providers*, Volumes 1–4
by High/Scope staff and field consultants

1995, 2002, & 2008   *Educating Young Children: Active Learning Practices for Preschool and Child Care Programs*
by Mary Hohmann, David Weikart, and Ann Epstein

2002   *You Can't Come to My Birthday Party! Conflict Resolution With Young Children*
by Betsy Evans

2003   *Preschool Child Observation Record (COR)*, 2nd ed.

2003   *Preschool Program Quality Assessment (PQA)*, 2nd ed.

2005   *Growing Readers Early Literacy Curriculum*
Andrea DeBruin-Parecki and Mary Hohmann, developers

2007   *Essentials of Active Learning in Preschool: Getting to Know the High/Scope Curriculum*
by Ann Epstein

The High/Scope Preschool "Wheel of Learning"

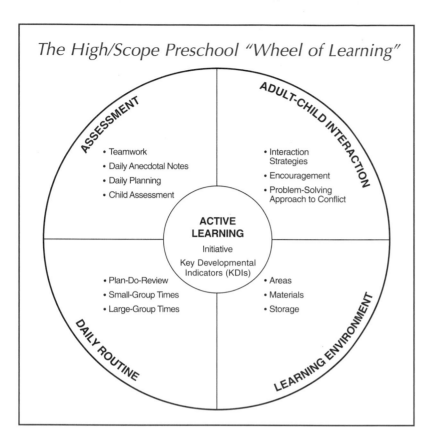

tional, social, and physical abilities. KDIs occur during children's creative, ongoing interactions with people, materials, events, and ideas, for example, when they are *pretending and role playing, having fun with language, building relationships with other children and adults, moving to music, sorting and matching, counting objects, fitting things together and taking them apart,* and *anticipating events.* The extent to which adults support children's initiative and understand children's actions in terms of the KDIs determines the adults' success in implementing the High/Scope Curriculum. Clearly, active learning experiences influence every aspect of our work with children and form the core of the preschool curriculum.

Adult-Child Interaction

Active learning depends on positive adult-child interactions. Mindful of the importance of providing a psychologically safe climate for young learners, adults using the High/Scope preschool approach strive to be supportive as they converse and play with children. Throughout the day, guided by an understanding of how preschool children think and reason, adults practice positive interaction strategies—sharing control with children, focusing on children's strengths, forming authentic relationships with children, supporting children's play, and adopting a problem-solving approach to social conflict. This interaction style enables the child to express thoughts and feelings freely and confidently, decide on the direction and content of the conversation, and experience true partnership in dialogue. Adults rely on encouragement and use a problem-solving approach to deal with everyday classroom situations rather than a child-management system based on praise, punishment, and reward.

Learning Environment

Because the physical setting has a strong impact on the behavior of children and adults, the High/Scope Curriculum places a strong emphasis on planning the layout of the preschool or center and selecting appropriate materials. An active learning environment provides children with ongoing opportunities to make choices and decisions. Thus, adults organize play space into specific interest areas to support preschool children's abiding interest in such activities as sand and water play, building, pretending and role play, drawing and painting, "reading" and "writing," counting, sorting, climbing, singing, and dancing. The interest areas contain a wide and plentiful assortment of easily accessible materials children can choose and use to carry out their intentions and ideas for play. Natural, found, commercial, and homemade materials provide many opportunities each day for children to engage with curriculum content in creative and purposeful ways. Adults arrange storage for materials using low shelves, clear boxes, and picture labels children can "read," so all children can independently find, use, and return the items they need.

Daily Routine

In addition to arranging the setting, adults also plan a consistent daily routine that supports active learning. The routine enables young children to anticipate what happens next and gives them a great deal of control over what they do during each part of their preschool day. The High/Scope preschool daily routine includes the plan-do-review process, which enables children to express their intentions, carry them out, and reflect on what they have done. Adults set this process in motion by asking an appropriate question, such as "What would you like to do?" Children indicate their plans, then carry them out—for just a few minutes or for as long as

an hour. Pretending and role playing, building block structures, and drawing are common child-initiated activities during the "do" period, after which adults encourage children to review their experiences. The children may talk about what they have done or express themselves by drawing and "writing." Small-group time encourages children to explore and experiment with new or familiar materials adults have selected based on their daily observations of children's interests, the KDIs, and local events. During large-group time both children and adults initiate music and movement activities, story re-enactments, group discussions, and cooperative play and projects. Through a common daily routine focused around opportunities for active learning, children and adults build a sense of community.

Assessment

In the High/Scope preschool approach, assessment includes a range of tasks teaching staff undertake to ensure that observing children, interacting with children, and planning for children receive full adult energy and attention. Teamwork built on supportive adult relationships forms a solid base for adults doing this work together. Each day the teaching team members gather accurate information about children by observing and interacting with children and taking daily anecdotal notes based on what they see and hear. Before the children arrive, after the children leave, or while the children are napping, teaching team members engage in daily planning sessions in which they share their observations of children, analyze the observations in terms of the KDIs, and make plans for the next day. Periodically, the team

uses the child observations they have noted to complete a KDI-based child assessment instrument for each child—the *Preschool Child Observation Record (COR)* (2003a). Adults draw the data for the COR from their daily anecdotes and team planning discussions. Supervisors and teachers also periodically assess their curriculum using the *Preschool Program Quality Assessment (PQA)* (2003b). Assessment in the High/Scope approach means working in teams to support and build on children's interests and strengths, guided by the curriculum.

These five basic principles—active learning, positive adult-child interactions, a child-friendly learning environment, a consistent daily routine, and team-based daily child assessment—form the framework of the High/Scope approach. This book elaborates on each of these principles.

High/Scope Preschool Program Effectiveness

Over the years, researchers have tested the validity of the High/Scope approach to preschool education, gathering longitudinal data on both the High/Scope Perry Preschool Project and the High/Scope Preschool Curriculum Demonstration Project. Between 1989 and 1992, High/Scope researchers also conducted an evaluation of the High/Scope Training of Trainers Project to study the outcomes of High/Scope's training programs. This section reviews the results of these research studies and explains how the High/Scope approach to preschool education produces lasting benefits for children, families, *and* society.

Effects of the High/Scope Perry Preschool Program

The most recent data (Schweinhart, et al. 2005) on the effects of the High/Scope preschool approach come from interviewing and reviewing the records of the students who participated in the Perry Preschool Project from 1962 to 1967. In addition to information gathered directly from the students over the years (participants were age 40 at the time of their most recent interviews), research staff also examined their school, social services, and arrest records. They found major differences favoring the 40-year-olds who had been enrolled in the active learning preschool program.

• **Social responsibility.** By age 40, 36% of preschool program group members had been arrested five or more times as compared with 55% of the no-preschool program group, and fewer had been arrested for violent crimes (32% vs. 48%), property crimes (36% vs. 58%), and drug crimes (14% vs. 34%).

• **Earning and economic status.** At age 40, more of the program group than the no-program group were employed (76% vs. 62%), and the program group had higher median annual earnings than the no-program group ($20,800 vs. $15,300). At age 40 more of the program group owned their own homes (37% vs. 28%), owned their own cars (82% vs. 60%), and had savings accounts (76% vs. 50%).

• **Educational performance.** Almost a third again as many preschool program group members as no-preschool program group members graduated from regular or adult high school or received General Education Development cer-

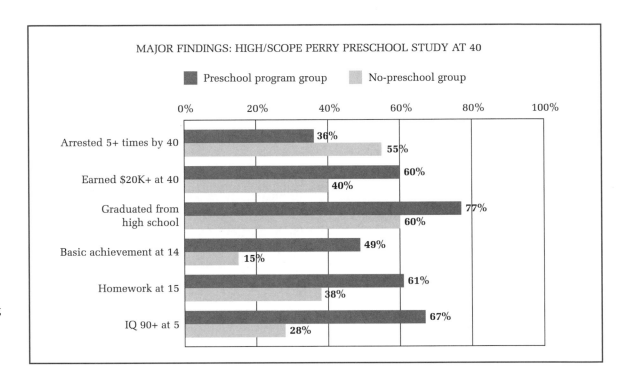

MAJOR FINDINGS: HIGH/SCOPE PERRY PRESCHOOL STUDY AT 40

Preschool program group   No-preschool group

- Arrested 5+ times by 40: 36% / 55%
- Earned $20K+ at 40: 60% / 40%
- Graduated from high school: 77% / 60%
- Basic achievement at 14: 49% / 15%
- Homework at 15: 61% / 38%
- IQ 90+ at 5: 67% / 28%

tification (77% vs. 60%). Earlier in the study, the preschool program group had significantly higher average achievement scores at age 14 and literacy scores at age 19 than the no-preschool program group.

• **Marriage and family life.** At age 40 more program than no-program males took responsibility for raising their children (57% vs. 30%), more program males were married (71% vs. 54%), and more had second or third marriages (29% vs. 8%). At age 40, more of the program group than the no-program group said they were getting along very well with their families (75% vs. 64%)

These findings indicate that a high-quality preschool program such as High/Scope's can significantly increase children's future success and contributions to families and society.

Consequences of Three Preschool Curriculum Models

Recent interviews of participants in the High/Scope Preschool Curriculum Demonstration Project (1967–1970) occurred when participants reached the age of 23 (Schweinhart and Weikart 1997). As mentioned earlier, this study compared three curriculum approaches. Both the **High/Scope** and **Nursery School** approaches emphasized child-initiated activities while the **Direct Instruction** approach focused on academics. Initially, all three curriculum approaches improved intellectual performance substantially, with the average IQs of children in all three groups rising 27 points (Weikart, Epstein, Schweinhart, and Bond 1978). By age 23, however, there were no significant differences in academic achievement or measured intelligence. On average, all three groups performed the same in all academic areas starting in kindergarten and continuing throughout the school years. Contrary to common expectations, two years of intense drill and practice on basic reading and math skills *did not* give the Direct Instruction group an academic advantage. Significant differences did appear in the area of **social responsibility.** At age 15 students in the Direct Instruction group reported almost three times as many acts of misconduct as students in the High/Scope group. Thirty-three percent of the students in the Direct Instruction group, 6% of the students in the Nursery group, and none of the students in the High/Scope group reported that their families "feel you do nothing worth much." In the Direct Instruction group 47% of the students were identified by the schools as emotionally impaired compared to 6% of the students who were so identified in the other two groups. By age 23, members of the Direct Instruction group had a police-reported arrest rate of one time per person, up to five times higher than the police-reported arrest rate of the other two groups (0.2 per person in the High/Scope group and 0.3 per person in the Nursery group).

All three groups received home visits every other week in which children, parents, and teachers engaged in learning activities consistent with their preschool program. However, home visiting and parent involvement *per se* were not significantly related to children's academic success and social behavior. Rather the specific curriculum model accounted for significant differences between the three groups of children. It thus appears that a preschool program such as High/Scope's that promotes child-initiated activities seems to contribute to the development of an individual's sense of personal and social responsibility.

Child Outcomes in the High/Scope Training of Trainers Evaluation

In the High/Scope Training of Trainers evaluation (Epstein 1993) research staff conducted a **trainer study** (an analysis of participant reports of 40 seven-week training projects involving 793 trainers, as well as surveys of 203 certified High/Scope trainers); a **teacher study** (surveys of 244 High/Scope and 122 comparison teachers); and a **child study** (systematic observations of 97 children in High/Scope classrooms and 103 children in comparison classrooms). Findings from the child study highlight advances in children's initiative, social relations, and cognitive and motor development.

• **Initiative and social relations.** High/Scope children showed significantly more initiative than comparison children. They engaged in more complex play and joined in more program activities; had significantly better social relations than comparison children; engaged in more social interaction and cooperation with their peers, and showed a greater adeptness at social problem solving.

• **Representation, language, and logic.** High/Scope children tended to outscore comparison children on measures of cognitive development, including representation, classification (sorting and matching), and language skills.

• **Movement.** High/Scope children did significantly better on measures of motor development. They were better able than comparison children to coordinate listening and movement skills and to focus their physical energies during activities.

Developmental Differences Between Children in High/Scope Preschool Programs and Children in Comparison Preschool Programs

• Children in High/Scope programs significantly outperformed children in comparison programs in the following areas:

  Initiative, including complex play, joining in program activities

  Social relations, including relating to peers, social problem solving

  Motor development, including music and movement, focusing energies during physical activities

  Overall development

• Children in High/Scope programs tended to outscore children in comparison programs in **cognitive development,** including *representation, classification,* and *language skills.*

• Comparison children showed no significant advantages over High/Scope children on any of the assessments.

Source: Epstein 1993, p. xx

In sum, the High/Scope approach to preschool education enables young children to take the initiative and develop their social, intellectual, and physical capacities.

Why the High/Scope Preschool Approach Works

Looking at High/Scope research outcomes, the best appraisal of why the High/Scope Preschool Curriculum works is this: Participating as active learners within a supportive classroom community, children develop a sense of initiative and pro-social dispositions that positively affect their subsequent learning and life decisions.

Since its beginnings, the High/Scope preschool approach has encouraged children to develop initiative within a supportive social context. During the daily plan-do-review process children express, carry out, and then reflect on their intentions. Throughout the day, children develop their own interests, generate ways to answer their own questions, and discuss their ideas with others. Supported by adults who are genuinely interested in what they say and do, children are able to construct their own understanding of the world around them and gain a sense of control and personal satisfaction. The High/Scope Curriculum works because its unflagging attention to children's strengths and abilities empowers children to follow through on their interests purposefully and creatively. In the process, children develop trust, initiative, curiosity, resourcefulness, independence, and responsibility—habits of mind that will serve them well throughout their lives.

The High/Scope Preschool Curriculum works because it empowers children to follow through on their interests purposefully and creatively.

References

Brickman, Nancy A., and Lynn S. Taylor, eds. 1991. *Supporting Young Learners: Ideas for Preschool and Day Care Providers.* Ypsilanti, MI: High/Scope Press.

Epstein, Ann S. 2007. *Essentials of Active Learning in Preschool: Getting to Know the High/Scope Curriculum.* Ypsilanti, MI: High/Scope Press.

Epstein, Ann S. 1993. *Training for Quality: Improving Early Childhood Programs Through Systematic Inservice Training.* Ypsilanti, MI: High/Scope Press.

Erikson, Erik. 1950. *Childhood and Society.* New York: Norton.

Graves, Michelle. 1989. *The Teacher's Idea Book: Daily Planning Around the Key Experiences.* Ypsilanti, MI: High/Scope Press.

High/Scope Educational Research Foundation. 2003a. *Preschool Child Observation Record (COR),* 2nd ed. Ypsilanti, MI: High/Scope Press.

High/Scope Educational Research Foundation. 2003b. *Preschool Program Quality Assessment (PQA),* 2nd ed. Ypsilanti, MI: High/Scope Press.

High/Scope Extensions: Newsletter of the High/Scope Curriculum. 1986–1995. Nancy A. Brickman, ed. Ypsilanti, MI: High/Scope Press.

Hohmann, Mary, Bernard Banet, and David P. Weikart. 1979. *Young Children in Action: A Manual for Preschool Educators.* Ypsilanti, MI: High/Scope Press.

Hunt, J. McVicker. 1961. *Intelligence and Experience.* New York: Ronald Press.

Katz, Lilian G., and Sylvia C. Chard. 1989. *Engaging Children's Minds: The Project Approach.* Norwood, NJ: Ablex.

Schweinhart, Lawrence J. 2004. *A School Administrator's Guide to Early Childhood Programs,* 2nd ed. Ypsilanti, MI: High/Scope Press.

Schweinhart, Lawrence J., Jeanne Montie, Zongping Xiang, W. Steven Barnett, Clive R. Belfield, and Milagros Nores. 2005. *Lifetime Effects: The High/Scope Perry Preschool Study Through Age 40.* Ypsilanti, MI: High/Scope Press.

Schweinhart, Lawrence J., and David P. Weikart. 1997. *Lasting Differences: The High/Scope Preschool Curriculum Comparison Study Through Age 27.* Ypsilanti, MI: High/Scope Press.

Schweinhart, Lawrence J., David P. Weikart, and Mary B. Larner. 1986. "Consequences of Three Preschool Curriculum Models Through Age 15." *Early Childhood Research Quarterly* 1: 15–45.

Sears, P. S., and E. M. Dowley. 1963. "Research on Teaching in the Nursery School." In *Handbook of Research on Teaching,* N. L. Gage, ed., 811–64. Chicago: Rand McNally.

Weikart, David P., Ann S. Epstein, Lawrence J. Schweinhart, and J. Terry Bond. 1978. *The Ypsilanti Preschool Curriculum Demonstration Project: Preschool Years and Longitudinal Results.* Ypsilanti, MI: High/Scope Press.

Weikart, David P., Linda Rogers, Carolyn Adcock, and Donna McClelland. 1971. *The Cognitively Oriented Curriculum: A Framework for Teachers.* Urbana, IL: ERIC–NAEYC.

Related Reading

Bereiter, Carl, and Sigfried Engelmann. 1966. *Teaching Disadvantaged Children in Preschool*. Englewood Cliffs, NJ: Prentice-Hall, Inc.

Bredekamp, Sue, ed. 1987. *Developmentally Appropriate Practice in Early Childhood Programs Serving Children From Birth Through Age 8*. Washington, DC: NAEYC.

Bredekamp, Sue. 1996. "25 Years of Educating Young Children: The High/Scope Approach to Preschool Education." *Young Children* 51, no. 4 (May): 57–61.

Center for the Future of Children. The David and Lucile Packard Foundation. 1995. *The Future of Children: Long-Term Outcomes of Early Childhood Programs* 5, no. 3 (Winter).

Consortium of Longitudinal Studies. 1983. *As the Twig Is Bent: Lasting Effects of Preschool Programs*. Hillsdale, NJ: Erlbaum.

DeVries, Rita, and Lawrence Kohlberg. 1987. *Programs of Early Education*. New York: Longman.

Forman, George E., and Catherine T. Fosnot. 1982. "The Use of Piaget's Constructivism in Early Childhood Education Programs." In *Handbook of Research in Early Childhood Education*, Bernard Spodek, ed., 185–214. New York: Macmillan.

Johnson, James E. 1993. "Evaluation in Early Childhood Education." In *Approaches to Early Childhood Education*, Jaipaul L. Roopnarine and James E. Johnson, eds., 317–35. New York: Macmillan.

Kağıtçıbaşi, C., D. Sunar, and S. Berkman. 1988. *Comprehensive Preschool Education Project: Final Report* (Report for International Development Research Center, Ottawa, Canada). Istanbul, Turkey: Bogazici University.

Karnes, Merle B., Allan M. Schwedel, and Mark B. Williams. 1983. "A Comparison of Five Approaches for Educating Young Children From Low-Income Homes." In Consortium for Longitudinal Studies, *As the Twig Is Bent: Lasting Effect of Preschool Programs*, 133–70. Hillsdale, NJ: Erlbaum.

Katz, Lilian. 1985. "Dispositions in Early Childhood Education." *EAC/EECE Bulletin* 18, no. 2: 1, 3.

As active learners, children develop their own interests, generate ways to answer their questions, and share their discoveries with others.

Kohlberg, Lawrence, and Rochelle Mayer. 1972. "Development as the Aim of Education." *Harvard Education Review* 42, no. 4: 449–96.

McKey, R. H., L. Condelli, H. Ganson, B. Barrett, C. McConkey, and M. Plantz. 1985. *The Impact of Head Start on Children, Families, and Communities* (Final Report of the Head Start Evaluation, Synthesis, and Utilization Project). Washington, DC: CSR.

Miller, Louise B., and Rondeall P. Bizzell. 1983. "The Louisville Experiment: A Comparison of Four Programs." In Consortium for Longitudinal Studies, *As the Twig Is Bent: Lasting Effects of Preschool Programs*, 171–99. Hillsdale: Erlbaum.

Piaget, Jean. 1952. *The Origins of Intelligence in Children*. New York: International Universities Press.

Piaget, Jean. 1973. *To Understand Is to Invent*. New York: Grossman.

Piaget, Jean, and Barbel Inhelder. 1970. *The Psychology of the Child*. New York: Basic Books.

Roopnarine, Jaipaul L., and James E. Johnson, eds. 1993. *Approaches to Early Childhood Education*. New York: Macmillan.

Schweinhart, Lawrence J., Helen V. Barnes, and David P. Weikart. 1993. *Significant Benefits: The High/Scope Perry Preschool Study Through Age 27*. Ypsilanti, MI: High/Scope Press.

Vygotsky, Lev. 1978. *Mind in Society*. Cambridge: Harvard University Press.

Westinghouse Learning Corporation. 1969. *The Impact of Head Start: An Evaluation of the Effects of Head Start Experiences on Children's Cognitive and Affective Development*. Vols. 1–2. Washington, DC: Clearinghouse for Federal, Scientific, and Technical Information.

Part 1
The Active Participatory Learning Approach

Secure in the knowledge that an adult is available to help if needed, this child solves the problem of how to make a tower taller and develops an "I can do it" feeling about herself.

Human Development as a Framework for Education

The cornerstone of the High/Scope approach to early childhood education is the belief that *active participatory learning* is fundamental to the development of human potential and that active learning occurs most effectively in settings that provide *developmentally appropriate learning opportunities*. Therefore, the overarching goal of our early childhood work is to establish a flexible, "open framework," operational model that supports

developmentally appropriate education in diverse settings. In doing so, we have made the following basic assumptions about human development:

• Human beings develop capacities in predictable sequences throughout their lives. As people mature, new capabilities emerge.

• Despite the general predictability of human development, each person displays unique characteristics from birth, which through everyday interactions progressively differentiate into a unique personality. Learning always occurs in the context of each person's unique characteristics, abilities, and opportunities.

• There are times during the life cycle when certain kinds of things are learned best or most efficiently, and there are teaching methods that are more appropriate at certain times in the developmental sequence than at others.

Given that developmental change is a basic fact of human existence but that each person is also developmentally unique, and that there are optimal times for particular kinds of learning, developmentally appropriate education can be defined by three criteria. An educational experience, procedure, or method—whether adult- or child-initiated—is developmentally appropriate if it . . .

1. Exercises and challenges the learner's capacities as they emerge at a given developmental level

2. Encourages and helps the learner to develop a unique pattern of interests, talents, and goals

3. Presents learning experiences when learners are best able to master, generalize, and retain what they learn and can relate it to previous experiences and future expectations

Active Participatory Learning: The Way Children Construct Knowledge

Knowledge arises neither from objects nor the child, but from interactions between the child and those objects.

— Jean Piaget

Furthermore, in the High/Scope approach, learning is viewed as a *social experience* involving meaningful interactions among children and adults. Since children learn at different rates and have unique interests and experiences, they are more likely to reach their full potential for growth when they are encouraged to interact and communicate freely with peers and adults. These social experiences occur in the context of real-life activities that children have planned and initiated themselves, or within adult-initiated experiences that afford ample opportunity for children's choice, leadership, and individual expression.

Learning as *Developmental Change*

The High/Scope Curriculum is grounded in child development theory and research, originally based on the pioneering work of Jean Piaget (1969) and his colleagues, and the progressive educational philosophy of John Dewey (1938/1963). Since then, it has been updated according to the results of ongoing cognitive-developmental research (Clements 2004; Gelman and Baillargeon 1983; Gelman and Brenneman 2004; Gelman and Gallistel 1978/1986; Goswami 2002; National Research Council 2005; Necombe 2002; Smith 2002). While Piaget and Dewey explained learning in terms of broad developmental stages, today's cognitive-developmental researchers study chil-

dren's **learning pathways or developmental trajectories** as they relate to specific content and tasks (for example, vocabulary and counting).

Many High/Scope teaching practices, particularly the notion that development occurs within sociocultural settings where adults scaffold children's learning, were first derived from the work of developmental psychologist and educator **Lev Vygotsky** (1934/1962). Vygotsky saw the social or cultural environment as being particularly crucial to the development of language and thought processes. The High/Scope teaching practices that come from this view also continue to be updated, based on the theory and research of those who have followed Vygotsky's lead (Rowe and Wertsch 2002).

Interestingly, current brain research validates the active learning approach favored by cognitive-developmental researchers and theorists (see Shore 1997; Thompson and Nelson 2001). In the view of all these experts, learning depends on **interaction.** By interaction, they mean a child's encounters with people, objects, events, or activities, and later, ideas. In other words, without experiences, the brain has nothing to work with.

In a cognitive-developmental model such as High/Scope's, learning is seen as a process of **developmental change**—that is, a process in which we learn by relating and adding new information to what we already know and, if necessary, even changing the way we thought before. For example, if we know how to care for a pet guinea pig—to give it

certain kinds of food and clean water—then we have a knowledge base to care for other pets, such as a cat or dog. However, a conscientious pet owner still has more to learn—such as what cats and dogs eat and drink that is different from what guinea pigs eat and drink. This ongoing process of developmental change, first identified by Piaget and upheld by current research, is called **assimilation** (using our existing knowledge and behaviors to explore new things) and **accommodation** (changing our mental models of how the world works to take new and sometimes contradictory information into account). It often takes many experiences of assimilation and accommodation before changes in thinking are fully formed and consistently applied in our actions.

Active Participatory Learning—A Complex Process

The learning process in the High/Scope model is seen as an *interaction* between the goal-oriented actions of the learner and the environmental realities that affect those actions. Children construct their own models of reality, which develop over time in response to new experiences and exposure to other viewpoints.

Children as Active Participatory Learners

Active participatory learning—the direct and immediate experiencing of objects, people, ideas, and events—is a necessary condition for cognitive restructuring and hence for development. Put simply, young children learn concepts, form ideas, and create their own symbols or abstractions through self-initiated activity—moving, listening, searching, feeling, manipulating. Such activity, carried on within a social context in which an alert and sensitive adult is a *participant-observer*, makes it possible for the child to be involved in intrinsically interesting experiences that may produce contradictory conclusions and a consequent reorganization of the child's understanding of his or her world.

In embracing the view of learning as a process of developmental change, High/Scope adopted the term **"active participatory learning"** to describe the central process of the High/Scope Curriculum. This is defined as learning in which the child, by acting on objects and interacting with people, ideas, and events, constructs new understanding. No one else can have experiences for the child or construct knowledge for the child. Children must do this for themselves.

In this book, "active participatory learning" stands for four critical elements: (1) direct action on objects, (2) reflection on actions, (3) intrinsic motivation, invention, and generativity, and (4) problem solving. Next, we discuss each of these elements as reflected in the activities of preschool children.

▶ Direct actions on objects

Active learning depends on the use of *materials*—natural and found materials, household objects, toys, equipment, and tools. Active learning begins as young children manipulate objects, using their bodies and all their senses to find out about the objects. Acting on objects

gives children something "real" to think about and discuss with others. Through these types of "concrete" experiences with materials and people, children gradually begin to form abstract concepts. As Flavell (1963) puts it, "Children perform real actions on materials which form the learning base, actions as concrete and direct as the materials can be made to allow" (p. 367).

▶ Reflection on actions

Action alone is not sufficient for learning. To understand their immediate world, children must interact *thoughtfully* with it. Children's understanding of the world develops as they carry out actions arising from the need to test ideas or find answers to questions. A child reaching for a ball is pursuing an internal question, such as "Hmm . . . wonder what this thing does?" By acting (grasping, tasting, chewing, dropping, pushing, and rolling) and then reflecting on these actions, the child begins to answer the question and to construct a personal understanding of what balls do. Put another way, the child's actions, and reflections on those actions, result in the development of thought and understanding.

Thus, active learning involves both the *physical activity* of interacting with objects to produce effects and the *mental activity* of interpreting these effects and fitting the interpretations into a more complete understanding of the world.

▶ Intrinsic motivation, invention, and generativity

In this perspective, the impetus to learn clearly arises from within the child. The child's personal interests, questions, and intentions

Active participatory learning starts as children manipulate objects—for example, maneuvering a mirror to just the right spot for their pretend play.

lead to exploration, experimentation, and the construction of new knowledge and understanding. Active learners are questioners and inventors. They generate hypotheses—"I wonder how I can get this block that I want to be my scuba diving air tank to stay on my back?"—and test them out by using and combining materials in a way that makes sense to *them*. As inventors, children create unique solutions and products: "I tried tying the block on with string, and it kept falling off,

---

The Importance of Independent Problem Solving

Experiences in which the preschool child produces some effect on the world (in contrast with, say, watching television) are crucial to the development of thought processes, because the child's logic develops from the effort to interpret the information gained through such experiences; interpretation of new information modifies the interpretative structures themselves as the child strives for a more logical internal model of reality. Therefore, if we want children to become intelligent problem solvers, the best way to do so is to give them many opportunities to work on problems of interest to them—that is, problems that arise from their own attempts to comprehend the world.

but the tape made it work." While children's creations may sometimes be messy, unstable, or unrecognizable to adults, the *process* by which children think about and produce these creations is the way they come to understand their world. It is also important to recognize that the errors children make ("The string won't hold the block on") are as important as their successes in providing them with essential information about their original hypotheses. Thus, active learning is an ongoing, inventive process in which children combine materials, experiences, and ideas to produce effects that are new to them. Although adults may take for granted the laws of nature and logic, each child discovers them as if for the first time.

▶ **Problem solving**

Experiences in which children produce an effect they may or may not anticipate are crucial to the development of their ability to think and reason. When children encounter real-life problems—unexpected outcomes or barriers to fulfilling their intentions—the process of reconciling the unexpected with what they already know about the world stimulates learning and development. For example, Roberto, a child pretending to cook soup, tries to cover the pot of "soup" (water) with a lid. He expects the lid to cover the pan, but instead it falls into the soup and water splashes on his hand. Roberto knows from experience that the lid is supposed to stay on top of the pan, so he decides to place several other lids on the pot until he finds one that fits properly and does not fall into the soup. Through repeated experiences like this, he will learn to consider the size of any cover in relation to the size of an opening.

Young Children and Adults Think Differently

Learning to understand the world is a slow and gradual process in which children try to fit new observations to what they already know or think they understand about reality. As a result, they often come to unique conclusions, conclusions that, from the standpoint of adult thinking, may be viewed as errors. Adults interacting with children should recognize that this type of thinking is part of the active learning process and acknowledge children's nonadult reasoning—in time, children's thinking will become more like adult thinking. Below are some of the ways preschool children think differently from adults:

It's alive! "It's running after me!" 4-year-old Erin exclaims as she runs away from a trickle of water. Erin is not being silly or cute. She is trying to understand her direct experience. At ages 3 and 4 children are only beginning to distinguish between living and nonliving things. They sometimes equate movement with life ("The butter's running! It's alive!") and wonder when dead pets or relatives will be alive again.

Interpreting words concretely. "I'm beside myself with excitement!" exclaims Mrs. Cantu.
"How you do that?" James asks, looking at her curiously.
"Do what?" Mrs. Cantu asks.
"You . . . be . . . be . . . beside you. How you do it?"
Young children base the meanings of words on their own experiences. To James, "beside" means "next to." He is trying to figure out how Mrs. Cantu can be next to herself.

Blending intuitive and scientific thought. "Look, my magnet catches nails," Wanda says to her friend, Topher.
"We catch nails 'cause our magnets have strong powers."
"But we can't catch these sticks. They don't have powers."
Wanda and Topher have constructed their ideas from careful observation (the magnets pick up nails but not sticks) and intuition or fantasy (the magnet "catches" some things because of special "powers").

One thing at a time. Because they generally focus on one thing at a time, young children usually don't make "both . . . and" statements. For example, when Corey asks his friend Vanessa if she has any pets, she says she doesn't. This doesn't stop Corey from asking her whether she has any cats (even though cats are included in the larger class of pets). When Vanessa says she doesn't have a cat, Corey asks her if she has a dog. Vanessa replies that she does have a dog, and Corey confides that he has a dog, too. Neither child is aware that Vanessa's dog is both a dog *and* a pet.

Judging by appearances. Young children tend to make judgments about "how much" and "how many" based on appearances. For example, young children reason that a nickel is more than a dime because it is bigger. They might also think that a cup (8 ounces) of juice in a small glass is more than a cup of juice in a bigger glass simply because the smaller glass is fuller.

"If I hold my hands out like this, will I go faster?"—As they play, active learners pose questions and seek answers.

Active participatory learning involves both interacting with objects and interpreting the effects of one's actions (what made the ball go in?).

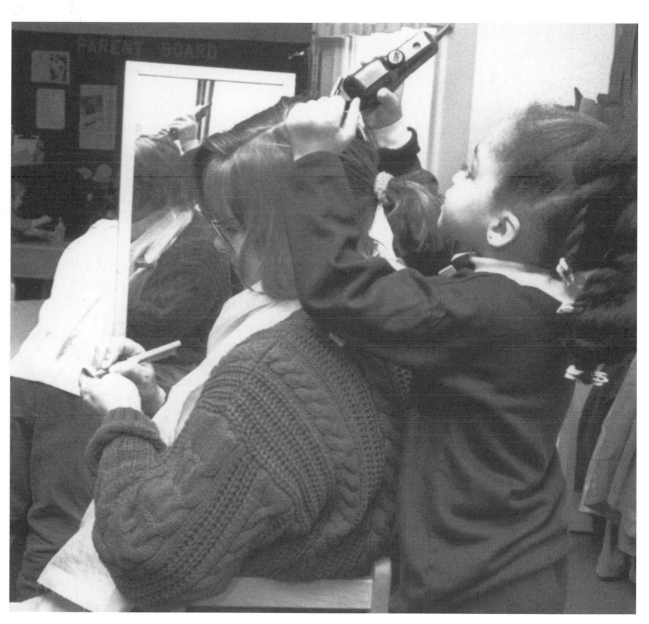

Children do most of the "work" of active learning while the teacher is a conscious participant-observer. Here, as she gets a "haircut," the teacher jots down an observation to discuss later with her teammate.

Adults as Supporters of Active Learners

Given that children learn through their own experiences and discoveries, what is the role of adults in the active learning environment? In the broadest sense, adults are **supporters of development,** and as such their primary goal is to encourage active learning on the part of the child. Adults both attend to what children learn and how they learn it, and they *empower* children to take control of their own learning. In carrying out this role, adults are not only active and participatory but also observational and reflective; *they are conscious participant-observers.*

While children interact with materials, people, ideas, and events to construct their own understanding of reality, **adults observe and interact with children to discover how each child thinks and reasons.** Adults strive to recognize each child's particular interests and abilities, and to offer the child appropriate support and challenges. This adult role is complex and develops gradually as the adult becomes more adept at recognizing and meeting each child's developmental needs. Basically, adults in High/Scope settings support children by . . .

- **Organizing environments and routines for active learning**

- **Establishing a climate for positive social interactions**

- **Encouraging children's intentional actions, problem solving, and verbal reflection**

- **Observing and interpreting the actions of each child in terms of the developmentally based curriculum content domains and KDIs**

- **Planning experiences that build on the child's actions and interests**

It is the major purpose of this book to describe in detail these aspects of the adult's role; therefore, specific examples of how adults support children appear throughout the text.

The Adult Role

Adults support active learning by

- *Organizing environments*

Play areas are clearly defined and stocked with interesting, age-appropriate materials.

- *Organizing routines*

The sequence of the day's events is carefully planned. Here, the teacher uses a message board to help children learn about variations in the day's routine. A chain of paper loops helps children count down the days until a vacation.

• Establishing a supportive social climate

Relationships among adults and children are relaxed and positive.

• Interpreting children's actions in terms of the curriculum content

Teams meet daily to discuss and interpret observations in terms of the curriculum content areas and key developmental indicators (KDIs).

• Encouraging children's intentional actions, problem solving, and verbal reflections

The adult focuses on the **children's** actions and goals.

• Planning experiences

The adults planned this activity to build on children's emerging writing skills.

Preschool Key Developmental Indicators

Approaches to Learning
- Making and expressing choices, plans, and decisions
- Solving problems encountered in play

Language, Literacy, and Communication
- Talking with others about personally meaningful experiences
- Describing objects, events, and relations
- Having fun with language: listening to stories and poems, making up stories and rhymes
- Writing in various ways: drawing, scribbling, and using letterlike forms, invented spelling, and conventional forms
- Reading in various ways: reading storybooks, signs and symbols, and one's own writing
- Dictating stories

Social and Emotional Development
- Taking care of one's own needs
- Expressing feelings in words
- Building relationships with children and adults
- Creating and experiencing collaborative play
- Dealing with social conflict

Physical Development, Health, and Well-Being
- Moving in nonlocomotor ways (anchored movement: bending, twisting, rocking, swinging one's arms)
- Moving in locomotor ways (nonanchored movement: running, jumping, hopping, skipping, marching, climbing)
- Moving with objects
- Expressing creativity in movement
- Describing movement
- Acting upon movement directions
- Feeling and expressing steady beat
- Moving in sequences to a common beat

Arts and Sciences

Mathematics

Seriation
- Comparing attributes (longer/shorter, bigger/smaller)
- Arranging several things one after another in a series or pattern and describing the relationships (big/bigger/biggest, red/blue/red/blue)
- Fitting one ordered set of objects to another through trial and error (small cup and small saucer; medium cup and medium saucer; big cup and big saucer)

Number
- Comparing the numbers of things in two sets to determine "more," "fewer," "same number"
- Arranging two sets of objects in one-to-one correspondence
- Counting objects

Space
- Filling and emptying
- Fitting things together and taking them apart
- Changing the shape and arrangement of objects (wrapping, twisting, stretching, stacking, enclosing)
- Observing people, places, and things from different spatial viewpoints
- Experiencing and describing positions, directions, and distances in the play space, building, and neighborhood
- Interpreting spatial relations in drawings, pictures, and photographs

---

Key developmental indicators (KDIs) are the building blocks of thinking and reasoning at each stage of development. High/Scope identifies 58 preschool KDIs organized under five content areas.

Science and Technology

Classification
- Recognizing objects by sight, sound, touch, taste, and smell
- Exploring and describing similarities, differences, and the attributes of things
- Distinguishing and describing shapes
- Sorting and matching
- Using and describing something in several ways
- Holding more than one attribute in mind at a time
- Distinguishing between "some" and "all"
- Describing characteristics something does not possess or what class it does not belong to

Time
- Starting and stopping an action on signal
- Experiencing and describing rates of movement
- Experiencing and comparing time intervals
- Anticipating, remembering, and describing sequences of events

Social Studies
- Participating in group routines
- Being sensitive to the feelings, interests, and needs of others

The Arts

Visual Art
- Relating models, pictures, and photographs to real places and things
- Making models out of clay, blocks, and other materials
- Drawing and painting

Dramatic Art
- Imitating actions and sounds
- Pretending and role playing

Music
- Moving to music
- Exploring and identifying sounds
- Exploring the singing voice
- Developing melody
- Singing songs
- Playing simple musical instruments

Key Developmental Indicators—A Framework for Understanding Active Learning

If a set of beliefs about how children learn, and how adults support learning, form the *process* of the High/Scope approach, then the **key developmental indicators** (KDIs) provide the *content* by which we can measure the progress of active learning as it takes place. The preschool KDIs are a series of statements that form a curriculum for **social, cognitive,** and **physical development** of children from the ages of 3 to 5 years. Each statement highlights an active child behavior that is essential for the development of the fundamental abilities that emerge during early childhood. The KDIs are not a set of specific topics and learning objectives; instead, they are basic concepts and skills that young children naturally use repeatedly, given the opportunity. Together, the KDIs define the kind of knowledge young children are acquiring as they interact with materials, people, ideas, and events.

Since the key developmental indicators describe activities that young children readily engage in, the role of adults is to create environments in which these behaviors can occur and then to recognize, support, and build on them when they do. *The creation of an environment rich with opportunities for KDIs, and the delivery of appropriate adult support, are critical elements in educating young children.* High/Scope KDIs are organized around these topics: **approaches to learning; language, literacy, and communication; social and emotional development; physical development, health, and well-being;** and **arts and sciences** (this last category is broken down into subcategories of **mathematics, science and technology, social studies,** and **the arts**). These content categories are discussed in Part 3 of this book.

The Adult's Role in Active Learning

"In our view, the role of the teacher remains essential but very difficult to gauge: it consists essentially in arousing the child's curiosity and in stimulating the child's research. It accomplishes this by encouraging the child to set his or her own problems, and not by thrusting problems upon the child or dictating solutions. Above all, the adult must continually find fresh ways to stimulate the child's activity and be prepared to vary his or her approach as the child raises new questions or imagines new solutions. In particular, when these solutions are false or incomplete, the role of the teacher will consist primarily in devising counter examples or control experiments so that the child will be able to correct his or her own errors and find fresh solutions through direct actions."

—*Jean Piaget, quoted in Banet
(1976, p. 7)*

"When education is based upon experience and educative experience is seen to be a social process . . . the teacher loses the position of external boss or dictator but takes on that of leader of group activities."

—*John Dewey
(1933, pp. 56, 59, 71)*

"Vygotsky referred to the *zone of proximal development* as the area between what children can accomplish on their own and what they can do with the help of an adult or another child who is more developmentally advanced. High/Scope teachers observe children carefully so they know when and how to enter this zone to scaffold learning to the next level. Children must be secure and confident in what they already know before they are ready to move to the next level. When High/Scope says adults support and extend children's learning, it means that the adults first validate, or support, what children already know, and then challenge them to extend their thinking to the next level."

—*Ann S. Epstein
(2007, p. 18)*

Adults use the High/Scope key developmental indicators (KDIs) as a window for understanding children's behavior. The KDI arranging several things one after another in a series or pattern helps adults interpret this child's actions.

What Happens in the Active Learning Setting

So far in this chapter we have outlined the perspective on learning that underlies the High/Scope Curriculum. We have introduced the concept of "active participatory learning" and have briefly described the adult's role in terms of supporting the active learning process. The next section illustrates how an active learning approach is implemented in classrooms, centers, or homes. We describe what children typically do in active learning settings, what adults do, how adults and children interact, and some of the short- and long-range benefits—for both adults and children—of participating in an active learning program.

Active participatory learners are focused on their own actions and thoughts.

What Children Do in the Active Learning Setting

▶ **Children initiate activities that grow from personal interests and intentions.**

How can we tell when children are truly engaged in active learning? One of the defining characteristics of active learners is that they are focused on their own actions and thoughts. At the art table, Jeff goes over to the easel to get the green paint; Vanessa stands up to press her elbows into her Play-Doh; Craig places his picture on the floor to have more room to work on it. These actions evoke discussion:

Craig: *Hey, Jeff. You didn't clean up.*

Jeff: *I'm still paintin'. I need some green.*

Craig: *I'm still paintin', too, and I need all the colors.*

Vanessa: *Look! Look! Holes! I did it!*

Active learners find plenty of things to do and often talk about what they intend to do. At first glance, adults who are expecting to see quiet groups of children doing the same thing at the same time may view an active learning setting as disorganized. But adults who understand the importance of supporting active learners realize that a child's *internal motivation* creates an effective organizing force both within the child and in the classroom or center. For example, if a child needs green paint, a smock,

another block, or a friend to help, he or she can generally meet the need independently because an active learning environment supports this type of decision making. Because children in active learning settings make choices based on their own interests and questions, and then have time to follow through on their plans, they are intensely involved with people and materials and freely share their ideas, findings, and observations. With appropriate adult support they thus become active agents of their own learning rather than passive recipients of adult-directed learning.

▶ **Children choose materials and decide what to do with them.**

One of the hallmarks of programs based on active learning is the many opportunities they provide for children to make choices. Young children are quite able and eager to choose materials and decide how to use them. Many materials are new to young children, so they often do not use the materials according to their intended function. Instead, children are inventive—manipulating the materials according to their own interests and abilities. One child might use tape, for example, to fasten pieces of paper together, while another might take the tape outside and use it for fastening acorns, flower petals, sticks, and stones together. Consider a group of children working with similar materials— paper, glue, yarn, and paper-towel tubes—at an art table. It is likely that each child will choose to do something different with the materials:

• Della cuts a piece of paper into little bits, which she puts inside a paper-towel tube. "Still need more," she says, getting up to peer down into the tube to see how full it is.

• Dan wraps yarn around his paper-towel tube and then puts glue on top of the yarn "to make the string stick."

When children are free to make their own choices, they often use materials in unexpected, creative ways—like painting with four brushes at once!

• Katie, spreading glue on her paper, watches Dan. "No, no," she tells Dan when he tries to roll his tube and string on her gluey paper.

• "I'm gonna make a long spying thing," announces Joey, as he cuts holes in two paper-towel tubes and ties them together.

• Kim Wan cuts a tube into rings and glues the rings in a row on his paper.

The freedom to make choices like these is essential to active learning because it is by making choices that children learn more about what interests them, what questions to answer, what contradictions to resolve, and what explanations to accept. Because adults in active learning settings understand the important role that children's choices play in learning, they strive to incorporate an element of choice in all of children's activities, even those—such as washing one's hands or zipping one's coat—that many adults might see as incidental to the "real program." Children, after all, do not make distinctions between the regular program and incidental events. They approach most situations with a desire for active involvement. By making choices available in all parts of a program, not just during "free play" or at "free-choice" times, adults increase children's active involvement and thus broaden their opportunities to learn.

▶ **Children explore materials actively with all their senses.**

The active learning process involves all the senses. A young child learns what an object is by experimenting with it—holding, squeezing, climbing on, crawling under, dropping, poking, smelling, and tasting it; viewing it from many angles; and listening to the sounds it makes.

When children explore an object and discover its attributes, they begin to understand how the different parts function and fit together, how the object "works," and what the object is really like rather than how it appears. When children discover that the outside part of a pineapple is hard and prickly while the inside part is sweet and juicy, they are beginning to understand that an object that looks forbidding may taste good. Even if they are told this, they still do not *learn* it unless they make their own observations and discoveries.

Through exploration, children answer their own questions and satisfy their curiosity. In active learning settings, adults respect children's

to the cardboard block tower?" "Pour sand from the milk jug into the strainer?" Two-year-old Barnie, for example, is not yet able to look at two cardboard boxes and tell which one is bigger, wider, deeper, or taller. To gain a sense of their relative proportions, he has to work with the boxes, fitting them together, stacking them, getting into them, standing them next to each other.

Adults in active learning settings give children like Barnie the time and space they need

desire to explore, recognizing that exploration is one of the most important ways young children learn.

▶ **Children discover relationships through direct experience with objects.**

As children become familiar with the objects around them and continue to experiment with them, they become interested in putting them together. In this way, children discover for themselves what objects are like in relation to other objects and how objects work together. Children learn about relationships between things by finding out the answers to their own questions, such as, "What happens when you put a long necklace on the teddy bear?" "Add a wooden block

This parent understands that active learning means exploring with all the senses: looking at an icicle up close, touching it, even tasting it.

Discovering How Objects Relate to Each Other

As they explore objects, children learn about relationships—that one box fits inside another, that juice can overflow a cup, that one block can be placed on top of another, that a truck fits inside a hollow block, that one tower is taller than another, that one truck goes faster than another. Simple discoveries such as these are the foundations for children's understanding of number, logic, space, and time concepts. Adults need to stand back and let children discover such relationships for themselves. This takes patience and an understanding of children's developmental needs:

Bonnie is fitting together large Lego blocks. One of the pieces is upside-down, so it will not fit on the one below it. As Mr. Bloom reaches over to help her, Bonnie pushes his hand away. "I do it. I do it," she insists. After considerable trial and error, she manages to fit the Lego block on top of the one below and then reaches for another block.

to discover relationships on their own. They resist the temptation to help children do something "right" or to show children what to do, knowing that this can deprive children of valuable opportunities for learning and discovery. Children need time to work at their own pace with materials in order to discover for themselves the relationships between things.

► Children transform and combine materials.

Changing the consistency, shape, or color of a material is another way children work with materials in the active learning setting. Consider Ahmed, who is playing in the sandbox. As he presses down on the sand to make a level panful, the sand becomes compacted and will no longer pour. When Ahmed adds some water to his pan of sand, he notices that the hard, dry, compacted sand has turned into a soupy liquid. As Ahmed molds the wet sand, the smooth, flat surface becomes a series of mounds and craters.

Sand play is just one of countless activities in which young children manipulate, transform, and combine materials. As children engage in this type of activity, they are learning about the less obvious, but essential, properties of materials. A child learns, for example, that the quantity of clay remains the same, whether it is clumped together in a ball or flattened out in a thin layer. Children are also learning about cause-and-effect relationships. For example, a child who ties a knot at the end of a string (cause) learns that this action keeps the beads on the string (effect). By providing materials that can take many forms and by valuing children's efforts to transform and combine the materials, adults in active learning settings are encouraging these kinds of important discoveries.

► Children use age-appropriate tools and equipment.

Opportunities to use tools and equipment designed for specific purposes are abundant in the active learning setting. By age 3, children can coordinate two or more actions and thus are capable of using a wide range of tools and equipment. These include both equipment designed for children—wheeled toys, climbers, swings—and such adult items as cameras, eggbeaters, food grinders, and staplers. As children use such simple machines, they are developing a range of movement and coordination skills. Consider the actions involved in riding a tricycle: the child must simultaneously grasp the handlebars, turn them to steer, and pedal. Similarly, when hammering, the child must grasp the hammer, steady the nail, aim, and pound. As they work with tools and equipment, children are developing skills and dispositions that will enable them to do more things on their own and to solve more complex problems.

Clearly, opportunities for problem solving are plentiful when children work with tools: one child searches for a nail that is long enough to connect two pieces of wood; another tries to find a piece of wood that is the right size to form one side of a birdhouse. Children also experience cause-and-effect relationships when using tools— sawing fast makes lots of sawdust and takes more effort; turning the handle of the eggbeater faster makes more bubbles.

Initially, just *using* a tool may be more important to the child than its intended function. For example, turning a vacuum cleaner on and off, pushing and pulling it, steering it, managing the cord, and fitting the machine under a table may be more important to a youthful vacuumer than actually cleaning the carpet.

► Children use their large muscles.

Active learning for a preschooler means learning with the whole body. Children are eager to stretch their physical strengths and capacities. They love to climb on top of blocks; move chairs and tables; lift up their friends; roll across the floor; mash clay with their elbows; turn around until they are dizzy; run, hop, jump, push, crawl, shout, whisper, sing, wiggle, throw, pound, kick, climb, twist. Such motions are an undeniable part of their youthful nature. Expecting young children not to move is like expecting them not to breathe. Therefore, in the active learning environment adults provide space and time for children to engage in activities that exercise the large

Preschoolers' Typical Transformations

Mixing paints

Adding food coloring to water

Blowing bubbles

Wringing out a wet sponge

Making a paper chain

Folding a doll blanket

Cracking open nuts

Sawing wood

Drilling holes

Shaking a tambourine

Fitting oneself into a doll cradle

Printing a mask created at the computer

Rolling a clay ball into a long coil

Putting on a wig

Twisting wire around a stick

The Essentials of Discovery

For the young child, *access* to materials, *freedom* to manipulate, transform, and combine them in his or her own way, and *time* to do so are the essentials of the process of discovery. Adults can provide these essentials.

muscles and also provide lots of things for children to push, throw, lift, kick, and carry.

Exploring materials, discovering relationships, transforming and combining materials, acquiring skills with tools and equipment, and using the large muscles are vital manipulative processes. Through such daily opportunities children gain a basic knowledge of the physical world—what it is made of, how it works, and the effect their actions have upon it.

▶ Children talk about their experiences.

In active learning settings, children talk about what they are doing (or have just done) throughout the day. Children are encouraged to set the agenda in conversations with adults, and as a result, what the child says often takes the adult by surprise. Listen to Jerry talking to Mrs. Gibbs about their field trip to a farm: "I left my lunch on the bus an' I had to share some of Toni's. His sandwich was flat. This flat! He sat on it 'cause his dad was late. Boy, was his dad mad, so Toni didn't tell him. It was in the bag, so it was okay."

Clearly, Mrs. Gibbs did not plan a trip to the farm so Jerry could have an experience with a flat sandwich. She thought he might talk about the goat he milked or the chicken feathers he collected, and she was mildly surprised that Jerry was so captivated by Toni's flat sandwich. Paula, on the other hand, describes the egg she found in the hayloft: "It was way down in there. It didn't break. The other one did." Whether children talk about sandwiches or eggs, however, the process of putting actions into words is the same. *But*—conscientious adults might ask—who learned more, Jerry or Paula? Each child was particularly interested in a different aspect of the trip. Perhaps Paula learned more about eggs and hay while

Working with snow at the water table helps children see how a common material can be molded, reshaped, and transformed.

Jerry learned more about what happens when one sits on a sandwich. What we can say with assurance is that both children were involved in memorable experiences that caused them some surprise, both had the opportunity to consciously reflect on their findings, and both were free to describe these reflections in their own words.

When children are free to converse about personally meaningful experiences, they use language to deal with ideas and problems that are real and important to them. As the children communicate their thoughts through language and listen to one another's comments, they learn that their personal way of speaking is effective and respected. In the active learning setting, where children's language reflects their personal perceptions, thoughts, and concerns, each child's voice is heard.

▶ **Children talk about what they are doing in their own words.**

What children say in the active learning setting reflects their own experiences and understanding and is often characterized by a logic that differs from adult thinking:

• "I didn't put any animals in my barn," Melissa says about a farm she made with blocks. "Just horses and cows."

• "That car can't go," Max giggles, pointing to a side-view picture of a car in a storybook. "It's got only two wheels!" "The other two wheels are on the other side," his dad points out. "No they're not!" Max exclaims, as he turns the page to look.

Why should an adult encourage children to say things in their own words when what they say is often incorrect? Because young children like Melissa and Max are using the best reasoning powers at their disposal. No matter how many

Using the large muscles is a key component of active learning.

times an adult tells Melissa that horses and cows are animals, until she develops the capacity to understand class inclusion, to her "a horse is a horse is a horse." Period. Max sees a car with two wheels. Since he is not yet able to imagine another spatial perspective, he thinks his father is joking when he explains to Max that the other two wheels are on the other side of the car. When Max looks on the "other side," he finds another picture, not the other side of the car. According to Melissa's and Max's best reasoning, their views and perceptions are correct. *They need the opportunity to share their observations, so talking about what they think and see becomes a natural part of their lives.* As they mature and experience new contradictions, their thinking will develop along with their self-confidence, and their observations will become increasingly more logical and realistic. In the meantime, they are developing the habit of talking about what they understand and what is important to them.

What Adults Do in the Active Learning Setting

▶ **Adults provide a variety of materials for children to work with.**

Observers new to active learning settings may be surprised by the wide range of materials that are available to children. Adults provide such a variety of materials to assure that there are plentiful opportunities for children to make choices and manipulate materials—key aspects of the active learning process. Materials may include any familiar or unfamiliar objects of interest to young children, except for things that are clearly dangerous (metal cans with sharp edges) or too difficult for this age group (a *Monopoly* game). In

Chapter 5 we describe specific materials and the play and learning they support, but following are some general types of materials that are typically offered to stimulate young children's active learning:

• **Practical everyday objects useful to adults.** Children enjoy using the same things that the important people in their lives use—a lunch box like dad's, hair curlers like big sister's, earrings like mom's, shaving cream like grandpa's.

• **Natural and found materials.** Natural materials like shells, acorns, and pine cones and found materials like cardboard boxes and toilet-paper tubes appeal to children because they can be used in many different ways for many different purposes. And they appeal to adults because they are easily accessible, plentiful, and often free.

• **Tools.** Tools are important to children for the same reason they are important to adults—they help "get the job done." Therefore, provide real tools—scissors, hole punches, construction tools like hammers and screwdrivers. (It is important that tools be in good condition and that safety procedures be followed consistently by both children and adults.)

• **Messy, sticky, gooey, drippy, squishy materials.** Touchable materials like sand, water, paste, paint, clay, and Play-Doh appeal strongly to many children because of the interesting sensory experiences they provide.

• **Heavy or bulky materials.** Children use their whole bodies, exercise their muscles, and gain a sense of their physical capacities when using large wooden blocks, shovels, wheeled toys, and other sturdy, heavy materials.

• **Easy-to-handle materials.** Materials that fit in their hands—buttons, toy figures, Lego blocks, and so forth—give children a sense of control because they can use such small objects successfully without adult assistance.

Some Materials for Active Learning

It is important to stock your classroom, center, or home with a wide variety of materials of interest to young children. The materials listed here are just a few examples of the kinds of materials that will support active learning experiences. Please refer to Chapter 5 for more details on selecting materials for an active learning environment.

Practical Everyday Objects
Pots and pans, eggbeaters, food grinders, mail, hammers, nails, staplers, pieces of wood, sheets, tires, boxes, books, paper

Natural and Found Materials
Stones, shells, leaves, sand, carpet scraps, paper-towel tubes, envelopes

Tools
Brooms, dustpans, mops, buckets, sponges; hammers, saws, hand drills, vices, nails, screws; staplers, hole punches, scissors, paper clips; car jacks, bicycle pumps; shovels, hoes, trowels, wheelbarrows, hoses, watering cans

Messy Materials
Water, soap bubbles, paste, clay, dough, glue, paint

Heavy or Bulky Materials
Boxes, tree stumps, wagons, shovels, piles of dirt, wooden planks, climbing structures, large blocks

Easy-to-Handle Materials
Blocks, beads, buttons, dry beans or pasta, toy cars, stuffed animals

Common Materials in Active Learning Settings

• *Practical everyday objects useful to adults*

• Natural and found materials

• Tools

• Messy, sticky, gooey, dripping, squishy materials

• Heavy or bulky materials

• Easy-to-handle materials

▶ Adults provide space and time for children to use materials.

To take full advantage of the materials in the active learning setting, children need an organized environment. Two key aspects of the adult's role in the active learning setting, therefore, are to *arrange and equip play areas* and to *plan a daily routine*. The specifics of planning the environment and routine are covered in detail in later chapters, but a few key elements of the environment and routine are introduced here.

First, adults divide the environment into distinct spaces organized around specific kinds of experiences, for example, house, art, block, toy, and sand and water areas. Each space is stocked with abundant materials related to that type of play.

Second, adults plan a consistent daily routine so children have opportunities for many different kinds of interactions with people and materials. **Plan-work-recall time** is a lengthy segment of the day allotted for children to work throughout the classroom or center with materials of their own choosing. **Small-group time** is the segment of the day in which children work in groups of six to eight in one location with similar sets of materials. (Even though the adult chooses a group of materials for children to use at small-group time, children are free to make choices among the materials provided, to add materials, and to use the materials in individual ways.) **Large-group time** is a segment of the day in which the whole group comes together for songs, movement activities, and other group experiences.

Outside time is usually the segment of the day allotted for children to play outside with swings, wheeled toys, outdoor art materials, materials from nature, and so forth.

By choosing materials, planning the arrangement of space, and offering a consistent daily routine, adults are able to set the stage for children's active learning. Once the stage is set, adults continue to be active and involved—observing children and supporting their initiatives throughout the day.

▶ Adults seek out children's intentions.

In active learning settings, adults believe that understanding children's intentions and encouraging children to follow through on them is essential to the learning process. By seeking out children's intentions, adults strengthen children's sense of initiative and control.

Adults are careful to *acknowledge children's choices and actions*. This lets children know that what they are doing is valued. Adults often let themselves be guided by the child's example, thereby demonstrating the importance they place on children's intentions. For example, Stony is crawling, so Mrs. Lewis crawls beside him. When Stony stops, Mrs. Lewis stops. When he crawls fast, she crawls fast to keep up with him. Stony laughs with delight at the game he has created, and Mrs. Lewis laughs right along with him.

Similarly, it is common for adults in active learning settings to *use materials in the same ways children are using them*—stacking blocks, flattening Play-Doh, packing sand. In this way they are nonverbally communicating to children that their activities are important, as well as offering opportunities for children to make thought-provoking comparisons.

To ascertain the intentions behind children's actions, adults *watch what children do with materials without preconceptions,* because children often use materials in unexpected ways. In the detailed example that ends this chapter, 3-year-old Callie is deeply involved in labeling envelopes with people's initials and then sealing them. Rather than assume Callie will use envelopes in the conventional way—enclosing something in them before sealing them—the adult observes Callie closely to discern her intention, then encourages her to use the envelopes *her* way.

In addition to seeking out children's intentions through observation, adults also *ask children about their intentions*. This gives children the opportunity to put their intentions into words and reflect on them. For example, an adult sees Scott sitting on the floor and sanding wood scraps, but she cannot tell whether Scott is sanding for its own sake or for some other purpose unless she talks with him. She sits down next to Scott and picks up several wood scraps he has sanded. Then she makes this observation:

Adult: *You've been doing a lot of work, Scott.*

Scott: *Yep . . . sanding. . . it's my job.*

Adult: *Oh, sanding is your job.*

Scott: (Continues sanding) *I sand these* (tosses sanded piece in a bucket). *Then I put 'em here, in the bucket. Billy's the wrapper. He's not here right now.*

Adult: *Oh, you sand and Billy wraps.*

Scott: *But he's getting more tape.*

For more information on conversing with children about their intentions and plans, see the discussion of planning with children in Chapter 6.

▶ **Adults listen for and encourage children's thinking.**

Children's **reflections** on their actions are a fundamental part of the learning process. Listening for and encouraging each child's particular way of thinking strengthens the child's emerging thinking and reasoning abilities. Adults *listen to children as they work and play* so they can understand from their spontaneous comments how they are thinking about what they are doing. Markie, for example, chants, "One for you . . . one for you . . . one for you" as he puts a block on each opening of his tower. His chant indicates that he is thinking out loud about matching blocks and openings in one-to-one correspondence.

Another way adults encourage children to reflect is to *converse with children about what they are doing and thinking.* In programs based on the High/Scope Curriculum, relaxed conversation between adults and children occurs through out the day. As they converse with children, adults *focus on the child's actions* rather than introduce unrelated topics. Instead of lecturing children or asking a lot of questions, adults make frequent comments that repeat, amplify, and build on what the child says. In the course of these conversations, adults pause frequently to give children ample time to think and gather their thoughts into words. Note, for example, how Mrs. Foster encourages Kurt's thinking in this conversational exchange:

Kurt: *I like that music. It's real fast.*

Mrs. Foster: *I think it's helping us put these blocks away real fast.*

Kurt: *I'm gonna put them on this truck and go really fast.*

Markie is thinking out loud as he puts a block in each opening of his tower in one-to-one correspondence. "One for you . . . One for you," he chants.

Mrs. Foster: *All the way to the block shelf?*

Kurt: *Yep. Here I go, just like my daddy.* (Drives off to block shelf, unloads blocks, returns for more.)

Mrs. Foster: *I saw your daddy's truck when he brought you this morning.*

Kurt: (Laughs) *But my daddy's truck is . . . big . . . too big for this room . . . . It wouldn't even fit in the door!*

Mrs. Foster: *No, it wouldn't fit in the door.*

Kurt: *The doors are big enough for . . . for . . . this one!* (Drives truck loaded with blocks to the door and then to the block shelf.)

Strategies for conversing with children are presented throughout this book. In particular, see the section in Chapter 7 on conversing with children at work time.

As noted earlier, adults in active learning settings understand that encouraging children's thinking means accepting children's answers and explanations—even when they are "wrong." Because children's thinking and reasoning skills are still developing, the conclusions children reach are often faulty by adult standards. However, if adults continually correct children, they encourage children to keep their thoughts to themselves. On the other hand, by accepting children's conclusions, adults encourage children to test their ideas. For example, consider Karla again, the child who made a Play-Doh ball and expected it to bounce. Karla finally concluded that the ball would not bounce because it was not round enough. The teacher accepted this conclusion, and Karla made another "very round" ball to test her idea. Many very round Play-Doh balls later, Karla finally observed, "This Play-Doh is too squishy to bounce." Again, the adult accepted Karla's idea. By accepting each new hypothesis Karla offered, the adult encouraged Karla's further reflection and testing:

Teacher: *It is squishy. Can you think of some way to change that?*

Karla: *Well . . . If I leaved it. Leaved it out . . . 'til tomorrow!*

Adults encourage children to talk about their thinking by listening to and accepting what they say rather than by correcting children or asking many questions.

Teacher: *If you left the ball out of the can?*

Karla: *Yeah! It would get hard!*

Teacher: *Would it bounce if it were hard?*

Karla: *Yeah! Then it would bounce. Leave it right here 'til tomorrow. Okay?*

▶ **Adults encourage children to do things for themselves.**

Adults in active learning settings are guided by a belief that encouraging children to solve

the problems they encounter offers them more learning opportunities than doing things for them or attempting to provide a problem-free environment. Therefore, they stand by patiently and wait while children take care of things independently—zipping a jacket, fastening a buckle, stirring juice, wiping up spills, moving the waste can, fitting the tricycle through the door, or finding a board that spans the space between two blocks. Adults can do most such things far more easily and efficiently than children can, but by waiting for children to

Give Children Time to Solve Problems Themselves

Mr. Mulla saw that Chad and Anil were having trouble cutting the long pieces of masking tape they needed for a box structure, because the tape kept getting stuck to itself. Although he could have come to their aid, Mr. Mulla waited while the boys came up with a number of ideas on their own. When one did not work, they simply tried something else. Finally, Chad taped one end of the tape to the table edge and held it there while Anil pulled the tape out as long as they needed it. Anil then cut the tape, and each boy held on to an end until they could attach it to their box structure in the place they wanted it. While it took quite a while for the boys to solve this problem, their solution worked, and in the process of solving the problem, they discovered something about the properties of tape. The boys felt good about their idea, especially when other children began to notice and copy it.

do these things for themselves, adults allow children to think of and practice ways of solving the everyday problems they encounter.

In an active learning environment, where children are constantly involved with materials and are encouraged to do things for themselves, spills and messes are inevitable and are actually important opportunities for learning. Dallas, for example, finds out what happens when he keeps pouring juice past the top of his cup. Juice gets on the table, the chair, the floor. To clean it up he has to get enough towels to soak up all the liquid. He also has to figure out a way to get the juice-soaked towels to the sink. In the active learning setting, *adults show understanding of such mishaps* because they view them as opportunities for children to gain the satisfaction of solving their own problems.

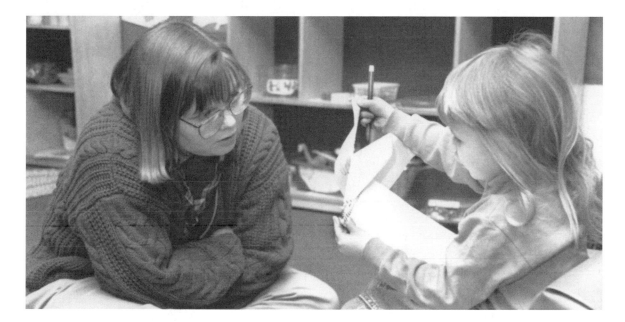

Another way adults encourage children to solve their own problems is to *refer children to one another for ideas, assistance, and conversation* so children come to rely on one another, rather than always turning to adults for assistance. For example, when Tess cannot remember how to print out the mask she just made on her computer screen, Mr. Wills suggests that she ask Mia (another child who had just printed out a mask) to show her how to do it.

Adults in active learning settings also *encourage children to ask and answer their own questions.* Generally, if a child knows enough to ask a particular question, he or she knows enough to have some idea of an answer. For example, following the incident with Tess and Mia, above, Tess came to Mr. Wills the next day with the same problem. Here is how Mr. Wills handled it:

Mr. Wills: *What did you do yesterday when Mia helped you?*

Tess: *Pushed this* (points to the print key).

Mr. Wills: *That's exactly what you did. What happened when you pushed that button?*

Tess: *It came out!* (She pushes the print key and watches the printer print out her mask.)

Providing a variety of materials, planning the play space and routine, seeking out children's intentions, listening for and encouraging children's thinking, and encouraging children to do things for themselves are key elements of the adult's role in active learning programs. More of these types of strategies are provided throughout this book.

How Adults and Children Interact in the Active Learning Setting

▶ **Children and adults are active and interactive.**

In an active learning environment, both children and adults act, think, and solve problems throughout the day. Children are active in choos-ing materials, activities, and playmates. Adults are active in supporting and participating in the learning experiences initiated by children as well as in planning group experiences and setting them in motion. Both children and adults take initiative and respond to one another's initiatives, building on one another's ideas, suggestions, and actions. These reciprocal give-and-take relationships are what drive both teaching and learning.

▶ **Adults and children form partnerships.**

In active learning settings, adults and children form partnerships. Whether joining in a child's play, working with a child to solve a problem, or conversing with a child about his or her experiences, the adult relates to the child as a *partner,* seeking out the child's intentions and helping the child carry out and expand upon his or her intended activity. Sita, for example, is rolling tennis balls under a chair. Mr. Bloom stretches out on his stomach on the other side of the chair, holding a tennis ball. "Wait," Sita instructs. "They have to go here," she says, indicating a path under the chair, "not out there." "Oh, in here," responds Mr. Bloom, rolling his ball along the path indicated by Sita.

The reciprocal give-and-take of a partnership relationship is more supportive of children's development than its alternatives—in which the adult assumes either a dominant or a passive role by directing, lecturing, diverting, or simply watching or ignoring the child's work and play. To form partnerships with children, adults in active learning settings *position themselves at the children's physical level, follow children's ideas and interests,* and *converse with children in a give-and-take style.*

Being a partner in children's play means following the child's lead.

By using these strategies to form a partnership with Sita, Mr. Bloom is letting her know that what she is doing is valued and accepted, and that he will be there to provide support as she expands on her explorations.

▶ **Children and adults invent and discover.**

Active learning is a process that *unfolds*, not a set of prescribed directives to be followed. In the active learning setting, children and adults invent, explore, and make unexpected discoveries. Although adults have set up the environment to support children's interests and activities, they cannot predict with accuracy what children will do or say or how they themselves will respond. Mr. Garcia, for example, is very pleased that he has finally been able to add a color printer to the computer system his preschoolers are using. He expects the children to print out the masks they are making on the computer screen in many different colors. Instead, they use the computer and printer exactly as they often use the easel—filling the whole piece of paper (computer screen) with one color. "Of course," Mr. Garcia realizes upon seeing the children excitedly clutching their pieces of paper filled with one color, "why didn't I think of that!" In the active learning setting, children and adults share the surprises and pleasures of teaching and learning.

The Effects of Active Learning

▶ **Choices for children provide an alternative to adult-child conflict.**

When children are free to make choices and decisions, potential adult-child conflicts are often avoided and are replaced with cooperative learning experiences. When adults understand children's need to be active, they become involved in supporting and extending children's self-initiated activities rather than trying to control children's behavior. For example, when adults expect children to talk about their choices and decisions, children who speak freely and express their intentions are not viewed as "disruptive." When children are free to decide how to use materials, adults are as willing to support the child who uses a material in an exploratory way (smearing paste on paper and arms, touching it, and smelling it) as they are to support the child who uses the materials in the expected way (using paste to fasten pieces of paper together in the course of making something). When adults eliminate long periods of waiting and listening in favor of active learning experiences, children direct their energies toward working with the materials they have selected rather than engaging in disruptive behavior.

By accepting children's exploratory behaviors as normal and desirable, rather than attempting to dispute or eliminate them, adults

A "Constructive" Learning Process

Active learning is the process through which children construct an understanding of things that interest them. For example, while most 4-year-olds are not yet able to construct an understanding of calculus because it involves abstract mathematical thinking beyond their capabilities, they are able to count objects, compare amounts, and construct 1-to-1 relationships—abilities from which their understanding of higher math will eventually evolve. And while most preschoolers are not yet able to read and write, they are enthusiastic about books, stories, their own names, and the process of invented writing.

make their own lives and children's lives more enjoyable, less contentious, and more conducive to learning.

▶ **Children and adults develop confidence.**

In an active learning setting, children are free to pursue their own interests. Adults stock the environment with developmentally appropriate materials and interact with children to support them in pursuing their intentions. Children are free to make errors as they gain an understanding of their world; adults do not correct children's errors, but when appropriate, they challenge children's thinking about what they are doing so children can begin to construct a more complete picture of reality. In this atmosphere, young children develop feelings of competence because they receive encouragement and support for their actions, choices, exploratory behaviors, and emerging thoughts and explanations. Adults feel more competent, too, because they find themselves supporting, rather than disputing, more of children's actions, and because each day they learn something new about the children in their group. As one adult put it, "I'm not yelling at the children anymore. I'm paying attention to *their* interests instead of trying to get them to sit still and pay attention to *me*."

▶ **Children draw on early active learning experiences in later school settings.**

Some adults worry that an "active learning" early childhood setting will put children at a disadvantage when they enter elementary school. What happens to active learners when they must remain seated at desks, follow detailed instructions, speak only when permitted to do so, and concentrate on paper-and-pencil tasks?

Active learners tend to adjust well to

elementary school because they identify themselves as "can-do" people who take care of their own needs and solve problems. In the best of circumstances, the elementary school setting will also encourage active learning. However, in settings that do not, children tend to use their problem-solving skills to adapt to the new style of teaching and learning, and continue to function as active learners outside of school. Since active learners have developed into self-confident decision makers, they often carry these attributes into whatever school settings they encounter.

Regardless of the setting or form of instruction in elementary schools, children continue to learn best by doing, thinking, speaking, and solving problems independently. Therefore, it is imperative that early childhood settings support active learning practices. Through their experiences in such active learning settings, children develop a strong sense of their own ability to affect and understand their world, a capacity which will serve them well throughout their lives.

The Practical Ingredients of Active Learning

To provide a practical frame of reference for adults interested in implementing programs based on an active learning philosophy, we have developed five **ingredients of active learning.** These ingredients capture the essence of the active learning process in summary form. They are easily understood and can be used by adults in any early childhood setting to evaluate whether an activity for children is truly a developmentally appropriate, active experience and to plan for activities that meet these criteria. As we explore

---

Denver Project Follows High/Scope Children Into Non–High/Scope Settings

The Clayton Foundation in Denver, Colorado, operates a High/Scope kindergarten program (Clayton Kids) and a High/Scope after-school program (Clayton Thinkers) for its kindergarten graduates in grades 1–3 in public schools across the city. In response to the question, "How well do Clayton Kids fare once they are in the public school system?" Clayton staff asked each elementary school for progress reports that included teacher comments on the 41 children who had graduated from the Clayton Kids kindergarten program and were currently enrolled in the Clayton Thinkers after-school program. Clayton staff were able to collect school progress reports and teacher comments on 34 of their 41 enrollees (Dalton 1991). They found that the elementary school teachers rated 88 percent of the Clayton after-school group as average or above in standard school subject areas (reading, writing, math, cooperation, and so forth); 38 percent were rated as average; 29 percent, as above average; and 21 percent, as well-above-average. The teachers also commented favorably on the children's social and intellectual abilities. For example, consider these excerpts taken from teacher reports on children's progress:

"D. is always willing to help on any project."
"I appreciate M.'s enthusiasm and creativity."
"J. is a real hard worker."
"T. is one of the best readers in the class."
"W. often sees unique solutions to problems."
"N. has many good ideas."
"E. has made great strides in her skills as a reader, writer, and leader this year."
"I'm enjoying watching A. grow and become more responsible and independent."
"C. is a pleasure to have in class."
"R. is a good group member and a hard worker."
"S. puts a lot into her assignments."
"V. is spontaneous, enthusiastic, straightforward in her thoughts, and lets everyone know what she is thinking. She enjoys learning and asking questions."

It is apparent from these findings that Clayton's active learners continue to do well in traditional elementary school settings. (For an account of a prekindergarten program based on the High/Scope Curriculum whose children's success in kindergarten and third grade has been researched and documented, see Hauser-Cram et al. 1991.)

the details of the High/Scope educational approach throughout the rest of this book, we will return again and again to the following active learning ingredients:

- **Materials**—There are abundant, age-appropriate materials that the child can use in a variety of ways. Learning grows out of the child's direct actions on the materials.

- **Manipulation**—The child has opportunities to explore, manipulate, combine, and transform the materials chosen.

- **Choice**—The child chooses what to do. Since learning results from the child's attempts to pursue personal interests and goals, the opportunity to choose activities and materials is essential.

- **Child language and thought**—The child communicates verbally and nonverbally, describing what he or she is seeing and doing. The child reflects on actions, integrating new experiences into existing knowledge, and modifies his or her thinking accordingly.

- **Adult scaffolding**—Adults support the child's current level of thinking, and challenge the child to advance his or her abilities to reason, problem-solve and create.

Using the Ingredients of Active Participatory Learning

Anyone caring for young children—parents, adults involved in home visits, adult teams in classrooms and child care centers, home child care providers, grandparents, babysitters—can use the active learning ingredients to provide developmentally appropriate experiences for young children. The active learning ingredients

When the ingredients of active participatory learning—materials, manipulation, choice, child language and thought, and adult scaffolding—are present, children are busy and focused.

apply to experiences and activities involving one child or two children as well as activities for small groups and large groups of children. Active learning opportunities are present throughout a formally structured day as well as in other daily events, such as trips in a car or visits to a park. **In the High/Scope Curriculum, the ingredients of active participatory learning guide every experience and activity adults and children engage in during their time together.**

Adults implementing the High/Scope Curriculum use the ingredients of active learning as a guide to observing children, planning for children's experiences, and interacting with children in any curriculum area. In the following example, we show how this framework is applied

Why Children Need to Make Choices

"The intrinsic motivation argument leads to perhaps the most common-sense rationale for allowing children to select learning experiences. A child will, like anyone else, learn best what he is interested in learning. If you allow him to choose, he will select what interests him. If he is interested in something, he will be an active agent in developing his understanding rather than a passive consumer of knowledge. Piaget's 50 years of research on children's thinking has led him to postulate that a child's active involvement in learning is at the heart of the developmental process. 'The child,' Piaget says, 'is the chief architect of his own mental model of the world.'"

—*Thomas Likona (1973)*

in the context of a writing activity undertaken by 3-year-old Callie. We describe how each active learning ingredient shapes the general decisions adults make in preparing for children's writing experiences as well as their specific decisions about how to interact with and support Callie. The teachers' observations of Callie are presented in italic type.

An Active Learning Experience: Observing and Supporting Callie

Materials. The adults in Callie's classroom have provided a wide range of materials to encourage and support young children's developing writing abilities. The materials available include writing tools and materials (crayons, markers, pencils, paints, brushes, stickers, many kinds of paper, envelopes), three-dimensional materials for letter play and letter-making (alphabet letter sets, sand, Play-Doh, clay), and a variety of print materials (favorite storybooks, children's dictated stories, word labels accompanying pictorial labels on classroom signs and storage containers, old magazines and catalogs). The availability of a wide range of writing materials has the stimulating effect intended by the adults, as Callie and several other children have chosen to work with some of the writing materials:

Callie got out some envelopes and markers.

Manipulation. The adults expect Callie and her classmates to manipulate the reading and writing materials in a variety of ways. For example, children might turn pages, point to and circle letters, draw, paint, print, and so on, as they explore for themselves the shape and feel of letters, or they might transform a variety of materials

into letters. In addition, since most of the children have observed that writing is used for important purposes in the world around them—for making shopping lists, taking restaurant orders, letter-writing, and so forth—the adults expect that some children will want to use (or pretend to use) writing for some of these same functions. Callie's use of the writing materials has the active, physical quality that we associate with young children's manipulations; it also shows her growing understanding of some of the functions of writing:

Callie seemed to be repeating a sequence of actions:

> *Put an envelope in front of herself on the table.*
>
> *Picked up the envelope in both hands.*
>
> *Licked it thoroughly three or four times.*
>
> *Pounded the envelope shut with her fist.*
>
> *Turned it over and drew on the front.*
>
> *Gave it to someone.*

Choice. In this classroom the children are free to use any of the writing materials they want to during the plan-work-recall segment of the daily routine:

None of the other children at the art table were working with envelopes and markers. (One was drawing, two were working with stickers; one was playing with wooden letters.) Working with the envelopes was obviously Callie's choice.

Child language and thought. As children work with writing materials, the teachers observe them and listen attentively, leaving room for the child to initiate conversation about what he or she is doing and taking care not to use

language to dominate or control the child's experience:

Callie was very quiet as she worked, but when she completed each envelope she would give it to someone, saying, "This is for you." I sat for a while at Callie's table, and soon she gave one to me, saying, "Here, Ann, I made this for you."

Adult scaffolding. The adults recognize that preschoolers are beginning to make a connection between spoken and written language and to realize that they can write things down for themselves. They understand that children's writing starts out as scribbles and drawings, and gradually, through trial and error, emerges as recognizable script. The adults in Callie's classroom, therefore, encourage children's early, creative interest in the writing process and support all children's attempts at writing, whether or not they use conventional forms:

I sat down at the art table to see what the children were doing. When Callie gave me an envelope, I saw that she had written lots of A's. I wanted to recognize her accomplishment so I said, "Callie, you made A's on my envelope!"

"That's your name!" she told me.

"A's for Ann," I replied. "A is the first letter in my name."

When Callie gave Linda an envelope, Linda threw it down on the floor saying "That's not how you write my name. It's L-I-N-D-A."

Linda is 5 and has been writing her name and other words for some time. I wanted to acknowledge both Linda's skill and Callie's, so I said, "That is the way you spell your name, Linda. Callie wrote the first letter of Linda. She used the letter L to stand for your whole name."

I also found when I started to open my envelope that Callie stopped me, saying, "No, I already did that!" Since I wanted to respect her intentions, I pressed down the part of the flap I had lifted and turned the envelope over so I could see the front again.

"Is this what you wanted me to have?" I asked, looking at the front of the envelope.

"Yep. That's what I made for you," Callie replied, before turning to another envelope and beginning the process again. Clearly what was important to Callie was sealing the envelope and writing on the outside. She had no intention of putting anything inside the envelope.

Active Participatory Learning: The Foundation of the High/Scope Curriculum

In the chapters that follow, the concept of active learning will continue to guide our discussions. In particular, the concept of active learning comes into play throughout discussions of how adults can create a supportive social climate (Chapter 2), work with families (Chapter 3), work as teams to make the active learning process effective in their particular setting with their particular group of children (Chapter 4), select and arrange materials for children to choose and manipulate (Chapter 5), develop the daily routine so children have many opportunities to initiate, plan, carry out, and discuss their actions and ideas (Chapters 6, 7, and 8), and use the High/Scope KDIs as a framework for planning activities (Chapters 9–22).

Essential Ingredients of Active Learning: A Summary

Choice: The child chooses what to do.
___ Children initiate activities that grow from personal interests and intentions.
___ Children choose materials.
___ Children decide what to do with materials.

Materials: There are abundant materials that children can use in many ways.
___ Children use a variety of materials.
  ___ Practical everyday objects
  ___ Natural and found materials
  ___ Tools
  ___ Messy, sticky, gooey, drippy, squishy materials
  ___ Heavy, large materials
  ___ Easy-to-handle materials
___ Children have space to use materials.
___ Children have time to use materials.

Manipulation: Adults encourage children to manipulate objects freely.
___ Children explore actively with all their senses.
___ Children discover relationships through direct experience.
___ Children transform and combine materials.

___ Children use age-appropriate tools and equipment.
___ Children use their large muscles.

Child language and thought: The child describes what he or she is thinking and doing.
___ Children talk about their experiences.
___ Children talk about what they are doing in their own words.

Adult scaffolding: Adults recognize and encourage children's intentions, reflections, problem solving, and creativity.
___ Adults form partnerships with children.
  ___ Put themselves on children's physical level.
  ___ Follow children's ideas and interests.
  ___ Converse in a give-and-take style.
___ Adults seek out children's intentions.
  ___ Acknowledge children's choices and actions.
  ___ Use materials in the same way children are using them.
  ___ Watch what children do with materials.
  ___ Ask children about their intentions.
___ Adults listen for and encourage children's thinking.
  ___ Listen to children as they work and play.
  ___ Converse with children about what they are doing and thinking.
  ___ Focus on children's actions.
  ___ Make comments that repeat, amplify, and build on what the child says.
  ___ Pause frequently to give children time to think and gather their thoughts into words.
  ___ Accept children's answers and explanations even when they are "wrong."
___ Adults encourage children to do things for themselves.
  ___ Stand by patiently and wait while children take care of things independently.
  ___ Show understanding of children's mishaps.
  ___ Refer children to one another for ideas, assistance, and conversation.
  ___ Encourage children to ask and answer their own questions.

References

Banet, Bernard. 1976. "Toward a Developmentally Valid Preschool Curriculum." In *The High/Scope Report, 1975–1976,* C. Silverman, ed., 7–12. Ypsilanti, MI: High/Scope Press.

Clements, Douglas H. 2004. "Major Themes and Recommendations." In *Engaging Young Children in Mathematics: Standards for Early Childhood Mathematics Education,* Douglas H. Clements, Julie Sarama, and Ann-Marie DiBiase, eds., 7–72. Mahwah, NJ: Lawrence Erlbaum Associates, Inc.

Dalton, Joanne. 1991. *State of Affairs Report of Clayton Thinkers.* Denver: The Clayton Foundation.

Dewey, John. 1938. *Experience and Education.* Reprint. New York: Macmillan, 1963.

Dewey, John. 1933. *How We Think: A Restatement of the Relation of Reflective Thinking to the Educative Process.* Boston: Heath.

Epstein, Ann S. 2007. *Essentials of Active Learning in Preschool: Getting to Know the High/Scope Curriculum.* Ypsilanti, MI: High/Scope Press.

Flavell, John H. 1963. *The Developmental Psychology of Jean Piaget.* Princeton: D. Van Nostrand Company.

Gelman, Rochel, and Renée Baillargeon. 1983. "A Review of Some Piagetian Concepts." In *Handbook of Child Psychology,* Paul H. Mussen, ed., 167–230. New York: John Wiley & Sons.

Gelman, Rochel, and K. Brenneman. 2004. "Science Learning Pathways for Young Children." *Early Childhood Research Quarterly* 19, no. 1: 150–58.

Gelman, Rochel, and C. R. Gallistel. 1978/1986. *The Child's Understanding of Number,* 2nd ed. Cambridge: Harvard University Press.

Goswami, Usha, ed. 2002. *Blackwell Handbook of Child Cognitive Development.* Malden, MA: Blackwell Publishers.

Hauser-Cram, Penny, Donald E. Pierson, Deborah Klein Walker, and Terrence Tivnan. 1991. *Early Education in the Public Schools: Lessons From a Comprehensive Birth-to-Kindergarten Program.* San Francisco: Jossey-Bass.

Interdisciplinary Council on Developmental and Learning Disorders (ICDL). 2000. *Clinical Practice Guidelines.* Bethesda, MD: ICDL.

Likona, Thomas. 1973. "The Psychology of Choice Learning." In *Open Education: Increasing Alternatives for Teachers and Children,* Thomas Likona, Ruth Nickse, David Young, and Jessie Adams, eds. Courtland: Open Education Foundation, State University of New York.

National Research Council. 2005. *Mathematical and Scientific Development in Early Childhood.* Washington, DC: National Academy Press.

Necombe, Nora S. 2002. "The Nativist-Empiricist Controversy in the Context of Recent Research on Spatial and Quantitative Development." *Psychological Science* 13, no. 5: 395–401.

Piaget, Jean. 1970. "Piaget's Theory." In *Carmichael's Manual of Child Psychology,* 3rd ed., Vol. 1, Paul H. Mussen, ed., 703–32. New York: John Wiley & Sons.

Piaget, Jean, and Barbel Inhelder. 1969. *The Psychology of the Child.* New York: Basic Books. (Originally published in French as *La Psychologie de L'Enfant.* Paris: Presses Universitaires de France, 1966.)

Rowe, S. M., and James V. Wertsch. 2002. "Vygotsky's Model Of Cognitive Development." In *Blackwell Handbook of Child Cognitive Development,* Usha Goswami, ed., 539–54. Malden, MA: Blackwell Publishers.

Shore, Rima. 1997. *Rethinking the Brain: New Insights into Early Development.* New York: Families and Work Institute.

Smith, L. 2002. "Piaget's Model." In *Blackwell Handbook of Child Cognitive Development,* Usha Goswami, ed., 515–37. Malden, MA: Blackwell Publishers.

Thompson, R. A., and C. A. Nelson. 2001. "Developmental Science and Media: Early Brain Development." *American Psychologist* 56, no. 1, 5–15.

Vygotsky, Len S. 1934/1962. *Thought and Language.* Cambridge, MA: MIT Press.

Related Reading

Ayers, William. 1986. "Thinking About Teachers and the Curriculum." *Harvard Educational Review* 56, no. 1 (February): 49–51.

DeVries, Rheta, and Lawrence Kohlberg. 1987. *Programs of Early Education.* New York: Longman.

Dowling, Jan Levanger, and Terri C. Mitchell. 2007. *I Belong: Active Learning for Children With Special Needs.* Ypsilanti, MI: High/Scope Press.

Epstein, Ann S. 2007. "What Is the Theory Behind the High/Scope Curriculum?" Chap. 3 in *Essentials of Active Learning in Preschool: Getting to Know the High/Scope Curriculum,* 15–20. Ypsilanti, MI: High/Scope Press.

Forman, George. 1992. "The Constructivist Perspective." In *Approaches to Early Childhood Education,* 2nd ed., Jaipaul L. Roopnarine and James E. Johnson, eds., 137–55. Columbus, OH: Merrill.

Forman, George E., and Catherine Twomey Fosnot. 1982. "The Use of Piaget's Constructivism in Early Childhood Education Programs." In *Handbook of Research in Early Childhood Education,* Bernard Spodek, ed., 185–211. New York: Macmillan.

Forman, George, and David Kuschner. 1983. *The Child's Construction of Knowledge.* Washington, DC: NAEYC.

Gelman, Rochel. 1978. "Cognitive Development." *Annual Review of Psychology* 29: 297–332.

Ginsburg, Herbert, and Sylvia Opper. 1979. *Piaget's Theory of Intellectual Development.* Englewood, NJ: Prentice-Hall, Inc.

Hohmann, Mary, Bernard Banet, and David P. Weikart. 1979. "Active Learning." Chap. 5 in *Young Children in Action,* 129–46. Ypsilanti, MI: High/Scope Press.

Kolb, D. A. 1984. *Experiential Learning: Experience as a Source of Development.* Englewood: Prentice-Hall, Inc.

Langer, Ellen J. 1997. *The Power of Mindful Learning.* Reading, MA: Addison-Wesley.

Post, Jacalyn, and Mary Hohmann. 2000. "Active Learning and Key Experiences for Infants and Toddlers." Chap. 1 in *Tender Care and Early Learning: Supporting Infants and Toddlers in Child Care Settings,* 21–54. Ypsilanti, MI: High/Scope Press.

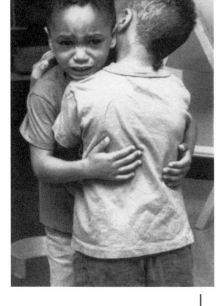

Children's self-confidence and friendships flourish in a setting where adults interact supportively with children throughout the day.

Understanding Supportive Climates

A supportive interpersonal climate is essential for active learning, because active learning is a social, interactive process. Therefore, one of the High/Scope Curriculum's major goals is to assist adults in establishing and maintaining settings where they can interact positively with children, so children can work and play with people and materials free of fear, anxiety, boredom, and neglect. This goal stems from the findings of psychological theory, research, and practice that **active learning** is the primary means by which children construct social, emotional, intellectual, and physical knowledge.

In an active learning setting children are free to manipulate materials, to make choices, plans, and decisions, to talk about and reflect on what they are doing, and to accept support from adults and peers as needed. Children who engage in these kinds of active learning experiences grow in their ability to think and reason, and also in their ability to understand themselves and relate well to others.

The purpose of this chapter is to clarify the meaning of **adult support** in an active learning classroom or center. This is done by defining the **building blocks of human relationships,** examining **contrasting interpersonal climates and their effects on children,** and focusing on the **elements of adult support** that contribute to a supportive active learning climate. The elements of adult support are *sharing control, focusing on children's strengths, forming authentic relationships, supporting children's play,* and *adopting a problem-solving approach to social conflict.*

The Child's Sense of Self: Development Through Interaction

From infancy, children's experiences with the significant people in their lives affect how they view themselves and, consequently, how they interact with people in various situations. A young child's sense of self develops gradually during these interactions—as the child progresses through a series of stages that have been described in a variety of ways.

From psychoanalyst Erik Erikson's (1950) perspective, children from infancy to preschool-age negotiate three major stages of social and emotional development—*trust versus mistrust, autonomy versus shame and doubt,* and *initiative versus guilt.* When children's experiences with adults lead to the development of trust, autonomy, and initiative rather than mistrust, shame, doubt, and guilt, children develop lasting feelings of hope, acceptance, willpower, and purpose.

Clinical infant researchers Stanley and Nancy Greenspan (1985) regard the period from infancy to age 4 as a time of six *emotional milestones—self-regulation and interest in the world, falling in love, developing intentional communication, emergence of an organized sense of self, creating emotional ideas,* and *emotional thinking.* The Greenspans believe that two basic tendencies guide children's development: *regulation and harmony,* and *exploration of new experience and practice.* Furthermore, they maintain that adult support of children's age-appropriate experiences is essential for building a social and emotional climate conducive to children's health and learning. In such a learning climate, children feel a sense of full emotional engagement, mastery, and control.

Establishing a Supportive Climate: The Basics of Positive Adult-Child Interactions

2

In practice, each child's self-understanding develops in collaboration with others. What, after all, is a child's real self? As adults, we have our views of the child's real self; the child, too, has views. Sometimes the child knows better than we do; other times we know better than the child. The goal is to collaborate with the child in the development of a self that is both valued and true.

—Nancy Curry and Carl Johnson, 1990

The hum of conversation is a normal feature of High/Scope settings because learning is a social, interactive process.

Research conducted by psychoanalyst John Bowlby (1969) and developmental psychologist Mary Ainsworth and colleagues (1978) revolves around the importance of *bonding*—the process by which a child becomes emotionally attached to his or her mother, father, and other significant caregivers. Bonding, or attachment, directly affects key aspects of the child's personality, including empathy, sympathy, problem solving, playfulness, and sociability. Related research (Lewis 1986, p. 15) describes the bonding process in similar terms: "Through the establishment of reciprocal and responsive interactions and the emergence of a sense of self, children are able to establish relationships that provide them with a secure base from which to explore their environment." Once firmly attached to their parent(s) or significant caregivers, the main emotional task of young children, according to psychologist Margaret Mahler and colleagues (1975), is to gain a sense of themselves as separate and distinct individuals—individuals who are still able to

maintain their strong emotional attachments.

Clearly, the ongoing support of attentive adults enables children to flourish—to grow, learn, and construct a working knowledge of the physical and social world.

Building Blocks of Human Relationships

While *sense of self* is a fairly abstract concept, it becomes clearer when considered in the context of five key capacities identified in child development literature as building blocks of children's social and emotional health. These capacities for **trust, autonomy, initiative, empathy,** and **self-confidence** provide the foundation for much of the socialization that occurs as the child grows to adulthood. These capacities are particularly apt to flourish within an active learning setting that supports the growth of positive social relationships.

Trust. Trust is the confident belief in oneself and in others that allows a young child to venture forth into action knowing that the people on whom she or he depends will provide needed support and encouragement. The development of trust begins at birth as parents and caregivers respond to their infant's needs—feeding, changing, cuddling, playing—making their baby feel safe and secure. By toddlerhood, the child's sense of trust has developed to the point where he or she can explore in the next room out of the adult's sight. But the toddler still needs to check back often to see that the significant adult is still there. Bolstered by trust, 3- and 4-year-olds leave

home for hours at a time to play with friends or attend preschool. Learning to trust a new set of people outside the family is an important step forward for this age group. In a supportive setting, young children extend the range of their trusting relationships to new adults and peers.

Autonomy. Autonomy is the capacity for independence and exploration that prompts a child to make such statements as, "I wonder

The process of bonding to important caregivers in infancy helps the child develop a sense of herself as a separate individual.

what's around the corner" and "Let me do it." While young children need to feel a strong attachment to their parents or primary caregivers, they also need to develop a sense of themselves as distinctly separate persons who can make their own choices and do things for themselves. An early example of independent thinking is an infant, Sam, cooing and gurgling to his little stuffed bear—Sam has discovered a simple way to entertain himself. Saying "no" indiscriminately is one way toddlers test their emerging sense of autonomy. Also, with toddlers' new-found mobility comes a feeling of independence that sometimes leads them into troublesome situations—stuck under a highchair, startled by the clatter of pots and pans they have pulled out of a cupboard, immobilized in a tangle of clothes they have decided to take off by themselves. By the preschool years, children are able to do many things on their own without putting themselves at such risk, and adults should encourage them to

do so. Preschool-aged children take great pride in dressing themselves, pouring their own juice, riding bikes, carrying big boxes, "reading" a book to a friend. These kinds of experiences enhance children's sense of autonomy, giving them the courage to reach out and explore new materials, situations, and relationships.

Initiative. Initiative is the capacity for children to begin and then follow through on a task—to take stock of a situation, make a decision, and act on what they have come to understand. From infancy on, initiative is evident as young children signal and act on their intentions. A toddler, Francie, for example, sees her mother's key ring on top of the stool. Her face lights up. She gurgles, and then says her all-purpose word for interesting objects, "Da-boo, da-boo." She

crawls to the stool and, gripping it with both hands, pulls herself to a standing position. Then she releases her two-handed grip on the stool to grasp the keys, loses her balance, sits back on the floor with a thump, but works her way back up the stool into a standing position. At this point Francie holds on to the stool with both hands—all the while gazing at the keys. With great care, she slowly removes one hand from the stool, grasps the keys with her free hand, puts them in her mouth, and then, using both hands, works her way down the stool into a sitting position. Once

The preschooler's trust in adults outside the home is tentative at first as the child takes on the challenge of widening her circle of relationships.

Preschool-aged children take great pride in doing things for themselves, reflecting their growing capacities for autonomy and initiative.

By encouraging young children to discuss their intentions and plans, adults help children act purposefully and feel confident about their choices and decisions.

The Beginnings of Empathy

"Seeing a child fall and hurt himself, Hope, 9 months old, stared, tears welling up in her eyes, and crawled to her mother to be comforted—as though *she* had been hurt, not her friend. When 15-month-old Michael saw his friend Paul crying, Michael fetched his own teddy bear and offered it to Paul; when that didn't stop Paul's tears, Michael brought Paul's security blanket from another room.

"Such small acts of sympathy and caring, observed in scientific studies, are leading researchers to trace the roots of empathy—the ability to share another's emotions—to infancy, contradicting a long-standing assumption that infants and toddlers were incapable of these feelings.

"In some of the most recent and surprising findings, researchers have identified individual neurons in primates that respond primarily to specific emotional expressions, a response that could be a neural basis for empathy. These findings are opening a new research area in which scientists are searching for the specific brain circuitry that underlies the empathic impulse."

—Daniel Goleman (1989, p. 20)

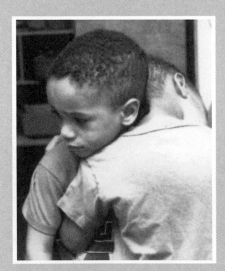

By the preschool years, children are often able to show their concern for others.

seated, she joyfully shakes, mouths, throws, and retrieves the keys she has worked with such determination to possess. Preschool-aged children are more ambitious and much more articulate than toddlers: "Play with blocks." "I'm gonna get some paper, lots of it, and cover up that box my daddy gave me, and cut some holes in it for windows, and that's gonna be my fort—me and Jamal, he's gonna help." It is important for adults to encourage preschool-aged children to describe their intentions in their own words. Doing so helps children act purposefully and feel confident in their ability to make choices and decisions—to make things happen—and to see themselves as competent, able people.

Empathy. Empathy is the capacity that allows children to understand the feelings of others by relating them to feelings that they themselves have had. Empathy helps children form friendships and develop a sense of belonging. The first glimmers of empathy appear in infancy. Psychologist Janet Strayer (1986) has this to say about an infant's capacity for empathy toward peers: "Although their cognitive understanding is limited, 6-month-olds react with interest and contact behaviors toward crying peers" (p. 50). In a group setting, for example, some infants and toddlers make a point of playing near peers for whom they have a special fondness, and they will gaze sadly at their special friends if they are crying—sometimes moving closer and patting their friends, or offering a toy as comfort. Strayer also reports that infants' concern extends to siblings as well as peers: "Mothers report that by 14 months of age, 65 percent of infants show empathic concern for their siblings" (p. 50). It is also true that infants reflect the feelings of their parents and adult caregivers. Consider, for example, Tony, an infant who smiles widely, gurgles, waves his arms, and kicks his legs when his dad

arrives to pick him up from child care. But, on the days when his dad arrives at the center feeling pressured and irritable, Tony's initial expressions of delight quickly become muted, mirroring his dad's irritability. By the preschool years, children are able to exhibit their concern for others in many ways. With their increasing language ability, preschool-aged children have a greater capacity to express their feelings and their empathy for the feelings of others—"Your mouth's goin' down. Why you so sad, little girl?" "Ricky's very sad 'cause he teared the picture for his mom." "Oh, boy. Shane's smiling 'cause he's gonna see his daddy."

Self-confidence. Self-confidence is the capacity to believe in one's own ability to accomplish things and contribute positively to society. Self-confidence is a core of inner pride that can sustain children through the difficulties and strife they are bound to encounter in their lives. Self-confidence develops when children spend time in supportive settings—developing their abilities and interests and having opportunities to experience success. Child development researchers Nancy Curry and Carl Johnson (1990) report that certain types of experiences influence one's self-confidence: "The available evidence suggests that it is protective to have a well-established feeling of one's own worth as a person together with a confidence and conviction that one can cope with life's challenges. The limited evidence suggests that two types of experiences are most influential: secure and harmonious love relationships, and successful accomplishment of tasks important to the individual" (p. 3).

Successful accomplishments, however, can be elusive if adults do not capitalize on children's problem-solving opportunities. It is understandable that adults may become annoyed with children who manage to put themselves in

"I did it!" Children develop self-confidence by accomplishing goals that are important to them.

troublesome situations—the infant stuck under the highchair, the toddler crying in the midst of a clutter of pots and pans, the preschooler pouring himself a glass of juice and spilling it all over a table. Ironically, however, potentially negative situations such as these often provide excellent problem-solving opportunities that can help children develop self-confidence. For example, with appropriate adult support and reassurance, the infant can find a way to remove herself from underneath the highchair; the toddler can be encouraged to put the pans back in the cupboard; and the preschooler can take responsibility for wiping up the spilled juice. When adults have the patience to look at these types of situations from the *child's* point of view, they recognize the importance of encouraging children to begin to solve their own problems, thereby laying the groundwork for learning experiences that build a child's sense of competence and self-respect.

Even very young children, however, are not fooled into self-confidence by adult manipulation and false praise. Consider David's experience, for example: David is sitting in his highchair happily throwing his spoon on the floor every time his mom hands it back to him. When saying "Don't throw your spoon, David" does not produce the result Mom desires, she removes David from the highchair and tells him to pick up his spoon. "No!" he says firmly. "Then Mommy will help you," says his mom, taking David's hand, guiding it to the spoon, curling his fingers around the handle, and holding her hand around his. "There. David was a good boy. He picked up his spoon," says his mom in tones of praise and approval. "No, *Mommy* do it," David replies matter-of-factly. Self-confidence develops as a result of one's own actions and decisions, and children seem to understand this and expect adults to understand it as well—and to act accordingly.

Who Is in Control? Contrasting Social Climates for Children

The qualities of supportive social climates in early childhood programs are better understood when viewed in contrast to the qualities of two other climates that are quite common in early childhood programs: the *laissez-faire climate* and the *directive climate*. We focus on these climates because many early childhood settings are

In supportive climates, the balance between the freedom to explore and the safety and security created by a predictable environment and appropriate adult support enables children to stay focused on their chosen activities.

distinguished by one or the other or by a combination of the two.

Laissez-faire climates. A laissez-faire, permissive climate is largely controlled by the children themselves. The daily routine and the physical environment are loosely structured, giving free reign to children's play, which adults in these settings view as the primary focus of the early childhood program. Adults purposely leave children alone so they may play with one another and with the materials provided, intervening only when asked, or to impart information, or to restore order when necessary.

This type of climate works well for independent-minded children who take leadership roles with their peers and who are able to obtain adult assistance when they need it. But, because of the relative lack of structure and adult involvement inherent in this type of approach, some children may become frustrated. For example, they may have difficulty finding things to do; they may give up in the face of problems; or they may feel anxious, bored, confused, or out of control. On a more positive note, a laissez-faire climate offers plenty of freedom for children and respects their need for play as a primary learning activity. Some adults believe such a climate mirrors the conditions of daily life, therefore preparing children to cope with reality and develop survival skills.

Directive climates. The directive approach to teaching and learning is characterized by adult-controlled activities. The daily routine and physical setting are tightly controlled by adults so they can lead children efficiently through adult-planned learning sequences. In short, adults talk; children listen and follow directions. Ideally, children remain subdued and attentive while adults, following skill-based objectives, show and tell them what they need to know. Then children drill

Even during an adult-initiated experience such as moving to music with paper streamers, children make choices about how they will use the streamers and respond to the music.

Contrasting Climates for Children

Laissez-Faire Climate	Supportive Climate	Directive Climate
• Children are in control most of the time, with adults as bystanders who provide supervision.	• Children and adults share control.	• Adults are in control.
• Adults intervene to respond to requests, offer information, restore order.	• Adults observe children's strengths, form authentic partnerships with children, support children's intentional play.	• Adults give directions and information.
• Curriculum content comes from children's play.	• Curriculum content comes from children's initiatives and is designed with key developmental indicators in mind.	• Curriculum content comes from learning objectives set by adults.
• Adults highly value children's play.	• Adults highly value children's active learning.	• Adults highly value drill and practice for children.
• Adults use various approaches to child management.	• Adults take a problem-solving approach to social conflict.	• Adults use correction and separation as predominant child management strategies.

and practice until they can duplicate the adult model or score adequately on an assessment instrument. Children who are not able to remain still and attentive during instructional sessions are publicly corrected or separated from their peers. This climate rewards children who enjoy following directions. They experience the feeling of success that comes from meeting adult expectations. But the range of acceptable behaviors in such a climate is so narrow that most children require ongoing adult supervision to keep them on task.

Supportive climates. The supportive climate advocated by High/Scope prevails in an early childhood setting where adults and children share control over the teaching and learning process. In this climate, adults provide an effective balance between the freedom children must have to explore as active learners and the limits needed to permit them to feel secure in the classroom or center. Adults create an orderly physical environment to support a broad range of children's interests, and they establish a daily routine within which children express and carry out their intentions. Throughout the day, children and adults initiate active learning experiences based on children's strengths and interests. Even during adult-initiated experiences, children make choices and decisions about materials and outcomes. Adults make their presence known by joining children as *partners* who are genuinely interested in and committed to watching, listening to, conversing with, and working with children; they encourage children and assist them as they solve problems that arise throughout the day. When conflicts arise, adults are not judgmental

Instead, they acknowledge children's feelings and engage children in problem solving so children experience the satisfaction of figuring out and being responsible for their own solutions. Adults and children alike view problems, mistakes, and conflicts as *active learning opportunities*.

We believe a supportive climate serves young children well. Children flourish in an active learning setting precisely because of the supportive climate; it enables them to focus on their own interests and initiatives, try out their ideas, talk about their actions, and solve child-sized problems in age-appropriate ways. A supportive climate stimulates and strengthens children's ongoing development of trust, autonomy, initiative, empathy, and self-confidence.

Shifting from climate to climate. In many early childhood settings, the locus of control shifts back and forth from one climate to another, from laissez-faire, to supportive, to directive, without conscious thought on the part of adults. Here, for example, is a typical instance of the shifting-climate syndrome from an imaginary child care center:

Tall Timbers Center

A supportive climate prevails as the day begins with greeting time. The children cluster around Miss Beale and Miss Lee, eagerly sharing tales about what they did at home, special outings, surprising occurrences, their pets, their siblings, their friends, the important things that have happened to them recently.

Next it's time for free play, and the climate becomes laissez-faire. The children play with materials, alone and together, while Miss Beale and Miss Lee work at record keeping and prepare the daily lesson. The adults take turns reminding the children to use their "indoor" voices and walking feet, and they intervene to settle disputes, such as restraining Max and Billy from throwing blocks.

At one point, Miss Beale summons five children over to a small table for the letter lesson of the day and the climate shifts to directive.

Since Miss Beale views this time as her true "teaching" time with the children, she directs this session like "real" school. She expects children to watch and listen as she explains and demonstrates how to print the letter G. Next she passes out worksheets and pencils so they can practice filling the whole page with G's. "Oh, Thomas, let me help you make another," she says pausing to guide his hand.

❧

While climate shift is a common occurrence in many early childhood settings and may at times be unavoidable, in the High/Scope approach adults consciously strive to maintain a consistently supportive climate throughout the day.

The Effects of a Supportive Climate

When adults maintain a consistently supportive climate for active learners, everyone benefits from the partnerships that emerge.

► **Children and adults are free to learn.**

When children and adults work together in an active learning setting with a supportive social climate, children are motivated to carry out their own intentions. Adults encourage children to use what they know to solve problems and initiate new experiences from which they gain new insights. In this open-ended approach, children learn through experience and construct their own understanding of their world. Adults also learn—about the capacities of individual children, about how to interact in a genuine way to support each child's development, and about their own potential for providing appropriate support.

In the Eye of the Beholder: Dressing in Two Different Social Climates

Below are two real-life stories about how two young children—Lyle and Gus—get ready for child care. As you read the stories, consider which social climate each story represents. Then decide what effect each climate has on these two children:

It's almost time to leave for the child care center. Four-year-old Lyle, still in his pajamas, is playing with his racing cars.

"Hurry up, Lyle," his dad calls, "or I'll be late for work."

"I'm waiting for mom to pick out my clothes," Lyle calls back. This brings his mom, who selects his clothes, dresses him, brushes his hair, and buttons his sweater.

"Don't you look smart," she says. And he does.

Meanwhile, down the block, Lyle's best friend, Gus, is also getting ready for child care. He opens his shirt drawer and finds his favorite shirt with cars all over it. He hesitates because it has buttons that are hard to fasten, but he decides to wear it anyway. He manages to get three buttons buttoned, and that seems like enough. "See," he says to his mom with pride.

"Those are hard to button," she comments "and you did them all by yourself!"

Next, he opens his pants drawer. But he can't see his pants because his pants drawer is underneath his shirt drawer, which is still open. When he tries to close his shirt drawer, only one side will go in; so he pulls the drawer all the way out. It falls into his pants drawer. Luckily, the handles are pointing up, so Gus pulls the shirt drawer out and most of the shirts stay in.

"Do you need some help, Gus?" his mother asks.

"Nope. I can do it myself." Gus picks out his favorite red plaid pants his grandma sent him for his birthday last year. They're a little short, but that's okay, he reasons, because then he can easily see his yellow Big Bird socks. "Look, I'm all ready," Gus announces a few minutes later.

"Yes, you certainly are," his mom agrees.

When adults are supportive and caring, children learn to be supportive and caring with others.

► **Children gain experience in forming positive relationships.**

When adults in an active learning setting share control, encourage problem solving, and invest a genuine part of themselves in their interactions with children, they model a positive interpersonal style. When adults are kind and patient, children learn to appreciate these qualities and, in dealing with others, may exhibit these same qualities themselves. When adults greet children with pleasure and respect, children often respond in kind. Of course, even in a supportive climate in which adults and children share control, positive interactions between individuals are not automatic. Rather, such relationships form over time under the influence of understanding and caring adult role models.

► **Adults see children's behaviors in terms of development.**

In a supportive active learning climate, adults view children's behavior in terms of *development*. As with individuals of all ages, young children will experience social conflicts. In settings where adults and children share control, however, adults tend to view social conflict as the result of young children's tendency to focus on their own intentions rather than of a desire to be naughty or mean. To understand this point more fully, consider the behavior of Vanessa, a very young 3-year-old. When Vanessa joined the program, she often hit children who intruded into "her" play space. Observing this behavior and understanding the partnership role of adults in supportive learning climates, Vanessa's teachers helped her find alternatives to hitting. But because they also understood Vanessa's strong desire to carry out her intentions, they studied the play activities she was attempting to defend—lining up rubber animals, balancing blocks, filling and emptying sand containers—and helped her find more protected spaces to play in until she was ready to play with others.

► **Children grow in their capacity to trust, be autonomous, take initiative, and feel both empathy and self-confidence.**

In a supportive climate, these building blocks for a healthy sense of self have a greater opportunity to flourish than in the other two social climates. In a directive climate, adults are in control and children have limited opportunities to interact with either people or materials. In a laissez-faire climate, children are largely on their

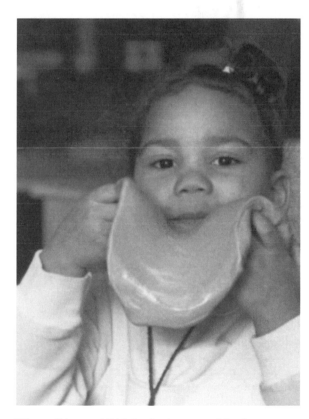

When adults see child behavior in terms of development, they accept children's exploratory behavior. No one says, "Don't use the clay that way!"

own and, while some children thrive, others are apt to feel lost or controlled by their more outgoing peers. In a supportive climate, adults strive to support each child's initiatives so each child gains a sense of self-control and competence in making choices and decisions.

Strategies for Creating Supportive Climates: Five Key Elements

By using five key elements of support as guidelines for working with children, adults create supportive climates that encourage the development of young children's capacities for trust, autonomy, initiative, empathy, and self-confidence. The elements of support are the following:

- **Sharing of control between adults and children**

- **Focusing on children's strengths**

- **Forming authentic relationships with children**

- **Making a commitment to supporting children's play**

- **Adopting a problem-solving approach to social conflict**

Adults can establish a supportive climate by incorporating these elements of support into any setting or program they share with children—homes, home visits, classrooms, child care centers, before- and after-school settings, recreation centers, playgrounds, field trips, and other outings. In the High/Scope Curriculum, the elements of support come into play throughout the day whenever adults and children are interacting. The following sections provide specific strategies adults can use to establish and maintain a supportive learning climate.

Sharing of Control Between Adults and Children

Sharing of control in a supportive climate calls for *reciprocity*—a mutual give-and-take between children and adults. In their joint interactions, both children and adults take turns being leader and follower, teacher and learner, speaker and listener.

Why should adults share control with children? Consider the alternatives. If adults give up control altogether, the hardiest children dominate, often at the expense of the others. If adults retain total control, children have little opportunity to develop the ability to control themselves or to make their own decisions and learn from the consequences. But when adults and children share power and control, an atmosphere of mutual trust, respect, and self-actualization prevails. Adults and children are willing to listen to and try out one another's ideas. Children feel secure, act independently, and take initiative. Since children are permitted to make and then discuss choices and decisions that affect themselves and the people around them, they develop a sense of their own powers and their own limits. Very early on, they come to understand that they do not have to wait for things to happen to them—they can make things happen themselves.

Adults can share control with children by adopting the following four effective strategies:

▶ **Take cues from children.**

Following children's cues in play and conversation gives children the opportunity to express their own ideas and follow through on them in the company of an attentive, cooperative adult partner—someone who can assist them without taking control of the experience or diverting them from their original quest. Here are three examples of adults sharing control by taking cues from children:

Gwen, an infant lying on her back and looking up at her mom, starts to make clicking noises with her tongue. When she stops, her mother answers, making clicking noises with her tongue. Now it is Gwen's turn again, and so forth. The dialogue continues until Gwen turns away, directing her attention to a little green rattle she can just reach with her hand.

∽

In a climate of shared control, there is a give-and-take between children and adults in which both children and adults take turns being leaders and followers.

Manuel, a toddler, wants to help with a grown-up task—carrying water to the water table. "Me help. Me do it," he says, tugging at the full water bucket Mrs. Alvarez is carrying. She puts the bucket down, but it is so heavy Manual cannot get it to budge. His eyes fill with tears.

"Manuel," she says. "What could you use to pull the bucket?" Manuel's face brightens. He gets the wagon, together they lift the bucket in, and Manuel pulls the wagon with the bucket in it to the water table. Together they empty the bucket. "Again," Manuel says, as he heads back to the sink with his wagon and bucket.

∾

Kimi and Reggie are the snack helpers for the day at their preschool. So they bring juice, bananas, cups, and napkins to the children at the snack table.

"Wait a minute," Reggie says, "These bananas can be telephones!" Reggie has caught the group's attention but they don't quite understand what to do. Observing the children's confusion, Ruth, Reggie's teacher, puts her banana "phone" up to her ear.

"Ring, ring. Hello, Ruth!" Reggie says into his banana phone, happy that someone understands his idea. "You want some juice?"

"Yes, please, and a cup, too," she responds.

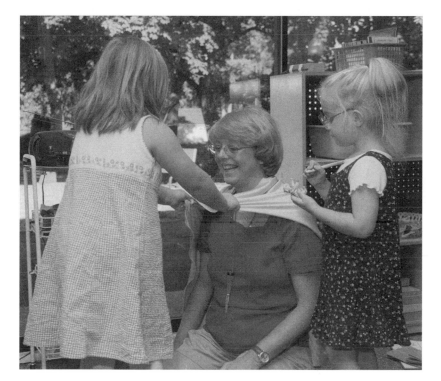

Letting the children be the play leaders, this adult assumes the pretend role they assign to her and wears a cape chosen by the children.

"Comin' right up. Bye." While Reggie gives his teacher the juice and a cup, Kimi calls Midori. The process continues until everyone is served.

▶ **Participate with children on children's terms.**

Adults are open to children's intentions, feelings, and ideas. They set aside the vision of themselves as all-powerful, all-knowing authorities to become partners with children. As partners, they share in children's interests, delights, and creative urges. To capture and build on children's natural enthusiasms, adults put themselves in children's hands as often as possible. They follow children's directions; willingly assume the pretend roles assigned to them by children ("Your leg is

To build on children's natural enthusiasms, adults put themselves in children's hands as often as possible.

broken, but I'm the doctor so I'll fix it"); and play games according to the child's rules.

▶ **Learn from children.**

Clearly, active learning is not a one-way street. In a climate of shared control, adults and children alike are both learners and teachers. Adults learn a lot from children's attitudes. For example, Mrs. Kim spent an evening learning a new computer program in which a mouse and touch pad were used to drive a car around a town. The next day, with some anxiety, she showed a group of children what she had learned. "Let me do that," said Jason, taking the mouse and in just a few minutes mastering the technique that had taken Mrs. Kim all evening to learn. As

Adults learn alongside children when they allow themselves to be captured by children's curiosity.

she watched and admired Jason's ease, she decided to try to approach the next new computer program with the same eagerness and lack of worry that Jason had exhibited.

Children can also teach adults about basic human needs. When a home child care provider's 4-year-old daughter became angry because the other children had gotten into her private things, the two of them talked about what had happened. After the mother had done all she felt she could, she left her daughter, who was still somewhat upset, and went into another room. The next thing she knew, there was her daughter, saying "You can't leave me just because I'm angry." "You're right about that," her mom agreed. She remembered this experience every time one of the children in her care

was angry or upset and she was tempted to walk away before the issue was resolved.

▶ **Relinquish control, consciously giving control to children.**

In the eyes of young children, adults are big and powerful. While there are times that call for the judicious use of this power to set and maintain reasonable limits so children can feel safe and secure, there are also times when adults should relinquish power so children may experience the impact and potency of their own ideas and intuitions.

Adults give control to children in conversation, for example, when they follow each contribution from a child with a contribution or an

acknowledgment rather than a question. Most of the time, when an adult asks a question, the adult retains control of the conversation because the question itself often shapes or limits the child's response. When the adult responds instead with a contribution or an acknowledgment, the child retains control of the conversation because the child is able to direct the conversation toward his or her particular interests. Consider the conversation between Karla and her teacher discussed in the previous chapter. Karla was unable to make a Play-Doh ball bounce:

Karla: *It doesn't bounce!*

Teacher: *I see. It doesn't bounce.* (Acknowledgment)

Karla: *It sticks to the floor. It's . . . it's . . . it's flat!*

Teacher: *When you throw it, it doesn't bounce. It sticks to the floor and it's flat.* (Acknowledgment)

Karla: *I'm going to make another one, a very round one, 'cause this one won't even work.*

Teacher: *Okay, I'll watch you make a very round one. I'm glad I came over to see what you were doing.* (Contribution)

(See also Sharing Conversational Control, p. 218.)

While many opportunities for children and adults to share control arise spontaneously throughout the day, adults can also plan some control-sharing activities. For example, at planning time (which is the time of day when each child decides what to do next), Miss Ricks started out the year by having each child relate his or her plans to her. Once the children had become very comfortable with the process of planning, Miss Ricks realized that they could ask one another about their plans. So, occasionally, the children took turns replacing Miss Ricks as solicitor of plans. At other times, she had the children form pairs and discuss their plans with their partners. While Miss Ricks also participated in this activity by being one child's planning partner and by joining any other pair that needed her, the children shared the responsibility for listening to and acknowledging one another's plans.

Sharing control is clearly a complicated matter. Psychologist Urie Bronfenbrenner (1979) believes that as children develop in a supportive climate, the balance of power between them and the significant adults in their lives gradually shifts, with children taking increasing control of their own actions. "Learning and development are facilitated by the participation of the developing person in progressively more complex patterns of reciprocal activity with someone with whom that person has developed a strong and enduring emotional attachment and when the balance of power gradually shifts in favor of the developing person" (p. 60). Our goal is

to empower children by giving them as much support and control as possible at each stage of their lives.

Focusing on Children's Strengths

Because learning occurs best when children are motivated by personal goals and interests, adults can create a supportive climate by discovering and building on children's interests, talents, capacities, and abilities. They start by observing young children in action so they can capitalize on children's natural desires and interests. This is in contrast to approaches in which adults look for children's weaknesses and prescribe activities designed to correct them. Generally, in this deficit-based approach, adults must motivate children to do things they have no desire to do. The more adults try to pressure children into action, the more defensive and anxious children become. By focusing on children's strengths, however, adults do not have to motivate children; the children have already motivated themselves. Discussed next are several strategies adults can use to focus effectively on children's strengths.

▶ **Look for children's interests.**

When adults seek out and support children's interests, children are free to follow through on interests and activities they are already highly motivated to pursue. They are also willing to try new things that build on what they are already doing. Consider Greg, for example. He loves to play with trucks. At first glance, he seems to be doing the same thing over and over again. By watching and listening, however, the adults in his child care center discover that Greg's repertoire of truck sounds is growing steadily

As the adult reads, she responds to what interests the child, pausing frequently for his questions and comments.

After a number of children talked about and acted out their camping experiences, teachers added real camping materials to the setting to support this interest.

and becoming increasingly elaborate. His pretend trucks have five gears, and the sounds he makes for each gear as the truck negotiates a "really steep grade" are astonishingly distinct and realistic. The adults conclude that Greg really enjoys making noises because he is so good at distinguishing and imitating sounds. This prompts them to add a music area to their child care center, in which Greg really becomes interested. In the music area he often makes up his own songs on the xylophone about trucks and "long hauls."

▶ **View situations from the child's perspective.**

Sometimes adults have a tendency to view children's strengths with mixed emotions because children's new-found enthusiasms can mean extra work for adults. It makes sense to look at these situations from the child's point of view, however, because the feelings of success the child gets from attempting a new activity are more important in the long run than the short-term inconvenience this may cause adults.

Jalessa, for example, is attempting to spoon tomato soup into her mouth, but soup is dribbling down her arm and onto the floor. Mrs. Dalgato, her child care mom, could express irritation because of the mess Jalessa is making. Instead, because she knows that Jalessa's intention is to feed herself rather than make a mess, Mrs. Dalgato chooses to focus on Jalessa's new-found skill. She watches and smiles as Jalessa continues. "Look at Jalessa," her older brother, Freeman, exclaims. "She's usin' a spoon just like us big kids!" "Yes, she is," says Mrs. Dalgato. "She's eating her soup with a spoon all by herself." She makes a note to share this new accomplishment with Jalessa's and Freeman's dad when he picks them up after work.

▶ **Share children's interests with parents and staff.**

The principle of attending to each child's strengths and interests rather than deficits also extends to interactions with colleagues and parents. When adults who work with children focus on children's deficits—all the things children cannot do or do not do very well—children and their parents often become defensive and discouraged. On the other hand, when adults focus on children's strengths, children feel successful and parents see their children as able individuals.

For example, consider Mrs. Hagen, the mother of very active twin boys. She is used to having other adults tell her what a handful the twins are, so she tries to keep a low profile when she comes to pick them up from preschool.

Today, Justin and Jerome are happily digging in the sandbox when their mom arrives. Even so, when their teacher comes over to talk with her, Mrs. Hagen has a sinking feeling that she is going to hear about some misdeed. "I'm so glad you're here," their teacher begins. "Justin and Jerome had such a busy work time this morning. They used boxes to make a robot and then made a house for the robot in the block area. Several other children saw what they were doing and asked Jerome and Justin to help them make robots, too. They were very patient as they worked with the other children. Pretty soon we had four robots in the block area!" Mrs. Hagen is relieved, grateful, and heartened to have someone else recognize and encourage the best in her boys. "Thank you," she says. "I have some boxes in the basement they might like to use when they get home."

▶ **Plan around children's strengths and interests.**

Most educators and adults who care for children believe that each child is unique and, consequently, they strive to individualize their approach to teaching. *Since children's strengths and interests are tangible manifestations of their uniqueness, focusing on children's strengths is a key to individualization in the High/Scope Curriculum.* In daily adult planning sessions, for example, the question "What do we want to plan for Vanessa tomorrow?" is coupled with a discussion about what Vanessa was engaged in today: "Today, Vanessa took all the big farm animals off the shelf and stood them up around herself. But as soon as some other children came to the block area, she put all the animals away and went to the quiet area. She did the same thing with all the little plastic animals for the rest of work time. Maybe we could build on her interest in animals and support her need for her own work space tomorrow by using the little plastic animals at small-group time." (For further discussion of planning around children's strengths, see Chapter 4.)

Forming Authentic Relationships With Children

Adults, like children, have strengths and interests. In a supportive climate, adults' unique capacities and enthusiasms enrich and enliven their interactions with children, laying the foundation for authentic relationships that allow honest, effective teaching and learning to occur. According to psychologist Carl Rogers (1983) *authenticity* is "a transparent realness in the facilitator, a willingness to be a person, to be and live the feelings and thoughts of the moment. When this realness includes a prizing, a caring, a trust, a respect for the learner, the climate for learning is enhanced. When it includes a sensitive and accurate empathic listening, then indeed a freeing climate, stimulative of self-initiated learning and growth, exists. The student is *trusted* to develop" (p. 133).

Since teaching and learning are socially interactive processes, it is imperative that adults share their best, most genuine selves so their effect on children is positive and sustaining. The immediate experience of the reciprocity and mutual respect inherent in authentic relationships supports and encourages *trust* ("I know Mrs. Finch is going to give me time to answer; I know she'll listen to me when I speak"); *autonomy* ("I can do it on my own because I know she'll be there to help if I need it"); *initiative* ("I can go up to Mrs. Finch and talk to her or show her something"); *empathy* ("Jimmy likes to swing; so do I"); and *self-confidence* ("What I have to say is important because the people at my table listen to me"). The memories of such relationships continue to guide children long after they have moved on to other relationships with adults and peers in other learning settings.

Since no prescribed set of behaviors will work for every adult and child, each adult improvises—bringing everything she or he knows into each interaction. In the following sections we

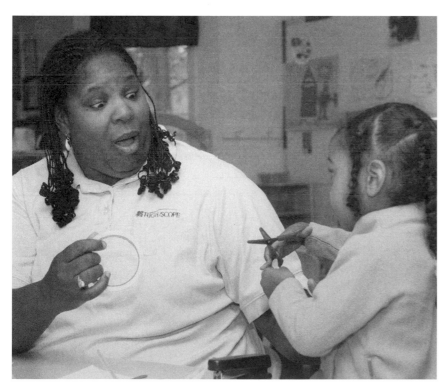

In authentic relationships, adults respond with genuine interest to what children say.

Adults share their genuine selves—their talents and interests—with children.

describe some effective strategies that will guide adults toward authenticity.

► Share yourself with children.

Adults working with children in a climate of support encourage and respect children's motivation to pursue their interests. They also draw upon their own interests. A visitor to one child care center was astonished by a group of 2-year-olds who sang songs together. "These little children sing so well. They're so involved they can't wait to suggest a new song! What's the secret?" he asked. "Why," answered the director, "it's simple. Mrs. Wiggens loves to sing. She sings every day with the children, so for them singing is the most natural thing in the world. With Mrs. Wiggens, even *I* can sing!"

► Respond attentively to children's interests.

Adults give children's interests their full attention out of the firm belief that what interests a child is the key to that child's learning: "Look what I found!" says Eddie, holding up a brilliant green leaf. "Well, look at that," says Mrs. Smith, squatting down to take a closer look, "there's a drop of water sliding around on it." "Where?" asks Eddie, bending very close to the leaf. "Oh, yeah. Here, let me hold it so it won't slide off. Hey, Willie, look! Look, a water drop."

► Give children specific feedback.

Adults speak in their own voices, sharing their own observations, laughter, and surprise in specific terms: "Look at how far your airplane flew this time, Teri! I had no idea that adding one paper clip could make such a difference." They also share their honest puzzlement: "I don't know what's making the door squeak so much, Ellie. Let's take a look at it."

Adults listen very carefully and patiently, never knowing what a child will say until the child says it, or how they will respond until the child has finished: "This is my song," Sylvie says, handing Miss James a paper full of pencil marks. Without saying anything, Miss James squats down so her head is level with Sylvie's. Holding the paper so they can both see it, she studies Sylvie's song. "See," says Sylvie, pointing to a mark in the middle of the paper, "it's about my dog. Here's where he's running very fast. Don't go in the road, little dog. The cars will hit you. Come back, come back! He runs to me and jumps and licks my face all over. You silly puppy. You stay with me. Stay right here. I will take care of you. Now let's sing it. Okay?" "Okay," Miss James agrees. "You start and I'll sing with you."

As Curry and Johnson (1990) remind us, "Authenticity and specificity in response to children should guide caregivers and teachers in their work with children. Honest feedback to specific behaviors helps children grow and change more than global comments such as 'good job'" (p. 3).

Adults look forward to personal conversations with children because they are unique and enjoyable. In a conversation with 4-year-old Rudy about his magnet, Mr. Oser uses words like *repel* and *attract*. Rudy offers a much more graphic explanation: "Look what my magnet caught!" Mr. Oser responds using Rudy's terms: "Your magnet caught lots of nails but my magnet isn't catching any of these toothpicks!" Through such dialogue focused on real interests and specific events, children and adults share opportunities to teach and learn. In this type of climate, children eventually develop the habit of sharing their interests with peers, as well as with adults:

Corey: *We love mud, don't we Jeff!*

Jeff: *Yeah, we love mud.*

Adults are attentive to the details of children's work, acknowledging it with specific feedback ("You put all the blue paint on this side") rather than vague praise ("Nice painting!").

Corey: *It gets all over the place.*

Jeff: *I got some in my hair.*

Corey: *Me, too. I got some on my shoe.*

Jeff: *I got some on both my shoes.*

► Ask honest questions and respond to questions honestly.

When questions arise between people in authentic relationships, they are honest questions—questions, very simply, to which the person asking the question does not have the answer:

• "Where is the stapler, James? Tanika needs it to staple her crown together."

• "Teacher, how you do this?"

• "I have never seen a shell like this, Loretta. Where did you find it?"

Honest questions reflect the questioner's real interest in hearing the answer, whatever it might be.

Similarly, authenticity requires that adults respond honestly to children's honest questions:

Clarita: *"Miss James, why do you have that stuff up there on your eyes?"*

Miss James: *"This green shadow on my eyelids?"*

Clarita: *"Yeah, why do you put it up there?"*

Miss James: *"Well . . . because I like it. It makes my eyes look greener. And it's fun, like I'm going to a party."*

Clarita: *"This isn't a party! This is . . . is . . . here!"*

Miss James: *"I think being here with you is fun!"*

Clarita: *"Like a party?"*

Miss James: *"Yes, fun like a party with lots of people I like."*

Clarita: *"I like Carter. He's my best friend."*

There is no rush to answer honest questions. The questioner pauses, waits patiently for a reply, and accepts the fact that sometimes there are no answers:

Miss James: *"Why did you put lots of colors on this side of your picture, LaRita, and no colors on this side?"*

LaRita: *"Because."*

By being authentic with children in these ways, adults help children form their own authentic relationships with others.

Making a Commitment to Supporting Children's Play

When young children are free from illness, malnutrition, neglect, and abuse they turn their considerable energies to play. Play is pleasurable, spontaneous, creative, and unpredictable. Whether it is noisy or quiet, messy or orderly, silly or serious, strenuous or effortless, children find play deeply satisfying, challenging, enjoyable, and rewarding.

When adults are asked about their pleasant childhood memories, their minds often fill with images of play: jumping rope, playing hopscotch, making mud pies, climbing trees, feeding chickens, playing kick-the-can and hide-and-seek, picking grapes in the back garden, playing dress-up, having fun with the water hose, hiding under the drapes in the dining room. Adults remember play because it is an activity they had control over and that consequently had a strong impact on them. The learning that emerges from active involvement in play is probably one of the main reasons both children and adults keep coming back for more.

Children play out of the need to construct meaning from their lives. They need to use all their senses to find out about things: "What does this odd thing on my highchair tray taste like? How does it feel, look, smell, sound? What will happen if I bang it or throw it on the floor?" Play is the way children explore what things do and how things work. It is also their way of making sense of personalities, social interactions, and the darker side of human existence: "You're dead. You can't move. We take you to the hospital and make you alive again. Now get in that ambulance, Joey."

Play in a supportive climate involves all the ingredients of active learning—**materials** to play with and **manipulate; choices** about what, where, how, and with whom to play; **child thought and language** as they play; and **adult scaffolding** for play that ranges from setting up an environment for play to actually participating in it. When children play under these supportive conditions, they have many opportunities to be aware of others; to watch and imitate what others do; to be adventurous; to concentrate on things that interest them; to work near and with others; and to converse about what they are doing and feeling. Consequently, there are many opportunities for trust, autonomy, initiative, empathy, and self-confidence to flourish. In the following sections we discuss ways adults act on their commitment to children's play in a supportive active learning setting.

▶ **Observe and understand the complexity of children's play.**

Since children communicate through play, it is important that adults commit themselves to learning the complex language of play. They can do this by watching and listening to children.

Adults who observe children carefully discover the many forms that play can take. Play develops in complexity as children themselves change and grow. Very young children engage in *exploratory play*—simple repetitive play experiences in which they explore the properties and functions of materials and tools, not for the purpose of making something, but simply for the pleasure of "doing it." This early play evolves into *constructive play*, the making of structures and creations, and *dramatic play*, in which children assume pretend roles and act out their own scenarios about people and animals. As they grow older, children begin to play *games with rules*, first playing by their own rather flexible rules and

Adults understand that play is the medium through which children construct their understanding of the world.

then by the official rules. To effectively support children's play without disrupting it, adults must be able to distinguish among and accept a variety of play forms. (For further discussion of play forms and how to support them, see the Work Time section in Chapter 7, pp. 196–224.)

▶ Be playful with children.

"More [adults] need to be joyful and playful as they work with young children, ready to accept the unexpected connection or alternative with good humor and patience" (Fromberg 1987, p. 60). Playful adults get down on the floor and build with blocks. They get "rescued" from the "burning house" and rushed to the "hospital" in the "ambulance." They eat pine-cone soup and blast off in rocket ships. They tell and read stories, make up and sing songs, play catch, slide, climb, dig in the sandbox, play tag and hide-and-seek. Some adults play quietly, others quite boisterously. Some love to sing,

Playful adults get down on the floor with children.

some to dance, some to play with glitter, some to make things that really work. Even adults who consider themselves to be serious people are quite able to understand and participate in the intensity of children's play, once they give themselves permission and understand the value of supporting play. Contradictory as it may seem, playing with children is something that adults in a supportive active learning climate do consciously, respectfully, seriously yet light-heartedly, and with great satisfaction. They play without teasing, belittling, or physical aggression. They understand that through play, they are supporting the active learning process and children's spontaneous desire to learn.

Adopting a Problem-Solving Approach to Social Conflict

In the course of children's play, conflicts arise—Jenni has the piece of wood that Tanya wants, Lyle and Hank come to blows because they both want to pretend to be the dad, and Vanessa hits anyone who invades her territory. In a supportive climate, adults know that children's desires are bound to conflict and that incidents like these are natural occurrences. They regard conflict situations as opportunities for children to develop skills in social problem solving. Although chidren's conflicts with peers can be annoying, adults focus their energies on enabling children to resolve the issues at hand rather than on punishing children for their immature social skills.

The problem-solving approach to social conflict is a long-term strategy supportive adults use with children from toddlerhood through high-

Adults see conflict situations as normal occurrences that offer opportunities for children to develop skills in social problem solving.

The Other Side of Play

Sometimes children's play is disquieting. William, a shy 4-year-old, is kneeling on the floor, stabbing a rubber doll in its stomach with a screwdriver. On one hand, his teacher would like to stop him because it is very painful to watch him play like this and she does not want children to hurt others, even in play. On the other hand, he is playing, pretending—he is not hurting anybody, destroying the tough rubber doll, or interfering with other children—and, in doing so, he seems to be expressing a side of himself that his shy, quiet manner generally obscures. As the teacher watches, another child comes over to William and recruits him to play with the construction tools at the workbench. William becomes completely absorbed in this new play activity with his friend. While the teacher is relieved that the direction of William's play has changed so easily and naturally, she also realizes that because William is so quiet she often over-looks him. Therefore, she resolves to observe William more carefully and to schedule a home visit, so she can find out more about him from his mom. In this case, William's teacher has the feeling that perhaps his play is telling her much more about him than she could ever learn through more direct means.

It takes time and patience to talk through a dispute, but the result is a sense of mastery and autonomy for children.

school graduation. As children grow in their ability to anticipate and resolve social conflicts, the conflicts they must confront become increasingly complex. However, when children practice resolving social conflicts from an early age, by the time they reach adulthood they have many of the social skills they need, the habit of using them, and the confidence gained from their years of experience and support.

When social conflicts arise, what guides adults? In the supportive climate of an active learning setting—in which adults are accepting, attentive, playful, and authentic—adults use the strategies described next to help children resolve conflicts and become more aware of themselves as capable problem solvers.

▶ **Approach social conflict calmly and acknowledge children's feelings.**

Adults calmly stop hurtful behavior and acknowledge children's feelings so children can let go of their emotions and clear the decks for identifying and solving the problem.

Adult: *Kneels between Lyle and Hank with an arm around each one. You look angry, Lyle, and you seem really upset, Hank. The boys nod in agreement.*

▶ **Gather information and restate the problem.**

It is important to hear both sides of the dispute without taking sides so each child's position is heard and acknowledged.

Adult: *What's the problem?.*

Lyle: *I want to be the dad. I said so first.*

Hank: *Well, you're always the dad. I want to be big.*

Lyle: *I'm the biggest, so huh! You can't be the dad. You're too little.*

Adult: *So the problem is, Lyle, **you** want to be the dad and Hank, **you** want to be the dad. Both boys nod in agreement.*

▶ **Ask for ideas to try, choose one together, and be prepared to give follow-up support.**

Curry and Johnson (1990) point out that this approach puts children in control. "THEY agree on the situation, THEY figure out what to do about it, and THEY choose what happens next. Mastery and autonomy are developed here!" (p. 117).

Adult: *What can we do to solve this problem? The boys look at her, thinking.*

Lyle: *I could be the dad today, and then you can be the dad the next day.*

Hank: *Well, I could be the dad today!*

Adult: *It sounds like you both want to be the dad today.*

Lyle: *We don't need two dads . . . Hank, you could be the ladder guy **and** wear the tool belt!*

Hank: *And the gloves?*

Lyle: *Ok, the gloves. Both boys look pleased.*

Adult: *So, Lyle, you're going to be the dad and Hank, you're going to be the ladder guy who wears the tool belt and the gloves.*

The boys nod "yes." The adult watches them get started and checks in with them as ladder guy and dad build a "swamp boat."

Finding alternatives to hurtful behavior, naming their feelings, and thinking of solutions are not easy to do, especially for young children

This adult listens carefully as children express their feelings and their needs.

"Uh-oh, Rachel. I'm Tellin' on You!"

Rachel is carrying two jars of paint from the easel to the art table, where she is painting a boat she made at the workbench. She very carefully sets both jars down, but one is so close to the table's edge that it tips over, spilling red paint on Brandon's tennis shoes.

Billy, who is making a walkie-talkie, sounds the alarm. "Uh-oh! Look what Rachel did! Paint on Brandon's shoes. It looks like blood! Brandon, your momma's gonna give you a spankin'!"

Brandon bursts into tears, and Rachel hides under the table.

Mrs. Williams takes in the situation as she looks up from the house area. She calmly walks over to the art table. "Brandon, you're upset and crying. What's the problem?" she asks.

"Billy says my momma's gonna give me a spankin'. . . 'cause of my shoes. . . . It's like blood."

"Nobody's spankin' me!" Rachel yells out from under the table.

"Nobody's getting a spanking," Mrs. Williams says calmly. "It looks like there's some red paint on the floor."

"I could use the mop like I did that other day," answers Rachel, coming out from under the table.

"You could use the mop," answers Mrs. Williams. (Rachel leaves to get the sponge mop.) "What about your tennis shoes, Brandon?"

"My momma washed 'em in the sink when me and Jimmy played in the mud!"

"You could wash them in the sink like your momma does," Mrs. Williams says.

"Then they'll be all wet!" Rachel cries.

"I know. Put 'em in the sun," answers Billy. "That's what my grandma does!"

"My mom put 'em in the dryer," Brandon chimes in. "They made a funny noise . . . like thumping!" (He takes off his shoes and turns on the cold water.)

who live in the present and often see things from their own point of view. Children need many real-life experiences in working through conflicts with peers and much ongoing support from adults to develop the capacity to anticipate and deal effectively with the conflicts they encounter. Given the opportunity to practice working through social conflict in a supportive climate, however, children learn to trust themselves as problem solvers, to trust adults to assist them when they need it, to be empathic and helpful to others, and to have faith in their individual and collective capacities to make relationships work. (For further discussion of supporting children's social problem solving, see the key developmental indicator **dealing with social conflict** in Chapter 12.)

These, then, are the five key elements of supportive climates: **sharing of control, focusing on children's strengths, forming authentic relationships, making a commitment to supporting children's play,** and **adopting a problem-solving approach to social conflict.** When these elements are in place, a supportive climate prevails, enabling children to grow in trust, autonomy, initiative, empathy, and self-confidence.

Using the Elements of Support: Moving a Group of Children From Place to Place

Adults can use the elements of support to help shape their interactions with children and deal with many kinds of interpersonal situations positively and supportively. Here is an example of how adults use the elements of support as a framework for planning experiences for children.

Most adults working with groups of young children face the task of getting them safely and smoothly from one place to another. In some programs, the task of moving children takes on major importance because of the physical layout of the setting—for example, the playground is on the opposite side of the building, or the bathroom or lunchroom is down the hallway. In programs housed in more child-oriented buildings, adults face the same issue whenever they leave the building for a walk or field trip. Lining children up and having them travel single file often seems, at first glance, to be the most efficient solution to such transport problems. However, since establishing and maintaining a quiet, orderly line of young children generally requires waiting on the part of children and constant adult vigilance, traveling in such a manner can quickly become a negative experience for everyone involved. By considering ways to incorporate the elements of support into the situation, however, adults can come up with some positive alternatives.

Sharing control. As much as we might think that young children ought to be able to walk in a line without talking or "bothering their neighbors," they usually show little natural inclination to do this, so if the adults choose this way of moving the group, the activity is of necessity adult-controlled. How, then, can adults shift the climate into a supportive one where adults and children share control? One strategy is to establish anchor points. For example, on a walk, placing one adult (or a designated child leader) at the starting point and one at the destination permits children to walk singly, with a friend, with several peers, or near an adult as long as they stay on the path between the two adults or designated anchors. When the only sink available for hand-washing is down the hall and around the corner, one adult can station herself in the bathroom while the other remains in the classroom sending and receiving small groups of travelers. What generally happens in anchored situations is that once adults shift some of the control back to children, children move quite appropriately from anchor to anchor. They know what is expected of them and enjoy the challenge of venturing between the two points on their own.

Focusing on strengths. Expecting children to line up and move silently in single file for any length of time is a policy that cannot help but highlight children's weaknesses. How can we approach the same situation with a focus on children's strengths? A good starting point is to think about what children like to do and do well. For example, they may be eager to play outside, even though it is quite a walk through and around the building to get there. They may enjoy carrying things. What if, then, they were to take things outside to play with, carrying things both singly and in pairs? This way, the journey from classroom to playground could focus on what they *can* do rather than on what they are not very good at.

Forming authentic relationships. Generally, the intent of silent lines is to prevent interactions both among the travelers themselves and between the travelers and the environments they are passing through. One way to shift toward authenticity is to think of traveling from place to place as a leisurely walk taken for pleasure and an opportunity to enjoy time with friends and acquaintances. The walk then becomes a time to chat, to notice things along the way, to stop in and say hello to neighbors. One preschool class, for example, frequently paused at the door of a neighboring class to see what they were doing and say hello. Another stopped at "Grandma Norton's" to look at her flowers and greet her if she was out on her porch or in the yard. (Once she knew their schedule, she almost always managed to be outside to greet them!) Traveling can be more than a means to an end. It can become a pleasant and rewarding process in itself, particularly for children who feel somewhat inhibited by the more formal atmosphere of the center or classroom. For these children, traveling can become a time for relaxation and intimacy.

Making a commitment to supporting children's play. A regimented line leaves no room for play. In fact, playful children in lines are generally reprimanded. How can adults shift from strict regimentation toward play, yet still provide limits within which children will be safe and secure and not disrupt others? One way to do this is to move in playful ways with anchors at either end—as a train; in wagons with some riders and some pullers; walking, holding streamers or scarves; as stealthy cats; wearing special traveling hats; not stepping on any lines or cracks; and so on. Children who are energetically focused on playful ways of moving are fun to travel with and require far fewer "reminders."

Adopting a problem-solving approach to social conflict. With encouragement, children themselves can think of ways to travel safely from place to place; when children are included in solving the problem, they are more committed to making the solution work. Mrs. Brads tried this at large-group time:

Mrs. Brads: *Today is our day to use the gym.*

Willis: *Yippee!*

Mrs. Brads: *You like going to the gym, Willis.*

Various other children: *I do . . . Me, too . . . So do I . . . I really, really like it. . . It's my best thing.*

Mrs. Brads: *Lots of people like to go to the gym.*

Katie: *My daddy goes to the gym. He gots very strong muscles.*

Mrs. Brads: *We can all have very strong muscles if we use them. Now, here's a problem. How can we get to the gym safely and quietly?*

Sarah: *Walk on our tippy toes. (She demonstrates.)*

Joey: *Crawl like a puppy and just make a tiny noise like this. (He yips very softly.)*

Beth: *I want to be a kitty.*

Mrs. Brads: *Okay. Let's try those ideas. Mrs. Hines will go first, and I'll be last. You can tiptoe or crawl like a puppy or kitty. (Mrs. Hines tiptoes to the door and everyone follows her either on tiptoes or their knees. Mrs. Brads crawls part way down the hall and then switches to tiptoeing.)*

Moving as a group from place to place can be viewed as a problem or it can be viewed as an appropriate opportunity for group problem solving. The choice is yours.

In supportive climates, adults and children enjoy one another.

How the Elements of Support Relate to the Rest of the Curriculum

The elements of support are guidelines adults use to establish and maintain supportive climates in which children generate and construct their own understanding and learning. Therefore, these key elements influence the implementation of every other aspect of the curriculum. In the next chapter, for example, we explore how the principles of sharing control, focusing on strengths, and creating authentic relationships relate to involving families in active learning settings. Similarly, the strategies for enhancing adult teamwork discussed in Chapter 4 are built on the premise that adult teams work most effectively in a supportive climate. Chapter 5, which focuses on arranging and equipping an active learning setting, examines ways adults can share control of physical space with children, so children can find, use, and return the materials they need. Through the daily routine and the plan-do-review process, discussed in Chapters 6, 7, and 8, children have numerous opportunities to initiate ideas and share control over teaching and learning. And finally, the key developmental indicators, discussed in Part 3 of this book, provide adults with a clearer understanding of the general kinds of abilities and interests typical of young children, so adults can accurately interpret and build on them. Thus, together with the ingredients of active learning, the elements of support provide a guiding framework for the discussion of the High/Scope Curriculum that unfolds in the following pages.

Strategies for Creating Supportive Climates: A Summary

Sharing of control between adults and children
___ Adults take cues from children.
___ Adults participate with children on children's terms.
___ Adults learn from children.
___ Adults relinquish control, consciously giving control to children.

Focusing on children's strengths
___ Adults look for children's interests.
___ Adults view situations from the child's perspective.
___ Adults share children's interests with parents and staff.
___ Adults plan around children's strengths and interests.

Forming authentic relationships with children
___ Adults share themselves with children.
___ Adults respond attentively to children's interests.
___ Adults give children specific feedback.
___ Adults ask honest questions and respond to questions honestly.

Making a commitment to supporting children's play
___ Adults observe and understand the complexity of children's play.
___ Adults are playful with children.

Adopting a problem-solving approach to social conflict
___ Adults approach social conflicts calmly and acknowledge children's feelings.
___ Adults gather information and restate the problem.
___ Adults ask for ideas to try, choose one together with the children, and are prepared to give follow-up support.

Given the opportunity to practice working through social conflict in a supportive climate, children learn to trust themselves as problem solvers, to trust adults to assist them when they need it, to be empathic and helpful to others, and to have faith in their capacities to make relationships work.

References

Ainsworth, Mary, D. Salter, Mary C. Blehar, Everett Waters, and Sally Wall. 1978. *Patterns of Attachment: A Psychological Study of the Strange Situation.* Hillsdale, NJ: Erlbaum.

Bowlby, John. 1969. *Attachment. Attachment and Loss,* Vol. 1. New York: Basic Books.

Bronfenbrenner, Urie. 1979. *The Ecology of Human Development.* Cambridge, MA: Harvard University Press.

Curry, Nancy E., and Carl N. Johnson. 1990. *Beyond Self-Esteem: Developing a Genuine Sense of Human Value.* Washington, DC: NAEYC.

Erikson, Erik. 1950. *Childhood and Society.* New York: Norton.

Fromberg, Doris P. 1987. "Play." In *The Early Childhood Curriculum: A Review of Recent Research,* Carol Seefeldt, ed., 35–74. New York: Teachers College Press.

Goleman, Daniel. 1989. "The Roots of Empathy Are Traced to Infancy." *New York Times* (March 28): 20–21 (Section B).

Greenspan, Stanley, and Nancy T. Greenspan. 1985. *First Feelings.* New York: Viking.

Lewis, Michael. 1986. "The Role of Emotion in Development." In *The Feeling Child: Affective Development Reconsidered,* Nancy E. Curry, ed., 7–22. New York: The Haworth Press.

Mahler, Margaret, F. Pine, and A. Bergman. 1975. *The Psychological Birth of the Human Infant.* New York: Basic Books.

Rogers, Carl R. 1983. *The Freedom to Learn for the 80's.* Columbus, OH: Merrill.

Schmoker, Mike. 1989. "The Sentimentalizing of 'Self-Esteem.'" *Education Week* (September 6): 34.

Strayer, Janet. 1986. "Current Research in Affective Development." In *The Feeling Child: Affective Development Reconsidered,* Nancy E. Curry, ed., 37–55. New York: The Haworth Press.

Related Reading

Brickman, Nancy A., ed. 1996. "Adult-Child Interaction." Chap. 1 in *Supporting Young Learners 2: Ideas for Child Care Providers and Teachers,* 3–56. Ypsilanti, MI: High/Scope Press.

Brickman, Nancy A., ed. 2001. "Supportive Adult-Child Interaction." Chap. 1 in *Supporting Young Learners 3: Ideas for Child Care Providers and Teachers,* 1–55. Ypsilanti, MI: High/Scope Press.

Brickman, Nancy A., Holly Barton, and Jennifer Burd, eds. 2005. "Supportive Adult-Child Interaction." Chap. 1 in *Supporting Young Learners 4: Ideas for Child Care Providers and Teachers,* 1–61. Ypsilanti, MI: High/Scope Press.

Dewey, John. 1938. *Experience and Education.* Reprint. New York: Macmillan, 1963.

Evans, Betsy. 2002. *You Can't Come to My Birthday Party! Conflict Resolution With Young Children.* Ypsilanti, MI: High/Scope Press.

Elicker, James and Cheryl Fortner-Wood. 1995. "Adult-Child Relationships in Early Childhood Programs." *Young Children* (November): 69–78.

Epstein, Ann S. 2007. "What Does Adult-Child Interaction Look Like in a High/Scope Program?" Chap. 5 in *Essentials of Active Learning in Preschool: Getting to Know the High/Scope Curriculum,* 25–37. Ypsilanti, MI: High/Scope Press.

Epstein, Ann S. 2007. *The Intentional Teacher: Choosing the Best Strategies for Young Children's Learning.* Washington, DC: NAEYC.

Goleman, Daniel. 1995. *Emotional Intelligence.* New York: Bantam Books.

Graves, Michelle. 2001. "A Child Development Approach to Rules and Limits." In *Supporting Young Learners 3: Ideas for Child Care Providers and Teachers,* 19–30. Ypsilanti, MI: High/Scope Press.

High/Scope Educational Research Foundation. 2003. *Preschool Program Quality Assessment (PQA),* 2nd ed. Ypsilanti, MI: High/Scope Press.

Hohmann, Charles and Warren Buckleitner. 1992. "Interactions That Promote Learning." Chap. 4 in *High/Scope K–3 Curriculum Series: Learning Environment,* 53–78. Ypsilanti, MI: High/Scope Press.

Levin, Diane E. 1994. *Teaching Young Children in Violent Times: Building a Peaceable Classroom.* Cambridge, MA: Educators for Social Responsibility.

Post, Jacalyn, and Mary Hohmann. 2000. "Supportive Adult-Child Interactions." Chap. 2 in *Tender Care and Early Learning: Supporting Infants and Toddlers in Child Care Settings,* 57–95. Ypsilanti, MI: High/Scope Press.

Related Media

The following materials are available from the High/Scope Press, 600 N. River St., Ypsilanti, MI, 48198-2898; to order, visit *www.highscope.org,* or call 1-800-40-PRESS.

Adult-Child Interactions: Forming Partnerships With Children. 1996. Color videotape, 60 min. Ypsilanti, MI: High/Scope Press.

The High/Scope Approach for Under Threes, U.S. Edition. 1999. Color videotape, parts 4–6 "Supportive Styles of Interaction," "Effective Communication," and "Social Conflict" 20 min. London, England: High/Scope Institute U.K. (Available from High/Scope Press, Ypsilanti, MI.)

It's Mine! Responding to Problems and Conflicts (The Tender Care Infant-Toddler Series). 2002. Color videotape or DVD, 40 min. Ypsilanti, MI: High/Scope Press.

Supporting Children in Resolving Conflicts. 1998. Color videotape or DVD, 24 min. Ypsilanti, MI: High/Scope Press.

PARENT BOARD

Children learn to value their own and others' family experiences when teachers build strong ties with parents and incorporate the materials and activities of family life into the preschool setting.

Family as a Frame for Understanding Children

From the day they are born, children live within a family that shapes their beliefs, attitudes, and actions. By striving to understand and respect each child's family, we encourage children to view themselves and others as valued, contributing members of society.

Educator Carol Brunson Phillips (1988) offers a compelling argument for making schools more like homes: "To grow and thrive as adults, children need skills to operate in two cultures—one that will provide them with power and productivity in mainstream America, and one that provides them with a sense of meaning in life, a history, and a home . . . . We must examine the values and beliefs that underlie childrearing practices and ways of being in the world and that influence children's learning styles. We need to figure out how to make our classrooms more like our homes" (p. 47).

Clearly, the impact of family life—in all its complexity—affects every aspect of a child's development. Phillips (1988) defines a family system or culture as involving "all the things that families do to enable their children to know and understand their group's shared ideas about values, beliefs, and behaviors. This participation in a home culture gives the child the power to influence his or her environment and to have an impact on the world" (pp. 46–47). According to Leslie Williams and Yvonne De Gaetano (1985), co-directors of a multicultural early childhood education program called "A Learning Environment Responsive to All (ALERTA)," a family's culture includes everything from food, dance, music, dress, and art, to lifestyle, recreation, social customs, medicine, history, holidays, and language, to religious beliefs, rules, education, attitudes toward others, and childrearing practices.

The High/Scope approach recognizes the important role families play in young children's development. We want children to know who they are—to be well rooted in their home cultures. If we do our jobs well as parents, educators, and caring adults, we will enable children to understand their own families and learn from others. We also want children to know that who they will become is ultimately their responsibility—the result of the choices and decisions they will make for themselves. To achieve these goals, adults implementing the High/Scope Curriculum support children's families by striving to . . .

- Understand children's home cultures

- Create open relationships among adults and children involved in the early childhood setting

- Positively influence the way children see, hear, understand, and learn from their peers

- Empower all children to act confidently and with respect for others based on their own decisions and understanding

In their homes children generally adopt their family's interaction styles and customs. Outside the home, however, where people may speak a different language or dialect, follow different customs, or exhibit different attitudes and behaviors, children may experience the setting as confusing or even hostile. To make children's transition from home to an early childhood

3

Involving Families in Active Learning Settings

The school should grow gradually out of the home life; it should take up and continue the activities with which the child is already familiar in the home . . . It is the business of the school to deepen and extend [the child's] sense of values bound up in his home life.
—John Dewey, 1954

Children are eager for the school day to begin when there is continuity between their preschool and home experiences.

setting as smooth as possible, adults using the High/Scope Curriculum are guided by a belief in the active learning process and the assumption that children develop best in a supportive climate.

Active Learning in Support of Family Involvement

The ingredients of active learning—*materials, manipulation, choice, child language and thought,* and *adult scaffolding*—not only guide High/Scope's approach to children but also to families.

▶ **Materials from home to manipulate**

Children are powerfully motivated to imitate parents and family members: farm children play on hay wagons, children from fishing communities play on boats, and so forth. By knowing about each child's family, adults in early child-hood settings can provide children with the tools and materials they see people using at home. Depending on what is familiar to the particular children in their care, adults can provide appropriate food containers, clothing and accessories, music, and art. If children see adults in their homes or communities weaving, beading, drumming, riding the subway, singing in choir, or playing cards, for example, adults will want to add looms, yarn, beads, drums, subway tokens, sheet music, and cards to the early childhood setting. They will also add carefully selected pictures, books, and magazines so children will see images of families like their own.

▶ **Choices reflecting family life**

Allowing and encouraging children to choose their own ways of buttoning, fixing, mixing, building, pasting, weaving, carrying, and arranging is one way to nurture their view of themselves as people who can do things for themselves and for others. When children make choices about what to play with and how to use materials, they will often make choices that reflect experiences they have had at home and in important family situations. "Here is where we walk and carry flowers," directed 4-year-old Benilda. Her grandmother had died recently, and she and several other children were playing funeral. "Here is where we put the flowers on the dirt and cry."

When children become independent doers and thinkers, they are in a good position to make their own judgments about what works best *for them* and to withstand pressures to accept the solutions of others without trying them out for themselves.

▶ **Home language from children**

Since young children learn best by putting their experiences into their own words, it is important that children be able to share their observations and enthusiasms in the language or dialect they already speak. Adults in early childhood settings make every possible attempt to converse with each child in his or

Stocking the preschool with the real tools children see adults using at home (such as this curling iron with the cord cut off) helps the child re-create home life in her play.

her home language. They can do this by. . .

- Hiring staff who speak the children's home languages

- Involving parents, grandparents, and older siblings as volunteers

- Spending time with non–English-speaking families to learn essential words and phrases

- Learning to speak one of the non-English languages used by children in the classroom

Since we want children to communicate, we want to make it as easy as possible for them to talk with peers and adults in whatever language they speak. Furthermore, the more conversant young children are in their home language, the more easily they will learn a second.

▶ **Respectful support (scaffolding) from adults**

Different families have different interaction styles. By closely observing children and

Adults in early childhood settings make every effort possible to communicate with children in their home languages.

talking with their parents, adults can begin to answer questions such as these:

How much space is enough space for each individual child?

How close or far away do I need to be to support rather than disrupt each child's play?

Which children rely on eye contact, body language, or stillness to gain attention?

Which children prefer little eye contact?

Which children seek out touch? Shun touch?

How do different children signal distress, confusion, sorrow, delight?

When 4-year-old Kera, for example, wanted Miss Kay's attention, she used the non-verbal attention-getting strategies that worked well with her family and relatives. She looked at Miss Kay and glanced down when Miss Kay looked in her direction; she moved very close to Miss Kay; she gently touched Miss Kay's clothing. Miss Kay, on the other hand, attended primarily to children's verbal requests. Often when Kera had worked patiently for 5 minutes to gain Miss Kay's attention, Miss Kay would turn instead to someone like Billy as soon as he called, "Miss Kay! Hey, Miss Kay! Come 'ere. You're not gonna believe this!" Eventually, Miss Kay realized that she was spending very little time with Kera and knew very little about her. When Miss Kay talked to her team member about this, they decided she should begin observing Kera more closely. The more she watched Kera and talked with her team member about what she saw, the more Miss Kay learned to recognize, appreciate, and respond to Kera's quiet communications. As she began to

Children's choices about using materials reflect their home experiences. This child chooses to make "blueberry pancakes" from clay. The children below help themselves to familiar foods at snack time.

All Kinds of Cooking Utensils

baskets	garlic presses	rolling pins
bread pans	graters	skillets
calabashes (gourds)	measuring spoons	stew pots
chopsticks	mixing bowls	tablecloths
clay pots	mortar and pestle	tortilla presses
coffee grinders	pastry molds	wooden spoons
deep fryers	pots and pans	
frying pans	rice bowls	

attend to Kera, Kera's comfort and confidence with talking increased.

It is also important to attend and respond to differences in children's conversational styles. Some children freely associate, jumping from topic to topic in their conversations: "My grandma broke her leg real bad. She was broke in all her money, too, so Auntie Lee, oh her hair is so beautiful, it goes like this, she won't be coming 'cause she lost her job. My daddy's got a job and once he taked me with him." Other children converse about one thing and then stop: "My brother fell on his head. He got stitches an' a spider ring. I didn't get one." It is important for adults to encourage and appreciate both the vitality of the first style and the focus of the second, and to attend to what children are saying regardless of how they say it.

A Supportive Climate for Family Involvement

Achieving comfort with children's families depends on establishing a supportive climate in the educational setting. In Chapter 2 we noted that a supportive climate has certain characteristics—characteristics that can be expanded to include children's families. A supportive climate for family involvement, then, is characterized by shared control between children and adults, a focus on children's and *families'* strengths, authenticity on the part of adults, and a commitment to children's *family-inspired* play.

▶ Shared control between children and adults

To the extent that adults share control with children, they allow children both to interact in familiar ways and to learn new ways of interacting from other children and adults in the early childhood setting. Sharing control allows children to express a variety of beliefs and attitudes. This means that adults do not always have the last word, as three young children in Mr. Levy's care demonstrated during their doll-baby play:

Jana: *I know where babies come from. The stork brings 'em an' then the mommy wakes up.*

Teri: *Oh, that's silly. They come from the mommy's tummy.*

Jana: *No, from the stork. My big brother told me.*

Beth: *Well, it's really like this. The baby gets borned from the mommy's tummy, but then the stork comes from heaven and brings the baby's soul.*

Jana: *Oh!*

Teri: *Okay. Now let's get these babies back to bed.*

▶ Focusing on children's and families' strengths

An emphasis on children's and families' strengths promotes children's self-respect and helps counteract social stereotypes. To understand this point, consider the experience of home visitor Sally W. who worked with a family in an isolated, rural area. Billy and Caroline M. and their children lived in a one-room wooden building with a cement floor

Pictures, books, magazines, and puzzles in the setting should include images of people and situations that children recognize as similar to their own family and community experiences.

and walls covered with newspapers. The yard was home to a variety of dogs and the rusted bodies of pickup trucks.

"When I first started visiting this family," Sally tells home visitors she trains, *"I was terrified. Their lives were so different from mine, I only saw negatives. As I continued to visit them, however, I began to learn how they coped with adversities that I have never had to face. I began to admire the family's strengths—their sense of humor, the way they worked together, their gardening ability, their trapping and hunting skills, and their strong commitment to educating their children. As I saw how these strengths were reflected in their children, I began to see how much each child was capable of and how much each had to offer. I wanted the children to feel strong and proud when they went to public school, and I wanted their teachers to see them as I did."*

In working with children, it is important that we focus on what they and their families *can* do. It is up to the adults who have daily contact with children to look for, inform themselves about, and promote both family strengths and individual strengths, so children, their peers, and the other adults in their lives recognize and value them.

▶ **Authenticity on the part of adults**

Rather than "brush-off" or minimize children's fears and concerns about the differences they notice in people, adults discuss them honestly and directly, in a matter-of-fact tone. This provides children with both a sympathetic listener and useful information about coping with the differences they notice. Adults' genuine attention to children alerts them to children's fears and concerns about differences and

provides children with an understanding conversational partner. The following scenario depicts just such a conversation between an adult and a child who is facing an unsettling situation. The adult seizes the opportunity to explain another child's appearance in terms that make sense to her peers and lead to acceptance.

Lerone: *I don't like that girl. She doesn't have any hair.*

Ms. Holmes: *Marla's hair came out because she was burned in a fire.*

Lerone: *She hurt bad?*

Ms. Holmes: *Yes, she was in the hospital for a long time. But now she can play with her friends again.*

Lerone: *She looks funny.*

Ms. Holmes: *We're used to seeing people with hair, but some people lose their hair.*

Lerone: *Hey! Chauncey [local NBA player] doesn't have hair!*

Ms. Holmes: *No, he doesn't, but he makes lots of baskets and has lots of friends.*

Lerone: *Yeah, he made a hook, then he hugged Rip and gave 'im five! I saw it on TV.*

Ms. Holmes: *Chauncey and Rip are friends.*

Later that day, Ms. Holmes noticed Lerone pushing Marla on the taxi.

▶ **Commitment to children's family-inspired play**

Young children's play often gets to the heart of their lives, reflecting such emotionally charged family situations as births, deaths (of pets and relatives), weddings, funerals, family gatherings, and religious observances.

Four-year-old Kalani's mother, for example, gave birth to Kalani's new brother at home. After her brother's birth, Kalani's doll-play reflected this experience. Another child, 5-year-old Bonnie Lou, often directed her playmates in "visiting daddy." This involved baking "cookies" and a "birthday cake," a long car ride to the "metal hospital," lots of unlocking and locking of "doors," bringing "cookies" and "cake" to daddy, singing Happy Birthday, playing cards, taking a walk to feed the "ducks," eating "clam chowder," and falling asleep on the long ride home "in the nighttime."

When the children asked Bonnie Lou what a "metal hospital" was and why people had to be locked up there, she explained, "It's metal so they can lock the crazy people up and they won't fall out the window and get runned over by a car."

"Is your daddy crazy?" they asked.

"No, he's my daddy!"

"Why's he at the metal hospital then?"

"So he won't be sad. . . . He's happy when he sees me."

"That's why you go visit and take him stuff?"

"Yep!"

The Effects of Valuing Families

When early childhood professionals value diverse family styles and traditions, everyone in the early childhood setting benefits. Some of these benefits are described in the sections that follow.

▶ **Children talk about their families.**

When adults respond positively to children's family experiences and ways of

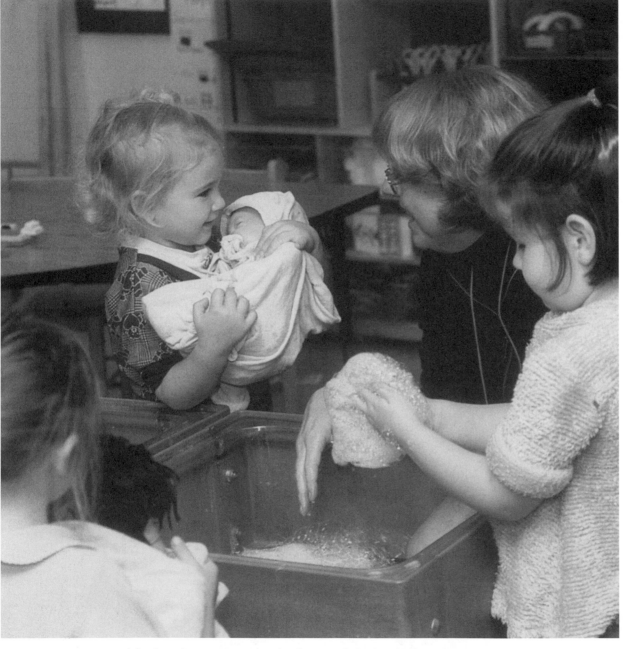

Adults show their commitment to family-inspired play by actively participating in it.

communicating about them, children have the opportunity to talk freely about their families:

- "I have a special way to write my Chinese name."

- "My grandma's gonna tell about that Br'er Rabbit. Can't nobody get him."

- "I miss my daddy at the metal hospital. I'm glad when he gets better and comes home."

▶ **Children explore and appreciate family differences.**

Ignoring differences with statements such as "People are really all the same" distorts reality and inhibits children's natural curiosity. When respect for family traditions is embedded in the early childhood setting, children have the opportunity to explore and appreciate the differences they notice:

Aaron: *We don't put a tree in our house! We light the candles and get presents for all the days we have the candles.*

Talitha: *Hey, I'm gonna tell my mom about that 'cause we only just get presents on one day!*

▶ **Children and adults see each other in a positive light.**

When adults recognize children's strengths, other children do so as well.

"I know who can help us," Nealey says to Villete. "Renata is real good at puzzles."

"That little tiny girl with the long black hair down to here?"

"Yeah, she can do puzzles faster than anyone. Hey, Renata . . ."

While children are free to express their fears about one another's differences, they also

Bringing Family Art to Early Childhood Settings

When Mrs. Lukosavitz discovered that 4-year-old An-Mei was learning the art of Chinese calligraphy and how to "hold the brushes very lightly," she arranged to call on An-Mei's grandmother and observe one of An-Mei's "lessons." Once Mrs. Lukosavitz found out what kinds of paper, inks, and pens were used, she added them to the art corner to support An-Mei and to encourage her to share her experiences with the other children.

∾

One day, Joseph told his child care mom, Maria, that "Uncle Tundye from Nigeria" was staying at his house with "all his big, big pictures." In talking with Joseph's mom, who was helping Tundye sell his paintings, Maria arranged to have Tundye visit. During his visit, he made the children a special painting and told them a story about anansi, the spider. For many days after, the children enjoyed painting large "anansi pictures" with lots of "big parts of black and red and yellow like Tundye's from Nigeria."

have the opportunity to appreciate each person's abilities—whether for painting pictures, building towers, helping on the computer, making up songs, being the mommy, or figuring out how to fit all the large Tinkertoys back in the box.

▶ **Children are free to use their energies on growth and development.**

Children's anxieties are diminished when adults greet children in their home languages, when children find similarities between their homes and

When materials reflecting family life are available in the setting, children learn about other children's family experiences (like tent camping) that are different from their own.

their early childhood settings, when adults concentrate on what children *can* do rather than on what they cannot, and when adults encourage children to observe and talk about differences matter-of-factly. In such a supportive atmosphere, they can attend fully to the matters at hand and enjoy the energy and camaraderie of the people around them.

Strategies for Supporting Family Involvement: Four Key Elements

Adults implementing the High/Scope Curriculum want children to feel comfortable and secure as they move between the home and early childhood setting. The following family support strategies will help adults ease this transition for children:

- **Knowing yourself and your family's roots, beliefs, and attitudes**

- **Learning from children and families about their particular styles and traditions**

- **Creating positive relationships with others**

- **Anticipating excellence from each child**

As with the ingredients of active learning, the elements of a supportive climate, and other strategies in this curriculum, the strategies presented in this section apply to adults whenever and wherever they find themselves teaching and caring for children. The strategies influence every adult-child interaction in these circumstances.

Knowing Yourself, and Your Family's Roots, Beliefs, and Attitudes

To understand the family practices, beliefs, and attitudes of the children we serve, we need to know who *we* are and what influences *our* perceptions of other families. We have found the following strategies to be helpful in setting such an examination in motion. Using these strategies on your own or introducing them at teacher meetings, workshops, or parent get-togethers can assist you in understanding the roots of your beliefs about yourself and others.

▶ **List family origins.**

One way to begin is with family origins. Where were you, your parents, grandparents, and great-grandparents born? You may be surprised by the regional and national diversity within your own family tree.

▶ **Examine your "whats, hows, and whys."**

To help you become aware of your own family's influence on you, Williams and De Gaetano (1985) suggest analyzing your own

Sharing personal "whats, whys, and hows" of one's own family life at a team meeting or inservice helps teachers be aware of how their family experiences can influence their values and daily behavior.

values, beliefs, customs, and daily lifestyle in terms of three simple categories: *what*, *how*, and *why*. Ask yourself the following questions:

What things are really important to me? What kinds of music, food, clothing, art, and dance make me feel comfortable, secure, "at home"?

How do I behave as a parent, family member, friend? How do I commonly act when ill, having fun, or celebrating holidays or special occasions like weddings? How do I express myself at home, at work?

Why do I behave a certain way, believe what I believe, adopt particular attitudes? What religious, educational, historical, legal, and social beliefs are important to me?

▶ **Be aware of personal filters.**

When we look closely at ourselves and our family experiences, we can begin to see that

who we are and what we believe influences the way we interact with both children and adults. One staff member, for example, realized that her fondness for wearing casual clothing to work so she could play comfortably on the floor with children might be taken as a sign of disrespect or personal laziness by some parents who were expected to dress more formally for their jobs. Once she realized this, she took more care about her appearance at the beginning and end of each day. She also realized that she tended to pay more attention to children who talked a lot. Therefore, she gradually learned to attend more often to less talkative children. She also decided that she wanted to be more patient with families who were more rushed or pessimistic than she.

By recognizing and appreciating our own strengths and personal filters, we can also begin to realize that most of the people with whom we have daily contact are guided by a slightly or radically different set of "whats, hows, and whys." By identifying the beliefs that shape our own lives, we can begin to seek out and understand the beliefs that shape the lives of the children in our care, and their families.

Learning From Children and Families About Their Styles and Traditions

It is not possible to "grow" people unless you nurture their roots. You cannot lead them into the future without treasuring the past.

—Martin Luther King, Jr.

As important as it is to know ourselves, it is just as important to understand the families of the children we serve. Understanding children's "whats, hows, and whys" enables adults to provide familiar materials and adopt comfortable

interaction styles that make children feel welcome and secure in early childhood settings. Here are some strategies for learning about children's families.

▶ **Conduct home visits.**

Visiting families in their homes is one of the best ways to learn about their values and the aspirations they have for their children. To fully appreciate the value of home visits, we return to Sally W., the home visitor introduced on page 72. Sally's visits to the M. family are part of a county-wide child development program in which home visits with young children and their families are the main program activity. Each week Sally drives to the family's home and spends an hour or so talking with parents Caroline and Billy (when Billy is available) about their immediate concerns for their children. She also engages the adults and the under-school-aged children in an active learning experience. The kinds of active learning experiences she chooses are increasingly shaped by what she learns about how the family lives and what they value.

"One of the first things I noticed," Sally recalls, "was that there were no 'typical' toys for the children to play with—no dolls, cars, crayons, wheel toys, puzzles. And yet, whenever I visited, the little ones were usually engaged in some play activity—for example, picking up rocks and stones, putting them in an old bucket, and then dumping the stones out again. Once when I arrived, everyone was watching $3\frac{1}{2}$-year-old Sammy write in the dirt. Of course, Sammy wasn't really writing, but he thought he was, just as any $3\frac{1}{2}$-year-old would write by making important-looking lines and squiggles.

"Realizing that the family had no money for commercial toys and that the children had a great capacity to play contentedly with whatever

was at hand, I decided to rely on 'found' materials and the children's ingenuity for my home visit activities. One day, for example, we made little dolls out of sticks and baling twine, and Caroline supplied some material scraps from her sewing basket supplies. The next week when I arrived, there were not only more stick dolls but also walnut dolls, and handkerchief dolls, and even a doll one of the older boys had whittled. We played for weeks with those dolls—building them houses out of boxes and newspaper. We added farm animals and furniture that we made from all kinds of odds and ends—matchboxes, toilet-paper tubes, cereal boxes. Billy even made a special shelf to store all these treasures.

"I also brought books for the family to read together from the county library, but the library was so far away that the family rarely got there on their own. Then, during one of my visits, the children persuaded Caroline to tell one of her stories about what she used to do when she was a little girl, so I could hear it. She told a spellbinding story about how she used to bring the cows home for her dad at milking time and how one time she was chased up a tree by the neighbor's bull. I was so excited, I asked her if I could record her story during my next visit. She agreed, and after I recorded her story, I took it home, typed it out on my computer in a big, kindergarten-sized font, and printed it out. On my next visit, I brought watercolor paints, brushes, and paper so the children could illustrate Caroline's story. When everything was finished, we punched holes and tied the story and pictures together into a book. After that, bookmaking became a regular practice with us. Sometimes even the older children got involved between visits."

On a home visit, this child shows her teacher photographs of her family.

Home visits provide enjoyable opportunities for children to share with their teacher things that are special to them—toys, books, pets.

It is clear that the more Sally learned about the family from her weekly visits, the more she was able to incorporate their strengths and interests into her active learning goals.

► **Build home visits into home child care and center-based programs.**

In contrast to home visit programs like Sally W.'s, most early childhood programs are conducted outside of children's homes. In these center-based programs, it is vital that the adults who teach and care for the children make a concerted effort to visit each family before or during the child's first few weeks in the program. Such a visit allows adults to see children at home where they are most comfortable and to learn about the things they particularly enjoy.

Center-based programs generally set aside time at the beginning and end of each enrollment period for home visits. Home visits often require scheduling flexibility, especially when children come from a distance and parents work. One child care provider resolved this problem by accepting only those children who had received a home visit. She found that when parents had this incentive, they usually found a mutually agreeable time for a home visit.

Once home-visit logistics are established, it is important to build rapport, put family members at ease, and find out about each family's strengths, values, and desires for their children. Each adult will approach these home-visit goals differently, depending on who they are and the techniques they use to put other people at ease. If you are new to home visiting, or you are anxious about meeting new families for the first time, think back for a moment to the strategies for establishing a supportive learning climate (see Establishing a Supportive Climate With Parents, p. 79). These strategies

can guide your interactions with parents as well as with children.

One High/Scope teaching team, Mr. Milton and Mrs. Ernal, carried out their initial home visits by setting aside two-and-one-half days to go together to each of the homes of the 18 children in their urban, center-based program. They called each family to ask if they could visit, explaining that they wanted to meet each child and family in the setting where they were most at home in order to help ease the child's transition from home to center. Through this call they were able to set up a 30- to 45-minute visit with each family.

Because they went as a team, once they had exchanged greetings and introductions, Mr. Milton was able to focus on the child (or children) and Mrs. Ernal, on the parent. After getting information and requesting help ("Can we include your address and phone number on the class list?" "Would you like to accompany us on field trips?" "Would you be able to care for the class guinea pig on weekends or holidays?"), they talked about things the family liked to do together and things the children liked to do. Whenever Mrs. Ernal made notes on a blank sheet of paper, she would say something such as, "What a good idea! Let me write that down" or "I'm going to jot that down so I won't forget." When she and Mr. Milton went with the children

When the teacher takes notes about the interests of the child and her family, she shows them to parents so they can see that she is not making judgments about the family's lifestyle.

to see where they usually played, Mrs. Ernal always left her page of notes out so parents could see for themselves that she really was only writing down what she said she was and not making judgments about their home or lifestyle. Here are some of the notes Mrs. Ernal made on this series of visits:

Kestin—Has been with her family for 6 months, being adopted. Likes dolls. (Make sure dolls are immediately visible.)

Athi—Has lots of toy vehicles. Likes to build, take things apart, and fix them with real tools. (Open construction area.) Dad plays guitar and sings. (Available to play for children on Friday mornings.)

Joel—Likes to dance. (Have CDs and player available.)

Alexis—Grandmother works at Terri's Bakery (close enough for field trip).

Boomer—Noodle-maker (mother will bring and make noodles with the children).

Knut and Bjarne—Grandmother raises chicks (will bring baby chicks in a few weeks).

Tara—Came out in sari, put on Indian music, and danced for us. (Add saris to house area, Indian music CD to music area.)

Juan—Just arrived from Colombia, speaks only Spanish. Family speaks Spanish, although father speaks English (he's from New York). (Speak Spanish with Juan and help interpret messages to and from other children.)

▶ **Participate in community life.**

After these initial home visits, Mr. Milton and Mrs. Ernal continued to learn about their children's families through potlucks, parent get-togethers and meetings, phone calls, talking with parents as they dropped off and picked up their children, and subsequent home visits. Since they both lived in the same community as the families they served, they also had the opportunity over the course of the year to meet families at

religious services, the gym, the grocery store, the farmers' market, local meetings, school meetings for their older children, the health clinic, the dentist, the library, the ice cream parlor, the bowling alley, the fishing dock, the pool, the roller rink, local restaurants, and the county fair. At the local Heritage Festival, for example, they watched Knut and Bjarne's dad and aunt dancing with a Swedish folk dance group and invited them to the early childhood center to dance with the children.

▶ **Observe children closely every day.**

Visiting homes and participating in community life are vital ways to learn about children's families, but they usually are not everyday activities. Observing children is something that adults who teach and care for children can do on a daily basis. Each day, adults can observe children's play and interaction styles, listen to how they express themselves and what they talk about, and learn about the specific things that interest each child. Mrs. Lukosavitz, for example, discovered

This father, an engineer, volunteered to show children how rope can be made from twisted tissue.

"I'll bring a salad!" Potlucks and other family events strengthen relationships with families.

A parent board is another way to reach out to families. Materials posted include a daily routine chart, children's art, announcements of events, requests for materials from home, and a sign-up sheet for volunteers.

An-Mei's knowledge of Chinese calligraphy by watching and listening to her as she worked with art materials (see Bringing Family Art to Early Childhood Settings on p. 75). One day An-Mei took a small watercolor brush and some black tempera paint to the table and began making very light and deliberate brush strokes. "What is that?" asked Anthony, who was sitting next to her and making a Batman mask. "That's my name," she replied. "That's not your name," laughed Anthony. "Your name starts with *A* like *Anthony*." "No," she said. "This is my Chinese name. My grandma is teaching me." "Oh," said Anthony, studying the lines closely. "What's my Chinese name?" "You don't have a Chinese name," replied An-Mei. Anthony paused in

concern and then brightened, "Well, ask your grandma if she can make me one." "Okay," An-Mei replied with a smile. When An-Mei's grandmother came to visit, she translated each child's name into Chinese characters.

▶ **Reach out to families.**

In addition to visiting families, participating in community life, and observing children each day, adults can also reach out to families to make them feel welcome at the early childhood setting. Here are some strategies that can help staff do this:

Share anecdotes. Begin conversations with family members with an anecdote or story that illustrates their child's abilities. For example,

"Mrs. Baines, let me tell you what Lynnette did today. She spent all of work time in the block area building a large building with lots of rooms for animals and people."

Plan family gatherings. Invite families to an open house or family potluck. Family members can see the early childhood setting and meet staff and other families.

Publicly acknowledge families' importance to your program. One full-day program in New York City did this by filling a bulletin board with photographs of each parent/guardian accompanied by a brief descriptive caption. For example,

Gloria Galeano, mother of Maria (toddler group) and Eduardo (preschool)—When she isn't working

or going to nursing school, she loves to sew. She made the beautiful animal quilt in the toddlers' doll corner. Thanks, Gloria!

❧

Jack Rizzo, father of Vince (preschool)—As you can see, Jack likes motorcycles and so does Vince. His job keeps him busy so he doesn't ride much anymore. Whenever he's in town he spends a few hours with us in the block area. He makes great car and truck sounds!

❧

Rayanne James, mother of twins Rayette and Rayelle (toddler group)—Another set of twins at home keeps Rayanne very busy. How does she do it! Rayette and Rayelle are very excited about their new brothers.

Converse with family members at drop-off/pickup. Make the most of the daily opportunities to speak with family members when they drop off and pick up their children. Staff members of one full-day program in Dayton, Ohio, for example, not only make a point of speaking to family members at these times but also encourage them to spend a few minutes with their child in the center at the end of the day to ease the transition from center to home. It is not unusual to see a father sitting on the floor working on one last puzzle with his daughter, a boy leading his mom to the sandbox to see his roads and bridges, and a mom in a rocking chair giving 7-month-old Jinnie her late afternoon bottle. "It makes it so much easier on both of us when I

feed Jinnie here," her mother says. "When we leave, we've already spent time together. I've already been able to feed and cuddle her, and we both arrive home comfortable and relaxed—instead of Jinnie screaming with hunger and frustration."

Encourage family members to join their children on their lunch hours. In a downtown Pittsburgh center, for example, parents come for lunch hour in their work clothes and, depending on their arrival time and the schedule of their child's group, they either feed their infants, have

Taking the time to talk with family members at drop-off and pickup times helps to build positive, trusting relationships.

lunch with their preschoolers, play on the playground, or read a naptime story. "I really feel cheated when I have to miss a lunch hour with Ricky," remarks one dad.

Send home brief anecdotal notes. One early childhood staff member in Milton Keynes, England, for example, developed what they call a *Home Link Book.* Made of $8\frac{1}{2}$" × 11" paper folded in half with a construction paper cover bearing the child's name, a copy of this book goes back and forth with each child each day. At some point during the day, a staff member makes a brief, dated entry like this one:

Monday 18th January. Stephen thought up the idea of turning the house area into a fish-and-chip shop. He used straws for chips and shells as fish. It was a brilliant idea, soon copied by the other children.

Stephen's mom writes back:

Stephen has been talking about his "zipper coat" and what he has been doing there at the house area. I have a suggestion for used Christmas cards. Stick them on a thin card [piece of cardboard] and make a jigsaw puzzle by marking them in four, six, or eight sections. Cut them out.

Send home a newsletter on a regular basis. Include specific anecdotes about each child. For example:

On our field trip to the apple orchard on Tuesday, Nicole found a bird's nest and said, "It's full of sticks and prickles." Ramon caught a cricket and carefully brought it back in his apple bag . . . .

Encourage family members to join you and the children on outings and field trips. This provides many opportunities for parents, children, and staff to converse, enjoy one anothers' company, and share active learning experiences.

Encouraging parents to participate in field trips is another way to build bonds with program families.

Creating Positive Relationships Between Yourself and Others

Knowing yourself, the children in your program, and their families paves the way for the creation of positive relationships. Although it may be easier to maintain such relationships with people who have views and experiences similar to your own, it is essential that adults in early childhood settings strive to relate openly and honestly to all children and families. Here are some strategies for building such relationships.

▶ Accept and trust others.

One way to build trusting relationships is to see yourself and others as members of the human family. Think of the people in your immediate or extended family—your mate, your child, your mother, your friend, your Aunt Lou. Now, as you look at people in a parent meeting or a staff meeting, imagine each one as someone else's mate, child, mother, friend, or aunt—someone who is as important to others as each of your family members is to you. From this perspective, it makes sense to approach the families of the children in your care with the respect and care you hope others would extend to your immediate family.

▶ Value human differences.

The array of human differences is vast. It is important to realize, however, that the way we respond to difference is partly a matter of choice. We choose, for example, how we respond to families that include people who are blind or deaf, use a wheelchair, have a different skin color, shave their heads, prefer people of the same sex, or eat foods we have never tasted. When we

choose to fear or ignore such differences, we build barricades. But if we choose to value differences, we allow ourselves to reach out to others and learn from them.

Adults can help children learn to value the differences they notice. For example, when 4-year-old Martin tried to rub all the brown off Waleed's skin, Waleed said, "No, I'm brown like my daddy." "You're right, Waleed," agreed Mrs. Rivera, supporting the interchange. "Every person has skin of a beautiful color. You get your skin color from your mom and dad when you are born." "Oh," said Martin, perhaps considering how to incorporate this new idea into his old way of seeing Waleed's skin.

▶ Focus on people's strengths.

When adults focus on strengths, children are encouraged to do the same. Mrs. Ernal and Mr. Milton, for example, viewed Juan, a child newly arrived from Colombia, as a lively, alert, social child. Yet Juan had become frustrated because he could not talk and joke with his preschool peers as he had done in Colombia. Mrs. Ernal and Mr. Milton wanted the English-speaking children to view Juan as an important member of their team of playmates. Therefore, in introducing him, they focused on Juan's intense desire to communicate rather than on his frustration with English. They spoke Spanish with him, translated for him, and encouraged the other children to use Juan's Spanish words and phrases. Eventually, Juan became more familiar with his new setting and the English language, and as his peers became more familiar with his Spanish language, Juan's ease with and enjoyment of preschool activities grew.

▶ Communicate clearly and honestly.

We communicate with our whole bodies. Therefore, it is important for children and families that we say the same thing with our words as we say with our facial expressions and actions. By being aware of what we say and how we act, we can convey positive messages to children about themselves and their peers. Monica, for example, spends a lot of time sitting on the floor playing with children, watching them, reading to them, singing, and so forth. Children often settle comfortably in her

The opportunity to play basketball at outside time, like their older siblings do in the driveway at home, communicates to children that family activities are valued at preschool.

lap. Because she wants to send the message that all children are equally welcome, she is very conscious of cuddling and attending to each child she holds. Whoever sits in her lap receives the same unspoken message: "I'm glad you're here with me." In the same manner, whenever Monica meets parents, she gives them her full attention and lets them know she is glad to talk with them about their children.

Anticipating Excellence From Each Child

Since children are influenced by adult expectations, it is our responsibility to anticipate the very best from each child in our care. Here are some strategies to consider in helping children excel:

▶ Avoid labeling and stereotyping children and families.

As early childhood educators, it is important from the start that we focus on, encourage, and alert others to children's strengths rather than burden children with labels that limit their own and other people's belief in their innate capacities and abilities.

Avoid referring to children as "disadvantaged," "developmentally delayed," "not ready for kindergarten," "immature," "aggressive," "language-impaired," "quiet little girl," "rowdy boy," "wild," "deprived." Choose positive, specific, descriptive words— words that highlight children's strengths—"active," "involved in role play," "detailed story teller," "problem solver," "effective nonverbal communicator," "inter-

ested in letters," "able planner," "rhymer," "wagon puller."

▶ Regard each child as competent.

By regarding each child as a capable individual, adults help unlock the child's potential. It is our responsibility to look for and recognize each child's special gifts and, to the extent possible, to help each child develop these special skills.

▶ Assume that each child will succeed.

Expect children to be capable individuals— successful planners, decision makers, role players, explorers, block builders. Maintain a supportive active learning setting where children can succeed. In a special education program in Marysville, Michigan, some preschoolers used wheelchairs, some crawled, some wore hearing aids, some were mute. Their teacher's initial response to the High/Scope approach was skeptical: "Active learning, shared control, problem solving—these approaches will never work with my kids!" By focusing primarily on the children's disabilities, the teacher was not recognizing their potential for

Parents are welcome to join in as adults read with children at the beginning of the day.

success. However, once she gave the children materials to manipulate, the opportunity to make choices and to talk in whatever way they could about what they were doing, she was overwhelmed by their enthusiasm, involvement, and excitement. Language, or as close as each child could come to it, poured out of the children (whereas before, when language learning was approached mainly through drills, very few children had shown much inclination to communicate verbally). Once she opened the door to active learning, the teacher learned from the children themselves about their many strengths and abilities.

Understanding our own motivations and attitudes, learning about children and families, creating positive relationships, anticipating excellence in others as well as ourselves—these are the elements of family support. These elements enable adults and children to think well of themselves and their peers, to appreciate the contributions and strengths of others, and to proceed in the knowledge that they are unique and valued members of the human family.

Using the Elements of Family Support: Two Examples

Here are two examples of how to use the elements of family support to (1) deal with *conflicting approaches to setting limits for children,* and (2) guide *observations of children.*

▶ **Example 1: Setting limits for children**

In any learning environment, children need adults to set clear and reasonable limits, so they can carry out their plans and ideas safely and enjoyably. It is not unusual, given our family differences, for adults to disagree on how to set and maintain such limits. For example, a teacher may be committed to a problem-solving approach to setting limits for children, while a child's family relies on a more traditional punishment-and-reward approach. How can the elements of family support help in this type of situation?

Review your own definition of "setting limits." Recall your childhood experiences. How were limits set for you as a child? Who set them? Who enforced them? Were they consistent? Unpredictable? How did you respond? An examination of these types of childhood experiences makes you aware of the origins of your expectations about setting limits. It also enables you to reconstruct the thoughts and feelings behind the choices about limit-setting you have made as an adult and early childhood professional.

Learn how children's families set limits. On a home visit or at a parent meeting, find out from parents how they set limits, how *their* parents set limits for them as children, and how they responded. You will probably find that as children, the parents in your program were punished, left to set their own limits, or experienced some kind of help in sorting out conflicts.

Create positive relationships with families over the issue of limit-setting. Once you recall your own experiences and have learned about the experiences of the parents of the children in your care, you are on the way to creating a positive relationship with parents around the issue of setting limits. Once you have conversed with parents and know something about their upbringing, perhaps even sharing some similar childhood experiences, parents are no longer on "the other side of the issue." Instead, you can begin to appreciate and comment on their strengths—their concern for their children's well-being, their advocacy on the children's behalf, their willingness to talk about difficult issues, their honesty in sharing their own experiences. You can also be clear and honest about why your approach to limit-setting focuses on problem solving—you want to give children opportunities to learn from their mistakes and feel good about resolving their own conflicts, cleaning up their spills, and finding alternatives to annoying behavior.

Although you and the parents may never achieve universal agreement, talking together honestly about limit-setting allows you all to share your views and the reasons behind them, and to begin to trust that both of you want what is best for the children.

Anticipate excellence from children and families. Assume that your relationship with parents will continue to develop positively. Keep them up to date on the children's interests and accomplishments. Instead of thinking of a particular parent as "difficult," or "uninformed," think about his or her strengths—a quick mind, a willingness to try new things, a sense of humor, generosity. Focus on these strengths and assume that by working closely together you will succeed in bringing out the best in his or her child.

▶ **Example 2: Observing and supporting a child's family experiences**

Each time you learn something about the "whats, hows, and whys" of a child's family, write it down and share it with your team members so you can begin to incorporate your knowledge into your daily plans and interactions. Here are the notes one team made about Billy's family experiences:

8/30   Father from Nigeria. Mother and Billy born in South Carolina. Moved here so parents could teach and do graduate work at the university. Billy has traveled to Nigeria with his parents and has also lived in Washington, DC. Parents value education highly. Want Billy to be stimulated and allowed to work at his own fast pace.

9/11   Brought in recording of "drum music to play for cleanup time." This stimulated a lot of conversation about drums. Billy showed how you played these drums with your hands, not with sticks.

10/4   Although he is very verbal and imaginative, Billy is very attuned to other children's nonverbal behavior. "Hey, Mrs. Millete, Kera needs you. Look at her face lookin' at you that way."

10/20   He and Joey mixed brown, black, and white paint to get the color that was the same as their skin.

11/6   Drew a picture for his momma and dictated, "This is me eatin' greens. And this is my baby brother with no teeth yet. No greens for him, just milk and mushy stuff."

11/9   Very excited about getting his Chinese name from An-Mei's grandmother. Spent a long time learning to make the Chinese characters.

12/5   At snack time, Billy told about how his grandma is coming in on his birthday to tell the story of Bruh Alligator and Bruh Rabbit. "Bruh means brother in Gullah," he translated when he saw the puzzled look on Vanessa's face.

The Elements of Family Support and the Rest of the Curriculum

The elements of support for family involvement—*knowing yourself, learning from others, creating positive relationships*, and *anticipating excellence from each child*—expand a supportive climate and influence every other aspect of the High/Scope Curriculum. Chapter 4, Working in Teams, focuses on how teamwork is guided by these very elements: self-awareness, knowledge of others, positive relationships, and anticipation of success based on mutual respect. As teams plan for children, they consider everything they know about each child's family, what makes her or him comfortable and secure, and what things each child enjoys doing. In Chapter 5, Arranging and Equipping Spaces for Active Learners, adult teams take children's families into account so children will find familiar materials as well as pictures and books about people like themselves in the learning environment. Chapters 6, 7, and 8, which deal with the High/Scope daily routine, illustrate many natural opportunities for children to work and play with other children—some of whom are similar and some of whom are different. Adults learn how to support and encourage children's interest in their peers throughout the day. Chapters 9–22 describe High/Scope key developmental indicators and discuss how adults may encourage children to follow their own interests and talk about their pursuits in the language and style that makes the most sense to them.

An understanding of the important influences of the family on children's education, along with the ingredients of active participatory learning and the elements of support, is integral to understanding the rest of the curriculum as it unfolds in the following chapters.

In an early childhood environment that is welcoming to families, parents feel comfortable pausing to chat at the beginning of the day.

Strategies for Supporting Family Involvement: A Summary

Knowing yourself and your family's roots, beliefs, and attitudes

___ List family origins.

___ Examine family "whats, hows, and whys."

___ Be aware of personal filters.

Learning from children and families about their styles and traditions

___ Conduct home visits.

___ Build home visits into home child care and center-based programs.

___ Participate in community life.

___ Observe children closely every day.

___ Reach out to families.

Creating positive relationships between yourself and others

___ Accept and trust others.

___ Value human differences.

___ Focus on people's strengths.

___ Communicate clearly and honestly.

Anticipating excellence from each child

___ Avoid labeling and stereotyping children and families.

___ Regard each child as competent.

___ Assume that each child will succeed.

At drop-off time, this father is comfortable staying to read for a few minutes with his children and knows he is welcome to take part in the message board activity that follows.

References

Dewey, John. 1954. "John Dewey." In *Three Thousand Years of Educational Wisdom: Selections From Great Documents*, Robert Ulrich, ed., 615–40. Cambridge: Harvard University Press.

Hale-Benson, Janice E. 1986. *Black Children: Their Roots, Culture, and Learning Styles*. Baltimore: Johns Hopkins University Press.

Phillips, Carol Brunson. 1988. "Nurturing Diversity for Today's Children and Tomorrow's Leaders." *Young Children* (January): 42–47.

Williams, Leslie R., and Yvonne De Gaetano. 1985. *ALERTA: A Multicultural, Bilingual Approach to Teaching Young Children*. Menlo Park, CA: Addison-Wesley.

Related Reading

Adams, Marilyn, and Bonnie Freeman. 1991. "Multicultural Education." In *Supporting Young Learners*, Nancy A. Brickman and Lynn S. Taylor, eds., 47–52. Ypsilanti, MI: High/Scope Press.

Banks, Nita. 2001. "Involving Parents in Curriculum Planning: A Head Start Story." In *Supporting Young Learners 3: Ideas for Child Care Providers and Teachers*, Nancy A. Brickman, ed., 333–40. Ypsilanti, MI: High/Scope Press.

Brickman, Nancy A., ed. 2001. "Collaborating With Parents." Chap. 7 in *Supporting Young Learners 3: Ideas for Child Care Providers and Teachers*, 307–42. Ypsilanti, MI: High/Scope Press.

Brickman, Nancy A., ed. 1996. "The Family Connection." Chap. 4 in *Supporting Young Learners 2*, 145–74. Ypsilanti, MI: High/Scope Press.

Bronfenbrenner, Urie. 1979. *The Ecology of Human Development: Experiments by Nature and Design*. Cambridge: Harvard University Press.

Center for the Future of Young Children. The David and Lucile Packard Foundation. 1993. *The Future of Young Children: Home Visiting 3*, no. 3 (Winter).

Derman-Sparks, Louise. 1989. *Anti-Bias Curriculum: Tools for Empowering Young Children*. Washington, DC: NAEYC.

Elkind, David. 1995. "School and Family in the Postmodern Work." *Phi Delta Kappan* (September): 8–14.

Epstein, Ann S. 2007. "How Do High/Scope Programs Work With Parents?" Chap. 8 in *Essentials of Active Learning in Preschool: Getting to Know the High/Scope Curriculum*, 81–88. Ypsilanti, MI: High/Scope Press.

Graves, Michelle. 2000. *The Teacher's Idea Book 4: The Essential Parent Workshop Resource*. Ypsilant, MI: High/Scope Press.

Hale, Janice E. 1994. *Unbank the Fire: Visions for the Education of African American Children*. Baltimore: Johns Hopkins University Press.

High/Scope Educational Research Foundation. 2003. *Preschool Program Quality Assessment (PQA)*, 2nd ed. Ypsilanti, MI: High/Scope Press.

Hill, Robert B. 1972. *The Strengths of Black Families*. New York: Emerson Hall.

Hilliard, Asa G. 1989. "Cultural Style in Teaching and Learning." *The Education Digest 55*, no. 4 (December): 21–22.

Hohmann, Mary, Bernard Banet, and David P. Weikart. 1979. "Working With Parents." In *Young Children in Action*, 20–31. Ypsilanti, MI: High/Scope Press.

Kendall, Frances E. 1983. *Diversity in the Classroom: A Multicultural Approach to the Education of Young Children*. New York: Teachers College Press.

Kruse, Tricia S., with Polly Neill. 2006. *Building a High/Scope Program: Multicultural Programs*. Ypsilanti, MI: High/Scope Press.

Markley, Carol. 2001. "Preparing for Successful Parent Conferences." In *Supporting Young Learners 3: Ideas for Child Care Providers and Teachers*, Nancy A. Brickman, ed., 325–32. Ypsilanti, MI: High/Scope Press.

Marshall, Beth. 1996. "Classrooms That Reflect Family Experiences." In *Supporting Young Learners 2*, Nancy A. Brickman, ed., 137–42. Ypsilanti, MI: High/Scope Press.

Morrow, Robert D. 1987. "What's in a Name? In Particular, a Southeast Asian Name?" *Young Children* (September): 20–23.

Neugebauer, Bonnie, ed. 1987. *Alike and Different: Exploring Our Humanity With Young Children*. Redmond, WA: Exchange Press.

Olmsted, Patricia P., and David P. Weikart. 1994. *Families Speak: Early Childhood Care and Education in 11 Countries*. Ypsilanti, MI: High/Scope Press.

Olmsted, Patricia P., and Marilyn Adams Jacobson. 1991. "Parent Involvement: It's Worth the Effort." In *Supporting Young Learners*, Nancy A. Brickman and Lynn S. Taylor, eds., 237–48. Ypsilanti, MI: High/Scope Press.

Phillips, Carol Brunson. 1994. "The Movement of African-American Children Through Sociocultural Contexts." In *Diversity and Developmentally Appropriate Practices: Challenges for Early Childhood Education*, Bruce Malloy and Rebecca S. New, eds., 137–54. New York: Teachers College Press.

Polakow, Valerie. 1993. *Lives on the Edge*. Chicago: University of Chicago Press.

Post, Jacalyn, and Mary Hohmann. 2000. "The Caregiver Team and Their Partnership With Parents." Chap. 5 in *Tender Care and Early Learning: Supporting Infants and Toddlers in Child Care Settings*, 295–355. Ypsilanti, MI: High/Scope Press.

Ramsey, Patricia G. 1987. *Teaching and Learning in a Diverse World: Multicultural Education for Young Children*. New York: Teachers College Press.

Romero, Martha. 1981. "Multicultural Reality: The Pain of Growth." *The Personnel and Guidance Journal* (February): 384–86.

Rosegren, Karl, Douglas Behrend, and Marion Perlmutter. 1993. "Parental Influences on Children's Cognition." In *Emerging Themes in Cognitive Development*, Vol. 2: *Competencies*, Robert Posnak and Mark L. Howe, eds., 103–27. New York: Springer-Verlag.

Saracho, Olive, and Bernard Spodek. 1983. *Understanding the Multicultural Experience in Early Childhood Education*. Washington, DC: NAEYC.

Schweinhart, Lawrence, and Shannan McNair. 1991. "Using Anecdotal Notes With Parents." *High/Scope Extensions* (November/December): 4.

Simonson, Rick, and Scott Walker, eds. 1988. *The Graywolf Annual Five: Multicultural Literacy, Opening the American Mind*. St. Paul, MN: Graywolf Press.

Ongoing adult teamwork sets the stage for children's participation in an active and cooperative community.

4

Working in Teams: Adult Collaboration to Promote Active Learning

Understanding Teamwork

In implementing the High/Scope Curriculum, adults work in teams to support children's active participatory learning. Team members share a commitment to the educational approach and work together to exchange accurate information about children, design curriculum strategies, and evaluate the strategies' effectiveness. Team members strive to deepen their understanding of the curriculum and of individual children so they can provide a setting that is both consistent with their goals and beliefs about learning and consistent in implementation from one adult to another.

In applying the High/Scope Curriculum, effective teamwork . . .

• Creates a supportive climate for adults so the support and trust they feel among themselves pervades their interactions with the children

• Meets adults' needs for belonging, achievement, recognition, and curriculum understanding so when they are with children they can concentrate fully on the children's interests and intentions

• Results in a unified approach to curriculum implementation, enabling all adults working with the same group of children to provide each child with consistent, appropriate adult support

The purpose of this chapter is to look at what teamwork entails in a High/Scope early childhood setting, including the nature of the teamwork process, the effects of teamwork, steps in forming the team, and the practical strategies that enable adult teams to support children's active learning on a daily basis.

Teamwork: An Interactive Process

Teamwork is an interactive process. In working as a team, adults use many of the same curriculum principles and strategies that they use in working with children. **At its best, teamwork is a process of active participatory learning that calls for a supportive climate and mutual respect.** In this section we briefly discuss some of the ways teamwork relates to the basic curriculum principles presented in the first three chapters for supporting active learning, establishing supportive climates, and involving families.

▶ **Teamwork is active.**

As adults work closely together to implement the High/Scope Curriculum, they are active learners who are constructing a new understanding of how best to support each child's development. To do this, adults must call upon a common set of curriculum principles and strategies as well as the knowledge gained from their individual observations of children, past experiences, and training. Team members make choices—about how to interpret what they see children doing; about when, where, and how to build on children's abilities; about which of their current practices to shift, retain, improve upon, discard. As they work together, team members put their observations of children and events

A successful organization, even a relatively small one, is a complex social system. It takes more than hiring competent personnel, planning well, and issuing orders to achieve outstanding performance. A complex set of interdependent, cooperative relationships exist between the manager and the staff, and among the staff in successful enterprises.

—Rensis Likert, 1967

In a High/Scope program, active participatory training experiences help to build a strong teaching team.

into their own words so, collectively, they can use and build on what they know. Team members give and receive support, taking turns talking and listening to each other's ideas so together they can incorporate these ideas into new strategies for working with children. Adult collaboration in a High/Scope program, then, is an *active, participatory process.*

► Teamwork is supportive.

Effective teamwork draws on the same elements of support that adults use as they work

with children. Team members share control rather than follow the directives of one person. Team members share responsibility for promoting teamwork, setting curriculum goals, raising issues, and solving problems. In talking about and planning for children, each team member takes initiative and serves the team as both a leader and a participant. Team members also focus on strengths—they look for ways to use one another's abilities and interests, and concentrate on what *can* be done rather than dwell on problems and obstacles. In addition, they strive for relationships with each other that are based on honesty, attentiveness, open dialogue, and patience. Because of their commitment to play as the primary path to early learning and development, they exhibit a sense of humor in their interactions with others. Also, their adoption of a problem-solving approach to conflict enables them to deal with one another calmly, patiently, and with kindness, in the belief that such situations are opportunities for personal and collective growth.

► Teamwork is respectful.

Each member of the team appreciates and respects the experiences, understanding, and beliefs of the others. Team members work hard to create mutual trust, to engage in honest communication, and to know both themselves and their collaborators. Rather than say "She can't understand me, she's not from here" or "I don't want *him* on my team—he's too young" team members anticipate success, avoid labeling others, and

assume that by working diligently together they will be able to provide high-quality learning environments for the children in their care. Respect for one another frees team members from a fear of judgment and allows them to focus their collective energies on children.

Clearly, teamwork calls for mutual respect and an understanding of the principles of active learning and supportive climates. In the next section, we discuss some of the beneficial effects of such collaboration.

The Effects of Teamwork

When adults work together to establish and maintain active learning environments for children, the effects are far-reaching. By working together, team members gain recognition, a sense of accomplishment, and a feeling of belonging to a group of like-minded individuals. They come to value having colleagues with similar curriculum goals with whom to talk and solve problems. They find they can provide a more consistent approach to the children in their care because together they have set goals and have devised strategies for implementing them. When adults share control with their team members, they often find it easier to share control with young children.

► Team members grow in curriculum understanding.

By focusing on children's actions and interests, team members develop a better understanding of child development and the ways the curriculum can be used to guide their daily interactions with children. Through observation, reflective thinking, and problem solving, team members come to see themselves as people who

become increasingly aware of and articulate about child development issues as they *specifically* apply to individual children. They are able to voice and pursue their thoughts and intuitions so when they find something that works, they can repeat or build on this strategy in related situations.

▶ **Team members teach and learn from one another.**

On a daily basis, team members share what they are learning about children and curriculum strategies. Therefore, collective learning is an ongoing process. As educator Rensis Likert (1967) found in his studies of teams, "The important skills are not bottled up in a particular individual but are rapidly shared and cooperatively improved" (p. 57).

Forming the Team

▶ **Identify daily team teaching and planning partners.**

Identifying team members in your particular early childhood setting is the first step toward effective teamwork. The type of setting and the agency with which it is connected influence who is readily available for daily team teaching and planning.

If you work in a *center-based early childhood program*, you probably already work in teaching teams when children are present, although your team may not meet regularly to plan together for children. If yours is a full-day program in which children come and go throughout the day and staff work in shifts, coordinating team efforts will be complicated because it requires communication between staff

can make and test curriculum decisions. They discover or reaffirm an adventurous sense of teaching and learning, an eagerness to learn from shared observations, and the challenge of building on and improving what they know. Team members, together, wrestle with curriculum and teamwork issues and enjoy the ongoing process of generating new ideas and strategies.

▶ **Team members are empowered.**

Team members see that they are able to solve problems and make decisions that have a positive effect on their own lives and the lives of

the children in their care. They also develop the ability to welcome the challenge of change rather than be overwhelmed by it.

▶ **Team members develop a problem-solving approach to teaching and learning.**

What exactly did Vanessa do with the blocks? What do her actions signify? What would happen tomorrow if . . . ? How else can we support her emerging ability to stack and balance? What happened when we tried that strategy with Vanessa? What modifications can we make? As team members discuss questions like these, they

A Time for Planning

In a High/Scope program, teaching team members meet daily to share observations of children, examine children's work, and plan what to do the next day based on their findings.

at changeover times. And, if you work in a laboratory school setting, the logistics of collaboration become even more complex. The large number of people—college students, student teachers, work-study students, regular staff—who regularly or periodically work in such settings complicates the mechanics of collaboration, calling for a firm public schedule of staff meeting time.

Home-based programs present their own special teamwork issues. You may be a home child care provider working by yourself. Finding another home child care provider, family member, or student volunteer to collaborate with will probably require you to reach into your personal store of initiative and ingenuity. On the other hand, if you are a home child care provider who employs one or two staff members, your team is already formed. If you are a home visitor, you already have an ideal circumstance in which to form a team with parents.

▶ **Designate a daily, uninterrupted time for the team to meet.**

Because most early childhood programs are not initially established with adult teamwork

in mind, almost everyone working with young children has to make some effort to find time to meet as a team on a daily basis. To work most effectively in the High/Scope Curriculum, teaching team members need *daily, uninterrupted adult meeting time* so they can share observations of children and plan what to do next. If you have not already done so, you will want to look closely at your current schedule and, with administrative support, identify a daily adult evaluation and planning time—before children arrive, after they leave, or while they are napping. This may entail starting your program for children later than it currently starts, ending it earlier, or hiring additional staff.

▶ **Include support staff on the team as needed.**

In an agency setting, it is also important to enlist the support staff as collaborators—the speech therapist, health coordinator, home visitor, psychologist, parent specialist, education coordinator, curriculum assistant, lead supervising teacher, student-teacher coordinator, trainer, social worker, nutritionist, and so forth. These are the people who *periodically* join the immedi-

ate staff team in training sessions, staff meetings, or "on the floor" to work with specific children or to contribute from their particular area of expertise.

The collaboration of immediate staff and support staff ensures that all the adults within the agency who come in contact with children work toward the same goals and carry out common strategies for reaching them. Such teamwork avoids the confusion and frustration that result when, for example, the immediate staff members are focusing on active learning and supporting children's strengths; the home visitors are focusing on children's deficits and ways to overcome them; the speech therapist is taking children to labs for drill and practice; the parent specialist is responding to parents' push for academics by advocating worksheets as preparation for kindergarten; and the psychologist is instituting a child-management system based on behavior modification. While each person may be acting independently with the best of intentions, the conflicting strategies and demands of this eclectic approach are apt to confuse the children while at the same time immobilize staff who work with the children every day. However, when immediate staff members have a regular daily evaluation and planning time, support staff can generally arrange their schedules to join them periodically or as needed to wrestle with issues of mutual concern. This way they can work together rather than at cross purposes.

Hiring New Team Members

A preschool administrator in Kansas supports her staff by using a careful hiring process to look for new staff members who are philosophically compatible with the High/Scope educational approach and will work well with other team members. She follows a four-step hiring process:

1. Preliminary interview: Talk to the candidate to gather information about his or her experiences and approach to working with children. To what extent, for example, does the candidate share control with children and other adults?

2. Written questions: Ask the candidate to describe in writing how he or she would respond to a typical situation such as the following: *It's cleanup time, and Joey wants to save his block building to show his mom. How might you respond?* Ask the candidate to design an early learning environment. Give the candidate a blank floor plan on which to draw in interest areas, materials, and equipment.

A careful hiring process can lead to the selection of new staff members whose educational philosophy is compatible with the program's approach to children. This ensures that all adults who come in contact with children work toward the same goals and carry out common strategies for reaching them.

3. Meet the staff: Other staff members casually interview the candidate. This gives the candidate and staff members a chance to assess whether they might work comfortably with one another. Later, staff members who may be working closely with the candidate share their observations.

4. Observe the candidate: Observe the candidate with children. Does he or she tend to be supportive? Overly permissive? Highly directive?

Through this process, the director reports, she is generally able to hire staff who support the active learning program she administers.

Parents Join the Team

The Montgomery County Community Action Agency (MCCAA) Head Start Program in Dayton, Ohio, not only encourages on-site parent-staff collaboration but also conducts a formal program for interested parent volunteers called Parent Education Participation Program (PEPP). The program is designed to give parent volunteers job experience and training that will qualify them later on to apply for staff positions within the MCCAA Head Start program.

Interested parents volunteer for at least one 3-hour session per week for 32 weeks. During the 32 weeks, parents attend training sessions with staff and gradually take on increasing amounts of responsibility, according to a cumulative ten-step sequence. Step one, for example, includes four sessions of observing children using the active learning checklist (Chapter 1, p. 40) and sharing these observations with staff.

Strategies for Daily Teamwork: Four Key Elements

Adult teams implementing the High/Scope Curriculum meet daily to discuss their observations of children and relate them to general curriculum strategies. They use the following elements of collaboration to guide their joint efforts:

- **Establishing supportive relationships among adults**
- **Gathering accurate information about children**
- **Making group decisions about children: interpreting observations and planning what to do next**
- **Making group decisions about teamwork**

The following sections describe strategies for implementing each of these elements.

Establishing Supportive Relationships Among Adults

An early childhood team is a small but complex social system formed for the purpose of generating ways to support active learners. To be successful, team members need to build supportive relationships among themselves through open communication, respect for differences, and patience. Following are some strategies for building such relationships.

Effective team members communicate together in an open, honest, straightforward manner. They say what they mean. Their words, facial expressions, body positions, and voice tones are in harmony. They identify issues and describe how they interpret or approach them as clearly and specifically as possible.

▶ **Communicate openly.**

Supportive relationships depend on specific, honest, straightforward communication. Psychologist Virginia Satir (1988) calls open communication "leveling," in contrast to the four crippling patterns of communication listed next. When people fear rejection ("I'm afraid she won't like me. She'll think my field trip idea is stupid"), they often use one of these negative communication strategies to hide their fear:

• *Placating:* "No matter what I think or feel, I'll agree with whatever she wants."

• *Blaming:* "I'll find fault with her idea so she'll know that I'm not someone she can push around."

• *Computing:* "I'll use a lot of jargon so she'll really be impressed by how much I know."

• *Distracting:* "I'll change the subject so we don't have to deal with this uncomfortable issue."

On the other hand, when people choose to level with one another, they say what they mean. Their words, facial expression, body position, and voice tone are in harmony rather than in opposition to one another. According to Satir (1988), levelers are people you trust: "You know where you stand with them, and you feel good in their presence" (p. 94). Further, Satir says, "Being a leveler enables you to have integrity, commitment, honesty, intimacy, competence, creativity, and the ability to work with real problems in a real way . . . . People are hungry for straightness, honesty, and trust. When they become aware of leveling and are courageous enough to try it, they diminish their distance from other people" (p. 98).

Open communication occurs when team members identify issues and describe how they interpret or approach them as clearly and specifically as possible. Barriers to communication occur when one or more people withhold feelings or relevant information by placating, blaming, computing, or distracting.

Suppose, for example, that you and your team are planning to make pancakes with the children tomorrow. You are concerned that the activity as it currently stands does not include the ingredients of active learning. Here are examples of five different ways you might communicate your concerns. In our view, only the fifth one, leveling, is helpful:

• *Placating:* "I'm really sorry to ask such a dumb question. Promise you won't get mad at me. Making pancakes with kids is great. They each get a chance to stir the batter. Maybe I don't understand. Is this active learning?" or [looking down at the table, sighing] "Sure, making pancakes is fine with me."

• *Blaming:* "What's the matter with you? Don't you remember anything about active learning? You've missed the boat with this pancake activity!"

• *Computing:* "The ingredients of active learning provide the parameters of any developmentally appropriate process we engage in with preoperational children. Let us consider these critical factors. Any comments?"

• *Distracting:* "Pancakes. Grandad used to make them at our house. I'll look in the kitchen to see if we have everything we need. [Calls from the kitchen.] We're out of juice and napkins. I'll stop at the store on my way home."

• *Leveling:* "So far the only action we have children doing is stirring the pancake batter. How can we give them materials to manipulate, choices, and opportunities to talk about what they are doing?"

Leveling is not easy, especially if it involves breaking old communication patterns. And while leveling results in honest, useful communication, it does not shield you from being human—from making mistakes, being criticized, affecting others, exposing your imperfections. On the other hand, leveling also allows you to grow, to learn from your mistakes without being devastated, and to respect yourself as a person and a team member.

▶ **Respect individual differences.**

Rather than avoid differences, supportive team members wrestle with different ideas, values, experiences, and views of the curriculum. Likert's (1967) management studies show, for example, that a major human asset in productive teams is the "capacity to use differences for purposes of innovation and improvement, rather than allowing differences to develop into bitter, irreconcilable, interpersonal conflict" (p. 135).

Similarly, human resource developer Gordon Lippitt (1980) points out that "in an effective group, persons are willing to express their differences openly. Such expressions create authentic communication and more alternatives for a quality decision" (p. 14). For example, in the team of adults planning to make pancakes with children, Sue is an experienced cook, Shawna is well versed in the ingredients of active learning, and Melany is an engaging storyteller. Together, they come up with a sure-fire plan for the activity that includes an easy pancake recipe; materials and ingredients so each child can make and fry her or his own batter; and plans for the group to eat the pancakes and listen to an Indian folk tale about runaway batter that Melany will tell using the baking tools as props.

While some individual differences may make other team members uncomfortable, each team member makes a choice about how to respond. A team member can choose to see individual characteristics either as barriers to collaboration or as opportunities for growth. For example, the chart presented on page 96, Breaking Down Barriers to Collaboration, illustrates some contrasting choices a team member might make in response to interpersonal differences.

In supportive team relationships, adults *choose to collaborate.* They view one another as valuable resources for gaining a broader perspective on educating young children and working with others.

▶ **Have patience with the teamwork process.**

Establishing an honest dialogue about specific curriculum issues, leveling with people, getting to know team members in a more than superficial way, learning from one another's strengths and differences—all these processes take time. Therefore, be patient with yourself, your

Children's cooperative play reflects the supportive approach that effective adult teaching teams demonstrate in their ongoing interactions with children and with each other.

team members, and the teamwork process. Though the process of developing supportive relationships may appear inefficient and time-consuming, in the long run it allows early childhood teams to work effectively together through the daily ups and downs of life with children.

Gathering Accurate Information About Children

Early childhood teams work together each day to gather accurate information about children to guide their daily interactions and plans. As team members interact with children, they are constantly observing and collecting factual information about them. Team members also briefly document findings about children as the first step in the process of deciding what to do next to support them.

Breaking Down Barriers to Collaboration

Individual Characteristic	Choice to Erect Barriers	Choice to Collaborate and Grow
Speaks in dialect.	It is too hard to figure out what this person means.	It is worth the effort to try to understand this person.
Speaks negatively of women.	He is a jerk to avoid.	I can counter his negative comments firmly, matter-of-factly.
Wants everyone to do things her way.	She's a tyrant to fight.	I can propose alternatives that make sense to me.
Uses a wheelchair.	I am afraid I will do or say the wrong thing so I will not say anything.	He is a person, first of all, so I will approach him as I approach others.
Lives with her "significant other" who is a woman.	I do not want anything to do with a woman like that.	Maybe she can help us understand children who live in nontraditional families.
Believes in faith healing.	I know better than that!	Maybe his faith will help us when we are in a fix. Who knows?
Lives on "the wrong side of the tracks."	Why should I associate with her? My neighborhood is better.	We can learn from her about the children and families in her neighborhood.
Father is in jail.	Like father, like son. Stay away from him.	He has faced hard times and survived. That quality can help the team.
Never finished school.	She must not be very smart.	She can help us understand why children leave school.
Close to retirement.	Forget about him. He's leaving soon. What does he care?	How can we learn from his experience?
Unusual hair style.	She must disrespect people like me. I'll be on my guard.	She is willing to take a stand. We need risk-takers on our team.

A pen is always handy for note taking when you wear a necklace pen! Children also help by "writing" notes along with you.

▶ **Observe children throughout the day.**

"Observation," John Dewey (1933) reminds us, "is exploration, inquiry for the sake of discovering something previously hidden and unknown" (p. 193). Through observation and interaction, adults get to know children. They watch and listen closely to children as they work and play with them to find out what interests them, what holds their attention, and what they understand about their world. Guided by the ingredients of active learning, they ask themselves questions such as these:

What materials does Eli enjoy playing with?

What exactly does he do with materials?

What problems does he encounter? How does he solve them?

What are Eli's interests? What does he like to do?

What choices does he make?

With whom does he like to play?

What kind of play does Eli choose?

How does he communicate verbally? Nonverbally?

What language or dialect does he speak?

What does he say?

What kinds of experiences does Eli share? Re-enact? Re-create in models, drawings, paintings?

What kinds of questions does he ask spontaneously?

Who supports him? How?

With whom does he feel at ease?

As team members learn about the High/Scope plan-do-review process and the High/Scope

As adults observe children, they briefly jot down what they see and hear. Gathering accurate information about children is the first step in the daily team planning process. Today, their teacher notes, the two children on the left carry their interest in "writing" from the typewriter to the computer.

key developmental indicators (KDIs), they ask themselves additional questions, such as these:

What kinds of plans does Eli make?

What does he enjoy doing during each part of the day?

Does he pretend? Does he use one thing to stand for something else?

To what extent does Eli use language to describe events, observations, feelings, and problems? Tell stories?

How is he involved with sorting and matching? Comparing? Fitting things together and taking them apart?

By asking such questions and searching for answers, adults gradually begin to understand and anticipate how each child might act in specific situations. This information guides adults in planning experiences for children and in interacting with them from moment to moment.

► **Briefly note observations.**

It is easy to forget the details of even the most vivid experiences. Therefore, it is important for team members to document in some way what they observe about children. This enables team members to recall, report, and build on their discoveries.

There are many ways to record observations. Some adults jot notes to themselves on cards or slips of paper they carry in their pockets. Others make brief entries in spiral notebooks or on clipboard pads strategically placed around the space used by children. Capturing events with a digital camera works well for some adults, especially those with an aversion to pencil and paper. Setting aside a "recall prop basket" is a memory strategy that works for one child care teacher. Whenever she wants to remember something, she tosses a representative item labeled with the child's name into a basket. For example, a peg with the masking tape label "Miko and Karleen" might stand for a game these two girls devised with the pegs and pegboard.

Whatever the documentation method, it is important for each team member to collect observations of individual children to share later with the rest of the team.

► **Suspend judgment.**

Team members observe and document children's actions from a neutral, matter-of-fact perspective. Here, for example, are two contrasting observations of the same situation:

• **Matter-of-fact anecdote or observation.** *Lynnette stacked cardboard blocks. Next to them she stacked square, hollow blocks. Worked by herself without talking for 15 minutes.*

• **Judgmental anecdote or observation.** *Lynnette built a castle out of cardboard blocks and square, hollow blocks. Worked by herself for 15 minutes. Is not a sociable child.*

While the first anecdote states that Lynnette stacked blocks, the second anecdote jumps to the conclusion that the stacks are a castle. The only way to confirm this, however, is to talk with or listen to Lynnette. As to whether or not Lynnette is a sociable child, neither anecdote provides enough information to draw any conclusion. Playing alone is as fundamental to children's play as playing with others. Playing alone for 15 minutes in itself may signify nothing other than Lynnette's great concentration and interest in the task at hand.

It is important that we describe children's actions as objectively as possible so we do not unwittingly undervalue children who, for example, explore rather than build models or who work alone rather than with others. (For a system of recording observations of children based on the High/Scope KDIs, see the *Preschool Child Observation Record [COR] [2003]*, an early childhood assessment instrument available from High/Scope Press.)

Daily Team Planning Leads to Appropriate Assessment: The Preschool Child Observation Record (COR)

Staff of many early childhood programs are required to do formal child assessments. Frequently, their agencies ask that they use a test-based assessment instrument that often presents some of the following problems:

• The assessment instrument may require teachers to pull children out of their daily routine and present them with a set of standardized tasks that have no relationship to their ongoing interests and play activities. Children, understandably, are often confused by the demands of the test and do not perform as expected.

• The assessment process is time-consuming, taking time teachers would prefer to spend working directly with children or planning with other team members.

• The assessment instrument is often incompatible with the goals of a developmentally appropriate program and overemphasizes formal academic or pre-academic skills.

• The information gathered through this kind of testing does not present a well-rounded picture of children's emerging abilities and thus is not very useful in guiding teachers and caregivers as they work with children, plan program activities, or report on child progress to parents.

The Preschool Child Observation Record (COR) (2003), presents a validated child-observation-based alternative to conventional, test-based assessment systems. The Preschool COR is designed to address common assessment concerns such as those listed above by providing a practical and meaningful assessment system for developmentally appropriate early childhood programs. With COR assessment, early childhood staff observe children and, as they support and interact with children throughout the day, gather the information to complete COR forms. If you follow the daily team observation and planning process described in this chapter, completing the COR once or twice a year for each child in your program will require little additional effort. The child anecdotes you discuss and record daily will enable you to assess children's development on items such as the following from the Initiative section of the COR:

B. Solving Problems With Materials

Level 1. Child expresses frustration when encountering a problem with materials.

Level 2. Child identifies a problem with materials and asks for help.

Level 3. Child tries one way to solve a problem with materials.

Level 4. Child tries two ways to solve a problem with materials.

Level 5. Child tries three or more ways to solve a problem with materials.

Preschool COR materials, which are available in software, online, and paper-and-pencil versions from High/Scope Press, include the **COR instrument** (*Observation Items*), a **user guide,** a set of **booklets for recording daily observations** of each child's behaviors, various **forms for reporting progress, parent report forms,** a set of **parent guides,** a **desk poster** for handy reference use, and a **wall poster** highlighting the major observation categories. **COR training,** available on site or online, may be arranged through the High/Scope Foundation.

Making Group Decisions About Children: Interpreting Observations and Planning What to Do Next

Once team members have gathered information about children, they must next decide: "What does this information mean? How do we act on it?" Through collective reflection on the available information, the team generates strategies to support each child's development.

► **Reflect on the significance of children's actions.**

Reflective thinking about child observations is an open-ended process in which adults explore their observations, add overlooked details, relate new information to what they already know about the child, and speculate on possible meanings. Suspending judgment throughout this process makes it far easier for adults to fully explore alternative explanations of children's behavior and to generate a variety of corresponding support strategies.

For example, one teaching team decided they needed to observe Vanessa, a young 3-year-old who had just joined their program. They gathered these observations about three of Vanessa's play episodes:

Vanessa: Play episode 1.

– Piled six large hollow blocks on top of one another.
– Stacked four small hollow blocks end to end. Called, "Look it! Look it!"
– Stacked nine cardboard blocks end to end.
– Said, "Look it! Look it!"
– Looked at Erin's block structure.

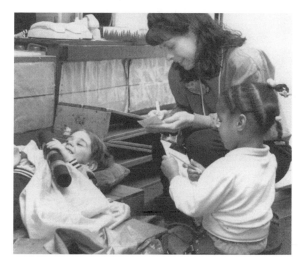

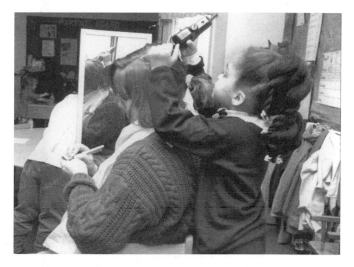

Being part of children's play puts adults in a good position to make notes about what they see and hear. Sharing child observations and reflecting together about what they mean enables team members to generate strategies to support children's interests and intentions.

– Climbed up the ramp, balanced, jumped off.
– Repeated this three times until Erin said, pointing to her block structure, "My truck."
– Watched Erin pretend to drive her truck.
– When Erin left, Vanessa tried the same thing. From her seat, she saw the ramp again and slid down it.

– Climbed back up on the ramp, balanced, and jumped off.

Vanessa: Play episode 2.

– In the art area, got paste, piece of paper.
– Saw Eliot's box of paper scraps. Said "I want some of that."
– Tried to take Eliot's box. He said "NO."

- Got another box of scraps from the shelf.

- Covered paper with paste. Put paper scraps on top. Left some paste areas uncovered.

- Ilana, Jeff, and Michael talked about their moms coming to get them. Vanessa said, "My mommy's picking me up."

- Said, "Look it! Look it!" to Karl [adult].

- He asked her about her paper. She said, "For Mommy."

- Put away paste, got sponge, wiped off the table and her pants.

Vanessa: Play episode 3.

- In the toy area, sat next to Karl.

- Lined up small blocks.

- Said, "Look it! Look it!"

- Moved small plastic bear along line of blocks.

- Stacked small blocks and stood two bears on top.

- To Karl, "Look it! Look it!"

- Karl asked, "What did you make?"

- Vanessa raised her hands to the height of her stack.

- Karl said, "You stacked the blocks that high!"

- Vanessa nodded, adding, "I do it!"

After the team shared these observations, they wrestled with a number of questions: "What do these observations signify? What do they tell us about Vanessa?" Here are the conclusions they reached as they continued their discussion:

What Vanessa's actions tell us about her.

- Enjoys stacking blocks.

- Balances big and small, heavy and light blocks skillfully.

- Understands pasting sequence.

- Enjoys physical activities—stacking, climbing, balancing, jumping, sliding, wiping table.

- Chooses different blocks and different ways to stack them.

- Is engaged in what she is doing.

- Concentrates on materials she selects.

- Solves problems (got own paper scraps, used block structure as truck and climber).

- Uses language to call attention to her accomplishments ("Look it!"), voice her needs ("I want some of that"), and share important events ("My mommy's picking me up").

- Seeks out Karl's acknowledgment; feels comfortable with him.

- Understands questions.

- Uses gestures effectively.

- Creates gestures when she needs them.

- Plays by herself.

- Is attuned to people and materials around her.

- Watches and imitates others (Erin).

- Mom is important to her.

▶ Generate support strategies to try.

After documenting what they know about children's interests and abilities, the next question for teaching teams to resolve is, "What do we do tomorrow based on what we learned today?" Here are the strategies Vanessa's team generated based on their knowledge of Vanessa, active learning, the daily routine, and the key developmental indicators. They decided to try these strategies during the following few days:

Support strategies to try with Vanessa.

Throughout the day.

- Be attuned to Vanessa as she plays so when she looks for adult acknowledgment, an adult is there to converse with her.

- Watch for further instances of Vanessa imitating other children.

- Pause to include Vanessa in conversations.

- Continue to give Vanessa time to solve her own problems.

At outside time.

- Add loose materials Vanessa can stack and balance to the outdoor play area—boxes, boards, logs, lumber scraps, cans, plastic foam packing pieces.

- Watch for Vanessa climbing, sliding, and jumping.

- The stationary slide may be too high for Vanessa. Add removable sliding board and sawhorse pieces.

- Bring out things for Vanessa to jump off of—balance beam, tree stumps, upside-down rocking boat, railroad tie.

At planning time.

- Keep Vanessa in Karl's group for planning and small-group time.

At small-group time.

- Use paste, paper scraps, paper-towel tubes at small-group time tomorrow. Watch to see how Vanessa and others use them.

- Plan additional small-group times around other sticky, gooey materials—Play-Doh, real dough, finger-paints, mud pies.

At large-group time.

– Provide opportunities for imitation by suggesting group games: Have children take turns choosing a motion for others to imitate in "Everybody Do This."

At cleanup time.

– Continue to count on Vanessa as an able cleanup person.

▶ **Try out the strategies and talk about how they are working.**

Strategies like those the team generated for Vanessa are a starting point. When adults try such strategies, however, they find that some work well while others do not. Some strategies do not work at first but eventually become effective as team members learn to adjust them to the actual situations they face with children. Some strategies that appear very promising, however, turn out to be useless. The only way to discover a strategy's effectiveness is to try it out. Here, for example, are highlights from a conversation the team had after trying out some of the strategies they had generated for Vanessa:

Strategy: Watch for further instances of Vanessa imitating other children. "I was surprised to see two examples of Vanessa imitating. In the block area she watched Jeff pretending to be a lion and she made her hands into claws just like he was doing. Then, at large-group time, she was the first one there. She sat down and started to pat the beat, just like we had done yesterday, so it seemed to me that she was imitating Karl from yesterday!"

Strategy: Continue to give Vanessa time to solve her own problems. "At one point this morning I was afraid this idea wasn't going to

After observing this child's intense interest in filling and emptying containers at the water table, the adults in her program supported her play by adding containers and loose materials to each interest area as well as to the outdoor play area.

work. Vanessa went into the block area and hit Zach. But then Jeff turned around and said, 'Tell Zach what you want.' So Vanessa told Zach, 'I want to play over here.' Zach moved his cars away from the front of the block shelf, and Vanessa began stacking the cardboard blocks."

"That reminds me. Vanessa went to wash her hands after painting, came out of the bathroom and said to me, 'Soap.' I got the liquid-soap dispenser down off the high shelf and was ready to give her a squirt, but she stopped me. 'I

do it.' she said. I gave her the bottle so she could do it herself. And she did!"

Strategy: Add loose materials Vanessa can stack and balance to the outdoor play area—boxes, boards, logs, lumber scraps, cans, plastic foam packing pieces. "These were great strategies except that today Vanessa was on the swings the whole time we were outdoors! Ilana, Jeff, and Michael used lots of the new materials to build a great house, though. I think we should bring out some sheets and blankets tomorrow for them, because they wanted something to use to make a roof. With Vanessa, we should just keep watching. She is very active and well-coordinated."

Strategy: Be attuned to Vanessa as she plays, so when she looks for adult acknowledgment, an adult is there to converse with her. "It seemed to me that Vanessa didn't say 'Look it! Look it!' as much today. I still heard her saying it, but not as often—probably because one of us was generally near her. I know that I was much more aware of trying to see where she was and trying to keep myself close to her if I saw that no other adult was in her vicinity."

As they review the effectiveness of the strategies they have developed on a daily basis, teams fine-tune their plans and generate further strategies to support children's growth and development. (See Suggestions for Adults after each KDI in Chapters 10–22 for specific support strategies to try with children in various circumstances.)

Making Group Decisions About Teamwork

How are we doing as a team? What expectations do we have for ourselves as team members? Who does what? When? Are we sharing responsibilities equitably?

The processes of building supportive relationships, gathering accurate information about children, and generating strategies to support children's learning call for a consciousness of how the team is functioning. This involves discussing roles and expectations, sharing responsibility for team functioning, and making curriculum decisions as a team.

▶ **Discuss team members' roles and expectations.**

It is important for all teams to consider the roles and expectations that lay the groundwork for day-to-day interdependence. While each early childhood team is different, some general starter questions are useful for guiding most team discussions; these are presented in Discussing Team Members' Roles, below. You can add other questions as needed to address the particular concerns of your group.

▶ **Share responsibility for team functioning.**

As they work together, team members periodically take time to consider their own roles as *collaborators*. They ask and discuss such questions as the following:

What are our strengths as a team?

To what extent are we using open communication? Relying on and valuing each other? Sharing responsibility? Collecting

---

Discussing Team Members' Roles

Planning for children

When do we meet each day as a team to discuss child observations and plan for the next day?

How do we record our plans for ourselves? For others (parents, visitors, support staff)?

Getting ready for children

Who opens the building?

Who takes the chairs off the tables?

Who restocks paint, paste, glue, tape, paper, staplers, nails, lumber scraps, sand, etc.?

Who checks on guinea pig food? Fish food?

Who makes sure there are enough food and utensils for snacks and meals?

Who sets up special materials for the day?

Who checks out and returns library books?

Who empties, cleans, and refills the water table?

How and when do we rotate these responsibilities?

Working together for smooth transitions

Who meets the bus?

Who greets parents who bring their children?

Who greets the children?

Who deals with bumps and bruises? Children who become ill? Medications?

Who goes outdoors with the first group of children? Waits inside with those who need more time to put on boots, coats, mittens?

Who takes children to the bus?

Who talks with parents as they pick up their children?

How and when do we rotate these responsibilities?

Supporting each other while working with children

How can team members maintain contact with one another while maintaining their focus on children?

What if a team member needs to leave unexpectedly?

What if a team member needs to focus all her attention on one or two children for some length of time?

What if a team member becomes really angry or upset with a child or team member?

What can team members do when a child's favorite adult is absent?

How can team members support one another in the event of unexpected visitors? Last-minute plan changes?

What can team members do when an adult expects to talk with one of them during the time they are working with children?

How do team members divide responsibility for the group on outings and field trips?

and designing strategies around our observations of children? Sharing decision making?

To what extent are we collaborating with support staff, parents, administrators? How are we maintaining contact with all parents? Our agency? The community?

To what extent do we have contact with the other programs our children are currently enrolled in? The ones they will enter when they leave our program?

► **Make curriculum decisions as a team.**

As team members continue to wrestle with and implement curriculum ideas, they continue to address curriculum issues as a team. Here, for example, are some general curriculum questions teams must consider:

How shall we arrange our active learning environment? What changes can we make

now? Later? Whose support do we need to make these changes?

What materials do we want to add? Eliminate? Supplement?

What common limits and expectations do we want to set for children?

How can we incorporate the plan-do-review process into our daily routine?

To what extent do our small-group times include the ingredients of active participatory learning? What do we understand about the key developmental indicators. How do we fashion a curriculum around them?

How can we incorporate opportunities for children to recall their experiences by re-enacting them, talking about them, and drawing pictures?

There are as many answers to these questions as there are teams. More important than the answers, however, is the team's willingness to wrestle with each issue in terms of the curriculum and to come up with strategies to try.

fact, collaboration strengthens each person's capacity to act. "Teamwork develops security in interpersonal relationships and better understanding of one's functions and contributions to the group. Thus, an individual gains the respect of the group for contribution, with the result that the group is better able to sanction individual action" (Lippitt 1980, p. 15).

On the other hand, some adults are very comfortable acting alone and have little experience with collaboration. Drawing such a person into the team can be difficult but rewarding. Here is how the elements of daily teamwork might be used by an early childhood team to involve a new team member:

An early childhood agency works closely with a senior citizen's group. Recently, one of its members, Virginia Jones, has joined your early childhood team. She works with you and the children three mornings a week and on those days stays for the daily team meeting. She is energetic and warm with the children, encouraging them to call her "Grandma Jones." Recently, she made 4-year-old Chris her special project. Chris has

As team members implement the High/Scope Curriculum, they continue to wrestle with curriculum issues. Together they ask and answer questions such as "How can we make planning time more active for children?"

Using the Elements of Daily Teamwork: Involving a New Team Member

Collaboration among early childhood team members rests on establishing supportive adult relationships, gathering accurate information about children, and making group decisions regarding curriculum-related strategies and teamwork.

While teamwork is ongoing among adults, it does not preclude individual action. In

Involving a new team member depends on a commitment to supportive adult relationships and a willingness to value each team member's strengths.

cerebral palsy, uses a wheelchair, and communicates with gestures, noises, and facial expressions. Chris and Grandma Jones clearly enjoy each other. However, in her desire to help Chris, Mrs. Jones does things for him that he can do for himself. "Chris, you're my boy," she tells him affectionately. "Grandma will do that for you." While you appreciate Mrs. Jones's enthusiasm, you are concerned that she is thwarting Chris's sense of autonomy and initiative.

Establishing supportive relationships among adults. Open communication with Mrs. Jones during the daily team meeting is one important way to begin working on this situation. In reviewing the morning together, a team member might begin the discussion with reflections on a specific situation, in this case, for example, a small-group experience using stickers. Here is how the conversation might go:

Janet: *One goal we had for small-group time today was that each child would choose colored paper, stickers, and other decorations, and decide how to arrange them. We wanted children to use the stickers any way they wanted to. I know that this was a challenge for Chris. What did he do himself?*

Mrs. Jones: *Well, when I asked him if he wanted green paper, he nodded and smiled. I asked him if he wanted the duck stickers and he nodded, and he nodded "Yes" again when I asked him if he wanted the ducks in a row. So he made lots of choices.*

Janet: *Yes, he certainly agreed with you about the paper, the duck stickers, and their position. Did he actually touch or handle any of the materials?*

Mrs. Jones: *No. It would have been just too hard for him.*

Myron: *Which part was too hard for him?*

Mrs. Jones: *Well, the stickers were too small, and getting the paper off the backs would have been too frustrating for him.*

Myron: *You know, I noticed that a number of children really struggled with getting the sticker backing off. What I did with Alyse and Ryan who were quite frustrated was to pull the backing off just a little way, giving it a little start so they had an edge to grab on to. That worked for them. Do you think this might work with Chris?*

Mrs. Jones: *Well, yes, it might. And I also think we should get some bigger stickers.*

Janet: *Yes! That might help a lot of the children. What if we had big and little stickers tomorrow, and for Chris and other children who have trouble, we can pull the backing just a little bit to get them started.*

Mrs. Jones: *That just might work with Chris!*

Myron: *Let's try it and see. I know where we can get some big stickers . . . .*

In addition to such open communication, it is also important for team members to seek out, understand, and respect Mrs. Jones's uniqueness, using the special resources she brings to the team. For example, she has lived through the Depression and World War II, events other team members may only know about from books, has persevered and remained optimistic through many personal and political changes, and has reared her

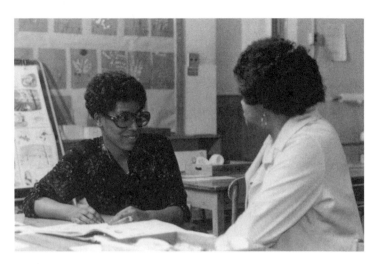

When interviewing a potential new team member, inquire about the candidate's views on partnership and sharing control with both children and adults.

own children and grandchildren. Along the way, she has collected a trove of stories about people she has known and places she has lived, and she loves to tell stories to anyone who will listen. In addition, she never throws anything away and makes clothing, toys, and games from everyday materials. Along with communicating openly about active learning as an alternative to doing things for children, it is equally important for team members to find as many opportunities as possible to put Mrs. Jones's storytelling and toy-making strengths to use.

Mrs. Jones, like any other adult, will probably not change overnight, or after one discussion with team members about Chris and active learning. It will take time, some successes with storytelling and toy-making, support from team members, and further discussions about active learning for her to see for herself that she can help Chris most by encouraging him to do things for himself, even though most physical acts require an enormous effort from Chris.

Gathering accurate information about children and making group decisions about strategies to try. It is important that Mrs. Jones take part in observing Chris and other children to discover their interests and abilities, especially since she may be more accustomed to seeing what children cannot do rather than what they can do. As she participates in discussions that focus on accurate information about children and as she becomes involved in developing strategies to support them, Mrs. Jones will find examples of strategies she used or saw others use in the past but had never thought about in terms of active learning. Being a member of a curriculum-centered early childhood team puts Mrs. Jones in the position of translating her experiences with children and people into a new language and culture—that of shared control. And, for Mrs. Jones or anyone else, learning a new language and way of doing things takes time, persistence, and a chance to practice and make mistakes in a supportive setting.

Making group decisions about teamwork. Scheduling periodic discussions about team members' roles and expectations, shared responsibility for team functioning, and curriculum decisions on the days when Mrs. Jones is present for team meetings will enable her to become involved in understanding and contributing to team functioning. As she participates in this process, Mrs. Jones will come to realize that others value her observations and contributions, and she, in turn, will be more likely to value and attempt to implement the ideas of her teammates.

Looking Ahead: The Relationship of Adult Teamwork to the Rest of the Curriculum

The elements of daily teamwork—establishing supportive relationships among adults, gathering accurate information about children, making group decisions about children, and making group decisions about teamwork—are integral to the way adults work together to implement the specific curriculum principles. These are described in the upcoming chapters on *arranging and equipping spaces for active learners*, conducting the High/Scope *plan-do-review* sequence (as well as the other elements of the *daily routine*), and identifying and building on *key developmental indicators (KDIs)*.

The ongoing daily teamwork of immediate staff and the support staff who are able to join them from time to time makes the effective implementation of this curriculum possible. Teamwork builds bridges among adults who make a difference in children's lives, uniting them as they support the development of children's strengths and emerging skills and abilities. Adult teamwork also models for children a way of interacting with others that relies on **cooperative relationships, constructive problem solving,** and **personal initiative.**

Teamwork, such as conducting large-group time as partners, builds bridges among adults who make a difference in children's lives.

Strategies for Supporting Daily Teamwork: A Summary

Forming the team
___ Identify daily team teaching and planning partners.

___ Designate a daily, uninterrupted time for the team to meet.

___ Include support staff on the team as needed.

Establishing supportive relationships among adults
___ Communicate openly.

___ Respect individual differences.

___ Have patience with the teamwork process.

Gathering accurate information about children
___ Observe children throughout the day.

___ Briefly note observations.

___ Suspend judgment.

Making group decisions about children: Interpreting observations and planning what to do next
___ Reflect on the significance of children's actions.

___ Generate support strategies to try.

___ Try out the strategies and talk about how they are working.

Making group decisions about teamwork
___ Discuss team members' roles and expectations.

___ Share responsibility for team functioning.

___ Make curriculum decisions as a team.

This teacher uses the Preschool Child Observation Record to help her interpret anecdotes about children that she records as she interacts with them. She and her team member use these as a starting point for planning activities to support children's developing abilities.

References

Dewey, John. 1933. *How We Think: A Restatement of the Relation of Reflective Thinking to the Educative Process.* Boston: Heath.

High/Scope Educational Research Foundation. 2003. *Preschool Child Observation Record (COR),* 2nd ed. Ypsilanti, MI: High/Scope Press.

Likert, Rensis. 1967. *The Human Organization: Its Management and Value.* New York: McGraw-Hill.

Lippitt, Gordon. 1980. "Effective Team Building Develops Individuality." *Human Resource Development 4,* no. 1: 13–16.

Satir, Virginia. 1988. *The New People Making.* Mountain View, CA: Science and Behavior Books.

Related Reading

Brickman, Nancy A., ed. 1996. "Child Observation, Team Planning, Assessment." Chap. 7 in *Supporting Young Learners 2,* 267–302. Ypsilanti, MI: High/Scope Press.

Brickman, Nancy A., and Lynn S. Taylor, eds. 1991. "The Team Process: Child Observation, Team Planning, Assessment." Chap. 5 in *Supporting Young Learners,* 187–225. Ypsilanti, MI: High/Scope Press.

Brickman, Nancy A., ed. 2001. "Meeting the Needs of All Children." Chap. 5 in *Supporting Young Learners 3: Ideas for Child Care Providers and Teachers,* 217–73. Ypsilanti, MI: High/Scope Press.

Brickman, Nancy A., ed. 2001. "Team Planning, Assessment, and Staff Development." Chap. 8 in *Supporting Young Learners 3: Ideas for Child Care Providers and Teachers,* 343–93. Ypsilanti, MI: High/Scope Press.

Brickman, Nancy A., Holly Barton, and Jennifer Burd, eds. 2005. "Child Observation, Team Planning, and Staff Development." Chap. 5 in *Supporting Young Learners 4: Ideas for Child Care Providers and Teachers,* 283–365. Ypsilanti, MI: High/Scope Press.

Brickman, Nancy A., Holly Barton, and Jennifer Burd, eds. 2005. "Meeting the Needs of All Children." Chap. 6 in *Supporting Young Learners 4: Ideas for Child Care Providers and Teachers,* 367–446. Ypsilanti, MI: High/Scope Press.

Bryant, Bridget, Miriam Harris, and Dee Newton. 1980. *Children and Minders.* Ypsilanti, MI: High/Scope Press.

Comer, James P. "Educating Poor Minority Children." 1988. *Scientific American* 259, no. 5 (November): 42–48.

Epstein, Ann S. 2007. "How Do Staff in High/Scope Programs Work Together?" Chap. 9 in *Essentials of Active Learning in Preschool: Getting to Know the High/Scope Curriculum,* 89–100. Ypsilanti, MI: High/Scope Press.

Gerecke, Katie, and Pam Weatherby. 2001. "High/Scope's Approach for Children With Special Needs." In *Supporting Young Learners 3: Ideas for Child Care Providers and Teachers,* Nancy A. Brickman, ed., 231–39. Ypsilanti, MI: High/Scope Press.

Graves, Michelle. 1996. *The Teacher's Idea Book 2: Planning Around Children's Interests.* Ypsilanti, MI: High/Scope Press.

Graves, Michelle. 2001. "Toys From Home: One Teaching Team's Dilemma." In *Supporting Young Learners 3: Ideas for Child Care Providers and Teachers,* Nancy A. Brickman, ed., 357–64. Ypsilanti, MI: High/Scope Press.

Hayden, Jacqueline. 1995. "Applying Early Childhood Principles in Extraordinary Circumstances." *Child Care Information Exchange* (July): 64–66.

High/Scope Educational Research Foundation. 2003. *Preschool Program Quality Assessment (PQA),* 2nd ed. Ypsilanti, MI: High/Scope Press.

Hohmann, Mary, Bernard Banet, and David P. Weikart. 1979. "Teaching in a Team" and "Planning in a Team." Chaps. 3 and 4 in *Young Children in Action,* 100–125. Ypsilanti, MI: High/Scope Press.

Killion, Joellen P. 1988. "Parallels Between Adult Development and Trainer Development." *Journal of Staff Development* (Summer): 6–10.

Lehman, David. 1989. "Authority, Aggression, and Building Community in Alternative/Free Schools." *Holistic Education Review* 2, no. 2 (Summer): 5–11.

Lieberman, Ann. 1981. "Teachers and Principals: Turf, Tension, and New Tasks." *Phi Delta Kappan* (May): 648–53.

Mathes, Katheryn W. 1988. "Promoting Adult Growth in a Doctoral Program in Staff Development." *Journal of Staff Development* (Summer): 12–16.

Miller, Louallen F. 1986. "Creativity's Contribution to a Liberal Education." *The Journal of Creative Behavior 4,* no. 20: 248–57.

Post, Jacalyn, and Mary Hohmann. 2000. "The Caregiver Team and Their Partnership With Parents." Chap. 5 in *Tender Care and Early Learning: Supporting Infants and Toddlers in Child Care Settings,* 295–355. Ypsilanti, MI: High/Scope Press.

Ranweiler, Linda. 2001. "Mentoring in the High/Scope Preschool Classroom." In *Supporting Young Learners 3: Ideas for Child Care Providers and Teachers,* Nancy A. Brickman, ed., 383–93. Ypsilanti, MI: High/Scope Press.

Ratzki, Anne. 1988. "The Remarkable Impact of Creating a School Community." *American Educator* (Spring): 10–42.

Schon, D. A. 1983. *The Reflective Practitioner: How Professionals Think in Action.* New York: Basic Books.

Tertell, Elizabeth A., Susan Klein, and Janet Jewett, eds. 1998. *When Teachers Reflect: Journeys Toward Effective, Inclusive Practice.* Washington DC: NAEYC.

Part 2
The Active Learning Environment

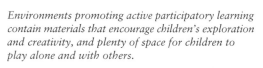

Environments promoting active participatory learning contain materials that encourage children's exploration and creativity, and plenty of space for children to play alone and with others.

Ideas That Shape Settings for Active Learning

Young children in action need spaces that are arranged and equipped to promote active participatory learning. To capture the spirit of such spaces, try recalling the pleasurable things you did as a young child. Perhaps you played in water, made mud pies, curled up in a cozy chair with a picture book, climbed trees, collected bottle caps, or played hide-and-seek. Many of the activities you remember as enjoyable were probably noisy and messy. As you think about how to plan spaces for a new generation of active, inquisitive children, keep in mind your own favorite play experiences.

Young children need space to use materials, explore, create, and solve problems; space to spread out, move around in, talk freely about what they are doing; space to work alone and with others; space to store their belongings and display their inventions; and space for adults to join them in support of their intentions and interests.

Environments for Children and the Active Learning Ingredients

To understand how the physical setting contributes to the learning experiences that occur there, it is helpful to look at High/Scope settings in terms of the **ingredients of active learning: materials, manipulation, choices, child language and thought,** and **adult scaffolding.**

Materials that interest children are essential for active learning. The setting, therefore, includes a wide variety of materials that children can explore, transform, and combine. The materials are arranged to promote **manipulation**— children's direct use of materials—as opposed to being arranged primarily for demonstration or display. To enable children to manipulate materials freely, without disturbing or being disturbed by others, the setting has enough materials for each child and plenty of work and play space.

Choices for children is another principle that governs the arrangement of the setting. The space is divided into well-defined interest areas that offer visible and accessible storage of materials so children can see the choices available and easily reach the materials. The commitment to provide choices also implies *flexibility*—that is, materials children can use in a variety of ways in the pursuit of different types of play and interest areas located so children can move easily from one to another as the focus of their play dictates.

To encourage **child language and thought,** the interest areas are stocked with interesting materials that engage children and inspire them to learn and communicate in both verbal and nonverbal ways. To encourage experiences with written language, the setting is also "print rich"—it includes many books and other print materials as well as tools children can use to make their own written material.

Children's play is enriched by **adult scaffolding,** which can best occur when spaces are easily accessible for adults as well as children. This means there is room for adults to watch and comfortably join children's play at the children's physical levels. Adult support also implies that the environ-

Arranging and Equipping Spaces for Active Learners

When an object or environment is open to many interpretations and uses, the child holds the power to tell it what it is to be or do, rather than it giving the child some preconceived "correct" way to perceive or act.

—James Talbot and Joe L. Frost, 1989

Interest areas are easily accessible for adults as well as children, so adults can comfortably join in play at children's physical levels.

Active learning settings are arranged to promote choice. Children have easy access to a wide range of interesting materials and can move easily from one interest area to another as their play activities develop and change.

ment is planned to encourage children's sense of security and control. Materials are stored in the same locations so children can find and return materials as they need them and also feel in control of their environment; attention is paid to keeping the setting safe, clean, and inviting, thus creating an overall feeling of warmth and welcome. Yet cleanliness and order are not overemphasized. Adults understand that action is the norm for children. While the space may look cluttered as children work, times of play and intensive use of materials are followed by cleanup times when

materials are sorted and put away, and order is restored.

In summary, adults using the High/Scope Curriculum promote children's active learning by establishing settings where children can . . .

• Engage in a wide range of play, alone and with others, including exploring, building, pretending, painting and drawing, and playing simple games

• Find, use, and return materials of particular interest to them as they pursue their own plans and intentions

• Feel safe, valued, adventurous, and competent

Our purpose in this chapter is to present general guidelines for organizing space and materials for active learners, discuss the effects of such organization, and offer practical strategies for arranging and equipping specific interest areas for children.

General Guidelines for Organizing Space and Materials

Adults using the High/Scope approach organize space for children so children have as many opportunities for active learning and as much control over their environment as possible. The following guidelines influence adults' decisions as they arrange and equip early childhood centers and child care homes:

- The space is inviting to children.

- The space is divided into well-defined interest areas to encourage distinctive types of play.

- The space incorporates places for group activities, eating, napping, and storing children's belongings.

- Interest areas are arranged to promote visibility and easy movement between areas.

- Interest areas are flexible to accommodate practical considerations and children's changing interests.

- Materials are plentiful and support a wide range of play experiences.

- Materials reflect children's family lives.

- The storage of materials promotes the find-use-return cycle.

▶ The space is inviting to children.

Do children and adults respond favorably to the overall physical environment you have created? Certain design elements, which are listed next, can make your early childhood space comfortable and welcoming.

Softness. To create comfortable play surfaces, use carpets, throw rugs, easy chairs, cushions and pillows, mattresses, beanbag chairs, futons, curtains or drapes, and wall hangings. Such soft materials not only are cozy and inviting but also absorb sound. To create a comfortable outdoor

play space, provide grass, sand, shrubbery, trees, wood, water, flowers, foliage, and hammocks.

Rounded corners. Large potted plants, hanging plants, easy chairs, pillows, and fabric hangings placed or hung in corners round out sharp edges.

Pleasing colors and textures. Some colors and textures soothe and invite; others do not. Examine your walls, ceilings, and floor coverings. If they make you want to move in, they are fine; if not, you might want to consider alternatives.

Natural materials and light. The use of wood and outdoor light from windows and skylights is another way to soften the environment by bringing a bit of nature inside.

Cozy places. A loft, nook, or window seat with pillows and books gives children a place to pause, be by themselves, observe and take things in without having to respond socially (Phyfe-Perkins and Shoemaker 1986). Cozy places are especially important to children in full-day programs who need a break from ongoing interactions.

In this preschool center, a child-sized stuffed chair is a cozy place to read together.

▶ The space is divided into well-defined interest areas to encourage distinctive types of play.

An active learning setting is designed to support the types of play that young children enjoy—sensory exploration, building, creating things, pretending, using books, and playing simple games. To support these pursuits, a High/Scope setting is divided into areas with simple names that make sense to young children—for example, the

Architectural Elements of Active Learning Settings

Whether renovating an existing area or designing and building a new space for children, consider the following architectural issues:

Amount of space. Active learning requires space for children to move, experiment, and work undisturbed either alone or with others. When assessing a potential space, imagine it with the number of children who will be using it as well as the furniture, materials, and equipment you expect it to hold. In a space that is too small, children have a difficult time moving and making things, and they may spend more time than necessary in territorial disputes. In a space that is too large, children tend to cluster together, using only parts of the space rather than spreading out over the entire area. It is generally easier, however, to make a large space comfortable and intimate than to work within a very restricted space.

The overall shape of the space. Each kind of space has its own particular advantages. In an open space, children and adults can see and find materials and each other easily. In a space spread over several rooms, children can play in a particular spot with a minimum of disturbance. In a multilevel space, children enjoy going up and down stairs or ramps and using the stairs or ramps themselves as play areas. Space in a house helps children feel at home. Outdoor space promotes messy play.

While some spaces are more challenging to arrange and equip than others, almost any space can be organized to promote active learning.

Utilities and fixtures. The following fixed elements of the setting support children's active learning activities and also their health and safety:

- *Water*—within easy reach of children for washing hands, brushing teeth, drinking, dampening cloths for cleaning, mixing paints, washing brushes, filling and emptying buckets, bathing dolls, washing dishes and toys.

- *Toilets*—child-sized and child-level, close to where children play so children can get to and use them on their own as the need arises. In child care homes with standard fixtures, step stools allow children to use toilets independently.

- *Electrical outlets*—either above children's reach or covered so children cannot stick their fingers or toys into them.

- *Flooring*—that children and adults can easily clean and on which they can comfortably sit and play.

- *Permanent display space*—within the children's reach, on which they can hang and see their work. Cork-board wall-covering makes it easy for children to hang up their pictures with thumbtacks. Clear plastic wall-covering over wood or plaster makes it easy for children to tape their pictures to the wall for display. In child care homes, refrigerators, low cupboards, and closet doors can provide display space.

- *Windows*—low enough for children to see outside and to admit light so children can see what they are doing. The more natural lighting available, the more children notice the daily and seasonal rhythms of their surroundings. In homes or buildings with high windows, broad, sturdy steps allow children to reach the windows and see outside.

- *Doors to the outdoor play space*—so children and adults can move from inside to outside with ease. Glass sliding doors make it easy for children to see outside and move in and out of the building.

Spaces not used for play. In every center, the bulk of the space is allocated for children's interest areas and for the storage of materials within these areas. However, it is also necessary to consider spaces, such as the following, that are needed for auxiliary activities:

- *Outdoor clothing space*—in climates where children come in boots and snowsuits. When children dress for cold weather, they need a

separate space—benches or a dry patch of floor—where they can sit comfortably to take off and put on their garments, as well as hooks and racks they can reach to hang or spread their clothes to dry.

- *Outdoor storage space*—for materials used outdoors: wheeled toys, loose materials for sand and water play, gardening tools, balls, ropes, tents, boards, balance beams, ladders. An outdoor storage shed saves adults the trouble of hauling all this equipment in and out each day.

- *Storage space for adults*—away from children's sight and reach for materials and supplies not needed for children's everyday use. In a child care home, this space may be the top of the refrigerator if all the closet space is claimed.

- *Adult meeting space*—separate from children's play space with comfortable adult-sized furniture for team meetings and conferences, and file cabinets to hold children's artwork, emergent writing samples, adult observation notes, team plans, and so forth.

Since the display space is well within reach, this child can hang up her own picture.

Designing Classroom Space

sand and water area, block area, house area, art area, toy area, book and writing area, woodworking area, music and movement area, computer area (for programs with computers), and the *outdoor area.* These interest areas are defined by low boundaries and the child-accessible materials stored in them—blocks in the block area, paints in the art area, and so forth.

While the amount of space available varies from program to program, the play spaces for children take first priority in the distribution of space. Each interest area needs adequate space for materials and for the number of children who wish to play there at any given time. Using most of the overall space for the interest areas means moving to other parts of the building such space gobblers as office desks and tables used only for meals.

Establishing well-defined interest areas is one concrete way to foster children's capacities for initiative, autonomy, and social relationships. Because the areas are accessible on a daily basis, children know what materials are available and where to find them. The consistent and therefore

dependable organization of the space gives children the opportunity to anticipate where they would like to work and what they would like to do with the materials there. Since they can depend on the availability of materials, children are free to focus on the process and interactions of play. In fact, research has demonstrated that "in pro-

grams where children made choices and worked at their own pace in a variety of well-defined activity settings, children exhibited high levels of social interaction, child-initiated behavior, and child involvement in activities" (Phyfe-Perkins and Shoemaker 1986, p. 184).

▶ **The space incorporates places for group activities, eating, napping, and storing children's belongings.**

In a large space, it is helpful to locate the interest areas around the perimeter. This provides an open central space for *group activities,* such as morning greeting and movement experiences, and easy access to all the areas. If your program is located in a small or oddly shaped space, or in a series of adjoining rooms, consider alternative ways of providing group meeting space and

Plants and a low wooden fence create a boundary that adds the homelike feeling of a back garden to this house area in northern Portugal.

A Label for David's Tub

One morning, David arrived wearing a new belt. After he showed it to his friends, he took it off because, as he said, "I want to keep it new."

"Here, David," said Mrs. Hill, "I'll put that in your tub so you'll know where it is when it's time to go home." David gave her his new belt, she put it in his tub, and David continued to play.

When Ricky came in late and joined David in his play, the first thing David said was, "Ricky, wanna see my new belt! Mrs. Hill put it in my tub." With great anticipation, the two boys headed for the tubs, but stopped short in front of two shelves of 18 tubs each. David looked perplexed. "Which one's mine?" he wondered aloud, although all 36 tubs were clearly labeled with each child's name. David thought for a moment, then went to the first tub on the top row, pulled it out carefully to see if it held his belt, pushed it back again, and tried the next tub. After checking 20 tubs or so in this manner, David found his belt, showed it to Ricky, and put it back on. "I ain't losin' it again!" he said.

Shortly after David lost and found his belt, the adults in David's program cut out a different symbol for each child. David chose the green tree. He put it on his tub himself. "This is my tub, the one with the green tree, and these letters say my name, D-A-V-I-D, David." He never lost his belt or any of his special things again. At least not when he remembered to put them in his tub!

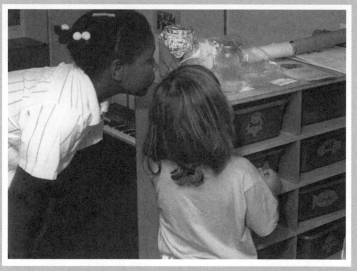

Children can find their own personal storage tubs when the tubs have labels children can "read." Even David's friends know that his tub is the one with the "green tree."

To avoid filling potential play space with tables that are used only for eating, adults in this center use the work tables in the art and house areas for snack and meal times as well.

routing traffic from one area to another. For example, make the block area large enough for group meetings.

When it comes to *eating* and *napping*, child care homes have an advantage over center-based programs because they already have a table for family dining and beds and couches for sleeping. In center-based programs, it is important to incorporate spaces for eating and napping in such a way that they do not take space away from the interest areas. For example, to avoid filling up potential interest areas with tables that are used only for eating, consider eating on the tables that serve as work surfaces in the art, toy, and house areas. On the other hand, if space is plentiful, and especially if children spend the whole day in your program, designating a separate room for eating—with child-sized tables and chairs and a pleasant view—will provide a natural and beneficial change of scene. The same advice is true for napping. If nap time is part of your program and if there is space for napping that is separate from the interest areas, children can rest without being distracted by toys and materials. But if space is limited, consider having children set up their cots in the meeting space or passageways between areas.

By providing storage space for each child, you allow children to have a space to call their own in which they can keep track of per-sonal belongings. Along with a place to hang outdoor clothing, each child needs a personal storage container he or she can reach independently and readily identify by "reading" the label (the child's name and symbol or his or her letter link—see pp. 344–345). In some centers, for example, children's personal storage space is a shelf near the coathooks that contains an appropriately labeled tub, box, basket, or cubbyhole for each child. In one child care home, a closet contains buckets for each child, with the youngest children's buckets stored on the lowest shelves and the older children's, on the higher shelves.

▶ **The interest areas are arranged to promote visibility and easy movement between the areas.**

Visibility between areas means arranging the entire space so, when standing, children can observe their peers in other areas and adults can quickly scan the space to locate each child. Low boundaries between areas accomplish this goal. In multiroom settings, visibility from room to room is increased by keeping doors open and, when possible, cutting openings in interior walls between rooms.

Children should be able to move freely from interest area to interest area—they should be able to move to the art area, for example, without going through the house area. If the block and house areas share one room, locate the areas on the sides of the room so as people enter they can go into the block area or the house area without having to walk through either one to get to the other. If you must pass through one room to get to another, establish a passageway so children can play in either room undisturbed by the traffic flow. Establishing passageways around the areas allows children easy access and the opportunity to play in relative peace. Wide passageways and area entrances accommodate children who are carrying blocks or their own creations. If children's play often spills over from one area into another—for example, when the pretend play in the house area continues into the block area—it makes sense to put these areas close together to encourage interrelated play and reduce traffic problems.

▶ **The interest areas are flexible enough to accommodate practical considerations and children's changing interests.**

In arranging the interest areas, flexibility is essential. Adults make changes in space arrangement and equipment throughout the program year to accommodate children's evolving interests, the over- or under-use of certain interest areas, unforeseen traffic patterns, field-trip experiences and re-enactments, new materials, and the

In northern Portugal, preschool children personalized this smock storage rack by creating, drawing, and taping their own symbols next to their coathooks.

Since children's house-area play often spills over into the block area, it makes sense to locate these two areas close to each other.

need for novelty. Here are some examples of how adults in one center adapted the areas and materials in response to what they saw children doing:

Dory and Sammy have been building robots in the block area, so the adults add boxes, foil, wire, and a bucket of old radio parts to the art area. Dory and Sammy use these materials to make big robots with moving parts.

☙

The adults conclude that children are not using the toy area because, if they do, they cannot see over the two tables, or get to the toy shelves, or find a place on the floor to play. Therefore, the adults decide to take out one table, move the other against the wall, and turn one shelf so it is more visible. Children respond to these changes by playing in the area as if it were totally new.

☙

Now that the weather is nice and the sand table is just outside the door, which is next to the book area, the adults decide to move the book area to the other side of the room. As a result, children can enjoy the books without being disturbed by the traffic to and from the sand table.

☙

After a trip to the grocery store, the adults and children rearrange the house area to make room for children to build grocery store shelves and set up a checkout counter.

If your program operates in a very small space, you may decide to rotate the areas: that is, set up only two or three areas at a time—the house, block, and book areas, for example, followed by the art, toy, and woodworking areas. While this is not an ideal way to arrange a setting, rotating the areas is preferable to having a little bit of everything out all the time but not having enough space or materials to allow children to really build, paint, and so forth.

Regardless of why you change your play space, *involving children in making changes in the environment* gives them a sense of control over their world. Treating space arrangement and equipment issues as opportunities for problem solving involves children positively in changes that might otherwise upset their sense of consistency and security. For example, in Andrea's child care home, the children themselves wheel out toy storage carts, take down the toy storage boxes, and help set up the areas on a daily basis. In another setting, children help make the decisions about where new materials and equipment should go. In establishing an area for a new workbench and construction tools, for example, children carry the books and the bookrack to the other side of the room to make a suitable space for the workbench, which they have brought from the storage closet. After sorting the wood and Styrofoam pieces into tubs, the children make and attach their own labels.

If your program is housed in either a church or your own home, the *sharing of space* that is necessary calls for another kind of flexibility. Setting up and taking down interest areas on a weekly or daily basis is an ongoing chore and calls for creative thinking and the conviction that space for active learning is well worth the effort. Here are some storage strategies for programs that use shared space:

• Casters or wheels on interest area storage shelves that make them easy to turn and move against the wall for storage

• Hinged storage shelves that close up like boxes

• Storage tubs that fit under beds, sofas, and easy chairs

• Storage tubs or boxes that stack behind couches or in closets, hallways, and entryways

• Toy baskets and containers stored on wheeled carts

Weather changes may also require flexibility in the use of space. When rain, wind, smog, snow, or temperature extremes keep you inside, you and the children may decide to move storage shelves, tables, chairs, and sofas to convert part of the indoor space into an obstacle course or an open space for wheeled toys or running games. On the other hand, when the weather is nice, you and your hardy band of movers may decide to move entire interest areas (house, art, block, water table) outdoors.

Finally, flexibility means *multiple usage.* For example, a sofa can be a comfortable place to sit with a book, a place to store things under and crawl behind, a puppet stage, a make-believe hospital bed, or a fort. A table can be an eating space, a work surface for painting or rolling Play-Doh, a platform for a block city, a place to work under, or a structure to pretend with (covered with a blanket, it becomes a house, or pushed against another table, it becomes an obstacle-course tunnel). In the High/Scope Curriculum, it is important for *both* adults and children to realize that the interest areas and the things in them can be used in many different ways, depending on children's needs and imaginations.

▶ **Materials are plentiful and support a wide range of play experiences.**

By plentiful we mean that there are enough materials in each area so a number of children can play there at the same time. For example, there are enough sets of big blocks for several children to build a structure that they can play in together, and enough sets of small blocks that children can use them for filling and emptying as well as building. Whenever possible, there are at least two of everything—dump trucks, hammers, staplers, dress-up shoes. There are also many "found materials," including recycled paper and containers, corks, bottle caps, and paper-towel tubes.

Materials in each area support a wide range of play suitable to the interests and emerging abilities of the children in the program—there are materials for sensory exploration, building, making things, pretending, and playing simple games; materials that encourage children's interests in art,

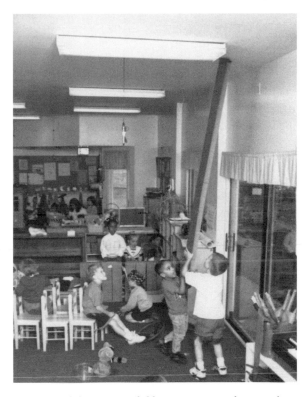

One way adults support children's interests is by providing "found materials" such as this long cardboard box, which these children used to make a "big long ramp" for their toy cars.

Identifying Children's Family Cultures*

High/Scope consultant Beth Marshall provides some examples of how teachers she works with learn about children's home experiences and then incorporate this knowledge into their early childhood settings:

"**Parents** are an invaluable source of information about their home cultures. Making a home visit is an excellent way to learn about a child's family setting and experiences. For example, when one teaching team visited Efrat's home, they discovered that although her mom is a chemist, she used to be a concert pianist. Jazz was playing in the background while they visited, and when one recording ended, Efrat went over and expertly put another CD in the CD player. After the visit, the team decided to add a CD player and music CDs to the music and movement area. They also decided to ask Efrat's mom if they could borrow some of Efrat's favorite selections.

"Talking with parents informally as they drop off and pick up their child is another way of keeping in touch with the children's families. One day, for example, a child care director told Kenneth's mom that Kenneth had been using the tools in the construction area regularly. Kenneth's mother then explained that Kenneth's dad liked to tinker in his workshop and often fixed broken appliances for friends. She also mentioned that her husband often found ways for Kenneth to help him with these activities. In a subsequent planning session, the teaching team decided to change the construction area to a 'take-apart-and-put-together area' to build on Kenneth's interests and support his home culture. In this area they placed small used appliances such as toasters and hair dryers, along with screwdrivers, pliers, and safety goggles. Kenneth and the other children enjoyed taking the appliances apart and looking at what was inside.

"The **community** may also give us important insights into children's cultures. Look at the community from the child's viewpoint. If you do not live in the community around your school or center, try to visit it often. What are the neighborhood's colors, sounds, and smells? What are people wearing? What types of goods are sold in the area stores? What occupations seem to be typical of the area? What types of vehicles do you see? Are there special events or celebrations in the community? Looking and listening as you visit the community will give you ideas for materials to add to your classroom. The teacher in Jessica's program, for example, knew that many of the children in her group lived in an urban area and sometimes rode buses around town. So she placed toy buses in the block area.

"Of course, we can also learn about culture from the **children** themselves. Adults can watch what children do with materials and listen to their comments about them. Hearing about Bradley's interest in imitating his grandfather, a baker, his teachers decided to add additional baking tools to the house area in their classroom. After hearing Corrin talk about the special letters in her home, one of the teachers relayed the anecdote to her mom. Her mom laughed and explained that there were lots of press-on letters laying around the house right then. She had just gone back to work as an architect and was able to do most of her work at home. The teachers decided to add some press-on letters to the art area—Corrin enjoyed using them and demonstrating them to the other children.

"The examples of Efrat, Kenneth, Jessica, Bradley, and Corrin illustrate how the experiences children have in their families and communities can be incorporated into the classroom or center by adding materials and making changes in the setting to encourage children to build upon those experiences. When this happens, learning about cultural diversity becomes a natural part of classroom life."

---

*This section was written by High/Scope consultant and teacher, Beth Marshall. It first appeared in a slightly different version in the High/Scope Extensions curriculum newsletter, September 1992.

In a house area in a northern Portugal preschool, a bedside table with a wind-up clock, an electric lamp, and a religious statue reflect the furnishings in children's homes.

music, drama, writing and storytelling, numbers, and the physical world; and materials that support children's key developmental indicators in language and literacy, creative representation, social relations, similarities and differences, ordering and patterning, number, space, movement, and time. This calls for many materials that are fairly simple in themselves but that children can use in many different ways, depending on their interests, abilities, and experiences—materials such as balls, blocks, paper, and scarves.

▶ **Materials reflect children's family lives.**

Finally, materials and the images they convey reflect children's everyday family life. The way we arrange and equip spaces for children says, in effect, "This is who we are and what we value." Therefore, it is important that homelike items, books, magazines, pictures, photographs, dolls, and play figures accurately portray the realities of the families and communities of the children in the program.

► **The storage of materials promotes the find-use-return cycle.**

The most important idea governing how materials are stored is to make it possible for children to find and return the materials they need on their own. In a sense, the interest areas are a series of attractive open storage units, each stocked with materials that support a certain kind of play. Children move from area to area, locating the things they need to make bottle-cap soup, write a letter, put on a show, build a boat, and so forth. As they play, children use materials freely, wherever they need them. Play-Doh may be carried to the house area to be used as "food for babies" and to the block area to become "snakes in the river." Blocks may be carried to the toy area to make a puppet stage. At cleanup time, however, all the blocks, all the Play-Doh, and everything else children have used are returned to their original storage spaces so children can find them when they need them again. While the storage of materials is consistent, the use of the materials is flexible.

As children play, they use materials freely, wherever they need them. For example, this child uses Play-Doh from the art area, a plate from the house area, and plastic shapes from the toy area in a house he and his friends have built in the block area.

Family Experiences Classroom Checklist

How well does your classroom or center reflect children's home settings? To evaluate your setting, here is a checklist that is organized by several interest areas.

Art area
___ Paint, crayons, and paper mirror skin colors of people in the school community. (Note: crayons designed to reflect actual skin tones are now available.)
___ Other art materials representing the art and crafts of the community are available (for example, weaving supplies, clay).

Block area
___ Toy people are multiracial and without sex-role stereotyping.
___ Animal figures simulate those found in your area (for example, house pets).
___ Toy vehicles represent those found in the community.

Book area
___ Books written in children's home languages are included.
___ Books depict a variety of racial, ethnic, and cultural groups, focusing on modern lifestyles and including natural-looking illustrations of people.

___ References to color in books are nonstereotypic (avoid books that associate black with evil, white with purity and goodness).
___ Books represent a variety of family situations, including single-parent families, two-parent families, biracial couples, step-parents, gay and lesbian parents, children cared for by extended family members.
___ Books portray women and men in realistic situations, with both girls and boys playing active roles and both women and men seen as independent problem-solvers.
___ Books show children and adults with various disabilities. Characters with disabilities are portrayed as real people who live with handicapping conditions rather than as objects of pity.

House area
___ There are multiracial girl and boy dolls with appropriate skin colors, hair textures and styles, and facial features.
___ Contents and arrangement of the house area reflect homes found in the community (for example, patio area in the Southwest).
___ Kitchen utensils, empty food containers reflect what children see their family members using.

___ Dress-up clothing is reflective of the community, including occupations of the children's parents.
___ Whenever possible, child-sized wheelchairs, crutches, glasses with lenses removed, and other assistive devices are available.

Music and movement area
___ Recorded music and instruments reflect children's cultures.
___ A variety of instruments are available for children's use.
___ Movement games that are characteristic of families' cultures are played.

Toy area
___ Puzzles reflect the community atmosphere (for example, rural or urban).
___ Puzzles represent occupations of the parents and others in the community.
___ Toy figures, puzzles, and so forth depict multiracial people and avoid sex-role stereotyping.

Materials are stored so preschoolers can find and return them independently.

Store similar things together. Storing similar materials together—the blocks in the block area, the art supplies in the art area, and so forth—helps children find and return the things they need in their play. Within each interest area, placing materials with similar functions close together helps children see alternatives and think about different ways of accomplishing tasks. In the art area, for example, the various drawing tools—crayons, markers, chalk, colored pencils—might occupy one shelf, and fasteners—tape, paper clips, staplers, string, yarn, glue—might be stored on another shelf.

Use containers children can see into and handle. Open, easy-to-handle containers help children see and find what they need. These containers should be stored on low, open shelves. Clear plastic containers (shoe and sweater storage boxes, gallon milk jugs with the upper part cut off, refrigerator storage containers) will hold small, loose materials and provide a clear view of

them. Low, flat containers, such as egg cartons and silverware trays, also provide highly visible storage for small materials. Baskets with handles, dish tubs, ice cream tubs, sturdy boxes, and milk crates may be used to store larger materials. Children can handle such containers on their own. Some large materials, however—hollow blocks, boxes, buckets, boards—do not need containers and can be stored directly on the floor.

Label containers in a way that makes sense to children. Labeling the container, or the place on the shelf (or floor) where the material goes, provides a regular storage space that children can count on to find what they need and then return the material, even if it is scattered during play. Labels that are understandable to young children include those made from the material itself as well as tracings of the material, drawings, catalog pictures, photographs, photocopies, or any of these along with a word.

Picture labels provide a map that children can "read" on their own. At cleanup time, chil-

Even the youngest preschool children can "read" picture labels or labels made from the objects themselves.

dren enjoy sorting materials into their containers and matching things to their labels on the shelves. They also enjoy deciding where new materials should go and making their own labels for them. One team member, new to the idea of labeling, noted, "If I had known it would help children to be so in control and independent of me, I would have labeled the center a lot sooner!"

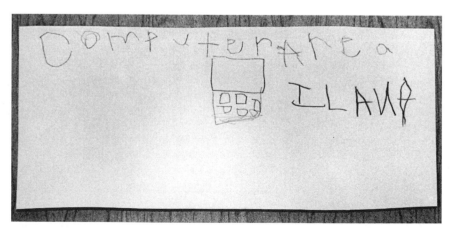

Using the letters on the computer area sign as her guide, Ilana made her own sign for the computer area.

Acquainting Children With the Names of Areas and Materials

Knowing the names of things gives children a sense of control and ownership over their space. Here are some strategies to help children learn these names:

- Use the interest area names as you converse with children: "Oh, Miguel, I see you're in the block area with Sanjay!"

- Use the names of materials in conversation with children: "You're using the sifter, Yvette."

- Play a train game in which you and a train of children travel from area to area. Have children take turns being the leader and deciding which area you will travel to next.

- Play a simple version of "Simon Says." Have children take turns being Simon and deciding which area to go to and how to get there. For example, "Simon says, crawl to the art area!" "Simon says, hop to the toy area!"

Storing Materials in Child Care Homes

In the videotape *The High/Scope Curriculum: Its Implementation in Family Child Care Homes* (High/Scope 1989), California home child care providers Ruby Brunson, Darlyn Johnson, and Andrea Scheib illustrate some of the ways they have planned for materials storage in homes already filled with the furnishings of family life. Ruby, for example, emptied the lower level of her house and set it up solely for children, while Darlyn and Andrea incorporated areas for children into their families' living space. Here are some of their storage methods:

- A shelf of labeled cardboard boxes is stored along one living room wall. Each box contains smaller labeled boxes of materials from each interest area. The first children to arrive each day enjoy getting down the big boxes and setting up the block, house, art, and toy areas.

- Labeled baskets of toys are stored overnight behind the couch on wheeled carts. At the beginning of the day, pairs of children wheel out the carts and set up the house and block areas.

- Art area materials are stored overnight in baskets on top of the refrigerator. When the children arrive, the baskets go on the counter next to the kitchen table, which doubles as the art table.

For many young children, labels made from the objects themselves (an actual paintbrush taped to the paintbrush storage can, for example) make the most sense. For visually impaired children, use labels made from the objects themselves or labels with a lot of texture (such as a unit-block tracing cut from sandpaper) to help them read with their fingertips. For children who show an interest in letters and words, it is appropriate to provide written labels, but always provide picture or object labels as well—for example, add the word *stapler* next to the drawing of the stapler.

Covering labels on both sides with clear contact paper or clear tape makes them easy to attach to shelves or containers with loops of masking tape, and easy to move to another shelf when it is time to make room for new materials.

Some teams make labels for each interest area and call them *area signs*. The block area sign, for example, might be a large poster hung or displayed in the block area where children can see it. It may include the words *Block Area* along with some actual blocks and pictures, drawings, or photographs of block-area play. Area signs help adults new to the setting learn area names and are interesting to beginning writers who enjoy copying words.

The Effects of Arranging and Equipping Space According to High/Scope Guidelines

When adults arrange or rearrange a space for children using the guidelines just presented, they will notice many positive effects.

▶ **Children engage in active participatory learning.**

It is difficult for children to play and learn in an environment lacking materials, but children spring into action when adults organize and equip appealing interest areas. Children can explore, build, pretend, and create because they have a variety of engaging materials to choose from, manipulate, and talk about with peers and adults. In well-equipped, well-organized settings, where adults provide ongoing attention and support, children are motivated to pursue their own ideas and interests with vigor and enthusiasm.

▶ **Children take the initiative.**

Areas for active learning are set up so children can be initiators, doers, and problem-solvers. They get their own blocks down, find the paints, water the plants, fill the water table, print out the masks they made on the computer, get the glue, fasten the clamp to the workbench, and drape a blanket over the house area table. By encouraging children to find, use, and return things themselves, adults foster children's independence, competence, and success. Children

In an active learning environment, children choose the materials they need for their own particular purposes.

develop the habit of saying and believing, "I can do that!"

▶ **Adults are free to interact and learn.**

Areas arranged for active learning enable adults to observe and interact with children. Since the environment itself is set up to engage children in play of their own choosing, adults are freed

from managing, entertaining, or directing children. Instead, they can concentrate on supporting children's play and problem solving.

Strategies for Arranging Active Learning Settings

In the first part of this chapter, we discussed the general principles and guidelines that govern the arrangement of active learning settings. In this section, we present strategies for setting up interest areas for specific kinds of play and conclude by examining the principles of space arrangement in relation to the other elements of the High/Scope Curriculum.

Arranging and Equipping Specific Interest Areas

▶ **The sand and water area**

From infancy to adulthood, people enjoy sand and water. Young children like to play with sand and water and find such play satisfying. They enjoy mixing, stirring, heaping, dumping, digging, filling, emptying, pouring, patting, sifting, molding, and splashing, as well as making pretend cakes, houses, roads, and lakes for floating boats. Children in the sand and water area play by themselves, next to others, with a friend, or in a play group.

Location. Under the most natural conditions, the sand and water area is a shallow outdoor pond surrounded by sand where children can dig trenches, make mud pies, float sticks, wade, and splash. An outdoor sandbox and a hose or hand-pump serve the same purpose.

Indoors, the sand and water area generally centers around a table with its own water spigot, or a wheeled table lined with plastic with a stoppered hole for drainage. Locating this table close to a sink makes it easier for children to add water, and positioning it away from a wall allows children to play on all four sides. For an inexpensive alternative to a sand and water table, put several dishpans or baby bathtubs on a low table or on the floor. A tile floor aids cleanup. Otherwise, you can cover the floor with a sheet of heavy plastic or a shower curtain.

Children tend to work around the sand and water table with their backs to the surrounding play space. Therefore, physical boundaries are not essential to give the children a sense of being in a specific area. On the other hand, low shelves on one or two sides of the table protect children from traffic interference and also provide storage space for sand and water play materials.

Materials. Sand and water play materials include containers, tools, and toys for filling and emptying, floating, and pretending; alternatives to sand and water; waterproofing gear; and cleanup tools. (See the materials list on p. 125 for details.) Children will also bring things to the sand and water area from other areas, such as rubber dolls from the house area to bathe and boats they have made at the workbench.

Accessible storage. One of the easiest ways to store sand and water play materials is by sorting them into labeled tubs. Put the buckets and other containers in a tub labeled with a picture of containers, put the shells in a basket labeled with a shell, and so forth. If the sand and water table is next to a wall, it may be possible to hang some materials on hooks attached to the wall or a pegboard. For example, you might hang the whiskbrooms and dustpans over tracings of each one.

At the water table, children enjoy the sound and feel of pouring and splashing water.

Packing and molding sand are satisfying and absorbing experiences for young children.

One winter day, these children filled the sand and water table with snow and played until the snow "melted into water."

Sand and Water Area Materials

Fill-and-empty materials
Buckets
Plastic food containers
Plastic pump and squeeze bottles, poultry basters
Measuring cups
Plastic tubing
Strainers, colanders, funnels
Cake pans, muffin tins, plates, spatulas
Shovels, trowels
Scoops, spoons

Floating materials
Corks, sponges
Popsicle sticks, twigs
Styrofoam bits and pieces

Pretend-play materials
Rubber animals and people
Plastic dishes
Boats
Cars, trucks, and construction vehicles

Alternatives to sand and water
Chestnuts, leaves, pine needles
Shells
Pebbles and stones
Pea gravel
Marbles
Snow
Water and soap bubbles
Shaving cream

Waterproof gear and cleanup materials
Waterproof smocks
Rubber boots and waders
Towels, sponges
Whiskbroom and dustpan
Battery-operated hand-held vacuum

▶ The block area

Almost all children enjoy playing in the block area and can find something to do with blocks, whether or not they have ever played with them before. Young children with little prior experience enjoy taking blocks off the shelves, heaping them into piles, lining them up, stacking them, loading them into cartons, dumping them out, carrying them, and fitting them carefully back on the shelves. After they have had plenty of time to explore blocks, children begin to build all kinds of structures. With increasing thoughtfulness, they begin to experiment with balance, enclosure, patterns, and symmetry. They also combine blocks with little people, animals, and vehicles in make-believe play. Structures become houses and barns; lined-up blocks become roads and fences. As children play on their own and with others, adults recognize and support their exploration, imitation, spatial problem solving, sorting, comparing, and pretending.

Space for quiet and vigorous block play. Many children play very vigorously in the block area, taking up lots of space. A road race may extend from one end of the block area to the other, for example, and hospital play may involve numerous patients, hospital staff, and beds. Such highly social play is normal and important. At the same time, other children play very quietly with blocks, exploring and arranging them by themselves in their own space. This quiet, solitary block play is equally valid and necessary. Since the vigorous, more social block players often take over the space they need at the expense of the quiet block players, it is important to provide space for both kinds of play. Here are some strategies to consider:

• Enclose part of the block area to create a nook for quiet block play.

• Take blocks outside where there is more space for both quiet and vigorous block play.

• Help quiet block players find a spot outside the block area where they can take their blocks and play undisturbed—for example, under a table, in a tent, inside a large box.

Location. Because of its popularity, the block area works best when located in a spacious area. Setting up the area so it opens onto a central space allows block play to extend outward on particularly busy days. Locating the block area away from the area for wheeled toys and the general traffic flow allows children to balance their structures undisturbed and keeps accidental topplings to a minimum.

Children's block play is often highly social, requiring room for vigorous movement.

Young children with little block-play experience begin with exploration—taking blocks off the shelves, stacking or lining them up, and putting them back on the shelves.

Plentiful blocks and vehicles allow children to carry out their plans for block play.

Since role play often extends from the house area to the block area, locating the block area next to or across from the house area allows children to use both areas simultaneously without disrupting children working in other areas. In the house area, blocks become beds, walls, telephones, dishes, and cars, while pots and pans, tablecloths, mirrors, and dolls add realistic details to the structures children build in the block area.

If your block area is small, try one or more of the following strategies to make it more spacious:

• Eliminate extra furniture (adult-sized desks, file cabinets, unused tables, storage cabinets).

• Use hallways for coats, cubbies, and extra storage.

• Add a loft and move one of the interest areas from the floor level to the loft.

• Move blocks and building materials outside.

Low shelves and storage containers can create boundaries in the block area. A flat, tightly woven carpet helps to define the area, reduces noise, and provides a comfortable work surface.

Materials. Block area materials include all kinds of things to build with, put together and take apart, fill and empty, and pretend with. (See the materials list on this page.) When space permits, the block area also includes materials children can test their strength against, such as logs, tree-stump rounds, and a real gate. Since the block area has wide appeal and a number of children often plan to play there at the same time, it is important to have plenty of materials. This often means supplementing commercially made blocks with homemade and found building materials.

Accessible storage. Big heavy blocks, large boxes, boards, carpet pieces, wooden vehicles, and large Tinkertoys can be stored on the floor in clearly labeled containers or spaces. Before you begin labeling block area materials, look at how you have arranged them and decide which materials will work best with individual labels, and which with group labels. For example, you might put all the small, multicolored blocks in a basket or tub labeled with a picture, photograph, or one or two of the blocks themselves. You might store the unit blocks by size, with one label for all the square blocks, one for all the rectangles, and so forth. You might put all the medium-sized cars on one shelf, all the trucks on another, and all the little metal cars in a tub.

Block Area Materials

Building materials
Large hollow blocks, ramps, boards
Unit blocks (as many shapes and sizes as possible)
Small blocks (multicolored and/or plain)
Cardboard blocks
Blocks made from boxes or milk cartons, covered with cloth or contact-paper
Pieces of carpet, cardboard, Plexiglass, Styrofoam
Sheets, blankets, tarps, tents
Packing boxes
Boards, sticks, logs, stumps and tree-stump rounds,
Cardboard, metal, or plastic tubes
Rope and pulleys

Take-apart-and-put-together materials
Wooden or plastic "take-apart" trucks and cars (some that snap, some that screw)
Large Tinkertoys
Interlocking blocks and boards
Clip-on wheels and blocks
Interlocking train tracks
Plastic plumbing pipes and connectors

Fill-and-empty materials
Dump trucks, pickup trucks
Boxes, cartons, baskets, cans, buckets, crates, picnic baskets
Small blocks
Small vehicles, people, animals
Dollhouse furniture
Empty sewing spools
Stones, pea gravel

Pretend-play materials
Cars and trucks (scaled to blocks)
Construction and farm vehicles
Planes, helicopters, boats, trains, buses
Multiracial dollhouse people, dollhouse furniture
Wooden, rubber, or plastic animals familiar to children
Steering wheel

Reference photos
Photographs of children's homes, neighborhoods, farms
Photographs or drawings of children's block structures

► The house area

The house area supports both individual and cooperative play. Many children spend considerable time in the house area—stirring, filling, emptying, pouring, shaking, mixing, rolling, folding, zipping, buttoning, snapping, brushing, trying things on and taking them off. They may imitate cooking sequences they have seen at home or pretend to feed a doll or stuffed animal.

Children involved in exploring, imitating, and pretending in the house area are often content to play by themselves or alongside others. Other children play there with friends, acting out familiar roles—moms, dads, stepparents, babies, brothers and sisters, aunts and uncles, grandparents, firefighters, store clerks, babysitters, pets.

In the house area, children play with the real utensils and food containers they see important people using at home.

Children also re-enact events they have experienced or heard about—visiting the dentist, going to the emergency room, moving, going shopping, talking on the phone, cleaning up after a flood, visiting daddy, having a birthday party, dressing up to "go out," celebrating holidays, going to church, and attending weddings, funerals, picnics, and movies. By providing a setting for role play, the house area allows children to make sense of their immediate world. Children have numerous opportunities to work together, express their feelings, and use language to communicate roles and respond to one another's needs and requests.

Location. Since house area play often extends into the block area, locating the house area next to, or across from, the block area, as noted earlier, allows this interaction to occur with a minimum of distraction to children working elsewhere. Providing space for more than one kind of role play is another important consideration in arranging the house area. Allocating enough space so one part of the house area can be defined as a kitchen, for example, while leaving another part open, allows children to set up a living room, bedroom, back yard, garage, workshop, doctor's office, spaceship, store, fire station, stage, or whatever setting they need for the particular role play they have in mind. One early childhood team converted a small alcove into an additional role-play space by covering the alcove opening with a piece of plywood into which they cut a door and two windows.

In the house area, children re-enact important events, such as getting dressed to visit a sick friend in a block-area "hospital."

Children in this preschool painted fabric pieces, sewed them together, and stuffed them to make pillows for the house area.

Low storage shelves, child-sized appliances or sinks, a refrigerator, storage boxes, and a free-standing mirror or door can all serve as house area boundaries. In one house area, a puppet stage that often becomes a store counter helps to define the area. In another, a loft house facing into the center of the room provides a boundary as well as a versatile role-play space. Depending on the children's play, the loft becomes a boat, a hideaway, a pet store, a castle, a spaceship, or a "gingerbread house."

Materials. House area materials include cooking and eating equipment and all kinds of materials for dramatic play. The list of house area materials on page 131 includes many things adults can purchase at garage sales, flea markets, thrift shops, and discount stores. When they are aware of the need, some businesses will donate items they no longer use. For example, a hotel that is phasing out key locks may donate the old keys, and a fabric store may donate fabric remnants.

As you equip the house area, it is important to provide child-sized appliances and adult-sized utensils. A child-sized sink, stove, and refrigerator are built so young children can comfortably reach and use them. A child-sized sink, for example, could be a real sink built on a small scale or a wooden unit including a tub for water. We recommend adult-sized utensils and dishes because they are generally more durable than the toy utensils made for children; they allow for larger motions, and they hold more

With their teacher's help, these children use a real blender to make a blended fruit drink.

"Realness"

"Children sense the difference between toys and real objects. In many situations, especially where size is not a problem, they prefer the real thing over the sham. Perhaps it has to do with physical attributes—a greater and more minute degree of its detail, its weight and heft, its strength and longevity, or its being constructed of denser materials. Or maybe it has to do with association— 'This is the hammer my dad uses'—that magically imparts attributes of the original user to the novice. Or perhaps its value, in terms of materials or time spent in creating it, gives it a quality that a mere copy can never have. It might also be its actual usefulness; i.e., it will do more things better, longer, or easier.

"For instance, a real fire engine in a playground will have a much more profound impact on children than a climber made to remind children of one, especially if it has its original bell, hoses, gauges, chrome plating, tires, and other details still intact. Things that actually *do* something help so much to create its rich character. In fact, the more working or mechanical parts it actually has that children can either control or relate to, the better. This gives it a specialness that no copy can match; and by association with both its original purpose and its history, it endows the new users with special capabilities."

—James Talbot and Joe L. Frost (1989, p. 13)

Miguel Seeks the Comfort of Familiar Things in the House Area

It is a cold December day. Miguel and his family have just moved from Puerto Rico to New York City, and this is Miguel's first day of preschool. He has never seen snow and ice before, or such tall buildings. Where are the beach, the ocean, the palm trees, the warm sun, he must wonder. At work time in the toy area, Miguel chooses the small lock-together blocks and takes them to the house area where a CD of salsa music is playing. He finds a seat at the kitchen table, which is decorated with a bright red tablecloth and a bouquet of flowers. There, surrounded at last by familiar sights and sounds, Miguel builds an "areoplano para regresar a Puerto Rico" ("airplane to take me back to Puerto Rico").

House Area Flexibility in Action

One morning in the house area of a Pittsburgh preschool, some girls and boys decide to "go out." The girls dress up in pantyhose, long gloves, and big hats, and spray themselves with "perfume" from empty perfume bottles. The boys shave with real shaving cream and bladeless razors, and put on ties, colorful suspenders, vests, and hats. After the "party," the children decide to move. They pack all the dress-up clothes in boxes and suitcases; tie the refrigerator together with a rope and lift it onto a small, wheeled dolly; unscrew the knobs from the stove with a screwdriver "so they won't get knocked"; load everything that will fit into a shopping cart; move everything they have packed to the center of the room; and then move back into their "new" house. At the end of the move, one of the boys hands his "wife" a newspaper saying "You look for the sales, honey. I'll get this stove fixed and stir us up something hot."

"food." Children seem to prefer the "real thing," probably because they see adults using spoons, mixing bowls, strainers, and so forth at home and the urge to imitate adult actions is powerful.

Props—collections of materials related to particular roles—are also important house area equipment. Some props come from field trips. A farmer, for example, might contribute an empty feed sack, a piece of rope, or a bale of straw. Special role-related articles of clothing are often stored in prop boxes—the hospital box contains a lab coat; the farmer box, a pair of overalls. Other "everyday" dress-up clothes (hats, dresses, pants, scarves) are always available.

A child-height table with chairs in the house area accommodates real and pretend cooking, real and pretend family-style meals and snacks, and small-group projects.

In this house area, dress-up clothes hang on child-level hooks or are stored in a child-sized dresser. Outline labels help children find and return the cooking utensils they need.

Making the house area homelike. You can welcome children to the house area by making it as much like children's real homes as possible. This may mean, in one center, having a brightly colored tablecloth and flowers on the table or, in another, earth-colored mats and candles. The house area might include futons, hammocks, woven mats, or quilts, depending on what children are familiar with. In some parts of the country you might see kindling, logs, and the outer casings of a wood-burning stove. Suitcases may figure prominently in the house area in a community where children move or travel a lot. Depending on the population, the empty food boxes may have original labels in English, Spanish, Japanese, Chinese, Thai, Korean, Arabic, or Croatian. Dress-up clothes may include saris, obis, multilayered skirts, or wide sashes.

Accessible storage. Many odd-shaped, one-of-a-kind materials in the house area present storage challenges. Here are some strategies that might help:

• Hang pots, pans, and utensils on pegboard or wall hooks, tracing their outlines as they hang, and fastening the labels behind the hanging objects.

• Use the space organizers people use in their homes—silverware trays, cup racks, spice racks, plate racks, and canisters. Canisters labeled with a picture or an object can be used to store loose items for cooking, such as stones, buttons, seeds, and beans.

• Store clothing and accessories as they are stored in people's homes—on hooks (easier than hangers), in drawers, and in boxes (with labels). Sometimes the container itself serves as its own label—a hanging shoe holder for shoes, a jewelry box for jewelry, a towel rack for towels, a bed or chest for blankets.

• Position labels in the same way in which an item is stored. For example, trace the outline of a coffeepot and attach the tracing to the wall directly behind the spot on the shelf where the coffeepot is stored.

Dolls and Diversity

Educator Louise Derman-Sparks, author of *Anti-Bias Curriculum* (1989), uses a set of 16 dolls to tell children stories, often about things that are happening in their daily lives. In her stories, the doll Zoreisha is African-American, speaks English, and lives with her mom and grandmother. David is an American of European descent who speaks English, has weak legs because of a spinal defect, uses a wheelchair, and lives with his mom and dad. May is Chinese, speaks Cantonese, is learning English, and lives with her father and sister because her mom died. While these special dolls are always at hand for adults and children to use, children discuss their plans for playing with them with an adult because the dolls are so "real" and treated with great respect.

House Area Materials

Cooking and eating equipment
Child-sized sink, stove, refrigerator
Adult-sized forks, spoons, knives, chopsticks
Cooking containers—pots, pans, wok, rice cooker
Cooking tools—
    barbecue cooking utensils
    slotted spoons, spatulas, ladles
    eggbeater, whisk, food mill, mortar and pestle
    sand timer, bell timer
    teapot, coffeepot
    colander, sieves
    ice-cube trays
    cookie press and cutters
    hamburger press, tortilla press
    can opener
Baking equipment—
    cake pans, muffin pans, loaf pans
    mixing bowls and lids
    measuring cups and spoons
    rolling pin
    sifter
    canister set
Dishes—plates, bowls, cups, saucers
Sponges, dishcloths, towels, potholders
Tablecloths, placemats, napkins
Things to cook and serve—seeds, seed pods, beans, nuts, shells, stones, pine cones, chestnuts, acorns, macaroni, noodles, buttons, bottle caps, poker chips, Styrofoam packing pieces, fabric squares for wrapping
Empty food containers—boxes, cans, cartons, jars, and bags, with original labels in English, Japanese, Arabic, Spanish, and so forth to reflect children's home languages

Pretending and role-play materials
Dolls—female and male, commercial and home-made, to reflect the skin colors, hair styles, facial features, and special needs of children in the program
Stuffed animals
Doll beds, blankets, stroller, front/back pack
Baby rattles, bibs, bottles, diapers, clothes (pants and dresses)
Broom, dustpan

Toaster (wooden or de-electrified), clocks (wind-up or de-electrified)
Mirror
Two phones (land-line and cell)
Small stepladder
Dress-up clothes and accessories—hats, shoes, purses, wallets, briefcases, scarves, head wraps, jewelry, masks, neckties, belts, suspenders
Lunch boxes, picnic basket, laundry basket
Toolbox and tools
Envelopes, canceled stamps, seals, stickers, junk mail, newspapers, magazines
Typewriter, computer keyboard
Sturdy cardboard boxes
Low, movable partitions
Props—
    home-builders' props: toolbox, tools, empty paint cans, brushes, pipe fittings, blueprints
    doctors' props: lab coats, Band-Aids, gauze, stethoscope, cloth bandages
    farm props: overalls, pail, straw, animal brush, empty feed bag
    gas-station props: empty oil can, hose, rags, empty paste-wax can, jack, lug wrench, steering wheel, hubcaps, maps
    fire-station props: hats, raincoats, boots, hoses
    restaurant props: hats, aprons, cups, straws, napkins, menus, order pads and pencils
    fishing props: fishing poles, nets, heavy boots, sou'westers, buckets, oars, gas can, buoys

Homelike materials
Rocking chair or easy chair
Blankets, sheets, quilts, pillows, beach towels, sleeping bags
Photos of program's children and their families
Wall hangings reflecting local community
Real plants, watering can

Real cooking equipment *(stored out of children's reach and used only with an adult present)*
Hotplate, toaster oven
Electric frying pan
Popcorn popper with clear lid

Reference photos and recipes
Cookbooks, picture recipes
Field-trip photos (for role-play ideas)

► The art area

For some children, the art area is a place to explore materials. Here they stir, roll, cut, twist, fold, flatten, drip, blot, fit things together and take them apart, combine and transform materials, or fill up whole surfaces with color, fringes, paste, or paper scraps. Other children use art materials to make things—pictures, books, weavings, movie tickets, menus, cards, hats, robots, birthday cakes, cameras, fire trucks. In a well-stocked art area with plenty of work space, children exploring materials work alongside children who are using the same materials to make something they especially want or need.

Location. In the art area you will need water, adequate lighting, easy-to-clean flooring, plenty of work surfaces, and spaces for drying and displaying projects:

• *Water.* Children working with art materials need water for mixing paints and washing up. A low sink in the art area allows children to use water without disturbing children in other areas. If you do not have a sink in the art area, consider these alternatives: adding buckets or dishpans and a water cooler, large thermoses with spigots, or pitchers of water. If the art area is outside, try a hose and bucket. Keep a supply of towels and sponges nearby for cleanup.

• *Light.* Putting the art area near windows or under a skylight provides children with natural light by which to work, see colors, and notice the interplay of light and color. "Hey, something changed," Michael, a preschooler, exclaimed, as a cloud passed over the sun while he was painting.

• *Easy-to-clean flooring.* An outdoor art area avoids this problem altogether. Indoors, a smooth tile floor works well. If neither option is possible, consider covering the art area floor each day with newspaper, a drop cloth, or a tarp. Putting down a floor covering, like putting on a smock, can become part of children's art area routine.

• *Work surfaces.* Children need space to spread out and work undisturbed on their own art projects: low sturdy tables, low countertops, smooth floor space, or easels. Think also about locating the art area so it opens into a central area, thus allowing children to spread out on the floor with their projects, if necessary.

The art area table was crowded, so this child decided to work on the floor.

• *Drying space.* Children need a place to dry their artwork. Clotheslines, folding clothesracks, and flat paper racks are some of the possibilities. Hooks mounted on a wall or shelf backs can hold smocks.

• *Display space.* Low bulletin boards and the backs of shelves can be used to display pictures, while the tops of shelves can hold structures and models.

In the art area, children use materials to carry out their ideas. Here, one child experiments with long strips of paper while another child makes the "spy things" he needs for his role play.

The placement of the easel allows children to work alone or discuss their paintings with others. When their artwork is completed, a child-level clothesrack enables children to hang up their own paintings to dry.

Materials. Art area materials include all kinds of paper, painting and printing materials, fasteners, drawing and cutting tools, modeling and molding materials, and collage materials. (See the materials list on p. 135.) Unlike the block and house areas, in which the same blocks and dishes can be used year after year, the art area, with its consumable supplies, must be restocked continually. Recycling is one way to ease replacement costs—putting construction scraps in a scrap box instead of throwing them away, using office and computer paper with one blank side, saving catalogs, junk mail, yarn ends, fabric scraps, Styrofoam packing bits, egg cartons, boxes, and paper-towel tubes. Here are some other ideas:

• Partially fill small glue bottles so children can squeeze all they want without using up all the glue in one day. At the same time, provide other squeezing experiences with garlic presses, ricers, and squeeze bottles of water.

• Fit gallon jugs of paint with gallon pumps (available from school supply catalogs). Place jugs with pumps where children can easily reach them and pump the paint they need.

• Use heavy-duty materials when possible. Office-type tape dispensers and staplers, for example, last longer and are easier for young children to use than household-sized tape dispensers and staplers.

Sometimes adults look at the suggested list of art area materials and wonder whether it is wise to have all these things available for children on a daily basis. On one hand, as with any other work area, the art area should provide a variety of materials to choose from. On the other hand, children also need time to work and experiment with particular art area materials to discover their purpose and how they work best. Therefore, it makes sense to set up the art area with an initial supply of basic art materials and to supplement these with other materials as children become familiar with what is already there.

Accessible storage. Paper is best stored in a flat rack where it takes up little space, is

After moving the art area table, these children spread out on the tile floor to work together on a big painting.

• Clear a tabletop for finger painting.

• Provide rope and large items for stringing, such as paper-towel tubes, plastic pipe fittings, and funnels.

Outdoor art. The outdoors is a natural place for experimenting with art materials and working on large-scale art projects. Here children can paint with oversized paintbrushes and rollers on walkways, steps, fences, play structures, and tree stumps, and then hose their creations away if necessary. Children can make footprints and handprints with either paints or mud on large paper or natural surfaces. They can also print with objects they gather, such as sticks, grass, leaves, flowers, stones, bricks, cans, and tires. Fence posts and heavy twine strung from tree branches serve as looms where children can weave in vines, sticks, hoses, long grasses, branches, and twine.

One group of young children in Seattle worked outside each day for several weeks making a totem pole "about us." They decided to make the totem pole after looking at, touching, and hearing stories about real totem poles they had visited. One child reported that the city was cutting down damaged trees near her house "to make it more safe in the park." With the help of parents and a pickup truck, they got one of these "whole" tree trunks, stripped off the bark, and then set about adding things and painting. One section of the tree, for example, was a collection of wood pieces and bottle caps nailed in the pole. Another section was ringed with special "writing" that "helps us with magic." Another was wrapped with multicolored yarn and string. Pieces of clay made eyes and ears; yarn and ribbons streamed down for hair. One idea led to another, and everyone who was interested was able to contribute.

Art gallery art. Just as they like to sing and hear stories, children also enjoy looking at art created by others. Here are a few ways to bring young children and art together:

• Bring in masks, weavings, quilts, sculptures, carvings, baskets, pots, and mobiles for children to examine close up.

somewhat protected and contained, and is easily reached by children. Small loose items such as crayons, pencils, chalk, scissors, markers, paper clips, and toothpicks store well in clear plastic containers, lidless cigar boxes, or hanging shoe pockets.

Big art projects. Many art area experiences, such as drawing a picture or rolling Play-Doh strands, involve working with fairly small objects in a relatively small space. This is enjoyable for many children, but here are some ideas to consider for those children who usually choose vigorous physical activity and who might be more inclined to work in the art area if they could be as vigorous there:

• Provide large appliance boxes and Styrofoam packing pieces for children to paint, decorate, turn into houses, robots, dinosaurs, and so forth.

• Cover an art area wall with large sheets of butcher paper for large-scale painting, printing, and collage-making.

Creative Display Space

Chrissy had just spent work time on the art area floor making a long banner using the large, ink-filled, roller-tipped markers adults use in bingo games and a roll of shelf paper. "Bob," she said to her teacher, "where can I hang this?"

"Well, I don't know, Chrissy, where do you think? It's very long." Bob admired her work and waited while Chrissy looked around the room at walls already covered with children's work.

"Up," she finally decided, pointing to the ceiling. Bob climbed on a chair and attached one end of the banner to the ceiling. "What about this end?" he asked as they looked together at the end still on the floor. "Over there." Chrissy indicated a spot on the wall across the room. Together they walked the free end over to see if it reached. It did, so Bob climbed up on the chair again and fastened the free end to the wall. The next day Chrissy made and hung another banner. So did Lemar and Angie. The room looked quite festive!

- Hang paintings, prints, and photographs where children can look at them. Many museums and bookstores sell posters and prints, and some libraries lend framed prints.

- Include pairs of art-print postcards in the toy area.

- Invite local artists to share their work with children. In one program, for example, a weaver brought in a multicolored hanging she had made, her table loom with a piece she was working on, and some very simple looms for the children to try on their own.

- Observe with children *natural outdoor art*: shadows, clouds, bare trees, rocks, leaves, flowers, insects.

A child uses sticks and a blunt knife to create pretend-play props.

Art Area Materials*

Paper
White drawing paper, recycled computer/photocopying paper
Graph paper, lined paper
Newsprint
Finger-paint paper
Wrapping, butcher, or shelving paper (large roll)
Tissue paper, wrapping paper, foil, cellophane
Construction paper (many colors)
Wallpaper samples
Cardboard and mat board pieces
Cardboard boxes and tubes (large and small)
Contact-paper pieces and scraps
Paper plates, grocery bags
Used greeting cards, postcards, stationery
Catalogs and magazines (with pictures reflecting the children and families in your program)

Painting and printing materials
Tempera paints (primary colors, black, white, and brown)
Paint pumps
Watercolor paints
Finger paints (or liquid starch and soapflakes to add to tempera paints)
Ink pads and stamps
Paintbrushes (small ones for watercolors and large ones for tempera paints)
Easels
Jars with lids, squeeze bottles for mixing and storing paints
Plastic plates or food tins to hold paint for printing
Smocks or paint shirts
Sponges, towels, newspaper

Fasteners
Heavy-duty staplers, staples
Hole punch
Paste, liquid glue, glue sticks
Masking tape, clear tape
Paper clips, butterfly fasteners
Rubber bands, elastic
Pipe cleaners, wire
String, yarn, ribbon, shoelaces
Needles with big eyes, thread

Modeling and molding materials
Moist clay, modeling clay
Play-Doh (including black and shades of brown)
Beeswax
Plaster of Paris
Modeling accessories—rolling pins, thick dowel rods, cookie cutters, plastic knives, hamburger or tortilla press

Collage materials
Cardboard tubes, egg cartons, small boxes and cartons
Empty thread spools, clothespins
Wood and balsa pieces
Cloth, felt, carpet scraps
Old stockings and socks
Feathers, cotton balls, fringe
Buttons, straws, sequins
Yarn, ribbon
Styrofoam packing pieces
Looms, weaving loops

Drawing and cutting materials
Crayons (including a range of skin-tone colors)
Block crayons
Colored pencils
Marking pens, markers (of varying sizes)
Chalk
Oil pastels
Charcoal sticks
Scissors

---

*See also art materials listed in the High/Scope publication Supporting Young Artists by Ann S. Epstein and Eli Trimis, 2002.

► The toy area

The toy area is a place where children play with simple games, puzzles, and sets of manipulatives that can be used in a variety of ways. Working on their own or near others, children use the materials in both simple and complex ways; they may explore new materials, fill and empty containers, put together and take apart small structures, sort and match, make patterns. Some children spend time repeating and expanding new skills. Children who have mastered a puzzle may do it again and again, and then challenge themselves by putting it together outside the puzzle frame. Some children play simple matching or make-believe games together. For example, they may use the pegs and pegboard to make a birthday cake, or build a fence of dominoes for the rubber farm animals.

Location. Consider locating this area away from the house and block areas. While many children ignore the sounds of vigorous play, others are distracted by them, and almost all children need a relatively calm place to play sometimes. Although many of the materials in the toy area are small, children will still need ample space to spread out with their cards, beads, and interlocking shapes. Therefore, allow for plenty of comfortable floor space, especially next to the toy shelves where children often prefer to play. When space permits, include a table and chairs as an alternative work surface.

Walls and low storage shelves help define the toy area. However, if this area is too enclosed, children may tend to overlook it simply because they cannot see the small toys available. To avoid such situations, consider enclosing the toy area on three sides and leaving the fourth side open.

Toy Figures Attract Children

Ruth Strubank, a High/Scope certified trainer, reported the following toy area experience when she was a teacher in the High/Scope Demonstration Preschool:

"After noticing that our children were not paying any attention to the plants on a low table in the toy area, I asked a visiting 6-year-old if she could think of a way to make the large and small pine cones, basket of rocks, aloe vera plant, and Norfolk Island pine plant more interesting to children. 'We have gnomes at my school,' she offered. Taking her advice, the next day I added nine small, flexible figures called Pocket Pals (made of wood, wire, and brightly colored felt) to the branches of the pine and aloe plants. I purposely did not introduce the new toy figures during the greeting circle because I wanted to see if and how the children would discover and use them on their own.

"Sure enough, when Maxwell finished in the computer area (next to the toy area), he noticed the Pocket Pals hanging from the plants. Discovering that they were flexible, he began bending them, hanging them in different positions, and making up conversations between them.

"Donnette and Christopher joined him, asking questions and offering suggestions. They used the rocks to make a path between the pine and the aloe plant and turned the rock basket over to make a house. They added a Tinkertoy pole so the Pals could slide from the table into their swimming pool on the floor. Will joined the play group, and gathering construction paper, tape, and scissors from the art area, built a bridge from the table to a chair. Maxwell brought over a basket of wood scraps, and Christopher colored two of them green for 'mean crocodiles' under the bridge.

"The children invited me to the toy area again and again as they added materials, expanded their ideas, and told stories aloud. I was very excited that such small additions made such a big impact on their play."

Space for explorers and pretenders. Sometimes the toy area becomes a supply area for role play initiated in another part of the room. Children come in to get beads for the "soup," pegs for their "birthday cake," cards for their "party," scales for their "store," and so forth. At other times, the toy area itself becomes the stage—for the dance program the children are putting on, for example, or for the "movie" for which they have made "tickets" and "popcorn."

The toy area cam be a place to work alone—with stacking "bracelets" and Mr. Potato Head.

In the toy area, children also play games they make up together.

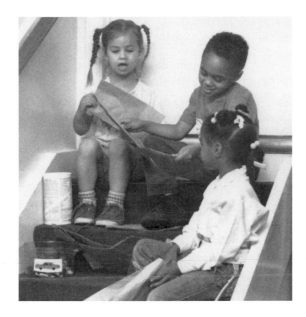

The actors may bring in extra chairs for the audience and large blocks for the stage. While all this activity is appropriate for the role players, it is also important to consider ways of preserving play space for children engaged in other activities in this area. Here are some strategies to consider:

• Include different toy area levels (lofts, platforms) that children can play under and on top of to help separate individual and social play.

• Include a toy area nook for individual play.

• Tip an appliance box on its side so children can work inside undisturbed.

Materials. An inviting toy area is amply stocked with fit-together-and-take-apart toys, sorting materials, small building materials, pretend-play materials, and games. (See the materials list on this page.) As you select toy area materials, look for sets of things that children can use in a variety of ways. Since active learners are creative problem-solvers, a child in the toy area may make a house for counting bears by using a puzzle for the floor

and dominoes for the walls. Remember, too, that natural materials and homemade games are generally quite satisfactory and even preferable to some commercially made items. You can also save money by not buying battery-powered toys, which children tend to watch rather than manipulate.

Accessible storage. Sort sets of toys into suitable containers (clear plastic shoeboxes, baskets, refrigerator storage containers, silverware trays) and label each container with a picture or the actual object fastened to the outside of the container. Storing games in their original boxes works for as long as the boxes last. (It helps to reinforce the corners.) When the box falls apart, pictures from it make familiar labels for the new container. Puzzles store well in racks.

For objects such as pegboards, sewing boards, scales, and balances that simply rest on a shelf (rather than in a container), attach labels to the shelf to indicate where the object is stored.

Drawing children into the toy area. At the beginning of the year, many children tend to overlook the toy area, perhaps because the toys on the shelves are small and less immediately visible than the blocks, dolls, and easels. Here are some strategies to consider if this happens in your setting:

• Store some of the larger toy sets on the floor or on top of a low toy shelf where children can see them from different parts of the room.

• Add different levels to the toy area, both for storage and play. A loft works well. Using this idea on a smaller scale, one teaching team added a low, carpeted platform with pillows to a corner of the toy area and stored the games there.

• If space permits, encourage children to use some of the large hollow blocks to arrange for their own play surfaces.

Toy Area Materials

Sorting and small building materials
Beads and strings (large and small)
Buttons, marbles, corks
Shells, stones, pine cones, seed pods
Building cubes
Parquetry blocks
Attribute blocks
Nesting cups, boxes, rings
Cuisenaire rods

Take-apart-and-put-together materials
Washers, nuts, bolts
Pegs and pegboards (large and small)
Stacking rings and post
Small Tinkertoys
Interlocking blocks
Interlocking shapes
Connecting straws
Puzzles (including ones with diverse images of people)
Magnets
Shape sorters and shapes
Scales, balances
Gear sets
Sewing boards
Geoboards and rubber bands
Dowel rods with Velcro connectors

Pretend-play materials
Counting bears
Miniature animal collections
Little people, gnomes
Wooden village/city/farm sets
Puppets (animals and multiracial people)
Wooden train sets

Games
Simple card games, such as "Snap," "Go Fish," "Old Maid"
Memory card games
Dominoes (picture, texture)
Picture lotto games
Simple board games, such as "Candyland"

▶ The book and writing area

Here, children look at and read books, simulate reading books from memory and picture cues, listen to stories, and make up and write their own stories in their own way. For many children, this area is a cozy spot where they can look at books or magazines, either by themselves, with friends, or with an older person who has agreed to read aloud to them. Some children use story props to re-enact and retell stories in their own words, while others write and illustrate their own books and stories. Although preschool children generally "write" using scribbles, drawings, and letterlike marks rather than letters, expressing themselves in such unconventional forms is important because such experiences are the beginnings of literate behavior.

Location. The book and writing area is often near the art area so children can easily obtain additional writing supplies whenever they need them. It is important that this area be located in a quiet spot away from areas of vigorous play. Windows add natural light and a window seat makes a cozy reading spot.

One team with limited space turned a storage closet into a booknook. They removed the door and the lower shelves, built forward-facing bookracks along the three closet walls, and covered the floor with pillows. They placed the writing table outside next to the nook. They added a sofa, forward-facing bookrack, large sturdy potted plants, and a low storage shelf for writing supplies to serve as boundaries and make the area inviting.

Materials. This area includes all kinds of commercially published, homemade, and

child-made books along with magazines, photo albums, story props, and writing materials. (See the materials list on p. 139.) As you select books from the library and bookstore, and make your own, look for the following:

In the book and writing area, children "read" books on their own and to each other.

• Books with illustrations (drawings, paintings, or photographs)

• Stories and pictures showing people of all races, ages, and physical abilities in positive, caring roles

• Stories and alphabet books in the languages spoken by the children in your program

• Stories and pictures reflecting the experiences of single-parent, two-parent, and extended families

Accessible storage. Forward-facing bookracks (as opposed to bookshelves) make it easy for children to see and reach books. Writing materials can be stored and labeled in the same manner as art area materials.

A Book Area at Home

"Sit, Mommy, sit," said Jamie, guiding her mom to the sofa. "Read, Mommy, read," she instructed, handing her mom the book *Caps for Sale,* by Esphyr Slobodkina, which she had selected from a collection of books on the coffee table. "Wait for me," called her sister Jessie, leaving her blocks and settling herself in on her mom's other side.

Preschoolers Jamie and Jessie M., aged $2\frac{1}{2}$ and 4 years, are part of a weekly home visit program. When Paula, their home visitor, first started visiting them and their mom, she ended each visit by asking Mrs. H. to read to the girls on the couch. Paula would then leave the book on the coffee table until her next visit. Between visits, Jamie and Jessie would persuade their mom to read them the story again and again. This eventually led to a trip to the library where the girls were really excited about picking out their own books and having six books to choose from!

As their library visits continued and story-reading habits grew, Jamie and Jessie claimed the top of the coffee table for their books. If their mom put her magazine or coffee cup on their table, they reminded her, "No, Mom. This is where the storybooks go. You put your things over there." Mrs. H. related this incident to Paula, concluding, "Well, at first I was a little miffed, but then I thought how glad I am that the girls like stories so much they want their own library table. I never would have thought of such a thing when I was their age!"

Children's literacy develops naturally in settings where reading with children is an intimate, homelike experience and writing materials are freely available.

Book and Writing Area Materials

Books

Picture books, for example,
  Where the Wild Things Are by Maurice Sendak
  Follow the Drinking Gourd by Jeanette Winter
  Gilberto and the Wind by Marie Hall Ets
  When I Was Young in the Mountains by Cynthia Rylant

Wordless books, for example,
  Bored, Nothing to Do by Peter Spier
  Anno's Counting House by Mitsumasa Anno
  The Snowman by Raymond Briggs
  Pancakes for Breakfast by Tomie De Paola

Folklore, for example,
  *Gingerbread Boy, The Three Billy Goats' Gruff, The Three Bears, The Three
    Pigs,* all by Paul Galdone
  Anansi and the Moss-Covered Rock by Eric A. Kimmel
  The Tongue-Cut Sparrow by Momoko Ishii

Predictable-format books, for example,
  Brown Bear, Brown Bear, What Do You See? by Bill Martin and Eric Carle
  Have You Seen Mr. Bear? by Marjorie Flack
  "Pardon?" Said the Giraffe by Colin West

Poetry, for example,
  Sing a Song of Popcorn: Every Child's Book of Poems by Beatrice De Regniers
  The Three Bears Rhyme Book by Jane Yolen
  Talking to the Sun by Kenneth Koch and Kate Farrell

Concept books, for example,
  Rosie's Walk by Pat Hutchins
  Mouse Numbers by Jim Aronsky
  I Hate English by Ellen Levine

Alphabet books, for example,
  Alligators All Around by Maurice Sendak
  Alligator Arrived With Apples: A Potluck Alphabet Feast by Crescent
    Dragonwagon
  Eating the Alphabet: Fruits & Vegetables from A to Z by Lois Ehlert

Homemade and child-made books

Photo albums including photos of program children, their families and neighborhoods, children at work and play, field trips and special events

Photo books, for example,
  *Children of Many Lands, Children and Their Mothers, Children and Their
  Fathers,* all by H. Reich

Magazines
Click
Faces
Cricket
Chickadee
Ladybug
Ranger Rick
Your Big Backyard
National Geographic Kids

Storytelling props
Characters and props (commercially available and/or homemade) for
    re-enacting stories, for example,
  • Three billy goats, a troll, a bridge
  • Three bears, their chairs, bowls, beds, a little girl
  • Max and the wild things

Writing materials
Unlined paper of all colors, shapes, sizes
Memo pads, notebooks, folders, envelopes
Multicolored pencils, pens, markers, crayons
Pencil sharpener
Stickers, stamps and ink pads
A sturdy, working typewriter
Alphabet letter and numeral sets of wood, plastic

These young "writers" find lots to do at the shelf their teachers stocked with paper, note pads, pencils, markers, and clipboards.

▶ **The woodworking area**

Here, children can actually use the real tools they see adults and "big kids" using. They can exert real strength to pound a nail and saw through a piece of wood. Many children use the tools simply to understand how they work and for the satisfaction of pounding and sawing. Other children use the woodworking area to make things such as boats, walkie-talkies, guinea-pig beds, and birdhouses. In the process, they may incorporate such art area materials as glue and pipe cleaners; some children may actually carry their creations to the art area to paint.

Location. The woodworking area can be located outdoors in an area removed from the path of wheeled toys and from general traffic patterns. Indoors, locating it near the art area makes sense, because children use both areas as they work on a project. Within the area, provide

adequate space for a child-level workbench, tools, and wood storage.

As you plan the area, keep in mind that children will tend to gather around the workbench, focusing on the immediate task at hand. Low shelves or boxes for wood and tool storage can also serve as protective boundaries on at least two sides of the workbench.

Materials. Woodworking materials include a variety of tools, fasteners, and wood. (See the materials list at right.) You can buy tools and fasteners at discount stores, garage sales, auctions, and flea markets. Just make sure that hammer heads and saw blades are securely fastened to their handles. Lumber yards generally have a bin of free scrap lumber you can rummage through periodically. Other sources of free or inexpensive wood scraps are furniture and cabinet makers, building sites, and ladder factories. You can also look for wooden packing crates discarded behind discount, hardware, appliance, and motorcycle stores. And, you can buy a sturdy child-sized workbench or you can make one by bolting boards to low sawhorses or tree stumps.

Accessible storage. Hang the tools on pegboards with hooks, or store them on a low shelf or in a large toolbox with spaces for each

Woodworking Area Materials

Tools
Claw hammers (12-oz. heads)
Saws (crosscut, 10–12 teeth per inch, 16–18-in. blade)
Hand drill, brace, and bit
Screwdrivers (those with solid plastic handles are most durable)
Pliers (medium size)
Vises (mounted at either end of the workbench)
C-clamps
Sandpaper, sandpaper blocks
Safety goggles

Fasteners
Nails
Golf tees
Screws
Nuts, bolts, washers
Wire

Wood and building materials
Wood scraps and pieces (fir, white pine, balsa)
Styrofoam packing pieces
Bottle caps, jar lids (for wheels)
Dowel-rod pieces

kind of tool. Outlines and tracings make clear labels for tools. Fasteners store well in their own containers, labeled with pictures or with one of the actual fasteners. For example, you might store the medium-length nails in a butter tub, refrigerator container, small canister, or cookie tin. You can sort wood scraps and other building materials into labeled boxes, milk crates, ice-cream tubs, dishpans, or sturdy wastebaskets.

At the workbench, children use real tools to make their own creations.

► The music and movement area

Young children are music-makers. They like to sing, play musical instruments, make up songs, move to the beat, dance, and listen to music. Some children explore instruments, sounds, and motions, while others create their own songs, dances, and games: "You and Victor hold the scarves and move them up and down, okay? And me and Lolly go under them like this, see? Okay. Ready, go!"

Location. It makes sense to locate this area closer to the noisier areas, such as the house, block, and woodworking areas, and farther away from the book, writing, and art areas. If you can locate the music and movement area next to a central meeting area, music-makers can spread into this space to dance, play musical games, or engage in other movement activities. A nearby electrical outlet allows you to plug in music players rather than rely on batteries. A carpet on the floor

helps absorb some of the sound, as do pillows, wall hangings, and shelf backs covered with quilts, drapes, corkboard, egg cartons, or carpet squares. A protected outdoor music area is ideal. Walls, low storage shelves or cubbyholes, low pegboard partitions, and child-level potted plants make suitable boundaries.

Materials. The music and movement area includes percussion and simple wind instruments, recording equipment, and dance props. (See the list alongside. For one set of recordings made specifically for moving and dancing, see the *Rhythmically Moving* series listed on p. 149.) To maintain the sound quality and extend the life of these materials, it is important to clean the electronic equipment and wind instruments and to polish the wooden instruments regularly. Also, children need to know that while mallets are a must for the xylophone and metalophone, they will break the heads of drums and tambourines.

Accessible storage. Hang the instruments on pegboard hooks or store them on low shelves, labeling the shelves or pegboard with line drawings or tracings of the instruments. Label the CDs with pictures or drawings that children can identify— for example, a picture of people playing drums on a CD of African drum music or a picture of an Indian dance troupe on a CD of dance music from India.

The music and movement area contains instruments and other objects for making sounds, as well as accessories, such as scarves, that children can use for costumes or streamers when moving to music.

Music and Movement Area Materials

Percussion instruments
Drums, tambourines
Triangles
Maracas, gourds
Clavés, sandpaper blocks
Cymbals
Bells—hand-held, or wrist and ankle bells
Xylophones, metalophones
Thumb pianos, keyboard

Simple wind instruments
Whistles, slide whistles, kazoos
Harmonicas

Recording and music playing equipment
Video cameras, digital recorders, CD players, or digital audio players
CDs representing a variety of musical styles, traditions, and cultures

Dance props
Scarves, ribbons
Hoops
Limbo sticks

► The computer area

If your program has computers, choose a variety of computer programs designed especially for young children. Many software programs allow children to draw; make masks and jewelry; play matching, comparing, counting, and memory games; make up patterns; "drive" on-screen trains, cars, and boats; experiment with letters; and write their own stories. Don't forget that computers can also play music files and CDs. As you plan this area, keep in mind that social play is common at computers and that screens and keyboards should be arranged to permit more than one child to use a computer at a time. As children work at computers, they often share games, ideas, and discoveries, and rely on one another to solve problems. "Children who experience success at the computer will often, by their enthusiasm, attract others to join them in the computer activity. Anxious to demonstrate their expertise, these 'expert' children may offer to help other, more reticent children to use the computer" (Hohmann 1990, p. 9).

Location. The computer area should be large enough to accommodate one to three computers, each on its own table. (Adjust the height of the table so the computer screens are at children's eye-level and the keyboards are at children's elbow-level.) For example, with three computers, arrange the tables in a semicircle with the monitor screens facing toward the center of the semicircle; with this arrangement, children can help one another while focusing on their own activity, and adults can easily see all the screens at once. It is important to locate the computer area where windows and lights do not create glare or reflection on the monitor screens. Also, if the area is backed up against a corner, then wires, cables, power packs, and power cords will be safely out of the way. Since children often create things at the computer that they want to decorate, cut out, or add to, locating the computers near the art area facilitates the natural movement between these two areas.

In many cases, simply arranging the computer tables in a semicircle is adequate for defining the area for children. If you have fewer than three computers, however, you may wish to use low storage shelves or dividers for boundaries.

Materials. At a minimum, the computer area needs the following equipment:

• An up-to-date multimedia computer (with speakers if you want to play music)

• Software appropriate for young children

• A printer

For more information on computer activities for children, see *Children's Technology Review* (*www. childrenssoftware.com*).

Accessible storage. The computer, monitor, and printer are stationary pieces of equipment that remain on their own tables. Program disks should be stored elsewhere in a safe space.

Computers and Active Learning

When considering whether to use computer activities with young children, adults often find themselves caught up in a lively debate. At one extreme are those who believe that children must learn to use computers as early as possible to ensure their place in tomorrow's labor force. At the other extreme are those who believe that early exposure to computers will inhibit, if not destroy, their creativity, thinking, and interpersonal communication skills. Both these viewpoints, fraught with powerful emotions and reflecting opposing world views, make it difficult to be objective about the use of computers in preschool settings. The ingredients of active learning, however, provide a more objective context in which to consider computer experiences and to decide whether to make them available to young children.

Materials. The computer (keyboard, mouse, monitor, printer, and developmentally appropriate software programs) is a tool that can help children do things—find letters and numbers, draw, write stories, make masks, make birthday cards, drive cars through cities they have created, play music, estimate distances and amounts. Children who see adults using computers are drawn to computers just as they are drawn to telephones, typewriters, radios, real kitchen utensils, vacuum cleaners, and hair dryers. While adults often feel intimidated by computers, children do not. Since everything in the world is new to children, they have not formed preconceived notions about computers and are as interested in and curious about computers as they are about anything else.

Manipulation. Because of its uniquely interactive character, a computer equipped with developmentally appropriate software programs allows children many opportunities to discover relationships by controlling events on the screen. When a child pushes a button on the keyboard, something happens on the screen or at the printer—the car turns the corner, the letter "A" appears, the printer prints out the child's mask or story, the train stops in the middle of the tunnel. Many programs allow children to transform and combine colors, shapes, sizes, figures, facial features, articles of clothing, letters, numbers, and words to produce their own pictures, designs, cards, masks, crowns, and jewelry that they cut out, color, decorate, give away, or wear as they see fit.

Choice. First, as with any material in an active learning setting, children choose whether, when, with whom, and for how long to work with a computer activity. Given some initial adult guidance with each new piece of software, children are quite able to take care of their own needs at the computer. Generally, they can operate programs and print out the results on their own and at their own pace. As soon as they have a repertoire of programs, they can choose the programs that particularly interest them. Within each program, children can make things happen. Depending on the program they can, for example, choose which key to push to get the letter on the screen to appear or disappear, decide whether to make the rider stay on his horse or fall off, select which pair of eyes goes with which nose, plan a route for ferrying several ducks safely to the beach while avoiding being capsized by a hippo. In addition, some programs allow children to print out a product, such as a drawing, story, card, or mask, providing each child with the additional choice of deciding whether or not the product needs cutting, folding, coloring, painting, gluing, or other refinements.

Child language and thought. Children who choose to use the computer typically have as much to say about what they are doing as they would about any other activity they have chosen. Because the link between cause and effect is so immediate in many programs, children are eager to tell others about the funny or surprising thing they just made the bird or the cat do, for example. Since children are just as likely to work with another child at the computer as they are to work by themselves, peer-to-peer conversations are common. When computer programs involve simple writing tasks, children are also engaged in putting their own words into print and reading them back and/or in having someone else read them back.

Adult scaffolding. One of the surprising things about computers is the extent to which young children can work on them independently and successfully. Even though computers are complex machines, with developmentally appropriate software they are easy to operate, quite robust, and tolerant of error. When a child makes a mistake, good software programs, like patient adults, give the child another chance, offer a clue, or simply present another problem.

As in any active learning situation, however, adult support is essential for computer activities. Adults provide and introduce developmentally appropriate software programs; they interact with children as they work at computers, using computers alongside children, observing what children are doing, conversing with children about their work, and referring one child to another. In other words, when interacting with children who are using computers, adults are guided by the same support strategies they use with other activities, such as building with blocks, playing with clay, or painting. Although the materials are different, the active learning process is the same.

Because using computers involves all the **ingredients of active learning—materials, manipulation, choice, language and thought,** and **adult scaffolding**—developmentally appropriate computer activities fit well in an active learning setting.

The computer area is a pleasant place for children to try out and talk about self-selected computer activities.

The outdoor area

The outdoors is a wonderful place for children. Here they are free to run, ride wheeled toys, push and pull wagons, throw balls, roll down hills, dig, swing, slide, climb, and do all the other things adults caution them against when indoors. Children demonstrate different abilities in the outdoor setting than they do inside. They may show themselves, for example, to be skilled climbers and balancers, or imaginative large-scale builders. It is essential to young children's growth and development to have time each day to play in a safe place outdoors.

Location. Although children can play vigorously in a spacious gym, no indoor space can match the sounds, sights, smells, and textures of the natural world. Outdoor play areas are best located on open land or in a yard immediately adjacent to indoor play areas so children can move quickly and safely from indoors to outdoors. In some urban locations, however, adjacent space may not be available for outdoor play. While there may be a public park within walking distance, this space will work only if children and adults feel safe. If there is no outdoor space available on ground level, consider the following:

• Develop a roof-top outdoor area.

• Share an outdoor area with a nearby church, school, YMCA, or business.

• Take a daily walk around the block with wagons, bikes, and strollers.

If you have your own ground- or roof-level outdoor space, consider planning the area so children can explore and appreciate a variety of landscape elements (hills, valleys, sunlit areas,

These children have found a quiet place under the climber to dig.

shaded areas, grass, rocks, gravel, water) and plant life (trees, shrubs, bushes, vines, and flowers). Include contrasts in shape, color, and texture—for example, a weedy area for exploration and a tilled bed for children's gardening. A fence or barrier around the entire perimeter of the outdoor area defines the play space, keeps children within safe limits, and provides a sense of security.

Within the outdoor area it is important to separate areas for physically vigorous play from areas of focused play—children should be able to dig in the dirt, for example, without having to watch out for children riding wheeled toys or children zooming off the slide. The sketch presented on page 145 may give you some ideas for an outdoor area layout. You can define various parts of the outdoor area by changes in surface materials (pea gravel under climbers, hard surfaces for wheeled toys) or actual physical boundaries (low shrubs around the swings, railroad ties around the sand).

Materials. Outdoors, children enjoy stationary structures for climbing, swinging, and sliding; wheeled toys for pushing and pulling; and loose manipulative materials for exploring, pretending, and building. (See the list on p. 145.) For safety guidelines, see *Let's Go Outside! Designing the Early Childhood Playground* (Theemes 1999).

In an outdoor tree house, small children have a unique opportunity to look down on the world.

A small shed provides a safe place for the overnight storage of items used for outdoor play.

Accessible storage. Wheeled toys need a safe, protected overnight storage space, preferably in an outdoor shed accessible to children (once it is unlocked). You can store loose materials in easy-to-carry tubs or buckets with handles. This enables children to easily locate and return these materials to their overnight storage space.

Outdoor Area Materials

Stationary structures
Climbers—
    jungle gym, net climber
    trees with low branches close
        together
High places—
    raised platform, low tree house,
        sturdy crates
    hills, boulders
    tree stumps, snow piles
Swings—
    commercial swing set, multi-
        person tire swing
    rope swing from tree,
        low hammock
    spring-based rocking toys
Slides—
    commercial slide, hill slide
    low ramp, low cable ride
    firefighter's pole, sleds for winter
Balances—
    balance beams
    rows of railroad ties, bricks, or
        rocks arranged in rows
        (including parallel rows,
        curving, and zigzag rows)

Within the outdoor area it is important to separate areas for physically vigorous play from areas of focused play—children should be able to dig in the dirt without having to watch out for wheel-toy riders.

(This sketch originally appeared in Esbensen 1987, p. 12.)

Wheeled toys
Tricycles
Scooters
Wagons
Wheelbarrow
Push vehicles with steering wheels
Strollers, carriages

Loose materials
Jumping equipment—
    inner-tubes, trampolines
    old mattress, leaf piles
    ropes (to jump over)
Equipment for throwing, kicking,
and aiming—
    balls (all sizes)
    beanbags
    low basketball hoop and net
    pails, buckets, boxes, bull's-eye
        targets

Building materials—
    boards of varying lengths
    slotted plywood pieces (sanded
        smooth)
    Styrofoam sheets, boards, packing
        pieces
    cardboard boxes
    twine, rope, pulleys
    old sheets, blankets, tarps
    small sawhorses
    tires, inner tubes
    workbench and tools
Sand and water materials (see p. 125
for additional materials)—
    sand pit, box, table or tubs
    sand, pea gravel, shells, sawdust,
        wood shavings, leaves, pine
        cones, snow

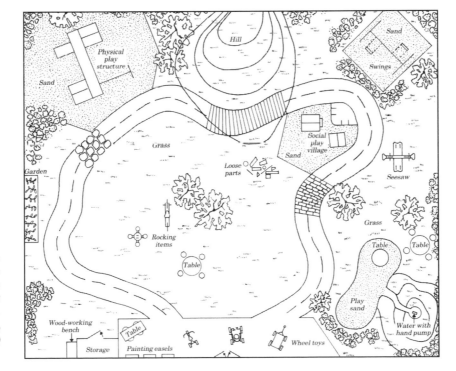

wading pool, spigot, hose, hand
    pump, flexible tubing
spoons, shovels, buckets
Gardening equipment—
    garden plot, window boxes, tubs
        with soil
    watering can or hose
    gardening tools
    seeds, bulbs, flowers, plants
Role-play props—
    boat, car, plane, train, spaceship,
        tractor, hay wagon
    dump trucks, bulldozers
    mounted steering wheel
    playhouse or enclosure (refrigera-
        tor box, dense shrubbery)
    telephone in playhouse or booth,
        or on pole
    mailbox
    low clothesline, clothespins
    small working flagpole with flags
    gas pump handle and hose, empty
        oil can and spout
    binoculars
    helmets, hats, goggles
    backpacks
Musical instruments—
    pipe chimes, wind chimes
    dinner bells, sleigh bells
    trash-can drums, hollow-log
        drums
    slatted fence (to run sticks across)
Art materials—
    painting canvases made from old
        sheets, paints
    paint rollers, large brushes
    bubbles and bubble wands
    large-scale weaving frame
    multicolored chalk
    clay for imprints of grass, stones,
        leaves, etc.
    food coloring, sand tools, boxes,
        cans for snow sculpture

The Relationship to the Rest of the Curriculum of Arranging and Equipping Space

The way adults arrange and equip space for children is guided by the ingredients of active learning and influences the way children and adults learn and teach. Because materials are plentiful and accessible, children can follow their own interests and intentions. A variety of well-organized, well-equipped interest areas lay the groundwork for the High/Scope plan-

A variety of well-organized, well-equipped interest areas lay the groundwork for the High/Scope plan-do-review process. Because materials are plentiful and accessible, children can follow their own interests and intentions.

do-review process and the other parts of the daily routine, which are discussed in the next three chapters. The interest areas are also equipped with materials that support the key developmen-tal indicators, discussed in Part 3 of this book, while the key developmental indicators, in turn, inspire the addition of new equipment and materials.

Guidelines and Strategies for Arranging and Equipping Spaces for Children: A Summary

Organizing space

___ The space is inviting to children. It includes
   ___ Softness
   ___ Rounded corners
   ___ Pleasing colors and textures
   ___ Natural materials and light
   ___ Cozy places
___ The space is divided into well-defined interest areas to encourage distinctive types of play.
___ The interest areas include some combination of the following:
   ___ Sand and water area
   ___ Block area
   ___ House area
   ___ Art area
   ___ Toy area
   ___ Book and writing area
   ___ Woodworking area
   ___ Music and movement area
   ___ Computer area
   ___ Outdoor area
___ The space incorporates places for group activities, eating, napping, and storing children's belongings.

Establishing interest areas

___ The interest areas are arranged to promote visibility and easy movement between areas:
   ___ The sand and water area is close to water.
   ___ The block and house areas are close to each other.
   ___ The art area is close to water.
   ___ The toy and book areas are located away from vigorous play areas.
   ___ The woodworking area is outdoors or near the art area.

___ The computer area avoids screen glare.
___ The outdoor area is close to indoor areas.
___ The areas can accommodate practical considerations and children's changing interests.

Providing materials

___ The storage of materials promotes the find-use-return cycle.
   ___ Similar things are stored together.
   ___ Children can see into and handle containers.
   ___ Labels make sense to children. They are made from
      ___ The materials themselves
      ___ Photographs, photocopies
      ___ Pictures
      ___ Line drawings, tracings
      ___ Written words in addition to any of the above
___ Materials are plentiful, support a wide range of play, and reflect children's family lives.
In the *sand and water area*
   ___ Fill-and-empty materials
   ___ Floating materials
   ___ Pretend-play materials
   ___ Alternatives to sand and water
   ___ Waterproof gear and cleanup materials
In the *block area*
   ___ Building materials
   ___ Take-apart-and-put-together materials
   ___ Fill-and-empty materials
   ___ Pretend-play materials
   ___ Reference photos
In the *house area*
   ___ Cooking and eating equipment
   ___ Pretending and role-play materials
   ___ Homelike materials reflecting children's family lives
   ___ Real cooking equipment (for use with adult supervision)
   ___ Reference photos and recipes

In the *art area*
   ___ Paper
   ___ Painting and printing materials
   ___ Fasteners
   ___ Modeling and molding materials
   ___ Collage materials
   ___ Drawing and cutting materials
In the *toy area*
   ___ Sorting and small building materials
   ___ Take-apart-and-put-together materials
   ___ Pretend-play materials
   ___ Games
In the *book and writing area*
   ___ Books
   ___ Magazines
   ___ Storytelling props
   ___ Writing materials
In the *woodworking area*
   ___ Tools
   ___ Fasteners
   ___ Wood and building materials
In the *music and movement area*
   ___ Percussion instruments
   ___ Simple wind instruments
   ___ Recording equipment, recorded music, and players
   ___ Props for dancing
In the *computer area*
   ___ Computer(s) that are multimedia and up to date (with speakers if you wish to play music)
   ___ Software programs appropriate for young children
   ___ Printer(s) (preferably color)
In the *outdoor area*
   ___ Stationary structures
   ___ Wheeled toys
   ___ Loose materials

References

Derman-Sparks, Louise. 1989. *Anti-Bias Curriculum: Tools for Empowering Children.* Washington, DC: NAEYC.

Epstein, Ann S., and Eli Trimis. 2002. *Supporting Young Artists: The Development of the Visual Arts in Young Children.* Ypsilanti, MI: High/Scope Press.

Esbensen, Steen B. 1987. *The Early Childhood Playground: An Outdoor Classroom.* Ypsilanti, MI: High/Scope Press.

The High/Scope Curriculum: Its Implementation in Family Child Care Homes. 1989. Color videotape, 19 min. Ypsilanti, MI: High/Scope Press.

Hohmann, Charles. 1990. *Young Children & Computers.* Ypsilanti, MI: High/Scope Press.

Marshall, Beth. 1992. "Providing Opportunities for Cultural Learning." In *High/Scope Extensions* (September): 1–3.

Phyfe-Perkins, Elizabeth, and Joanne Shoemaker. 1986. "Indoor Play Environments: Research and Design Implications." In *The Young Child at Play: Reviews of Research,* Vol. 4, Greta Fein and Mary Rivkin, eds., 177–93. Washington, DC: NAEYC.

Post, Jacalyn, and Mary Hohmann. 2000. *Tender Care and Early Learning: Supporting Infants and Toddlers in Child Care Settings.* Ypsilanti, MI: High/Scope Press.

Talbot, James, and Joe L. Frost. 1989. "Magical Playscapes." *Childhood Education* 66, no. 1 (Fall): 11–19.

Tegano, Deborah, James Moran, Alton DeLong, Janis Brickey, and Kris Ramanssini. 1996. "Designing Classroom Spaces: Making the Most of Time." *Early Childhood Education Journal* 23, no. 3: 135–41.

Theemes, Tracy. 1999. *Let's Go Outside! Designing the Early Childhood Playground.* Ypsilanti, MI: High/Scope Press.

Related Reading

Brickman, Nancy A., ed. 1996. "Arranging Environments for Children." Chap. 3 in *Supporting Young Learners 2,* 115–44. Ypsilanti, MI: High/Scope Press.

Brickman, Nancy A., ed. 2001. "Materials and Environments for Active Learning." Chap. 2 in *Supporting Young Learners 3: Ideas for Child Care Providers and Teachers,* 57–94. Ypsilanti, MI: High/Scope Press.

Brickman, Nancy Altman, and Lynn Spencer Taylor, eds. 1991. "Environments for Active Learning." Chap. 4 in *Supporting Young Learners,* 149–86. Ypsilanti, MI: High/Scope Press.

Church, Ellen Booth. 1985. "The Music Playground: A Place for Creative Thinking and Play." In *When Children Play,* Joe L. Frost and Sylvia Sunderlin, eds., 239–42. Wheaton, MD: ACEI.

Epstein, Ann S. 2007. "What Does the Learning Environment Look Like in a High/Scope Program?" Chap. 6 in *Essentials of Active Learning in Preschool: Getting to Know the High/Scope Curriculum,* 39–54. Ypsilanti, MI: High/Scope Press.

Gerecke, Katie. 1998. "Classroom Adaptations for Children With Special Needs." *High/Scope Extensions* (October): 1–3.

Golbeck, Susan L. 1992. "The Physical Setting: Ecological Features of Family Day Care and Their Impact on Child Development." In *Family Day Care: Current Research for Informed Public Policy,* Donald Peters and Alan Pence, eds., 146–69. New York: Teachers College Press.

Greenman, Jim. 1988. *Caring Spaces, Learning Places: Children's Environments That Work.* Redmond, WA: Exchange Press.

High/Scope Educational Research Foundation. 2003. *Preschool Program Quality Assessment (PQA),* 2nd ed. Ypsilanti, MI: High/Scope Press.

Hohmann, Mary, Bernard Banet, and David P. Weikart. 1979. "Arranging & Equipping the Classroom." Chap. 1 in *Young Children in Action.* Ypsilanti, MI: High/Scope Press.

Jones, Elizabeth. n.d. *Dimensions of Teaching-Learning Environments: Handbook for Teachers.* Pasadena, CA: Pacific Oaks.

Jones, Elizabeth. 1989. "Inviting Children to the Fun: Providing Enough Activity Choices Outdoors." *Child Care Information Exchange* (December): 15–19.

Kennedy, David. 1991. "Young Children's Experience of Space and Child Care Center Design: A Meditation." *Children's Environments Quarterly* 8, no. 1: 37–48.

Koepke, Mary. 1989. "Learning by the Block." *Teacher Magazine* 1, no. 3 (December): 52–60.

Marshall, Beth. 2001. "'My Way' — Children in the Computer Area." In *Supporting Young Learners 3: Ideas for Child Care Providers and Teachers,* Nancy A. Brickman, ed., 65–75. Ypsilanti, MI: High/Scope Press.

McLoyd, Vonnie. 1986. "Scaffolds or Shackles? The Role of Toys in Preschool Children's Pretend Play." In *The Young Child at Play: Reviews of Research,* Vol. 4, Greta Fein and Mary Rivkin, eds., 63–77. Washington, DC: NAEYC.

Moore, G. T. 1983. *The Role of Socio-Physical Environment in Cognitive Development.* Milwaukee: University of Wisconsin.

Olds, Anita Rui. 1988. "Places of Beauty." In *Play as a Medium for Learning and Development,* Doris Bergen, ed., 181–85. Portsmouth, NH: Heinemann.

Phyfe-Perkins, Elizabeth. 1980. "Children's Behavior in Preschool Settings—A Review of Research Concerning the Influence of the Physical Environment." In *Current Topics in Early Childhood Education,* Vol. 3, Lilian Katz, ed., 91–126. Norwood, NJ: Ablex.

Ramsey, Patricia G. 1998. "Physical Environment and Materials." Chap. 9 in *Teaching and Learning in a Diverse World: Multicultural Education for Young Children.* New York: Teachers College Press.

Ramsey, Patricia, and Rebecca Reid. 1988. "Designing Play Environments for Preschool and Kindergarten Children." In *Play as a Medium for Learning and Development,* Doris Bergen, ed., 213–39. Portsmouth, NH: Heinemann.

Spodek, Bernard, and Olivia N. Saracho. 1988. "The Challenge of Educational Play." In *Play as a Medium for Learning and Development*, Doris Bergen, ed., 9–22. Portsmouth, NH: Heinemann.

Sponseller, Doris. 1982. "Play in Early Education." In *Handbook of Research in Early Childhood Education*, Bernard Spodek, ed., 215–41. New York: Macmillan.

Sutton-Smith, Brian. 1988. "The Struggle Between Sacred Play and Festive Play." In *Play as a Medium for Learning and Development*, Doris Bergen, ed. 45–47. Portsmouth, NH: Heinemann.

Talbot, James. 1985. "Plants in Children's Outdoor Environments." In *When Children Play*, Joe L. Frost and Sylvia Sunderlin, eds., 243–51. Wheaton: ACEI.

Vogel, Nancy. 1997. *Getting Started: Materials and Equipment for Active Learning Preschools*. Ypsilanti, MI: High/Scope Press.

Related Media

The following materials are available from the High/Scope Press, 600 N. River St., Ypsilanti, MI 48198-2898; to order, visit *www.highscope.org*, or call 1-800-40-PRESS.

Classroom Area Signs. 2006. Colorful sets of large- or small-size signs with area names.

The High/Scope Approach for Under Threes, U.S. Edition. 1999. Color videotape, part 2 "The Learning Environment," 13 min. London, England: High/Scope Institute U.K. (Available from High/Scope Press, Ypsilanti, MI.)

The High/Scope Curriculum: Its Implementation in Family Childcare Homes. 1989. Color videotape, 19 min.

Rhythmically Moving 1–9. 1982–1988. Series of musical recordings, available on CDs (Phyllis S. Weikart, creative director).

Setting Up the Learning Environment. 1992. Color videotape, 20 min.

In a High/Scope early childhood setting, adults create a child-centered environment. Children such as this child have space in which to work with materials they choose based on their personal interests and initiatives.

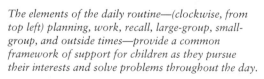

The elements of the daily routine—(clockwise, from top left) planning, work, recall, large-group, small-group, and outside times—provide a common framework of support for children as they pursue their interests and solve problems throughout the day.

The High/Scope Daily Routine— A Framework for Active Learning

Understanding the Daily Routine

"What happens now?"
"What do we do next?"
"When will we have time to . . . ?"
"When will we go outside?"

The High/Scope daily routine helps children answer these types of questions by providing them with a consistent schedule of events they can depend on and understand. It also helps adults organize their time with children to provide active, challenging learning experiences. In this sense, the parts of the daily routine are like stepping stones on a path. Along this path children engage in a variety of adventures and experiences that interest them and suit their playful, inventive natures. A consistent daily routine allows enough time for children to pursue their interests, make choices and decisions, and solve "child-sized" problems in the context of ongoing events.

As with all routines for children, the High/Scope daily routine consists of specific time segments allotted to certain activities— times for children to plan, to carry out their plans, to participate in group activities, to play outside, to eat, and to rest. Yet, as educators Caroline Garland and Stephanie White (1980) point out, "The nature of the experience cannot be deduced from the label on the activity" (p. 39). In the High/Scope Curriculum, a consistent routine is much more than a set of labels for a series of activities. **The daily routine provides a common framework of support for children as they pursue their interests and**

engage in various problem-solving activities. Next, we describe some of the ways the High/Scope daily routine supports children.

The Daily Routine Supports Child Initiative

While the **interest areas**, as described in Chapter 5, provide a structure for the *physical space* children use in High/Scope settings, the **daily routine** provides a structure for the *events of the day*— a structure that loosely defines how children use the areas and what types of interactions children have with peers and adults during particular times.

Though the routine breaks the day into recognizable blocks of time assigned to particular kinds of activities, it does not dictate the details of what children will do during each activity period. Instead, the routine is designed to support **child initiative.** As such, it provides time for children to express their goals and intentions; to follow through on these initiatives by considering their options, by interacting with people and materials, and by solving problems that arise; and to persist in these efforts until they are satisfied with the results.

In contrast to routines organized around an adult agenda of activities, the High/Scope routine is organized to allow

Learning and development are facilitated by the participation of the developing person in progressively more complex patterns of reciprocal activity with someone with whom that person has developed a strong and enduring emotional attachment and when the balance of power gradually shifts in favor of the developing person . . . . The developmental potential of a child care or preschool setting depends on the extent to which supervising adults create and maintain opportunities for the involvement of children in a variety of progressively more complex (ongoing) activities and interpersonal structures that are commensurate with the child's evolving capacities and allow [the child] sufficient balance of power to introduce innovations.
—Urie Bronfenbrenner, 1979

In an active learning setting, the daily routine encourages the formation of a supportive community in which children and adults share control.

children to build on their own plans, interests, and strengths. This focus on children's initiatives frees adults from constantly supervising children to keep them "on track." Released from the necessity of managing and doing things for children, adults become fully engaged in supporting and encouraging children to do and say things for themselves.

The Daily Routine Provides a Social Framework

As well as providing a structure for supporting daily events and activities, the High/Scope daily routine provides a **social framework** that creates

a community and sets the stage for the social interactions that develop. These social interactions, in turn, influence the ways learning experiences unfold. A High/Scope routine encourages the formation of a **supportive community** in which social relationships between adults and children are governed by the principle of **shared control.** This consistent commitment to shared control throughout the High/Scope daily routine distinguishes it from routines in which adults are always in control and routines in which adults control some events and children control others. The High/Scope daily routine both shapes and is shaped by all the persons participating in it. Such a daily routine relies on adults' careful daily team planning as well as their ability to respond quickly and appropriately to children's spontaneous interests and ideas.

The consistent social framework created by the High/Scope daily routine provides children with a **psychologically safe and purposeful environment.** As Garland and White (1980) note, the events involving children and adults throughout the day—making a plan, playing outside, meeting for a story—"break up the day into manageable blocks of time and provide a recognizable structure for the children" (p. 40). Knowing what to expect during each part of the day helps children develop a sense of security and control. The daily routine also maintains a balance between limits and freedom for children. Children feel safe because of the daily routine's predictable structure and clear, appropriate limits, within which

While children have little control over their parents' comings and goings, they have considerable control over what they themselves do in High/Scope settings while their parents are away.

they are free to work out their own ways of doing things. In a year-end progress report on their High/Scope educational program, educators Elizabeth Moore and Teresa Smith (1989) note the impact of a consistent routine: "The general picture with High/Scope is a sense of order and purpose—children taking a far more active part in their own learning, making their own decisions, and spending less time waiting to be told what to do, flitting, wandering aimlessly, or being disruptive" (p. 5). The High/Scope daily routine thus provides children with the security of **predictable sequences of events, smooth transitions** from one activity period to the next, and **consistency in adult expectations and support** throughout the day.

The Daily Routine: A Summary

The High/Scope daily routine is an operational framework that defines and supports daily events in the early childhood setting. It provides a supportive educational and social framework that is an appropriate alternative to either rigid structure or random activity. It is a regular sequence of events that loosely defines the use of space and how adults and children interact during the time they are together. Content and process are of equal importance and reflect an educational philosophy that values active learning, control shared by children and adults, and adult support of child-constructed knowledge.

The daily routine provides the operational framework for setting active participatory learning in motion.

The consistency of the routine is particularly important in early childhood settings because young children face, often for the first time, temporary separation from their parents or primary caregivers. This is a big step for children, and one that the High/Scope daily routine is designed to assist with its predictable sequences, clear expectations and limits, and emphasis on adult support for children's initiatives. While they have little control over their parents' comings and goings, children have considerable control over what they themselves do in High/Scope settings while their parents are away.

The daily routine eases children's transition from the home to the early childhood

setting by building a **sense of community**. The **collective expectations and procedures** embedded in the daily routine create a **social network—** *we all make plans, we all have work time, we all talk about what we did*. In particular, for children whose families may be changing and re-forming, the orderly, communal aspect of the daily routine may serve as an important emotional anchor.

The Daily Routine Provides a Flexible Structure

In the High/Scope Curriculum, the daily routine provides an alternative to rigid structure on one hand and to randomness on the other. It is neither an unchanging sequence of events about which adults make all the decisions nor a series of randomly evolving daily activities. The daily routine segments do occur in a predictable sequence and adults make general plans for each part of the day. Nevertheless, the routine is flexible in that adults understand they can never predict with exactness what children will do or say, or how the decisions children make will shape each experience. Indeed, for children, the daily routine provides many opportunities for following and expanding their own interests. Consequently, the daily routine has the potential for teaching adults something new about each child every day.

The Daily Routine Supports Curriculum Values

As a series of experiences that are predictable in sequence but varied in content and shaped by suggestions from children, the High/Scope daily routine framework enables adults to put into practice High/Scope's curriculum values and educational philosophy. Our belief that children learn best by following their own interests and by constructing knowledge through personal experiences and our commitment to the ingredients of active learning (materials, manipulation, choice, child thought and language, adult scaffolding) shape the process of each daily routine segment.

John Dewey on Community Life

"Most children are naturally 'sociable.' Isolation is even more irksome to them than to adults. A genuine community life has its ground in this natural sociability. But community life does not organize itself in an enduring way purely spontaneously. It requires thought and planning ahead. The educator is responsible for a knowledge of individuals and for a knowledge of subject-matter that will enable activities to be selected which lend themselves to social organization, an organization in which all individuals have an opportunity to contribute something, and in which the activities in which all participate are the chief carrier of control."

—John Dewey (1963/1938, p. 56)

In summary, the daily routine provides a stable framework within which children—assured of adults' full attention and supported by a secure social network—can safely initiate, reflect on, modify, repeat, and extend active learning experiences. While the High/Scope interest areas provide the *physical setting* for active learning, the High/Scope daily routine provides the *operational framework* for setting active learning in motion.

General Guidelines for Organizing a Daily Routine

By using the following guidelines, you and your team can establish and maintain a daily routine that works well in your setting:

- A variety of active learning periods provide children with a range of experiences and interactions. These active learning periods include the plan-work-recall sequence, small-group time, large-group time, outside time, transition times, and, if necessary, eating and resting times.

- Active learning periods occur in a reasonable, predictable sequence that meets the particular needs of the setting.

- Experiences take place in an appropriate physical setting.

- Each period involves children in active learning experiences in a supportive climate.

- The daily routine provides a range of learning experiences.

- The daily routine flows smoothly from one interesting experience to the next.

A Variety of Active Learning Periods Provide Children With a Range of Experiences and Interactions

In High/Scope settings, teaching teams construct the daily routine from the following time segments:

▶ **Plan-work-recall**

This three-part time block is generally the longest and most intense block of the day. It is designed to build on and strengthen children's natural interests, capacity for initiative, and problem-solving skills.

Planning: Each child begins by deciding what to do and sharing these ideas with an adult who understands the planning process. The adult

The plan-work-recall sequence builds on children's interests, capacity for initiative, and problem-solving skills.

watches and listens, asks for clarification or elaboration, and often records the child's plan in some way. Planning by children encourages them to connect their interests with purposeful actions.

Working: Children begin what they have chosen to do with the appropriate materials and people, and continue until they have completed their plans or changed them. Work time encourages children to focus attentively on both play and problem solving. As children work, adults pay close attention and move easily among the children—observing, supporting, and assisting them as needed. After about 45–55 minutes, children clean up by storing their unfinished projects and putting away materials.

Recalling: Children meet (usually with the same person with whom they planned) to share and discuss what they have done. Adults listen carefully and converse with children about their work-time experiences. Recalling helps children reflect on, understand, and build on their actions.

▶ Small-group time

This time is reserved for children to experiment with materials and solve problems in an activity adults have chosen for a particular purpose. Small groups of 5–10 children and one adult meet in a variety of locations—on the floor, outdoors, or around a table—to experiment with materials, pursue an expressed interest, or use materials to solve a problem. Although the

In this small-group time, children made hand puppets from foam pieces (with hard backing), colored paper strips, Popsicle sticks, and bits of scrap materials.

Sample Daily Routines

	Half Day	Full Day
Children Arrive & Depart at the Same Time	Greeting time, message board	Greeting time, breakfast, message board
	Planning, work, cleanup, recall	Large group
	Snack	Planning, work, cleanup, recall
	Large group	Small group
	Small group	Outside
	Outside & depart	Lunch
		Books & rest
		Snack
		Outside & depart
Staggered Arrivals & Departures	Small group for early arrivers	Breakfast & free play/outside as children arrive
	Greeting time, message board	Greeting time, message board
	Planning, work, cleanup, recall	Planning, work, cleanup, recall
	Snack	Outside, snack
	Outside	Small group
	Large group	Large group
	Small group for late departers	Lunch
		Singing, rest
		Outside, snack
		Plan, work, recall with parents
Variations for Special Events	Small group for early arrivers	Breakfast & free play/outside as children arrive
	Greeting time, message board	Greeting time, message board
	Ballet /Outside	Planning, work, cleanup, recall
	Snack & planning	Outside & snack
	Work, cleanup, recall	*Visiting artists*
	Large group	Large group
	Small group for late departers	Lunch
		Singing & rest
		Outside & snack
		Plan, work, recall with parents

"Let's kick our feet up in the air!" At this large-group time, children try out their own ideas about how to move to the music.

At outside time children have the opportunity for vigorous, noisy, physical play.

adult introduces a common activity and set of materials, each child is free to work with the materials creatively. Adults encourage children to make choices and decisions about how to use the materials and describe in their own words what they are doing. In this small-group setting, children use materials and encounter problems they might not experience on their own, while adults have the opportunity to observe, join, support, and challenge children and learn new things daily about each child.

► Large-group time

Large-group time builds a sense of community for children. Children and adults come together for singing, movement and music activities, storytelling, and re-enactments of stories and events. While adults initiate many large-group experiences and maintain a fairly rapid sequence of events, children initiate countless variations as well as offer new ideas: "Now it's Susanna's turn to be the leader," "Let's try Tommy's idea," "Look what I can do," "Do my idea" are typical comments at large-group time. Participating in large-group time gives children and adults a chance to work together, enjoy one another, and build a repertoire of common experiences.

► Outside time

This time of day is designed for vigorous, noisy, physical play. Children and adults spend at least 30–40 minutes outside once or twice a day. Without the restraint of four walls, many children feel freer to talk, move, and explore. Adults join in children's play, converse with them, and assist with pushes and pulls as needed. Outside time enables children to play together, invent their own games and rules, and become familiar with their natural surroundings. It also enables adults to observe and interact with children in what for many children is a very comfortable setting.

► Transition times

Transitions are times when children move from one time period or experience to the next. Transitions occur as children move from home to the early childhood setting (greeting time and message board) and back (departure time), and as they move through the segments of the routine in the classroom or center. Transitions are important because they create an atmosphere for the subsequent experience. Therefore, our

To make the transition from large-group time to outside time interesting and enjoyable for children, the teachers asked them to choose a way to move to the door.

goal is to make these potentially disruptive changes as peaceful and interesting as possible for children. For example, the day may begin with a greeting time that children join as they arrive, during which they may share information from home, read a book with a friend, or show a parent a special toy or picture. This would be followed by gathering around the message board, which uses words and pictures to let everyone know about new materials, visitors, or other special events of the day. How children begin, move through, and end each day affects them, their peers, and the adults in their lives. Ongoing adult support and planning for transitions can increase the quality of these experiences.

▶ **Eating and resting**

Meals and snacks are times for children and adults to enjoy healthy food in a supportive

social setting. Resting is a time for sleeping, or quiet, solitary, on-your-own-cot play. These home-life activities, transported of necessity to the early childhood setting, are ones around which children and their families have built particular habits, customs, and preferences. While we recognize and respect family customs, our goal at these times is to assure that children continue to experience, as much as possible, the active learning approach.

Quite simply, plan-work-recall time, small-group time, large-group time, outside time, and transition times are the building blocks of the High/Scope daily routine. These time segments designate a *process* or *place* rather than *content*—large-group time rather than story or music time, for example, and small-group time rather than table-toys time—because the content for each time period is set by children and adults. Consequently, children and adults read stories and become involved with art, music, movement, woodworking, computers, play acting, and building throughout the day in a variety of social and physical contexts. Rather than confining movement, for example, to a specific time of day, such as "exercise time," children and adults can build movement experiences into each part of the daily routine. (See Building Blocks of the Daily Routine, p. 159, for an example.)

When Can I Do . . . ?

Over the years, people have asked "If we follow a High/Scope daily routine, when can we do the XYZ program we're already committed to?" Special projects and experiences you want to provide for all the children generally fit well into small- or large-group times because these are times children are used to having the initial ideas come from adults. Even more important than how you fit these programs into the day, however, is how you *adjust them to include the ingredients of active learning.* **The challenge is to turn adult-initiated activities into experiences through which children can construct their own understanding of dance, art, math, science, or whatever the subject of the special program is.**

One center, for example, wrote a grant with the city ballet company and was funded to employ a ballet teacher for one hour each week. As it worked out, the ballet teacher came to the center from 9:00 to 10:00 on Wednesday mornings. Since this was generally the work-time segment of the daily routine, the first thing the staff did was adjust the Wednesday schedule by eliminating small- and large-group times and having plan-do-review follow the ballet period. After the first two sessions, they realized that an hour was too long for the entire group of preschoolers to work together at the same thing, so they divided the group of children in half. From 9:00 to 9:30, the first group of children had ballet while the second group had outside time. At 9:30 the two groups switched. The early childhood staff also worked closely with the ballet teacher to reduce waiting time, change from French movement pattern names to names that made sense to the children, and give children time to try particular movement patterns and variations on their own. Through this give-and-take process, the ballet teacher began to focus on her young dancers' developmental levels and to adjust her expectations and teaching style accordingly. At the same time, the early childhood staff began to see opportunities throughout the week when they and the children could incorporate ballet movements into other parts of the daily routine.

Active Learning Periods Occur in a Reasonable, Predictable Sequence That Meets the Particular Needs of the Setting

The order of the daily routine—the sequence of the time segments—varies from setting to setting and team to team, depending on the length of the program day, children's arrival and departure patterns, program location, and climate. This section discusses how each of these factors may affect the team's decisions about the daily routine.

▶ Program length

A major scheduling difference between half-day and full-day programs is the amount of time children spend eating and resting. Half-day programs generally include a snack and/or one meal and no time for rest, while full-day programs generally include 1–2 meals, 1–2 snacks, and an hour or so of rest. Full-day programs also permit more scheduling flexibility. A full-day program, for example, may include a longer plan-work-recall period in the morning and may delay small-group time until after rest time. Or, a full-day program might include a plan-work-recall period in the morning and another one in the late afternoon. How much time you spend with children each day influences how much time you can allot for each type of experience.

▶ Children's arrival and departure patterns

Many programs, especially half-day programs, have specific arrival and departure times so most children arrive and leave at approximately

Parents and Children Together

The Kenan Trust Family Literacy Model (Brizius and Foster 1993) program provides the High/Scope daily routine and curriculum for children. The program also provides high school and vocational classes and parenting discussion groups for the children's mothers. On three mornings each week, children and their mothers arrive on the bus and begin their day with breakfast together. While the children carry on with planning, work, recall, small-group time, and so forth, their moms divide their time between attending adult classes and working with their children in the center—reading to their children and supporting their active learning experiences. At the end of the day, children and moms leave together with many common enthusiasms and experiences.

Reading a book with mom is an important part of this child's preschool day. In this High/Scope program, as in the Kenan Trust Model, teachers have planned a daily routine that offers opportunities for parent-child reading.

the same time. This means that the children's day can officially begin and end at the same time for everyone and that all children can participate in each time period. In other programs, children's arrivals and departures are staggered over a one- to two-hour period so the mid-part of the day is the only part that is common to every child. There are also programs for children whose parents are themselves in school. Many of these children participate in the early childhood setting only during the times their parents are attending classes. Some children may come for plan-do-review and then leave. Others may be present only for small-group

and outside time, and so forth. Children's arrivals and departures heavily influence the kinds of experiences you and your team will plan for the beginning and end of each day.

▶ Program location

For programs located in buildings serving a large number of children or adults, the arrangement of the daily routine may be influenced by the availability and location of the gym, playground, pool, kitchen, or cafeteria. If the outdoor play space is a public park, it may be important to plan to use it when traffic is light

Building Blocks of the Daily Routine

The time segments of the High/Scope daily routine designate a *process* or *place* rather than *content,* because the content is set by both children and adults. For example, here is how Mrs. Ballou, Mr. Andrews, and their children included movement experiences throughout their daily routine one day in the fall.

Greeting time— Max shows Mrs. Ballou how he climbed up the ladder into his new bunk bed. Mrs. Ballou and the other children imitate his actions—-stretching, reaching, lifting their legs and pretending to climb.

Message board— Looking at Mrs. Ballou's drawing, the children guess there is a new tricycle in the outdoor storage shed. "I know how to steer," says Gina, demonstrating with her arms.

Planning— Mr. Andrews and the group of children he plans with form a train and travel from area to area to have a look at all the choices before making their plans.

Working— The children in the house area have "sold" their "house." They fill a big carton so full of household goods that it takes all of them together to push it to their "new house."

Recalling— Mr. Andrews pats his knees to a steady beat and starts a recall chant: "I worked with the blocks today. This is what I have to say. I built them tall and that is all. Now it's Peter's turn to tell, what he did and did so well. . . ."

Small-group time— Mrs. Ballou and the children in her small group use blocks to set up an obstacle course for the toy tumbling gnomes. She listens to children tell the gnomes where they should go and what they should do along the course: "Go up, up, up this side and then down to the bottom, right over here," Sophia tells her gnome.

Large-group time— Each child and adult has a plastic milk jug partially filled with water, which they swing, push, and carry in many different ways. Everyone seems to have a new idea to demonstrate.

Resting— As children settle down on their cots, Mr. Andrews has them close their eyes and then quietly asks them to move their arms or legs like a gentle wind . . . like rain softly falling . . . like a bird flying home to its nest . . . like a little bear curling up for a long winter's nap . . .

Following a consistent routine helps children feel secure and independent, making it easier to relax at rest time.

Boys and Girls Together

Swedish researcher Gunni Karrby (1988) has found that children in Swedish preschools respond differently to half-day and full-day programs, depending on whether they are female or male:

> Girls in full-time preschools were found to have more dialogues with the adults favoring their sexual identity, while girls in part-time preschools were more passive and silent. Boys in part-time preschools had relatively more verbal interaction with the adults and got more attention from adults than boys in full-time preschools who were found to have more peer interaction (p. 45).

> In the part-time group, where a more formal educational structure is dominant, girls adjust in the same way as in school, that is, by being silent and doing what is expected. Boys, on the other hand, use more active strategies, making themselves visible by talking and obtaining attention from adults (p. 51).

According to these and similar findings (see *A Delicate Balance . . .* on p. 160), if the day is rushed and regimented, girls retire and boys command adult attention. If, however, the day is informal, girls command adult attention and boys stay with their buddies.

What we desire in this regard is *balance* and *equity.* In a High/Scope program, whether it is half-day or full-day, we assume that *all* children are active learners, that both girls and boys are engaged and talkative, and that they receive appropriate support from adults. These research findings, however, caution us to look very carefully at our interactions with girls and boys, at how we share control with children of both sexes throughout the day, and what kinds of social messages we communicate to the children through our attentions and actions.

"It is our impression that girls were more likely to engage in activities in which adults were present, and that boys showed an equal tendency to engage in unsupervised activities . . . . We could not, of course, tell whether the boys were attracted towards the active games or away from adults; and similarly, whether the girls were attracted towards the finer motor skills or towards the adults. However, it would seem worth attempting to provide a balanced diet of activities with or without adults for both sexes, bearing in mind the tendencies of each" (Garland and White 1980, p. 46).

Questions to ponder:
What kinds of activities do I prefer?
How much time do I spend interacting with girls? With boys?
How can I balance the time I devote to supporting vigorous and quiet play?

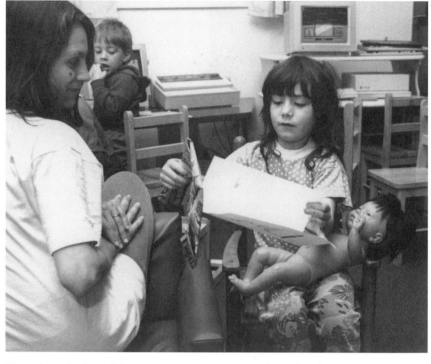

Throughout the day, adults strive to maintain an atmosphere of trust so children feel secure enough to try new things and freely speak their minds.

and older children are most likely to be in school. Home settings often involve planning the daily routine around walking school-aged children to the bus or school and meeting them again at the end of the school day.

► Climate

In many climates, weather influences scheduling. In a half-day program, for example, it may make sense to begin or end the session with outside time during the winter to minimize the number of times the children have to deal with snowsuits and boots. In very warm climates, outside time may be scheduled during the cooler parts of the day.

It is clear from this discussion that the daily routine *sequence* will vary from program to program. **Nevertheless, whatever order of events you and your team devise based on your particular situation, once a routine is established that works for your setting, it is important to maintain it.** A stable, predictable daily routine sequence gives children the sense that they have some control over what is going to happen next. They know, for example, that after recall time they will go outside,

that after large-group time they will go home. This consistency not only helps children feel secure but also assures children who are making a transition from one part of the routine to another that there will be time again tomorrow to play in the sand, hear a story, or swing. The cyclical nature of the daily routine allows children the opportunity to say "I can do the things I like again tomorrow."

Another advantage of a consistent daily routine is that children and adults can join the program at any point in the day, or year, and quickly make sense of how the day works. In this way, the daily routine is like a script for a play, with a certain number of acts each day. The standard "script" is repeated daily, enabling newcomers to quickly learn the order and requirements for each act (or time block) and to play their unique roles. Children whose first language

is different from the setting's predominant language find the consistency of a daily routine an invaluable aid in understanding the program and what is expected of them.

Experiences Take Place in an Appropriate Physical Setting

The room arrangement strategies presented in Chapter 5 will help you establish appropriate settings for each segment of the daily routine. The *plan-work-recall* time block, for example, calls for interest areas that are well stocked with materials children can choose, use, and return on their own. Small-group time works best when conducted in a cozy meeting place—with enough materials for each child. Large-group time works best when conducted in a space that is large enough for the whole group to meet together and be active. Outside time requires a safe outdoor area equipped appropriately for vigorous play.

Each Period Involves Children in Active Learning Experiences Within a Supportive Climate

A High/Scope daily routine is distinguished by each time period's focus on the ingredients of active learning—materials, manipulation, choice, child language/thought and adult scaffolding. While the setting changes from indoors to outdoors, from large group to small group to individual play—and while the experiences change from quiet to noisy, from music to art, from exploration to role play—the interactions between children and adults, children and children, and children and materials all involve the ingredients of active learning. Throughout the day, children make choices and decisions about materials and actions, and they talk about what they are doing and experiencing in their own words. Adults attend and listen to, support, encourage, and gently challenge children as they move from one experience to the next.

This consistent approach to interacting with children throughout the daily routine distinguishes High/Scope programs from programs in which the adult's role is not as clearly defined. In such programs, the adult's role shifts from monitoring, to teaching, to preparing for the next segment, to restoring order, to relaxing, to teaching again. As adults shift their roles, children's interactions reflect this inconsistency, as they shift from playing on their own and with peers to following (or not following) adult directions. In a sense, the ingredients of active learning enable children and adults to act as *partners* in the ongoing adventure of education, and the daily routine segments provide adults with ongoing opportunities to engage children's natural interests and promote children's initiatives.

It is important to note that the *emotional climate* for each period is just as important in sustaining active learning as are the ingredients of active learning. Throughout the day, adults strive to maintain an atmosphere of trust in which children feel secure enough to try new things, speak their minds, identify problems, and attempt solutions. Adults set clear limits within which children are free to engage in purposeful, spontaneous, and inventive play. Rather than alternate between taking control of children's activities or turning away from them, adults try to *share control* with children during each time period so children can assume increasing control of themselves and their learning within appropriate bounds of adult attention and support.

Attending to group dynamics is another important aspect of maintaining a supportive climate during each time period. For example, adult teams may put children who often play together in the same planning and recall group so playmates can collaborate on developing and reviewing their plans. And, adults may put all the quiet children in one small group, as one team did, so these children have an opportunity to speak up without being interrupted by their more assertive peers.

Beginning the Day With Support

"Though it is an inevitable part of becoming independent, the experience of separating from a parent can be very challenging. . . Here are some suggestions that will help.

"Reassuring greetings. Plan for one teacher or caregiver to be at the door to greet children and their parents, and the other to be with the rest of the children. Greetings may seem like an obvious ritual, but being fully greeted in a conscious, sincere way sets a positive tone for a child's day . . .

"A predictable routine. Each child's greeting should be followed by a predictable routine, which is calming for children because they know exactly what they will do next. For example, right after being greeted, children know they will hang up their coats and go to the breakfast table, where another teacher is offering cereal and milk and talking with children about their plans. Or, the routine may be to go to the book area where the other teacher is reading stories and exploring books with children, while the first teacher continues to greet children (and parents) as they come in. Parents who want to stay to read for a few minutes with children are welcome."

—*Betsy Evans (2000, p. 2)*

In spontaneous groups such as this one that formed at work time, adults enjoy sharing control with children.

The Daily Routine Provides a Range of Learning Experiences

Assuring balance in the daily routine means assuring that children engage in a wide variety of learning experiences. Here are some examples of the kinds of experiences the daily routine should promote:

• Children interact with peers and adults in spontaneous groupings (at work time, outside time), in small groups (planning, recall, small-group time), and in large groups (large-group time, meals).

• Children play vigorously and quietly both indoors and outdoors.

• Children engage in activities that continue over time as well as those that end within the day.

• Children engage in both repetitive play and play that presents new challenges.

• Children are actively involved with sensory exploration, imitation and role play, stories, art, music, movement.

Maintaining this kind of balance in the daily routine also means balancing control between children and adults throughout the day. (How to do this is explained in some detail in the following chapters.) The overall concept to keep in mind, however, is that rather than taking control of certain parts of the daily routine and relinquishing control during others, adults in a High/Scope setting strive to share control with children *throughout the day.*

In practical terms, this means that children initiate some experiences: "I'm going to the wood area and make a racer with fat wheels." Adults initiate some experiences: "Here are some shells and sand. What do you think you could do with them?" And children and adults jointly initiate some experiences:

Adult: *Today I'm going to read the story about the three pigs.*

Anton: *Don't use the book. Tell it like you did that other time.*

Valencia: *Yeah, and we all be the pigs and the wolf.*

Eddie: *And we blow like this . . . .*

Whoever initiates the activity, both children and adults have the opportunity for the respectful addition of ideas and variations.

The Daily Routine Flows Smoothly From One Interesting Experience to the Next

Moving smoothly from one part of the day to the next is also important so children are neither stressed and hurried nor bored with waiting and pointless repetition. The general idea behind assuring smooth transitions is to recognize that when a daily routine on paper comes to life in an early childhood setting, different children will finish whatever they are doing at different times. Smooth transitions help to maintain flow and momentum, while respecting each child's individual pace and work style. When children recognize the consistency of the daily routine, they can anticipate upcoming events and move toward them.

Therefore, it is generally important to start the next part of the routine while some children are still involved in the last, secure in the knowledge that they will join in as they are ready.

To help you make the most of the High/Scope daily routine, the remaining two chapters in Part 2 focus specifically on the plan-do-review process (Chapter 7) and the other parts of the routine (Chapter 8).

A consistent daily routine enables children to anticipate upcoming events. Because their teacher has given them "the five-minute warning," these children know they have time for "one more ride" before "it's time to go home."

Daily Routine Basics: A Summary

The daily routine supports child initiative.
___ Provides time for children to express and follow through on their goals and intentions
___ Enables adults to become fully engaged in supporting and encouraging children to do and say things for themselves

The daily routine provides a social framework.
___ Provides children with a psychologically safe and purposeful environment
___ Eases children's transition from the home to the early childhood setting by building a sense of community

The daily routine provides a flexible structure.
___ Provides an alternative to rigid structure and randomness
___ Has the potential for teaching adults something new about each child every day

The daily routine supports curriculum values.
___ Enables children to construct knowledge
___ Includes the ingredients of active learning in each segment

The daily routine provides a social framework in which children periodically come together to share experiences before setting off to pursue their own initiatives.

General Guidelines for Organizing a Daily Routine: A Summary

___ A variety of active learning periods provide children with a range of experiences and interactions. These periods include plan-work-recall, small- and large-group times, and outside time.
___ Active learning periods occur in a reasonable, predictable sequence that meets the particular needs of the setting.
___ Experiences take place in an appropriate physical setting.
___ Each period involves children in active learning experiences within a supportive climate.
___ The daily routine provides a range of learning experiences.
___ The daily routine flows smoothly from one interesting experience to the next.

References

Brizius, Jack A., and Susan A. Foster. 1993. *Generation to Generation: Realizing the Promise of Family Literacy.* Ypsilanti, MI: High/Scope Press.

Bronfenbrenner, Urie. 1979. *The Ecology of Human Development: Experiments by Nature and Design.* Cambridge: Harvard University Press.

Dewey, John. 1938. *Experience and Education.* Reprint. New York: MacMillan, 1963.

Evans, Betsy. 2000. "'Bye Mommy!' 'Bye Daddy!' Easing Separations for Preschoolers." *High/Scope Extensions* (September): 1–3.

Garland, Caroline, and Stephanie White. 1980. *Children and Day Nurseries.* Ypsilanti, MI: High/Scope Press.

Karrby, Gunni. 1988. "Time Structure and Sex Differences in Swedish Preschools." *Early Child Development and Care 39*, no. 1: 45–52.

Moore, Elizabeth, and Teresa Smith. 1987. *High/Scope Report 2: One Year On.* London: Volculf.

Related Reading

Brickman, Nancy A., ed. 1996. "Designing Routines for Active Learners." Chap. 2 in *Supporting Young Learners 2: Ideas for Child Care Providers and Teachers,* 57–114. Ypsilanti, MI: High/Scope Press.

Brickman, Nancy A., ed. 2001. "Exploring and Learning Through the Daily Routine." Chap. 3 in *Supporting Young Learners 3: Ideas for Child Care Providers and Teachers,* 95–141. Ypsilanti, MI: High/Scope Press.

Brickman, Nancy A., Holly Barton, and Jennifer Burd, eds. 2005. "The Daily Routine." Chap. 3 in *Supporting Young Learners 4: Ideas for Child Care Providers and Teachers,* 63–113. Ypsilanti, MI: High/Scope Press.

Buckleitner, Warren, and Sue Terdan. 1991. "Day One: What We Did When the Children Arrived." In *Supporting Young Learners,* Nancy A. Brickman and Lynn S. Taylor, eds., 143–47. Ypsilanti, MI: High/Scope Press.

Corsaro, William A. 1988. "Peer Culture in the Preschool." *Theory Into Practice 27,* no. 1 (Winter): 19–24.

Dowling, Jan Levanger, and Terri C. Mitchell. 2007. *I Belong: Active Learning for Children With Special Needs.* Ypsilanti, MI: High/Scope Press.

Doyle, Walter. 1986. "Classroom Organization and Management." In *Handbook of Research on Teaching,* M. Whittrock, ed., 392–431. New York: MacMillan.

Elkind, David. 1981. *The Hurried Child: Growing Up Too Fast Too Soon.* Reading, MA: Addison-Wesley.

Epstein, Ann S. 2007. "What Is the High/Scope Daily Routine?" Chap. 7 in *Essentials of Active Learning in Preschool: Getting to Know the High/Scope Curriculum,* 55–80. Ypsilanti, MI: High/Scope Press.

Evans, Betsy. 2007. *Teacher's Idea Book: "I Know What's Next!" Preschool Transitions Without Tears or Turmoil.* Ypsilanti, MI: High/Scope Press.

Freeman, Bonnie, Mary Hohmann, and Susan Terdan. 1991. "Planning a Daily Routine for Day Care Settings." In *Supporting Young Learners,* Nancy A. Brickman and Lynn S. Taylor, eds., 137–39. Ypsilanti, MI: High/Scope Press.

High/Scope Educational Research Foundation. 2003. *Preschool Program Quality Assessment (PQA),* 2nd ed. Ypsilanti, MI: High/Scope Press.

Hohmann, Mary, Bernard Banet, and David P. Weikart. 1979. *Young Children in Action.* Ypsilanti, MI: High/Scope Press.

Katz, Lilian G. 1987. "Early Education: What Should Young Children Be Doing?" In *Early Schooling: The National Debate,* Sharon L. Kagan and Edward Ziegler, eds., 151–65. New Haven: Yale University Press.

Post, Jacalyn, and Mary Hohmann. 2000. "Establishing Schedules and Routines for Infants and Toddlers." Chap. 4 in *Tender Care and Early Learning: Supporting Infants and Toddlers in Child Care Settings,* 191–294. Ypsilanti, MI: High/Scope Press.

Schweinhart, Lawrence J. 2004. *A School Administrator's Guide to Early Childhood Programs,* 2nd ed. Ypsilanti, MI: High/Scope Press.

Related Media

The following materials are available from the High/Scope Press, 600 N. River St., Ypsilanti, MI 48198-2898; to order, visit *www.highscope.org,* or call 1-800-40-PRESS.

The Daily Routine. 2007. Color videotape or DVD, 40 min.

The High/Scope Curriculum: Its Implementation in Family Child Care Homes. 1989. Color video, 19 min.

High/Scope for Children With Special Needs. 2006. Color videotape or DVD, 60 min.

During work time, this child dresses up "like a ballerina." The High/Scope daily routine provides children with a predictable sequence of time periods during which they can carry out their own plans and try out the ideas of others.

The plan-work-recall sequence enables children to act with purpose and to re-create their most memorable experiences. For this child, one day's sequence involves "writing" a plan in his planning book; making a drawing and hanging it up; talking over plans for further activities with friends; and recalling the highlights of these activities with the aid of a cloth path labeled with the symbols of the interest areas.

The High/Scope Plan-Do-Review Process

The plan-do-review process is the centerpiece of the High/Scope active learning approach. It encompasses all the elements of active learning—materials, manipulation, choice, child language and thought, and adult scaffolding. Moreover, the plan-work-recall sequence is the central element of the High/Scope daily routine and is the longest segment of the day—lasting approximately $1\frac{1}{2}$ hours.

In making daily plans, following through on them, and then recalling what they have done, young children learn to articulate their intentions and reflect on their actions. They also begin to realize they are competent thinkers, decision-makers, and problem-solvers. They will carry their self-confidence and independence into subsequent school settings and continue to benefit from these characteristics throughout their lives. We cannot emphasize enough the importance we place on the plan-do-review process in assuring successful implementation of the High/Scope active learning approach.

This chapter highlights the three key elements of the sequence—**planning time, work time, recall time**—and offers specific strategies adults can use to assist children in making the most of these important times in the daily routine. In addition, many scenarios are presented throughout this chapter to illustrate the dynamics of the plan-do-review process. These scenarios are based on actual events that have occurred in the High/Scope Demonstration Preschool and in other settings that have adopted the High/Scope approach.

Understanding Planning Time

In a High/Scope setting, children plan every day, both at the designated time for planning and throughout the day as they think about what they want to do. Thus, it is important that adults understand all aspects of the planning process: the role planning plays in an active learning setting, where planning occurs, what children do as they plan, and how best to support children at this time. The following plans, made by 3- and 4-year-olds in High/Scope programs, illustrate ways young children typically express their intentions.

"I'm making a kitty house. Maggie's helping."

"Me and Justin are buildin' a road so our racing cars can go reee-al fast!"

"Make a mask. On the computer."

"Dance in the big skirts for Cinco de Mayo."

"Make a cream factory with sticks and glue like Chris did. It will be real big for lots of cream. I'll show you how."

"Play in the sand. Pour water!"

The occurrence of a desire and impulse is not the final end. It is an occasion and a demand for the formation of a plan and method of activity.

—John Dewey, 1968

Plan-Work-Recall: A Summary

Planning — Each child states, in gestures or words, a plan of action.

Work Time — Children carry out their initial plans and other self-initiated activities, working and playing alone or with others. Adults interact with children to support their activities. At the end of work time, children put away materials.

Recall Time — Children reflect on, share, and discuss their work-time experiences.

What Is Planning?

Planning is a thought process in which internal goals shape anticipated actions. When young children plan, they start with a personal intention, aim, or purpose. Depending on their age and capacity to communicate, they express their intentions in actions (getting a block), gestures (pointing to blocks), or words ("I'm gonna play with blocks"). Because they participate in the planning process each day, children grow accustomed to indicating their intentions before acting on them. This helps children become conscious of their capacity to shape and control their own actions.

Planning is a thought process in which internal goals shape anticipated actions. "I'm going to make a writing table with blocks," this child tells his teacher, and then he does so.

▶ The roots of planning

The High/Scope practice of encouraging young children to make and carry out plans is based on the theories and observations of researchers (Case 1985; Bullock and Lütkenhaus 1988; Fabricius 1984; Berry and Sylva 1987), child development and educational theorists (Piaget 1962/1951; Piaget and Inhelder 1969/1966; Smilansky 1971; Smilansky and Shefatya 1990; Dewey 1933 and 1963/1938; Erikson 1950), and *our own experience* in preschool education over the past 30 years.

The child's capacity to plan emerges during what Erikson (1950, p. 255) calls the stage of "initiative versus guilt" about self-initiated actions. This means that preschoolers have many ideas they want to try out. When they are able to follow through on their intentions successfully, they develop a sense of initiative and enterprise. However, when their attempts to follow their interests are often thwarted, young children tend to feel guilty about taking the initiative.

The ability to plan develops along with the young child's growing capacity to use language and form mental pictures of actions, people, and materials that are not actually present. Preschoolers are able to imagine and talk about something they want to do but have not yet begun. So, planning in the High/Scope daily routine builds on what developmental psychologist Robbie Case (1985, p. 68) describes as the child's *executive control structures:* "By definition, an executive control structure is an internal mental blueprint that represents [the child's] habitual way of constraining a particular problem situation, together with his or her habitual procedure for dealing with it." (See Planning Mirrors Development, p. 172, for an illustration of Case's view of child development as a series of planning strategies children construct to solve immediate problems.)

Psychologist Sara Smilansky and educational theorist John Dewey have also commented on the important roles planning and reflecting on actions play in learning and development. Dewey (1963/1938) articulates the view that education revolves around *goal-directed activity* and the *child's participation* "in the formation of the purposes which direct his or her activities in the learning process" (p. 67). In 1964, Smilansky, a close observer and long-time proponent of the value of children's play and a consultant to the High/Scope Perry Preschool Project, urged High/Scope curriculum developers to incorporate a *recall process* into the planning and work-time sequence to strengthen children's ability to reflect on their plans and actions.

▶ The process of planning

When children make plans, they undertake a variety of mental tasks. Next we describe some of these tasks, or components, of the planning process.

Establishing a problem or goal. Children decide what they are going to do based on their own interests:

- "I'm going to make a boat . . ."
- "I wonder what's in that box . . ."
- "I want to find my mom . . ."

Planning Supports Initiative

"A child whose self-directed learning is encouraged will develop a sense of initiative that will far outweigh a sense of guilt about getting things started. On the other hand, a child whose self-directed learning is interfered with, who is forced to follow adult learning priorities, may acquire a strong sense of guilt at the expense of a sense of initiative."

—David Elkind (1987, p. 111)

For Case (1985), "The overriding image of the young child [is of one who] is endowed with certain natural desires, encounters certain natural barriers to their realization, but who also has the capability for overcoming these barriers" (p. 59). High/Scope early child-

hood educators support and encourage this capability.

Imagining and anticipating actions. As children plan, they imagine something that has not yet happened, and they begin to understand that some set of their own actions can make it happen. The child who wants to make a boat says, "I'll get some wood and nails and a hammer." The child who wonders what was in the box thinks, "If I push the stool right next to the box, I might be

high enough to see in." The child who wants her mom says to herself, "I heard singing on the porch. I'll look for Mom there." Thus, children begin to see their own actions as a means to an end. They also develop the desire and ability to remain task oriented long enough to act on their desires. According to psychologists Merry Bullock and Paul Lütkenhaus (1988), such task orientation calls for "resisting distractions, overcoming obstacles, correcting actions, and stopping activities when a goal is reached" (p. 664).

Expressing personal intentions and interests. It is important to emphasize that it is children's *own* intentions—their interests and desires—that impel them to engage in a series of actions that lead them toward a goal. This is true whether their intentions are relatively simple (to pick up the stuffed rabbit under the chair) or fairly complex (to build an outdoor pen for a real bunny). When children act on their intentions, they generally exhibit the energy, enthusiasm, and desire that make effective teaching and learning possible. *Children become most involved in learning experiences when adults acknowledge and support children's intentions rather than attempt to stifle or divert them.* Effective planning starts with children's spontaneous interests—*it comes from within the child.* As Dewey (1963/1938) reminds us, "Interests are the signs and symptoms of growing power. I believe that they represent dawning capacities. Accordingly, the constant and careful observation of interests is of the utmost importance for the educator" (p. 14).

Shaping intentions into purposes. As Dewey stated in the quotation that begins this chapter, a child's desire and impulse present the occasion for planning. When a child plans, he or she pauses between impulse and action to shape an intention into *purposeful* action. Appropriate

As children plan, they imagine something that has not yet happened. They also begin to understand that through their own actions they can make it happen.

adult support at planning time helps children formulate such purposeful plans.

Deliberating. Young children are initially more concerned with success (having their ideas work) than with efficiency (having their ideas work the best way possible). As young children develop their capacity to plan, however, they also become increasingly involved in learning from experience: "The last time I rolled a ball at my stuffed rabbit, it hit the rabbit but the rabbit didn't move very much . . . ." Through this type of deliberation, children's actions become more strategic and efficient as they become increasingly able to build on previous actions and their outcomes.

Making ongoing modifications. Children make initial plans—"I'm gonna play in the rocking boat with Kevin. We're catchin' fish!"—then often modify their plans as they play—"Let's pretend crocodiles are all around. We better make a

bridge or they'll bite our legs off!" Children construct new ideas and encounter unforeseen problems as they play. Therefore, we view planning as a *flexible process* occurring both *before* and *during* the play sequence.

Planning, then, is a problem-setting process involving imagination, deliberation, and ongoing modifications through which children turn intentions, desires, and interests into purposeful actions. Planning is well within the range of what young children can do because they have the requisite capacities to solve problems, form mental images, express intentions, deliberate, and make changes. Planning on a conscious level, however, is not something that most young children are in the *habit* of doing. Therefore, it is a process that requires daily adult support and attention.

The chart on page 171 is another way of looking at planning and the process children follow in turning ideas into coherent actions; it compares what happens when children do or do not plan.

Why Is Planning Important?

In any setting, there are many reasons for adults to encourage young children to express their intentions before carrying them out.

▶ **Planning encourages children to articulate their ideas, choices, and decisions.**

Putting their plans and observations into their own words helps children think about and clarify their intentions. Articulating their plans

also enables children to add detail to the mental pictures they are forming of what they are about to do. Further, children who articulate and act on their interests, choices, and plans gradually come to realize that they are ultimately responsible for their own decisions and actions.

▶ **Planning promotes children's self-confidence and sense of control.**

By planning, children come to rely on their own capacities to make choices and decisions and on their own ideas and direction. In contrast, psychologist Daniel Jordan (1976) points out that "children who grow up having no experience in setting their own objectives and pursuing the steps required to achieve them never become fully independent, responsible, and self-reliant human beings" (p. 294). Clearly, planning gives children opportunities to experience in concrete terms the relationship between their intentions and actions, and the results of their actions. They see themselves as people who can do things and make things happen. Jordan describes the benefits of child planning this way: "Being able to decide what it is one wants to accomplish and then being able to achieve it are vital to the maintenance of mental health and stability of personality. It is the wellspring of reality-based confidence, one of the fundamental sources of self-encouragement" (p. 296).

Parents of children in High/Scope settings report that their children have become "more independent, self-confident, and less subject to frustration or temper tantrums" (Moore and Smith 1987, p. 9). In a study conducted in Britain of the plan-do-review process in High/Scope settings, psychologists Carla Berry and Kathy Sylva (1987) found a relationship between child planning and

The Impact of Planning on Children's Actions

Internal Ideas	Expressing Intentions		Actions		Outcomes
No Planning					
No particular interest or intention	→		Aimlessness and wandering.		
Impulse	→		Impulsive activity.		Next impulse.
Planning					
Intentions	→	Reflect and observe.	→	Carry out purposeful sequence of actions.	→ Achievement of intent, goal.
Desires		Deliberate.		Concentrate on tasks.	Success.
Interests		Postpone immediate action.		Overcome obstacles.	Achievement of satisfying experience.
		Recall past actions.		Encounter and solve problems.	
		Connect actions and outcomes.		Deal with contingencies.	Process or product to share.
		Foresee goal and means of reaching it.		Stop upon reaching goal.	
		Anticipate problem(s) and alternatives.			
		Imagine whole and select a part to start on.			
		Organize an action sequence.			

children's increased sense of efficacy, control over events, and self-worth.

▶ **Planning leads to involvement and concentration on play.**

Psychologist Thomas Likona (1973) stresses that much social and educational literature supports the notion that people become more committed to and involved in tasks they choose for themselves. Further, Berry and Sylva (1987) found that children who planned concentrated on their play for longer periods than did children in settings where they did not plan.

▶ **Planning supports the development of increasingly complex play.**

In their study of the plan-do-review process, Berry and Sylva (1987) found that "children played with more imagination, concentration, and intellectual complexity during the time they carried out their plans than during more spontaneous, unplanned play" (p. 34). Planning, therefore, has the potential for drawing children into the kinds of increasingly challenging play defined in the following chart developed by Kathy Sylva and her colleagues Carolyn Roy and Marjorie

Painter (1980, p. 60) in the Oxford Preschool Research Project:

Ordinary Play	Challenging Play
Familiar, routine, stereotypical, repetitive, unproductive	Novel, creative, imaginative, productive
Cognitively unsophisticated, not involving the combining of elements	Cognitively complex, involving the combination of several elements, materials, actions, or ideas
Performed in an unsystematic, random manner with no observable planning or purposefulness	Carried out in a systematic, planned, and purposeful manner
Not directed toward a new, challenging goal, "aimless" and without structure	Structured and goal-directed—working toward some aim, whether the result is a tangible end-product or an invisible goal
Conducted with ease, little mental effort, and not much care; the child is not deeply engrossed, his attention may not be entirely on the task	Conducted with care and mental effort; the child devotes a great deal of attention, is deeply engrossed, takes pains
Repeating a familiar, well-established pattern without seeking to improve upon it and without adding any new component or combination	Learning a new skill, trying to improve an established one, or trying novel combinations of familiar skills

Planning Mirrors Development

According to Case (1985), development from birth onward involves an increasingly complex series of problems humans encounter and solve. People at all ages have natural desires, encounter obstacles, design strategies for overcoming them, and in the process, stretch their understanding of their world.

The process through which children move from interests to planning to purposeful actions to intended outcomes relates closely to Case's executive-control structures, a model of human thinking, which he illustrates thus: *The child encounters a problem, decides to overcome it, and formulates a strategy for doing so.*

PROBLEM SITUATION ➚ OBJECTIVE

STRATEGY

Here, for example, is how Case (p. 162) illustrates one of a preschooler's control structures for social interaction and role taking. In the situation below, the preschooler figures out how to get a basket to collect the grass a sibling is raking, to help the parent who is cutting the grass.

PROBLEM SITUATION		OBJECTIVE
Parent mowing lawn with lawnmower.	⇄	Join in activity.
Sibling already has rake.	→	Help with raking of grass.
Grass normally raked into basket.	↙	Go get basket.

STRATEGY
1. Retrieve basket.
2. Hold it near place where grass is accumulating.

The planning process, then, mirrors the development process. Children express spontaneous interests (problem situation), imagine outcomes (objectives), and plan a series of actions (strategies) to reach intended outcomes. Planning helps draw this internal process up to the level of the child's everyday consciousness. Once children become conscious of their efficacy as planners, they begin to see themselves as active agents in their own lives.

While children need opportunities to engage in both challenging and ordinary play, one goal of the High/Scope Curriculum is to encourage children to take on appropriate challenges that stimulate and support their emerging capacities. Child planning enables children to remain in control of the challenges they take on and the manner in which they deal with them.

What Children Do as They Plan

Understanding what children do as they plan helps adults appreciate and support the wide range of planning behaviors children develop over time. These behaviors include indicating intentions through gestures, actions, and words; making vague, routine, and detailed plans; and making perfunctory and real plans.

 Children develop the capacity to express their intentions.

Children are natural planners and problem solvers. In infancy, children face and overcome problems in a world where everything is new to them. As Case (1985, p. 273) notes: "The 2-month-old infant who has just experienced the sensation of having its finger in its mouth will actively work towards reinstating this pleasant state, experimenting with various possible arm movements that might enable it to do so."

Toddlers are increasingly able to work toward a goal without becoming distracted. Psychologists have noted that toddlers begin by focusing "more on the flow of activities than on the ends or consequences their activities lead to" (Bullock and Lütkenhaus 1988, pp. 671–72). By the age of 2, most children begin to shift their attention toward attaining outcomes that require

some effort. They may decide to use blocks, for example, to make a stack and stop when they have a stack that satisfies them. They may knock their stack down and build it again, but if stacking is their intention, 2-year-olds remain quite determined to create stacks and are not easily distracted by other possibilities.

Preschoolers can solve problems by planning a course of action in advance. Psychologist William Fabricius (1984) found that while 3-year-old children can keep a goal in mind, they generally work their way toward it one step at a time. Thus, as they work toward a goal, they generally deal with problems as they encounter them rather than anticipating and planning for them in advance. Very gradually, however, children between

Planning often draws children into complex play—such as this "barbershop" play—that is novel, creative, imaginative, and absorbing.

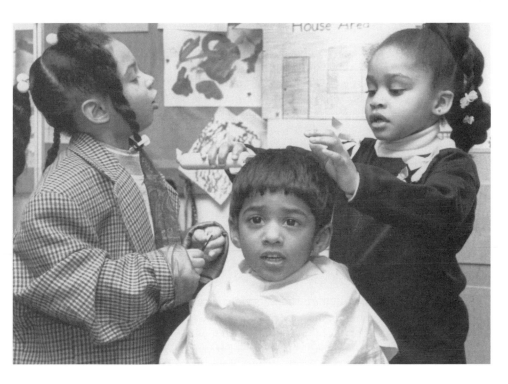

the ages of $3\frac{1}{2}$ and $5\frac{1}{2}$ gain the ability to plan a more complex course of action. They begin to foresee problems and ways around them before they launch into action, rather than dealing with each problem along the way in a trial-and-error fashion.

Being aware of how children's planning capacities develop helps adults see that planning takes various forms and is present in a variety of behaviors, depending on each child's growing capacity to identify, mentally picture, and work toward the solution of personally interesting problems. For example, for some children, planning consists of simply indicating a starting point: "Play over there." "Play with Play-Doh." Other children plan by listing several beginning points: "Read in the cozy area, paint, and play with magnets." Other children plan by outlining several steps beyond the beginning of their plan: "Make a robot. Get a big box. Tape on a smaller one for the head. Find something long for the arms." Still others can envision a fairly complex sequence of events: "We're putting on a show so we need to make a stage with the big hollow blocks, and make tickets, and put chairs up in front so people can see. And we need to practice our dance, and then everybody can get their tickets and watch." Once adults understand that children's capacity to plan develops over time and with experience, they can support all sorts of child planning in ways that make the most sense to each child.

▶ **Children indicate their intentions through gestures, actions, and words.**

From the outset, it is important to realize that young children indicate their plans both non-

verbally and verbally. Many people associate planning solely with talking, and they view planning time as an opportunity for children to build expressive language skills. For many children this is the case, but, for others, planning begins with nonverbal communications.

Expressing intentions through gestures and actions. When asked what they would like to do, some young children respond by pointing to someone or something, looking at a friend or toy, or simply starting their activity (for example, going to the block area, touching a red cardboard block, and looking back for adult acknowledgment). Other children may bring the animals or truck they want to play with back to the person they are planning with. They may also take that person by the hand and lead him or her over to the desired play area. These are all legitimate expressions of intent, conveyed by gesture and action, that adults can duly acknowledge and support:

The Development of Young Children's Planning

Infants — Work to repeat pleasant random actions.

Young Toddlers — Follow their intentions but focus on doing rather than on outcomes.

2-year-olds — Focus increasingly on outcomes; not easily distracted.

3-year-olds — Work purposefully toward a goal one step at a time.

$3\frac{1}{2}$- *to* $5\frac{1}{2}$-*year-olds* — Gradually gain the ability to plan a multistep sequence of actions to reach a goal.

• "Oh, you're pointing to the book and writing area, Katie. What will you do there?" (Katie gets the book *Mr. Gumpy's Motor Car.*) "You're going to read *Mr. Gumpy's Motor Car.*" (Katie nods and heads back to the book area to begin.) Often, when nonverbal children feel assured that adults understand their gestures and are not pressuring them to talk, they begin to add words on their own. Vanessa, for example, points to the block area and after a second shouts out, "Block area!" with great gusto. "What will you do in the block area?" Karl asks. Vanessa then acts out building a tower, then raises both arms and says "Big!"

• Six children in Andrea's child care home gather around Andrea on the living room rug. After the preschool- and kindergarten-aged children plan, 2-year-old Tessa makes her plan. To an outsider, her speech would sound like babbling, but her brother Rusty interprets: "She's saying she's gonna play with the blocks." Tessa babbles her assent and toddles off to the block corner.

• In a center for preschoolers with special needs, a group of children sit at a table with a clear view of their newly arranged interest areas stocked with toys, blocks, and books. Most of them cannot talk, many of them have trouble moving, but when Mrs. Manet asks them what they would like to play with, they have no trouble indicating their choices with gestures, sounds, and actions. Mrs. Manet, convinced until this moment that these children cannot plan, changes her mind. Children with even limited ability or no ability to talk prove to be enthusiastic choice makers and planners.

Expressing intentions in words. Most children respond to the question "What would you like to do?" by saying aloud what they

When asked what she planned to do, this child left the planning group and returned several minutes later with a book and a bag of socks. With these materials in hand, she was ready to talk about her plan.

intend to do. They describe their plans in single words ("Cars" or "Hammer"); in phrases ("In the glitter and glue" or "Over there by David"); in brief sentences ("Make something for my mom" or "I'm gonna play the ducks game on the computer"); and in whole paragraphs ("First me and Lena are gonna play dentist again. I'm being the dentist and she's the little girl. She doesn't want her teeth fixed 'cause she thinks it's gonna hurt, but, see, I'm the Doc, and I give her special stuff in her mouth. Then I read her a story"). Whether young children plan in words, phrases, sentences, or paragraphs is not as important as the fact that they are putting

anticipated actions into their own words. Whatever language children use and however they speak, it is our job to listen attentively, asking for clarification if necessary.

While language is highly important (child language and thought is an essential ingredient of active learning), it is also important to build on children's other skills and dispositions. If we equate planning solely with talking, we may bypass many *nonverbal* planners. For most children, planning ultimately does become a springboard for thoughtful conversation, but we must take our cues from children and value planning in both its nonverbal and verbal forms.

For many children, planning begins without talking. These two children need time to observe other children playing before they can decide what to do. And the children next to them have already started to play together before putting their intentions into words.

▶ **Children make vague, routine, and detailed plans.**

In the study cited earlier, Berry and Sylva (1987) noted that the clarity of children's plans depends on the extent to which they can mentally picture what they are about to do. Their classification of children's plans as "vague," "routine," or "detailed" (pp. 9–10) is useful for adults to keep in mind as they listen to children plan.

Vague plans. These are minimal plans in which children just barely indicate a choice or beginning point in response to the question "What are you going to do today?" For example:

- "Go over there."

- "House area."

- "Make something."

Children who make such ambiguous plans seem to have an unclear picture in their minds of what they actually want to do. They often end up doing one of three things: (1) going to a safe, unoccupied spot, picking up something such as a doll or stuffed animal, and watching other children; (2) wandering from place to place; or (3) seeking out an adult to join and follow. These children may be indicating that they need time to take in all the possibilities, time to see what other children are doing, or time to grasp the fact that they can make choices. In their own way, they may be trying to tell us, "I want to watch for a while before I decide what to do" or "I want to do something really safe before I risk something new."

Routine plans. These are simple plans in which children mention an activity, process, or material as a beginning point:

- "Play with blocks."

- "Cutting. Lots."

- "Wear the bells. I'll be jingling!"

These children seem to have a clear picture in mind of themselves engaged in a particular experience or with a specific material. They have a clear place to begin and generally get started right away unless someone else is using the materials they have in mind.

Detailed plans. These are more complex plans in which children mention an activity, process, or material as a beginning point, goal, or outcome and often outline one or more steps or accessories for getting from beginning to end:

• "Make a Robin Hood hat. With a feather, a real one like Michael's."

• "Be a doggie with Gutrune in the house area. I'll have a bowl for drinking and food."

• "Use the Construx. Make a telephone truck with a very tall ladder. (Pause) And I think I'll put balancers on the sides so it won't tip over, and a cab for the driver."

• "I saw birds at the beach with my dad. Hey, I bet I could make a beach with birds on it! Three birds—the mama, the dad, and the little boy bird. (Pause) And a nest for 'em. (Pause) Oh, yeah, and some water, too. You want to see it? I'll tell you to come over and look, okay?"

These children seem to have quite an extensive mental picture of what they want to accomplish and how they plan to go about it. They are generally quite persistent in spite of problems that arise, and they make modifications as necessary along the way.

► **Children make perfunctory and real plans.**

It is also important to attend to the *spirit* in which children plan. Generally, children are enthusiastic planners. You can hear it in their voices and see it in their motions and gestures as they lean in to tell you their ideas, pause to gather their thoughts, or gesture toward the place, person, or things they are talking about. There are times, however, when children just seem to go through the motions of the planning routine. They realize it is time to plan and they

do so, but their plans are perfunctory. One observant adult described this type of planning in this way: "Sometimes Jimmy just says something—anything—because I think what he really wants to do is play with his buddies, and they haven't arrived yet. When they come, they all get together and that's when Jimmy makes his *real* plan." Once adults can recognize children's perfunctory planning, they can accept statements such as "I can't make my plan now. I want to play with Chris and he's not here yet."

These children make their real *plans as soon as they find each other at arrival time.*

► **Children make a variety of plans over time.**

Children's plans change as they become familiar with available materials, their peers, and their own ability to make plans and think about how to carry them out. Here are some examples of how specific children's plans changed over time:

Teri: Planning Theme and Variations

Sept.
- "Make a house with blocks."

- "Make a house with long blocks and cardboard blocks."

- "Play with Cassie in our house. Use the big pillows for beds."

Oct.
- "Make a house with the giant Tinkertoy building blocks. It will have a roof, too."

- "Build a big Tinkertoy house and put sheets over it so no one can see us."

- "Me and Cassie are gonna make another house with sheets and Tinkertoys, and the gate will be the door."

Nov.
- "Paint in the art area. Make a picture of a house. It's for my grandma. She's at my house."

- "Look at my box from my new shoes my grandma got me! I'm gonna cut holes for windows and doors. One of those tube things for a chimney. Then I'm gonna paint it blue."

Jan.
- "Make a birdhouse like Joey's at the workbench."

- "Still workin' on my birdhouse. Put on the roof, but I need a big enough board or something else big."

- "Paint my birdhouse in the art area. One color for one side and another color for the other side, and one for this side, and one for this side, and then on the top. That's one color, two colors, three colors, four colors, and five colors!"

William: From Nonverbal to Verbal Planning

Aug.
- Looks at the boys playing in the block area.

- Points to the block area.

- Goes to the block area, stands next to Ricky and Joey, looks back with a smile.

Sept.
- Brings a car from the block area back to the planning table.

- Brings a car and long block back to the planning table and inclines his head toward the boys in the block area.

- Brings a long block back and moves his hand up and down the blocks, making a very quiet "Rrum, rrum" noise.

Oct.
- Says very quietly, "Blocks and cars" and points to the block area.

Nov.
- Brings the container of small metal cars from the toy area and says quietly, "Make a road."

► **Children engage in the planning process at home.**

Over the years, parents with children in High/Scope preschool and child care programs have been reporting on their experiences at home with the child planning process. Here are some parents' reports of these experiences:

- "Tina told me her plan while she was getting dressed this morning."

This child continues the planning process at home as he shows his dad how he will work with the pipes and fittings he watched his dad use.

- Children develop the capacity to express their intentions.
- Children indicate their intentions through gestures, actions, and words.
- Children make vague, routine, and detailed plans.
- Children make perfunctory and real plans.
- Children make a variety of plans over time.
- Children engage in the planning process at home.

- "Ricky made his plan in the car. He already knows what he wants to do."

- "When she came home yesterday, Tanya told me her plan was to look at books during her nap, and then after nap to play in the sandbox with Teri. I said, 'What about going to see Grandma?' 'We'll do that after the sand,' she said. She was very firm about it. And that's exactly what she did. Read the books, played in the sand with her friend, and then we went to my mother's. This child knows her mind!"

- "On Saturdays we all have to make a plan. Klenton is so used to planning each day with you, Ruby, that I guess he just brings it home with him. So now we *all* plan! Even Mona who has always been so scatterbrained. I think she does it because she is so surprised her little brother would come up with such an idea. It's fun to find out what everyone has in mind."

- "The other day, I heard Ollie telling his friend Fred, 'Okay, first we gotta make a plan. Then we'll get all the stuff we need.' I don't think Fred even knows about planning, but he went along with it!"

How Adults Support Children's Planning

It is planning time at the beginning of the program year. Ruth, an adult, is sitting at the house-area table with a group of nine children. She holds a cardboard tube to one eye as a spyglass, looks around the areas, and says. . .

Ruth: *I see blocks. I see books. I see paints on the easel. I see lots of things to play with!* (Looks at the children through her tube.) *I have enough spyglass tubes for each of you, so you can look for things you'd like to play with today at work time.* (Ruth gives a tube to each child, and they all begin to look through their tubes. Some stand up for a better view; others comment spontaneously on what they see.)

Chris D.: *Steering wheel.*

Ruth: *You see the steering wheel.*

Chris D.: *I'm going to use it.*

Ruth: *What will you use it for?*

Chris D.: *A fire truck!* (He leaves to get started.)

Kathryn: (Looks toward the art area.) *Ruth, I'm going to make two things. A birdhouse with scissors and paper, and then a wasp nest.* (Kathryn heads for the art area without waiting for Ruth's response.)

Colin: (Swings his tube toward the art area.) *I'm going to make a wasp nest—with baby wasps.*

Ruth: *You made some baby snakes yesterday.*

Colin: *Yes, but the wasps will be paper.* (Colin goes off to join Kathryn.)

Ruth: *What do you see, Will?*

Will: *Blocks!*

Ruth: *What will you do with the blocks?*

Will: *Build a boat.* (Leaves to get started.)

Ruth: *Caroline, I see you're looking at lots of different things.*

Caroline: *Well, I'm going to the computer to make a crown first. Then I'm going to color it with the pastels, and then be a princess.*

Ruth: *You'll be the princess with the pastel crown!*

Caroline: *No, it will be gold with jewels!*

Ruth: *Oh, gold with jewels.* (Caroline heads for the computer.) *What about you, Chris?*

Chris W.: *Sand area.*

Ruth: *You see the sand area.*

Chris W.: *Yep, I'm gonna use the tubes to make poison, and I'm giving it to you!* (He grins.) *Then I'm going to the computer.* (He leaves for the sand area, taking several tubes with him.)

Sara: (Puts her tube down.) *Ruth, that's where I'm going.*

Ruth: *You're going to the sand area, Sara?*

Sara: *No, silly, the computer. I'm playing the playroom game.*

Ruth: *Oh, the program where you make the animals move.*

Sara: *I'm going to do that and that other room where the letters come up.* (Sara heads for the computers.)

Ruth: *What do you see through your tube, Max?*

Max: *I see Will. I'm playin' with him.*

Ruth: *Why don't you find out what Will is doing. Perhaps you can make your plan with him.* (Max joins Will.)

Donnette: *Ruth, I'm reading you a story in the book area!*

Ruth: *Okay!* (They move toward the books.) *I wonder which story it will be.*

Donnette: *It's a surprise! Close your eyes.*

∽

As this scenario illustrates, planning time is a fairly brief period that involves focused, enjoyable exchanges between each child and an adult. It is important for adults to conduct planning as Ruth did, in ways that engage children and encourage them to make their plans as completely as possible. Adults can support children's planning in five important ways:

- **Examining their own attitudes about child planning**

- **Planning with children in an intimate setting**

- **Providing materials and experiences to maintain children's interest at planning time**

- **Conversing with individual children about their plans**

- **Anticipating changes in children's planning over time**

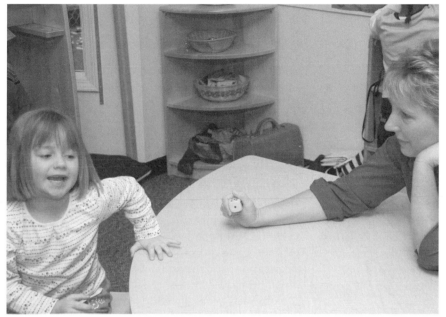

Like the other children in her planning group, this child rolls a die to get a number, talks about that number of things in her plan, then leaves to get started.

Adults Examine Their Beliefs About Child Planning and Their Personal Interaction Styles

To support child planning effectively, adults must be aware of their attitudes about the child planning process. Many adults approach the child planning process with enthusiasm because they understand that children learn best by following through on their special interests. These adults enjoy discovering children's thoughts and intentions and can easily incorporate the child planning process into the daily routine. Other adults, however, may be skeptical about the value of a planning process. They may be reluctant to change a comfortable routine or fear losing control of the situation: "What if there's

pandemonium? What if the children say one thing and do something else? What if all the children plan something in the block area? What if they never plan to do art projects? What if they don't plan for an experience I think they should have? What if children don't make the right choices?" **It is important for adults to realize that "worst-case" fears like these are rarely confirmed by reality.** You will find that once children have a consistent time and place to plan, and actually begin the planning process, they will prove to be competent planners and decision makers.

In addition to being conscious of their attitudes toward planning, adults must also be aware of their personal interaction styles. Some adults may favor a hands-off approach to planning time: "This is the children's time, so I won't interfere." Other adults may unwittingly impose their choices and decisions on children. For example, they may ask a child what he or she would like to do, and then counter the child's response with such inappropriate statements as these:

- "You did that yesterday, Juan. Think of something else for today."

- "The house area is full, Shanti. Where else could you play?"

• "I really think you should start in the art area today, Alex, because you haven't been there for a long time."

• "Why don't you paint your boat today, Kerry, and make some people for it while it's drying."

While statements such as these are intended to be helpful, they actually undermine the decisions we have already asked children to make for themselves. Once we become aware of our personal interaction styles, we can move toward an approach to child planning characterized by these key words: *authenticity, attention, dialogue, careful listening, honest questions,* and *support for the child's spirit of discovery.* We can view each planning session with children as a challenging adventure in which we support the course children set for themselves.

Adults Plan With Children in an Intimate Setting

Planning with children can occur in a variety of settings—at the art area table, in the block area, in a circle on the floor, in the middle of the room. Intimate settings such as these will help the planning process.

▶ **Plan in a place where intimate conversations can occur.**

Wherever it occurs, planning should involve a thoughtful conversation between the child planner and a supportive adult. The child talks about or in some other way indicates an intention, and the adult enters into a dialogue with the child about how to carry out the intention. Since planning with a group of children involves a series of such one-to-one conversations, the smaller the group of children sharing their plans with one adult, the more intimate and unhurried each planning exchange will be. In their study of the plan-do-review process, Berry and Sylva (1987, p. 16) indicate that children in smaller, more intimate planning groups tend to make more detailed plans:

Number of Children in Planning Group	Percentage of Detailed Plans
1–4	60
5–7	42
8–10	15

"We wonder," the authors relate, "whether the staff become more concerned in larger planning groups with 'getting through' and not losing the attention of the group than with the quality of each child's plan." Nevertheless, Berry and Sylva also point out that group size is not the only factor that influences the quality of children's plans: "Staff expectations and priorities also influence the sophistication of the planning process and the children's plans which emerge from it" (1987, p.16). In other words, while planning in a small group contributes to intimacy and detail, and is therefore preferable, an atmosphere

Wherever it occurs, planning involves a thoughtful conversation between the child planner and a supportive adult.

Overview of Ways Adults Support Children at Planning Time

Adults examine their beliefs about child planning and their personal interaction styles.

Adults plan with children in an intimate setting.

Adults provide materials and experiences to maintain children's interest at planning time.

Adults converse with individual children about their plans.

• Adults elicit plans.

• Adults listen attentively.

• Adults converse with nonverbal and vague planners.

• Adults converse with routine and elaborate planners.

• Adults encourage playmates to plan together.

• Adults value children's plans.

• Adults note plan-do connections.

Adults anticipate changes in children's planning over time.

of intimacy is one that adults can foster regardless of planning-group size. For example, one way to foster intimacy is to converse with children at their physical level. Another way is to provide interesting materials for the whole planning group to use while you converse with each child in turn.

▶ **Plan in a stable pair or group.**

Planning flourishes in a secure setting in which the adult, the other children in the group, and the actual physical space remain fairly constant. Such stability gives children the feelings of security and internal control they need to take on the challenge of planning. When changes do occur, it helps to alert children in advance: "Tomorrow, Bob and I are going to switch planning groups so we have a chance to plan with everyone. Bob is coming to the house area to plan with you, and I'm going to plan with the children in the art area."

▶ **Plan where people and materials are visible.**

The younger the planners, the more they need to be able to see the materials available to them. When materials are easy to see, children are reminded of all the objects they can choose from as they formulate their plans. For example, planning in a place that allows children to easily see the materials in the house area helps them to imagine what they might do with the dress-up clothes. In most early childhood settings, however, there will be some materials children cannot see as they plan, no matter where planning occurs. Adults can overcome limited visibility problems during planning by changing the planning setting from time to time, and by having children tour the areas just before they make their plans.

Adults Provide Materials and Experiences to Maintain Children's Interest at Planning Time

The challenge we accept at planning time is to keep a small group of young children engaged so we can plan individually with each child. When children have interesting materials to use, they do not mind waiting for their turn to plan. Once children are engaged, adults feel less pressure to rush through planning and are comfortable taking the time needed to talk with each child in turn.

▶ **Provide special games and experiences.**

A variety of special games and experiences have evolved over the years as ways to provide an enjoyable group setting for planning. These include *visibility* and *group games, props and partnerships,* and *representation activities* (see Planning Games and Experiences, p. 182). Such activities rely on playfulness and novelty to keep planning from becoming routine, and they challenge children to stretch their abilities to picture and describe their intended actions as completely as possible. They also help children see the many possibilities of planning time.

▶ **Children take charge.**

As children become familiar with the planning process, they are able to assume increasing control over planning time. They do this by adding their own spontaneous variations to planning games, taking over the adult's role of plan elicitor, and planning on their own, in pairs, or in small groups. For example, when one adult introduced the "Jingle, jingle, jingle" name rhyme

at planning time ("Jingle, jingle, jingle, jallie. It's your turn to plan if your name is Callie!"), the children in her planning group made it more fun and more active by pounding on the table to the beat, anticipating the name from the initial rhyme, and pointing with great gusto to the child with the rhyming name. Because the adult listened to and appreciated their ideas, the children expanded a planning rhyme into a playful movement experience.

Children also become quite adept at planning with each other, whether they are using props such as telephones or simply planning face to face. Often, children who tend to make fairly vague plans with an adult will make more detailed plans with another child, and the two will often carry out their plans together.

Over time, children assume as much control over making plans as adults are willing to relinquish. Ultimately, as children take more control, adults become less central to setting the planning process in motion and more important as attentive resource persons and facilitators.

Adults Converse With Individual Children About Their Plans

After they have set a playful context for planning, adults focus on *one-to-one planning conversations* with each child. In these intimate conversations, adults elicit children's plans, listen attentively, converse sensitively with both nonverbal and verbal planners, encourage co-workers to plan together, value children's plans, and note the connections between children's plans and actions. In the planning-time scenario on page 178, for example, the adult gives each child a spyglass and

Planning Games and Experiences

Visibility games

These games can help young planners see the choices available to them. They can also help children to feel comfortable in a new setting or to understand a change in the interest areas.

• **Guided tours**—Children tour the interest areas in pairs; a child familiar with planning and with the setting is paired with a new child. When they find something interesting, they begin playing. *Variation:* Children bring something they have found to an adult and have a brief planning conversation.

• **Displays**—The planning table (or spot) displays a variety of materials the adult has gathered from the interest areas. The children handle the materials, talking about which ones they would like to play with. When they have made a choice, they get started.

• **Train**—The children and an adult make a train and "chug" to all the interest areas—looking at the materials and the play possibilities as they move about the room. Children leave the train as they see things that interest them. *Variations:* (1) Children take turns being the leader. (2) The train travels around all the interest areas once with everybody on it. As the train makes its second tour, children "disembark" when the train nears the interest area and materials they want to explore.

• **Collections**—Ask each child the simple question: "What are you going to do today?" But instead of pursuing planning conversations at this point, give each child a bag, basket, or box. Ask children to collect some of the things they need to carry out their plans. As children return with their unique collections, continue planning conversations with each child about the materials selected and how he or she will use them. *Variation:* Offer collection containers of varying sizes (from cups to boxes) and ask children to select the specific container they think will best suit the materials they will be using.

Group games

Games that involve group suspense about who will plan next can hold children's interest in anticipation of their turn to plan.

• **Hula hoop**—Mark one spot on a hula hoop by wrapping it with a piece of colored tape or masking tape. Five or six children sit in a tight circle, each one holding on to the hoop with both hands. As everyone sings a short song, the children turn the hoop in a circle so the marked spot passes from hand to hand. When the song ends, the child whose hand is either touching or closest to the marked spot plans with the adult. Repeat until all children have planned. *Variation:* In place of a hula hoop, tie scarves together in a circle. Tie one large knot. Have children close their eyes and sing a familiar song. At the end of the song, the child with the large knot plans.

• **Ball**—Children sit in a circle. Either a child or the adult rolls the ball to a child who then plans with the adult. When the child has finished planning, that child rolls the ball to another child, who then plans, and so forth, until every child has made a plan. *Variation:* Do the same thing with a ball of yarn.

• **Spinner**—Children sit in a circle. Using a bottle or block for a spinner, one child gives it a spin. When it stops spinning, the child it points to plans with the adult. Upon completing the planning conversation, the child spins the spinner to designate which child will plan next.

• **Symbols**—Put each child's symbol in a box or bag (symbols are distinctive cut-out shapes bearing the children's names and photographs). A child draws a symbol from the box without looking. The child whose symbol is drawn plans with the adult, then draws the symbol of the next child to plan, and so forth.

• **Rhymes**—Make up a name rhyme like this one, for example: "Jingle, jingle, jingle jerry. It's your turn to plan if your name is Kerry." Kerry then discusses her plan. When she has finished, repeat with another child's name: "Jingle, jingle, jingle jax. It's your turn to plan if your name is Max."

Props and partnerships

Using a variety of props and forming planning pairs helps to hold children's attention while other children are planning.

• **Spyglasses**—Give each child a cardboard tube and have him or her look around the play space to see things to do or play with. As children are spying and talking among themselves, plan with each child. (See example on p. 178.)

• **Telephones**—Using two telephones, the adult "calls up" a child, and they have their planning conversation over the phone. At the end of the conversation, the child gives his or her phone to another child. The adult calls that child (or that child calls the adult), they plan over the phone, and so forth until each child has planned. *Variations:* (1) Have two children on the phones—one child plans and the other takes the adult role of supporter and questioner. (2) Have enough phones for each child so the other children can converse with one another while one of them is talking with the adult.

• **Puppets**—The adult wears a hand puppet who converses with each child in turn about his or her plan. After a child has planned, he or she tells the puppet which child to plan with next. *Variations:* (1) The adult uses one puppet and the children use another puppet so planning takes place between two puppets. (2) Each child has a puppet.

• **Voice recorder**—As the adult and child converse, they pass the microphone back and forth between them. At the end of the conversation, the child pushes the "stop" button and passes the microphone to another child. That child then pushes the "play" button while the adult pushes "record" and they proceed with their planning conversation. (The button pushing is simpler if the recorder has a "pause" button.)

• **Child pairs**—Two children plan together. One describes a plan while the other takes the sup-port role. Then they change roles. This works well once young children have planned often enough with adults to understand the planning process.

Representations

Sometimes photos, pantomime, drawing, and writing can help children *represent* (that is, visualize and describe) their plans more fully. These strategies also give each child something to do or explore while others are planning with the adult.

• **Pictures**—Put together a collection of clear, contact-paper-covered or laminated photos, catalog pictures, and drawings of all the materials in your setting, sorted into boxes by area. First, ask each child a quick "What are you going to do today?" Then ask children to select pictures of the materials they will be using. Finally, talk with each child in turn about the pictures and how they relate to his or her plan. *Variations:* (1) Have the children tape their pictures onto their symbols to refer to at recall time. (2) Encourage children to sequence the pictures in the order in which they think they will be using the materials.

• **Pantomime**— Say "*Show* me what you plan to do today. Pretend with your body but do not use any words. The rest of us will try to guess." After the child has acted out some or all of his or her plan, converse with the child about details, then go on to the next child's pantomime.

• **Map**—This strategy calls for a large map of the interest areas, including pictures or drawings of some of the materials in each area. Ask each child a quick "What are you planning to do today?" Then give each of them a plastic bear or other play figure and ask them to walk their bear to the places on the map where they plan to play. You might say "Show and tell me with your bear on the map what you plan to do." This strategy is appropriate for experienced planners who can interpret such a map. *Variation:* For children not ready for a map, try a planning path—a length of fabric or butcher paper divided into sections representing each interest area. Children stand on the interest area they would like to work in and then plan what they will do among themselves or with an adult.

• **Drawing and writing**— Provide paper and a variety of drawing and writing tools. Ask children to draw or write what they plan to do. Talk with each child in turn about his or her plan. This strategy works well when adults anticipate and appreciate a variety of drawing and writing styles, including scribbles, tracings, outline shapes, forms, designs, figures, common symbols, and letters in any combination.

This child enjoys talking about her plan while pointing to where she will play on a planning map.

"What would you like to do today?" is a straightforward way to begin a one-to-one planning conversation with a child.

• "Yesterday you said you wanted to work on your house again today, Teri. What do you think about that idea today?"

Once children become familiar with planning and understand the meaning of the word "plan" through their own experience, you can use this word in opening questions and statements. For example . . .

• "What is your plan today, Omondi?"

• "Tell me about your plan, Cindy."

• "Your mom said you already made your plan at home, Jeff. What do you plan to do?"

• "What are you planning to do today, Joseph?"

• "I see you've brought something with you that you plan to work with, Angie."

• "Joanie, you started to talk about your plan at breakfast. What else have you thought about it?"

▶ **Adults converse about children's concerns that might be impeding planning.**

When we ask "What are you going to do at work time?" we never know how a child will respond. In the case described below, Barry's sad news from home eventually leads him to his plan, but the adult does not pressure Barry to plan while he talks about his more immediate concerns:

Adult: *Barry, tell me, what are you going to do at work time?*

Barry: *My cousin's dog got runned over.*

Adult: *Oh dear. That's too bad. I'm sorry to hear that.*

then converses with each child in turn, using the strategies described next.

▶ **Adults elicit children's plans by asking "what" questions.**

To begin, put yourself at the children's physical level to engage in a real dialogue about an important subject. Then, the most direct way to elicit a child's plan is simply to ask, "What would you like to do today?" This open-ended question invites many possible responses, and a child can answer it without prior understanding of the meaning of the word "plan." Other variations include . . .

• "What would you like to do during work time?"

• "What are you going to do next?"

• "Tell me about what you're going to do today, Bill."

• "I see you have some magnets, Sharee. What are you going to do with them?"

• "Your dad told me that you already know what you're going to do today, Kwame!"

Barry: *My cousin, she cried and cried and so did my aunt and my mama.*

Adult: *That's what people do when they're very sad. They cry.*

Barry: *He should have stayed on his leash, but he didn't. He ran away into the street.*

Adult: *Dogs like to run, and sometimes they run into places that are dangerous for them.*

Barry: *I wish he didn't run into that street. (Pause) Well, maybe I'll make a house with a big fence around it. Yeah, that's what I'll do.*

Adult: *You're going to make a house with a big fence around it?*

Barry: *Yeah, I'll make it with the little blocks and the little animals. And I'll make them a house, too, where they can be away from danger.*

► **Adults elicit children's plans by "talking story."**

Some children are so eager to get started on their ideas that they do not wait to be asked. They get the attention of the adult they are planning with, announce their intentions, and begin while other children are still deciding what to do. Some children seem to need an opening question or statement to set their planning processes in motion. Still other children seem to linger at planning time, almost as if they are waiting until they can have the adult they are planning with entirely to themselves. Often, these children are more comfortable approaching the planning process indirectly, on their own terms, rather than in answer to an adult's question. **"Talking story"** (a native Hawaiian term involving co-narration and overlapping speech) is more apt to elicit a plan from these children than questioning them. Basically, "talking story" involves narrating what

you see and making supportive comments based on the child's responses. Here is an example:

Adult: *I'm sitting right next to a little girl named Lou. She's watching her friend Betsy.*

Lou: *I'm watchin' Betsy wash that baby.*

Adult: *She's washing her baby so she'll be clean and happy.*

Lou: *She'll be happy in her clean nightie. My baby's cryin'.*

Adult: *Oh, dear. Your baby's crying!*

Lou: *She's cryin' for her bath.*

Adult: *She wants a bath, too.*

Lou: *I better give her one.*

Adult: *Yes, you'd better give her a bath.*

Lou: *I'm gonna give her a bath and a clean nightie.*

Adult: *Okay, you're going to give her a bath . . .*

Lou: *And a clean nightie.*

Adult: *And a clean nightie.*

A Caution About Asking "Where" Questions

Encouraging children to describe the actions they intend is at the very heart of the High/Scope planning process. Questions such as *"What* will you do?" *"How* will you do it?" encourage children to anticipate actions.

Conversely, asking *"Where* are you going to work?" may help adults monitor children's use of the interest areas at work time, but it does not encourage children to anticipate and describe a plan of action. Here, for example, is what can happen:

Adult: *Where are you working today, Nick?*

Nick: *In the block area.*

Adult: (Later during work time) *Nick, what are you doing in the house area? Your plan is in the block area and that's where you belong!*

This last statement is not appropriate. Perhaps Nick was finished in the block area. Perhaps he was getting something from the house area he needed for his block play. Perhaps he was consulting a friend. Planning is meant to help children picture and think about what they want to do before they do it, not to confine them to a particular area for the duration of work time.

In their study of the High/Scope plan-do-review process, Berry and Sylva (1987, p. 32) found that asking "where" and leaving planning at that level leads to fairly minimal plans. Therefore, if you do initiate planning by asking "Where will you play today?" be sure to follow the child's response with *"What* will you do there?" Furthermore, if you ask "where" be prepared for such answers as these: "Everywhere," "All over the place," "In a whole bunch of places."

Adult: *Where will you work?*

Child: *All around.*

Adult: *All around! What will you do all around?*

▶ **Adults listen attentively to children's responses.**

There is no reason to rush through planning and cause children to feel hurried and anxious. Whether you elicit a child's plan with an open-ended question or by "talking story," it is important to pause and give each child ample time to respond. Whatever they say or do next tells you something important about each child's planning process. Listen for and be aware of both nonverbal and verbal planning. This tells you whether you will be translating the child's non-verbal communication into words or engaging in a dialogue about the child's intentions. Listen for vague, routine, and detailed plans to gain some idea of how much the child is able to imagine an action sequence and to what extent you might be able to help him or her picture it more completely. Listen for both perfunctory and genuine plans so you can assure children that it is okay to wait for their friends, take more time to plan, or talk about something more pressing.

One child, for example, came to planning time and sat as close as possible to the adult. When it was her turn to plan, she told about a fight her mommy had with her boyfriend and how she was afraid of the other adult in the program, because he looked like her mom's boyfriend and maybe he would hurt her as the other man had hurt her mom. After she and the adult talked about these frightening things, this child, who often made plans for elaborate art projects, planned simply to stay by this adult. The adult, in turn, spent as much time as she could in the art area so the child could draw some of the scary things she had witnessed.

Watching and listening carefully to children as they plan allows you to respond appropriately to each child. As you become familiar with the **High/Scope key developmental indicators**

When children plan, adults listen attentively. This child chooses to whisper her plan directly into her teacher's ear!

(KDIs) in early learning (presented in Part 3 of this volume) you will add a new dimension to your understanding of each child's plans. The KDIs will shed light on how the activities children choose and their particular ways of thinking about their plans relate to the important abilities they are developing.

▶ **Adults converse in a conscious "turn-taking" manner with nonverbal and vague planners.**

After an adult elicits a child's initial plan and listens to his or her response, the next step is to continue the conversation.

With nonverbal and vague planners, who do not state an initial plan in words or who do so only sketchily, the main idea is to explore the child's plan as far as possible without badgering or pressuring the child. The conversational "turn-taking" strategies, which are described and illustrated next in specific examples, are

useful for eliciting more detailed plans from non-verbal or vague planners. Using this turn-taking approach, the adults in the examples make a statement, then pause for the child to respond. After the child responds, the adults comment on the *child's* idea rather than introduce new ideas of their own. The strategies illustrated here enable adults to share control with children during planning conversations.

Interpret gestures and actions. With nonverbal planners, one effective strategy is for the adult to translate the child's gestures and actions into words. This calls for close attention to the child and verbal restraint. We are often tempted to jump in with our suggestions rather than wait patiently and respect the child's ideas, as this adult does:

Adult: *What are you going to do today, Katie?*

Katie: (Points to the book and writing area.)

Adult: *You're pointing to the book and writing area.*

Katie: (Nods yes.)

Adult: *Show me what you'll do there, Katie.*

Katie: (Goes to the bookshelf and brings back *Mr. Gumpy's Motor Car.*)

Adult: *Oh, you're going to read* Mr. Gumpy's Motor Car.

Katie: (Nods yes and walks to the beanbag chair with her book.)

Ask an initial open-ended question. This strategy works well with very young planners if the adult listens and offers comments afterward instead of responding with another question to each statement the child makes:

Adult: *How about you, what's your plan today, Pattie?*

Pattie: *Make somethin'.*

Adult: *You're going to make something.*

Pattie: *Like hers.* (Points to Donna.)

Adult: *Like Donna's.*

Pattie: *A crown. On the computer.*

Adult: *You'd like to make a crown like the one Donna made on the computer.*

Pattie: *But I don't know how to do that one.*

Adult: *Well, I bet Donna would help you get started on the crown-making program.*

Narrate what you see and comment on what the child says. This strategy helps adults match the child's pace of communication. Also, as with the previous strategy, it allows the child to direct the conversation. The inexperienced planner feels less pressure and anxiety because the adult simply makes comments rather than asks questions that demand an answer. Here is an example:

Ike: (Pounds on the table.)

Adult: *I saw you pound like that yesterday.*

Ike: *Play-Doh. I pounded it real hard.*

Adult: *Hard and loud!*

Ike: *Yeah, it was loud. I maked it flat all right!*

Adult: *Flat as a pancake!*

Ike: *Flat as **two** pancakes even! I'll show you how I can do it.*

Adult: *All right. I'll be over to see how flat you can pound the Play-Doh.*

Offer alternatives when the child does not respond. As you get to know each child, you will be able to offer alternatives suited to each child's particular interests. The adult cited here (on three different days) knows that Wendy has

Many of these children are excited about a new way of indicating their plans on a picture planning form. Their teacher understands, however, that some children may prefer to skip the form and simply talk about what they want to do.

played with beads and dolls. The adult offers these materials, and her own presence, as secure and familiar starting points for Wendy's planning. Also, when questions and comments fail, she offers actions.

Adult: *What would you like to do, Wendy?*

Wendy: (Long pause. No response.)

Adult: *Yesterday you strung lots of beads.*

Wendy: (Nods and smiles slightly.)

Adult: (Waits.)

Wendy: (Takes adult's hand and heads to the toy area.)

Adult: *Let's see what we can find.*

❦

Adult: *What would you like to do, Wendy?*

Wendy: (Long pause. No response.)

Adult: *Sometimes you point to something you'd like to work with.*

Wendy: (Sits in adult's lap.)

Adult: *Maybe you'd like to stay with me and watch for a while.*

Wendy: (Nods yes.)

❦

Adult: *What would you like to do, Wendy?*

Wendy: (Watches children playing with dolls.)

Adult: *Jill and Anna are playing with the doll babies.*

Wendy: (Continues to watch.)

Adult: *I'm going to feed my doll baby in the house area. You can help me if you'd like.*

Wendy: (Nods yes.)

► **Adults converse with routine and elaborate planners.**

Routine planners, who state simple but clear plans, and elaborate planners, who articulate plans of more complexity, also need adult support to continue the planning dialogue. Sometimes, however, in an effort to finish planning time, adults rush through planning conversations with such children and then try to talk with and question them during work time. At planning time, children are generally willing to stop and think about what they are going to do because they have not yet started to play. During work time, however, in the midst of their play, questions may annoy children and disrupt what they are doing. Therefore, it is important to converse with these able planners at *planning* time, to engage them in the challenge of thinking *before* doing.

Interestingly, Berry and Sylva (1987) report that while adults tend to question nonverbal and vague planners extensively, they seldom question routine and elaborate planners. Their findings suggest that adults tend to persist in questioning vague planners until they arrive at a more complete picture of what they might do, but pass up the opportunity to converse with and question children who have the potential for thinking through and articulating even more elaborate plans. Perhaps this tendency stems from a focus on what children *cannot* do rather than on what they *can* do. Whatever the cause, it is important to encourage both routine and elaborate planners to think through their plans as much as they can. Respectful listening and turn-taking strategies are important for these more experienced planners, just as they are for nonverbal and vague planners. In addition, using the following strategies will help routine and elaborate planners further develop their ideas.

As you review the strategies and accompanying conversational examples, note again how the adults work to give the child control in each planning dialogue by asking an opening question, waiting for a response, and reflecting children's ideas in their comments and responses.

Converse about space and materials. This can help children anticipate and solve problems that might otherwise prevent them from carrying out or even getting started on their plans:

Adult: *What's your plan today, Pete?*

Pete: *Make a really big monster house. Really big!*

Adult: *How will you make a really big monster house?*

Pete: *With all the blocks. The cardboard ones, the big wooden ones, and those other ones you can reach inside of.*

Adult: *That sounds like almost all our blocks to me.*

Pete: *Yep! I'm usin' all of 'em.*

Adult: *You know, I see some other kids already using the big hollow blocks and some of the big wooden blocks.*

Pete: *Aw, darn it! I need those!*

Adult: *Well, there are still some blocks left.*

Pete: *(Looks around.)*

Adult: *Sometimes people make houses out of other things.*

Pete: *I could use the pillows.*

Adult: *The pillows.*

Pete: *Maybe those boxes we had yesterday!*

Adult: *The boxes we used at small-group time.*

Pete: *Yeah, they're even bigger than the blocks. Ha! I'm gonna have an even bigger monster house now!*

∾

Adult: *How about you, Maria, what's your plan?*

Maria: *Paint at the easel. Make a rainbow.*

Adult: *Paint a rainbow at the easel.*

Maria: *But there's no room!*

Adult: *There are already some kids using the easel.*

Maria: *Well, but I want a big paper.*

Adult: *Yes.*

Maria: *And room for all the colors.*

Adult: *You need room for all the colors and a big piece of paper.*

Maria: *I could put it on the table.*

Adult: *Yes, you could. There's no one using the table.*

This child has drawn his plan. Using words to fill in the details, he explains that he will work at the computer to make some "magic tools" for "spy guy" play.

Talk about details. Talking about details gives a child the opportunity to put a fairly extensive mental picture into words and to think through and describe some of the steps needed to accomplish the task he or she has in mind:

Adult: *What will you do today, Jeff?*

Jeff: *Make an exercise machine.*

Adult: *Oh, an exercise machine. That sounds like a hard thing to do.*

Jeff: *Well, I'm going to use the big giant Tinkertoys and make some of those lifter things.*

Adult: *A lifter thing like a bar with weights on the ends?*

Jeff: *Yeah, I'll get a long Tinkertoy for the lifter and then put the round wheel things on for the weights.*

Adult: *So your exercise machine will have a lifter with weights.*

Jeff: *I'll make a part for your feet where you put them under and then lift them like this.* (He lies on the floor and shows where the bar goes over his feet.)

Adult: *I see.*

Jeff: *I'll have to make a holder for it, maybe with blocks . . . some on one end and some on the other.*

Talk about sequence. Sequence conversations allow children to organize multiple intentions. Such children generally follow these "maps across time" quite rigorously once they have described them in their own words and set themselves the challenge:

Adult: *Well, Mira, what's your plan?*

Mira: *Play in all the areas.*

Adult: *All the areas. That's a lot of places. What will you do first?*

These children are very interested in a planning board their teacher has created to experiment with the idea of sequence in planning. She encourages children to draw lines between their symbols and pictures of the interest areas where they will carry out their plans.

Mira: *Go to the art. Make a card for my mom.*

Adult: *Ah, make a card.*

Mira: *A Happy Birthday card 'cause it's her birthday. It's gonna have flowers.*

Adult: *First you're making a birthday card with flowers for your mom.*

Mira: *Then put it in my cubby and read a book.*

Adult: *Make a card, put it in your cubby, read a book.*

Mira: *Then I think . . . the block area. Yeah, make a house in the block area and then go to the house area for some stuff for soup.*

Adult: *I don't know if I can remember all that.*

Mira: *Write it!*

Adult: *You tell. I'll write.*

Mira: *First, card for my mom, put it in my cubby, then read, then make a house and soup.* (Adult writes down Mira's words.)

Adult: *That's a lot to do, Mira!*

These two children make their plans together because they plan to play together.

Tonio: *Okay! An' I'm gonna make a police car with the steering wheel and blocks and put all my stuff in it.*

► **Adults encourage playmates to plan together.**

When children play together, it often makes sense for them to plan together. This gives them a real-life setting for teamwork and cooperative problem solving:

Adult: *What will it be for you today, Linda?*

Linda: *Play with Jan and Rita.*

Adult: *Play with Jan and Rita.*

Linda: *Play with the dress-ups like we did the other day.*

Adult: *Maybe you and Jan and Rita can make a plan together.*

Linda: *We'll tell you!*

► **Adults value children's plans.**

Adult interest and responsiveness supports children's development. Speaking at a pediatric roundtable discussion, psychologist Paul Chance (1979) noted that institutionalized infants, when compared with other infants, were "just as capable of standing in their cribs, but were far less likely to do so. The reason . . . was that the institutionalized children got nothing for their efforts: nobody paid any attention" (p. 31). Children in High/Scope settings are very likely to express and carry out their intentions *because adults value their efforts to do so.* Although we have already discussed the following ways in which adults demonstrate that they value children's planning, we summarize them here:

- Setting aside a time for planning each day

- Asking children open-ended questions that call for actions

Remind children about related prior work. Reminders help children build on their previous play and begin to see that the plans they make from day to day can be related:

Adult: *Hi, Tonio. What do you think you'll be doing today?*

Tonio: *Being a policeman.*

Adult: *You made some policeman things yesterday.*

Tonio: *Yep. I made me a police badge. I gotta get some tape to hold it on my jacket. An' handcuffs, too.*

Adult: *I remember you tied two bracelets together with yarn for handcuffs.*

Tonio: *Now I need a belt 'cause when you're carryin' the handcuffs you put 'em over your belt.*

Adult: *Today you need a belt?*

Tonio: *There's that one in the house area. An' I need a map that says where to go. You know, one of those folding ones.*

Adult: *I have a map like that in my car you can use.*

- Listening attentively to children's responses

- Conversing with children about their plans

- Building on children's ideas and intentions

- Giving children time to respond, then following children's cues

- Accepting children's unique responses, rather than expecting children to express their ideas according to a formula.

Following are some additional strategies for showing the value we place on children's plans.

Encourage rather than praise children's ideas. Adults can more appropriately communicate the value they place on children's intended actions through interest and specific encouragement rather than praise. High/Scope educational consultant Mark Tompkins (1991) notes that "praise, well-intentioned as it might be, has been shown through research and practice to invite comparison and competition and to increase the child's dependence on adults. Too much praise can make children anxious about their abilities, reluctant to take risks and try new things, and unsure of how to evaluate their own efforts" (p. 1). Adult *encouragement*, however, puts children in control and makes them the evaluators of their own work.

At planning time, adults encourage children's ideas by attending to them and by commenting specifically on some aspect of a particular plan. Here are some examples:

Barry: *I wish my cousin's dog didn't run into that dangerous street. (Pause) Well, maybe I'll make a house with a big fence around it. Yeah, that's what I'll do.*

Adult: *Building a fence will keep a dog safe. So that's your plan, Barry, to make your house with a big fence around it?*

Adult: *Ah, make a card.*

Mira: *A Happy Birthday card 'cause it's my mom's birthday. It's gonna have flowers.*

Adult: *A card with flowers you draw is a way to tell your mom "Happy Birthday."*

Adult: *Sometimes people make a house out of other things.*

Pete: *Maybe I could use those boxes we had yesterday.*

Adult: *Yes, the boxes we used at small-group time are big and sturdy.*

Pete: *They're even bigger than the blocks! . . .*

Linda: *Play with the dress-ups like we did the other day.*

Adult: *Linda, you made some very colorful hats with the scarves and feathers.*

Linda: *Maybe we'll use some ribbons this time, too . . .*

Write down children's plans. Writing down a child's plan is another way adults show they value children's planning. This act says to the child, "Your plan is so important that I'm going to save it by writing it down." Some adults write down what each child says, word for word, while others take notes. Whatever the method, children see adults writing and know that adults value their ideas and intentions. By writing down children's plans, adults also encourage children interested in writing to write their own versions of their plans.

Writing down a child's plan is one way adults show that they value children's planning.

▶ **Adults note the connection between children's plans and actions.**

Planning time ends for children when they have reviewed their plans with an adult and leave the planning group to get started. At this point, adults note the connection between the child's actions and what he or she has just planned. Does Katie read *Mr. Gumpy's Motor Car*? Does Ike get started with the Play-Doh? Does Patti get help from Donna starting up the crown-making program? Briefly observing each child as he or she leaves the planning group gives adults a clue about the child's understanding of the planning process and who might need some help getting started at the beginning of work time.

Adults Anticipate Changes in Children's Planning Over Time

The dynamics of planning time change as children and adults get to know one another, become familiar with the interest areas, and become increasingly confident in their ability to make and support choices and plans. From a quiet, low-key beginning, planning time grows into an exciting time when children talk about their ideas with assurance and devise ways of carrying them out.

Ruth Strubank, who has served as head teacher at the High/Scope Demonstration Preschool in Ypsilanti, Michigan, contributes the following account of how planning changes over time:

To make planning concrete for the children in her planning group, this teacher asked the children to bring something to the planning table that they wanted to use at work time.

Beginning the Planning Process

In the beginning, it is very important not to make planning time difficult for children or adults. For many children, the concept of making choices is new. Therefore, we focused on helping children become familiar with materials and the interest areas where they were located. The children needed to know what materials were available before they could tell us what they planned to do with them. With this in mind, these are some of the ways we initiated planning with children:

• On the first day, we involved new planners with experienced planners by asking each experienced child to take a new child to an interest area to look at what was available. Our subsequent planning conversations with new children were quite informal and occurred after the children had started to play. Generally, we said something such as, "Max, I see you've decided to play with the trucks in the block area." New planners simply told us what they were going to play with and where they were going to play.

• On the second day of planning, we all sat down in a circle together. Ann (my team member) and I had gathered things from all the interest areas and put them in the middle of the circle. As children handled and talked about the materials, they got ideas about what they would like to do. Some children shared their ideas with Ann or me at this point, while others simply went to the areas to get started. We talked with these children as soon as we could get to them. Since most children didn't know the word "plan," we asked, "What would you like to do today?" or "You're holding a paintbrush. There are paint and paper in the art area if you'd like to paint today." We also referred new planners to experienced planners for help in getting started. The experienced children felt good about knowing where things were and how to use them, and we relied on their help.

• By the end of the first week of planning, we divided the children into two planning groups, one with me and one with Ann. We put their signs around the two planning tables to help them find the planning group they belonged to. In these small groups we played a variety of visibility games—a train to the interest areas, walking tours of the interest areas, displays of new and familiar materials from each area. Planning conversations with each child were simple and brief.

One key to introducing planning time is finding a balance between visibility games and planning conversations. On one hand, we often get so carried away with making a train, or playing with materials from the interest areas, that we lose sight of planning conversations. On the other hand, planning conversations that occur in the absence of materials and knowledge of what is available make little sense. We need to take our cues from the children, doing things that help them become aware of materials and choices, and conversing with children in a way that is supportive rather than burdensome.

When children are new to planning, they tend to plan fairly rapidly. Children often have little to say until they become familiar with the interest areas, the materials, and the other children. They will often simply indicate one thing they want to use, one person they want to play with, or one place where they want to work. Many children make similar plans at first because they like the comfort of repetition and familiar things. Their experience with materials is limited and they need additional opportunities to use the materials in different ways.

Planning After Two Months

By now, planning time is part of the routine children anticipate and expect. Children are ready for more planning games and longer planning conversations. They often arrive at planning time with a plan in mind, make plans for more than one activity, describe in some detail what they are going to do, and as a group, make a greater variety of plans.

Planning After Five or Six Months

By this time, children often describe what, how, where, and with whom they will work and are apt to make several connected plans. Christopher, for example, planned to make a screwdriver using the pegs in the toy area, then to get dressed up and use the screwdriver to repair the house area's refrigerator and stove. He did all this, and then went on to repair the boat Will had made in the block area.

Because children now feel more competent about making decisions and have had more experience using materials in several different ways, they are making a wider variety of plans. Planning time also lasts longer because children are more involved with their ideas at this stage and have more details to share, and sometimes more than one plan to consider. They are also more aware of one another and may engage in cooperative or team planning. With five or six months of planning experience, children can plan in pairs rather successfully and enjoy adding to each other's ideas.

∾

Planning is a child-adult partnership. Child-adult cooperation is the key to successful planning experiences. The child supplies the intentions and ideas for carrying them out; the adult encourages the child to think about and discuss his or her plans. In their study of early education programs, Rheta DeVries and Lawrence Kohlberg (1987) make this observation about the importance Piaget placed on child-adult cooperation: "Piaget emphasized that ego development necessitates liberation from the thought and will of others. Lack of this liberation results in the inability to cooperate. How does this liberation come about? For Piaget, it is through the child's experience of being respected by the adult who offers to cooperate with the child. Learning

Planning is an adult-child partnership—the child supplies the ideas, the adult provides the support to carry them out.

to understand others begins as [adults] show that they understand the child's inner feelings and ideas" (p. 35).

Planning is just a beginning. The whole point of making a plan is to carry it out—turning intentions into actions. Now that we have looked closely at what it means to plan, we are ready to move on to *work time*, the "do" part of the High/Scope plan-do-review process.

Common Adult Concerns About Planning Time

What if all the children plan to play in the block area?

Adults new to the child planning process worry that if they allow children to decide for themselves what to do during work time, the children will all choose the most popular area and chaos will occur. First, be assured that when given a choice most children will follow their own interests. When the interest areas are well stocked, children plan to work with a variety of materials, not just with those in one area. If, for some reason, a number of children plan to play in the block area and it does become rather crowded, children have the opportunity to solve a real problem. Among themselves or with adult support, if needed, they will figure out ways to share space and materials or move some of their block play to a less crowded spot. Adults can calm their own fears of overcrowding by having faith in the breadth of children's interests and their ability to solve their own problems.

Adults can also make sure that all the interest areas are arranged and equipped so children will want to do things in every area. If the block area is full of interesting materials, but the house area consists of one table and one doll, most children will choose the block area over the house area. To avoid overcrowding in one area, make all the interest areas irresistible!

One strategy we do not advocate is setting limits on the number of children who can play in an area at one time. This "administrative" approach to potential overcrowding deprives children of important opportunities to solve real space and material problems, and it allows adults to ignore play space arrangement issues. Furthermore, limiting access to interest areas undermines the child planning process.

What if some children never make a plan to work with certain materials?

When you give children choices, some children will want to try everything, and eventually they will, while other children will prefer to stay with a favorite material or activity for extended periods of time. Ricky, for example, may build with blocks, boxes, Tinkertoys, Lego blocks, and sand, and be involved in role play, but will never plan to paint, draw, cut, or glue. While we want children to work with a variety of materials, including art materials, planning time is not the time to force choices on children or manipulate their choices to fit our expectations. For example, we do not want to say to Ricky, "Ricky, today you have to make a plan to paint or glue before you can build with blocks." Giving children planning choices means respecting their ideas and interests. Nevertheless, we can make sure that Ricky works with art materials by using them at small-group time and by providing art materials at outside time (see Chapter 5 for more information on setting up interest areas). Using art materials at other times of the day gives Ricky the chance to see their potential for his work-time projects, and gradually he will incorporate them into his plans. He may begin, for example, by using paper, tape, and crayons to make road signs.

What if a child makes the same plan every day?

Noting the connection between plans and actions is important. While children may say the same thing over a period of time at planning time, careful observation generally reveals that, in fact, children vary and build on what they do from day to day. For a number of days, Margo, for example, planned to be a doggy with Donna. While they did play doggy each day, their role play expanded to include making dog dishes, dog food, reading stories before dog naps, making dog jewelry and dog toys, making dog houses from large boxes, decorating the walls with pictures, and so forth. Although her plans remained rather brief, at recall time, Margo talked about the new things she did each day. For other children, play variations are less dramatic. Michael, for example, often planned to play in the sand and water area. Once there, however, he used a variety of containers and scoopers for filling and emptying and imitated other children who also played there. Some days he concentrated on molding, on other days, Michael worked to keep the water in his sand holes. One day, he brought the small plastic animals over for a swim and a "jungle farm." While children may say the same thing at planning time, it is up to adults to look for, appreciate, and acknowledge the variety in their actual play.

How Adults Support Children's Planning: A Summary

Adults examine their beliefs about child planning and their personal interaction styles.

Adults plan with children in an intimate setting.
___ Adults plan in a place where intimate conversations can occur.
___ Adults plan in a stable pair or group.
___ Adults plan where people and materials are visible.

Adults provide materials and experiences to maintain children's interest at planning time.
___ Visibility games
___ Group games
___ Props and partnerships
___ Representations
___ Children take charge

Adults converse with individual children about their plans.
___ Adults elicit children's plans by asking "what" questions.
___ Adults converse about children's concerns that might be impeding planning.
___ Adults elicit children's plans by "talking story."
___ Adults listen attentively to children's responses.
___ Adults converse in a conscious "turn-taking" manner with nonverbal and vague planners.
　　___ Interpret gestures and actions.
　　___ Ask an initial open-ended question.
　　___ Narrate what you see and comment on what the child says.
　　___ Offer alternatives when the child does not respond.

___ Adults converse with routine and elaborate planners.
　　___ Converse about space and materials.
　　___ Talk about details.
　　___ Talk about sequence.
　　___ Remind children of related prior work.
___ Adults encourage playmates to plan together.

___ Adults value children's plans.
　　___ Encourage rather than praise children's ideas.
　　___ Write down children's plans.
___ Adults note the connection between children's plans and actions.

Adults anticipate changes in children's planning over time.

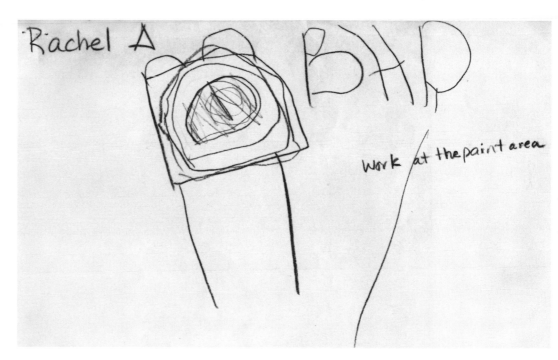

At planning time, children express their intentions in a variety of ways—through gestures, actions, and words. Here is a plan Rachel made by drawing a picture of what she intended to do. Her teacher wrote down what Rachel said as she explained her plan.

Understanding Work Time

Work time is the time of day during which children carry out their intentions, play, and solve problems. In this section we explain why work time is such an important part of the High/Scope daily routine, where children play during this time, what children do during work time, and how adults support them effectively. The following re-creation of several minutes of an actual work time in one High/Scope preschool program illustrates the dynamics of this part of the plan-work-recall sequence.

It is work time. Donnette is "reading" a story to Ruth, an adult. Kathryn is folding a cardboard roof for her birdhouse. Nearby, Colin searches for just the right paper for creating baby wasps, while Dom "writes" out tickets for a show Linda and Kerry are staging in the block area. Will and Max have converted the rocking boat into a "net fishing" boat, and they are talking with Ann, an adult, about what they might use for their net. "It's got to have holes," Will says, "but not too big holes or the fish will get out."

∼

Joseph adds more blocks to his house. "No fire, yet," he tells Chris D. and Athi. "It's not ready." Athi and Chris have propped the steering wheel between three cushions for their fire truck. Since Joseph's house isn't ready for a fire, they consult a road map for other fires. Over in the sand, Ali pauses to watch Chris W. fill cardboard tubes.

∼

"Hey! Watch this, Caroline!" Caroline turns from her computer screen to Sara's and laughs with Sara as she makes a balloon come out of a drawer pictured on the screen. Hearing their laughter, David and Chris M. look up from arranging their small blocks. In doing so, David glances at a set of tumbling gnomes, decides to use them in his play, and then gathers up some pipe cleaners and a kaleidoscope to complete his selections.

At work time, children carry out their plans ("We're going to play Batman!"), play, and solve problems they encounter ("What can we use for leg protectors?"). On this day, "Batman" and "Robin" have dressed up in capes made from scarves they have borrowed from the music area. They are "driving" a Batmobile they built using two large wedge-shaped hollow blocks, a steering wheel, and large half-tunnel blocks for "leg protectors."

What Is Work Time and Why Is It Important?

At work time children carry out a **purposeful sequence of actions** they have thought about and described during planning time, while also following through on new ideas and plans that arise as they play. As they work independently and with other children and adults, children play with purpose and concentration, solve problems they encounter. During these activities, their developmental progress is reflected in observable behaviors called **key developmental indicators (KDIs)**, which are described in Part 3 of this book.

▶ **Children carry out intentions.**

Work time in the High/Scope Curriculum is the "doing" part of the plan-do-review process. Children transform their initial plans into concrete actions, discover new ideas, make choices, select materials, and finish what they have started. The most obvious reason for work time is to provide children with the immediate opportunity to put into action the ideas they have indicated at planning time. Making plans is just the beginning; at work time, children select materials, find a place to start, and get started, critical steps that lead children to view themselves as *doers*.

▶ **Children play with purpose.**

While work time is *purposeful*, it is also *playful*. John Dewey (1933) recognized the value of playfulness in the education process: "To be playful and serious at the same time is possible, and it defines the ideal mental condition" (p. 286). Similarly, educator Michael Ellis (1988) discusses the significance of play as a medium for learning and development: "The propensity to play is a

While work time is purposeful, it is also playful. These children enjoy a nose-pinching game they have created together.

biological system for promoting rapid adaptation to threats to survival that cannot be predicted. . . . Playfulness is a critically important characteristic of humans. . . . Play has brought us to where we are now both as a species and as individuals and will be the basis for our future adaptation to the unpredictable future" (pp. 24, 25).

It is clear that children discover and make sense of their world through playful pursuits. High/Scope's work time promotes children's innate desire and need to explore, experiment, invent, construct, and pretend—in short, *to play*. Through the High/Scope planning process, children give conscious direction to their play. When children carry out their plans at work time, their activities have both the concentration and seriousness of work, and the enjoyment and spontaneous creativity of play.

► **Children participate in a social setting.**

The social context of work time becomes evident as we observe children working in self-selected pairs and groups. Even children working alone are generally aware of others. Because of its social nature, work time may be noisy, even boisterous, at times. As children carry out their plans and comment on the pursuits of their peers, there is a constant, comfortable hum of conversation, laughter, and noise brought about by children's industrious use of materials.

► **Children solve problems.**

Children's work-time pursuits are self-generated, influenced by new ideas, and likely to lead to unforeseen events and problems—the baby doll is too big for the bed, the paint drips, the sand runs out through the holes in the cup, the blocks topple. Further, what children *think* is going to happen often does not—the marker will not mark on foil; the roof board that fits over one part of the house does not fit over another; Bettye wants to be the doctor, not the mommy. As educator Doris Fromberg (1987) notes, in these situations children may be caught "between surprise and familiarity, partial resemblance and partial difference, what they expect and what they find" (p. 45). Encountering and dealing with such unexpected difficulties can lead children to a new and more complete understanding of physical and social realities.

► **Children construct knowledge as they engage with curriculum content, as described by the KDIs.**

The KDIs for early learning fall under five major categories: **approaches to learning; language, literacy, and communication; social and emotional development; physical development, health, and well-being;** and **arts and sciences** (which is broken down into the four subcategories of **mathematics,**

science and technology, social studies, and **the arts**). The KDIs are described fully in Part 3, but it is important to note here that they generally occur as a natural part of children's self-initiated activities at work time. The KDIs reflect what children are learning about themselves and the people, materials, ideas, and events of their world:

• "Hey, 'sock' rhymes with 'clock.' So does 'knock, knock!'" (*Having fun with language*—a KDI in **language, literacy, and communication**)

• "Let's pretend I'm the mom and you're the baby, and we're going to the farmers' market." (*Pretending and role playing*—one of the **dramatic art** KDIs)

• "Look where I climbed. I'm taller than even you!" (*Experiencing and describing positions*—a **mathematics** KDI)

• "No, not that button. I need one that's just the same as this one for her other eye." (*Sorting and matching*—a KDI in **science and technology**)

• "He's cryin' 'cause Ellie's got the truck, and he wants it for his garage." (*Being sensitive to the feelings, interests, and needs of others*—a KDI in **social studies**)

In other words, at work time preschool children construct their own knowledge. They initiate active, hands-on experiences that enable them to construct the kinds of knowledge and capacities represented by the High/Scope KDIs.

► **Adults observe, learn from, and support children's play.**

By observing, supporting, and entering children's play in the appropriate spirit, adults have the opportunity to discover the special interests of individual children: how they think and reason, whom they like to play with, how they use what they know to solve problems. **In fact, the insights adults gain about children at work time guide them in their interactions with children throughout the day.** Research on children's play

---

At Work Time, Children Construct Knowledge

Through their work-time pursuits, children's self-initiated plans become self-educating experiences:

• Building social relations—"Joey let me play with him. He's my friend."

• Developing initiative—"I can mix the paints I need."

• Finding out about how things work—"Watch me! I can put this wheel right back on!"

• Discovering mathematical relationships—"There's one for this kitty and one for this kitty but, oops, this kitty doesn't get one. Wait, I will find you another one, kitty."

• Learning to represent one thing with another—"This block is my bed."

• Using language to communicate—"Be quiet, baby, while I read you this story 'bout Jack and the big beans."

The insights adults gain about children at work time guide them in their interactions with children throughout the day.

backs up this claim: "The development of a child's play ability parallels development in all developmental areas; thus, observation of a child's play can give insight to overall development" (Sponseller 1982, p. 232).

What Children Do at Work Time

To support children appropriately at work time, it is important for adults to understand what children *do* in relation to plans, social settings, types of play, and conversations.

▶ **Children are involved in initiating, working on, modifying, completing, and changing their plans.**

After children have indicated a choice or talked about a plan with an adult, they are very likely to get started immediately. *The transition from gestures or words to action marks the beginning of work time for each child.*

The way young children carry out their plans varies from child to child. Some children stay in one spot, while others move from place to place. For example, Kathryn works very intently at the art table making a wasp's nest, while Kevin sits on the floor putting together a puzzle. They work for a long time at their projects until each is satisfied with the results. Other children make plans that take them from area to area: "We made cookies, and now we're takin' them around to everybody." Still other children start working in a fairly empty interest area but move when they feel crowded. Darien, for example, lines up all the animals in the block area but moves to the animals in the toy area when several other builders enter the block area.

Some children begin to carry out their ideas—making a fishing-net boat, for example—but then run into a problem, such as what to use for a net. They may modify their original idea, "Let's pretend it's a *pole* fishing boat," or they may figure out how to make a fishing net. Depending on how long it takes them to come up with a satisfactory net, children may or may not get to use it on their fishing-net boat that day.

Some children start working on their plans, stop to watch or join another child or group, and then return to what they were doing originally. When Linda, Kerry, and Dom are ready to put on their show, they recruit an audience of children who obligingly interrupt their own plans to watch and applaud.

Watching young children pursue their plans at work time, we can often see that while choices and plans shape children's initial actions, they can also lead children to actions and problems they did not anticipate. One experience leads to another, and children's play expands beyond

Children's actions at work time generally serve a purpose. The children at the art table are carrying out their plans to work with glitter and glue. The children under the table are carrying out their plans to play "doggy."

their initial plans. Athi and Chris, for example, planned to put out the fire in Joseph's house, but when Joseph's house was not ready for the fire, they returned to the "planning road map" to choose another place to put out a fire. Colin could not find any "wasp" paper that suited him, but he found some great "bee" paper, so he decided to make bees instead.

Children spend varying amounts of time executing their initial plans—from 2 minutes, to 15 minutes, to all of work time, to two or three consecutive work times. During one work-time session, some children may make and complete several related plans. Caroline, for example, made a crown, colored it, and even assumed the role of a princess. Other children may begin and complete their initial plan and then go on to something entirely different. Donnette, for example, read a book to Ruth, then joined Ali in the sand, and then painted.

Observed as a whole, a group of 18 children at work time can exhibit what looks like a lot of random movement. Observed individually, however, each child's actions generally fit an internal logic that is related to the child's particular purpose. So, while children move from place to place and talk with one another along the way, their actions more often than not serve some purpose they have set for themselves— to get a book to "read" to their "sick baby," to take Play-Doh cookies to everybody, to get the right kind of yarn for their nets, to gather up an audience, to put the birdhouse outside for the birds, to find something to stand on to tie the streamers up over their house.

Research and experience have shown that once children start their plans, they are very likely to complete them. In their study of the plan-do-review process, Berry and Sylva (1987) report that "31 of the 34 children who made plans completed them (91%). Furthermore, of these 31 children, 30 immediately started an activity related to their stated plan. Thus, children are purposeful and get down to work right away" (p. 20).

► **Children play in a variety of social contexts.**

During work time, children are involved with others to varying degrees. They watch others, play by themselves, play next to others, and in pairs and groups. These categories of social interaction are similar to those described by Mildred Parten (1932). Parten reported that young children are involved in *onlooking, solitary play, parallel play, associative play, and cooperative play.* She observed that younger preschool children tend to watch and play by themselves, while older preschool children tend to play with others. The research of Rubin, Fein, and Vandenberg (1983) supports Parten's finding that as preschool children grow older, solitary play tends to decrease while interactive play tends to increase. In the face of these important observations, adults must recognize that "solitary play does not necessarily mean a child lacks social ability" (Sponseller 1982, p. 218). It may simply mean that the older preschool child sometimes chooses to play alone and has the confidence to do so.

It is also interesting to note that playing in pairs seems to lead preschool children into more complex play. For example, early childhood researchers have noted that "$4\frac{1}{2}$- to $5\frac{1}{2}$-year-old children achieve their highest levels of play when in the company of adults, whereas younger children ($3\frac{1}{2}$ to $4\frac{1}{2}$ years old) have higher proportions of challenging play when playing in child-child pairs or in parallel to others. In the company of adults, children in both age groups are more likely to engage in complex play when the adult is actually interacting with them rather than merely being present" (Sylva, Roy, and Painter 1980, pp. 71–73). Further, children playing alone rarely change their level of play, but each child in a pair is more likely to shift toward more complex play, while a child playing in a group is more likely to shift toward simpler play.

► **Children engage in different types of play.**

Based on their emerging capacities and interests, children play with people and materials in ways that involve a range of interactions—from simple exploratory manipulation to complex social and imaginative play. The types of play that preschoolers are typically involved in include **exploratory play, constructive play, pretend play,** and **games.**

Exploratory play. This relatively simple type of play involves manipulating materials, trying out new actions, and repeating them, all of which enable the child to practice what Smilansky and Shefatya (1990) describe as "physical capabilities and the chance to explore and experience the material environment" (p. 2).

At work time, children involved in exploratory play spend time manipulating materials to see what will happen—squishing and patting Play-Doh, filling and emptying containers, cutting paper into little strips, standing all the blocks on end, running their hands through a tub of buttons, smearing glue all over a piece of paper. In these explorations, many of the key developmental indicators will be seen—*recognizing objects by sight, sound, touch, taste, and smell; exploring and describing the similarities, differences, and attributes of things; fitting things together and taking them apart; changing the shape and arrangement of objects;* and *moving with objects.*

Constructive play. The development from exploratory play to constructive play is "a

Exploratory play involves simple actions, such as filling and emptying containers at the water table.

Children involved in constructive play use materials to create things such as "birthday cakes" made from Play-Doh and popsicle sticks.

progression from manipulation of a form to formation; from sporadic handling of sand and blocks to building something which will remain even after the child has finished playing. The child expresses activity through these 'creations' and recognizes himself or herself as 'creator'" (Smilansky and Shefatya 1990, p. 2).

Children involved in constructive play build towers, roads, bridges, and buildings; make birthday cakes out of clay and pegs; hollow out rivers in the sand; make up songs and dances; nail together boats and birdhouses; create structures and figures out of Tinkertoys, straws, pipe cleaners, and wire; cut out, staple, glue, and tape together kites, hats, masks, collages; draw and write pictures, designs, cards, and books. As they do these things, children exhibit a variety of KDIs, particularly those that involve using oral and written language, making representations, and learning about relationships in the physical world. For example, during constructive play, children are *fitting things together and taking them apart; making models; drawing and painting; writing in various ways; exploring and describing similarities and differences; sorting and matching; using and describing things in several different ways; comparing; arranging several things one after another in a series or pattern; experiencing and describing positions, distances, directions, and rates of movement; expressing creativity in movement;* and *solving problems encountered in play.*

Pretend play involves acting out "what if" situations: "What if the baby is sick and needs some medicine?"

Preschoolers invent their own cooperative games, such as a race to dress up the "babies."

Pretend play. This type of play involves pretending and acting out "what if" situations: "What if I were the mom and you were the baby?" Children imitate the actions and language of others, using objects as make-believe props and taking on a variety of roles. One child puts on a chef's hat and says to himself, "I'm makin' burgers." Another group of children play dentist. As the mommy and daddy drive their baby to the dentist, their car (made of blocks) has a flat tire. While mommy and daddy change the tire, the dentist drills and brushes the baby's teeth with dental equipment made from Tinkertoys. "Now sit real still and this won't hurt," he advises.

Many KDIs are seen in children engaged in role play, especially KDIs that involve relationships with other people—*building relationships with children and adults; creating and experiencing collaborative play; pretending and role playing; talking with others about personally meaningful experiences; having fun with language; and anticipating, remembering, and describing sequences of events.*

Games. Preschoolers enjoy playing conventional games such as dominoes, cards, board games, hide and seek, and catch. Generally, they play games cooperatively rather than competitively and with little concern for sticking closely to the rules. Their aim is not to win but to have a good time hiding and looking for people, spinning the spinner and moving the pieces around the board, or picking up and trading cards with one another. Preschoolers are also beginning to invent their own simple games,

such as "jumping bears"—one child pushes a plastic counting bear off the big block into the box, then another child pushes another plastic bear off the block into the box. They take turns repeating this pattern until all the bears have "jumped." As they play these simple games, key developmental indicators occur: *participating in group routines; reading in various ways; distinguishing between some and all; arranging several things in order; fitting one set of ordered objects to another; counting; interpreting spatial relations in drawings, pictures, and photographs; starting and stopping an action on signal; describing movement; and acting upon movement directions.*

When preschool children can freely choose their play activity, as at work time, they are most likely to be involved in constructive play, followed by exploratory and pretend play, and finally, by simple games whose rules they have adjusted or invented to suit themselves (Bergen 1988).

▶ **Children carry on conversations.**

The characteristic elements of work time—intimate settings, pretend play, shared goals, a common focus, and sympathetic partners—encourage children to converse with peers and adults. When children converse among themselves at work time, they often talk in quiet, enclosed spaces—for example, under a blanket draped over two chairs that then becomes a tent or secret hiding place. Many conversations between children at work time occur when children are involved in pretend or role play, which by its very nature depends on dialogue and shared imagination.

What Children Do at Work Time: A Summary

- Children are involved in initiating, working on, modifying, completing, and changing their plans.

- Children play in a variety of social contexts.

- Children engage in different types of play.

- Children carry on conversations.

How Adults Support Children at Work Time

What adults do at work time is based on what children do, their understanding of children's actions, and the questions these actions raise: "What is Christopher doing with the blocks? Does he need my support? What should I do?" Supporting children at work time is a reflective process that involves taking stock of one's own beliefs about learning and teaching, observing children, interacting with children and examining these interactions, recording findings, and eventually bringing work time to a close.

Adults Examine Their Beliefs About How Children Learn at Work Time

It is important for adults to understand their beliefs about how children learn and how this influences their interactions with children at work time. For example, an adult who believes that children learn primarily by listening and following directions would probably tend to manage and direct children during work time. In contrast, an adult who believes that children learn best on their own would probably tend to withdraw from children at work time to pursue adult tasks. Adults guided by an active learning approach, however, believe that children learn best through active involvement with people, materials, ideas, and events, and that the adult's role is to interact thoughtfully with children throughout the day to support and encourage their development.

At work time, adults are guided by the support strategies that encourage active learning

and build supportive climates. These support strategies are discussed at length in Chapters 1 and 2, but the general principles behind them are summarized as follows:

- Supportive relationships with children are more conducive to learning than managerial, directive, distant, or punitive relationships.

- Playing and communicating with children in a "partnership" relationship is a more effective way for adults to support children's learning than managing them or lecturing to them.

- Valuing children's interests encourages children's initiative, control, and competence more effectively than ignoring, subverting, or redirecting children's interests.

Overview of the Ways Adults Support Children at Work Time

Adults examine their beliefs about how children learn.

Adults provide work places for children.

Adults scan the interest areas to find out what children are doing.

Adults choose children to observe, gain children's perspectives, and form on-the-spot interaction plans.

- Adults offer children comfort and contact.
- Adults participate in children's play.
- Adults converse with children.
- Adults encourage children's problem solving.

Adults examine their interactions with children as they occur.

Adults record their child observations.

Adults bring work time to an end.

Adults can form supportive partnerships with children, encouraging them to solve the problems they encounter as they carry out their plans. This child is figuring out how to cut a hole the size he needs in his box. His teacher remains close by, but the child does the work!

- Accepting children's nonadult ways of thinking and reasoning is more likely to encourage the thinking and reasoning process than expecting them to think and reason like adults.

- Encouraging children to solve problems they encounter generates more learning opportunities than solving problems for them or attempting to provide a problem-free environment.

- Ensuring that the information and activities offered are appropriate to the child's level of development is essential to effective learning experiences.

- Experimentation and problem solving are the primary processes through which children develop an understanding of concepts and relationships.

- Encouraging peer-to-peer play and problem solving promotes children's independence and sense of competence.

Research has shown that what adults believe about learning and teaching directly affects both their own actions and children's. When adults are warm, friendly, encouraging, and attentive to individuals and small groups, when they relate in a nondirective fashion with large groups, and when they encourage children to make decisions, the children they work with are very likely to exhibit high "task involvement, language comprehension, social participation, constructive use of materials, spontaneity, creativity, sympathy, and independence" (Phyfe-Perkins and Shoemaker 1986, p. 186). Furthermore, adults who interact with children as partners find that children will turn to them for *interaction,* while adults who manage children find that children turn to them for *management* (Wood, McMahon, and Cranstoun 1980, pp. 47–48). Also, these "managed" children seem to exhibit less ability to talk and communicate than children with whom adults interact as partners (Wood et al. 1980, p. 10).

Adults Provide Work Places for Children

Adults in the High/Scope Curriculum understand that work time, like planning time, occurs wherever preschool children have easy access to materials and people.

► **Children work in the interest areas.**

In a High/Scope program, work time generally occurs in **interest areas** (the block area, house area, art area, and so forth—the areas that are described in Chapter 5). Adults stock interest areas with materials that attract young children. However, they also realize that children's work-time pursuits may spread beyond the interest areas—for example, to an old rowboat outside, a garden setting, a staircase, a kitchen sink.

► **Children work in cozy and open spaces.**

Wherever children carry out their intentions, it is important to note that the type of play children engage in is influenced by the size, layout, and location of the physical space. Some children will seek small, cozy places in which to play, while the play of others may call for the expansiveness and flexibility of a more open space. For example, two or three children may use the coatroom as a "health clinic" where they take their doll babies for their "shots."

Adults Scan the Interest Areas to Find Out What Children Are Doing

Sometimes adults begin work time by joining a child who requests help in getting a plan started: "I want to make a dinosaur out of big boxes, but I need you to help me make some of that sticky paste stuff to hold the newspaper on." Or, "Come on, Ruth, I'm reading you a story!"

To identify children who do not make such clear requests, adults should periodically scan the interest areas and check the status of children's plans. They should also take note of the social interactions, types of play, or the KDIs in which children are involved. In effect, as they scan, adults are thinking, "I am going to interact with children in a supportive way. I need to decide whom to interact with and how. Scanning will help me find out what children are doing, what plans and play I might support, and who might be most open to support at this moment."

▶ **Look for the status of children's plans.**

As you scan the play space, observe each child and ask yourself these kinds of questions:

Is Jimmy starting a plan?

Does he have a plan well under way?

Is he focused on what he is doing?

Has he interrupted his work on his plan? If so, why? To watch or join someone else? Because he is stuck? To get something he needs?

Is he completing a plan? Changing his plan?

Answers to such questions will help you decide which children need support. For example, you may notice that Jimmy has stopped working on his "space machine" because he has used up all the available shiny cardboard. He may be willing to consider alternative materials, if prompted.

▶ **Look for children's individual and social interactions.**

As you scan, ask yourself these kinds of questions:

Which children are watching others play?

Which children are engaged in solitary play?

Which children appear to be playing next to someone else without any particular association with them?

Which children are playing in pairs? In groups?

The answers to these questions may lead you to a child such as Crystal, who seems to be hanging about the fringes of a group of children who are playing beauty parlor. Perhaps she could use your support to join the beauty parlor play.

▶ **Look for specific types of play.**

To identify specific types of play, scan the setting and ask yourself such questions as these:

Who is exploring, manipulating, practicing something?

Who is constructing or making something?

Who is pretending, carrying out a role, role playing with others?

Who is playing a game of some sort?

These questions may lead you to a child such as Sammy, who is filling sand containers. Perhaps if an adult plays next to Sammy, she will find out more about his play and thinking.

▶ **Look for the High/Scope KDIs.**

Scanning for High/Scope KDIs involves asking such questions as these:

As adults scan the interest areas at work time, they may see children watching others play. With adult support, perhaps the child on the left might join the block play he is watching.

Is an activity going on right now that could be identified as a KDI?

How are children using movement (language, number, classification . . .) as part of their play?

What KDIs might be occurring as Brenda works at the workbench?

Might Leroy be frustrated because he needs more pegs that match the ones he has been using?

Might Cerise be upset because she was having fun with language but no one will listen to her?

The answers to these and similar questions about KDIs might lead you to give Leroy an additional box of pegs so he can continue his pegboard pattern, or to make eye contact with Cerise to acknowledge her word play.

The chart at right summarizes what an adult might hold in mind in scanning the interest areas to find out what children are actually doing.

Adults Choose Children to Observe, Gain Children's Perspectives, and Form On-the-Spot Interaction Plans

Scanning helps you select children to observe. *Close observation* helps you gain children's perspectives and figure out an *interaction plan* to support them.

▶ **Choose children to observe.**

As you periodically scan the interest areas, particular children and play situations may draw your attention:

- A child hesitating at the beginning of his plan
- A child who is stalled in her work
- A child changing his plan
- A child soliciting help

Scanning the Interest Areas: What to Look for at Work Time

KDIs	Play Types	Social Contexts	Children's Plan Status
Approaches to Learning	Exploratory Play	Onlooking	Starting a Plan
Language, Literacy, and Communication	Constructive Play	Solitary Play	Continuing a Plan
Social and Emotional Development	Pretend Play	Parallel Play	Interrupting a Plan
Physical Development, Health, and Well-Being	Games	Group Play	Completing a Plan
Mathematics			Changing a Plan
Science and Technology			
Social Studies			
The Arts			

- A child carrying out a novel or long-term plan
- A child enjoying what she is doing
- A child watching others for a long time
- A child talking to himself
- A child repeating the same activity
- A child hesitating near or trying to join an ongoing play activity
- A child exploring materials
- A child making something complex
- A child playing a game others can join
- A child having an experience that you recognize as a KDI
- A quiet or withdrawn child
- An upset or frustrated child

▶ **Observe to gain each child's perspective.**

Once you have selected a child with whom you might interact in a supportive manner,

move closer to the child. Put yourself on the same physical level—on the floor if the child is on the floor, on the climber if that is where the child is playing, or on your knees by the sand table. Positioning yourself at the child's level enables you to see what the child sees and establishes you as an available partner. Maintaining silence enables you to listen carefully and give your full attention to the child's actions and words. It also allows the child to be aware of your interest and support without being interrupted by your unsolicited questions, comments, and suggestions.

▶ **Form on-the-spot interaction plans.**

As you observe, focus your full attention on the child to find out more about the situation that first caught your attention—the child's plan, social interactions, play type, or particular KDI. Your interaction plan starts with what you already know about (1) the child you are observing, (2) what typically happens at work time, and (3) what is possible at work time, given the available play space, materials, and human support systems. An interaction plan includes a hoped-for goal or outcome (for

Positioned on the floor where she can see and hear the children jumping off the stairs, this adult gathers information about the intent of their pretend play and forms an on-the-spot plan for supporting them.

example, supporting the child's plan, play, or train of thought; or finding out what the child is doing and thinking) and some possible steps for reaching it. Following are sample work-time interaction plans, as formulated throughout work time by one adult in our demonstration preschool. Although the sample interaction plans are in written form (for the sake of illustration),

it is important to note that your actual interaction plans are ideas you formulate "on the spot" based on your observations.

Brent seems hesitant to begin his plan to play with the Lego blocks because the box of Legos isn't on the shelf where he thought it would be. I remember that yesterday Shasha

put the Legos in the refrigerator to represent ice cubes. I'm going to suggest to Brent that he look there so he can find and play with them as he planned.

❧

Jimmy has been working very intently on his "space machine," but now he is hitting a juice can with a block, and he seems to be trying to get the metal bottom separated from the cardboard. If I say to him, "Jimmy, you're banging that can pretty hard," maybe he will tell me what he is trying to do and if and how his actions are related to his "space machine."

❧

Crystal seems to be hanging about the edges of the beauty parlor play as if she would like to join in. She's holding a purse and some rollers and she's watching the "beauty lady" and the lady in the chair getting her hair done. Maybe if I get a purse and some rollers I could say to her, "Hi. I'd sure like to get my hair fixed up, too." Depending on her response, maybe we could go together to the beauty parlor so she could become part of the play.

❧

Sammy seems to be enjoying himself in the sand area. He started filling a baby bottle using his hand as a scoop, then a cup as a scoop; then he turned the baby bottle over and used it as a scoop. Now he is using a funnel as a scoop and noticing that the sand can run out both ends of the funnel into the bottle. Maybe if I get a container and funnel and use them in the same way, he will say something to me about his play.

❧

Brenda seems very intent on sawing pieces of wood. After she cut the first piece, she laid it on top of the length of wood she was cutting from as if to guide where she wanted to make the next cut. I'm going to watch for when she finishes sawing and then say something like, "Brenda, you were cutting your wood pieces very carefully" to see if she might explain to me in her own words what she was doing.

We can summarize these five on-the-spot interaction plans in this way: Once adults have scanned the interest areas, observed a child to gain the child's perspective, and formed an on-the-spot plan of interaction, the next step is to join a child or play group and to use the interaction strategy that is appropriate—either offering comfort and contact, playing with children, conversing with children, or encouraging children's problem solving. These strategies are discussed next.

Adults Offer Children Comfort and Contact

There are times when children need immediate adult reassurance and acknowledgment of their feelings or efforts. Here are some strategies to help you identify and work with such children so they can regain their composure.

▶ **Look for children in need of comfort and contact.**

Children will express their need for comfort and contact in a variety of ways. Barry, for example, was not able to talk about his plan until he talked about the death of his cousin's dog. Donna, normally outgoing, clung to the female adults in her program for a number of days and shunned the males, saying of each one that "he looks like the man who hurt my momma." Some

The presence of a friendly adult adds to this child's comfort as he hunts for the letters in his name on a keyboard.

children are more subdued than usual. When Billy's parents were getting divorced, he tended to work quietly by himself. He barely acknowledged other children, as if focusing all his attention on materials over which he had control could temporarily make up for his lack of control over his home life. Other children become less focused, finding it difficult to concentrate on one activity for long. After her baby sister was born, Laura began to move from one material to the next, giving up any sustained activity in favor of being with adults. Some children may pout and wait for an adult to notice their feelings, while others call out incessantly—"Look it!" "Come here!"— as if to reassure themselves that the adults in this setting are still present and responsive.

As you scan the interest areas, be aware that children in the following situations may need comfort and contact:

• Children expressing anxiety or discomfort through looks, gestures, actions, or words

• Children watching play

• Solitary children

• Children moving rapidly from one material to another

• Children asking frequently for adult acknowledgment

• Children needing ongoing adult presence to start and continue their plans

► **Offer reassuring physical contact.**

Sitting next to Kristina, waiting quietly in the same spot for Kwame to return from saying goodbye to his mom, touching Chavon's hand or Misao's cheek, rocking Jodi—such reassuring physical contacts are sometimes the most important interactions an adult can have with a child. While it is important to respect children's growing need for independence and autonomy, it is equally important to be there when children need a hand to hold or a lap to curl up in. Experiencing a moment or several minutes of physical comfort seems to "re-fuel" some children, enabling them to re-enter the more autonomous world of plans and play.

Some children will signal their need for your warmth and comfort by clinging to your leg, tugging at your arm or sleeve, hugging you, or climbing into your lap. Other children will not initiate physical contact so overtly, but will ask for reassurance through their expressions and postures, responding positively when it is offered. And some children pull away from physical contact, but respond well to an adult who is calm and nearby. Keep in mind that the type of contact that feels comfortable to adults and is well received by children varies from adult to adult, child to child, and situation to situation.

► **Offer simple acknowledgment.**

Sometimes children need adult acknowledgment of their efforts and feelings:

Nestling close to their teacher, these children receive comfort, contact, and the story they have requested!

"Look it! Look it!" Vanessa calls out every few minutes. "I see, Vanessa," an adult responds each time with a smile, looking at Vanessa's block pile or line of animals or painting. Vanessa quickly returns to her play.

William stands quietly at Mrs. Elkin's side. She puts her arm around him. "Are you feeling a little bit lonely for your sister?" she says. He smiles and returns to his building. A little while later William is back. Mrs. Elkin gives him a hug, and he then returns to his tower. The next time William seeks Mrs. Elkin out, he says quietly, "Come here." He takes her hand and leads her to his tower. Mrs. Elkin kneels down next to him. He leans against her. "It's tall," William says. "Yes, it is," she agrees. He begins to build another tower next to the first. Mrs. Elkin watches for a while before joining a child at the workbench.

Nobody Paid Attention to Me When I Pouted!

Why Adults May Avoid Giving Comfort and Contact

From a distance, Michael, a preschooler, watches some children play with blocks. He has an unhappy expression on his face. Seeing him, an adult remarks, "He's just trying to get my attention!" While young children need comfort and contact from time to time, adults are sometimes reluctant to give it for a variety of reasons. Here are some examples:

• "I wasn't allowed to pout when I was a child, so I'm going to ignore him when he pouts."

• "Her sad look is so annoying. I know she wants me to feel sorry for her, but I'm not going to be manipulated by her needs. She needs to learn to overcome self-pity."

• "She's just being stubborn. She could talk if she wanted to. If she wants me to talk to her, she has to talk to me."

• "He could join in the block play if he really wanted to. He just wants me to help him, but I'm not going to because he has to learn to be independent."

• "I'm not her mom! Pulling a long face may work at home, but it won't work with me! That's a habit she'll have to break if she wants to succeed here."

• "He can sulk all he wants as long as he's quiet and not causing trouble. I see no reason to interact with him at this time."

Many young children rely on nonverbal communication to convey their need for contact and comfort. Such children may not yet be able to verbalize their feelings or describe what is bothering them, but they can perceive whether an adult is willing to comfort them through their own ups and downs. As mature professionals committed to educating children, it is up to us to be aware of our prejudices and to set them aside so we may provide children with the support they need to carry out their intentions.

Adults Participate in Children's Play

Participating in children's play is one way adults can demonstrate that they value and support children's interests and intentions. When children are playing or starting to play, and are receptive to other players, adults can sometimes join them in a nondisruptive, respectful manner. They can do this by looking for natural play openings, joining children on *their* physical level, engaging in parallel play with children, playing as a partner, referring one child to another, and suggesting new ideas within children's ongoing play activities.

▶ Look for natural play openings.

In general, it is easier for adults to join some types of play than others. For example, an adult can usually join children's exploratory play without disrupting it simply by exploring the same materials in a similar manner. Moreover, pretend play, by its very nature, depends on others joining in and taking on supportive roles. And children's games also require more than one player. *Generally, it is more natural and less disruptive to join children's exploratory play, pretend play, or games, rather than their constructive play.* (Constructive play may include building a Tinkertoy house, painting, or making a birthday card. In these types of activities, children focus so much energy on the task at hand that they have little left for adults.)

In scanning the interest areas for children whose play you might join, you might pick out children doing these sorts of things:

• Children creating and experiencing collaborative play

• Children pretending and role playing

• Children moving to music

• Solitary children wanting to join others' play

• Children engaged in parallel play

• Children exploring, manipulating, or repeating actions

• Children playing games

• Children having difficulty starting a plan

• Children whose plans are interrupted

▶ Join children's play on the child's level.

Joining children's play successfully depends on seeing it from the child's perspective and allowing the child to retain control over the play situation. Here are some examples:

• A child is sitting on the floor, beating a tambourine and singing "Hopa, hopa, hopa." You sit on the floor near her, hold a tambourine, and wait for her signal to play your tambourine and sing "Hopa, hopa, hopa." When she gives you the go-ahead, you play and sing softly enough so you can hear her voice and tambourine above your own. When she signals you to stop, you stop.

• "Here's some hay for you, horse," says a child, walking a rubber horse to a green bead of "hay" he has put in a "stall" built of cardboard tubes and Lincoln Logs. Sitting near the child,

This adult joins these children on the floor so he can see the road and tunnel from their point of view and they can retain control over the play situation.

Parallel play—using the same materials the children are using in a manner very similar to theirs—allows this adult to join their play in a way that allows their play to continue smoothly in the direction they have established.

you make your rubber horse "walk" near the stall and then quietly whinny ("Neigh, neigh").

Sometimes children invite adults to join their play, and sometimes adults take the initiative: "I am going to join the beauty parlor play to see if I can help Crystal participate." The success of the adults' initiatives, however, depends on their responsiveness to the specific play situation: "Since Crystal is holding a purse and some rollers, I'll take my cue from her. I'll get a purse and rollers and pretend I want to go to the beauty parlor, too." Interestingly, the more adults take the initiative for joining children's play in a respectful manner, the more children are apt to

invite them in. Researchers report that when children see adults assume the role of players, they learn that adults are willing to play: "The children learn that the adult is approachable and not a remote authority figure, and they may come to trust her more" (Wood et al. 1980, pp. 157–158).

▶ **Play in parallel with children.**

This strategy can be effective with children who are involved in exploratory play—using materials for their own sake without really trying to make something or pretend with them. These children often play by themselves but are receptive to the supportive presence of others.

In parallel play, adults play near the child using the same materials the child is using in the same or a very similar manner:

Child: (Fills a bucket with sand, empties it out, fills it up again, empties it into a bowl.)

Adult: (Fills a margarine tub with sand, empties it, fills it again, empties it into a saucepan.)

The adult may introduce variations in the play; for example, she may fill a sieve or funnel with sand. It is important for the adult to realize, however, that the child may not notice these variations. And, furthermore, if the child does notice them, he may or may not incorporate them into the play.

Conversation in parallel play may be minimal:

Child: *I need that* (indicating the saucepan the adult is using).

Adult: (Hands the saucepan to the child.)

On the other hand, because exploratory play is relatively undemanding, the presence of an adult may inspire child-initiated chats about personally meaningful topics:

Child: *My mommy's picking me up.*

Adult: *Yes, she is.*

Child: *Not my daddy like the other days.*

Adult: *Usually your daddy comes, but not today.*

Child: *He's at his work.*

Adult: *He's at his work so your mommy's coming.*

Child: *Yep! We're goin' someplace, too, an' I know where!*

Adult: *You're going someplace with your mom.*

Child: *Yeah, my Grammy's!*

As a play partner, this adult takes her cues from the children, riding in the seat they have assigned to her on the "train."

▶ **Play as a partner with children.**

This strategy can work well with children involved in pretend play and games—play that by nature depends on more than one person. The key is *partnership*—adults functioning as equals and followers. As partners, adults enter into the spirit of the play, adjust their speech and actions to the pace and theme of the play, accept or assume a play-related role, follow rules established by the children, and take direction from children. Here are two brief examples:

(Two boys stand in front of the mirror putting on and taking off their sunglasses.)

First child: *Cool.*

Second child: *Bad! Real bad.*

Adult: (Puts on a pair of sunglasses.)

First child: (To adult) *Hey, you bad!* (Both children giggle.) *Look at you in the mirror!* (Adult moves in front of the mirror.)

Second child: (To adult) *Hey, man, wanna see our stuff?*

Adult: *Okay, man, sure.*

Second child: *Come on.* (Takes adult by hand.) *Sit here. We'll get the stuff.* (Adult sits on the pillow as indicated.)

First child: *Close your eyes. Don't open till we tell you.*

Adult: (Closes eyes.) *I'm scared!*

First child: *Don't worry. We'll be right back!* (The children return with a grocery bag full of picture books and small, multicolored blocks.)

∽

(Two children are playing with hand puppets.)

First child: (Lowers puppet behind shelf, raises puppet up.) *Boo!*

Second child: (Repeats same actions with her puppet.) *Boo!*

First child: (Repeats actions.) *Goo!*

Second child: (Repeats actions.) *Woo!*

Adult: (Does the same thing with her puppet.) *Moo!*

Second child: (Repeats actions.) *Achoo!*

First child: (Repeats actions.) *Boo hoo!*

Adult: (Repeats actions.) *Garoo!*

First child: (Repeats actions.) *Kangaroo! Hey, I know. Let's each have two puppets!*

▶ **Refer one player to another.**

In the role of partner or follower in play rather than boss or leader, the adult should, whenever possible, refer one child to another for play support and expansion. This enables children to recognize each other's strengths, regard each other as valuable resources, use their abilities for the benefit of others, and play cooperatively:

Tim: (To adult) *How do you get these all mixed up?* (Tries to shuffle a deck of "Go Fish" cards.)

Adult: *Joe had a good way to do it.*

Joe: (Takes a few cards.) *See. First, you have to put 'em all like this.* (He stacks the cards carefully.)

▶ **Suggest new ideas within ongoing play situations.**

Adults working with young children often express a desire to extend children's play. In a sense, playing respectfully in parallel and as partners with children can and often does extend the length and even the scope of some play episodes. Beyond this, however, adults may also wish to challenge, in a gentle way, young children's thinking and reasoning to expand the breadth of their play, and, consequently, their understanding. When adults attempt this type of play extension, it is important that they offer new ideas within the context of the ongoing play. From her long-term study of dramatic and sociodramatic play, Sara Smilansky (1971) suggests some strategies for doing this:

Offer suggestions within the play theme.

Adult: *I brought my baby's thermometer.* (Hands the "doctor" a wooden Tinkertoy.)

∽

What? **Me** Play! You've **Got** to Be Kidding!

Playing with children does not come easily for some adults. Wood et al. (1980) report that reluctant adults come up with all kinds of reasons to avoid playing with children:

Play is for children, not adults.

Adults upset the delicate balance of children's play.

It is wrong for adults to intrude. They spoil things.

Playing with children is too repetitive and boring.

Adult ideas destroy children's creativity.

It is more important for children to play with other children than with adults.

It is too embarrassing. What if someone sees me!

I would lose my authority with children if I did what they wanted me to do.

It is important for adults who are uncomfortable playing with children to be aware of their feelings and weigh them against the benefits of playing respectfully and joyfully with children. When adults play with children, the children experience adults as supporters and resources, people who want them to succeed.

Address the role person rather than the child.

Adult: *Doctor, can you check my neighbor's arm? She hurt it at the fire.* (Rather than "Sandy, let Gina play with you.")

Respect the child's reaction to your idea.

Adult: *Doctor, her temperature's going up. She's warm.*

Child: *I'll check her after lunch. Here.* (Hands her a magazine.) *Look at this till I get back.*

Adult: *Thanks.*

Child: *Want me to bring her some milk and fries?*

Adult: *Yes, please, doctor.*

Adults Converse With Children

There are moments when conversation is a natural outgrowth of children's work or play. Adults look for these opportunities to converse with children as partners, following their leads and asking questions sparingly so children retain control of the dialogue. The more children converse, the more they put into words their own thoughts and experiences, and the more involved they are in interpreting and understanding their world.

▶ **Look for natural opportunities for conversation.**

The relative simplicity of exploratory play sometimes inspires young children to talk either about what they are doing or about an apparently unrelated topic. Pretend play relies heavily on role-related conversation, and games often involve verbal negotiations over rules and process. There are times during constructive play when children pause to take a look at what they have done so far or to consider a problem. A conversation is more likely to occur at these times than when children are wholly involved in making something. Also, children who have interrupted, completed, or changed their plans may find that conversing with an adult can help them clarify what they have done or intend to do next. Here are some examples of work-time situations that may lead to such conversations:

- Children describing what they are doing

- Children pretending and role playing

- Children exploring, manipulating, or repeating actions

- Children pausing during play

- Children talking during games

- Children interrupting, completing, or changing their plans

▶ **Join children at their level for conversation.**

At its best, conversation is an intimate exchange between trusting people. For such conversations to occur, adults position themselves near the child *at the child's physical level,* so children are not "looking up" to adults and adults are not "looking down" on children. For the most part, this means that adults spend a lot of time squatting, kneeling, sitting, and occasionally even lying on the floor. Adults must "shrink" to the children's size so children and adults can converse easily and comfortably.

What About Superheroes and War Play?

In "Superheroes and War Play in the Preschool: Let Them In or Lock Them Out?" High/Scope consultant and teacher Ann Rogers (1990) points out that "historically, the themes of power, control, anger, helplessness, and fear have always, in one way or another, been part of children's play—and for very good reasons. They are issues in the lives of all preschool children, and play is the medium they use to find out the meaning of these issues" (p. 61).

After outlining the pros and cons of banning such play or limiting it to outside time, Rogers offers a third approach that allows war and superhero play: "Stay involved in it yourself so you can attempt to move children beyond the endless repetitive quality in a way that will make the play more useful to them" (p. 62). Although this is the most difficult alternative for adults, it is ultimately the most constructive one for children who need and appreciate support in working with these potentially volatile issues. To make this approach work, Rogers (1990, pp. 62–63) offers these suggestions:

"1. Help children bring familiar experiences and materials into play.

"2. Strongly support and encourage any original ideas the children have.

"3. Help children learn how to 'keep the lid on' their war play so they won't be hurt or frightened.

"4. Limit or forbid the use of commercial war toys and figures. Instead, encourage children to create their own war-play props with many kinds of open-ended materials.

"5. As children get older, help them learn to compare war-play products as they are advertised with how they really are."

Working with children on these issues *as they arise* in play situations makes more sense in the long run than banning or ignoring them.

▶ **Respond to children's conversational leads.**

When adults make themselves available for conversation with children during natural pauses in their play, and when they are silent yet attentive, listening patiently and with interest to ongoing conversations, children are likely to address adults directly or make the first move toward involving them in conversation:

Child: (Wipes hands on smock and studies collage she is making.)

Adult: (Squats down next to child and looks at collage.)

Child: *This is for my mom.*

Adult: *Ah, something for your mom.*

Child: *It's a . . . It's not done.*

Adult: *Oh.*

Child: *I'm gonna put some of that twisty stuff on right here and those things he's got.*

Adult: *You mean acorn tops like Ryan's using?*

Child: *Yeah! Acorn tops. We picked 'em up didn't we?*

Adult: *Yes. We found the acorn tops on our walk.*

Child: *An' Linda found that stick, and you jumped over it!*

Adult: *You did, too!*

Child: *Yep!* (Pauses) *I'm gonna put a stick on and those tops. A lot!* (Turns back to her work.)

Adult: *I'll come back to see what it looks like with the twisty stuff and the stick and the acorn tops.* (Moves toward another child.)

▶ **Converse as a partner with children.**

As partners in dialogues with children, adults resist taking control of the conversation. Instead, they try to pass conversational control back to the child at every opportunity. Adults do this by sticking to the topic the child raises; making personal comments or affirmative utterances that allow the conversation to continue without pressuring the child for a response; waiting for the child to respond before taking another conversational turn; and keeping their comments fairly brief.

Adults often wait for the child to open the conversation, but may also initiate conversation, leaving it up to the child to decide whether to continue the

This teacher kneels at the bean table so she can converse at the children's physical level, establishing a climate of trust and intimacy.

The children are in charge of this conversation. They have instructed their teacher to choose the magic marker they have designated as the "right one."

exchange. An appropriate way to open a conversation with a child is to begin with a comment or an observation. This gives the child control over his or her response and, consequently, over the direction of the conversation. In the following examples, note how the adults give conversational control to the child by opening with an undemanding comment, and then leaving the direction of the conversation to the child:

Child: (Brushes the coat of a fluffy stuffed dog.)

Adult: *My dog Stanley likes to have his coat brushed.*

Child: *So does my doggy. He hates baths.*

Adult: *Stanley doesn't like baths, either.*

Child: *Sometimes, I have to put him in the tub.*

Adult: *I bet he tries to get out.*

Child: *He tries to get over the side, and then he shakes the water all over the place!*

❧

Tyson: (Standing at the workbench with a car he has made.)

Adult: *You made a very long car, Tyson.*

Tyson: *I got this long piece and this 'nother piece on top.*

Adult: *Yes.*

Tyson: *These are the wheels.*

Adult: *They really turn.*

Tyson: *It's gonna be a speed racer.*

Adult: *A speed racer.*

Tyson: *It's gonna have speed racer stripes right here and here.*

Adult: *Then it will really go fast.*

Tyson: *Yeah. Red stripes. That's the fastest color.*

Adult: *I didn't know that.*

Tyson: *Yeah, 'cause my brother's is red, and it's the fastest one.*

Adult: *I see.*

Tyson: *I'll show you how fast when I put on the red.*

Adult: *Okay!*

► **Ask questions responsively.**

While asking questions is a commonly accepted teaching method with older children, questioning younger children can be tricky. Our questioning styles can either dampen conversations or stimulate them, depending on how responsive our questions are to young children's play and interests. Questions that dampen conversation tend to be questions about facts that are obvious ("What color is that?" "Which board is longer?" "Is that a house?") and questions unrelated to the situation at hand (such as asking a child who is coloring, "Have you had your juice yet?"). According to Wood et al. (1980), these "test-type questions are a violation of normal conversational etiquette and the child seems

This child interrupts the story she is "reading" to talk about the caps the monkeys are wearing. Her teacher listens with attention and enjoyment.

intuitively aware of this fact. Adults tend to resort to test-like questions when they focus on topics and tasks beyond the child's comprehension or interests. Furthermore, in a drive for answers, they fail to share their own views and reactions with the child" (p. 178).

A string of adult questions also tends to put the adult in control of the conversation. As Wood et al. (1980) point out, "If the adult maintains the dialogue largely through questions, children's answers tend to be terse. [In such cases,] once the adult has the conversational bit between her teeth, her questions may even override the spontaneous offerings of the children. Indeed, the tendency to ignore children, talk over them, and generally dominate the proceedings prevents rather than encourages children's thought and conversation" (p. 65).

On the other hand, questions that tend to stimulate conversation have the following characteristics: *They are used sparingly, they relate directly to what the child is doing, and they ask about the child's thought process.*

Ask questions sparingly.

Adult questions are a conversational tool to be used with care. Such questions can help children contemplate, describe, and become more aware of their own thought processes. Nevertheless, it is important to remember that our main purpose is to support the children's desire to ask and answer *their own questions.*

An adult may ask a question to start a conversation but then should follow the course set by the child. Wood et al. (1980) characterize this style as "asking a question to get the child to say something, and then stepping back, taking the pressure off, either by making a contribution or by making an utterance that effectively fills your turn in the dialogue. [This style enables the child to] . . . elaborate on the theme and to take off in a direction that he chooses himself, presumably along the line he feels most interesting" (pp. 67, 69).

Child: (Watching the fish in the fish tank.)

Adult: (Watches next to the child for a while.)

Child: (Points to one fish.)

Adult: *What's that fish doing?*

Child: *He's waiting for his daddy.*

Adult: *Oh, he's waiting.*

Child: *See that big one down there? He's the daddy, and he's waitin' for him so they can go around together.*

Adult: *I see.*

Child: *They both have those tails like that. Kinda pointy. That's how you know.*

Adult: *Oh, the pointy tails mean they go together.*

Child: *Yeah, that means they're the boy and the daddy. Once I got lost.*

Adult: *Oh, dear!*

Child: *I couldn't find my daddy. He finded me.*

Adult: *He didn't want to lose you.*

Child: (Pointing to fish.) *Now they're together.*

Adult: *Like you and your daddy.*

Child: *Uh huh. There they go.*

Curiously enough, the fewer questions we ask young children and the more we listen and converse with them as partners, the more likely they are to see us as sympathetic listeners and, hence, to ask *us* questions of particular interest to them:

Child: (Rocks her stuffed dog.)

Adult: (Rocks a stuffed dog next to child.)

Child: *Does your father live with you?*

Adult: *No, he lives in Canada with my mom.*

Child: *Well, does that man, Bill, live with you?*

Adult: *Yes, Bill is my husband. He lives with me and Stanley.*

Child: *Stanley's a boy dog, right?*

Adult: *Right!*

Child: *My doggy's a boy dog, too. His name is Sky Star.*

Relate questions directly to what the child is doing. This strategy is another way of following the child's lead. Even though the adult is asking the question, it is based on everything she understands about the child at that moment. When the question grows out of the immediate situation, it is more likely to add to rather than take away from the conversation. For example, in the conversation about fish, the adult asks about the fish the child is pointing to. As the conversation continues, the adult asks another question that grows out of the exchange:

Child: *That fish only gots one eye.*

Adult: *How can you tell?*

Child: *'Cause look. That's all you can see.*

Adult: *I see. You can see only one eye.*

Child: *Yeah, one eye right on the side up by his nose.*

Ask questions about the child's thought process. Questions that stimulate conversation focus on *thought processes* rather than *facts*:

In the book and writing area, these two children and their teacher pause to converse about the card the child on the left has just made.

"How many eyes does the fish have?" demands a factual answer, which by the way, the adult already knows. In contrast, the adult asks the question, "How can you tell?" in response to the child's observation that the fish has one eye and encourages the child to describe how he arrived at the conclusion. *Only the child has the answer to this question, so it is a question well worth asking.* Furthermore, in the process of answering the question the child has the opportunity to consolidate what he knows and recognize how he knows it. Questions that inquire about children's thinking and reasoning include these:

"How can you tell?"

"How do you know that?"

"What do you think made that happen?"

"How did you get (the ball) to . . . ?"

"What do you think would happen if . . . ?"

Again, ask these questions sparingly and in relation to what the child is doing. Also, be alert for answers the children give to their own unspoken questions:

Child: (Building a block tower.) *It's getting higher!*

Adult: (Watches and nods in agreement.)

Child: *It's higher than even me!*

Adult: *Yes, it is!*

Child: *Uh oh. It's moving.* (Tower falls.) *Oh, no!*

Adult: *Oh, dear!*

Child: (Studies the fallen tower.) *It was too heavy. Up there.* (Holds hand out, indicating where the top of the tower had been.)

Adult: (Supplying what she thinks might be the child's unspoken question.) *That's why it fell?*

Child: *Yeah. It couldn't keep that big block up.*

Adult: *It couldn't keep the big block up.*

Child: *It wasn't strong enough. I know what!* (He begins to rebuild the tower.)

Adults Encourage Children's Problem Solving

Throughout the day in any stimulating environment, young children encounter physical problems ("This piece won't fit!") and social conflicts ("He took my truck!"). Adults who support children's active learning encourage them to grapple with child-sized problems rather than give up in frustration or turn to adults to patch things up.

Not all adults encourage young children to solve their own problems. In fact, some adults attempt to provide a trouble-free environment. They admonish children not to argue, and step in at the first sign of trouble to provide whatever direction is needed to keep things running smoothly. For example, a child making a book hits the stapler, but no staples come out. Noticing the situation, a nearby adult says, "Here, let me fix that for you." She opens up the stapler, sees that the staples are jammed, pulls out the jammed staples, and hands the stapler back to the child, saying "Now it will work." Other adults attempt to mediate disputes and problems so wrongs are recognized and punished. In such a setting, when a child making a book hits the stapler and no staples come out, a nearby adult says, "You've hit the stapler so hard, the staples are jammed." She then proceeds to unjam the stapler and puts it up on a shelf beyond the child's reach. "Maybe you can have another try with it tomorrow after you've had time to think about using it properly."

In a High/Scope setting, adults encourage children to solve their own problems. They believe that as young children work through the

---

Sharing Conversational Control

Based on their observations of adults and children, Wood et al. (1980, p. 73) devised a framework for identifying who controls a conversation. In conversational moves 1–3 below, the speaker retains control of the conversation. In moves 4–5, the speaker offers control to the listener:

- **Speaker retains control**

    1. Enforced repetition ("Say 'Night, night' to baby.")

    2. Closed question ("Is your baby crying?")

    3. Open question ("Where are you taking your baby?")

- **Speaker passes control to listener**

    4. Contribution ("I used to take my baby to the park.")

    5. Acknowledgment ("I see.")

As they observed, recorded, and analyzed the recordings of adult-child conversations, the researchers came to these conclusions:

- "The adult with the least controlling style on our particular measure asked relatively few questions and made a high proportion of contributions.

- "The adult who exercised least control over children was much more likely to be questioned and to hear unsolicited ideas from children, and was far more likely to have her questions not simply answered but elaborated upon.

- "Generally speaking, all children followed contributions and phatics [acknowledgments] with contributions of their own. In other words, each child responded conversationally to noncontrolling adult moves, so adult questions are not the only device for keeping a child involved in dialogue.

- "By leaving the child more turns that are not directly controlled, the adult provides an opportunity for the child to put his own ideas into words and, on occasion at least, a chance to ask the adult questions.

- "By leaving the child time to think and periodically taking the pressure off to reveal something of her own thoughts, she is most likely to see the child at his or her linguistically most active" (pp. 79–81).

problems they encounter, they learn firsthand about how things work, begin to see things from a variety of perspectives, and develop self-confidence. Consider how the stapler episode would evolve in a High/Scope setting: A child making a book pounds on the stapler and notices that no staples come out. He shakes the stapler and tries again without any luck. He leans on the stapler with both hands but it still doesn't work:

Child: (Addressing a nearby adult) *Hey, this thing's not working.*

Adult: *Sometimes, if you open it up, you can see what's the matter.* (The child does this.)

Child: *They're in there, but this one is . . . is . . . is going the wrong way.* (He tries to pull out the jammed staple with his fingers, then gets a pair of blunt-edged scissors, which he uses to pry off the staples.) *There. I got it! Now let's see.* (He tries the stapler once again. This time it works.)

▶ **Look for children involved in problem situations.**

Problems may arise in any type of children's play, and it is important for adults to be looking for children in need of support. In particular, children involved in constructive play, more so than those engaged in exploratory play, may encounter problems simply because they generally have a clear goal in mind and may have to overcome unexpected obstacles to achieve it. Also, children who have stopped working on their plans may have done so because they are having difficulty solving a problem. Here are other examples of some problem-solvers in work-time situations who may need your assistance and support:

• Children recognizing and solving problems ("How many do I need?" "What will fit?"

"What will go with this?" "How can I make this look right?" "What goes next?")

• Children developing strategies for dealing with social conflict

• Children whose project is not working

• Children who have interrupted or are changing their plans

▶ **Allow children to deal with problems and conflicting viewpoints.**

Children are, by nature, problem-setters and problem-solvers. They can and do solve many problems on their own. Sometimes adults, who are more efficient problem-solvers than children, have to restrain themselves from interfering prematurely with children's problem-solving attempts. Here are some strategies to help adults practice such restraint.

Sit down with children. Do this as often as possible rather than remaining highly mobile throughout work time. While you must remain alert to what is going on in as much of the play space as possible, by having to get up and walk over to the problem-solvers, you give children more time to sort things out on their own or generate their own solutions to try.

Give children time to use their own problem-solving skills. Even if you move close to problem-solvers, wait to offer assistance until children ask, or until they have made an attempt at a solution and seem about to abandon the effort.

Refer one child to another. Whenever possible, refer problem-solvers to other children who have the skills to help them at the moment. This empowers the child who assists and enables the problem-solver to view peers as resources:

Child: *Darn! I can't get this open!*

Adult: *Yesterday, I saw Reeny open her glue bottle. Maybe she could help.*

Child: *Hey, Reeny! How you do this?*

Reeny: *I'll help you. See, you push this up like this.*

Listen to conflicting viewpoints.

Children frequently disagree with each other. Some adults may want to keep children from arguing, but a more appropriate response would be to listen to the conflicting views and encourage children to elaborate these views:

Adult: (Reading the story of how the elephant got his trunk. Stops to look at the picture.)

First child: *He's a nice elephant.*

Second child: *No he's not, he's bad.*

Whenever possible, adults refer children to each other for the help they need at the moment, such as tying a necktie.

Adult: *What makes you say that?*

Second child: *'Cause he went down to the river when he wasn't supposed to.*

Adult: *Yes, he went down to the river.*

First child: *No, he's nice. He's just a nice little baby elephant.*

Adult: *Yes, he's a baby.*

Second child: *Read some more.*

Adult: *Okay. Let's see what else we find out about the baby elephant at the river.*

▶ **Interact with rather than manage children.**

When adults *interact* with children, they play and converse with them as partners. When adults *manage* children, they retain the upper hand by passing out instructions and warnings: "You need to go wash your hands." "You need to find something else to do. It's too crowded for you to play here." "That's too much glue. Take just a little bit." "Three more minutes till you have to get off the trike." Not only does adult management prevent children from confronting and working with child-sized problems it also limits or curtails more beneficial and enjoyable adult-child interactions. Here is an example of two adults approaching the same situation in different ways, the first through interaction and the second through management:

First child: *Yip, yip, yip.*

Second child: (Pretends to eat out of "dog" dish.)

First adult: (Patting both "dogs.") *Nice doggies.*

First child: (Sits up and "begs.") *Yip, yip.*

First adult: *Let me see if I have a bone for you.* (Finds a pretend bone in her pocket.) *Here, doggy.*

(Several other "dogs" join the play. The play continues with the "dogs" finding ways to make themselves "dog beds" and rearranging them so there is room for each new "dog.")

Second adult: (Across the room, flicks lights off and on.) *There are too many children playing dogs and there's too much yipping. You two can stay in the block area, but the rest of you will have to find something else to do.*

The children who are encouraged to work together to find space for their dog beds have a very different experience from those being shooed out of their play space. While prevention of the problem may be a more efficient short-term approach, encouraging children to solve the problem for themselves accomplishes more in the long run because of the opportunities it provides. However, supporting children through the problem-solving process will require a greater degree of adult involvement than solving the problem for them.

Furthermore, as Wood et al. (1980) noted in their observations of adult-child interactions, "[Adult] management seemed to breed more management, [adult] interactions, more interactions. Where an adult herself usually initiated contact with children for purposes of management, children often came to her for similar purposes. Their spontaneous overtures took the form of requests for turns and arbitration, questions about when story time was and other basically managerial functions. However, where the adult was holding a conversation with children or playing with them, the opening from a 'new' child was much more likely to be a request for her to play with them, help them with something, or simply to talk" (pp. 47–48).

This adult calmly helps these children with a conflict they cannot resolve on their own. She listens patiently as each child talks about the problem and offers ideas for ways to solve it.

▶ **Calmly assist with unresolved conflicts.**

When conflicts arise that children are unable to solve on their own, approach calmly, use the following problem-solving strategies, and be prepared to give follow-up support:

Acknowledge children's feelings.

Adult: *You both look pretty upset.*

First child: *I'm pretty steamed!*

Second child: *This is getting me mad!*

Adult: *So you're steamed and you're mad.*

Gather information.

Adult: (Pause.) *Tell me what's happening here.*

First child: *I need that big, big box.*

Second child: *I had it first.*

First child: *You weren't using it!*

Second child: *I was going to use it.*

Restate the problem.

Adult: *It seems that both of you need a box.*

First child: *I need it for my house so I can get into it.*

Second child: *Well, I need a big box to put all these papers in.*

Third child: *Box! Me!*

Adult: (To third child.) *You need a box, too.*

Third child: (Nods in agreement.)

Ask for ideas for solutions and choose one together.

Adult: *So we have one big box and each of you wants to use it. How can we solve this problem?*

First child: (Thinks.) *I could use it first and you could use it the other days.*

Second child: *I need it now.*

Third child: *No. Mine.*

Adult: *Everybody needs the box now, today.*

Second child: *We could all get in.*

First child: *Yeah!*

Second child: *But don't sit on my papers.*

First child: *We could put 'em in a bag and then put 'em in.*

Third child: *Me, bag.*

Second child: *Let's all have bags, okay?* (The other children nod yes.)

Adult: *So, you're all getting in the box and each person has a bag to put papers in.* (Again, the children nod yes as they move into action.)

Adults Examine Their Interactions With Children as They Occur

As they offer comfort and contact, play, converse, and support children's problem-solving efforts, adults in a High/Scope setting also maintain an awareness of their *own* actions and the effect they are having on the situation. They do this by asking themselves these types of questions:

"What is happening to Jenny's play as I interact with her?"

"What am I learning about Jenny?"

"What should I do next with Jenny? Continue what I am doing with her? Change what I am doing? Withdraw?"

No matter how well we know a child, we cannot always predict how the child will respond to our words and actions. By interacting with children on their level, that is, by playing with children, examining what we are doing as we do it, and reflecting on how our actions support children's active learning, we assume the role of learners ourselves even as we support children's learning.

Adults Record Their Child Observations

So much goes on at work time that it is easy to lose track of all the things you learn about individual children—how they play, whom they play with, how they carry out their plans, what interests them, what KDIs can be identified. Recording this information enables adults to share and analyze their findings at the end of the day so they can plan for the next day.

Different recording techniques work best for different people. If you do not already have a way of recording work-time findings, here are some ideas to consider:

• Take mental "snapshots" of children's actions and words. As soon as children are napping or have left for the day, file through your mental pictures, and jot down specific notes about what individual children said and did.

• Take photos with a digital camera. Children enjoy seeing themselves and the photos will serve as reminders as you talk over the day with team members.

• Jot down the child's name or symbol and key words or phrases about specific things a child did and said. Some adults leave clipboards or pads and pencils in the areas for this purpose. Others put file cards or sticky notes in their pockets. Often, children become interested in what adults write and offer to add their own comments in whatever form of writing they are currently practicing—scribbles, pictures, letters, their names, invented spellings, actual words, and so forth. When children see adults writing about them, they understand both that adults value what they are doing and adults depend on the act of writing to remember important things.

Adults Bring Work Time to an End

Putting toys and materials away creates a transition from working to recalling in the plan-work-recall sequence. Adults generally alert children a few minutes before the end of work time so they can come to a natural stopping place in their play. Cleanup time, as with the

At cleanup time, these children enjoy using wet sponges to wash the table.

rest of work time, is a time for problem solving, playfulness, and realistic expectations.

► **Encourage problem solving.**

At the end of work time, some children deal with the problem of how to continue play that is not quite finished. They figure out on their own, or with the support of adults, how to complete what they are doing—either at the moment, later on in the day, at home, or during work time the next day. For example, at the end of one work time, two children continue working on a large puzzle they have almost finished so they can bring

it to recall. Then they help put other puzzles and toys away. Another child puts the special materials he needs to finish his dinosaur inside the box he is using so he can continue to work on it at home. He puts some of the paper he has been using in his dinosaur box, then puts the rest on the art shelf.

Figuring out how to save what they are working on is another problem some children face at the end of work time. For example, several children have built a "cave" out of blankets and rocks. Instead of taking it down and putting the blankets away, they want to save it to play in after nap time. They discuss their plan to save the cave with an adult who supports their idea; then they make a "Please do not disturb" sign to hang on their cave.

Putting toys and materials back in their containers or on the shelf so they can find them the next time they need them is another problem children solve at the end of work time—a situation that generally calls upon their sorting and matching skills.

Children enjoy figuring out how to use mops, vacuum cleaners, brooms, and sponges because they get to use the real tools that grown-ups use. For example, two young children run a tank-type vacuum cleaner. One guides the hose while the other pushes the tank. Although it takes some time for them to coordinate their efforts, the two children are pleased with their accomplishments, and the house-area floor is free of the pine cone bits and sand left over from "dinner."

▶ **Play put-away games.**

Some children derive a great deal of satisfaction out of stacking blocks back on a shelf, hanging up dress-up clothes, washing paintbrushes, and sorting stones and shells; other children do not. At the end of work time these children are ready for a change of pace. They see no particular problems to solve, they have completed their plans to their satisfaction, and now they are happy to cruise the areas and engage in rough-and-tumble play with other like-minded children. Sometimes, these children will join and contribute enthusiastically to physically active put-away games such as tossing all the inch cubes into the inch-cube box, seeing how many big blocks can be carried at once, racing against the sand timer to put all the dollhouse furniture back on the shelf, setting

up a "fire brigade" line in which items are passed from child to child until they reach their shelf or container, or playing peddler and gathering stray toys into a sack.

▶ **Maintain realistic expectations.**

For many adults, cleanup time is not a favorite segment of the day. In fact they worry that some materials will not be put away, that some children will not help, that putting away toys will take too long, that they will tend to direct rather than interact with children, and that if another adult is observing this time of day, that person will find fault in all these areas of concern. In fact, some or all of these situations probably will occur on any given day. Here are some strategies to help you cope with them:

• Focus on supporting children's problem solving and play. Approach cleanup time, like any other time of the day, from the child's viewpoint.

• Remain calm and optimistic. Generally, within ten minutes the interest areas will be in decent shape.

• Work along with the children to put toys and materials away and to keep the spirit of play and problem solving alive. Enjoy children's energy and ingenuity.

• Begin recall time even if there are still materials left to put away. It makes more sense to go on to recall than to prolong the end of work time. Sometimes the remaining materials can serve as useful recall reminders. (For additional information on the transition between work time and recall time, see the end of Chapter 8.)

As this adult joins the children in putting away the blocks, she enjoys the children's energy and teamwork.

How Adults Support Children at Work Time: A Summary

Adults examine their own beliefs about how children learn at work time.

Adults provide work spaces for children.
___ Children work in the interest areas.
___ Children work in cozy and open spaces.

Adults find out what children are doing.
___ Look for children's plan status.
___ Look for children's individual and social interactions.
___ Look for specific types of play.
___ Look for key developmental indicators.

Adults choose children to observe, gain children's perspectives, and form on-the-spot interaction plans.

Adults offer children comfort and contact.
___ Look for children in need of comfort and contact.
___ Offer reassuring physical contact.
___ Offer simple acknowledgment.

Adults participate in children's play.
___ Look for natural play openings.
___ Join children's play on the child's level.
___ Play in parallel with children.
___ Play as a partner with children.
___ Refer one player to another.
___ Suggest new ideas within ongoing play situations.
 ___ Offer suggestions within the play theme.
 ___ Address the role person rather than the child.
 ___ Respect the child's reaction to your idea.

Adults converse with children.
___ Look for natural opportunities for conversation.
___ Join children at their level for conversation.
___ Respond to children's conversational leads.
___ Converse as a partner with children.
___ Ask questions responsively.
 ___ Ask questions sparingly.
 ___ Relate questions directly to what the child is doing.
 ___ Ask questions about the child's thought process.

Adults encourage children's problem solving.
___ Look for children involved in problem situations.
___ Allow children to deal with problems and conflicting viewpoints.
 ___ Sit down with children.
 ___ Give children time to use their own problem-solving skills.
 ___ Refer one child to another.
 ___ Listen to conflicting viewpoints.
___ Interact with rather than manage children.
___ Calmly assist with unresolved conflicts.
 ___ Approach calmly.
 ___ Acknowledge children's feelings.
 ___ Gather information.
 ___ Restate the problem.
 ___ Ask for ideas for solutions and choose one together.
 ___ Be prepared to give follow-up support.

Adults examine their interactions with children as they occur.

Adults record their child observations.

Adults bring work time to an end.
___ Encourage problem solving.
___ Play put-away games.
___ Maintain realistic expectations.

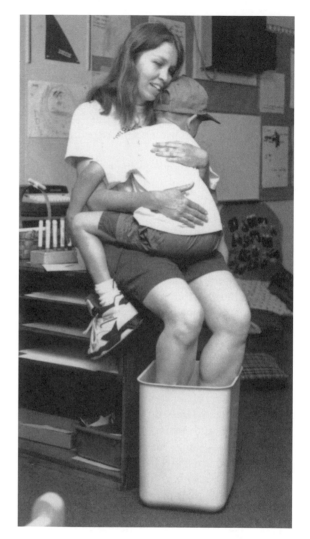

At work time, this teacher provides comfort and contact in a play situation devised by the child she is holding on her lap.

Understanding Recall Time

Recalling takes place both in the *recall* segment of the daily routine—the final element in the plan-work-recall sequence—and throughout the day as children reflect on their work. This chapter examines the recall process—why it is important, where it occurs, what children do at this time, and how adults can best support them. The following examples from an actual recall time in a High/Scope program illustrate the various ways preschool children talk about what they have done.

"I got dressed up and went to a wedding! Scott went. Kelly went. They got dressed up."

"I was the mommy, and Carol was the baby."

"Me. Carol." (Carol thumps her chest with the flat of her hand on each word.) *"Baby."*

"I made a pizza-thrower car this high." (Scott holds his hand up to his waist.) *"I sat on it and throwed pizzas to people. Then it turned into a dump truck."*

(Jessa brings a plate to Becki, an adult.) *"I saw you using this plate today, Jessa,"* Becki says. *"It looked like you were cooking."* (Jessa nods in agreement.)

> "Learning involves purposeful memory."
> —Donald Norman (1988)

"Namen and me made a boat. With the big blocks and those red blocks. We wanted more, but Kerry already had some for her house."

"French fries. We cooked lots. I took some to the block area and gave them to Linda to eat!"

"See this!" (Shows a toothpick and clay structure.) *"This keeps the giants out. And the ugly trolls. Dogs bark down here. The princess locks the door. Up, up to the top of the tower. Faster than a motorcycle. 'You leave me alone, you had giants.' That's why she has this tower."*

What Is Recall and Why Is It Important?

During recall time, children reflect on, talk about, and exhibit what they have done at work time. While the *planning process* involves children in forming a purpose and anticipating a course of action that leads to active learning experiences, the *recall process* helps children make sense of these actions. At recall, children are involved in several important processes—drawing on memories, reflecting on experiences, associating plans with outcomes, and talking with others about their discoveries and actions.

▶ **Remembering and reflecting on actions and experiences**

For young children, the recall process involves much more than the straightforward retrieval of facts and figures stored away in the brain. During recall, children engage in an active, story-forming process. They literally *construct* memory, which in the words of Edmund Bolles (1988) "is a living product of desire, insight, and consciousness" (p. xiv). When children recall their work-time experiences, they form a mental version of their experiences based on their ability to understand and interpret what they have done. They select and talk about the parts of their experiences that have a special meaning to them: "We made mud! We love mud, don't we Jeff!" As psychologist Roger Schank (1990) points out, "We need to tell someone else a story that describes our experiences because the process of creating the story also creates the memory structure that will contain the gist of the story for the rest of our lives. Talking is remembering" (p. 115).

As children engage in this process of selecting events to talk about and then interpreting what happened, they develop a better understanding of their experiences. Writing, talking, storytelling, painting, sculpting, dancing, composing music—these are all ways we as adults organize and make sense of what we know. We have an experience, feeling, or idea that we attempt to give form to or describe by using words, notes, numbers, formulas, brush strokes, or movements. Similarly, weavers in the Middle Ages wove great tapestries that depicted their particular understanding and interpretations of nature, myth, religion, and everyday court life.

Preschoolers have the same need as the rest of us to remember and make sense of what

At recall time, children reflect on, talk about, and exhibit what they have done at work time. Brendan, for example, has drawn and is describing a "chair plane" he traveled on at work time. "I went there and back!"

Here is Brendan at work time "flying" on the "chair plane." Note how the curved lines of his recall drawing suggest the curved block he holds in his lap.

they know. In fact, their own words and gestures are their primary tools for shaping and understanding past events:

Reeny: *I was . . . I was playin' in the sand but . . . it was too dry!*

Adult: *Too dry?*

Reeny: *It wouldn't stay in a cake so I . . . I, um . . . made it very muddy!*

Adult: *Oh . . . How did you do that?*

Reeny: *I put in lots of water!*

Adult: *I saw you put in lots of water.*

Reeny: *Then it sticked in a cake . . . and . . . it sticked* (looks at hands) *on me, too!*

As children reflect on what they have done, they begin in their own deliberate fashion to consider the meaning of their experiences and ideas, turning them over in their minds. They thus begin to think about what they have done *in the abstract.* Moreover, by thinking things through, they begin to understand that they can make things happen, learn new things, and solve their own problems: "The paint knocked over. I put my hand down fast to catch it. I held it on the edge of the table. (Demonstrates.) Then Timmy got paper towels. It didn't even go on the floor, only just a little bitty drop."

Berry and Sylva (1987) underscore the importance of recall time for young children's

development in this succinct observation: "Recall provides a rich potential for language use, discussing means-ends relationships, and exploring connections" (p. 35).

▶ **Associating plans, actions, and outcomes**

As children recall their work-time experiences, they gradually begin to associate what they did with the plans they made before they started. They begin to develop a consciousness of purpose, realizing that planning prior to doing gives them control of their actions through the entire plan-work-recall sequence: "I planned to be a kitty with Sabrina. And we were kitty cats all the whole time. Even at cleanup time!"

▶ **Talking with others about personally meaningful experiences**

Recalling involves social interaction on a very personal level—reflecting on experiences and finding the words, actions, and gestures to convey their meaning to others: "I made a . . . a . . . paper with lots (acts out squeezing a glue bottle) . . . lots of drippy glue! I'll show you. (Gets paper.) It's here (points to patches of glue) and here. It's . . . it's . . . you can touch it. It's not sticky!"

Such recall experiences are an opportunity for children to engage in personal story-telling in which they, as narrators, are the major characters. The dramatic, exciting, or puzzling aspects of work-time experiences provide the raw materials that children use at recall time to construct a story for others. Clearly, the social aspects of planning, doing, and recalling directly support children's emerging literacy. Through this process, children become conscious of themselves and their peers as people with interesting thoughts to relate. This awareness contributes to their readiness to relate their experiences in emerging print forms and to interpret the printed narrations created by others. Put another way, *during planning time children turn their interests into purposeful actions, while at recall time children turn their purposeful actions into narratives that capture the striking features of those actions.* Educators who help children capture these moments meet the educational challenge described by educator Elliot Eisner (1990) as "finding a way of helping children acquire the language they need while at the same time keeping a playful attitude toward language alive" (p. 47).

Recalling also makes children's experiences public. Since recalling is a social phenomenon

taking place between two or more people, it has the effect of opening up personal experiences to public scrutiny. Children have the opportunity to present their experiences in such a way that others not only listen to them but also add their observations and ideas:

Carlie: *I played with Jack.*

Kevin: *You played with me, too.*

Tim: *And you drived me, remember?*

Carlie: *We all played and played!*

Public discourse, even at this very simple level, is an essential part of any culture. Eisner (1990) explains this function in these terms: "The public representation of ideas and images is a way to share them with others. We usually take this function for granted, but unless the private is made public there is no way to participate in the experience of others . . . The process of representation is a way to enter the lives of others and to begin to understand what others have thought and felt. Without representation, culture itself would not be possible" (pp. 53–54).

Children who engage in the recall process are offering their experiences for public examination. Catherine, for example, displays the banner she has made, and over the next week or so, other children, intrigued with the idea, experiment with banner-making in a variety of forms. Clearly, as children become interested in and experiment with one another's projects and experiences, these ideas and ways of doing things are gradually assimilated into the culture of their early childhood setting.

At recall time children turn their work-time pursuits into narratives that capture the striking features of what they did. "And all of us got under the table!" this child says, spreading her arms for emphasis.

Recalling—What and Why: A Summary

What It Is and Why It Is Important

- Remembering and reflecting on actions and experiences
- Associating plans, actions, and outcomes
- Talking with others about personally meaningful experiences
- Forming and then talking about mental images
- Expanding consciousness beyond the present

▶ **Forming and then talking about mental images**

Preschoolers have the capacity to picture in their minds real and imagined past and future experiences. This capacity for forming mental images and symbols enables them to use both language and movement to recall, imagine, talk about, and describe people and objects in forms that others can comprehend. In other words, they can *represent* experiences. The recall process provides an opportunity for children to exercise their emerging representational abilities. As they turn their memories into concrete words and gestures, children form their own understanding of their work-time experiences: "I, um (gestures with hands as if using the mouse) worked in the computer . . . area today. I made pictures! Then I cutted . . . a, um (holds an imagined page with one hand and makes scissor-like motions with the other) I cutted a, um . . . the . . . pictures apart!"

▶ **Expanding consciousness beyond the present**

In their new-found capacity for engaging in pretend play with others, preschoolers use what educator Anthony Pellegrini (1986) describes as the "language of absence": "Language that takes people away from their immediate surroundings" (p. 83). Children also use the "language of absence" as they recall their work-time experi-

ences: "I got Will money and that's all I can tell. And I played with those two guys. And I drove the cars and they broke out our windows!" As children recall, they consciously look back in time and search for the images and words to express their interpretation of their immediate past:

Adult: *What happened when you broke out the windows?*

Kyle: *We'd be dead!*

Adult: *You were dead, Kyle?*

Ben: *So were me!*

Thus, as they recall, children come to understand what they have done and develop the ability to relate their actions and outcomes to others who can then explore and modify them. Remembering and reflecting on their original intentions, associating plans with actions and the outcomes of these actions, and talking with others about meaningful experiences are important to the intellectual and social-emotional development of all of us, not just children. These mental and social processes allow us to search through the past for clues to the present and future. Recalling events and experiences is a skill that will benefit children throughout their lives. For this reason, the recall process is an essential element of the High/Scope daily routine.

What Children Do as They Recall

As fledgling storytellers, preschoolers recall in unique ways. Adults should be aware of the characteristics of preschoolers' personal storytelling

As children recall, they search for the images and words to express their interpretations of their immediate past. This child talks about a painting he made at work time.

styles to understand what to expect during their recall conversations with children.

▶ **Children grow in their capacity to recount past events.**

As toddlers, children develop the capacity to talk about the past. In one study, Peggy Miller and Linda Sperry (1988) observed 2-year-old children to find out how they talked about past events they had personally experienced. The authors report that "during this period (2.0–2.6 years of age) the children talked primarily about negative past events, especially events of physical harm; the rate of talk about specific past events doubled; temporally ordered sequences increased dramatically; and the children became better able to accomplish such talk independently. In addition, one of the most striking findings is the extent to which these 2-year-olds were able to communicate their attitudes toward the past event, with speech about the past containing five

Children select experiences to recall. Even though Brendan also tied knots to make a string "trap" and played the marker guessing game at work time, at recall time he decided to draw and talk about his ride on the "chair plane."

times more evaluative devices than other speech. These results suggest that (1) by 2.6 years of age, stories of personal experience emerge in incipient form, and (2) the roots of this genre lie not only in cognitive skills and social interactional support but also in the emotional significance of the depicted event" (p. 293). As this statement illustrates, even children as young as 2 years of age are inclined to talk about personally meaningful experiences, often experiences that have caused them some sort of pain or confusion.

In examining 3- and 4-year-olds' ability to recall personal experiences, Miller and Sperry (1988) note that "preschool-aged children also tell stories about events that happened to them or their associates—a fight with another child, a ride at the Fair, an accidental injury, a trip to the swimming pool" (p. 294). Berry and Sylva (1987) found that "children [in High/Scope programs]

were able to recall what they had done, and often with considerable detail. They frequently included comments indicating that they were aware of the difference between activities they had planned and others they had not planned" (p. 16).

Clearly, while the ability to talk about their own experiences is evident very early, children are often able to add more details to these discussions as they grow older. The more they understand about what they have done, the more they are able to talk about it in detail:

Ben (3 years old): (Pretends to type.) *I played with the computer.*

Linda (4 years old): *Me and Chelsea played wedding. We danced on the steps and then we went home. And then we had dinner . . . and had dessert . . . and then pretended that we were playing downstairs . . . and then . . . and then we played again!*

A common thread that seems to run through most stories about the past is a personal emotional investment in the original experience. Children, indeed persons of all ages, are most apt to recall experiences in which they themselves were actively and emotionally engaged.

▶ **Children select experiences to recall.**

Throughout most of work time, 4-year-old Trina was engaged in an elaborate role-play

sequence that eventually involved several other children. The children decided to dress up as ballerinas. Once dressed in their tutus, the children built a stage for their show, set up chairs for the audience, made tickets, and recruited everyone they could to sit in the chairs and watch. At recall time, the adult recalling with Trina anticipated a detailed report, because Trina had been so focused on the play sequence that had involved almost every other child and adult at one time or another. What Trina actually talked about at recall, however, had nothing to do with dressing up, building a stage, or dancing. Instead, she told about something she had done after the show, in the last 10 minutes of work time: "I made a card for my daddy . . . for his birthday. It's this day! . . . I sended him one card but . . . but this card's for when . . . for when . . . he's home!"

It is often difficult to predict what, out of all the things they have done at work time, young children will choose to talk about at recall time. What impresses an adult about a child's work-time experiences may or may not be what a child decides to share. Children rarely give a strictly chronological account of their work-time experiences. Instead, they tend to select one or two things that are of particular significance to them, regardless of how much time they actually have spent on the activities. They may talk about the last thing they did during work time. They may show a picture that took them five minutes to paint or a workbench construction that took all of work time to complete. They may simply recount who they played with, if playing with their friends was more significant than anything they actually did together. The point is, *recalling is a selective experience.* Children choose what they want to talk about based on their own interests and ideas. Having the opportunity to say something about their own experiences is more important than which experience they actually recall.

▶ **Children construct their own understanding of what they have just done.**

"We remember things according to our understanding of what happened, not according to the way something really occurred" (Bolles 1988, p. 72).

First child: *We made mud. The water . . . it jumped out . . . out of the hole . . . so we made mud.*

Adult: *It jumped out of the hole!*

First child: *Yeah, just like this.* (Makes a jumping motion with his hand.)

Second child: *We love mud, don't we Jeff?*

First child: *Yeah, we love mud!*

As children's understanding of experiences increases, they are able to construct memories that are closer to actuality. When children understand what they have done, the recall stories they construct are fairly accurate and straightforward:

Child: (Shows a pair of tin-can stilts.) *These are my stilts. I made 'em.*

Adult: *I saw you pounding holes in the tops.*

Child: *Well, I pounded . . . I pounded a nail . . . One here . . . here . . . here, here* (points to four holes). *It's hard to poke this string through . . . It kept slipping back out. I stopped it with this tape, see, right here . . . You can walk on 'em. Like this.* (Demonstrates.)

▶ **Children recall experiences in a variety of ways.**

While the recall process generally involves discussions, young children also use

At recall time, this child put something he had used at work time into a bag and had his teacher guess what it was!

motions and gestures, re-enactments, drawings, and written accounts to describe their work-time experiences.

Gesture and re-enactment. Some children, especially young children who are new to the plan-work-recall sequence, simply point to a person or object they played with or to one of the places where they played. They may also get

something they used or act out something they did. Three-year-old Tara, for example, uses all of these strategies:

Adult: *What did you do today, Tara?*

Child: (Points to the sand and water table.)

Adult: *Ah, you played in the sand.*

Child: (Nods in agreement.)

- Children grow in their capacity to recount past events.
- Children select experiences to recall.
- Children construct their own understanding of what they have just done.
- Children recall experiences in a variety of ways.

Adult: *I saw you.*

Child: (Gets a bucket from the sand table.) *This!*

Adult: *This bucket.*

Child: (Makes scooping motions.)

Adult: (Makes scooping motions.)

Child: (Laughs and turns bucket over.) *All gone!*

Adult: *All gone!*

Talking. It is very common for pre-schoolers to talk as they recall. As they remember and reconstruct past events, their speech is often punctuated by pauses during which they search their minds for words to express their understanding. Older, more experienced recallers will include more details in their stories and, as well, are likely to add to other children's recall narratives.

Drawing and writing. As noted earlier, children also draw and write about their experiences in a variety of forms, including scribbles, simple and more detailed drawings, letters, and words. While some children can write and draw about their work-time experiences from the images they have in their minds, other children need the actual object to trace or refer to.

How Adults Support Children at Recall Time

*I*t is recall time in Becki's program. Becki and the children have been planning and recalling for about three months. Five of the nine children in the recall group talk with Becki about what they have done. Please note that Becki's recall interchange with each child is quite short—lasting from 35 to 50 seconds:

Becki: *Scott, what did you do at work time?*

Scott: *Ah, I played with . . . Will played with me.*

Becki: *Will played with you.*

Scott: *And I played with Will.*

Becki: *And you played with Will.*

Scott: *We were movers.*

Becki: *You guys were movers?*

Scott: *Yeah, we moved all the food!*

Becki: *You moved all the food from there.*

Linda: *Did you guys put it all back?*

Scott: *No.*

Becki: *You moved it all from off that shelf?*

Scott: *Yeah . . . And even that basket.*

Becki: *Even that basket. You sure did.*

Scott: *Even the chocolate milk!*

Becki: *Even the chocolate milk! And what happened when you were done moving?*

Scott: *We cleaned it up!*

Becki: *You cleaned it up. (To the other children) You know what, guys? They surprised me. They cleaned up after they moved the food. I turned around, and it was like magic. It was all clean!*

❧

Becki: *What did you do, Chelsea?*

Chelsea: *Ummm . . . Played with all these things.*

Becki: *You played with all those what?*

Chelsea: *Fruit.*

Becki: *All that fruit. What did you do with all that fruit?*

Chelsea: *I ate it all up.*

Becki: *All by yourself?*

Chelsea: *Yeah.*

Becki: *You ate it all up all by yourself! Did you do anything else?*

Chelsea: *Nope.*

Becki: *Nope.*

Chelsea: *That's all I did!*

Becki: *That's all you did!*

❧

Linda: *Me!*

Becki: *Linda, what did you do today?*

Linda: *Me and Chelsea played wedding. We danced on the steps and then we went home. And then we had dinner . . . and had dessert . . . and then we pretended that we were playing downstairs . . . and then . . . and then we played again.*

Becki: *You did all that, and then you played wedding again!*

Linda: *And lots of kids danced on the steps.*

Becki: *I saw you on the steps. There were lots of kids on the steps today.*

❧

Becki: *Ben, your plan was to work with blocks.*

Ben: *I worked with Kyle.*

Linda: (Making a rhyme) *Kyle and style.*

Becki: *What did you do with him?*

Ben: *I worked with um . . .* (talking among children). *Callie was with me. And I worked with Will.*

Kyle: *Callie worked with me.*

Becki: (To Ben) *And you worked with Will. What did you do when you worked with Kyle and Callie and Will?*

Ben: *I got Will money and that's all I can tell. And I played with those two guys. And I drove the cars, and they broke out our windows.*

Becki: *They broke out your window?*

Ben: *Me and Kyle.*

Becki: *You broke out of the windows in the car?*

Ben: *Uh huh.*

Becki: *What happened when you broke out of the windows?*

Kyle: *We'd be dead.*

Becki: *You were dead, Kyle?*

Ben: *So were me!*

Becki: *And you were dead, too! Oh, dear!*

❧

Becki: *Callie, what did you do in the block area?*

Callie: *Played with stacks.*

Becki: *Played with stacks.*

Callie: (Talks with other child in the group.)

Becki: *You played with Kyle, too?*

Callie: (Points.)

Becki: *You played in that area.*

Callie: *Block area.*

Becki: *You played in the block area.*

Callie: *We played.*

Becki: *You played.*

Callie: *And that's it!*

Becki: *That's it!*

In High/Scope active learning environments the adult's role at recall time is similar to the adult's role at planning time and grows out of work-time observations, conversations with children, and participation in children's play. These shared work-time experiences become the basis for recall stories and conversations. As at planning time, adults can best support children's recall by adopting the following five strategies:

- Examining their beliefs about how children learn at recall time

- Recalling with children in a calm, cozy setting

- Providing materials and experiences to maintain children's interest at recall time

- Conversing with children about their work-time experiences

- Anticipating changes in the way children recall over time

> "Memory is a creative act of construction and imagination."
>
> — *Edmund Bolles (1988)*

Adults Examine Their Beliefs About How Children Learn at Recall Time

If adults approach the recall-time segment as another obligatory time period to "get through," the results tend to be perfunctory, drill-like, and not particularly enjoyable. Using recall to hold young children accountable for their original plans and where they worked or expecting children to give a chronological account of their work-time pursuits generally undermines the spirit and purpose of recalling.

For adults implementing the High/Scope educational approach, recalling with children is an opportunity to find out how children think about and share their thoughts and observations about what they have just done. Adults who are most comfortable supporting children's recall efforts have come to understand that children are most likely to recall when they are able to tell their own stories in their own words about work-time experiences they choose to interpret. Children are comfortable participating in recall experiences in a way that is playful, gives them control over the stories they tell, and encourages them to contribute to one another's narratives.

Adults Recall With Children in a Calm, Cozy Setting

Effective recall experiences are more likely to occur in calm, cozy settings under the guidance of adults who are willing to follow the child's lead.

▶ **Recall in intimate groups and places.**

Young children seek out and benefit from full adult attention as they try to recall and describe their activities in their own words. Thus, small and intimate recall groups result in more satisfying recall times for both children and adults. Nevertheless, 5- and 6-year-old children are increasingly able to recall in whole-group settings, especially if their peers are willing to listen to them with genuine interest. While adults cannot always control the size of recall groups, they can make them as intimate as possible by adopting the following practices, some of which are also used at planning and work times:

• Converse with each child at the child's physical level.

• Provide materials at recall time to engage all children as each child recalls individually (see suggestions on p. 235).

• Physically separate recall groups as much as possible so the natural noise or enthusiasm of one group does not distract another.

• Consider cozy alternatives to sitting in chairs around a table. For example, recall in a block building made during work time, under a table draped with a blanket, outside under a tree, or on cushions in the book area.

▶ **Recall with those who shared the experiences children are recalling.**

Because preschoolers are relatively new at consciously constructing memories and expressing their thoughts in ways that are comprehensible to others, they appreciate recalling with adults who know what occurred at work time. As children recall, particular objects,

Gathering on the floor around a large sheet of paper for group drawing provides a cozy, intimate setting for recall.

sounds, smells, and actions may suddenly remind them of work-time experiences. These spontaneous recollections may often seem out of context to listeners who have not shared the same experiences, unless they realize that the child has linked the present with the past. Berry and Sylva (1987) confirm the value of shared experiences at recall time: "Recall was especially detailed when it was conducted by the staff person who had been in the activity area where the child worked, rather than by an adult who had participated in planning but was ignorant of what the child actually did during work time" (p. 18). Consider this example of recalling shared experiences:

Recalling child: *I played with Callie.*

Adult: *You played with Callie.*

Recalling child: *Played baby.*

Adult: *I saw you had a crib over there.*

Contributing child: *I played baby too!*

Recalling child: *We went to the store . . . We . . . we went . . . huntin'.*

Adult: *You went hunting?*

Recalling child: *For toys! Baby toys!*

Adult: *I saw you hunting for toys in the toy area.*

Recalling child: *Yeah, we got lots. We had to have a bag to carry 'em all! That many!*

Adults Provide Materials and Experiences to Maintain Children's Interest at Recall Time

When recalling with more than three or four children at a time, it is important to provide materials that children can use during one another's recall narratives or to play games that make waiting for a turn to recall enjoyable rather than tedious for children.

The ideas presented in Recall Games and Experiences, page 235, are similar to the planning-time games and experiences suggested on pages 182–183 because they serve a similar purpose—to hold the interest of small groups of children while one child recalls. When trying out these ideas, be alert to the possibility that the game or material may take over, rather than support, the recall process. Sometimes, for example, children using telephones may recall in a fairly perfunctory manner because what they really want to do is choose the next person to use the phone and dial their number!

Adult: *Hello, Ivan. What did you do today?*

Ivan: *I made a boat and played diver. Now I'm calling Yuri. Get ready, Yuri, I'm calling . . . one . . . two . . . two . . . That's your number . . . Ring . . . ring . . . ring!*

Sometimes, too, if the recall materials or game require much adult explanation, the game itself may command all the children's attention and interest and recalling may feel to them like an imposition. If these types of situations occur, take note, follow the children's interests, and try simplifying the strategy the next time you use it.

Children enjoy telling their recall stories "on TV." The use of this simple prop draws children's attention as if the recalling child really were on camera!

Adults Converse With Children About Their Work-Time Experiences

Once adults have incorporated materials and games that engage all the children in their recall group, they can turn their attention to conversing with individual children about what they have done. The following suggestions are similar to the suggestions we offer for conversing with children about their plans. In planning, however, children look forward to what they *might do;* in recalling, the children reflect on some aspect of what they *have done.* In either case, adults support children's anticipated actions and construction of memory in the same attentive, responsive fashion.

▶ **Adults take an unhurried approach to recall.**

In their observations of recall time, Berry and Sylva (1987) note that the benefits of recall are often missed in the daily pressure on the adult to get through all the members of the group. One way to avoid rushing is to recall in small groups of three or four children. If this is not possible, it may be more relaxed for children and adults to recall with half the children in each recall group each day. One benefit of slowing down appears to be that when recalling with fewer children each day in a more leisurely fashion, children feel less pressured and more inclined to add to one another's narratives:

Recalling child: *We were movers!*

Adult: *You guys were movers?*

Recalling child: *Yeah, we moved all the food!*

Adult: *You moved all the food from there.*

Contributing child: *Did you guys put it back?*

Recalling child: *No.*

Recall Games and Experiences

Tours

The games and experiences presented here allow children to go to places where they have played and to things they have made during work time. Thus, children can move around for recall rather than being confined to one place.

- **Visits to structures**—The recalling child leads the rest of the recall group to a structure he or she has made (and that has not been taken apart and put away during cleanup). Gathering around (and in, when possible) a block house, a Tinkertoy tower, or a sand castle, for example, reminds the recalling child of what she did and the adventures she had. In addition, the rest of the children may become very interested too, because they can see and touch the structure for themselves. Often they ask their own questions, such as "How do you get inside, Malek?" "What are these big things for?" "How'd you make that stick on?"

- **Gallery visits**—Similar to visits to structures, during gallery visits the recalling child leads the rest of the group to a picture on a wall, artwork drying on a rack, a banner hanging from the ceiling, a collage, mask, or workbench piece in progress.

- **Collections**—At the beginning of recall, all the children gather one or two things they have played with during work time and bring them back to the recall place. Children take turns talking about and demonstrating what they have chosen to gather.

- **"Let's be . . ." or "Let's take the . . ."**—This strategy changes with children's interests. If children have been playing ghost, for example, you might say "Let's be ghosts and fly with Amir to something he played with at work time." Or, if children are spending a lot of time building police cars, you might say "Let's drive in our police cars, following Nikki to something she wants to tell us about."

Group games

These recall games, like the planning games, provide children with enjoyable things to do or anticipate while other children are recalling.

- **Photographs**—During work time, take and print a number of digital photographs of each child in your recall group. At the beginning of recall, spread the photos out on the floor and have each child collect the photos in which he or she appears. As children talk among themselves about what they see, move from child to child for individual recall conversations.

- **Musical chairs or carpet squares**—Set up a circle of chairs, carpet squares, or blocks. Mark one seat as the recall seat, for example, the seat with the red bow, or the one with the airplane taped to it. Play a musical selection, stopping the music at unexpected intervals. The children walk (crawl, swim, hop) around the circle until the music stops, then sit on the nearest seat. The child who sits on the recall seat has a turn to talk about work time. If you have the children move around the inside of the circle, they will end up facing toward the center of the circle and one another as they recall.

- **Hula hoop, ball, spinner, symbols, rhymes**—See the descriptions of these games on page 182. Modify them for recall time by substituting the word "recall" for the word "plan."

Props and partnerships

These recall experiences center around materials children can use together as they recall and as they await their turn to recall.

- **Spyglasses, telephones, puppets**—See the descriptions of these games on page 182. Modify them for recall time. Or modify them by giving one spyglass, telephone, puppet (or stuffed animal) to each child so children can talk with each other as you move from child to child for individual recall conversations.

Representations

Pantomime, mapping, and drawing enable children to construct and represent recall memories in media other than words.

- **Pictures, pantomime, map, drawing, and writing**—See the descriptions of these strategies on page 183. Modify them for recall time.

- **Group work-time story**—Hang up or lay out a long piece of butcher paper. Ask each child to use a part of it to draw and write about what he or she did at work time. Children who played together may wish to share a space or work next to each other.

- **Recall books**—Sometimes children enjoy collecting their recall drawings and writings into a book they can take home and share with their families. For example, if you ask children to draw and write their recall stories once a week, at the end of a month or so, you might bring all their drawings to recall time along with a variety of fasteners children could use to make them into a book. Or you might assemble paper into a book and have children draw and write their recall stories until all the pages are full.

❧

These ideas for tours, games, props and partnerships, and representations at recall time are just a beginning. As you recall with children, you and your team will devise your own strategies for making recall time an active learning experience for the children in your care.

▶ **Adults invite children to talk about what they have done.**

After putting yourself at or below the child's eye-level, there are several ways to begin the recall experience.

Pick up on children's opening comments. Sometimes a child begins a recall conversation with a comment he or she is eager to share, or one that is inspired by a particular material:

Child: (Looking at a work-time photo) *That's me . . . over at the . . . the . . . the books!*

Adult: *That's you over at the books!*

Child: *The story about the trees.*

Comment on a child's play. An adult can also begin a recall conversation with a personal comment or observation about a child's work-time experience:

Adult: *I saw you driving, Denise.*

Denise: *Marshall didn't want to go to the clinic, but I told him, "You get in that car!"*

Ask an open-ended question. For example, "What did you do today, Sam?" "What happened with you and Ricky in the sand, Lenore?" or "What were you doing with all that tape, Larry?"

Opening questions are fine as long as children respond to them with interest, but try to avoid an over-dependence on adult questions to begin recall conversations. Note which children respond most naturally to comments and which children respond to open-ended questions.

▶ **Adults watch children and listen attentively.**

When you take time to recall with children in an unhurried manner, you will often be surprised by what children choose to talk about and how they construct their memories in words:

Adult: *What did you do, Namen?*

Child: *Oh, I went to . . . I played next to . . . I was in the water table!*

Adult: *You were in the water table.*

Child: *I worked with . . . with sand . . . and water.*

Adult: *It looked like you took about three or four bottles of water over there.*

Child: *Uh, huh. I took tons of it.*

Adult: *You took tons of it!*

Some children may use gestures and actions rather than words. By watching carefully and knowing what the child was doing at work time, you can incorporate these actions into your conversation:

Adult: *I saw you with lots of stuffed animals, Bethany.*

Bethany: (Giggles. Gets as many stuffed animals as she can carry and brings them back to the group.)

Adult: *Here they are!*

Bethany: (Makes each animal lie down. Pats each one.)

Adult: (Pats an animal.)

Bethany: (Smiles. Puts her finger to her lips.) *Shh!*

Adult: *Shh!*

At recall time, this adult watches and listens very carefully to the child's description of what he made.

As with planning, it is important to follow the child's lead in recall conversations whether or not they are related to a work-time experience:

Child: *I'm not telling what I did.*

Adult: *Oh?*

Child: *That boy messed with me.*

Adult: *That boy messed with you at work time?*

Child: *No! That . . . that big boy . . . on the bus.*

Adult: *A boy on the bus. This morning?*

Child: *No, that 'nother day . . . tomorrow.*

Adult: *Oh, the other day.*

Second child: *Did'ja tell your momma?*

Child: *I told my momma. She said, "You quit messin' with little kids." Then she told his daddy, an' he gave him a whoopin.*

Adult: *He got a whoopin', and he didn't bother you today.*

Child: *He looked at me . . . but he's scared of his daddy.*

Adult: *Getting whooped is scary.*

Child: *I don't want him messin' with me. He pushed me down.*

Adult: *Being pushed on the bus is scary too.*

Sometimes, particularly after three or four other children have recalled, children who initially were eager to recall are ready to move on to the next part of the routine. Consider this recall time during which the children are talking to one another through a pretend TV screen:

Adult: *Chris, you've been waiting to talk on the TV.*

Chris: *I don't want to anymore.*

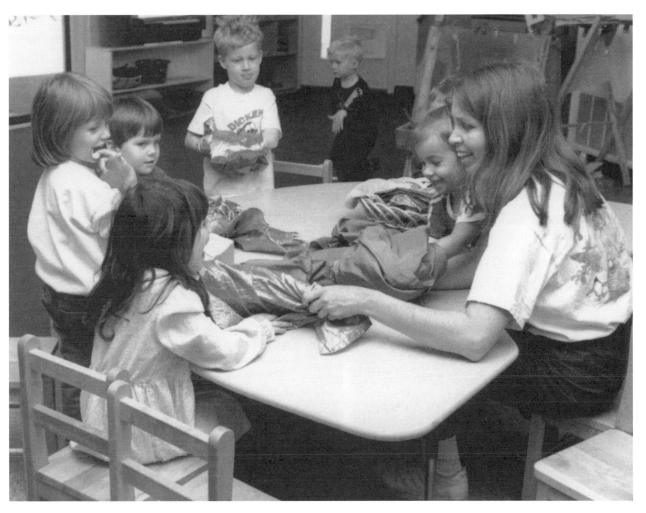

"Guess what I have!" These children talk excitedly about the work-time materials they have chosen, wrapped in colorful scarves, and brought back to their recall group. "A block! Me and Emma made a bear house!"

Adult: *You don't want to anymore. Do you want to recall some other way?*

Chris: *No.*

Adult: *No . . . What do you want to tell us?*

Chris: *I want to do snack! Pass out the cups!*

Adult: *Okay! We'll start with you tomorrow at recall time. But now it's time for you to pass out the cups for snack.*

▶ **Adults contribute observations and comments to keep children's recall narratives going.**

Some children rely on responsive adult contributions and acknowledgments to help them spin their narrative thread. Note how the adult's neutral comments help this child keep his recall narrative going:

Antoine: *I worked on the computer.*

Adult: *I saw you.*

Antoine: *I worked on the mask program.*

Adult: *Oh! The mask program.*

Antoine: *I made it again and again and again . . . On the printer.*

Adult: *You made it again and again and again!*

Antoine: *Yeah, a big long . . . banner . . . for the school.*

Adult: *For the school.*

Antoine: *You could hang it from the ceiling.*

Angelette: *I know. We could hang right . . . up . . . there!* (Points above their heads.)

Children: *Yeah, let's.*

▶ **Adults use questions thoughtfully and sparingly.**

While you may use a question to begin a recall conversation, it is important to remember that, in general, when an adult asks a child a question, the adult rather than the child retains control of the conversation. When you do ask questions during recall, ask them sparingly rather than bombarding the child with one question after another. Also, ask questions that encourage children to describe and explain, such as "How did you do that?" and "Why did you decide to add the string?"

Adam: *I maked it real, real tall.*

Adult: *It was tall. How did you get it to stay up?*

Adam: *We put that big board up and . . . and Brian stood on the other side like this.* (Demonstrates.) *And I put that other board on. And then he didn't have to stay there anymore.*

Adult: *Brian didn't have to stay on the other side any more.*

Adam: *No, 'cause then it stood up, and he didn't even have to hold it!*

▶ **Adults support children's co-narratives and conflicting viewpoints.**

When children share their work-time experiences and adults listen and contribute, other children often add their own questions, observations, and opinions. These extended conversations can be very enjoyable, even though they may become heated at times and stray from the original topic. Here, for example, is the full conversation that followed from Bethany's rather brief recall narrative presented on page 236:

Adult: *I saw you with lots of stuffed animals, Bethany.*

Bethany: (Giggles. Gets as many stuffed animals as she can carry and brings them back to the group.)

Adult: *Here they are!*

Bethany: (Makes each animal lie down. Pats each one.)

Adult: (Pats an animal.)

Bethany: (Smiles. Puts her finger to her lips.) *Shh!*

Adult: *Shh!*

Markie: *She's puttin' 'em to sleep!*

Children: *Shh! They're sleeping.* (Whispering.) *We better whisper, okay?*

Adult: (Whispering.) *Bethany played with the animals and put them all to sleep.*

Bethany: *And I gave 'em peaches.* (Pretends to feed a cat.)

Joey: (Out loud.) *Cats don't like peaches. They like cat food!*

Bethany: *Peaches!*

Erika: *My dog likes bananas.*

Joey: *That's dumb. Dogs aren't supposed to eat bananas. They like bones.*

Margo: *My cat likes chicken bones, but my mom says he'll choke. But he just coughs up hair. Like this.* (Demonstrates.)

Joey: *Yeeck! That's gross.*

Adult: *Some cats like peaches, some like cat food. Some dogs like bananas, some like bones.*

Margo: *And chicken bones.*

Adult: *And chicken bones. Some cats like chicken bones.*

Bethany: *Peaches.*

Joey: *Oh, brother!*

▶ **Adults acknowledge (rather than praise) children's work-time experiences.**

It is important to acknowledge children's work-time experiences rather than praise them. It is more beneficial to children in the long run if we avoid phrases such as "I *liked* the way you . . ." "You really did a *good job* on . . .," however well-intentioned these comments may be. Instead, comment on a specific aspect of a child's play:

Adam: *We put that big board up and . . . and Brian stood on the other side like this.* (Demonstrates.) *And I put that other board on. And then he didn't have to stay there anymore.*

Adult: *Brian didn't have to stay on the other side anymore.*

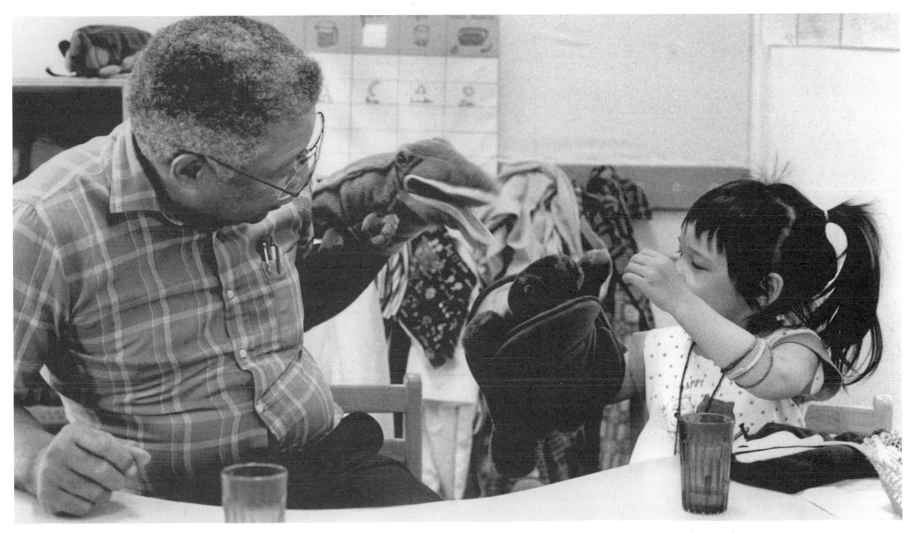

Whether conversing through puppets, on "TV," or around a group mural, creating recall stories helps children bring closure to their work-time experiences.

Adam: *No, 'cause then it stood up and he didn't even have to hold it!*

Adult: *Your tower stayed up because Brian held it up while you leaned the long board against it.*

Adam: *Yeah! That's how we did it!*

Writing down what children say as they recall is another way to acknowledge the importance of children's recall narratives. Recording

recall narratives serves the same purpose and also allows adults to listen to themselves. As they listen, adults can evaluate which conversational strategies—such as contributing, commenting, repeating, acknowledging, and questioning—they use most often in recall conversations and how children are responding. While recordings take time to transcribe, once you can hear what you have said, you can gain a clearer picture of how

effectively you are supporting children's construction of memory.

▶ **Adults note connections between children's recall narratives and plans.**

It is instructive for adults to note connections between children's plans and what they choose to talk about at recall time. Often, experienced planners and recallers make these connections on their own—"I planned to play with Barbara, and we played baby with Gwen and Eva." Other children make a plan, complete it, and move on to something else. They may talk about this second activity in their recall narrative rather than discuss the activity they first anticipated and carried out. This is perfectly natural. As children grow in their ability to articulate what they want to do and construct memories in words, their understanding of the connections between their plans and recall narratives becomes increasingly apparent.

Adults Anticipate Changes in the Way Children Recall Over Time

Over time, bolstered by daily experience, children's ability to recall increases. While preschoolers may still need to see or hold on to something they used at work time to spur their memories, they also . . .

• Become increasingly able to add detail to their recall stories—what they used, how they worked or played, with whom they played.

• Tell longer stories: "First we played wedding, and then . . ."

• Add to the recall narratives of their friends.

• Become aware of similarities between what they did at work time and what others did: "I did that too!"

• Include more detail in drawings of what they did.

• Anticipate how the activities of one work time might lead to further play at work time the next day.

It is noteworthy, too, that once children become accustomed to talking about what they have done at work time, they depend on the recall process to give a sense of closure to their work-time experiences.

In the final chapter of this discussion on the elements of the High/Scope daily routine, we examine the purpose and meaning of other special parts of the routine—group times, outside time, and transition times. We also offer suggestions to help adults make the most of these important active learning experiences.

At recall time, Zach drew a picture of one of the things he did at work time. "It's a necklace," he said when he completed his drawing. "That's me wearin' it!"

How Adults Support Children's Recall: A Summary

Adults examine their beliefs about how children learn at recall time.

Adults recall with children in a calm, cozy setting.

___ Recall in intimate groups and places.
___ Recall with those who shared the experience children are recalling.

Adults provide materials and experiences to maintain children's interest at recall time.

___ Tours
___ Group games
___ Props and partnerships
___ Representations

Adults converse with children about their work-time experiences.

___ Adults take an unhurried approach to recall.
___ Adults invite children to talk about what they have done:
    ___ Pick up on children's opening comments.
    ___ Comment on a child's play.
    ___ Ask an open-ended question.
___ Adults watch children and listen attentively.
___ Adults contribute observations and comments to keep recall narratives going.
___ Adults use questions thoughtfully and sparingly.
___ Adults support children's co-narratives and conflicting viewpoints.

___ Adults acknowledge (rather than praise) children's work-time experiences.
___ Adults note connections between children's recall narratives and plans.

Adults anticipate changes in the way children recall over time.

Adults meet with children in a cozy setting every day so children can recall—through words, actions, and drawing—interesting things they have done at work time.

References

Bergen, Doris. 1988. "Stages of Play Development," and "Methods of Studying Play." In *Play as a Medium for Learning and Development,* Doris Bergen, ed., 27–44, 49–66. Portsmouth, NH: Heinemann.

Berry, Carla F., and Kathy Sylva. 1987. *The Plan-Do-Review Cycle in High/Scope: Its Effect on Children and Staff.* Unpublished manuscript. (Available from High/Scope Educational Research Foundation, Ypsilanti, MI.)

Bolles, Edmund Blair. 1988. *Remembering and Forgetting: An Inquiry Into the Nature of Memory.* New York: Walker and Company.

Bullock, Merry, and Paul Lütkenhaus. 1988. "The Development of Volitional Behavior in the Toddler Years." *Child Development* 59, no. 3 (June): 664–74.

Case, Robbie. 1985. *Intellectual Development: Birth to Adulthood.* Orlando, FL: Academic Press.

Chance, Paul. 1979. *Learning Through Play.* New York: Gardner Press.

Dewey, John. 1938. *Experience and Education.* Reprint. New York: Macmillan, 1963.

Dewey, John. 1933. *How We Think: A Restatement of the Relation of Reflective Thinking to the Educative Process.* Boston: Heath.

Dewey, John. 1968. "My Pedagogic Creed." In *The World of the Child,* Toby Talbot, ed., 387–97. Garden City, NY: Anchor Books.

Eisner, Elliot W. 1990. "The Role of Art and Play in Children's Cognitive Development." In *Children's Play and Learning: Perspectives and Policy Implications,* Edgar Klugman and Sara Smilansky, eds., 43–58. New York: Teachers College Press.

Elkind, David. 1987. "Early Childhood on Its Own Terms." In *Early Schooling: The National Debate,* Sharon L. Kagan and Edward Zigler, eds., 98–115. New Haven: Yale University Press.

Ellis, Michael J. 1988. "Play and the Origin of Species." In *Play as a Medium for Learning and Development,* Doris Bergen, ed., 23–25. Portsmouth, NH: Heinemann.

Erikson, Erik. 1950. *Childhood and Society.* New York: Norton.

Fabricius, William Van. 1984. *The Development of Planning in Young Children.* Doctoral dissertation, University of Michigan. Available from UMI Dissertation Publishing (*www.proquest.com*).

Fromberg, Doris P. 1987. "Play." In *The Early Childhood Curriculum: A Review of the Current Research,* Carol Seefeldt, ed., 35–74. New York: Teachers College Press.

Jordan, Daniel C. 1976. "The Process Approach." In *Curriculum for the Preschool-Primary Child: A Review of the Research,* Carol Seefeldt, ed., 273–303. Columbus, OH: Merrill.

Likona, Thomas. 1973. "The Psychology of Choice in Learning." In *Open Education: Increasing Alternatives for Teachers and Children,* Thomas Likona, Ruth Nikse, David Young, and Jessie Adams, eds. Courtland: Open Education Foundation, State University of New York.

Miller, Peggy J., and Linda Sperry. 1988. "Early Talk of the Past: The Origins of Conversational Stories of Personal Experience." *Journal of Child Language* 15, no. 2 (June): 293–315.

Moore, Elizabeth, and Teresa Smith. 1987. *One Year On: High/Scope Report 2.* London: Volculf.

Norman, Donald A. 1982. *Learning and Memory.* San Francisco: W. H. Freeman.

Parten, Mildred B. 1932. "Social Participation Among Preschool Children." *Journal of Abnormal and Social Psychology* 27, no. 3: 243–69.

Pellegrini, Anthony D. 1986. "Communicating in and About Play: The Effect of Play Centers on Preschoolers' Explicit Language." In *The Young Child at Play: Reviews of Research,* Vol. 4, Greta Fein and Mary Rivkin, eds., 79–91. Washington, DC: NAEYC.

Phyfe-Perkins, Elizabeth, and Joanne Shoemaker. 1986. "Indoor Play Environments: Research and Design Implications." In *The Young Child at Play: Reviews of Research,* Vol. 4, Greta Fein and Mary Rivkin, eds., 177–93. Washington, DC: NAEYC.

Piaget, Jean. 1951. *Play, Dreams, and Imitation in Childhood.* Reprint. New York: Norton, 1962.

Piaget, Jean, and Barbel Inhelder. 1966. *The Psychology of the Child.* Reprint. New York: Basic Books, 1969.

Rogers, Ann. 1990. "Superheroes and War Play in Preschool: Let Them In or Lock Them Out?" In *Fourth Annual High/Scope Conference Proceedings,* Kerry Teegen, Polly Neill, and Mary Vardigan, eds., 61–63. Ypsilanti, MI: High/Scope Press.

Rubin, Kenneth H., Greta G. Fein, and Brian Vandenburg. 1983. "Play." In *Socialization, Personality, and Social Development, Handbook of Child Psychology,* Vol. 4, E. Mavis Hetherington, ed., Paul H. Mussen, series ed., 698–744. New York: Wiley.

Schank, Roger C. 1990. *Tell Me a Story: A New Look at Real and Artificial Memory.* New York: Scribners.

Smilansky, Sara. 1971. "Can Adults Facilitate Play in Children? Theoretical and Practical Considerations." In *Play: The Child Strives Toward Self-Realization,* 39–50. Washington, DC: NAEYC.

Smilansky, Sara, and Leah Shefatya. 1990. *Facilitating Play: A Medium for Promoting Cognitive, Socio-Emotional and Academic Development in Young Children.* Gaithersburg, MD: Psychosocial & Educational Publications.

Sponseller, Doris. 1982. "Play in Early Education." In *Handbook of Research in Early Childhood Education,* Bernard Spodek, ed., 215–41. New York: Macmillan.

Sylva, Kathy, Carolyn Roy, and Marjorie Painter. 1980. *Childwatching at Playgroup & Nursery School.* Ypsilanti, MI: High/Scope Press.

Tompkins, Mark. 1991. "In Praise of Praising Less." *High/Scope Extensions* (September): 1–3.

Wood, David, Linnet McMahon, and Yvonne Cranstoun. 1980. *Working With Under Fives.* Ypsilanti, MI: High/Scope Press.

Related Reading

Bronfenbrenner, Urie. 1979. *The Ecology of Human Development: Experiments by Nature and Design.* Cambridge, MA: Harvard University Press.

Bruner, Jerome. 1980. *Under Five in Britain.* Ypsilanti, MI: High/Scope Press.

Casey, M. Beth. 1990. "A Planning and Problem-Solving Preschool Model: The Methodology of Being a Good Learner." *Early Childhood Research Quarterly* 5, no. 1: 53–67.

Cassidy, Deborah J. 1989. "Questioning the Young Child: Process and Function." *Childhood Education 65,* no. 3 (Spring): 146–49.

Clark, Christopher M., and Penelope L. Peterson. 1986. "Teachers' Thought in Process." In *Handbook of Research on Teaching,* M. Whitrock, ed., 255–96. New York: Macmillan.

DeLoache, Judy S., and Ann L. Brown. 1987. "The Early Emergence of Planning Skills in Children." In *Making Sense: The Child's Construction of the World,* Jerome Bruner and Helen Haste, eds., 108–30. New York: Methuen.

Egan, Kieran. 1989. "Memory, Imagination, and Learning: Connected by the Story." *Phi Delta Kappan 70,* no. 6 (February): 455–59.

Egan, Kieran, and Dan Nadaner, eds. 1988. *Imagination and Education.* New York: Teachers College Press.

Epstein, Ann S. 2007. "Plan-Do-Review." In *Essentials of Active Learning in Preschool: Getting to Know the High/Scope Curriculum,* 60–67. Ypsilanti, MI: High/Scope Press.

Evans, Betsy. 1992. "Helping Children Resolve Conflicts and Disputes." *High/Scope Extensions* (May/June): 1–3.

Evans, Betsy. 2002. *You Can't Come to My Birthday Party! Conflict Resolution With Young Children.* Ypsilanti, MI: High/Scope Press.

Graves, Michelle. 1991. "Child Planning: Why It's Important, How to Get Started." In *Supporting Young Learners,* Nancy A. Brickman and Lynn S. Taylor, eds., 115–19. Ypsilanti, MI: High/Scope Press.

Graves, Michelle. 1989. *Teacher's Idea Book: Daily Planning Around the Key Experiences.* Ypsilanti, MI: High/Scope Press.

Graves, Michelle. 1996. *Teacher's Idea Book 2: Planning Around Children's Interests.* Ypsilanti, MI: High/Scope Press.

Graves, Michelle. 1996. "Work Time: Teacher Habits That Are Hard to Break." In *Supporting Young Learners 2,* Nancy A. Brickman, ed., 61–68. Ypsilanti, MI: High/Scope Press.

Haynes, Vernon F., and Patricia Miller. 1987. "The Relation-ship Between Cognitive Style, Memory, and Attention in Preschoolers." *Child Study Journal 17,* no. 1: 21–33.

High/Scope Educational Research Foundation. 2003. *Preschool Program Quality Assessment (PQA),* 2nd ed. Ypsilanti, MI: High/Scope Press.

Hohmann, Mary. 1996. "Let Them Speak! Conversing With Children." In *Supporting Young Learners 2: Ideas for Child Care Providers and Teachers,* Nancy A. Brickman, ed., 7–14. Ypsilanti, MI: High/Scope Press.

Hohmann, Mary. 1991. "The Many Faces of Child Planning." In *Supporting Young Learners,* Nancy A. Brickman and Lynn S. Taylor, eds., 120–28. Ypsilanti, MI: High/Scope Press.

Jones, Elizabeth. 1986. "Perspectives on Teacher Education: Some Relations Between Theory and Practice." In *Current Trends in Education,* Vol. 6, Lilian Katz, ed., 123–41. Norwood, NJ: Ablex.

Kessel, Frank, and Artin Goncu. 1984. "Children's Play: A Contextual-Functional Perspective." In *Analyzing Children's Play Dialogues,* Frank Kessel and Artin Goncu, eds., 5–22. San Francisco: Jossey-Bass.

Kohn, Alfie. 1993. *Punished by Rewards: The Trouble With Gold Stars, Incentive Plans, A's, Praise, and Other Bribes.* Boston: Houghton Mifflin Company.

Lay-Dopyera, Margaret, and John Dopyera. 1987. "Strategies for Teaching." In *The Early Childhood Curriculum: A Review of the Current Research,* Carol Seefeldt, ed., 13–33. New York: Teachers College Press.

Lubeck, Sally. 1984. "Kinship and Classrooms. An Ethnographic Perspective on Education as Cultural Transmission." *Sociology of Education 57,* no. 4 (October): 219–32.

Marshall, Beth. 2005. "TRUST in Children's Play." "Overcoming Roadblocks to Playing With Children." In *Supporting Young Learners 4: Ideas for Child Care Providers and Teachers,* Nancy A. Brickman, Holly Barton, and Jennifer Burd, eds., 287–98. Ypsilanti, MI: High/Scope Press.

Oken-Wright, Pamela. 1988. "Show and Tell Grows Up." *Young Children 43,* no. 2 (January): 52–58.

Post, Jacalyn and Mary Hohmann. 2000. "Establishing Schedules and Routines for Infants and Toddlers." Chap. 4 in *Tender Care and Early Learning: Supporting Infants and Toddlers in Child Care Settings,* 190–293. Ypsilanti, MI: High/Scope Press.

Reifel, Stuart. 1988. "Children's Thinking About Their Early Education Experiences." *Theory Into Practice 27,* no. 1 (Winter): 62–66.

Spidell, Ruth A. 1985. *Preschool Teachers' Interventions in Children's Play.* Doctoral dissertation, University of Illinois at Urbana-Champaign. Available from UMI Dissertation Publishing (*www.proquest.com*).

Spodek, Bernard, and Olivia N. Saracho. 1988. "The Challenge of Educational Play." In *Play as a Medium for Learning and Development,* Doris Bergen, ed., 9–22. Portsmouth, NH: Heinemann.

Tompkins, Mark. 1991. "A Look at Looking Back: Helping Children Recall." In *Supporting Young Learners,* Nancy A. Brickman and Lynn S. Taylor, eds., 129–36. Ypsilanti, MI: High/Scope Press.

Vogel, Nancy. 2001. *Teacher's Idea Book 5: Making the Most of Plan-Do-Review.* Ypsilanti, MI: High/Scope Press.

Weiss, Rita S. 1981. "INREAL Intervention for Language Handicapped and Bilingual Children." *Journal of the Division of Early Childhood 4,* no. 1: 40–51.

Yang, Ok Seung. 1985. *The Effect of Verbal Plan and Review Training on Preschoolers' Reflectivity.* Doctoral dissertation, University of Southern California. Available from UMI Dissertation Publishing (*www.proquest.com*).

Related Media

The following materials are available from the High/Scope Press, 600 N. River St., Ypsilanti, MI 48198-2898; to order, visit *www.highscope.org,* or call 1-800-40-PRESS.

The Daily Routine. 2007. Color videotape or DVD. 40 min.

The High/Scope Curriculum: The Plan-Do-Review Process. 1989. Color videotape, 20 min.

How Adults Support Children at Planning Time. 1997. Color videotape, 19 min.

How Adults Support Children at Recall Time. 1997. Color videotape, 19 min.

How Adults Support Children at Work Time. 1997. Color videotape, 25 min.

Supporting Children in Resolving Conflicts. 1998. Color videotape, 24 min.

At small-group, large-group, transition, and outside times, children work with people and materials, make choices and decisions, and talk about what they are doing. In short, they are **active participatory learners.**

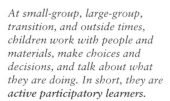

Although the **plan-do-review** process is the centerpiece of the High/Scope daily routine, regular times are also allotted for other important experiences. These regularly scheduled events are **small-group time, large-group times, outside time,** and **transition times.** Other recurring events are **greeting time** and **message board;** most programs also include **snack or meal times.** Each of these times has distinctive features that create special opportunities for active learning. At **small-** and **large-group times,** children participate in adult-initiated experiences in which they interact with others and encounter new activities, concepts, and materials. Play experiences at **outside time** differ from those available in the indoor setting. During this time, children can experience outdoor sights and sounds, use outdoor play materials and equipment, and play vigorously and noisily (or quietly, if they prefer). During **transition times,** children move from one activity to the next. Transitions are not incidental events; rather they provide children with opportunities for choice-making, movement activities, and a variety of learning experiences.

Though each of these times has distinctive features, they share a common goal: **to encourage children's active involvement with materials, people, ideas, and events.** Active learning is the guiding philosophy, just as it is during the plan-work-recall sequence. Throughout these activities, children make choices and decisions, learn through direct experience, and talk about what they are doing. This chapter presents the unique features of each of these parts of the daily routine and the ways adults implement an active learning philosophy throughout these times.

Special Features of Group Times

Small- and large-group times are adult-initiated— they are planned and set in motion by the adult. At *small-group time,* the adult meets with the same group of children each day. The adult provides common sets of materials children can use for exploring, creating, experimenting, or building. The same small group typically eats together at snack or meal time. At *large-group times,* adults meet briefly with the entire group of children to discuss upcoming events using the message board, sing songs, do fingerplays, tell stories, move to music, or participate in action games or other group activities. Because these group times are initiated by adults, they present an opportunity to introduce various concepts, activities, and materials to children. At large-group time, for example, the adult might interact with children to create a new variation of a familiar song or game. At small-group time, the adult might introduce new materials or new combinations of materials to children—a computer program, counting bears and small blocks, or toy farm animals. Sometimes, the materials the adult sets out at small-group time have already been available in the classroom; the small-group time, however, allows children who have not yet used the materials to explore them in a comfortable setting.

8
Group Times, Outside Times, Transition Times

. . . The small group can afford the opportunity for a qualitatively different and valuable experience in which the participants may unite in pursuing a common goal . . . and willingly articulate, however hesitatingly, their own discoveries.

—Caroline Garland and Stephanie White, 1980

Group times also offer special social opportunities. During the child-initiated parts of the routine, children can choose how solitary or sociable they wish to be—working by themselves, with a friend or adult, or with a group. Since some children will choose not to play with others during these times, the group times offer additional opportunities for them to participate in a social experience. At small-group time, for example, where everyone is working with the same materials, children often share and discuss what they are doing, learn from one another, and help one another. At large-group time, where everyone is engaged in a common action-game or song (all of which are safe, low-risk social experiences), children have opportunities to contribute and demonstrate their ideas to the group as well as imitate and learn from their peers.

Briefly, then, group times in High/Scope settings are not times for rigid routines, complicated games, or teacher-led lessons. Instead, the hallmarks of group activities are the *ingredients of active learning* (materials, manipulation, choice, child language and thought, adult scaffolding), *flexibility,* and *openness* to children's signals, interests, initiatives, and ideas.

Understanding Small-Group Time

Small-group time in a High/Scope program provides children with opportunities to use materials, experiment with these materials, talk about their discoveries, and solve problems they encounter. To illustrate the dynamics of small-group time, we have re-created two actual small-group times from High/Scope programs.

The "Pineapple Connection"

Carol and Elaine have taken their children to a farmers' market where the children are particularly intrigued by a basket of pineapples. The adults buy four of the pineapples, and the next day these pineapples become the focus of Carol's and Elaine's small-group times. Here is a sample of what happened in Carol's group:

Carol cuts one pineapple into slices and gives a slice to each child. Joanie licks her slice. Antoine watches her intently and then takes a tentative lick of his own slice. Jeff matter-of-factly takes a bite. "I like it. It's . . . sweet."

"I'm gonna cut the stickers off mine," announces Teresa.

"Me, too," says Felix.

Both children go to the house area for some table knives. This idea catches on and soon many children are cutting their pineapple pieces, "making juice," and examining the "pineapple string."

"Watch out. It sticks. It's tangled into my teeth!" warns Jeff.

Carol leaves the second uncut pineapple in the middle of the table.

"I don't want to touch that. It's got stickers," says Teresa.

"Let me feel it. Let me feel it," says Sammy. *"Ouch!"* He draws his hand back.

"It's prickery to me, too," says Pepe.

"Look at me! I'm holding it by the leaves! It's not prickery to me!" says Jennifer.

"See, I can make it roll," says Kadith. *She rolls it across the table to Pepe.*

"It goes kind of crooked," Pepe notices.

❧

All the Colors of the Rainbow

Becki has prepared materials for the children in her small group to color eggs. The table is

At small-group time, this child very carefully squeezes several drops of the water she has colored onto her "mixing" spoon.

covered with newspaper, and a plastic cup holding a small amount of vinegar awaits each child.

"What is this?" someone asks.

"Well, see if you can tell by using your nose," Becki replies.

"It's gross!"

"If you drink it you'll get sick!"

"Mine spilled!"

"Just what happened with mine."

"It stinks, yewee! It stinks!"

"It does stink," says Becki. *"It's vinegar."*

"Vinegar, yuck!"

"I'm giving you each a color tablet, then water, then eggs," Becki says, giving each child a

"If you squeeze hard like this, it gets full!" the child on the right tells his small-group-time buddy, who is watching his colored water spread out on the white paper towel that lines the bottom of his basket.

tablet. The children drop their tablets in their vinegar.

"Colors!"

"It turned a color!"

"Mine is turning green, Becki!"

"It is turning green," Becki acknowledges.

"Mine is coming into orange!"

"Mine is turning to yellow."

"Mine is turning to red."

"Mine turned to orange."

"Watch that. That turned to yellow!"

"Does the green really go to the bottom?"

"It's spreading."

"It is spreading," Becki says to Catherine, who has been looking at the bottom of her cup.

"It's really, really green! Even on the bottom."

The children talk excitedly about the colors they see emerging and pour water from a small pitcher into their colored vinegar. Becki gives each child three hard-boiled eggs in a small berry basket. "When you put them in gently," she says, "they won't crack."

"Drop it in gently!"

"Mine's on top."

"Look, I did it gently."

There's a lull in the conversation as children concentrate on putting their eggs into the dye. Some use their hands, others use spoons.

"I think I need a little bit more water," Amy says.

"You get it on your fingers," says Boomer.

"I'm keepin' mine in for a long time!" says Namen.

"What will happen to it in a long time?" Becki asks.

"It'll catch more color," Namen answers.

"Oh, the egg catches the color," Becki says.

"Yeah, if you put it in just a little bit, just a little bit gets on there," he answers.

"Would you like to trade colors?" Catherine asks Caleb.

"Mine turned something . . . red!" Kyle says.

"Mine spilled again," says Namen. (Becki passes him some towels.)

"Becki, I need another color," says Namen.

"Catherine and Caleb traded colors," Becki says. "Maybe someone will trade with you."

"Can I use your color?" Namen asks Amy.

"Want to trade colors?" she replies.

"Here, guys, blue!" Max says.

"I'm gonna make mine two different colors, red and yellow!" Namen says.

"I want red now," Catherine says to Kyle. "Can I have your spoon, too?"

"Look at mine, look at mine!" says Namen.

"Look at yours, Namen!" Becki says.

"I need orange," Boomer says.

"Kyle has orange," says Max.

"Becki, don't take it out. It needs more green," Caleb advises.

"Okay," Becki agrees.

Two children pour their dyes together. "It looks like dog doo but it isn't. I made mine all different colors."

"I need more eggs," says Catherine.

"We only cooked enough eggs for each person to have three," Becki says.

"Mine cracked," Boomer says.

"Sometimes that happens," Becki says.

"But that's okay," Max says.

"It sure is," Becki agrees.

"I'm done," Catherine says. She goes to the window ledge and gets another basket she has decorated (at an earlier small-group time) with real grass (planted several weeks before). She puts her three colored eggs in on top of the grass.

"Look what Catherine did," Becki says, holding up Catherine's basket. "Here's her basket with her grass and her three eggs."

The children talk together as they add their eggs to their baskets. "We can take them home today, can't we Becki?"

"You sure can," she agrees.

The children admire their baskets, help clean up the table, and gather with Becki again for planning time.

What Is Small-Group Time?

As illustrated in the foregoing examples, at small-group time the same group of children meet each day with the same adult. In this intimate setting children are given their own materials, make choices about how to use them, and talk with one another and the adult about what they are doing.

▶ An unchanging group of children with the same adult

During small-group time, the children are divided among the adults on the teaching team. If there are 20 children and 2 adults, each small group includes 10 children and 1 adult. If there are 12 children and 3 adults, small groups consist of 4 children and 1 adult, and so forth. Whatever the group size, the same children meet with the same adult each day for several months at a time.

▶ Active learning in a supportive setting

At small-group time, adults introduce the activity but then allow children to work with the materials in their own way and at their own rate. Children make choices and decisions about what to do with the materials, talk with one another and the adult about what they are doing, and receive appropriate adult support and encouragement. Small-group time provides children with a daily opportunity to try out their own ideas as well as others' in a safe setting with an attentive adult close by. Children often carry small-group ideas into their work-time play.

▶ An adult-initiated learning experience based on children's interests and development

While adults plan and introduce small-group-time learning experiences, such as building with blocks, working in the garden, and making collages from materials collected on a walk, their inspiration for each small-group experience comes from their understanding of what children like to do and what children are learning as they pursue their interests. Here are some examples of how small-group time originates:

• Several children were very enthusiastic about tossing blocks into the block box at cleanup time, so Beth planned a small-group time around beanbags and baskets. Some children stood very close to their "targets" while others challenged themselves by tossing their beanbags into the box from farther and farther away.

• Knowing how excited children were about Halloween and realizing that many would stay up late that night, Becki and Beth planned a small-group time for the day after Halloween that involved using Play-Doh and "slime." They had decided that this tactile experience would satisfy the children's interest in Halloween-related play without taxing their patience. Indeed, after their trick-or-treating adventures, the children were happy to return to a familiar material they could easily shape and control.

• Since the children in her small group often requested the story *Caps for Sale* and were also involved in role play at both work time and outside time, Becki planned a small-group time around re-enacting the story using different colored caps for props. The children took turns being "the peddler," but their favorite role was "being monkeys." They decided the hollow blocks could be their tree "because we need to climb up and throw the caps down."

In these small-group times, the children were involved in activities that are described as KDIs in Part 3 of this volume. The beanbag tossers *experienced and described positions, directions, and distances* (a **space** KDI), the Play-Doh and "slime" players *changed the shape and arrangement of objects* (a **space** KDI), and the *Caps for Sale* players *pretended and role-played* (a **dramatic art** KDI).

Why Is Small-Group Time Important?

Small-group time builds on children's strengths, introduces children to materials and experiences they might otherwise miss, and provides adults with an intimate setting in which to observe and learn about individual children on a daily basis.

▶ An opportunity to build on children's strengths

By planning small-group activities around children's emerging abilities, adults can help children consolidate what they are learning and develop related skills. "Alex, Audie, and Sarah are really involved in cutting, so I'm going to plan a small-group time using scissors and construction paper. It's not too thick and it's not too flimsy, so everyone in my group can be successful." Small-group times planned with children's interests in mind encourage children to do things they can do and like to do. As they gain confidence in their abilities, children are willing to take on new challenges: "I don't want this paper," says Julia. "I'm gonna get some magazines to cut."

▶ An opportunity to provide new materials and experiences

"Kacey, Frances, and JoJo like to play in the water. I'm going to plan a small-group time with water and introduce turkey basters and short lengths of hose." At small-group times adults can present children with new materials—a computer program, saws and wood, a set of interlocking blocks—as well as "old" materials children may be overlooking—toy farm animals and blocks, beads and strings, sticky-backed foam scraps and paper-towel tubes. Thus, for children who choose to play with blocks at work time, small group may be a time to try out scissors, musical instruments, sand and water. For children who choose to draw and paint at work time, small-group may be a time to build with blocks, act out stories, and wash bicycles. In this manner, children discover new ideas to incorporate into their play at work time, at outside time, and at home.

▶ An opportunity for regular peer contacts and interactions

Small-group time draws a little band of children together to explore the same materials. Because of their close proximity, children have lots of opportunities to interact and communicate with one another. Children who play by themselves at work time will play next to other children at small-group time. In fact, children may team up to help each other out: "Megan, will you take the wrappers off my Band-Aid?" Alex

Small-group time introduces children to active learning experiences, such as mixing salt, flour, and cooking oil to make dough and then coloring it with food coloring.

asks. "Namen, can I use your orange egg dye?" Kyle asks.

Small-group time also provides children with the opportunity for *immediate feedback from peers* on their work: "Hey, look what Louie did!" "See, mine stays up all by itself!" In this way, children comment on one another's discoveries and learn from their peers. Such interactions are important, report developmental psychologists Rheta DeVries and Lawrence Kohlberg (1987): "When the child has the experience of others who react to what he says, he begins to feel that the truth is important" (pp. 30–31). The consistency of the small-group-time community provides a *social anchor* for children and an important contrast to the openness of work time when children play alone or in spontaneous groups throughout the interest areas.

▶ An opportunity for adults to observe and interact daily with the same children

Adults can observe children's development over time, appreciate individual differences, and begin to predict how children in their groups will respond to small-group experiences they plan. As Linda plans a small-group time using glue, for example, she imagines how each child in her group might respond: "I think Corey and Joanie will just want to squeeze their glue bottles and watch the glue dribble out on the paper. Lynnette and Tracy will probably glue scraps and shapes to their paper, and Wendy and Erica may have a plan in mind of a particular thing they want to represent. Wendy's been drawing horses lately, so she might try to make a horse out of shapes and scraps. I'll have some yarn available, too. She might use it for a tail or mane."

▶ An opportunity for adults to practice support strategies in a stable setting

Watching and listening to children at small-group time gives adults an excellent opportunity to practice support strategies. In the following example, Mrs. L., aware that her habit of asking too many questions sometimes inhibits children's conversations, practices repeating and commenting on children's observations as an alternative to questioning:

Rita: *See my Play-Doh. It's flat.*

Mrs. L.: *Your Play-Doh is flat.*

Rita: *I know. My hands are stronger . . . stronger than Play-Doh.*

Mrs. L.: *Oh, your hands are stronger than Play-Doh.*

Rita: *Yeah. That's why it squeezes out. See, I'll show you.*

Mrs. L.: *I see.*

Rita: *And if you stand up it's even stronger!*

Another adult, Mr. P., takes the opportunity to practice referring one child to another rather than doing things for them:

At this small-group time, children gather around a bowl of tadpoles one of the children brought from home. The other children ask him how he and his sister caught the tadpoles.

Alice: (Says to Mr. P.) *How do you get this . . . all . . . all spread on the table?*

Mr. P.: *It looks like Rahima has figured out a way.*

Alice: (Watches Rahima) *How you do that?*

Rahima: *Like this.* (She demonstrates.)

Where Small Groups Meet

When planning a place for each small group to meet, designate a consistent gathering place, but do not confine yourself to experiences that can only be done in that place. Be willing to move to wherever the relevant materials are located.

▶ **Gather together in a consistent place.**

Pick out places in your setting where each small group can gather and work comfortably—on the floor in the block area, at the table in the art area, or outside under a tree. A designated gathering place for each small group gives children a sense of belonging and control. If Anna knows that her small group gathers at the house-area table, she can go there every day on her own at small-group time and know that she will meet with Beth, her teacher, and the same seven children.

▶ **Go to the relevant materials.**

While a consistent gathering place is important, it is equally important not to be limited by your location. Often, you will spend small-group time in the place where you gather, but other times, after gathering, you will go together as a small group to the sandbox, the garden, the workbench, the butcher paper on the floor, or the totem pole outside.

At the beginning of the year, teachers Beth and Becki chose the art-area table and the house-area table as their small-group time gathering places. As they talked with children at planning time, they realized that many of the children were not aware of what was in each interest area, and their lack of knowledge limited their work-time plans. Therefore, the adults planned small-group times that would explore the interest areas. For example, after Becki's group gathered at the house-area table, they went together to the block area "to find all the things there are to play with." There, Becki's children discovered the steering wheel and the large blocks. Meanwhile, Beth's group gathered at the art-area table: "Let's 'sneak' to the house area (her children liked to 'sneak') and see what we can find to play with." They found poker chips, bottle caps, and chestnuts inside canisters, a stack of diapers, and dishes for setting the table. Later, the children incorporated some of these "new" materials into their work-time play.

What Children Do at Small-Group Time

The discussion of small groups began with examples of small-group times in which children cut up pineapples and colored eggs. Here is another account of the egg-coloring small-group time from the perspective of one child, Catherine:

Catherine is one of the first children to arrive at her teacher Becki's small group. Catherine converses with Amy across the table. Then she listens as the other children talk about the smell of the vinegar, and she watches Namen mop up his spill. Catherine is very interested in watching what happens when the children add

Small-Group Time—What, Why, Where: A Summary

What It Is
- An adult-initiated learning experience based on children's interests and development.
- The same group of children with the same adult.
- Active learning in a supportive setting.

Why It Is Important
- Builds on children's strengths.
- Introduces children to materials and experiences they might otherwise miss.
- Provides children with regular peer contacts and interactions.
- Lets adults observe and interact daily with the same group of children.
- Enables adults to practice support strategies in a stable setting.

Where to Meet
- Gather together in a consistent place.
- Go to the relevant materials.

their pellets to their vinegar. When she adds her own pellet she says, "Mine is turning green, Becki!" "It is turning green," Becki acknowledges. After watching the color spread through the vinegar, Catherine asks, "Does the green really go even to the bottom?" She lifts her cup over her head to look at it from the bottom. "It's spreading," she says. "It is spreading," Becki acknowledges. "It's really, really green, even on the bottom," Catherine says.

Next, Catherine pours water into her cup of green-colored vinegar, watches Becki balance an egg on a spoon, and then puts her first egg into the dye using her fingers. Her hands get a little wet and green. She shakes the water drops off,

What Children Do at Small-Group Time: A Summary

• Children explore, play, work with materials, and talk about what they are doing.
• Children solve problems they encounter.

their eggs, the other children follow Catherine's lead. While Catherine watches, Amy fills her basket with three colored eggs, and they talk about their work-time plan to play together with Sarah.

then leaves the table to get a towel from the bathroom. When she returns, she takes her egg out with a spoon, looks at it, returns it to the dye solution, takes it out again after a short while, puts it on the table in front of her, and wipes her fingers on the newspaper covering the table. Turning to her peer Boomer, she asks, "Would you like to trade?" Boomer doesn't respond, so she turns to Caleb, and asks, "Would you like to trade?" "Sure!" Caleb takes her green solution and she takes his yellow solution. Catherine tries to explain to Caleb that the spoon goes with the dye, but he wants his original spoon, so she keeps her "green-dye" spoon. Suddenly, Caleb under-

stands the purpose of the exchange request, gives Catherine the yellow-dye spoon, and takes the spoon for the green dye.

Catherine stirs the yellow dye, adds her second egg, turns it over occasionally with her spoon, watches Caleb spoon a red-dye solution over his green egg, and then takes out her yellow egg, placing it on the table next to her green egg. "I want red now," she says to Kyle. "Can I have your spoon, too?" They make the trade. She dyes her last egg. "I need more eggs!" she says. "We only cooked enough eggs for each person to have three," Becki tells her.

Catherine informs Boomer that one of his eggs is cracked, then says, "I'm done." She goes to the window ledge, gets her grass basket, and carefully puts in her three dyed eggs, parting the grass for each egg. She then takes the basket to Becki. "Look what Catherine did," Becki says to the other children, who are still working. "Here's her basket with her grass and her three eggs." As they finish dyeing

► **Children explore, play, work with materials, and talk about what they are doing.**

Catherine's varied experiences and interactions during this one small-group session illustrate the diverse learning opportunities these times offer. To support children appropriately at small-group time, it is important for adults to realize that children use small-group time to explore, play, work with materials, and converse. Thus small-group time offers a range of active learning experiences. Children use materials in a variety of ways guided by their imagination, creativity, and personal intentions. They explore with all their senses ("This pineapple tastes yucky!"), discover relations through direct experience ("Look, it's yellow! Mine turned yellow!"), transform and combine materials ("I'm gonna put some beans in my dough"), and acquire skills with tools and equipment ("This beater makes the bubbles really big. Bigger than ever!"). They make choices about what to do with materials ("I'm pushing down on my pineapple; the juice comes out") and materials to add ("This glue doesn't stick—I'm getting some tape"). They talk about what they are doing with other group members ("Hey, everybody, there's a worm in my dirt!"), and they think and reason out loud ("It won't bounce 'cause . . .'cause it sticks to the floor!"). Each small-group time presents many active learning challenges as children work with materials,

This small group meets with one child's mother on the floor where there will be plenty of room to try carding and spinning raw wool.

select additional materials, talk about their work, solve problems, and comment on the work of others.

▶ **Children solve problems they encounter.**

As they work with materials, solving a problem presented by an adult ("Let's see what we can do with these tubs full of snow"), children also form their own goals and discover problems they need to solve to accomplish them: "I'm making my snow into a house . . . But the roof? . . . It gots to go over this hole . . . I know. Sticks!" Caleb and Namen decide to make their eggs two different colors. Caleb does this by dyeing his egg yellow and dripping red dye over it. Namen goes about it a different way. He dips one end of his egg in green dye and the other end in orange dye. For young children, solving small-group problems

means looking to see what other people are doing and experimenting with their own ideas.

When small-group time involves a new material (chestnuts picked up on a walk, or cardboard packing boxes, or a set of large Tinkertoys), children also solve the problem of where these materials should be stored so they will know where to find them at work time: "I know . . . let's put these [chestnuts] in a can over there [points to the house area] . . . then we can make soup!"

How Adults Support Children at Small-Group Time

Above all, small-group time is supposed to be an enjoyable event in which an adult brings a small group of children together to use a common set of materials according to their own interests and understanding. Adults support children at small-group time by . . .

- Examining their beliefs about how children learn
- Forming well-balanced small groups
- Planning small-group experiences ahead of time
- Preparing for small groups before the children arrive
- Setting small groups in motion—the beginning
- Supporting each child's ideas and use of materials—the middle
- Bringing small-group time to a close—the end

Adults Examine Their Beliefs About How Children Learn at Small-Group Time

Adults in High/Scope settings view small-group time as another important opportunity for children to construct knowledge through meaningful interactions with people and materials. While small-group time is focused in one place around a specific set of materials and an open-ended problem set by the adult, adults also realize that each child will respond to the materials and the challenge in his or her own way. *It is the adult's job to support each child accordingly.*

In some non–High/Scope programs, adults use small-group time to drill children in concepts such as the names of letters, numbers, colors, shapes, and the days of the week; in some programs, children fill out dittos or reproduce art projects following the teacher's model: "Color the pumpkin orange. Color the stem green and stay inside the lines." Dittos and adult-directed drill-and-practice activities, however, have no place in High/Scope small-group times, in which children construct knowledge at their own level of development through hands-on explorations. Small-group time is an opportunity for children to work with concepts related to the KDIs: **approaches to learning; language, literacy, and communication; social and emotional development; physical development, health, and well-being; and arts and sciences** (which are broken down into subcategories of **mathematics, science and technology, social studies,** and **the arts**). (See examples on pp. 254–255.) In small groups the emphasis is on *experiencing* rather than drilling, *conversing* rather than listening to adult explanations, *solving problems* rather than following directions, and *obtaining additional materials* as needed rather than waiting for an adult to pro-

One Teacher's Thoughts About a Small-Group Time Using Found Materials

In the following account, High/Scope teacher Ruth Strubank discusses a small-group time she planned around new collage materials from a local recycling center. She thought these materials might encourage children to experience and describe the positions of things (a **space** KDI).

I made a trip to The Scrap Box where I found laminated pieces of white cardboard with four holes in them. I also picked up some cardboard tubes and some two-sided plastic stickers. Back at the center, I stapled each laminated cardboard piece with holes to a sheet of green construction paper using four staples, one in each corner. I also filled a baggie of stickers for each child in my small group.

At small-group time, I gave each child a cardboard/green paper piece and a cardboard tube and asked them what they could do with them. I thought they might try to fit the tubes into the holes, but they ignored the tubes and began by putting their hands through the holes and opening up the sides of the paper. When I gave them the two-sided stickers, some children used them to stick the green and white sheets together, some stuck them through the holes onto the green paper, some stuck them on the back (the green side without holes). Children made statements like these: "Look, I stuck mine together." "Now it won't open, see?" "I put mine in the middle." "Mine are side by each."

Eventually, Joseph pulled the sides of his paper open and put the paper over his head. He looked out of the holes one at a time. Chris watched and then tried the same thing, except that he pulled the narrow sides of his cardboard piece open. When his head did not fit he said, "My head is too big!" Then Joseph showed him how to turn the paper around the long way so it would fit on his head. Chris then looked through the holes in his paper so he had one hole in front of each eye. "I am a robot," he said in a robot-like voice. "Put a sticker on this white part," he continued. "It's the on/off button. Push it to make me walk." I followed his instructions and pushed his "on button." He began to move around the table making stiff, jerky movements. This inspired Kerry, Caroline, and Noah. They, too, became robots, only Kerry said her button meant "hot and cold." Meanwhile, the rest of the children continued filling up their papers with stickers.

At outside time, Chris and Kerry took their creations outside and continued to play robots until it was time to go home.

While I had hoped the children would become involved in describing where they were sticking their stickers, which they did, I was amazed at their ability to turn an experience I had introduced only for its spatial potential into pretend play and make-believe experiences.

A Sample Small-Group-Time Plan: *Making Play-Doh Models*

Originating idea:
Visual art KDI—*making models out of clay.* The children in my small group often make block models of houses and things, but I have never seen them make clay or Play-Doh models.

Materials:
A sizable piece of home-made Play-Doh for each child, a heavy piece of cardboard for each child to work on and save model on. Uncooked spaghetti and noodles in various sizes and shapes sorted onto Styrofoam trays.

Possible KDIs:
Visual art—*making models out of clay.*
Space—*changing the shape and arrangement of objects.*

Beginning:
Give each child a lump of dough and a cardboard base. Say "Here's some Play-Doh and a board to work on. I wonder what you could make that would fit on your board."

As children begin, put trays of noodles in the center of the table where everyone can reach them.

Middle:
Watch to see what children do with their dough. Some may make "cakes." Perhaps the children who usually draw people will make people. Move from child to child to watch and listen.

End:
Have each child share what he or she has done, take it to the window ledge to dry, and help put remaining noodles back in trays.

Follow up:
(1) Add noodle collection to the art area.
(2) At next small-group time, have children check to see if their models are dry.
(3) When they are dry, have children put their models in boxes to take home.

A Sample Small-Group-Time Plan: *"Writing" Thank-You Cards*

Originating idea:
Local traditions—After a trip to a local dairy farm, we need to thank Farmer Gerry.

Materials:
Farm-visit photographs, construction paper, markers, large manila mailing envelope addressed to Farmer Gerry.

Possible KDIs:
Visual art—*drawing and painting; relating photographs to real places and things.*
Language, literacy, and communication—*writing in various ways; reading in various ways; dictating stories.*

Beginning:
Have photos on the table for children to view. Listen briefly to what children say. Then say "Today we need to make Farmer Gerry thank-you cards for all the things he showed us at his farm." Bring out paper and markers. "Whatever you draw and write to Gerry, I'll send to him in this big envelope so he'll know how much we liked our visit."

Middle:
Move from child to child as they draw. Watch and listen. Some children may want to give dictation. Others will want to do their own form of writing.

End:
Have children "read" their cards, put them in the envelope, put the caps back on their markers, and put their markers back in the basket.

Follow up:
(1) Tomorrow walk to the mailbox around the corner at the beginning of outside time.
(2) Put dairy farm photos in album in book area. Write a message on the message board to remind the children that it is there to view.

A Sample Small-Group-Time Plan: Exploring Coconuts

Originating idea:
New materials—The children have been reciting a rhyme about coconuts but are not sure what coconuts are.

Materials:
Nine coconuts, plastic tablecloth, board with a coconut-sized hole in it, hammer, goggles, table knives, one coconut with two holes pounded in it for pouring out "milk," nine cups, plastic bucket.

Possible KDIs:
Language, literacy, and communication—*describing objects, events and relations.* **Classification**—*exploring and describing similarities, differences, and attributes of things.*

Beginning:
Have children help spread plastic tablecloth on floor and sit around the edge. Give each child a coconut and ask "What can you find out about your coconut?"

Middle:
Listen and support children's observations. When a child mentions juice or milk, show them the coconut with the holes and have them pour a little bit into their cups to taste. Have one child (maybe Donna, since she works a lot at the workbench) try opening her coconut by putting on the goggles, putting her coconut in the hole board, and hammering it until it splits open. Pass board, goggles, and hammer around until everyone who wants to open a coconut has the opportunity. Have table knives available for children with open coconuts.

End:
Collect coconut pieces in plastic bucket and ask children, "What could we do with these pieces tomorrow at work time?" Listen to children's ideas. Together gather up the plastic tablecloth so the coconut milk stays in the middle. Have children take cups and knives to the dishpan next to the sink and wash their hands before outside time.

Follow up:
(1) "Write" a message on the message board about coconut pieces to remind children of their work-time ideas. (2) Bring a grater and some big coconut pieces to snack time tomorrow. (3) Recite the coconut rhyme at large-group time. Listen for children's comments about real coconuts.

A Sample Small-Group-Time Plan: *Jumping*

Originating idea:
Children's interests—For several days, Ricky, Joey, Markie, and Lynnette have been playing "monster" at work time, jumping off blocks, chairs, and the sofa.

Materials:
Tire-swing pit (since it is a safe jumping place). The pit is filled with pea gravel and surrounded by rubber-padded ledges of varying heights—from just about ground level to about three feet.

Possible KDIs:
Physical development, health, and well-being—*moving in locomotor ways: running, jumping, hopping, climbing; describing movement.* **Space**—*experiencing and describing positions, directions, and distances.*

Beginning:
Meet in the block area as usual. Tell children, "Today we're having small-group time outside so we can do some jumping. Think of how you could jump all the way from the block area to the tire swing." Jump with children to tire-swing pit. At the pit say "When nobody is swinging, this is the place for jumping. You can jump from a low ledge or a high one."

Middle:
Stay in the middle as children jump. Listen for their comments and observations. They may mention distance, direction, height, how they are going to jump. Some children may want to jump to me and give instructions about how close to them I should stand.

End:
Give a warning: "Two more jumps, and then it's time to go in for large-group time." Ask children to think of a way to jump back to large-group time.

Follow up:
At outside time, some children may want to jump while others may want to swing on the tire swing. Listen for and be ready to support children as they work to solve this problem.

These children enjoy jumping into the tire-swing pit at small-group time.

vide them. Adults who take these beliefs to heart are most likely to plan and carry out small-group experiences that support children's learning.

Adults Form Well-Balanced Small Groups

As much as possible, teaching teams form each small group from a cross section of the children in their program. They balance small groups by sex, age, and energy level so children can interact with a wide range of peers in each small group.

While balance is important, however, there are no hard and fast rules for achieving it.

For example, some younger children speak and work together more when the $2\frac{1}{2}$- to 3-year-olds are in one group and the 4s and 5s are in another. Other younger children really enjoy their older peers. Some children tend to talk more in a group composed of other quiet children. Some work-time buddies like to remain together for small-group time while other children are ready to interact with a different group. Each teaching team forms small groups based on their knowledge of what works best for their particular children.

Once you have formed small groups that are balanced in ways that make sense to you, maintain the groups for at least a month or two (preferably several months) so children get to

know one another and can depend on being in the same group of people each day, thus developing a sense of belonging to a particular group.

Adults Plan Small-Group Experiences Ahead of Time

The key to successful small-group times is planning experiences that appeal to children's interests and support their development. Ideas for active small-group times originate from several sources: the **interests of individual children, new and unexplored materials, the High/Scope KDIs,** and **local traditions.**

At this small-group time, children construct their own understanding of what happens when they cover a marble with paint and role it around on a piece of paper.

► **Plan around the interests of individual children.**

Many small-group times originate from observations and anecdotes that team members share about individual children at daily team planning time: "This is the second day Brianna has asked me for a Band-Aid to patch up a 'tiny cut' on her hand," Barbara reported at daily team planning. "Audie also told me that the masking tape he was using looked like a Band-Aid, so I think I'll provide Band-Aids for small-group time tomorrow since the children really seem interested in them."

Following are other examples of small-group sessions that teaching teams have planned around their observations of individual children's interests:

• On a neighborhood walk, Carol's and Elaine's children were very excited about the long freight train that went by. So Carol and Elaine planned their small-group times for the next day around providing children with small wooden trains and blocks to see how they might talk about or re-create their experience.

• At work time, Ann noticed that several children working in the art area were really involved in squeezing glue onto pieces of construction paper. This prompted her to plan a "squeezing" small-group time using plastic ketchup and mustard bottles at the water table.

• At outside time, Betsy helped four children figure out together how to push a wagonload of sticks and tires around the playground. As she described their interaction at daily team planning, Betsy decided to plan a cooperative-play small-group time using long planks and boards that were too heavy for one child to manage alone.

• Becki noticed that the children in her small group liked to say rhymes, so she planned a small-group time around reading a picture book that repeated several short rhymes the children could easily anticipate and learn by "reading" the pictures.

• When a group of children in their classroom began playing "pizza making" and "pizza delivery," Becki and Beth planned a small-group time in which children made individual pizzas (using English muffins for crusts and a selection of toppings) for snack time.

► **Plan around new and unexplored materials.**

Often small-group-time plans originate from the teaching team's desire to introduce children to new materials or draw their attention to materials they may be overlooking: "Several children—Alex, Trey, Sarah, and Audie—have been painting with tempera paints. I'd like to introduce them to watercolors," Barbara says at daily team planning. "I think that's what I'll use at small-group time tomorrow." The next day Barbara provides watercolor paper, brushes, water, and blocks of watercolor paints for each child at small-group time. The children pour their own "brush water" from a small watering can into their plastic cups, select their colors, and begin.

Here are some additional examples of small-group times that teaching teams have planned around new and unexplored materials:

• At small-group time, Carol and Elaine took turns introducing a computer program featuring trains to support their children's continuing interest in trains. Prior to the computer activity, the adults gave children small wooden trains and block tunnels to explore so they would be familiar with the type of situation they would encounter on the computer screen.

• One team introduced children to a new combination of materials—golf-ball tees (which the children had been inserting in Play-Doh) and pieces of Styrofoam (which they had been using at the workbench). Some children filled pieces of Styrofoam with golf-ball tees. Others made "cakes" and "walkie-talkies."

• Linda planned a small-group time around the materials children had gathered on a walk around the block—stones, chestnuts, leaves, twigs, an old windshield wiper, a hubcap, and hedge clippings. In response to Linda's question "What can we do with these things we found on our walk?," children got tape and clay and made musical instruments, collages, and people.

• Noticing children's interest in "writing messages," Beth introduced stamps and ink pads at small-group time: "Mine says 'Bunnies come home for supper,'" Alana said, reading her stamped message consisting of several lines of bunnies, the letter B, and a house. At the end of small-group time, the children decided to add the stamps and pads to the book and writing area.

• Becki introduced nine new rubber playground balls at a small-group time she held outside. The children rolled, kicked, threw, and bounced their balls. At the end of small-group time they put the balls in the storage shed "for outside time."

► **Plan around the High/Scope KDIs.**

Sometimes teaching teams look back through their observations and anecdotes about children and realize that they have not observed very much about a particular KDI (the High/Scope KDIs are described in Part 3 of this volume), so they plan a small-group time around materials and actions around a particular key developmental indicator. "We haven't recorded any anecdotes for Frances, Julia, or Douglas about the **space KDI**—*fitting things together and taking them apart*," Peter said at daily team planning. "I think I'll plan to give children the plastic stacking pegs and pegboards at small-group time and see what kind of fitting together and taking apart they do." At small-group time the next day, Frances filled her pegboards with pegs, took the pegs out, and started over again. Julia made four stacks of pegs, counted them up to 20, and then made a startling observation: "Look, I have one, two, three, **four** towers—twenty pegs in four towers!" Douglas fit all his pegs together in one tower that got so tall he had to stand on his chair to complete it. He then decided to take the whole tower out of the pegboard without taking it apart.

Following are other small-group times teaching teams have planned around the High/Scope KDIs:

• For several days, Michelle took photographs of children at work time. After she had printed the photos, she planned a small-group time around the **visual art** indicator—*relating photographs to real places and things*. She gave each child several photographs, listened to their comments about what they saw, and encouraged them to find and compare the objects to the photos.

• Noting children's interest in playing musical instruments, Beth planned a small-group time around the **time KDI**—*experiencing and describing rates of movement*. Each child chose an instrument and together the group played along to fast and slow musical selections: "Let's play another fast song."

• Since she wanted to give the children in her small group an experience with "materials

Noticing that several of the children in her small group were beginning to recognize letters and write their names, this teacher planned a small-group time using letter stamps. Each child chose the letters he or she wished to use.

that stretch" (**space** KDI—*changing the shape and arrangement of objects*), Linda planned a small-group time using rubber bands and pieces of elastic with geoboards and small looms as stretching frames: "Look, mine goes all the way across." "I can stretch this to hold two together."

• Keeping in mind the **physical development** KDI—*moving with objects*—Sam planned an outdoor small-group time around walking on tin-can stilts. He provided children with a choice of stilts in a variety of heights (from tuna cans to

coffee cans) so each child could find a comfortable height.

• Interested in the **seriation** KDI—*arranging several things one after another in a series or pattern*—Ann provided each child in her small group with lengths of wide, flat ribbon in several colors along with paper and a glue stick. "What could you do with these ribbons?" she asked, and then she watched to see if any patterns emerged in the children's creations. Amy made a border on her paper that repeated the pattern red-white-red-white. Namen made a "wild man" with alternating green and blue ribbon hair.

▶ **Plan around local traditions.**

Some small-group times originate from children's interest in local traditions. During outside time in the fall, for example, Ruth's children often heard the local high school marching band practicing their music. "The children are so excited when they hear the marching band and see it on the day it marches down our street," Ruth said one day at daily team planning. "I think I'll plan my small-group time around having our own band. We'll take the musical instruments outside and play and march around the playground." The next day at small-group time, the children gathered as usual with Ruth at the art-area table, then went together to the playground where they chose their instruments and traded off being "the leader of the band." When it was Brian's turn, he marched the parade along the fence. Alana marched everyone through the sandbox and up and down the hill. Douglas led the parade under the slide, the climber, the climbing net, and the tree house.

Here are some other small-group times that teaching teams have planned around children's responses to local traditions in which they had participated with their families:

• After Mardi Gras, a major community celebration, teachers Helena and Sarah noticed that their children were very interested in costumes. So, they planned costume-making small-group times. They provided children with butcher-paper smocks (with head and arm holes), crepe paper, scissors, and tape so they could make their own colorful costumes like the ones they had seen in the parade. Some children taped small pieces of

As these children create with yarn and sticks, they are engaged in the space KDIs **changing the shape and arrangement of objects** and **fitting things together and taking them apart.**

crepe paper to their smocks while others preferred long streamers.

• At one center it was a holiday tradition for all the children to prepare a meal for their families on a day between Thanksgiving and Christmas. Each classroom took responsibility for preparing one dish. One class was in charge of the mashed potatoes, so teachers Cathy and Evelyn planned a small-group time of potato peeling. Each child was very excited to have his or her own peeler and lots of potatoes to peel. "Did we do all these?!" they said when they finished, surrounded by a table filled with peelings and mounds of peeled potatoes. (Although some adults might worry about preschoolers peeling potatoes, this group of children and adults peeled potatoes with care and enthusiasm.)

• In a center where one of the children's parents was a weaver, the teaching team planned a small-group time around outdoor weaving. The weaver mom set up two simple outdoor looms and went back and forth between the two groups helping children weave in streamers and materials they found outside, including sticks, leaves, grass, and even a sandbox shovel.

• Following up on children's interests in a local kite-flying weekend, a teaching team planned small-group time around making kites to fly at outside time. They provided the children with a variety of kite-making materials, including fabric, tissue paper, construction paper, crepe paper, balsa wood strips, and string. The children who had made kites at home with their parents and siblings offered advice and assistance.

• After a trip to a nearby pumpkin patch, teachers Ruth and Ann planned their small-group time around exploring the pumpkins the children had gathered. Since the weather was still nice, they spread newspapers outside, helped the children cut the tops off their pumpkins, and provided spoons for "scooping out the insides." Many children preferred to use their hands to dig out the "yucky slime and seeds."

Adults Prepare for Small Groups *Before* Children Arrive

Once adults have a plan firmly in mind, small-group time requires adult preparation before the children arrive. Two strategies that help adults get ready are gathering materials for each child and putting them within easy reach of children.

▶ **Gather materials for each child.**

Since children learn from their own interactions with materials (as opposed to watching someone else), small-group time works best when each child has a set of materials to use. This means providing children with their own collection of small blocks and cars, paintbrushes and jars of paint, slices of pineapple, or whatever materials the small-group experience involves.

▶ **Have materials ready.**

Gather materials before children arrive and put them in a spot close to your small-group meeting place. This allows you to get small groups started as soon as children gather. One team started the day with small-group time, setting out materials on the table in the art area and house area each day before the children arrived. Another team scheduled small-group time right after recall time. In the morning, before the children arrived, they sorted small-group materials into bags, boxes, or baskets that they stored close to their meeting places so they could pass them out quickly at the beginning of small-group time.

Adults Set Small Groups in Motion: *The Beginning*

Children come to small-group time eager to begin. Here are two strategies that allow them to get started with a minimum of delay.

▶ **Give children materials as they arrive.**

Often adults set small-group time in motion simply by having materials out when children assemble. When presented with a pile of blocks, markers, and paper, or a hat full of little animals, a child will generally begin to build, draw, or play.

▶ **Make a *brief* introductory statement.**

Sometimes you will want to offer a simple challenge at the beginning of small-group time. Make your statement brief: "What can you do with ribbons, glue, and paper?" During one small-group time, teacher Ruth held a hat filled

This teacher gives a brief introduction to small-group time: "I wonder what we can do with these sticks."

with animals and made this brief statement: "Today we have hats, and animals to jump in and out of the hats. We'll also try a computer program with magic hats and animals that jump out of them." Then she gave each child his or her own hat full of animals.

Adults Support Children's Ideas and Use of Materials: *The Middle*

Once children have their materials and are involved in cutting paper, stacking blocks, filling and emptying squeeze bottles, cutting and tasting pineapples, or pounding nails into soft pine, it is up to adults to support their efforts. The following strategies will help you do so.

► **Move to the children's physical level.**

If children are sitting on the floor, sit on the floor with them. If they are kneeling around a large piece of butcher paper, kneel around it with them. If they are marching in a parade, march with them. Joining children at their physical level gives you an idea of what they are seeing and experiencing and makes you easily accessible for conversation and play.

► **Watch what children do with materials.**

This gives you an idea of how each child interprets the initial challenge. Frances fills her whole pegboard with pegs, Kacey makes a pattern, Julia counts her pegs, and Douglas sees how high he can stack his pegs. Adults will observe a range of responses within their groups—from Megan who watches other children get started before painting with her watercolors, to Alex who covers his paper with green and blue, to Julia who

After a trip to the pumpkin patch, this child scoops the seeds out of his pumpkin and carves a "scary face" of his own design using a table knife from the house area.

mixes colors for "pea soup." Adults will also see various **key developmental indicators** emerge as Audie counts the number of steps he takes on his stilts (*counting objects*), Sarah talks about the noise the stilts make (*exploring and identifying sounds*), and Alex fills his stilt cans with pea gravel (*filling and emptying*). Using this kind of information, adults can begin to see how they might interact to support each child appropriately.

► **Listen to what children say.**

By listening attentively to children, you learn what they find interesting and what they are thinking about: "Mine is coming into orange!" "I'm keeping mine in [the egg dye] for a long time." "How do you keep the can part on?"

Their language gives you a clue about what the small-group experience means to them and what they might find meaningful to talk about.

► **Move from child to child so all children receive attention.**

Even with a small group of children, it is difficult to attend to every child at once. By moving from child to child, you will see and hear each child and, by your actions, show children you will come to them when they need you. Your willingness to move about allows children to focus exclusively on their work; they can just call you over if they need your assistance.

► **Imitate children's actions.**

Often at small-group time, children's intense focus on materials takes up all their energy, and *conversation* takes a back seat to *action*. At these times, adults may wish to join in and support children's work by using a set of materials themselves and imitating what children are doing. Imitation puts adults into partnership with children without interfering with children's intentions.

► **Converse with children, following their leads.**

When children are ready to talk, follow their conversational leads. In this way, you operate at their level of understanding:

Catherine: *Mine is turning green, Becki!*

Becki: *It is turning green.*

Catherine: *It's spreading.* (She looks at her cup from the bottom.)

Becki: *I see the green spreading.*

Catherine: *It's really, really green. Even on the bottom.*

The child in the middle has stuck a curved piece of paper with two black balls on either end between his fingers "like wigglers." His teacher tries this idea and makes "wigglers" just like his. "I made wigglers, too!" says the child at right.

▶ **Encourage children to do things for themselves.**

Children learn through their own actions, so the more they can do for themselves at small-group time, the more opportunities they have for learning and gaining a sense of their own competence. When children spilled their dyes, Becki handed them a towel. They matter-of-factly wiped up their spills and went on with their egg coloring. Their own experiences enabled them to sympathize with other spillers: "Just what happened with mine!" When Catherine got dye on her fingers, she went to the sink, washed her hands, then returned to color her other two eggs.

Even though we may like to do things for children at small-group time, we will be more effective teachers if we allow children to do things for themselves.

▶ **Refer children to each other for ideas and assistance.**

This helps children learn that other children are valuable resources. Small-group interactions such as the following can strengthen children's beliefs in themselves and their peers:

Boomer: *Becki, I need another color.*

Becki: *Catherine and Caleb traded colors. Maybe someone will trade with you.*

Boomer: (to Amy) *Can I use your color?* (Amy and Boomer exchange colors.)

▶ **Ask questions sparingly.**

In general, the most relevant questions are the ones children ask themselves: "Does the green really go even to the bottom?" Catherine wonders, after she drops her color pellet in the vinegar. When you do ask a question at small-group time, make sure it is part of an ongoing conversation and is directly related to what the child is doing or thinking. Questions that probe the child's thought process are useful:

Namen: *I'm keepin' mine in for a long time.*

Becki: *What will happen to it in a long time?*

Namen: *It'll catch more color.*

Becki: *Oh, the egg catches the color.*

Namen: *Yeah, if you put it in just a little bit, just a little bit gets on there.*

Adults Bring Small-Group Time to a Close: *The End*

Adults strive to bring small-group time to a close without rushing children or holding them to a task in which they are no longer interested. Here are some strategies that can help.

▶ **Realize that children finish at different times.**

In an active-learning small-group experience, children proceed at their own pace and finish at different times. While all the children in Becki's small group received their egg-coloring materials at the same time, Catherine finished first. She stayed with the group, put her materials away, and helped Amy clean up. Namen, on the other hand, was still coloring his last egg as the other children put their colored eggs in their baskets. Becki began planning time with the children who were finished. Namen continued working and was the last person to plan.

In another setting, large-group time followed small-group time. Children joined the large-group activity individually, as they finished with small group. Basically, one adult started large group as soon as several children gathered. This accommodated children who finished small group early and allowed others to take the time they needed to carry out their small-group ideas.

▶ **Give children a warning near the session's end.**

Sometimes a small group needs to end at a set time. Under these circumstances, it helps to give children a warning several minutes before they need to stop working and put materials away. Advance notice lets children know ahead of time that they may have

to stop working before they are finished. It also gives them an opportunity to modify their plans so they can come to a natural stopping point.

▶ **Support children's concluding observations.**

Children often like to share their work or observations about what they have done. This happened in Becki's egg-coloring group as the children gathered around the window ledge, gently parted the grass to make a place for their eggs, and talked together about their eggs and baskets. Becki joined them to hear and take part in the conversation: "We can take them home today, can't we Becki?" "You sure can," she assures them.

▶ **Tell children that materials will be available at work time.**

This strategy enables children to incorporate small-group-time ideas into their play at other times of the day. It also assures children who may not have finished that they can return to these materials at work time or

When this child completes his shell painting at small-group time, his teacher talks with him about what he has done. She listens carefully to what he says and follows his conversational lead. She uses these strategies so she can support his thinking rather than impose her point of view.

outside time. Children may also suggest where new materials can be stored and even make labels for them.

▶ **Ask children to put away materials.**

As children finish, ask them to put their materials away. Have a trash can handy for scraps and newspaper table coverings, a bucket for emptying containers of liquids, a box for the scissors (or other loose materials), and sponges or cloths for wiping the table.

Small-Group-Time Ideas

For additional small-group-time ideas, see the High/Scope KDIs chapters in Part 3, as noted:

*Gathering together, this small group listens as their teacher reads **Harold and the Purple Crayon** by Crocket Johnson. Next, they select crayons and draw their own pictures.*

How Adults Support Children at Small-Group Time: A Summary

Adults examine their beliefs about how children learn at small-group time.

Adults form well-balanced small groups.

Adults plan small-group experiences ahead of time.
___ Plan around the interests of individual children.
___ Plan around new and unexplored materials.
___ Plan around KDIs.
___ Plan around local traditions.

Adults prepare for small groups before children arrive.
___ Gather materials for each child.
___ Have materials ready.

Adults set small groups in motion: the beginning.
___ Give children materials as they arrive.
___ Make a *brief* introductory statement.

Adults support each child's ideas and use of materials: the middle.
___ Move to children's physical level.
___ Watch what children do with materials.
___ Listen to what children say.
___ Move from child to child so all children receive attention.
___ Imitate children's actions.
___ Converse with children, following their leads.
___ Encourage children to do things for themselves.
___ Refer children to each other for ideas and assistance.
___ Ask questions sparingly.

Adults bring small-group time to a close: the end.
___ Realize that children finish at different times.
___ Give children a warning near the session's end.
___ Support children's concluding observations.
___ Tell children that materials will be available at work time.
___ Ask children to put away materials.

Understanding Large-Group Time

Large-group time is a time for the entire group to share important information and to participate in activities that are suitable for a large group. Typically programs have one of their large-group times, called **message board,** early in the day so important news and announcements can be shared. To illustrate the dynamics of large-group time, we have re-created two actual experiences from High/Scope programs. The first is an example of message board; the second re-creates a large-group movement and music experience.

The Information Exchange

It is the beginning of the day. Two adults, Beth and Sam, and 16 children gather in the middle of the toy area and together "read" the messages for the day "written" by adults and children on the message board that hangs on the wall low enough for everyone to reach and see:

During message board, a large-group time at the beginning of the day, children and adults share important information, such as who is riding in which vehicle on a field trip to a greenhouse.

The first message leads to a discussion about a friendly neighborhood kitty who has been joining the children at outside time. Yesterday, the children had asked about bringing the kitty inside with them. Beth had promised to talk with their neighbor, "the kitty's mom."

"We can't bring him inside," Beth tells the children, "because if we let him in, he won't go back to his house at night for food. But our neighbor says we can play with him when we're outside."

"He's a nice kitty."

"I wish he could come inside."

"My kitty at home is orange . . . with stripes."

Next, the group talks for a few minutes about Becki, another adult, who is away. They count the number of balloons left on the wall, one for each day Becki will be absent. Then Alana pops today's balloon. Before she does, however, several children note that "the pop's gonna be loud. I'm covering my ears!" Others announce, "Not me." "It's not too loud for me."

The third message, written and read by Max, a child, leads to a brief discussion about the fact that Sam is the teacher while Becki is away.

The last message on the board focuses the attention of all 16 children on Beth, who is holding the camera the children have been using at work time for the past several days. Beth tells them that she has added new batteries to the camera so now "when you push the button the flash goes off." She pushes the button to demonstrate.

"Does it take pictures now?" one child asks.

"No, the film still gets stuck."

"But we can pretend to take pictures!" says Callie.

Beth agrees, and everybody announces at once that they want to use the camera at work time.

"What can we do so everyone can have a turn?" Beth asks.

Several children understand that some kind of turn-taking will be necessary, but it takes the group another five minutes of discussion to finally put the turn-taking procedure together: a list of people who want to use the camera, and a timer to tell how long each turn is. Throughout this discussion, the children remain huddled around Beth, leaning in, intently focused on the camera, which is obviously of great interest to them. Once the camera-using problem is solved and the list is actually started, the children pull back, and Beth asks Ben how they should move to small-group time. "Pop!" he says, jumping up like a flashbulb going off, and everyone "pops" to small-group time.

❧

Moving and Singing Together

Later in the day, the entire group gathers in the middle of the block area for large-group time. As the children arrive, Sam sits down and leans back on his hands, bending his knees and lifting his feet up and down. "Tap, tap, tap your feet, tap them on the rug," he sings to the tune of "Row, Row, Row Your Boat." "Tap, tap, tap your feet, tap them on the rug." The children join in sitting like Sam, singing, and tapping their feet.

"I've got an idea," says Anna at the end of the verse, "your nose!" She sings and demonstrates, "Tap, tap, tap your nose, tap it with your fingers."

Sam, Beth, and the other children join in. Petey, Callie, and Bryant offer variations for everyone to try—"Pound your hands," "Clap your knees," and "Shake your head."

After the last variation, Beth says, "I've got a new song with four motions. The first one is marching. See if you can do some **marching**." The children and Sam march in various directions about the block area.

"Okay, marchers," says Beth. "The next movement is **up**. Try stretching up tall."

The children try this out on their own. "Look, I can go really high," says Kenneth. "Me, too!" "Me, too!"

After the children have tried stretching up, Beth says, "The next movement is **down**. Try bending and reaching way down to the floor." Some children bend and touch the floor, others crouch.

"The last movement is **halfway-up**," Beth says. "It's in between down and up. See if you can make yourself halfway-up." She waits to see how children will interpret this idea. When some have decided on a crouching stand and others are bending over, Beth says, "Here's the song that goes with these movements," and she sings "The Noble Duke of York." The children and Sam join in with words and phrases during the next several rounds of the song. The last time, they try out the motions as they sing.

When they are finished singing "The Noble Duke of York" Sam says, "When I turn on the 'boing-boing' music, you can move any way the music makes you want to move." He turns on a musical selection that sounds like rubber bands stretching and contracting.

"This is funny jumping music," Jana says, as the children laugh and bounce, bend, jump, and stretch.

When the music ends, several children say, "Let's do it again."

"Okay," says Sam, "but this time, think of a way to move to the coatrack so we can put on our coats for outside time." He plays the music again, and he, Beth, and the children hop, bounce, stretch, and "boing" over to the coatrack.

❧

Children and adults in a High/Scope program gather together at large-group time for companionship, sharing, and the pleasure of doing things as a community.

What Is Large-Group Time?

Since ancient times peoples of all cultures have gathered around fires or hearths to sing, dance, tell stories, and exchange information. In a similar spirit, children and adults in a High/Scope program gather together at large-group times for companionship, sharing important information, and the enjoyment of doing things together as a community.

▶ **Children and adults together**

Large-group time involves the entire group of children and all the members of the adult teaching team. Everyone participates, usually for about 10 minutes, in singing, movement experiences, storytelling, or a brief discussion about a topic important to the children.

Experiences such as singing together at large-group time build a sense of "we" and "us."

▶ **Active learning in a communal setting**

At large-group time, children actively *manipulate materials,* such as storytelling props, musical instruments, balls, or scarves, or move their own bodies in a variety of ways. Children make *choices* about how to play their instruments, how to move with their scarves, how to make themselves into pretend animals, what songs to sing, and how to change the words of songs. They *talk* about their ideas and observations and receive *adult support* for their initiatives.

▶ **Enjoyable shared experiences**

Adults plan and initiate participatory large-group experiences that are active rather than passive, move swiftly from one experience to the next, involve brief rather than lengthy introductions, and accommodate children's interests and initiatives. In general, enjoyable large-group experiences involve singing and music-making, moving and dancing, storytelling and re-enacting, cooperative group games and projects, and "reading" and discussing messages on the message board. Here are some examples:

• Linda, an adult, begins singing the "Run Around the Circle" song to the tune of "Blue Bird, Blue Bird, Fly Through My Window." Carole, another adult, and the children join in by running around in a circle and singing: "Run around, run around, run around the circle. Run around, run around, run around the circle. Run around, run around, run around the circle. Run around and stop." "I've got an idea. Jump!" says Joey. Everyone begins the action song again, this time substituting jumping for running. The children suggest and try out other actions, including marching, flying, popping, and wiggling.

• Beth, an adult, tells "The Mitten," a story about forest creatures who huddle inside a mitten to stay warm in the winter. A large red sleeping bag serves as the mitten. Children get into and out of it as they pretend to be the mice, chipmunks, hedgehogs, squirrels, rabbits, foxes, and bears in the story. At the end, everyone "pops" out when the mitten finally bursts at the seams.

• Aware of children's interest in numbers and counting, Becki, an adult, initiates a fingerplay based on the rhyme "Five Little Monkeys Sitting on the Bed." Everyone says the first verse together: "Five little monkeys jumping on the bed. One fell off and bumped his head. The doctor came and this is what he said, 'No more monkeys jumping on the bed!'" Before the next verse Becki asks, "How many monkeys this time?" "Lots," says Alana. "What are lots of monkeys doing?" Becki asks. "Climbing up a tree," suggests Andrew. The next verse goes like this. "Lots of monkeys climbing up a tree. One fell off and bumped his head (some children said "knee" to rhyme with "tree"). The doctor came and this is what he said. No more monkeys climbing up a tree." The fingerplay continues with "Seven little monkeys making popcorn soup," "Two little

monkeys playing in the mud," and "Twenty-seven monkeys knocking on the door." The children use their fingers to express their idea of "lots," 7, 2, and 27 and also make up hand motions for climbing, making soup, playing in mud, and knocking on the door.

Why Is Large-Group Time Important?

Large-group time brings children and adults together for brief periods to exchange information and do things as a group. This experience builds a sense of "we" and "us."

▶ A repertoire of common experiences

Children draw on large-group experiences as they play at other times of the day. For example, outside on the tire swing, Julia and Andrew sing "The Mud Song" then change some of the words, making up their own variations: "Ponds, ponds, we love ponds for floating boats and floating on." "Listen to this," Jalessa says, joining Julia and Andrew when the swing comes to a halt: "Dirt, dirt, we love dirt, on your face and on your shirt." Singing together as they swing is a natural experience for these children because all three have learned and sung "The Mud Song" many times at large-group time. They are com-

fortable singing together and readily accept new singers and new verses to their songs.

▶ A sense of community

Large-group time briefly draws everyone together—to look at a new camera, try out a new way of moving, sing a favorite song, or act out a story. The underlying message of this time of day is togetherness. It is a time to sing, dance, pretend, and talk with everyone. When the day begins or ends with large-group time, parents can also participate. When their parents are present, children often nestle in their parents' laps. In fact, one-child-one-lap is probably a preschooler's ideal for singing and storytelling at large-group time.

▶ Group membership and leadership

In a High/Scope large-group time, it is common for children to say, "I've got an idea!" and then assume a leadership role to change a song, introduce a movement, add to a story, or modify a game. At times, adults facilitate this process with statements such as "We'll try your idea, James, after Erica's and Trey's ideas." Because children have many opportunities to contribute to large-group time, they take turns presenting their own ideas and trying out the ideas of others. At large-group time, then, children have many opportunities to be both *participants* and *group leaders*.

▶ Group problem-solving experiences

Sometimes, children have more ideas for songs to sing than time allows. In such instances, an adult might pose a question: "Three of you have suggested songs but there's only time for one before the bus comes. What should we do?" A child responds, "I know. Close my eyes and pick." Large-group time provides many such opportunities for adults and children to solve preschool-level problems together.

Where Large Groups Meet

Large-group meetings call for a space flexible enough for both vigorous action and cozy intimacy as well as the enactment of young children's ideas about when and how to move and where and how to sit.

▶ **Gather in a spacious location.**

Large-group meetings often take place in the most spacious interest area. To make enough space available, you may have to move a shelf or a large piece of equipment. One teaching team used the block area for large-group meetings. When they added a music area at one end of the block area, they moved the instrument shelf each day for large-group time to make enough space for everyone to move freely. In warm climates and seasons, large-group time might take place outside under a tree or on a patio or deck.

▶ **Let the large-group-time experience determine the formation of the group.**

Some large-group games call for a circle formation. Some movement activities confine children to individual carpet squares or the inside of their hoops. In other experiences children move about the whole area. When they re-enact stories, children like to build and perform on a platform stage assembled out of blocks. For important information, children draw as close as they can to the speaker or object of interest. Rather than expecting children to always sit in a circle for large-group time, adults in a High/Scope program understand that the positions children assume will vary depending on what they are doing.

What Children Do at Large-Group Time

Returning to the earlier account of Sam's and Beth's large-group time, consider the experiences of one child, Kenneth:

Kenneth joins the singing game in progress at the end of the "tap your feet" verse.

Large-Group Time— What, Why, Where: A Summary

What It Is
- All children and adults are together.
- Active learning occurs in a communal setting.
- Provides enjoyable shared experiences.

Why It Is Important
- Gives children a repertoire of common experiences.
- Builds a sense of community.
- Encourages group membership and leadership.
- Provides children with group problem-solving experiences.

Where to Meet
- Meet in a spacious location.
- The large-group-time experience determines the formation of the group.

He has just gotten his feet going when Anna changes the verse to "tap your nose." He keeps his feet tapping for a few beats, then switches to tapping his nose with three fingers on each hand while looking at his friend Bryant. "What if a giant tapped his nose!" he says to Bryant, as Petey talks to Sam about changing the verse to "pounding the floor." When Petey's verse begins, Kenneth leans over and pounds the floor with both fists. At the end of this verse, he and Bryant continue their conversation about giants. "A giant could pound through the floor." "And he wouldn't get hurt." "Yeah, he has special powers." For the "clap your knees" verse Kenneth pounds his knees, then shakes his head "like a giant" from side-to-side during the last verse.

Kenneth is still shaking his head as Beth encourages the group to try the marching movement for the new song. When other children begin to march, Kenneth gets up and marches after Bryant. "We're giants, aren't we, Bryant," he says. They lift their legs as high as they can as they weave in and out among the other marchers. "Look, I can go really high," Kenneth tells Beth after she describes the second movement, "Go high." He stands on his toes and stretches toward the ceiling. Beth nods and smiles in acknowledgment then asks the children to go "down." Kenneth falls to the floor on his hands, then crouches with his arms wrapped around his knees. For "halfway-up," he watches Bryant, then assumes a standing crouch. When Beth begins to sing, Kenneth falls to the floor on his hands again, crawls over to Beth, sits down, and leans comfortably against her, singing along from time to time. When it is time to sing and move, Kenneth jumps up and marches with Bryant, reaches up, falls to the floor, then stands in a crouch. He sings some of the words and goes

and process of large-group gatherings.

▶ **Children actively participate.**

At large-group time, as at other times of the day, children use both materials and their own bodies in creative ways. For example, they march, fall to the ground, wave and jump over streamers, dance their own interpretation of popcorn popping, line up blocks for a stage, shake tambourines and hit them against different parts of their bodies, make up movements for others to try, and assume the shape and motions of rats to act out "The Rats in the House" story. They make choices about how to move, what songs to sing, what stories to re-enact, what words and actions to change, what music to dance to, what instruments to play first, what games to play, and whom to sit near. In the process, they voice their own opinions ("A giant could pound through the floor!") and observations:

Adult: (telling a story) *And he cried and cried and cried.*

First child: *Whaaaaa, whaaaa.*

Second child: *Maybe he cried "Boo hoo, Boo hoo."*

Third child: *My baby cries like this, "Eeeee, eeeee."*

Fourth child: *"Maaa, maaa." He wanted his mom.*

They also tell their own stories ("Once there was an old man and he walked around with his hands in his pockets, like this . . .") and make up their own songs ("The bird flew up the tree, the bird flew up the tree, the bird flew up the tree, and then it went to sleep.").

▶ **Children initiate ideas, offer suggestions, and generate solutions.**

Throughout large-group gatherings, children initiate their own ideas: "We're giants." "Let's sing that Donkey song!" They make suggestions: "I've got an idea. Pat your nose." "I think the bells should have their own turn." They offer solutions. For example, the children are discussing the "ownership" of carpet squares in a musical game: "I know—if you want to come back to your same square, just tell everybody and they won't get on yours. But the other kids can change, 'cause they like to go to different squares." In a High/Scope large-group time, both adults and children shape what happens.

> ### What Children Do at Large-Group Time: A Summary
>
> • Children actively participate.
>
> • Children initiate ideas, offer suggestions, and generate solutions.

back to marching until Sam puts on the "boing-boing" music. "This is the funny jumping music!" Kenneth says, as he jumps up and down. "Let's do it again," he says when the music stops. Kenneth is the first to reach the coatrack when Sam plays the tape a second time. As soon as he gets his coat on, he resumes jumping until the music stops. "Bryant," he says on the way out the door. "Let's be giants, okay?"

As Kenneth's experiences illustrate, in an active learning setting, children's actions and ideas play a major role in shaping the content

How Adults Support Children at Large-Group Time

The adults' role at large-group time is similar to their role at small-group time: Adults initiate experiences and support children's initiatives. The following strategies help them to do this:

- **Examining their beliefs about how children learn**
- **Planning large group experiences ahead of time**
- **Preparing for large groups before the children arrive**
- **Setting large-group experiences in motion—the beginning**
- **Supporting children's ideas and initiatives—the middle**
- **Bringing large-group time to a close—the end**

Adults Examine Their Beliefs About How Children Learn at Large-Group Time

Adults in active learning settings view large-group times as opportunities for the whole group to come together for common experiences that support and extend children's individual and small-group pursuits. Adults seek out experiences that appeal deeply to children and structure them so children can shape and influence what happens.

For some adults, adopting an active learning approach to large-group times means giving up the notion of the adult as the center of attention, the "star" performer who reads a story, leads a discussion, or directs an activity.

Adults committed to an active learning approach to educating young children have realistic expectations of young children's interests and behaviors. They realize that children need to communicate and move about and that large-group time will involve energetic action and conversation. Believing in their obligation to create opportunities for children to take an active part in shaping their experiences, adults using the High/Scope approach accept the challenges and rewards of planning for and supporting children's initiatives at large-group time.

Adults Plan Large-Group Experiences Ahead of Time

While children make major contributions to large-group experiences, adults set each large-group time in motion around a plan they make relating to the children's current interests, the music and movement KDIs, cooperative play and projects, or events that are currently meaningful to their children.

▶ **Plan around children's interests.**

Building large-group times around things children enjoy is one way to ensure their enthusiastic participation. For example, a teaching team, composed of adults Ann and Ruth, observed that Linda, David, and Kerry often planned to dance with scarves at work time. As they discussed their observations during their daily team planning session one day, Ann said, "Let's use the scarves at large-group time tomorrow. I bet lots of children would like to see how they move."

"We could play music they haven't heard before, maybe 'Oh, How Lovely Is the Evening,' because it's kind of slow and floaty. We could ask them to move with their scarves to the music," Ruth added.

The next day at large-group time, Ruth passed around the basket of scarves for the children to select. Ann put on the music and the children danced, waving their scarves with one hand or two hands, making them go "up like a parachute," tying them on their arms, and draping them over their heads as they twirled, waved their arms, and moved slowly to the music.

Here are some other examples of large-group-time plans that arose as adults thought about their particular children's interests:

- Teachers Barbara and Michelle heard Julia sing "Do Your Ears Hang Low" several times during work time, so they planned to have Julia help them teach this song and its motions the next day at large-group time.

- Teachers Peter and Becki watched Audie and LJ throw beanbags to each other, so they planned a large-group time with beanbags. The next day at large-group time the adults gave a beanbag to each pair of children to toss and catch. Some children stood very close to each other while tossing their beanbags, while other, more experienced throwers stood farther apart.

- Erin and Markie had new baby sisters at home and played "babies" a lot at work time, so teachers Linda and Carole planned a large-group time around being "tiny babies who can't crawl yet." They asked the children to lie on

After observing several children playing with streamers at work time, this teaching team planned a large-group time around streamer dancing. For the children, selecting and unwinding their streamers was just as important as dancing with them to the music!

their backs and move their arms and legs around "like tiny babies" to a slow musical selection and then to one with a faster tempo.

• One spring day, teachers Ruth and Ann observed that several of their children liked to play tag, so they planned an outdoor game of tree tag for large-group time. They made the rules very simple: When the drum is beating, run. When the drum stops, run to a tree for "safety." No one was "It," and adults and children took turns beating the drum.

▶ **Plan around music and physical development KDIs.**

Many large-group experiences originate when members of a teaching team relate the High/Scope indicators in **music** and **physical development** to the observations they make of

their particular children. (Part 3 of this volume describes the High/Scope KDIs.) One day during work time, for example, Deola and Corrin sang the phrase "We all live in a yellow submarine" over and over again as they worked at the art table.

"They seem to be *developing melody*," Beth, their teacher, said to her teammate Becki, referring to one of the **music** KDIs during daily team planning. "Let's plan to use this phrase at large-group time tomorrow."

"Okay," Becki agreed. "Maybe we could add an ending to it." She sang what she meant: "We all live in a yellow submarine, a yellow submarine, a yellow submarine. We all live in a yellow submarine, a yel-low sub-ma-rine."

The next day when they sang this song with the children at large-group time, the children invented new verses, including "We all live in my

grandpa's pick-up truck." "We all live in a green pickle jar." "We all live in a red choo-choo train."

Here are examples of other large-group experiences adult teams have planned for their particular children around the **music** and the **physical development** KDIs:

• Thinking about two **music** KDIs, *moving to music* and *playing simple musical instruments*, teaching teammates Sam and Peter planned a large-group experience around dancing with wrist and ankle bells. At large-group time, the children chose how to wear their bells and danced to the drum beat Peter played. He was ready to trade the drum for bells so other children could play the drum, but that day all the children wanted to dance with their bells.

• Here is one way Beth and Becki planned around the **music** KDI *singing songs*.

One Teacher's Thoughts About Large-Group Time

When planning large-group times, I [High/Scope teacher Beth Marshall] think about the beginning, the middle, and the end with a transition to the next activity, which in our daily routine is outside time. For the beginning of today's large-group time, I planned to start playing the "Run Around the Circle" singing game with the children who finished their snacks first. I think it is important to begin large-group time with an active experience because (1) the children have been sitting for snack and (2) large-group time should be attractive to children who are still eating. My co-teacher, Becki, agreed that I would start large-group time and that she would stay with the children still eating snack, then join the large group when most of the children were finished.

For the middle of large-group time, I wanted to sing "The Depot Town Song," which we had written with the children earlier in the week at large-group time after walking to our neighborhood farmer's market (in Depot Town). As the children suggested ideas for verses, we recorded them on a sheet of butcher paper using words, drawings, and the children's symbols. Becki and I both noticed that the children went to the song sheet to "read" and sing "The Depot Town Song" during work time the next day. "Great," we said to each other, "They're *reading in various ways,* a **language, literacy, and communication** KDI!"

Finally, I wanted to end large-group time with a child's work-time idea. During our daily team planning session, Becki and I discussed and recorded an anecdote about Anna's "hopping stones." Anna had gotten several sheets of colored paper from the art area and placed them on the floor in the block area. She then hopped from paper to paper, going back to the art area several times to get more paper to add to her spreading collection. When Callie and Ben asked her what she was doing, she said the floor was "hot lava," and she could only step on "these safe hopping stones." Ben and Callie quickly got on a piece of paper so they would be "safe" and joined her game. I decided to incorporate this new play into large-group time by using carpet squares and adding some hopping music. I was interested in two things: would children pick up on Anna's hopping from "stone" to "stone" idea, and would some children *feel and express steady beat,* a **physical development, health, and well-being** KDI.

Thinking about the transition to outdoor time, I wanted to end the "stone" activity and get the children across the room to the door. I thought that if Becki picked up her carpet square toward the end of the hopping music and hopped with it over to the door, perhaps the children would follow her lead. They could then stack the carpet squares by the door and go outside.

Today, before the children arrived, I prepared for large-group time by putting the song "Bele Kawe" (a musical selection on the High/Scope *Rhythmically Moving 3* recording) in the CD player, making sure we had enough carpet squares for each child plus a few extra. When snack was almost over, I joined the children who had already gone to the large-group-time space. We sang and moved to the "Run Around the Circle" song we made up:

> *"Run, run, run around the circle.*
> *Run, run, run around the circle.*
> *Run, run, run around the circle,*
> *Until you want to stop."*

The children suggested other ways to move—tip-toeing, rolling, walking backward, and jumping. As we sang and moved, the rest of the children joined us as they finished snack.

When all of the children were present, we sat down and sang "The Depot Town Song." The children enjoyed "reading" and singing each verse. When we got to Mikey's butterfly symbol, Mikey patted himself on the chest and said "That's me! I did the train," as the rest of the group sang "Mikey saw the fast train." When we sang the verse "Alana saw a bunch of carrots," Alana ran to the house area and got the plastic carrots!

After "The Depot Town Song," I got a carpet square from the pile and said that I had some "hopping stones" for everyone. The children quickly helped themselves to the carpet squares, and Becki spread out the rest while I turned on the music.

I was amazed at the variety of things the children did. Brian hopped from the rug to his square to the rug, over and over again. Rachel hopped on her square from corner to corner. Chelsea got a scarf, stood on her square, and slowly moved the scarf to the music. Ben sat by the window and watched what the other children were doing. Deola hopped all over the large-group area, landing sometimes on carpet squares, sometimes on the rug. Mikey ran around his carpet square. Anna and most of the other children hopped from carpet square to carpet square, even hopping to "the really 'farest' one." We noticed that some children hopped to the steady beat of the music.

Becki and I tried to support what individual children did by imitating their actions. We also mentioned what some children were doing when it seemed appropriate: "Alana, Chelsea's doing something different with her hopping stone." As we neared the end of the song, Becki picked up a square and hopped toward the door. I told the children that when they were ready to go outside, they could hop to the door with a "hopping stone," and we hopped to the door and hopped outside.

A Sample Large-Group-Time Plan: Playing Horses

Originating idea:
Children's interests—Wendy, Erin, Scott, and Troy have been playing "horses" at work time, walking about on all fours, rearing up on their "hind legs," neighing, and pawing the air.

Materials:
No materials are needed.

Possible KDIs:
Dramatic art—*pretending and role playing.* **Language, literacy, and communication**—*having fun with language: making up stories.* **Physical development**—*expressing creativity in movement.*

Beginning:
Start with a variation of "Run Around the Circle":

> "*Horses run, horses run, run around the circle.*
>
> *Horses run, horses run, run around the circle.*
>
> *Horses run, horses run, run around the circle.*
>
> *Horses run, then stop.*"

Ask children for other ways horses can go around the circle. Sing and do these variations.

Middle:
Tell a simple repetitive story about horses that the children can act out along the way. To introduce it say "Here's a story about horses just like you who have been running around the circle":

> "*Once upon a time there were eighteen little horses who had run about all day long, so they walked slowly to their barn and went to sleep. Good night, horses (pause for the horses to go to sleep). The next morning they woke up refreshed and rested. They stretched their long legs (pause for leg stretching). They stretched their long necks (pause for neck stretching). They felt hungry so they went out to the pasture to eat grass (pause for grass eating). They ate grass all day long (pause for more grass eating). When night-time came, they were tired, so they walked slowly back to their barn and went to sleep. Good night, horses (pause for sleeping).*
>
> "*The next morning the eighteen little horses woke up refreshed and rested. They stretched their long legs (pause for leg stretching). They stretched their long necks (pause for neck stretching). They felt like neighing and pawing their feet in the air, so they went out to the pasture (pause for neighing and pawing). They neighed and pawed their feet in the air all day long (pause for more neighing and pawing). When night-time came, they were tired, so they walked slowly back to their barn and went to sleep. Good night, horses (pause for sleeping).*
>
> "*The next morning the eighteen little horses woke up refreshed and rested. They stretched their long legs (pause for leg stretching). They stretched their long necks (pause for neck stretching). They felt like—What did they feel like doing? (get action from children)—so they went out to the pasture to _____ (pause for action children suggest). They _____ all day long. (Pause for more of the action children suggest.) When night-time came, they were tired, so they walked slowly back to their barn and went to sleep. Good night, horses (pause for sleeping).*"

(Repeat as long as the children are involved and offer actions.)

End:
End the story with a transition to outside time:

> "*The next morning the eighteen little horses woke up refreshed and rested. They stretched their long legs (pause for leg stretching). They stretched their long necks (pause for neck stretching). They felt like playing outside like girls and boys so they trotted over to the coatrack to put on their girl and boy coats for outside time.*" (Trot over to coatrack with the children.)

Follow up:
Continue to watch children's "horse" play for other actions to build into this story. Plan a field trip to a local horse farm to see what horses do and how they move.

A Sample Large-Group-Time Plan: Singing Favorite Songs

Originating idea:
Music KDI—*singing songs.* The children know more songs than they probably realize.

Materials:
Song cards, masking tape, message board, bag of children's symbols

Possible KDIs:
Music—*singing songs.* **Physical development**—*feeling and expressing beat.* **Number**—*counting.*

Beginning:
Put on tape, "Gaelic Waltz" (a musical selection on the High/Scope *Rhythmically Moving 1* recording), and sway to the beat as children arrive. They will probably think of other ways to move on their own. Follow children's movement ideas. To get in position for singing, initiate a sitting movement on the final time through.

Middle:
Spread out the song cards face up. Ask a nearby child to pick a child's symbol out of the bag. Then say to the child whose symbol has been drawn, "Devon, it's your turn to pick the first song we're going to sing." Tape the song card Devon chooses and his symbol next to each other on the message board. Have another child draw a second symbol from the bag. Have the second child pick the second song and tape that song card and child's symbol next to each other on the board underneath the first song card and symbol. Repeat this process until there are five song cards on the board.

Sing the songs in order. Have the child who chose the song pick a way for everyone to move to the beat as they sing (rocking, swaying, tapping a body part).

End:
Ask children to think of a way to move to small-group time humming the last song we just sang.

Follow up:
Leave the song cards and symbols up and repeat this process at large-group time later in the week until we have sung all the songs we know and the children can see how many songs they can sing. Watch to see if the children stop to "read" the song list on their own during the day.

A Sample Large-Group-Time Plan: Moving Sand

Originating idea:
Cooperative play and projects—We have a new sandbox with no sand in it and a pile of sand that was just delivered and dumped about 20 feet away from the sandbox.

Materials:
Sand, shovels, nine good-sized buckets with handles, camera

Possible KDIs:
Social and emotional development—*experiencing collaborative play.* **Space**—*filling and emptying.*

Beginning:
As children gather, to the tune of "Row, Row, Row Your Boat," sing "Fill, fill, fill your buckets, fill your buckets with sand. Fill, fill, fill your buckets, fill your buckets with sand." Do filling motions along with the song. Sing other verses—"Carry, carry, carry your buckets . . ." "Dump, dump, dump your buckets . . ." Ask children for additional ideas.

Middle:
Say something like this: "For large-group time we're going outside to move the sand from the sand pile into the sandbox. Here are some buckets and shovels we can use." Respond to children's comments and questions. Distribute buckets and shovels and go outside. Watch to see how children fill the buckets, what they do when they find that a full bucket is too heavy for one person to carry, and if they think of using other containers such as the wagon. Support children's problem solving and observations about this task. Take pictures so, later, the children can see themselves at work, and they can see the sand pile growing smaller and the pile in the sandbox getting bigger.

End:
When all the sand is in the sandbox, go to the sandbox and start singing (to the tune of "Row, Row, Row Your Boat"), "We moved all the sand, we moved all the sand. We moved all the sand, we moved all the sand." Ask children for additional verses and sing them. Conclude with a statement such as, "Now it's outside time and we can play in the sand or with anything else on the playground."

Follow up:
Leave buckets and shovels out for sand play. Print the pictures and introduce them at morning greeting circle or small-group time.

"Let's make a big pile!" These children and their teacher enjoy their new sandbox.

A Sample Large-Group-Time Plan: Exploring Helium Balloons

Originating idea:
Currently meaningful events—The children have been exploring balloons (blowing them up, tying off some, and releasing others so they zoom around the room) because Sanna brought balloons for everyone on her birthday. The children have been wondering "How do those other kinds of balloons stay up in the air?"

Materials:
Heavy-duty balloons (one for each child), long strings with loops on one end to fit over children's wrists (if they want to use the strings), a small tank of helium

Possible KDIs:
Language, literacy, and communication—*talking with others about personally meaningful experiences.* **Physical development**—*moving with objects.* **Space**—*experiencing and describing positions and directions of things.*

Beginning:
Fill balloons with helium, tie on long strings and distribute to children as they gather. Listen for and support children's observations and conversations.

Middle:
When everyone has a balloon, say "See how many things you can do with your helium balloons. Then when you hear the music, bring your balloons back to the circle." Watch and listen to the children. Support their experiments. (They may let their balloons go up to the ceiling and pull them back down. They may try tying them to various objects around the room to see if they will lift them.)

End:
Ask the children to wear the loops at the end of their balloon strings over their wrists. Put on "Irish Washerwoman" (a musical selection on the High/Scope *Rhythmically Moving 3* recording). Tap your head with both hands to the beat of the music and watch the balloons move to the beat. Ask children to suggest other body parts or things to tap to the beat and continue to watch the balloons move. At the end of "The Irish Washerwoman," ask "Where can we park our balloons for the night before we go home?" Once children settle on a balloon storage location, say "When you hear the music, put your balloon in _____ and move any way you like to the music to get your things for going home." Play "Sliding" (a musical selection on the High/Scope *Rhythmically Moving 1* recording) as children park their balloons and get ready to go home.

Follow up:
Talk with children at greeting circle tomorrow about what they notice about the balloons. Also, let them know that the balloons are available for them to use at work time.

At large-group time, these children sing a favorite song and do the motions on their own while their teacher accompanies them on the Autoharp.

After the children had learned "Twinkle, Twinkle," "Row, Row, Row Your Boat," "Muffin Man," "Are You Sleeping?" and "Jingle Bells," Beth and Becki made a song card for each song (the song title and a simple drawing to represent the song covered with clear contact paper). At large-group time they showed children each card and had them "read" the name of the song. Then they turned the cards face down and asked a child to pick a song card. After they sang that song, another child selected a card and so forth until all the cards were face up again.

• After they had made popcorn several times with their children at small-group time, teachers Becki and Peter, with the **music** KDI *moving to music* in mind, planned a large-group experience around "Popcorn" (a musical selection on the High/Scope *Rhythmically Moving 1* recording). "This is music about popcorn popping," Peter

said, introducing the experience to the children. The children decided to start out "as little kernels." "Put salt on me," Alana requested before Peter started the music. Peter and Becki "sprinkled" salt on the "kernels" who then wiggled and sizzled and popped with the music.

• Thinking of the **physical development** KDI *moving with objects* and several children's expressed interest in playing pickup sticks, teachers Yvonne and Karen planned a large-group experience around moving with large Tinkertoy sticks. At large-group time they asked each child to select a large Tinkertoy piece and move with it to the music played so the Tinkertoy did not touch anybody. When the music stopped, they asked the children to put the sticks down and walk to the music around the block area without touching the sticks as they walked.

▶ **Plan around cooperative play and projects.**

Some large-group experiences arise from the teaching team's desire to promote cooperative play and projects. At daily team planning, for example, teachers Helena and Sarah discussed the stories their children told. They decided to plan a large-group experience around cooperative storytelling:

"I'd like to start with a simple story the children could add to along the way," Helena said, "but I wonder how we could keep them all focused on the story."

"Well, they like puppets, so maybe they could each have a puppet," said Sarah, thinking out loud. "We have enough puppets, but then we'd end up with eighteen different characters in the story!"

"What if we gave each child two pieces of cloth they could attach to their wrists with rubber bands and use as puppets," said Helena. "We could tell a really simple version of 'Little Red Riding Hood' and then give each child a red cloth and a grey cloth for Little Red Riding Hood and the wolf."

The next day at large-group time, Helena and Sarah tried out their idea. It took a while for the children to get their puppets on, but they finally managed, helping one another with their rubber bands. Once the storytelling began, the children made their puppets walk, run, and skip through the woods, sing, pick flowers, and talk to the wolf. "These guys need eyes!" several children observed, and they decided to make them some eyes at work time the next day.

Here are some other examples of large-group experiences teaching teams have planned around cooperative play and projects:

• Adults Karen and Jeanne planned a cooperative large-group time around Maypole dancing. Since their children enjoyed dancing to music with streamers, they thought this idea might work, but first they needed to find a sturdy pole. They finally decided to tack nylon streamers to a pole outside that held up their bird feeder. At large-group time, everyone went outside, found the end of a streamer, and danced around the pole to selections of recorded music. "Look what's happening to the pole!" the children exclaimed when the music stopped, "it's getting colors!"

• Another cooperative storytelling idea Helena and Sarah used with their children involved musical instruments. They made up simple stories with lots of sounds in them to mimic: crying babies, barking dogs, walking up stairs, ringing telephones, and running water in a bathtub. As they told the story at large-group time, the children provided the sound effects, using their voices as well as instruments from the music area.

• Teachers Linda and Carole planned a simplified version of "Hot Potato" to play with their children. At large-group time, each child selected a potato. When the music played, they passed the potatoes around the circle; when the music stopped, they held on to their potatoes. Some children talked to their "potato babies" during the pauses. After several rounds, Joey had the idea of passing the potatoes with his feet, which everyone tried with much laughter and lots of straying potatoes.

• Teachers Cindy and Bob planned a large-group time around making a mural together. They laid a long piece of butcher paper on a paved part of the playground. At large-group time, each child selected a brush and a jar of paint, and everyone gathered around the paper and painted a mural to hang on the playground fence. To get the project started, Bob said, "Paint any way you want to make a big picture to hang on our fence."

This group of children enjoys a large-group train game.

▶ **Plan around events currently meaningful to your children.**

Finally, some large-group-time experiences originate from children's ongoing interest in events they find particularly meaningful. For example, in January, teachers Peter and Sam noticed that many of their children were singing "Jingle Bells" as they played. "Let's plan to sing 'Jingle Bells' at large-group time tomorrow," Peter said at daily team planning time, "and use the bells again. Everyone can wear bells on their wrists or ankles and jingle while we sing." The next day, the children liked doing this so much

that they asked to repeat the activity at the next large-group time and then made more requests throughout the winter and well into spring.

Here are some other examples of large-group experiences that teaching teams have planned around events that children found meaningful:

• In the days following Halloween, teachers Helena and Sarah observed that several of their children continued to play "trick or treat." So, they planned a stopping-and-starting large-group experience in which the children "trick or treated" every time the music stopped. They played "Arkansas Traveler/Sailor's Hornpipe/Turkey in the Straw" (a musical selection on the High/Scope *Rhythmically Moving 1* recording). When the music stopped, the children knocked on any surface they could find and said "trick or treat." The children enjoyed finding different places to knock on (blocks, windows, shelves, tables).

• After a trip to a local apple orchard, teachers Michelle and Barbara planned a large-group experience around looking at and talking about the pictures they had taken of children picking apples, eating them, riding on the wagon, looking at bugs in the grass. As the children sat on the floor and looked at the pictures, they talked with one another about what they saw.

• One weekend, the streets of town where most of Gwen's and Betsy's children lived were "taken over" by a basketball tournament that raised money for local charities.

On Monday, the adults watched and listened to the children talk about the tournament. That day at team planning time, Gwen and Betsy decided to incorporate "basketball" into large-group time the next day. Using duct tape, they taped hoops at fairly low levels along the fence on the playground (using quite a bit of tape to secure the hoops as tightly as possible). At large-group time each child selected a rubber playground ball and had the opportunity to shoot baskets. Several children invented a game of standing inside the hoops, catching the balls, and throwing them back to "their team." (The teachers left the hoops up so children could use them at outside time, too.)

• After a trip to the gas station around the corner, teachers Carole and Elaine planned a large-group experience around making up a song about what the children saw on their trip. Elaine played a simple tune on her guitar while the children made up words and motions for the verses. The children's verses included "We saw the windshield wipers," "We saw the car go up," "We saw the candy machine," "We saw the piles of tires," "We saw the mom and her baby," "We saw the dog digging."

Adults Prepare for Large-Group Time Before Children Arrive

Active large-group experiences such as the ones just described require well-prepared adults. Here are some strategies that help adults plan for these sessions.

▶ **Modify songs and games to fit children's development and specific events.**

In singing games like "Hokey Pokey," change references from "right foot" and "left foot" to "one foot" and "the other foot." In "Musical Chairs," do not remove any chairs so all children can participate throughout the game. After a trip to the farmer's market, change the words of "Old MacDonald" to "Farmer Karpo went to market . . . In the market he had some apples . . ."

▶ **Practice ahead of time.**

At daily team planning, sing "Farmer Karpo" or "The Noble Duke of York" with your team member so both of you know the words, the tune, and the motions (if there are any). Listen to the "boing-boing" music, "Popcorn," or "Oh, How Lovely." Find and listen to the fast and slow selections you plan to play for "pretending to be babies on their backs." Practice the story you plan to tell about Little Red Riding Hood and the Wolf, and so forth.

This adult begins large-group time with "Run Around the Circle," an active singing game children can easily join as they finish eating their snack.

▶ **Have materials ready.**

Before the children arrive, draw messages on the message board, put the music you plan to use in or next to the player, gather the streamers you need for dancing and put them on a shelf near your large-group meeting place. Having materials gathered and ready ahead of time allows you to start large-group time as soon as children begin to gather.

Adults Set Large-Group Time in Motion: *The Beginning*

Here are some strategies for getting large-group time off to a smooth start.

▶ **Draw children to the group with a simple, easy-to-join activity.**

Plan to begin large-group time with an enjoyable activity children can easily join. This might be moving to a song such as "Run Around, Run Around, Run Around the Circle," or singing a favorite song, such as "Jingle Bells," "The Mud Song," "Row, Row, Row Your Boat," or doing an often-requested fingerplay such as the "Five Little Monkey" variations. By going to the large-group meeting spot and starting an activity, adults (and children) signal that large-group time has begun. When adults consistently start large-group time with an easy-to-join activity, children will begin to imitate the adults, as Vanessa did one day when she came to the circle first and began singing "Row, Row, Row Your Boat."

▶ **Start right away with the children who have gathered.**

This strategy minimizes delays for the children who arrive first and encourages children who are still busy with the previous activity (snack, small-group time, or hanging up their coats) to finish so they can join the fun. As you begin, do not worry about children who linger at the previous activity; they will participate more readily when they do arrive if they can join at their own pace. Some children, for example, find particular satisfaction in watching large-group time begin while they finish snack.

Adults Support Children's Ideas and Initiatives: *The Middle*

Once you begin a large-group experience and involve children in singing, moving, or storytelling, they will offer their own variations and modifications. Here are ways you can support children's ideas and initiatives at large-group time.

▶ *Briefly* **introduce the next experience.**

At the conclusion of the activity you have used to draw children to large-group time, go right on to the next experience you have planned. Give a *brief* explanation if one is needed:

• "I've got a new song with four motions. The first one is marching. See if you can do some marching."

• "When I put on the boing-boing music, you can move any way the music makes you want to move."

• "Today we have balls to take outside for shooting baskets."

▶ **Participate on the children's physical level.**

If the children are sitting on the floor, sit on the floor with them. If they decide to crawl to the music, crawl to the music along with them. If they are dancing around a Maypole, grab a streamer and join the dance. Being at the children's physical level gives you a better idea of what they are saying and seeing. Trying out their suggestions lets them know that you value their ideas and initiatives.

▶ **Turn props and materials over to children.**

When your large-group experience involves storytelling props, such as Little Red Riding Hood and wolf puppets, or materials, such as instruments, streamers, balls, potatoes, cloths, or rubber bands, get them into the children's hands as rapidly as possible. If adults are the only ones using props, or if you spend a long time passing them out, children will become distracted.

▶ **Watch and listen to children.**

This gives you an idea of how each child is making sense of the experience you have planned. During the "Pass the Potato" game, teachers Carole and Linda noticed that Joanie and Corey, two of their youngest children, did not pass their potatoes, although they passed along the potatoes that others passed to them. In musical carpet squares, their teachers recalled, Joanie and Corey were also the children who stayed on or next to their own squares the entire time.

Linda and Carole understood that keeping "their" possessions was still very important to Corey and Joanie and that both activities could accommodate their particular requirements.

Attending closely to children also gives you a clue about how they are fitting an experience into the context of their own lives. In the earlier example, when teachers Becki and Peter played the "Popcorn" music and Alana requested salt, they later heard LJ say "Give me some hot sauce," Nathan say "Give me some pepper," and Julia say "I need some cheese." They sprinkled on these toppings and were pleased at the range and flexibility of the children's thinking.

▶ **Follow up on children's suggestions and modifications.**

While adults plan for large-group time each day, they are also prepared to modify their plans to accommodate children's ideas. This is a way to support and encourage children's thinking, creativity, and initiative. Generally you can incorporate children's suggestions ("Let's do it again fast!" "I know! We all live in a yellow school bus!") into the activity you are already doing. Other times, children suggest favorite activities you have not planned for that day. ("Let's play that game where we pretend to be different animals." "Let's play that tree game again.") If there really is no time to accommodate children's suggestions, write them down on the message board to remind you and the children that you will do them the next day at large-group time. Flexibility is a hallmark for adults conducting large-group meetings with active learners.

▶ **Let children be the leaders.**

Children are quite able to stop and start the music for a game, tell a story, demonstrate a motion for others to try out, and suggest a song to sing. Being the leader puts children in the position of thinking clearly about what they are doing so other children can do it as well. And, the other children are usually very responsive to peer leaders.

Adults Bring Large-Group Time to a Close: *The End*

By planning large-group time ahead of time, adults can end the session with a transition to the next part of the daily routine.

▶ **Make the final large-group experience a transition to the next part of the daily routine.**

Before Sam, an adult, played the boing-boing music for the last time, he said, "This time, think of a way to move over to the coatrack so we can put on our coats for outside time." The children had been moving around the block area. Now they used the same music and movement ideas as a transition to outside time.

When teachers Beth and Becki sang "Yellow Submarine" with their children, they used the last variation ("We all live in a red choo-choo train") as a transition idea. "This time, think of a way you could drive your red choo-choo trains to outside

time," said Beth. After they pretended to be "tiny babies," Carole said to the children, "This time, pretend you have grown into crawling babies. When I put the music on, see how you can go like a baby to small-group time!"

▶ **Put materials away as part of the transition activity.**

After teachers Helena and Sarah played the scary music for flying ghosts, they put on a lullaby and asked the children to fly their ghosts to snack time and "put them to bed" in the "ghost basket" on their snack table. After "Jingle Bells" and several other songs with bells, Peter, an adult, asked the children to "jingle over to the door for outside time. You could put your bells in the box by the door." Linda and Carol had the children toss their potatoes into a basket and then move to small-group time like "hot potatoes."

During this transition at the end of a large-group time, children freeze into "statues" and the teacher uses a pat on the head to "unfreeze" them and send them one by one to the next activity.

Large-Group-Time Ideas

For additional large-group-time ideas, see these KDI chapters:

After a vigorous large-group time, this child is ready for a rest!

How Adults Support Children at Large-Group Time: A Summary

Adults examine their beliefs about how children learn at large-group times.

Adults plan large-group experiences ahead of time.
___ Plan around children's interests.
___ Plan around the music and the physical development KDIs.
___ Plan around cooperative play and projects.
___ Plan around events currently meaningful to the children.

Adults prepare for large-group time before children arrive.
___ Modify songs and games to fit children's development and specific events.
___ Practice ahead of time.
___ Have materials ready.

Adults set large-group time in motion: the beginning.
___ Draw children to the group with an easy-to-join activity.
___ Start right away with the children who have gathered.

Adults support children's ideas and initiatives: the middle.
___ *Briefly* introduce the next experience.
___ Participate on children's physical level.
___ Turn props and materials over to children.
___ Watch and listen to children.
___ Follow up on children's suggestions and modifications.
___ Let children be the leaders.

Adults bring large-group time to a close: the end.
___ Make the final large-group experience a transition to the next part of the daily routine.
___ Put materials away as part of the transition activity.

Understanding Outside Time

At outside time in a High/Scope program, children pursue active physical play with the support of attentive, playful adults. Adults and children alike enjoy the sights, sounds, and vigor of play and exploring on the playground, at a nearby park, or in a neighboring wood. To illustrate the dynamics of outside time, we have re-created a portion of an actual outside time from a High/Scope program.

"Mud, mud, we love mud," sing Julia, Andrew, and Jalessa, swinging together on the tire swing.

~

LJ and Nathan hit Wiffle balls with short plastic Wiffle bats. Becki, an adult, is their pitcher. Brianna picks up the third bat and joins "batting practice." "What a hit," Becki says. "That was right to me!"

~

Mikey, Audie, and Brian are riding tricycles and watching the pinwheels they have taped to the handlebars.
"Look, Beth," says Brian to the other adult on the playground, "they're turning!"
"I see," Beth calls from under the climber, where Kacey, Erica, and Chrysten have placed her "under a magic spell." They are playing "Aladdin and Genie."

~

Trey and Douglas fill buckets with pea gravel and dump them into Alana's wagon. "I got more stones," Alana calls to Sarah, who is on the climbing net. They are dropping the pea gravel through the cracks in the tree-house deck.

~

What Is Outside Time?

Outside time is a daily opportunity for children to engage in vigorous, noisy outdoor play. Children continue their indoor play in a more expansive setting, examine their natural surroundings, gain a sense of their immediate neighborhood, and experience changing weather conditions and seasons. Adults join children's play and gain a broader understanding of children's interests and abilities.

► Energetic outdoor play

Outside, children have room to run, jump, throw, swing, climb, dig, and ride. Their pretend play ranges all over the play area: under the slide, up the climbing net into the tree house, down the hill in the wagon, and over to the sandbox. They can be galloping horses or rocketship explorers. They have space to make big paintings and chalk drawings, weave streamers into the fence, pound nails into a tree stump, and make forts from big cardboard boxes.

► Opportunities for social play

Outdoor play often brings young children together. Large pieces of equipment, such as slides, climbers, and tree houses, have a socializing effect because they accommodate more than one child at a time. Children try to do what they see others doing—sliding backward, climbing up the cargo net, twirling on the trapeze. Sandboxes also draw children together for filling and emptying activities and all kinds of pretend play. Even bike riding and swinging seem to invite conversational exchanges. While children also play by themselves, an exclamation such as "Look what I found!" from a lone explorer can attract curious children playing nearby.

► An outdoor setting for learning

Many outdoor activities are described by KDIs: **language, literacy, and communication** ("I know; let's do different words to the mud song, Julia!"); **social and emotional development** ("I'm gonna take one more ride, then you can have my bike, okay, Mikey?"); **physical development** ("Run, Erica, she's going to get you!"); **seriation** ("We need the biggest one for our dirt"); **number** ("You need leaves! Two handsful!"); **space** ("Look, I'm going twisty"); **classification** ("This house is for cats. No people allowed!"); **time** ("Okay, when I wave the flag, you go"); **dramatic art** ("We're ninja guys; follow me 'cause I'm the leader"); and **music** ("We're hitting stones together for our parade drums"). They construct and test knowledge about the people and things in their immediate outdoor world.

Why Is Outside Time Important?

Outside time allows children to express themselves and exercise in ways that are generally not available to them in indoor play. Although children in active learning settings move throughout the day, once outside, they engage in more invigorating, noisy play.

► Healthy, unconstrained play

Children breathe fresh air, absorb vitamins from the sun, exercise their hearts, lungs, and muscles, and see broader vistas. Children who are quiet and shy inside often become more talkative and adventurous outside. Some children play with children outside whom they may not play with inside. And children who like to make noise feel free to do so outside.

At outside time, children pursue active physical play with the support of attentive, playful adults.

Outside Time—What, Why, Where: A Summary

What It Is
- Energetic outdoor play.
- Opportunities for social play.
- An outdoor setting for learning.

Why It Is Important
- Outdoor play is healthy and unconstrained.
- Children have contact with nature.
- Adults continue to learn about children.

Where to Play
- On a playground designed for young children.
- In a neighborhood park.

Where Children Play Outside

► On a playground designed for young children

In most cases, children in active learning settings play on a playground designed and equipped to meet their particular needs and interests. (See Chapter 5, pp. 144–145, for information on equipping the outdoor interest area.) In such an environment they are safe, secure, and stimulated to try things that suit their inclinations ("I'm going to swing!") and challenge their physical abilities ("Let's hang upside down from the net!").

► In a neighborhood park

When programs do not have playgrounds of their own, children often play in neighborhood parks, taking loose materials, bikes, and wagons along to supplement the equipment that is already there.

► Contact with nature

At outside time, children experience the natural world in ways that make sense to them. They collect flowers, leaves, and nuts. They see the sky darken as the sun goes behind a cloud. They watch the motions of insects, birds, and squirrels. They dig in the dirt, plant gardens, and turn over logs to find bugs. They hang wet things in the sun to dry, feel the wind, and see rain making puddles. They make observations, "This bug's carrying something," and draw conclusions, "He must be moving to a new house."

► An opportunity for adults to learn more about children

At outside time, adults observe, converse, and play with children to learn more about what children can do and what attracts their interest. For example, teachers noted that as their children planted and tended a garden, they became increasingly attuned to seasonal changes. "Look! It's a baby flower!" "This is bigger than me!" "The flowers are changing. They're turning brown!" "Look inside! Tiny seeds!"

What Children Do at Outside Time

At one outside time, Douglas plays by himself because his best friend is absent. He climbs to the top of the tire tree. "I just like to look around from up here," he remarks to Beth, one of his teachers. After a while, Douglas climbs almost all the way down and then jumps to the ground. He walks to the tire swing where Alana is swinging, balances on the ledge that surrounds the tire swing pit, walks around the ledge, hangs from the tire arm, and jumps down into the pea gravel. From here he makes his way to the Wiffle ball and bat.

Becki, his other teacher, pitches and he hits or throws the ball back to her. After batting, he moves onto the scooter, pushing himself swiftly with one foot, then balancing on both feet for the glide. Finally, he climbs up the cargo net, carefully placing each foot until he reaches the tree house. He climbs onto the deck and scoots down the tree-house stairs, holding on to the handrails for balance. "Hi, Daddy!" he calls, seeing his dad and little brother who have come to take him home.

To support children at outside time, it is important for adults to understand that children take on physical challenges and continue indoor types of play in a vigorous way.

► **Children play, converse, and solve problems they encounter.**

Children engage in *exploratory* play—digging, looking under logs for bugs, figuring out how to bounce balls, and hanging upside-down from the trapeze. They engage in *constructive* play—making a tire tower, decorating the sidewalk or fence, making a pile of leaves or snow—and in *pretend* play—making sand and stick "cakes," playing "monster," giving people "taxi" rides. They also invent

In a nearby park, these children play in a stream, collect pebbles, look for fish, and watch the sticks and leaves that float by.

What Children Do at Outside Time: A Summary

- Children play, converse, and solve problems they encounter.
- Children try out and practice pumping, pedaling, climbing, jumping, steering, throwing, hitting, and catching.

games such as toss and catch, galloping horses, and streamer parades. They play alone, in pairs, and in groups. They carry on conversations:

> *"Don't get in there."*
> *"Why not?"*
> *"There's a spider."*
> *"Let's put grass on the spider."*
> *"They like grass."*

And they solve problems they encounter, such as drying a wet climber, stopping the bikes before running into the fence, and carrying the tires up the slide.

► **Children try out and practice pumping, pedaling, climbing, jumping, steering, throwing, hitting, and catching.**

Children take on these challenges inspired by their access to climbers, swings, pedal toys, sleds, and balls, as well as natural features like hills, boulders, and tree stumps. They approach experiences on their own time at their own pace. For example, on the swings, Callie likes gentle pushes, Julia likes strong pushes, and Alana prefers to pump for herself. At the beginning of the year in one center, the children found the slight incline on their bike path too steep to ride down. However, over time and with daily bike-riding experiences, the incline gradually became a challenge of just the right size, and finally it became just another bike path: "I wish we had a big hill," one bike rider said in the spring.

How Adults Support Children at Outside Time

The adults' role at outside time is very similar to their work-time role. They focus all their attention on children to understand and support children's outdoor initiatives in a playful, non-managerial way. The following strategies help adults to do this:

- **Examining their beliefs about how children learn at outside time**
- **Helping children obtain the materials they need**
- **Using work-time support strategies**
- **Observing nature with children**
- **Bringing outside time to a close**

Adults Examine Their Beliefs About How Children Learn at Outside Time

Adults in an active learning setting understand that children construct knowledge through their own initiatives and interactions with people and materials both indoors and outdoors. Children's social, physical, and cognitive learning is not restricted to certain places or times.

To adopt an active learning approach, many adults must give up the idea that outside time is their time to relax, chat with other adults, stay inside to prepare for the next time period, or sit on a bench while children take care of themselves in "free play." Other adults who see the teacher as a "playground manager"—whose job when outdoors is to organize games, oversee turns, and solve conflicts—must also rethink their roles. Rather than leave children on their own or direct their activities, adults on a High/Scope team join in and support children's outdoor play. In fact, adults in an active learning setting look forward to outside time as an opportunity to continue working and conversing with children, and through these interactions, to learn more about children's interests and development. Adults approach outside time with good-natured enthusiasm and dress in clothing that allows them to be active—climbing, rolling, digging, and so forth.

Adults Help Children Obtain the Materials They Need

While swings, climbers, slides, and tree houses are permanently situated, other materials, such as bicycles, sandbox dishes and shovels, scarves, pinwheels, chalk, paints, hammers and nails, balls and bats, and wagons are usually stored in a protected storage area or shed. It is up to adults to devise ways of getting these materials in and out of the storage area on a daily basis so children have a rich variety of props and objects to inspire and support their outdoor play. Here are some ideas to consider:

- As a team, take loose materials outside before the children arrive. Include early-arriving children and parents as helpers in this task.

- Store loose materials in milk crates or baskets with handles that children can easily carry outside by themselves or in pairs.

- Involve children (and parents) in gathering up loose materials at the end of the day.

- Place locked storage containers around the playground—one for balls, bats, and ropes; one for sand toys; one for dress-up materials; and so on. Unlock the containers at the beginning of outside time and have children help with cleanup at the end of the session.

Adults Use Work-Time Support Strategies

Once children are outside with the materials they need, adults use the same support strategies as used at work time. These strategies are described in Chapter 7, pages 203–224, and are summarized below:

▶ **Adults participate in children's play.**

To support children's outdoor play, treat it with the same attention and respect you grant to children's indoor play at work time. Consider the following strategies.

Look for natural play openings. Observe children filling and emptying buckets at the sandbox, singing on the swings, playing rocketship play on the climber, chasing one another in a game of tree tag or hide-and-seek.

Join children's play at the children's levels. Slide with children on the slide, climb up and under the climber, roll down the hill, jump in the leaf pile.

Play in parallel with children. Fill and empty your own container with water or nuts, run with a pinwheel, jump over sticks.

Play as a partner with children. For example, you might play toss and catch with a child, join a streamer parade, or look at things from the top of the climber with a child who is already up there.

Outside time provides children with the opportunity to take on physical challenges they set for themselves, such as learning to pedal and pump.

Refer one player to another. When Robert asked his teacher, "How you do that?" she replied, "Ask Brandon. He's the one who wove all these streamers into the fence."

Suggest new ideas for ongoing play. Julia was playing Aladdin and Genie and had lost her "magic lamp," at which point her teacher made a suggestion:

Julia: *Where's my magic lamp. It's gone!*

Adult: *Genie, here's a magic lamp you could use.* (Hands her a stone.)

▶ **Adults converse with children.**

Children who are quiet inside often find lots to say at outside time.

Look for natural opportunities for conversation. Conversations often occur when children are engaged in repetitive play such as swinging, filling cups with sand, or digging in the garden. Sometimes, children will come up to you with a discovery to share: "Hey Beth, look at this!"

Join children at their level for conversation. Sit on the climbing net, under a tree, on the tire swing; stand on the slide ladder or wherever the children are.

Respond to children's conversational leads. This allows you to pursue the child's topic:

Child: (Digging) *My daddy has a shovel.*

Adult: *Your daddy likes to dig and so do you.*

Converse as a partner with children. Offer comments and observations so the child retains control of the conversation. Here is how the digging conversation continued:

Child: *I can get a lot of sand in my shovel.*

Adult: *Yes, you can.*

Child: *I can fill up this whole bucket . . . but it's going to take a lot of shovels.*

Adult: *Yeah, that's a pretty big bucket.*

Child: *We have a really big one at home. It's for horses.*

Adult: *I didn't know you had horses at your house.*

Child: *No. It's for my sister's horse at Karen's barn.*

Ask questions sparingly. Use occasional questions to clarify your understanding of the child's thinking:

Adult: *You mean your sister has a horse but it lives in Karen's barn?*

Child: *Yeah, lots of horses live there. But you have to go and feed 'em and stuff.*

▶ **Adults encourage children's problem solving.**

As children play outside, they encounter all kinds of problems to solve, such as how to keep the balls inside the tires while they are rolling and how to keep the "robot sticks" on their backs while running.

Encourage children to deal with problems and conflicting viewpoints. Rather than solving problems for children (for example, taking away the toy that several children want), encourage children to find a way to proceed. Working out a system for sharing the job of steering a taxi is as important as the task of learning how to steer.

Interact with children rather than manage them. Playing and conversing with children supports children's learning more effectively than

spending outside time "policing" the use of the bikes and the swings.

Calmly assist with unresolved conflicts. When children seek your assistance or seem to need your support, acknowledge their feelings, listen to their descriptions of the issue, and ask them for their ideas about what to do. Do as little of the talking as possible. They are the ones who need the experience of putting their own thoughts and feelings into words. For examples of solving outdoor problems, such as sharing bikes, drying the climber, and emptying sandy shoes, see pages 315–316 in Chapter 10.

Adults Observe Nature With Children

Several children are smelling, holding, looking at, and breaking apart seed pods they have discovered. Julie, an adult, joins them and begins breaking apart seed pods herself and listening to the children's conversation. They all continue to collect and study the pods for about 15 minutes.

෴

Adults like Julie remain alert to natural things that attract children's attention—bugs and spiders that cross their paths, worms they dig up in the garden, playground plants and animals that catch their eye, birds that fly

Adults play as partners with children—for example, tossing the ball to young batters and joining a weaving project.

overhead, puddles, the sound of the wind. Adults look for opportunities to join children as they observe, experiment with, and draw conclusions

Adults Bring Outside Time to a Close

Before the end of outside time, adults give children a warning so they have a chance to bring their play to a timely end. "Five more minutes till it's time to put the bikes and toys away and then go inside for lunch," Julie says to each group of players as she tours the playground.

Adults also engage children in gathering up and storing the loose balls, sand toys, streamers, bikes, wagons, and scooters. When the day ends with outside time, storing loose materials can be a leisurely activity for everyone—children, parents, and teachers.

Outdoors, this teacher observes and takes notes on children's development, just as she does indoors.

about nature and the physical world. For example, in even the most urban areas planting a garden of any size—an 8' × 12' plot on the playground, containers on the roof, milk crates (lined with plastic bags) in the sun, window boxes, hanging pots—draws children, adults, and nature together to dig, plant, weed, water, make mud, pick, smell, eat, and observe. Flowers attract butterflies. Trees and bushes are home to insects, birds, and squirrels. A water garden, watercourse, swamp, or wetland area provide children with plant and creature life to watch, sticks to float, water to enjoy, and stones and rocks to gather, examine, carry, and rearrange. Such experiences shared with supportive adults encourage children to love, appreciate, and care for the earth and living things.

How Adults Support Children at Transition Times*

Throughout the day in every early childhood setting, there are many transitions for children—when a parent drops a child off in the morning, when children and adults walk down the hall on their way to the playground, when a small group of children stops recalling and starts eating their snacks. At these times, children experience one or more changes—of activity, location, caregiver, or playmates. Adults may think of these changeover times as incidental parts of their routine, but they are crucial events for

*This section (pp. 288–292) was written by High/Scope consultant and teacher Becki Perrett. It first appeared in a slightly different version in the High/Scope Extensions *curriculum newsletter, October 1992.*

children, who often react strongly to them: "I want my mommy!" "I don't want to clean up!" Well-planned transitions are often the difference between a difficult day and one that goes smoothly for both children and adults.

Adults Adjust Transition Times to Suit Children's Developmental Needs

To ease transition times for children, start by thinking about the preschooler's need for active learning and for a climate of support. Consider ways to adjust transition times to fulfill these needs.

▶ **Establish a consistent daily routine.**

Transitions go more smoothly for children when they are familiar with the daily routine and can prepare themselves for what comes next. A consistent daily routine not only helps children feel secure but also assures children, as they make the transition from one part of the routine to the next, that there will be time again tomorrow to continue their play.

▶ **Keep to a minimum the number of transitions between activities, places, and caregivers.**

In discussing the daily routine as a team, ask yourselves the following questions: Are there too many transitions? Can we coordinate our daily routine so there are fewer changes and smoother transitions? For example, adults in one Head Start program reduce the number of transitions in their day by having children plan individually as they finish breakfast, instead of regrouping children in another location to make their plans. In this program, an adult asks for each

child's plan at the breakfast table, as soon as the child has finished eating. Then the child moves directly into work time. This way, children make only one shift in location (from the breakfast table to the chosen play area) instead of two (from the breakfast table to the planning table to the play area). And, children do not have to wait for others to finish eating before they can make their plans. As this example shows, reducing the number of changes children have to make and eliminating waiting time are key principles for planning successful transitions.

▶ **Start new activities right away.**

At the beginning of small-group or large-group times, for example, children can become distracted if they have to wait—as the teacher prepares materials or as all the children gather. Therefore, it makes sense to start a new activity even if all the children are not finished with the one before it. At the High/Scope Demonstration Preschool one year, large-group time followed snack time. The children were assigned to two groups for snack, one group with each teacher. Children moved to the large-group meeting place one by one as they finished eating. As soon as a few children had gathered, the adult designated to lead the large-group activity that day would join them and start right in with a song, active game, or fingerplay. This way, adults did not have to tell children, "Let's wait until everyone is finished eating."

▶ **When waiting time cannot be avoided, plan ways to keep children actively involved.**

Waiting time can be reduced, but it cannot always be eliminated. If children have to wait for the school bus at the end of the day, plan to use this time with them for singing songs, learning

fingerplays, and talking or reading books together. Remember that children of this age do not like to sit still and keep quiet.

▶ **Plan enjoyable ways for groups of children to move from place to place.**

Keeping children mentally and physically active when they have to walk from place to place makes these transitions pleasant for children and adults. Instead of asking children to walk quietly, single-file, with their hands at their sides, encourage them to move in creative ways: "Which animal can we move like as we walk down the hall to the bathroom?" (Each child chooses an animal to imitate.) For further discussion of this topic, refer to Chapter 2, pages 64–65.

Adults Plan for Transitions With Individual Children in Mind

The strategies just described usually make transitions go smoothly for the group as a whole. There may be some children, however, for whom transitions are particularly stressful. These children may find it difficult to get involved in cleaning up after work time, resist leaving the playground when everyone else is going inside, or "hide" under the table at the beginning of small-group time. As you develop strategies for these children, it is especially important to keep in mind two of the ingredients of active learning—*choices* and *adult scaffolding*.

▶ **Decide where to position adults during transition times.**

During daily team planning, decide where adults can best position themselves as children change from one part of the routine to the next. At times, it may be helpful to designate a team member to assist a particular child. For example, if Jessica has trouble getting started with cleanup, choose an adult to be near her at the end of work time.

▶ **Offer appropriate choices to individual children before a transition.**

Choices may help children focus on a particular action they can take during an upcoming transition. Here are two examples:

"Mikey, when you finish your snack, it will be large-group time. Is there someone you want to sit next to when we sing?"

"Chelsea, it is almost time to go inside. Show me how you are going to move to get to the door."

▶ **Alert children to the upcoming change.**

If the end of work time or some other part of the routine is near and a child shows no sign of completing his or her activity, alert the child to the upcoming change. At the same time, give the child some control in deciding what to do. Here is an example:

"Deola, work time is almost over. When you finish the face on your drawing, it will be time to clean up. (Pause. Deola quickens the pace on her drawing.) *Where can you put your drawing so you can finish it tomorrow?"*

Changeover times are crucial events for children. Well-planned, comfortable transitions can make the difference between a difficult day and one that goes smoothly for children.

Adults Plan for Cleanup, the Longest Transition

Cleanup time is often the longest transition of the day. Further, cleaning up is an emotional issue for many adults who judge themselves by how clean and orderly their homes are. Teaching teams, too, may measure the day's success by how smoothly cleanup time goes. Following are strategies that can help adults relax in the face of this potentially stressful time.

▶ **Maintain realistic expectations of children.**

Cleanup is an adult-initiated activity; yet a child's need at cleanup is often to continue to play. Though we as adults may hate to clean, we expect children to clean up willingly and are surprised when this does not happen.

While it is natural for children to resist cleaning up, cleanup is a valuable learning experience. As they put toys and materials away, children are developing self-help skills and a sense of responsibility for their environment. In addition, they are engaging in many activities that are KDIs. For example, they are *sorting and matching* (a **classification** KDI) as they sort spoons from forks and place the utensils on the shelves; they are *pretending and role playing* (a **dramatic art** KDI) as they pretend to be airline pilots "flying" the toys to their boxes.

► **Label containers and shelves to indicate where materials are stored.**

Cleaning up is a lot easier if adults and children know where materials belong. Therefore, it makes sense to label shelves and containers with developmentally appropriate labels. Use *concrete labels*—the actual objects taped to the sides of their containers (for example, a Lego block); *pictures of the materials*—drawings, catalog pictures, photocopies, or photos taped to the containers or shelves; and *tracings*—outlines of objects taped to the exact places where the objects go on shelves, pegboards, or racks. (Chapter 5 contains more information on arranging and equipping your classroom or center.)

► **When possible, clean up throughout work time.**

Encourage children to put away the materials they are using before they start a new activity: "Tiffany, you're done playing in the house area. Let's put away the dishes and then you can tell me your next plan." This strategy reduces classroom clutter, making it easier for children to see the choices available to them. And there is less to do later at cleanup time if children pick up as they go along. There are occasions, however, when it is not appropriate for children to clean up immediately after they finish doing something. For example, if five children have built a stage out of blocks for a concert and one of them decides to paint, the block stage should be left out for the other children to use. Deciding if and when children should be expected to "clean as you go" is an issue for the teaching team to resolve through discussion. Further, encouraging children to put toys away throughout work time should not take precedence over playing and conversing with children and supporting problem solving.

► **Follow children's interests at cleanup time.**

Use what you know about individual children and build on it. If Petey loves to pretend he is a basketball star, hold out the trash can and encourage him to shoot baskets with paper scraps and other litter. Another way to follow children's interests at cleanup time is to **extend on their work-time activities.** If children are pretending to be "dogs" during work time, encourage the dogs to clean up: "Doggie Ben [hand the child a toy], here is a bone for you to put away." You might follow this by saying "Can *you* find another bone to put away?"

► **Remain flexible.**

Just because cleanup (or some other transition) is not going as smoothly as it might does not mean it cannot result in a worthwhile experience for children. (See "Ready or Not!" Cleanup-Time Games on p. 292 for more strategies for making cleanup an effective learning experience for children.)

Nevertheless, dealing with children's approaches to cleanup can push adults to the limits of their patience. We offer the following two vignettes of cleanup times from the High/Scope Demonstration Preschool to show how adults can respond calmly to unexpected cleanup-time situations, helping children to learn about the natural consequences of their actions.

Responding to the Unexpected

During one day's cleanup time, Sam, a teacher, asked three children to wash paintbrushes. They took the brushes into the bathroom, and Sam got involved with several other children putting blocks away. Shortly afterward, a child ran to Sam, reporting, "The kids are painting the bathroom!"

Sam walked into the bathroom. The children had indeed painted the toilets and the linoleum walls with red, green, and blue paint. Resisting the temptation to get angry, Sam calmly asked the children what had happened. "We're painting just like my dad does at home," Max said. Sam asked the children what they needed to do and several answered, "Clean up the bathroom." Sam found sponges and the children washed off all the paint.

Later, at their daily planning session, Sam and Becki decided to support the children's interest in painting by making large paintbrushes and buckets of water available at outside time the next day. They also decided to confine paintbrush-washing to the sink in the art area to help limit the temptation for children to paint the bathroom walls.

The next day, the children enjoyed painting with water—they painted the climber, the sidewalk, and the building. They never again tried to paint the bathroom.

One day near the beginning of the school year, Kenneth decided it might be fun to make a pile of toys in the house area. The idea

was contagious, and soon a small group of children were pulling toys off the shelves and adding them to the rapidly growing pile.

When it came time to clean up, Beth reminded the children that it was their job to put the pile of toys away. It took 45 minutes for the children who had made the pile to put the toys in their places. The teachers supported them throughout this process, using all the active learning strategies they could muster to help keep them involved in their task.

The next day, the teachers overheard Petey asking Kenneth if he wanted to make a pile again. "No way!" Kenneth replied. "If we dump out all these toys, we'll be cleaning up forever!"

In both these situations, which occurred early in the school year, children were "testing the boundaries" of appropriate behavior by making bigger-than-usual messes. However, in both cases adults resisted the temptation to scold children. Instead, they stepped back and looked for ways to turn the situations into active learning experiences with a lasting impact. Instead of squelching children's initiative, they built on it, but still made it clear they expected the children to clean up after themselves. These cleanup experiences gave children opportunities to learn about the natural consequences of their actions.

In this section we have presented ideas for smoothing transition times for children. You have probably noted that we approach transitions with the same general teaching approach we use during other parts of the daily routine. During transitions, just as at work time or small-group time, **remember to use the principles of active learning and the elements of support, and to build on children's interests.**

"Ready or Not!" Cleanup-Time Games

Once cleanup has begun, **look for ways to make the process active and enjoyable** for children. Here are some ideas to try:

• **Imitation.** Sometimes children enjoy carrying toys in unique ways. If you see a child carrying something behind his or her back, try imitating the child as you carry a toy to its place on the shelf. This will probably catch the attention of other children who will then imitate what they see the two of you doing.

• **Beat the clock!** Encourage children to clean up an area quickly before the sand in the sand timer runs all the way to the bottom, the timer (set for three to five minutes) rings, or the big hand on the clock gets to the four.

• **Paper bag.** Give each child a lunch sack or grocery bag. Ask the children to move around the room, filling up their bags with toys that are out. When the bags are full, ask them to return the toys to their places in the room.

• **Football game.** One adult pretends to be a football player, "hiking" a toy between her legs to a child behind her. The child then puts that toy away and returns for another one. Children will often line up behind the adult to play this game.

• **Statues.** Play music as children clean up, stopping the music occasionally. When the music stops, children pose as statues, resuming cleanup when the music begins again.

• **Music cleanup.** Music can be used in a variety of other ways during cleanup. For example, sing a cleanup song, with or without children's names in it. It is also fun to play selections at different tempos as children put things away—ask children to match their pace to the music, speeding up or slowing down as the music changes. Another idea is to put a familiar song in the CD player and ask children to clean up the room before the song is over.

These suggestions are intended merely as examples—-the same principles of adult support and active learning can be used in many other ways at cleanup time. Use these strategies as a starting point for brainstorming ideas of your own.

Sometimes at the end of work time, the biggest job is cleaning up yourself!

How Adults Support Children at Transition Times: A Summary

Adults adjust transitions to suit children's developmental needs.

___ Establish a consistent daily routine.

___ Keep the *number* of transitions between activities, places, and caregivers to a minimum.

___ Start new activities right away.

___ When waiting cannot be avoided, plan ways to keep children actively involved.

___ Plan enjoyable ways for groups of children to move from place to place.

Adults plan for transitions with individual children in mind.

___ Decide where to position adults during transition times.

___ Offer appropriate choices to individual children before a transition.

___ Alert children to the upcoming change.

Adults plan for cleanup, the longest transition.

___ Maintain realistic expectations of children.

___ Label containers and shelves to indicate where materials are stored.

___ When possible, clean up throughout work time.

___ Follow children's interests at cleanup time.

___ Remain flexible.

References

DeVries, Rheta, and Lawrence Kohlberg. 1987. *Programs of Early Education.* New York: Longman.

Garland, Caroline, and Stephanie White. 1980. *Children and Day Nurseries.* Ypsilanti, MI: High/Scope Press.

Perrett, Becki. 1992. "Shifting Gears Smoothly: Making the Most of Transition Times." *High/Scope Extensions* (October): 1–3.

Rhythmically Moving 1–9. 1982–88. Series of musical recordings, available on cassettes, or CDs (Phyllis S. Weikart, creative director). Ypsilanti, MI: High/Scope Press.

Zehnder, Becki. 1991. "Group Times: What Makes Them Work." *High/Scope Extensions* (October): 1–3.

Related Reading

Ansbach, Ursula. 2001. "Beyond the Blue Horizon: Promoting Outdoor Experiences." In *Supporting Young Learners 3: Ideas for Child Care Providers and Teachers,* Nancy A. Brickman, ed., 167–74. Ypsilanti, MI: High/Scope Press.

Boisvert, Christine, and Suzanne Gainsley. 2006. *Teacher's Idea Book: 50 Large-Group Activities for Active Learners.* Ypsilanti, MI 48198.

Brickman, Nancy A., ed. 1996. "Designing Routines for Active Learners." Chap. 2 in *Supporting Young Learners 2,* 57–114. Ypsilanti, MI: High/Scope Press.

Epstein, Ann S. 2007. "Group Times." In *Essentials of Active Learning in Preschool: Getting to Know the High/Scope Curriculum,* 67–79. Ypsilanti, MI: High/Scope Press.

Epstein, Ann S., and Suzanne Gainsley. 2005. *Teacher's Idea Book: "I'm Older Than You. I'm Five!" Math in the Preschool Classroom.* Ypsilanti, MI: High/Scope Press.

Evans, Betsy. 2005. "'Bye Mommy! Bye Daddy!' — Easing Separations for Preschoolers." In *Supporting Young Learners 4: Ideas for Child Care Providers and Teachers,* Nancy A. Brickman, Holly Barton, and Jennifer Burd, eds., 49–57. Ypsilanti, MI: High/Scope Press.

Evans, Betsy. 2007. *Teacher's Idea Book: "I Know What's Next!" Preschool Transitions Without Tears or Turmoil.* Ypsilanti, MI: High/Scope Press.

Graves, Michelle. 1997. *100 Small-Group Experiences: The Teacher's Idea Book 3.* Ypsilanti, MI: High/Scope Press.

Haraksin-Probst, Lizabeth, Janet Hutson-Brandhagen, and Phyllis S. Weikart. 2008. *Making Connections: Movement, Music, & Literacy.* Ypsilanti, MI: High/Scope Press.

High/Scope Educational Research Foundation. 2003. *Preschool Program Quality Assessment (PQA),* 2nd ed. Ypsilanti, MI: High/Scope Press.

Post, Jacalyn, and Mary Hohmann. 2000. "Establishing Schedules and Routines for Infants and Toddlers." Chap. 4 in *Tender Care and Early Learning: Supporting Infants and Toddlers in Child Care Settings,* 190–293. Ypsilanti, MI: High/Scope Press.

Rivkin, Mary S. 1995. *The Great Outdoors: Restoring Children's Right to Play Outside.* Washington, DC: NAEYC.

Theemes, Tracy. 1999. *Let's Go Outside! Designing the Early Childhood Playground.* Ypsilanti, MI: High/Scope Press.

Weikart, Phyllis S. 2003. *Movement in Steady Beat,* 2nd ed. Ypsilanti, MI: High/Scope Press.

Weikart, Phyllis S. 2004. *Movement Plus Music: Activities for Children Ages 3 to 7,* 3rd ed. Ypsilanti, MI: High/Scope Press.

Weikart, Phyllis S. 1997. *Movement Plus Rhymes, Songs, & Singing Games,* 2nd ed. Ypsilanti, MI: High/Scope Press.

Related Media

The following materials are available from the High/Scope Press, 600 N. River St., Ypsilanti, MI 48198-2898; to order, visit *www.highscope.org,* or call 1-800-40-PRESS.

Small-Group Times for Active Learners. 2007. Color videotape or DVD, 42 min.

Large-Group Times for Active Learners. 2006. Color videotape or DVD, 53 min.

Part 3

Curriculum Content in Early Childhood Development

The key developmental indicators (KDIs) help adults identify ongoing opportunities for learning—about investigating the properties of glue and Play-Doh and cooking "blueberry pancakes"; about "setting and styling" hair, writing a "secret message," and making a pattern with a hole punch and paper; about making friends and playing together. The indicators describe the kinds of discoveries young children make as they strive through their own actions to make sense of their world.

9

Introduction to High/Scope's Curriculum Content

What are young children like? What kinds of play experiences and activities do they seek out, no matter where they live? How do they make discoveries and achieve an understanding of their world? What kinds of support do they need to grow and prosper? As early childhood educators, our answers to these questions are embodied in the High/Scope curriculum's "content areas" and "key developmental indicators" (KDIs; Epstein 2007). These guideposts define both our *beliefs* about how children develop and the *actions* we must take to support that development.

High/Scope is a comprehensive curriculum model—it addresses all areas of development. In the High/Scope Curriculum the *content* of children's learning is organized into five major divisions that parallel the five dimensions of school readiness identified by the National Education Goals Panel (NEGP; Kagan et al. 1995) and widely accepted as the standard in the early childhood community. High/Scope's five categories are **approaches to learning; language, literacy, and communication; social and emotional development; physical development, health, and well-being;** and **arts and sciences.** High/Scope further subdivides **arts and sciences** into the subjects of **mathematics; science and technology; social studies;** and the **arts.** *Note:* The National Education Goals Panel uses slightly different wording to label the second, fourth, and fifth dimensions, namely: **language and communication; physical well-being and motor development;** and **cognition and general knowledge.**

The NEGP emphasizes that these five dimensions are related to one another; that is, a child's development in one area affects his or her growth in all the others. Therefore, all five dimensions are equally significant. It is also important to note that children's development varies widely within each age range. No two preschoolers are alike, and any individual child may be more or less advanced in each area. The objective of early childhood programs is to provide the kinds of experiences that support and nurture all these areas of learning and development in every child. High/Scope agrees with all these points and therefore finds the Panel's readiness model appropriate for organizing its own curriculum as well as for formulating the standards adopted by many states and school districts.

High/Scope further sees development as taking place in all five areas *throughout life.* That is, individuals continue to learn from infancy through adulthood when they actively engage with objects, people, events, and ideas. The early childhood "readiness" framework thus applies equally well to the Foundation's work with elementary-age students, youth, and training for adults. Readiness to learn, extended into youth and adulthood, becomes readiness to work. It is a widely held notion in early childhood that children learn through play and that play is a child's work. Adults also learn through playful exploration of ideas, and they work most effectively when they integrate and apply all the areas of their knowledge. High/Scope thus sees play, learning, and work as recurring along a lifelong continuum of personal and professional development.

KDIs—Guideposts for Child Development

Within each of the readiness content areas, High/Scope identifies **key developmental indicators** (formerly called "key experiences") that are appropriate to each age range. (See the list on p. 299). KDIs are the building blocks of thinking and reasoning at each stage

All children, not simply some, are entitled to early experiences that will foster their optimal development.

—National Education Goals Panel, 1995

of development. They pave the way for later schooling and eventual entry into the adult world. In terms of the two major types of learning objectives used by many educational theorists, these indicators include both "knowledge" and the application of this knowledge in "thinking." For example, preschoolers need to know color names (knowledge) in order to describe objects they sort (thinking) by color. (For further information on these terms, see *Designing a New Taxonomy of Educational Objectives*, Robert Marzano, 2001.) Now let's take a look at the components of the term *key developmental indicators*.

The word *key* refers to the fact that these are the meaningful ideas children should learn and experience. High/Scope acknowledges that young children need to master a wide range of specific knowledge and thinking skills—the list could be almost endless in scope and detail. To keep the list manageable, the content captured in the individual KDIs stresses the broader areas of knowledge and skills that lay the foundation for further learning.

The second part of the term, *developmental,* conveys the idea that learning is gradual and cumulative. Learning follows a sequence, generally moving from simple to more complex knowledge and skills. Moreover, *developmental* emphasizes that it is inappropriate, not to mention futile, to expect preschoolers to behave and learn as kindergarten or first-grade students do. Whatever level we are addressing, from infancy through youth, the curriculum must be consistent with what we know about human development in that age range.

Finally, *indicators* was chosen to emphasize that educators need evidence that children are developing the knowledge, skills, and understanding considered important for school and life readiness. To plan appropriately for students and to evaluate program effectiveness, we need

*In High/Scope's approach to curriculum content, the emphasis is on what children **can do and are doing,** such as whistling and shoveling—that is, on children exercising their abilities in varied contexts with interesting materials.*

observable indicators of our impact on children. Further, by defining these child outcomes in measurable terms, we can develop assessment tools that are consistent with the curriculum. In other words, the assessment system "indicates" whether the program is meeting its goals.

The continuity across content areas and KDIs allows for the fact that development occurs along a continuum and children of different ages and abilities cannot be pigeonholed into a single age-based category. This book focuses on the 58 KDIs that make up the High/Scope Curriculum's content for preschoolers, that is, children aged 3 to 5. However, children in this age range may exhibit behaviors characteristic of older toddlers or early elementary students. Hence, the preschool

indicators were developed with the entire early childhood spectrum from infancy to age 8 in mind. Furthermore, children with special needs can fall at different points along the continuum, without regard to age, so this flexible system for organizing content helps practitioners understand and plan for their development.

For children to learn the content contained in the KDIs, it is not enough for adults to simply pass along information. Children must experience the world firsthand. Adults can then support and help extend children's thinking, scaffolding their learning as the children progress to each new level of insight and knowledge. Moreover, true learning takes time and repeated exposure. It is not a one-shot affair.

The High/Scope KDIs are based on the latest child development research and decades of classroom practice. They are periodically updated as early childhood research reveals more about how preschoolers learn and how adults best support their development. To give an example, emerging statistics on the prevalence of childhood obesity is causing a reevaluation of how to promote healthy physical development in young children. As information accumulates in this and other areas, High/Scope will revise its content accordingly in future publications.

The KDIs are also written to be universal. Teachers and caregivers from different cultures in the United States and countries all over the world report that they see children engaging in these developmentally important behaviors. Researchers confirm these commonalities among children of all backgrounds. For example, children everywhere sort objects into containers and take things apart and put them together. The exact materials used may vary from culture to culture, but the activity and the resulting learning about the nature of things is essentially the same.

High/Scope Preschool Curriculum Content

Approaches to Learning
- Making and expressing choices, plans, and decisions
- Solving problems encountered in play

Language, Literacy, and Communication
- Talking with others about personally meaningful experiences
- Describing objects, events, and relations
- Having fun with language: listening to stories and poems, making up stories and rhymes
- Writing in various ways: drawing, scribbling, and using letterlike forms, invented spelling, and conventional forms
- Reading in various ways: reading storybooks, signs and symbols, and one's own writing
- Dictating stories

Social and Emotional Development
- Taking care of one's own needs
- Expressing feelings in words
- Building relationships with children and adults
- Creating and experiencing collaborative play
- Dealing with social conflict

Physical Development, Health, and Well-Being
- Moving in nonlocomotor ways (anchored movement: bending, twisting, rocking, swinging one's arms)
- Moving in locomotor ways (nonanchored movement: running, jumping, hopping, skipping, marching, climbing)
- Moving with objects
- Expressing creativity in movement
- Describing movement
- Acting upon movement directions
- Feeling and expressing steady beat
- Moving in sequences to a common beat

Arts and Sciences

Mathematics

Seriation
- Comparing attributes (longer/shorter, bigger/smaller)
- Arranging several things one after another in a series or pattern and describing the relationships (big/bigger/biggest, red/blue/red/blue)
- Fitting one ordered set of objects to another through trial and error (small cup and small saucer; medium cup and medium saucer; big cup and big saucer)

Number
- Comparing the numbers of things in two sets to determine "more," "fewer," "same number"
- Arranging two sets of objects in one-to-one correspondence
- Counting objects

Space
- Filling and emptying
- Fitting things together and taking them apart
- Changing the shape and arrangement of objects (wrapping, twisting, stretching, stacking, enclosing)
- Observing people, places, and things from different spatial viewpoints
- Experiencing and describing positions, directions, and distances in the play space, building, and neighborhood
- Interpreting spatial relations in drawings, pictures, and photographs

> **Key developmental indicators (KDIs)** are the building blocks of thinking and reasoning at each stage of development. High/Scope identifies 58 preschool KDIs organized under five content areas.

Science and Technology

Classification
- Recognizing objects by sight, sound, touch, taste, and smell
- Exploring and describing similarities, differences, and the attributes of things
- Distinguishing and describing shapes
- Sorting and matching
- Using and describing something in several ways
- Holding more than one attribute in mind at a time
- Distinguishing between "some" and "all"
- Describing characteristics something does not possess or what class it does not belong to

Time
- Starting and stopping an action on signal
- Experiencing and describing rates of movement
- Experiencing and comparing time intervals
- Anticipating, remembering, and describing sequences of events

Social Studies
- Participating in group routines
- Being sensitive to the feelings, interests, and needs of others

The Arts

Visual Art
- Relating models, pictures, and photographs to real places and things
- Making models out of clay, blocks, and other materials
- Drawing and painting

Dramatic Art
- Imitating actions and sounds
- Pretending and role playing

Music
- Moving to music
- Exploring and identifying sounds
- Exploring the singing voice
- Developing melody
- Singing songs
- Playing simple musical instruments

Teachers use the KDIs to guide all aspects of their program. They set up the classroom, plan the day, observe children and extend their thinking, and measure children's progress based on the general principles of active learning and the specific content in the indicators. Part 3 of this book presents an in-depth look at the KDIs in all areas of children's learning and explains the thoughtful and practical strategies High/Scope teachers use to promote them.

This chapter provides an overview of the KDIs. We examine them from several perspectives: how they have been derived; how they are organized; why they are important; how they relate to active learning, the learning environment, and the daily routine; and how adults use them as they work with children. More detailed examinations are presented in Chapters 10–22. These chapters look in turn at specific KDIs in major content groupings: **approaches to learning; language, literacy, and communication; social and emotional development; physical development, health, and well-being; mathematics: seriation; mathematics: number; mathematics: space; science and technology: classification; science and technology: time; social studies; arts: visual art; arts: dramatic art; and arts: music.**

The Evolution of High/Scope's Content Areas and KDIs

High/Scope's curriculum content areas and KDIs in early childhood development have been derived from the close observations of children by educational psychologists and early childhood practitioners and from the theories

formed through these observations. As they worked with and observed young children, High/Scope staff members tried out and modified their teaching plans and support strategies in light of ongoing experience, while simultaneously building an educational approach around a core theory (see Phillips 1975). These efforts have resulted in a more complete understanding of how children construct knowledge as they develop in early childhood and how adults can provide optimal support for children in this period of development.

The current list of KDIs, then, has evolved over the last 30 years through the integration of child development theory and the observations and experiences of teachers and others actually conducting programs with children (see Weikart 1974). The process of development can be divided into five phases, which are described next.

Phase 1: Starting With Levels and Content Areas

The High/Scope educational approach took shape through the High/Scope Perry Preschool Project (1962–1967) and the High/Scope Curriculum Demonstration Project (1967–1970). In these projects, an early version of the High/Scope approach, the *Cognitively Oriented Curriculum*, was developed and studied. The teaching teams, support staff, and researchers in these early settings organized their observations, interactions, and plans for children around three major concepts: the "levels of representation" (object, index, symbol, and sign levels); the "content areas" (classification, seriation, spatial relations, and temporal relations); and the "levels of operation" (motoric and verbal) (Weikart et al. 1971,

pp. 13–36).[*] These concepts helped adults "tune in" to the young child's way of looking at the world (Silverman and Weikart 1974, p. 17). They evolved from Piaget's description of the emerging abilities of preschool children (Banet 1976) and the discussion of Piaget's work by other developmentalists, including David Elkind (1974), John Flavell (1963), Irving Sigel and Frank Hooper (1968), Adrien Pinard and Monique Laurendeau (1969), and J. McVicker Hunt (1961).

Phase 2: Moving to Goal Sequences

In the early 1970s, as High/Scope staff became involved in program dissemination and training, they began reorganizing and expanding the levels of representation, content areas, and levels of operation into *goal sequences*—one sequence for preschoolers and another sequence for children in early elementary school. However, the term "goal sequences" did not serve well, because the "goals" being described—for example, sorting and matching, comparing along a single dimension, talking with others about personally meaningful experiences—were not goals and objectives that adults could readily teach children. Rather, as elements of development, they were among the least teachable aspects of learning. Also, the term "sequences," while distinguishing preschool development from the development of older children, implied that one goal led to another in stepwise fashion, when often this was not the case. Furthermore, it became clear

---

For a complete history of these projects, see Weikart et al. 1970; Weikart et al. 1978a; Schweinhart and Weikart 1980; Berrueta-Clement et al. 1984; Schweinhart et al. 1993; Weikart et al. 1978b; Schweinhart et al. 1988; and Schweinhart et al. 2005.

Filling and emptying, a space KDI, was added to the curriculum in 1995 in recognition of the satisfaction preschool-aged children derive from this activity.

that in a developmental approach it was not possible simply to define specific learning objectives and then plan a sequence of activities to teach each one in the listed order. No matter how well researched or "average" such ordering might be, it could not account for the uniqueness of each child's pattern of interests and strengths (C. Hohmann 1991).

Phase 3: Discovering "Key Experiences"

During the 1970s, it became clear to High/Scope staff members that what they were describing, organizing, introducing, and supporting were important **experiences** children sought out and needed to have over and over again with a variety of materials so they could construct their own understanding of the world. Thus, the term **"key"** *(essential)* **"experiences"** *(participatory, ongoing interactions)* was formulated. The evolution in terminology—from "levels and content areas," to

"goal sequences," to "key experiences"—reflected the staff's desire to make the child development principles behind the High/Scope approach as understandable as possible for practitioners. Staff also wanted to help shift the focus away from what children *could not do* (**goals**) toward what children *could do* and *were doing* (**experiences**). In adopting the term "key experiences," High/Scope staff placed the emphasis on children exercising their thinking abilities in varied contexts with new materials and challenging situations rather than on precisely timed interventions aimed at moving children from one level of development to the next (C. Hohmann 1991).

Once the concept of key experiences was clarified, staff members began to develop lists of key experiences for major areas of child development, such as language and spatial relations. For each major category, staff wanted a list that was short enough for adults to keep in mind when working directly with children, yet broad enough to embrace the full range of important learning experiences in each category

as well as to accommodate each child's preferences and level of functioning.

After having been used and circulated for several years in a variety of formats, the first key experiences were formally published (Banet 1976). These first key experiences were organized under the following major headings: active learning, experiencing and representing, language, classification, seriation, number concepts, temporal relations, and spatial relations. "Active learning" appeared at the top of the list because it was considered fundamental to all other key experiences. That is, all preschool experiences are built on the child's direct interaction with materials, people, and events, because *action* is the young child's preferred mode of learning as opposed to *mediated experiences* conveyed through words or pictures. "Experiencing and representing" and "language" were listed next because they were seen as the means of extending active learning experiences associated with classification, seriation, number, time, and space into the realm of *representation*—that is, one step away from direct interaction with objects and people and toward abstract thinking.

Phase 4: Expanding and Revising the Key Experiences

From the mid-1980s to the publication of the first edition of this volume—as the High/Scope approach spread through various High/Scope training projects—it became clear that the existing key experiences provided a useful but incomplete picture of child development. Advice from the field suggested that the early key experiences understated the importance High/Scope trainers and practitioners placed on *social learning and development*. Thus, the **initiative and social relations** key experience categories were developed in response to these concerns (see M. Hohmann 1991). The **initiative and social relations** key experiences presented in the first two editions were derived from the first set of *active learning* key experiences and also incorporated new key experiences derived from the work of Jean Piaget (1966, and Barbel Inhelder 1969), Erik Erikson (1950), John Bowlby (1969), Sherri Oden (1988), Howard Gardner (1983), Sara Smilansky (1968), and Stanley and Nancy Greenspan (1985). In addition, several **movement** key experiences (first published in P. Weikart 1987) and preschool **music** key experiences developed from the work of Elizabeth Carlton and Phyllis Weikart (1994) were added.

Also during this phase, High/Scope staff removed "active learning" from the formal key experience list to distinguish it as the most basic element of the High/Scope educational approach. In addition, two of the original active learning key experiences, *making choices and decisions* and *taking care of one's own needs*, were incorporated under the **initiative and social relations** key experience category.

The High/Scope key experiences were now organized under the headings of **creative representation; language and literacy; initiative and social relations; movement; music; classification** (working with similarities and differences); **seriation** (creating series and patterns); **number; space;** and **time.** The changes in the names of some of these headings—for example, from **experiencing and representing** to **creative representation**—reflected the common usage that had evolved among trainers and practitioners in the field.

Several other new key experiences also appeared in the first edition of this book. Under **language and literacy**, we added *writing in various ways: drawing, scribbling, and using letterlike forms, invented spelling, and conventional forms,* and *reading in various ways: reading storybooks, signs, symbols, and one's own writing*. These additions reflected a growing understanding of the emergence of literacy in young children. Under the **space** category, *filling and emptying* was added in recognition of the attraction this action holds for many young children even after the toddler years.

Further, many of the original **time** key experiences were combined in the first edition to reduce the number of experiences under this heading and thus de-emphasize the overall importance of time, which remains quite an abstract concept for preschool-aged children. Finally, *using conventional time units* and *observing that clocks and calendars mark the passage of time* were eliminated because over the years we observed that they seemed to encourage adults to stress clock and calendar time, which is developmentally inappropriate for preschool children.

Phase 5: Reorganizing Content

Since the publication of the second edition of this volume, High/Scope has reorganized the preschool key experiences into new categories and has replaced the term *key experiences* with the term *key developmental indicators* (KDIs). While the 58 KDIs are identical in wording and meaning to the former key experiences, they have been (as explained earlier in the chapter) regrouped in five major content categories that parallel the five school readiness dimensions identified by the NEGP. Some of the old categories have been split up or combined, while others are largely the same except for changes in wording.

High/Scope adopted the new content groupings and KDI terminology not only to bring

*While each child is an individual and comes from a unique culture, children everywhere, like these young "moms" carrying their "babies" on their backs, engage in **pretending and role playing**.*

the curriculum into closer alignment with professional standards and requirements but also to make the curriculum more accessible. Quite simply, many people did not understand the term *key experiences*, thinking these were experiences that teachers should provide children, that is, they were statements about what teachers do. As a result, High/Scope was sometimes criticized for not having content, that is, statements about *what children learn*. However, the curriculum always intended these statements to describe the content—the concepts and skills—young children should be learning as a result of their educational experiences. The term *KDI* better communicates this focus on children's learning.

Similarly, the language we had used to name the content areas was often not clear to our audiences. While the High/Scope Curriculum has always addressed content in all major areas of children's development, the terms the field commonly uses for these content areas has changed over time. For example, what was formerly called "language and literacy" is now typically referred to as "language, literacy, and communication," so we adopted this wording in our new category name. Similarly, the phrase "creative representation" was confusing to many people, but "the arts" is a universal term. Thus, we moved most of the key experiences/KDIs in the old **creative representation** category into a new **arts** subcategory, which is subdivided into *visual arts* (relating representations to real things; drawing, painting, and making models), *dramatic arts* (imitating and pretending), and *music*. Note, too, that the old **music** category was formerly positioned next to the old **movement** category to emphasize their interrelatedness. In the new list, they are separated, with the movement KDIs now listed under **physical development, health, and well-being.**

The new content categories are intended to communicate more clearly the connection between preschool experiences and later academic and social learning. Thus, in the new **arts and sciences** category, the old **seriation, number,** and **space** categories are now grouped as subcategories of **mathematics,** and the old **classification** and **time** categories are now subcategories of **science and technology.** The KDIs in the old **social relations and initiative** category have been separated and regrouped into three related but more specific categories—**approaches to learning, social and emotional development,** and **social studies**—to highlight the distinct abilities in each domain. (See the High/Scope Web site, *www.highscope.org,* for more information on the alignment of key developmental indicators and key experiences.)

The KDIs in this book, which are the latest evolution of High/Scope's curriculum content, are clearly not "the last word." Early childhood practitioners and researchers will continue to learn more about the process and sequence of young children's learning. And, by keeping current in the field, High/Scope staff members will continue to develop an approach to teaching and learning that revises or incorporates additional KDIs and promotes children's healthy growth and development (Schweinhart 1988).

The Significance of the KDIs

The content areas and the KDIs within them are significant for adults involved in the High/Scope preschool approach primarily because of their reality in children's activity. Children's active engagement with people and materials naturally involves them in using these key concepts and skills. As children play—fit things together, take them apart, make things, pretend—they construct knowledge and gain a sense of competence. For adults, the KDIs give meaning to what children are doing. Adults who understand the importance of the KDIs as tools for observing, describing, and supporting children's development can use them to shape their work with children—in the ways outlined next.

▶ **KDIs can focus adults' observations and interpretation of children's actions.**

Curriculum content provides adults with a child development "filter" for observing children and for choosing appropriate interactions. For example, through the filter of the KDIs, an observation such as "Johnny is playing in the sand" might expand to "Johnny is playing in the sand filling pots and colanders *(filling and emptying)* and watching to see what happens to the sand in each case *(exploring and describing similarities, differences, and the attributes of things)*." KDIs can help adults interpret what children do and say throughout the day and can shape adults' support strategies: "Perhaps if I sit down next to Johnny and start filling and emptying the sieve, he might begin to put his observations about what is happening to the sand into words." Or, "At recall time, I'm going to ask Johnny if he can show us what happened to his sand."

▶ **KDIs can serve as a cross-cultural reference for observing and interpreting children's actions.**

Practitioners from many different cultures and regions around the world report that they see their children doing such things as *having fun with language, sorting and matching, pretending* and role playing, and solving problems encountered in play. Each child is an individual, each culture is unique, and each community is idiosyncratic, yet child development occurs in similar progressions in all cultures and geographic locations. For example, although children may use different containers (depending on what is available in their setting), if they are given the opportunity they will spend appreciable amounts of time filling and emptying these containers, sorting them, using them to stand for whatever they need in their play, and describing in their own words what they are doing with them.

▶ KDIs can help adults maintain reasonable expectations for children.

We know, for example, that many young children are intrinsically motivated to write and that this process emerges slowly through a series of imitations—drawing, scribbling, and making letterlike forms—that are themselves as valuable and necessary as children's later attempts to make conventional letters. For example, adults who understand the KDIs in **language, literacy, and communication** are happy to listen to Mary Lynn "read" her story about a storm even though what she has "written" looks to the adults like a series of random squiggles and blobs. They are not concerned that Mary Lynn is not making conventional letters because they understand and expect her to be engaged in the kind of "writing" that is appropriate at her level of development.

Also, the KDIs can put the whole notion of children's mishaps into perspective for adults. Pouring juice at snack time, for example, becomes

a valuable experience for children because it gives them a real-life opportunity to engage in *filling and emptying*. However, pouring is an emerging capacity that takes lots of practice, since children in their excitement about pouring sometimes forget to stop. But that is a valuable experience, too, because cleaning up spilled juice provides children with the opportunity to *solve problems*.

▶ KDIs can answer questions about the legitimacy of children's play.

Play is a legitimate and necessary activity for young children. However, for adults who may be concerned that play prevents children from engaging in the "real work" of learning, the KDIs identify over 50 types of active learning experiences readily apparent in young children's

play. In fact, the KDIs can deepen adults' appreciation of the complexity of children's play.

▶ KDIs can guide decisions about materials and the daily routine.

The content areas and KDIs provide adults with a set of criteria for selecting appropriate materials for an active learning environment. They encourage teaching teams to ask themselves questions such as, What kinds of materials can we add for children to rearrange and reshape? Are there **music** KDIs that might occur more often or more broadly if we were to provide some additional materials? Since many children are involved in "building the longest train in the world," how can we rearrange the block area to make more floor space available?

This teaching team refers to a one-page curriculum content list as they share and record child anecdotes and make plans for the next day, based on their observations of children.

The KDIs also provide a window on the daily routine, that is, some indicators may tend to occur at certain times of the day. For example, in a well-organized setting, there are days when cleanup time is characterized by concentrated *sorting and matching*. On the other hand, if *dealing with social conflict* accelerates right before lunch, this may indicate that a change in the daily routine is in order.

► **KDIs enable adults to recognize and support children's emerging capacities.**

Knowledge of the content areas and KDIs guides adults in planning activities and supporting children's play. For example, Lisa made "pizza" in the house area and invited Beth, her teacher, to "sample" a piece. Beth exclaimed that the "pizza" was delicious and asked Lisa for the recipe. Hurrying to the art area, Lisa chose some writing materials and returned to the house area to write her recipe in scribble form. Beth knew from her previous observations that Lisa was beginning to write and, by asking her for the recipe, was able to create an occasion for her to use her emerging skill.

In summary, the High/Scope content areas and KDIs can broaden adults' understanding of what children do, think about, and enjoy. This appreciation of the complexity of children's pursuits enables adults to support children's emerging capacities with appropriate materials and interactions rather than to focus on children's mistakes and deficits.

Using the KDIs to Support Teaching and Learning

For all the reasons discussed thus far, the content areas and KDIs are useful tools for adults working with young children. Their daily usefulness, however, depends on accessibility. Since few people are likely to memorize the entire list of KDIs, it is important to keep the list where adults can easily refer to it:

• Post a large-print version of the KDI list in a central location where adults can glance at it throughout the day.

Providing Materials That Support Curriculum Content

One teaching team devised a form to assist with the selection of materials. They photocopied a batch of these forms, kept them in the daily planning log, then filled in the heading and a particular KDI as needed. Below is one of the forms as they filled it out.

Content Category: *Arts/Dramatic Art*   **KDI:** *Pretending and role playing*

Materials We Already Have	Materials We Want to Add
Block Area *Steering wheel, scarves, puppets, small vehicles*	*picnic basket, blankets*
House Area *dressup clothes, pots and pans, dolls, phones, food containers, barbershop props*	*stuffed animals, dog accessories*
Art Area	
Toy Area *doll house and people, counting bears and cats, train set*	*tumbling gnomes*
Sand/Water Area *coffee pot, dishes*	*rubber animals*
Outside *boxes, streamers, sand toys*	*row boat*

• Keep one-page lists of KDIs in places where team members can refer to them as needed—for example, with the daily team planning log, child anecdotal records, and parent conference folders, and on the parent announcement board. Lamination extends the lifetime of each list. (High/Scope Press offers an $8\frac{1}{2}$" × 11" laminated list of KDIs. Visit *www.highscope.org* to order.)

Some adults are hesitant to use the KDIs because they are not familiar with them. However, the best way to become familiar with them is to use them. Following are six ways to get started.

▶ **Use the KDIs as a basis for assessing materials available to children.**

To begin this process, select one of the sets of groups or subgroups of KDIs. Identify materials in the interest areas and on the playground that currently support each KDI in the set. If you come up with very few items or none at all for one particular KDI, brainstorm a list of materials to add. You might also skim the corresponding content area chapter in this book for materials to consider (and ask the children for their ideas, too). Repeat this process periodically, so over the course of the year you have systematically assessed and provided materials related to each of the content categories.

One teaching team, as they evaluated the materials they were providing to support **dramatic art,** particularly the *pretending and role playing* KDI, decided to consult their children. Accordingly, at greeting time the next day, they asked, "What do you think our house area needs that would make more children want to play there?" "A dog!" was the children's immediate response (not at all the one the adults anticipated). Nevertheless, taking their children's interests to heart, one team member arranged to bring her gentle family dog, Daisy, into the house area for several days along with her water and food dishes, leash, grooming brush, and bed. During her visit, Daisy was well cared for, and after she left, the children continued to play "doggy," making their own beds and dishes from blocks, boxes, and blankets.

▶ **Use the content areas and KDIs to organize and interpret observations of children.**

As you interact with children throughout the day, jot down specific, short observations about what they do and say. During daily team planning, share these anecdotes and together make an interpretation of them by deciding which of the KDIs they most closely illustrate. Then save the anecdote by recording it on a note form organized by the curriculum content categories. (See the sample section from a KDI note form on p. 307.) This way, you will be able to refer to it and other anecdotes during daily team planning, when filling out assessments such as the *Preschool Child Observation Record (COR),* and in meetings with parents.

More lengthy anecdotes of specific events are also useful for staff planning. One adult, for example, made the following observation of Jonah during work time:

Jonah selected all the black chess pieces from the box and put them next to one side of the chessboard. Then he went around to the other side of the board and dumped all the white pieces out.

He returned to the first side and placed all the black chess pieces on the black squares and then moved to the other side of the board and placed all the white chess pieces on the white squares.

∾

As the adult discussed this anecdote with her team member during daily team planning, they were both struck by the precision with which Jonah sorted the chess pieces by color and matched them with squares of the same color, and by his desire to place all the black pieces on one side of the board and all the white pieces on the other. They interpreted Jonah's actions as relating to his interest in and ability to classify by *sorting and matching.* Therefore, because Jonah was so intent on sorting and matching the chess pieces, they recorded this incident on Jonah's KDI notes form under the **classification** category. (See entry on p. 307.)

▶ **Use KDI-based child observations as a basis for daily team planning.**

After you have discussed your observations of children's actions during various times of the day and have interpreted them in light of the KDIs, use what you learn from your observations and discussions to plan support strategies and experiences to use with children the next day. You can also use these notes as part of the *COR* assessment process as described later in this chapter and in Chapter 4.

For example, after discussing Jonah's "chess playing," his teachers went on to consider how they could build on this insight about Jonah in their interactions with him the next day. If Jonah planned to play with the chess pieces again, they decided that one of them would try to be near him (1) to see if he said anything about what he was doing and (2) to make one of the teachers available if Jonah asked her to play. They also decided to add a set of colored marbles and a Chinese Checkers gameboard to the toy area next to the chessboard to provide another game-like sorting and matching opportunity. For small-group time, Jonah's small-group teacher decided to bring in four more checkerboards so each pair of children in her group could have one. For game pieces, she planned to provide a box of small, varicolored plastic "counting" bears to see what kinds of "chess games" the children might make up. She was particularly interested to see what Jonah would do with colored bears that were not the same color as the squares on the board.

For another discussion of this child-observation-based adult planning process, see the story of Vanessa (pp. 99–102).

▶ **Use the KDIs as a guide to planning small-group and large-group times.**

Building on your observations of what interests children, you can introduce activities at small- and large-group times that provide opportunities for children to engage in activities related to specific KDIs. For example, if box-elder bugs are swarming outside and have attracted the children's attention, you might plan for children to observe the bugs and draw them at small-group time (**visual art** KDI: *drawing and painting*). Or, if some children have recently talked about seeing circus clowns walking on stilts, you might plan an outdoor large-group time in which children try walking on tin-can stilts (**dramatic art** KDI: *imitating actions and sounds*; **physical development, health, and well-being** KDI: *moving with objects*).

▶ **Use the content areas and KDIs to guide on-the-spot interactions with children.**

As you talk with children and support their problem-solving efforts, observe what children are doing in terms of curriculum content. This type of observation will often give you ideas for ways to support and extend their play. Asking yourself, "What is Sally doing? What is she involved in at this moment? What KDIs are at work here?" will often yield clues about ways to enter children's play without disrupting it. Here are three examples of how this process works:

Joanie is in the art area having trouble using the tape dispenser. Your first impulse is to go over and get the tape untangled for her and into position over the cutting edge. But then you think of

---

*A page from one classroom's KDI notes form holds anecdotes about a child's progress in **mathematics** and **science and technology**.*

KDI Notes

Child: *Jonah*   Observers: *Betsy and Merrilee*

Remember to date all entries.

GC=greeting circle, PT=planning time, WT=work time, RT=recall time, SGT=small-group time, LGT=large-group time, OT=outside time

Mathematics

Seriation	Number	Space
1/29 At WT Jonah draws a spiral that starts out large and gets smaller and smaller. Several children become very interested and ask how he does it. Jonah shows them how to "start big and then small and smaller."	1/13 "I have a lot of teeth . . . more than my mom," Jonah says about the picture he is drawing of himself at WT. "And lots of mouths. Now I can talk a lot of times."	1/6 Jonah makes a picture about the zoo trip. "I saw ducks. See," he says, pointing to the ducks in his drawing. "There are a lot in the pool."
3/10 At WT, Jonah builds a nesting block tower, arranging the blocks in order from largest to smallest. Then he makes a series of balls out of modeling wax and puts the largest ball inside the largest block, the next largest ball in the next largest block, and so on until each block holds a ball of similar size.	1/26 "You know what?" Jonah says to Jacob as they draw at SGT. "My sister's older than both of us. She's seven!"	1/22 At RT, Jonah shows and talks about four drawings he made. "This one isn't a picture. It's a map."
	2/1 AT SGT, Jonah counts six sticks on his collage and seven pieces of foam. "There are more of those," he says, pointing to the foam pieces.	1/28 At WT, Jonah and Jason tie ropes to chairs, then climb up the climber holding the free ends of their ropes and begin pulling in an attempt to hoist the chairs onto the climber.
	2/1 At WT, Jonah strings beads and counts them up to 25, then counts "27, 29, 50, 60, 66."	2/16 At WT, Jonah fits Lincoln Logs together to make a tower.
	2/3 At WT, Jonah lines up and counts 12 blocks, then places one small bear on each block.	

Science and Technology

Classification	Time
1/12 "I almost made a circle track but it (marble) stopped at the corner," Jonah says at WT.	1/26 "We get candy on Hanukkah, Shabbat, and I think on Friday and Saturday," Jonah says to Amanda at lunchtime.
1/28 Jonah plays with bears and Play-Doh at WT. "Some bears are here and some bears are under (the Play-Doh). I can't fit all the bears (under the Play-Doh)."	2/28 Jonah plans a sequence of activities at PT: "Make a bow and arrow . . . With pipe cleaners and tape. And then a boat . . . but the boat will have sticks and paper and tape."
2/24 At WT, Jonah selects all the black chess pieces from the box and puts them next to one side of the chessboard. Then he goes to the other side of the board and dumps all the white pieces out. He returns to the first side and places all the black chess pieces on the black squares and then moves to the other side of the board and places all the white pieces on the white squares.	2/9 At GC Jonah says, "I only need one more day. One more day after today and I get a toy. I'm going to get a Ninja guy. I make 'em fight and kill all the bad guys."
3/4 "You know what?" Jonah says to Merrilee at RT. "I used all the flat ones."	3/11 "When the snow melts, it will be my birthday," Jonah says at snack time.
3/13 At WT, Jonah shakes a cup he has filled with paper and cloth pieces and taped closed. "It doesn't make a sound. It has quiet things in it," he says.	

the KDI *solving problems encountered in play*. So instead you silently sit down next to Joanie. She stops and you think she has given up, but then she comes back with a pair of scissors, cuts off the tangled part, and carefully puts the straight edge of the tape in place over the cutter. "There!" she says with obvious satisfaction. "You fixed the tape," you agree.

∾

At greeting circle, Sandra brings over a book and sits down in your lap, but instead of opening the book, she starts to tell you about the groundhog her father caught in a trap and how she and her brother and father "tooked the groundhog in the truck to a big, big field and then we letted him go." Several nearby children join the conversation with questions ("Did it get bloody?" "How did it get in there?"), comments ("I'm glad it was okay," "It would be sad if it got its leg hurt"), and their own animal stories. Although this is not a discussion you had planned on and

greeting circle is therefore taking longer than usual, you listen to and participate in the children's conversation about traps and animals because they are so earnestly involved in **talking with others about personally meaningful experiences** as well as **describing objects, events, and relationships** (two **language, literacy, and communication** KDIs). They are also **expressing feelings in words** (a **social and emotional development** KDI) and **being sensitive to the feelings, interests, and needs of others** (a **social studies** KDI).

∾

Jessa and Anna are building an elaborate "beehive" in the block area with blocks of all sizes and colored scarves. Later they come over to the art area (where you and several other children are playing with Play-Doh), press a small triangle block into your arm, and giggle while waiting for your response. At first you are taken by surprise, but then you remember the "beehive" and think of the KDI **pretending and role playing**. "Ouch, bees," you reply. "Please don't sting me!" The two giggling "bees" fly back to their hive. You have understood and entered into the spirit of their play.

∾

For a related discussion on KDIs and on-the-spot interactions, see Chapter 7 (pp. 206–208).

▶ **Use the KDI-based planning and assessment tool, the *Preschool Child Observation Record* (COR; 2003).**

Drawing on your ongoing observations of children and the anecdotes recorded daily on the KDIs you observe, you will have the information needed to fill out a *Preschool COR* on each child in your program one or two times a year. The

COR is a developmentally appropriate assessment instrument based on the High/Scope KDIs for preschoolers. To use the COR to assess child development, early childhood staff draw on the information gathered from daily child observations. The process of filling out the COR based on anecdotes gathered and recorded over several months will give your team an idea of where each child is developmentally, in terms of many of the KDIs, and will chart each child's growth from one part of the year to the next in the COR categories: *initiative, social relations, creative representation, movement and music, language and literacy,* and *mathematics and science.* For a complete discussion of the *Preschool COR* and how to use it, see the *Preschool COR User Guide* (2003).

🐾

The High/Scope curriculum content areas and KDIs are a set of tools designed to help adults understand young children and to use this understanding in their daily interactions with children. As adults use the KDIs to assess materials, interpret observations of children, plan for the next day, guide on-the-spot interactions, and assess children's development, they begin to appreciate their children's strengths and capacities and to expand their own repertoire of support.

The 13 chapters that follow are organized according to major High/Scope content categories. Each chapter provides the following information: (1) illustrative anecdotes teaching teams have noted in their KDI notes; (2) a brief discussion of the specific content category; and (3) suggestions for adults on how to support progress on each KDI throughout the day.

*Guided by an understanding of the **dramatic art** KDI **pretending and role playing**, this adult accepts a "baby shower present" wrapped and given to her by her "mom."*

References

Banet, Bernard. 1976. "Toward a Developmentally Valid Preschool Program." In *The High/Scope Report, 1975–1976*, C. Silverman, ed., 7–12. Ypsilanti, MI: High/Scope Press.

Berrueta-Clement, John, Lawrence Schweinhart, Steve Barnett, Ann Epstein, and David Weikart. 1984. *Changed Lives: The Effects of the Perry Preschool Program on Youths Through Age 19*. Ypsilanti, MI: High/Scope Press.

Bowlby, John. 1969. *Attachment. Attachment and Loss, Vol. 1*. New York: Basic Books.

Carlton, Elizabeth, and Phyllis S. Weikart. 1994. *Foundations in Elementary Education: Music*. Ypsilanti, MI: High/Scope Press.

Elkind, David. 1974. *Children and Adolescents*. New York: Oxford University Press.

Erikson, Erik. 1950. *Childhood and Society*. New York: Norton.

Flavell, John H. 1963. *The Developmental Psychology of Jean Piaget*. Princeton, NJ: Van Nostrand.

Gardner, Howard. 1983. *Frames of Mind: The Theory of Multiple Intelligences*. New York: Basic Books.

Greenspan, Stanley, and Nancy T. Greenspan. 1985. *First Feelings*. New York: Viking.

High/Scope Educational Research Foundation. 2003. *Preschool Child Observation Record (COR)*, 2nd ed. Ypsilanti, MI: High/Scope Press. (Includes *User Guide*.)

Hohmann, Charles. 1991. *The High/Scope K–3 Curriculum Series: Mathematics*. Ypsilanti, MI: High/Scope Press.

Hohmann, Mary. 1991. "Key Experiences: Keys to Supporting Preschool Children's Emerging Strengths and Abilities." In *Supporting Young Learners*, Nancy Brickman and Lynn Taylor, eds., 63–70. Ypsilanti, MI: High/Scope Press.

Hunt, J. McVicker. 1961. *Intelligence and Experience*. New York: The Ronald Press Company.

Kagan, Sharon L., Evelyn Moore, and Sue Bredekamp, eds. 1995. *Reconsidering Children's Early Development and Learning: Toward Common Views and Vocabulary. (Goal 1 Technical Planning Group Report 95–03)*. Washington, DC: National Education Goals Panel.

Marzano, Robert. 2001. *Designing a New Taxonomy of Educational Objectives*. Thousand Oaks, CA: Corwin Press.

Oden, Sherri. 1988. "Alternative Perspectives on Children's Peer Relationships." *In Integrative Processes and Socialization: Early to Middle Childhood*, T. D. Yawkey and J. E. Johnson, eds., 139–66. Hillsdale, NJ: Erlbaum.

Phillips, Paul. 1975. "Theory: Its Place in Curriculum Development." In *The High/Scope Report, 1974–1975*, C. Silverman, ed., 12–13. Ypsilanti, MI: High/Scope Press.

Piaget, Jean. 1966. *The Psychology of Intelligence*. Totowa, NJ: Littlefield, Adams, and Company.

Piaget, Jean, and Barbel Inhelder. 1969. *The Psychology of the Child*. New York: Basic Books.

Pinard, Adrien, and Monique Laurendeau. 1969. "'Stage' in Piaget's Cognitive-Developmental Theory: Exegesis of a Concept." In *Studies in Cognitive Development, Essays in Honor of Jean Piaget*, David Elkind and John H. Flavell, eds., 121–70. New York: Oxford University Press.

Schweinhart, Lawrence J. 1988. *A School Administrator's Guide to Early Childhood Programs*. Ypsilanti, MI: High/Scope Press.

Schweinhart, Lawrence, Helen Barnes, David Weikart, Steve Barnett, and Ann Epstein. 1993. *Significant Benefits: The High/Scope Perry Preschool Study Through Age 27*. Ypsilanti, MI: High/Scope Press.

Schweinhart, Lawrence J., Jeanne Montie, Zongping Xiang, W. Steven Barnett, Clive R. Belfield, and Milagros Nores. 2005. *Lifetime Effects: The High/Scope Perry Preschool Study Through Age 40*. Ypsilanti, MI: High/Scope Press.

Schweinhart, Lawrence, and David Weikart. 1980. *Young Children Grow Up: The Effects of the Perry Preschool Program on Youths Through Age 15*. Ypsilanti, MI: High/Scope Press.

Schweinhart, Lawrence, David Weikart, and Mary Larner. 1988. *Consequences of Three Preschool Curriculum Models Through Age 15*. Ypsilanti, MI: High/Scope Press.

Sigel, Irving E., and Frank H. Hooper. 1968. *Logical Thinking in Children: Research Based on Piaget's Theory*. New York: Holt, Rinehart, and Winston, Inc.

Silverman, Charles, and David P. Weikart. 1974. "Open Framework: Evolution of a Concept in Preschool Education." In *The High/Scope Report, 1973*, C. Silverman, ed., 14–19. Ypsilanti, MI: High/Scope Press.

Smilansky, Sara. 1968. *The Effects of Sociodramatic Play on Disadvantaged Preschool Children*. New York: John Wiley and Sons, Inc., 1968.

Weikart, David P. 1974. "'Devices of Art' or Strategies for Change?" In *The High/Scope Report, 1973*, C. Silverman, ed., 2–5. Ypsilanti, MI: High/Scope Press.

Weikart, David, J. Terry Bond, and Judy McNeil. 1978. *The Ypsilanti Perry Preschool Project: Preschool Years and Longitudinal Results Through Fourth Grade*. Ypsilanti, MI: High/Scope Press.

Weikart, David P., Dennis DeLoria, Sarah Lawser, and Robert Weigerink. 1970. *Longitudinal Results of the Ypsilanti Perry Preschool Project*. Ypsilanti, MI: High/Scope Press.

Weikart, David P., Ann Epstein, Lawrence Schweinhart, and J. Terry Bond. 1978. *The Ypsilanti Preschool Curriculum Demonstration Project: Preschool Years and Longitudinal Results*. Ypsilanti, MI: High/Scope Press.

Weikart, David, Linda Rogers, Carolyn Adcock, and Donna McClelland. 1971. *The Cognitively Oriented Curriculum: A Framework for Preschool Teachers*. Urbana, IL: ERIC–NAEYC.

Weikart, Phyllis. 1987. *Round the Circle: Key Experiences in Movement for Children*. Ypsilanti, MI: High/Scope Press.

Related Reading

Armstrong, Thomas. 1994. *Multiple Intelligences in the Classroom*. Alexandria, VA: ASCD

Epstein, Ann S. 2008. "Understanding High/Scope Curriculum 'Content Areas' and 'KDIs.'" *High/Scope ReSource* 27, no. 1 (Spring): 21, 31.

Epstein, Ann S. 2007. "What Is the High/Scope Preschool Curriculum?" Chap. 2 in *Essentials of Active Learning in Preschool: Getting to Know the High/Scope Curriculum*, 7–14. Ypsilanti, MI: High/Scope Press.

Graves, Michelle. 1996. *The Teacher's Idea Book 2: Planning Around Children's Interests*. Ypsilanti, MI: High/Scope Press.

Post, Jacalyn, and Mary Hohmann. 2000. "Key Experiences: What Infants and Toddlers Learn." In *Tender Care and Early Learning*. 35–54. Ypsilanti, MI: High/Scope Press.

Children's approaches to learning develop as they make plans and follow through on them. As they pursue their intentions, they solve problems and express unique learning styles and interests.

In this chapter we will discuss **approaches to learning**—how one goes about acquiring knowledge and skills—and how teachers can support and enhance children's motivation to learn.

The content area of approaches to learning is extremely important because it shapes children's educational experiences in all other content areas.

As central as it is to development, this area is hard to define and measure. The National Education Goals Panel (NEGP; Kagan et al. 1995) says approaches to learning includes the following components in the early childhood years: **curiosity, creativity, confidence, independence, initiative,** and **persistence.**

These components reveal themselves in behaviors or skills that adults can easily observe. For example, we can see whether children take the initiative to explore materials and ideas or whether they independently solve problems as they carry out their intentions.

Approaches to Learning and School Readiness

The NEGP emphasizes that school readiness is enhanced when young children are encouraged to explore, ask questions, and use their imaginations. These early experiences prepare them in a positive way to venture into the world.

High/Scope uses the term **initiative** to describe children's desire and ability to begin and then follow through on a task. Children **intentionally** decide to engage with the objects, people, events, and ideas they encounter—that is, they do so with a specific goal in mind. The goal can be simple (get the ball) or more complex (write my name with stones in the sand). By encouraging young children to follow their own interests, the High/Scope Curriculum supports the development of initiative and intentionality. Children's play is purposeful and confident. The difference between simply making a choice (red or blue beads?) and making a plan ("What shall I do at work time?") is that planning involves thinking about and expressing intent (see "planning" in Chapter 7).

Supporting Children's Approaches to Learning

Whether children perceive learning and problem-solving situations as positive challenges, insurmountable barriers, or even threats directly affects children's ability to benefit from their educational experiences. How young children approach learning carries long past their entry into formal schooling. In fact, it will likely shape their educational careers and adult lives. Therefore, it is important to provide young children with experiences that

10
Approaches to Learning

It is fundamentally misleading to think about a single mind, a single intelligence, a single problem-solving capacity.
—Howard Gardner, 2003

KDIs in Approaches to Learning
• Making and expressing choices, plans, and decisions
• Solving problems encountered in play

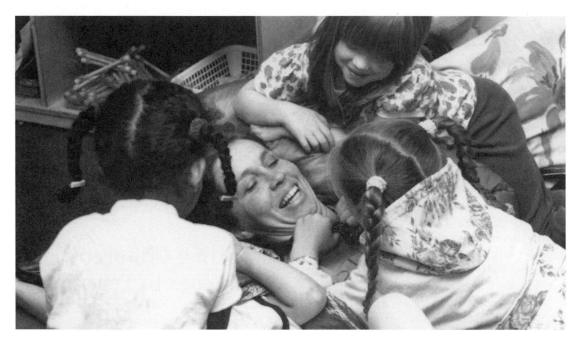

Adults support the development of children's initiative by exhibiting kindness, focusing on children's strengths, and enjoying children's play.

help them develop initiative and the skills needed to solve problems with confidence, flexibility, and persistence.

High/Scope has **two key developmental indicators (KDIs) in approaches to learning,** described below. The first reflects the curriculum's emphasis on initiative and focuses on how young children express their intentions (plans and choices) throughout various parts of the daily routine. The second looks at how children deal with the problems they encounter as they interact with materials, people, events, and ideas.

Key Developmental Indicator
Making and Expressing Choices, Plans, and Decisions

At greeting circle while the other children read books and talk together, Andrew and Alana sing "Row, Row, Row Your Boat."

∽

"I'm going to the climber and drive to Florida to feed the alligators," Amanda says at planning time.

∽

Petey plans to work at the computers. When he gets there, he sees that all of the computers are in use, so he goes to the house area. "I'm going to be the pizza delivery guy," he decides.

∽

Jonah plays with blocks and bears, then puts the blocks away and says, "Now I'm gonna use these bears with Play-Doh."

∽

Alana shows Peter a coffee can. "I'm thinking about what to do with this," she explains.

∽

Colin and Nicholas are playing fox and wolf, taking dolls and food from the children in the playhouse. "Why can't I be a good fox and you be a good wolf?" Colin asks. "No, I want to be bad," Nicholas says. "No, that's not a good choice," Colin tells him, " 'cause people don't like bad guys."

∽

Aimee puts a clay ball on a stick at recall time. "I want to recall with this," she states, speaking into "the microphone."

∽

At small-group time, Megan puts her stickers all the way around the edge of her paper.

Trey puts his stickers all over his paper, then connects them with a crayon line. Nathaniel puts all the bird stickers together and tells Audie about his friend's bird: "He flew right out of the cage and sat on my head!"

∽

"I have an idea," Julia says at large-group time. "We could all be hippos rolling in the mud!" Everyone enjoys being "muddy hippos."

∽

One night, lightning strikes the tree growing through the center of the tree-house tower. The next day, Mark and Daniel examine the scorched bark on the ground. "Me and Mark are going to climb up the big tower and look at the lightning hole in our tree," says Daniel. "We're going to be the big noise that made it happen. Bang! Bang!"

As children initiate personally interesting activities—such as the ancient art of face painting—they learn about the physical world, themselves, and their friends.

By nature children are inquisitive, enterprising, and motivated to take action to pursue their interests and ideas. Through such everyday choices, plans, and decisions as deciding to climb the tower to examine the effects of the lightning strike, children initiate personally interesting activities that enable them to learn not only about the physical world but also about themselves and others as learners and adventurers. By acting on these initiatives, children gain confidence in themselves as *capable persons* and in others as *supportive participants*.

Following are ways adults can support children's emerging sense of themselves as doers and initiators by acknowledging and affirming their choices, plans, and decisions.

Suggestions for Adults

▶ **Establish an option-rich environment and consistent daily routine.**

Supporting children's choices, plans, and decisions calls for an **inviting physical environment** that offers children a broad array of choices and opportunities for self-initiated play. Such an option-rich environment includes **well-defined interest areas** that encourage children to plan for distinctive types of play, a wide range and plentiful **assortment of materials** for children to select, and an **orderly storage system** that enables children to find, use, and return the materials they have chosen. (For ways to establish and maintain an environment that encourages child choice, see Chapter 5, pp. 112–124.)

Along with an orderly, child-accessible physical environment, it is equally important to establish and maintain a **consistent daily routine** that allows children to *(1) predict* what happens next, *(2) make, carry out, and recall plans* during

a daily plan-work-recall sequence, and *(3) make choices and decisions* during adult-initiated activities. With the support of knowledgeable adults, such a daily routine gives children ongoing opportunities for decision making and control over their own learning, and serves as a powerful force in building children's self-confidence and initiative. (For ways to establish a consistent daily routine that encourages children's initiatives, see Chapter 6, pp. 151–152.)

▶ **Express and maintain interest in the choices children make.**

While young children are natural decision-makers, they are new to the process and a little uncertain. They therefore depend on adults to acknowledge and take a genuine interest in the choices they make. Consider this example:

Daniel: *Me and Mark are going to climb up the big tower and look at the lightning hole in our tree. We're going to be the big noise that made it happen.*

Adult: *You're going to look at the hole up close and then be the lightning that made the hole!*

Once in the tower, Daniel and Mark call their teacher to come see the "sticky stuff" that "comes out of the hole" and the "bugs eating it!" She supports their plan to examine the lightning hole by acknowledging their decision and conversing with them about their discoveries.

In a sense, this approach makes children the leaders and adults the followers. For adults who are used to following prescribed lessons,

concentrating on children's expressed interests may take some practice. However, once adults make this shift in perspective, satisfying outcomes result. Children feel empowered and adults learn a great deal about children's interests, feelings, thinking, and reasoning, while simultaneously strengthening and enjoying their relationships with individual children.

▶ **Give children time to make choices, plans, and decisions.**

Many adults live with the constant pressure of tight schedules and, without realizing it, may pass the same pressure on to children: "It's time to make a plan—now." "It's time to think of a song to sing—now." "It's time to answer my question—now." Yet preschoolers need time to put experiences and intentions into words. It is important, therefore, for adults to wait patiently while children consider their choices, whether

Throughout the day, children make many choices about where to sit, what materials to use, and how to interpret adult requests.

the decision is what to do at work time or which song to sing at large-group time. When we step in with our suggestions in an attempt to speed up the decision-making process, we may frustrate rather than support children's initiatives. Although we may move things along, children may become anxious, resentful, or disinterested. Children are more apt to flourish as decision-makers and problem-solvers when they can take their time in reaching a decision.

▶ **Encourage children to make choices and decisions throughout the day.**

Though it is natural to associate choice-making with the plan-work-recall sequence, it is equally important for children to make choices during the other parts of the daily routine, even during activities initiated and planned by adults, such as group times. Following are some choices and decisions children make throughout the daily routine:

- **Greeting circle:**
  Whom to sit with
  What book to look at
  Whom to talk with
  What to talk about

- **Planning time:**
  What to do
  Whom to plan with
  What materials to use

- **Work time:**
  How to begin
  How to modify plans
  Whom to play with
  What materials to add
  How to solve problems encountered
  What to do next

- **Recall time:**
  What to share with others
  How to describe actions

- **Small-group time:**
  Whom to sit next to
  What to do with materials
  How to use the materials to carry out their own ideas
  What else to try with the materials
  What materials to add

- **Large-group time:**
  What songs to sing
  What new verses to add
  What motions to try
  How to be a horse, duck, gardener
  What happens next in a story
  How to interpret adult requests

- **Outside time:**
  What to do
  Whom to play with
  What materials to use

Making and expressing choices, plans, and decisions is fundamental to a child's developing sense of competence and equality. As daily planners and decision-makers, children acquire increased confidence in interacting with peers and adults. They come to see themselves as respected partners in shaping many of the ongoing events in their world. (For the role of choice as an essential ingredient of active learning, see Chapter 1.)

Key Developmental Indicator
Solving Problems
Encountered in Play

When Isaac accidentally tears his easel painting, he lays it on the floor, carefully tapes the torn parts back together, and hangs the painting up to dry.

Hannah tries gluing popsicle sticks together side-by-side. When they fall apart, she decides to tape them together. They still wobble, so she tapes the taped sticks to a piece of cardboard.

"Colin," says Jonah, "are you using this truck?" Colin says that he is. Jonah looks around the block area for another truck like Colin's. He can't find one, so he asks Betsy, his teacher, if there are any more. "Have you looked in the toy area?" she asks. Jonah goes there, finds a truck, and returns to play with it.

At outside time Alana plans to play on the climber. She puts her hand on the first rung, draws back in surprise, and wipes her hands on her jacket. "It's wet!" she says to Becki, her teacher. "It certainly is wet," Becki agrees. After touching another part of the climber as if to confirm her finding, Alana says, "I'm gonna get a towel to wipe off the water." She gets a towel and dries each rung. "Now I can climb!" she says.

Children who have the opportunity to pursue their own initiatives will inevitably encounter obstacles. When children are encouraged to solve problems they encounter in play—as do Isaac, Hannah, Jonah, and Alana—they are gaining valuable opportunities to deal thoughtfully and creatively with unanticipated situations. In the process, they come to see themselves as capable of solving everyday problems. Also, by routinely solving problems, 3- and 4-year-old children acquire the *problem-solving habit* as well as an image of themselves as *proactive*.

Note that Alana's teachers did not say at the beginning of outside time, "Let's all go out and dry the climber." Nor did they hose down the climber before the children arrived to create a problem. Instead, they stepped back and allowed the children to take the lead, knowing that the children would encounter meaningful problems as a natural part of pursuing their own initiatives. Following are ways adults can support young children's initiatives at these times.

Suggestions for Adults

▶ **Encourage children to describe the problems they encounter.**

Throughout the day when children encounter problems that sidetrack their intentions, it is important for adults to refrain from intruding on the child's thought process by offering an adult interpretation of the issue. Instead,

After tracing her hand and her foot, this child solves the problem of how to position herself on a piece of paper so she can trace all the way around her bottom!

wait. Give children the opportunity to formulate their own observations. Observing and describing a problem is the child's first step in acknowledging the situation, making some interpretation of it, and deciding what to do next.

One day, at the end of outside time, 3-year-old Jason stood by the door, with tears in his eyes. "What is it, Jason?" his teacher asked, crouching near him and thinking that he was missing his older sister who was absent that day. "I don't have any sand in my shoes," Jason said. Several children were emptying sand from their

Day after day, this child worked on a problem he found particularly absorbing—how to tie and untie knots in string, yarn, and laces.

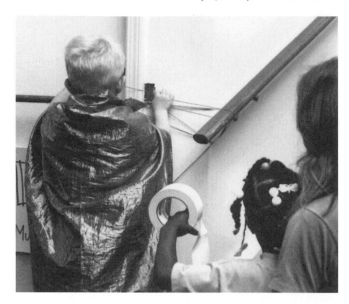

shoes into the box the janitor had built for this purpose next to the door. "Oh, you don't have any sand in your shoes," his teacher replied, glad she had not mentioned his sister. "I want to do like them," he continued. "You want to empty your shoes into the box?" the teacher asked. Jason nodded. "But your shoes don't have any sand in them." "Yeah." Jason thought for a while. "I know," he said, brightening. He headed for the sand pile, took off his shoes, filled them with sand, carried them back to the box near the door, and carefully emptied them alongside his classmates. In this example, Jason has enough time to identify and describe a problem (which the adult never would have guessed), think of a solution, and carry it out.

▶ **Give children time to generate their own solutions.**

Once children have identified the problems they are facing (a wet climber, no sand in their shoes) they also need time to decide what to do about them. Again, adults provide support at this time by waiting patiently. Offering efficient adult solutions may save time but will deprive

children of important learning opportunities as well as the satisfaction of developing and enacting their own solutions.

Consider Andrew's dilemma. One day, Andrew planned to play with the puppets and then planned to use a computer to draw. By the time he finished with the puppets, however, there were already two or three children at each computer, and all the chairs that would fit around them were filled. He studied the situation for a few minutes, then touched each of the chairs as if to verify that they were really occupied. "Well," he concluded matter-of-factly to an adult who was nearby, "I'll work with the snap-together blocks . . . then I can see when somebody leaves the computers."

▶ **Assist frustrated children.**

There are times when children need more than an adult's acknowledgment, supportive presence, and patience. At such times children have encountered a problem that impedes their plans, have tried some solutions that have not worked, and are about to give up in frustration. At this point, it is appropriate for adults to provide enough assistance to enable children to follow through on their intentions. Here are some examples of this strategy:

• Kacey likes to dress up by using some of the large silk squares. She has one tied around her shoulders like a cape and has been attempting to tie one around her waist, but no matter how hard she tries, the length is never quite what she wants. Becki, an adult, has been watching Kacey's efforts, and when Kacey appeals to her for help, she gives it readily, knowing that Kacey has tried a number of alternatives and wants to get on with her play:

"Becki, I want it to stay right here!" Kacey says, pointing to a place just below her knees. "Okay," Becki responds, "Let's try rolling up this part at the top," which they do, "and tying it in front." Kacey holds the scarf in place while Becki ties. "There—is that okay?" Becki asks. Kacey takes a few steps to check the length, decides it is satisfactory, and resumes her play.

• Peter is doing a puzzle. He has most of the pieces in place, but no matter how he turns them, he cannot make any of the remaining pieces fit the spot for the elephant's ear. Neenah, an adult, sees a puzzle piece behind Peter that he has overlooked. "Sometimes when I'm having trouble with a puzzle," Neenah says, "I look all around me for missing pieces." Peter looks on either side of himself, then turns around and finds another puzzle piece. He picks it up, twists it around, and after several tries, fits it in place. Then, through trial and error, Peter figures out the positions of the remaining pieces and finishes the puzzle. "I did it!" he proudly tells Neenah. "Yes, you did," Neenah agrees.

Approaches to Learning Strategies: A Summary

Making and expressing choices, plans, and decisions

___ Establish an option-rich environment and consistent daily routine.

___ Express and maintain interest in the choices children make.

___ Give children time to make choices, plans, and decisions.

___ Encourage children to make choices and decisions throughout the day.

Solving problems encountered in play

___ Encourage children to describe the problems they encounter.

___ Give children time to generate their own solutions.

___ Assist frustrated children.

References

Gardner, Howard. 2003, April 21. "Multiple Intelligences After 20 Years." Paper presented at the American Educational Research Association, Chicago, Illinois.

Kagan, Sharon L., Evelyn Moore, and Sue Bredekamp, eds. 1995. *Reconsidering Children's Early Development and Learning: Toward Common Views and Vocabulary.* (Goal 1 Technical Planning Group Report 95–03). Washington, DC: National Education Goals Panel.

Related Reading

Dowling, Jan Levanger, and Terri C. Mitchell. 2007. *I Belong: Active Learning for Children With Special Needs.* Ypsilanti, MI: High/Scope Press.

Epstein, Ann S. 2007. "What Is the High/Scope Curriculum in Approaches to Learning?" Chap. 10 in *Essentials of Active Learning in Preschool: Getting to Know the High/Scope Curriculum,* 103–108. Ypsilanti, MI: High/Scope Press.

Gardner, Howard. 1983. "The Personal Intelligences." Chap. 10 in *Frames of Mind: The Theory of Multiple Intelligences,* 237–76. New York: Basic Books.

Graves, Michelle. 2001. "Children's Problem-Solving: When to Step In, When to Stand Back." In *Supporting Young Learners 3: Ideas for Child Care Providers and Teachers,* Nancy A. Brickman, ed., 5–12. Ypsilanti, MI: High/Scope Press.

Graves, Michelle. 1996. *Teacher's Idea Book 2: Planning Around Children's Interests.* Ypsilanti, MI: High/Scope Press.

High/Scope Educational Research Foundation. 2003. *Preschool Child Observation Record (COR),* 2nd ed. Ypsilanti, MI: High/Scope Press.

Katz, Lilian, and Diane McClellan. 1997. *Fostering Children's Social Competence: The Teacher's Role.* Washington DC: NAEYC.

Kohn, Alfie. 1993. *Punished by Rewards: The Trouble With Gold Stars, Incentive Plans, A's, Praise, and Other Bribes.* Boston: Houghton Mifflin Company.

Oden, Sherri. 1993. "Implementing Research on Children's Social Competence: What Do Teachers and Researchers Need to Learn?" *Exceptionality Education Canada 3,* nos. 1 & 2: 209–32.

Related Media

The following materials are available from the High/Scope Press, 600 N. River St., Ypsilanti, MI 48198-2898; to order, visit *www.highscope.org,* or call 1-800-40-PRESS.

Initiative and Social Relations. 2001. Color videotape or DVD, 60 min. Ypsilanti, MI: High/Scope Press.

High/Scope for Children With Special Needs. 2006. Color videotape or DVD, 60 min.

Preschool children are powerfully motivated to communicate with others through conversation. They also enjoy such highly literate pursuits as "writing" and "reading" in their own particular ways.

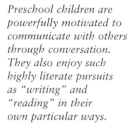

Early literacy is often cited as the most important academic skill in school readiness because most school learning depends on knowing how to read. Knowing how to read, in turn, is highly dependent on language skills, particularly vocabulary. In choosing the term "language development and communication," the National Education Goals Panel (NEGP; Kagan et al. 1995) emphasized that this area of school readiness should not be limited to learning how to read. The Panel noted that language is the means by which children convey their needs, describe events, interact with others, and express their thoughts and feelings. Language and communication are therefore intertwined with all areas of individual development, as well as also being essential to children's becoming members of their classroom and other groups.

During the past three decades, researchers have learned a great deal about how **language, literacy, and communication** develop in young children. These findings are reflected in the writings of the National Reading Panel (2000) and the National Early Literacy Panel (Strickland and Shanahan 2004), which emphasize four essential areas: comprehension, phonological awareness, alphabet knowledge, and concepts about print.

Comprehension is the process of deriving meaning from action, speech, and text by connecting what one is learning to what one already knows. **Phonological awareness** is recognizing the sounds that make up words. **Alphabet knowledge** is understanding the relationship between letters and sounds in oral and written language. **Concepts about print** is knowing how print is organized on the page and how it is used for reading and writing.

These research-based areas are embedded in the **six language, literacy, and communication key developmental indicators (KDIs).**

Basic Beliefs About Language, Literacy, and Communication

In 1979, when we published *Young Children in Action,* our approach to language development focused primarily on children's *oral* language. Except for dictation, we shied away from examining children's experiences with print, believing that symbols and letters were too abstract for young children to comprehend. Since then, however, studies conducted by educational researchers, including Susanna Pflaum (1986), Elizabeth Sulzby (1985, 1995), Catherine Snow (1991), David Dickinson and Miriam Smith (1994), Susan Neuman and Kathleen Roskos (1997), and Catherine Snow, Susan Burns, and Peg Griffen (1998), have expanded our knowledge about children's language and the many ways they are capable of communicating.

Consequently, in this manual we focus on the *interconnectedness* of spoken and written language during the early years. In particular, we draw on the work of educator Kenneth Goodman (1986, 1996), who describes curricula that integrate spoken and written language within the context of situations and experiences familiar to young children. We also use the term *emergent* or *early literacy* to describe the contemporary perspective in which educators and researchers see the devel-

11
Language, Literacy, and Communication

We are the meaning makers—every one of us: children, parents, and teachers. To try to make sense, to construct stories, and to share them with others in speech and in writing is an essential part of being human.

—Gordon Wells, 1986b

opment of children's ability to use the print forms of language as beginning in infancy and continuing to emerge throughout early childhood. These experts view emergent literacy as early, unconventional forms of writing and reading that precede conventional writing and reading. In discussing early language development in High/Scope programs, educator Jane Maehr (1991) embraces the concept of early literacy: "We see the emergence of language and literacy in children as a dynamic, ongoing process of discovery involving both children and adults in the early years" (p. 5). Maehr goes on to explain that in the integrated approach implemented in High/Scope programs, practitioners view language as a *communication process* in which both oral and written language—*speaking, listening, reading, and writing*—are bound together in a system that is useful and has meaning to young learners.

Clearly, from the integrated perspective, literacy—learning about all the print forms of language—develops in close relationship with oral language experience. While conventional writing and reading are still generally beyond the grasp of most preschoolers, they are nevertheless deeply involved in making sense of the writing and reading process in their own terms. In adopting the integrated approach and early-literacy terminology, we have relied on several basic assumptions about children's language development, and these are discussed next.

The primary function of language is communication between people.

We are social beings, and language helps us establish and carry on relationships throughout our lives. Infants and toddlers develop a communication system of coos, cries, gurgles, varied facial expressions, gestures, and short verbal utterances. By the time they are 3 or 4, most children are using language to make themselves understood and are interested in the print they encounter in their daily lives—in storybooks, on signs and cereal boxes, and as their families read the mail and the newspaper and write lists and letters. Young children who cannot yet read nevertheless realize that print means something, and they are powerfully motivated to create their own systems for conveying meaning

through print. Children want to communicate. They want to understand and be understood. In that spirit, it is important for adults to focus on *what* children are trying to communicate as well as on *how* they are trying to say or write it.

Language, literacy, and communication develop in young children.

Language is of great importance in our program. We want children to speak, listen, "write," and read. We see language and literacy as the outgrowth of social interaction and of children's active engagement with the environment.

In their desire to communicate, children's language becomes increasingly complex. It grows from one-word utterances ("Juicy") to sentences ("It's my turn to get the juice!"); from concrete subjects ("Look! Doggy!") to abstract ones ("Don't worry about the tornado. God has matters well in hand!"); and from the present ("Me play ball") to the past and the future ("I slept at my grandma's!" "When Noah comes, we're gonna be robots!"). The complexity of children's language evolves as a result of two-way conversations among children themselves, and between children and adults who listen attentively and share their interests. While adults naturally use language that is more varied and complex than the preschool child's, this need not interfere with the give-and-take of conversations, as long as adults support children's emerging grammar, word usage, or writing systems. In a climate rich in con-

Language develops in environments where children have experiences they want to talk about with responsive partners.

versation and print, the complexity of children's language will evolve naturally—at a different rate for each child. Psychologist and educator Charles Temple and his colleagues (1988, p. 10) summarize the process this way:

Children learn to talk by formulating tentative rules about the way language works, trying them out, and gradually revising them. At first, they make many mistakes in speech, but they gradually correct them. In writing we see errors of letter formation, spelling, and composition occurring as children make hypotheses about the rules that govern the writing system; errors give way to other errors before children arrive at correct forms.

Children do not start using correct forms of speech as a result of direct teaching; speech forms change only gradually. In writing, too, spelling forms and composition strategies

In High/Scope programs, adults encourage children to write in their own ways. Douglas, for example, started writing his name in the middle of the paper, ran out of room after the first three letters, then wrote the last four letters in the space at the left. While Douglas wrote the letters in his name in the correct order, he was not concerned about the unconventional arrangement of the letters on the paper.

may not be immediately improved by corrective teaching but through gradual conceptual learning that is controlled by the child as much as by the teacher.

Language, literacy, and communication develop through interactions. Maehr (1991) stresses that language is an *interactive process* rather than an *innate skill* or a *behavior* learned strictly through imitation. When children are immersed in an environment where oral and written communication are valued, they have a powerful desire to master language. Children learn to talk and write and read because they

want to communicate with the significant people in their lives. They learn to do these things because people sit down and talk with them in an unhurried manner, and listen to them and respond with interest to all their attempts, however halting, to put their own desires, thoughts, and experiences into words.

Language develops in an environment where children have experiences they *want* to talk about, and when they have a responsive partner engaging in the dialogue. These interactions with people and materials set the stage for children to construct an understanding of talking, reading, and writing—a process that begins at birth and continues to emerge throughout the preschool years.

Early childhood settings that value language, literacy, and communication are noisy and active. Since language development is an interactive process in which children learn to talk by talking freely about their experiences, it stands to reason that a preschool setting promoting language development will be distinguished by the constant hum of children's conversations. A setting where children are expected to be relatively quiet and where adults do most of the talking inhibits language development. One of the essential ingredients of the High/Scope active learning approach is *language from children,* that is, children forming and expressing thoughts and understanding in their own words. In the High/Scope setting, conversations among children and between children and adults are full of surprises; they are not scripted or perfunctory exchanges. Language arises from actions that children want to comment on and puzzle about; language development is an internal process and a noisy one, full of doing, talking, laughing, wondering out loud, debating, and discovering.

Supporting Language, Literacy, and Communication

The six High/Scope key developmental indicators (KDIs) in language, literacy, and communication present a picture of preschoolers as budding communicators. The first three indicators focus on *speaking and listening:*

- **Talking with others about personally meaningful experiences**
- **Describing objects, events, and relations**
- **Having fun with language: listening to stories and poems, making up stories and rhymes**

The remaining three focus on *reading and writing:*

- **Writing in various ways: drawing, scribbling, and using letterlike forms, invented spelling, and conventional forms**
- **Reading in various ways: reading storybooks, signs and symbols, one's own writing**
- **Dictating stories**

Maehr (1991) stresses the importance of the adult's role in an early childhood setting that supports the development of both oral and written language. The role of adults, Maehr maintains, is to encourage children throughout the day to speak freely in their own language and dialect, to write in their own way, and to read their own writing and the writing of others in their own emerging fashion.

The sections that follow on each KDI in language, literacy, and communication include specific suggestions for adults. These suggestions provide ideas for facilitating learning in ways that are appropriate and enjoyable for both children and adults. They also reflect strategies discussed in previous chapters on active learning, arranging and equipping a classroom or center for active learners, and establishing the daily routine.

Key Developmental Indicator
Talking With Others About Personally Meaningful Experiences

Jason knows that he and his mom are giving Robbie a ride at the end of the day: "If I tell Robbie I sit in the front seat, he'll think I'm a big kid," Jason says to Merrilee, his teacher. "I'm gonna tell him." He tells Robbie, then he returns to Merrilee. "I'm so excited we're bringing Robbie to his grandma's!"

❧

"Kangaroos don't need pockets," Alana says, as she takes off her mittens and puts them in her coat pockets. "'Cause they have pockets in their mommy's tummy."

❧

"Did you know that nuclear bombs die up a whole lake?" Douglas asks Kenneth as they build up their block tower again.

❧

"There's no such thing as ghosts," Hannah says to Evan. "When you see ghosts on Halloween, it's really people dressed up."

❧

Colin and Nicholas make a "fire" with bark and sticks. "These are our protectors," Colin says, indicating his gloves. "They're invisible," Nicholas adds. "Yeah, they're new, soft, and fuzzy!"

❧

"Bees get nectar from flowers," Corrin says to Sam. "They need it to make honey."

❧

"Nobody is stronger than Cathy," Jonah says to Betsy. "Cathy can pick up the whole house. She's stronger than anybody. Isn't she amazing! She's one of my invisible friends."

❧

"I have a cozy shirt. I love my cozy shirt, but I like my jumper and party shoes. I wish I could wear my party shoes to school," Abby says to Rachel. "Me, too," says Rachel.

❧

Jason and Laura play in the block area. "Everybody gather away from the dynamite," Jason says. "I feel a vibration. The earthquake's blowing up higher than a tree!"

As these anecdotes demonstrate, *talking with others about personally meaningful experiences* provides preschoolers with a solid base for language and literacy learning. Like everyone else, young children converse with others because they have something to say. They want to share their experiences with the significant persons in their lives, to make sense of discoveries and fit their observations into a personal framework of understanding. As they talk and listen, preschoolers are discovering that language helps people function. According to educator and researcher Joan Tough (1977), "All young children's learning is based on their own direct experiences. Learning to use language is no exception. Children learn to use language as they begin to communicate with others. Talking with others provides the model and the context and so forms the basis of experiences upon which the child's own disposition to use language will develop" (pp. 174–175).

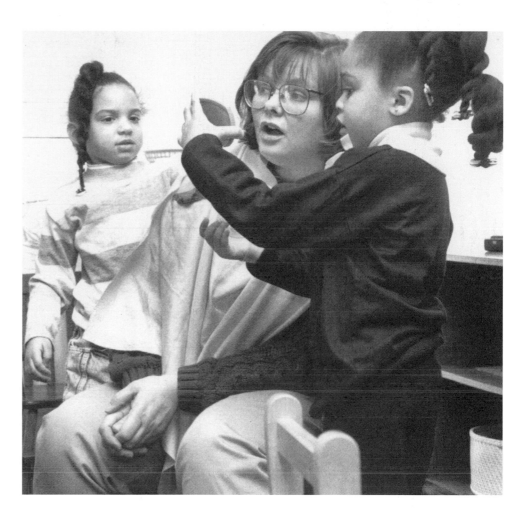

In a High/Scope setting, it is up to adults to encourage children to talk in their own ways about the things that interest them most. For example, the day after a trip to pick pumpkins at the local pumpkin patch, Ms. Flores asks the children in her small group to bring their pumpkins outside to the picnic table. The following discussion ensues:

Ms. Flores: *I wonder how we can find out what's inside these pumpkins.*

Timmy: *Cut!*

Liz: *Can I mark a line and cut? It might work.*

Victor: *My dad used a . . . a big . . . knife!*

Ms. Flores: *You could mark a line and we could cut it with a knife like Victor's dad.* (Victor goes to the house area and brings back some table knives.)

Timmy: *With that long part . . . that you stick with.*

Lisa: *Break it.* (She rolls her pumpkin off the table.) *It's . . . it's too strong!*

Ms. Flores: *It's too strong to break.*

Jeff: *Bet I could throw it.* (He throws his pumpkin on the ground.) *It . . . it broke in . . . in a little place.*

(As they get their pumpkins open, the children discover the seeds.)

Erin: *I'm gonna get a spoon.* (She goes to the house area.)

Sonya: *Look, Lisa's dumping hers over.* (Turns hers over too, and bangs on it.) *They're stuck!*

Jeff: *Ya gotta pull 'em.*

Sonya: *Ick! It's . . . it's on me!*

Jeff: *Timmy's has little hairs inside.*

Juan: *My mom said we can eat these seeds. They taste like peanuts.*

Liz: *Yuck! It tastes awful.*

Victor: *You cook 'em and then they taste like . . .*

Juan: *Peanuts!*

Victor: *No, they're seeds.*

Ms. Flores: *If we cooked some, we could taste them ourselves.*

Victor: *You put them in . . . a pan.*

Erin: *I'm gonna keep mine in my juice cup.*

As she works with the children, Ms. Flores does not focus on teaching them the names of pumpkin parts or impose her own ideas on how to proceed. Instead, she *listens carefully* to the children's observations and occasionally adds her own related comments. The children enjoy her respect and attention, and freely share their ideas. As they talk, they reveal their unique perceptions, interests, and concerns, so Ms. Flores comes to know each child a little better.

Here are some specific strategies adults can use to encourage children to talk about what they see, think, feel, and understand.

Suggestions for Adults

▶ **Establish a climate in which children feel free to talk.**

It is extremely important for adults using the High/Scope approach to create and maintain an environment in which children enjoy conversing with peers and adults *throughout* the day. It may be helpful to look back over the preceding chapters, which collectively describe how to establish such an environment and why doing so is essential. Specifically, review the elements of supportive environments discussed in Chapter 2:

- **Sharing control between adults and children**

- **Focusing on children's strengths**

- **Forming authentic relationships with children**

- **Making a commitment to supporting children's play**

- **Adopting a problem-solving approach to social conflict**

When you provide these elements of a socially supportive climate and plan a daily routine that builds on children's initiatives, you are well on the way to providing a setting where children's conversations flow freely.

▶ **Be available for conversation throughout the day.**

Children are more likely to talk with adults about personally meaningful experiences when they feel that adults desire and enjoy such conversations. Following are some ways adults can demonstrate their readiness to be partners in dialogue during each part of the daily routine.

Place yourself at the children's physical level. Since it is difficult to maintain a conversation when there is a major difference in the speakers' head or eye levels, it is important to sit, kneel, or crouch down so you are at the children's level. Assuming this position lets children know they have your full attention. It also makes you available for physical contact if

In supportive settings where the daily routine builds on children's initiatives, even sucking on a pacifier does not prevent children from talking.

a child so desires. In one preschool setting, the staff member responsible for greeting children and parents sits on the floor near the door when the children arrive. She greets the child first and later rises to talk directly with the parents. By her actions, both children and parents know they are important to her.

Listen carefully to what children are saying. It helps to look directly at a child and at the object he or she may be showing you. Allow plenty of time for children to organize their thoughts and choose the right words as they go along. While a child is talking, follow what he or she is saying rather than use this time to formu-

"Language exists only when it is listened to as well as spoken. The hearer is an indispensable partner."

—John Dewey (1958/1934, p. 106)

This adult watches and listens carefully as the children search for words to talk about the tadpoles in the fish bowl.

late your response. Otherwise, you may miss the child's meaning and the spirit of dialogue.

Give children control of conversations. You can do this by listening, focusing on what children say rather than on how they say it, following the child's conversational lead, taking turns with the child, and adding your own brief observations and comments, when appropriate.

Child: *Hey! Look at here! Look at my way-high-up boy.*

Adult: *He's very high!*

Child: *He's a lookin' and a lookin'. "There he is," he says, and his dad gets it in his truck and takes it home for the little boy. It's a little dog for the little boy.*

Adult: *Oh, I see. The boy got up high so he could find a dog?*

Child: *Yep. And his dad helps him, too, 'cause he wanted a little dog so much, but he couldn't see on the ground so he went way high up to see.*

Be prepared for any subject—the past, memorable events, speculations about the future, why events happen the way they do, why people are as they are, children's dreams. Responding to children's chosen topics with relevant comments and honest questions is more supportive than changing the subject or trying to get your own point across. Consider these examples:

• As he plays during work time, Jonah talks to a nearby adult:

Jonah: *The bear is getting ready for war. He's going to fight the bad guys.*

Adult: *Why are the bears having a war?*

Jonah: *The bad guys want to get the bears. The bears need to protect themselves.*

• Abby is "sick" in bed in the house area. While she is waiting for the "doctor," she turns to her teacher, who is also a "patient":

Abby: *My grandma was in the hospital. She was sick before she died. She threw up. Trout threw up and died, too.*

Adult: *I threw up when I was sick, then I got better.*

Abby: *I'm not really sick. I'm just pretending.*

Adult: *Me, too.*

As educational researchers Barbara Tizard and Martin Hughes (1984) found in the many conversations they recorded between children and adults: "The kind of dialogue that seems to help the child is not that currently favored by many teachers in which the adult poses a series of questions. It is rather one in which the adult listens to the child's questions and comments, helps to clarify the child's ideas, and feeds her the information she asks for" (p. 254). (For a summary of related research, see Sharing Conversational Control, Chapter 7, p. 218.)

Accept children's hesitations and non-verbal utterances. Sometimes children hesitate as they search for words to express a particularly difficult or novel idea. It is important to give them time to choose the words they need rather than jumping in with your own suggestions. Sometimes, too, children resort to nonverbal utterances when language suddenly seems inadequate. One normally articulate 3-year-old, for example, would often swoop down on his favorite people with a growl of recognition before speaking to them in the conventional manner.

Learn and remember each child's particular interests. This knowledge enables you to initiate conversations about things children might enjoy talking about. Ms. Adams, for example, knew that Tommy was particularly interested in farm equipment, so she brought in an advertisement for tractors she had received in the mail and asked him to explain the different tractors pictured on it. "This one's like my daddy's," Tommy began. Ms. Adams also knew that Petey was pleased whenever he wore new clothes. "You're wearing a new jacket today," she commented one morning, and thus initiated a conversation with Petey about shopping with his uncle.

▶ **Encourage children to talk with one another throughout the day.**

Talking with other children can be a socially satisfying interaction for a child as well as a way of sharing experiences and gathering new information. While some children talk with peers more readily than do other children, almost all young children need adult support at one time or another. Here are some ways adults can help children talk with one another.

Provide opportunities for cooperative projects and play. Some materials, by their very nature, appeal to children and bring them together for play and conversation at work time, small-group time, and outside time:

• **Heavy awkward things,** such as appliance boxes, logs, and boards, that require children to work together to move and position them. Children also want to see who is inside the box or get inside themselves.

• **Large items that can be filled and emptied,** such as wagons, wheelbarrows, and tents. Again, children want to see what is in the wagon, to get in for a ride, or to negotiate a turn to push or pull.

• **Water-related materials,** such as items for watering the garden, washing bikes and sand toys, soaping and scrubbing the art table, blowing bubbles, washing smocks and doll clothes, making a pond in the sandbox, floating boats, and playing in the rain.

• **Real utensils and tools,** including mops and buckets, computers, hammers and nails. One teaching team recorded this conversation between two 4-year-olds as they used a large tank-type vacuum cleaner:

Lynnette: *Okay, Markie. You push this metal thing.*

Markie: *Can't go. Stuck. Wait. I got it now. I got this hose thing. Now go.*

Lynnette: *There it goes. There it goes. Ohhh, eee!*

Markie: *The dirt goes up under. Here's some more.*

Lynnette: *Stop! Cut it off . . .*

Support children who wish to plan and recall together. "I'm playing with Callie." Often children know whom they want to play with, but they don't know what they are going to do until they have had a chance to talk with their buddies. In these situations it makes sense to encourage the children to plan together: "Corrin, when Callie comes you can talk with her about your plans. Then tell me what you have decided to do." Or if Callie and Corrin are in two different planning groups, an adult might say, "Corrin, it sounds like you need to go talk to Callie and make your plan together. Let me know what you have decided."

Sometimes, too, children make separate plans to use the same materials, such as blocks. This presents an opportunity for the children to talk together about how to proceed. It is important that adults support children in their efforts to talk about the situation ("We need these blocks for our house!" "Well, we need them for our roller coaster!") rather than solving the children's problem for them.

At recall time, children who have played together or even just near each other will often spontaneously add to each other's recall narratives. They may tell what they saw each other doing, ask each other questions, or offer suggestions and ideas. (For examples, see Chapter 7, pp. 234, 238.)

Refer one child's questions and problems to another child. When children ask adults for help at work time, small-group time, outside time, or any other time, adults can often step aside and refer them to other children. This puts children in contact with one another and shows them that they can turn to their peers for assistance. The underlying message is that children, not just adults, are competent:

Tim: (To Ann, an adult) *This thing won't work!*

Ann: *Tim, ask Noah. He knows how that computer program works.*

Tim: (To Noah) *It's stuck. I want it to go here.*

Noah: *Well, roll the mouse like this. See.*

Tim: *There it goes! Let me do it!*

Interpret and deliver messages. In almost every early childhood setting there are children who do not understand each other. Perhaps they speak a different language, like Roger and Aquiles in the scenario below. Or perhaps they pronounce the same words in different ways. Through close observation, as well as by trial and error, adults can learn to understand what children are trying to communicate and serve as their interpreters, as Mr. Yanez does in this episode:

Mr. Yanez: *Roger, I thought you were going to build a house in el rincón de los bloques.*

Roger: *I was gonna, but Totor and Jimbo have 'em all.*

Mr. Yanez: *Totor and Jimbo do have all the blocks.*

Roger: (Shakes his head in agreement, then looks at Aquiles.)

Mr. Yanez: *Hey, maybe Aquiles has an idea. Aquiles, podrias ayudarle a Roger? Quiere construir una casa pero los bloques ya estan ocupados. Que mas podriamos usar para hacer una house?*

These two children pause at snack time to talk about an important matter. (Note the example of scribble writing on the wall to the left.)

Aquiles: *Los Tinkertoys.*

Mr. Yanez: *Aquiles says you could use the Tinkertoys.*

Roger: *We could cover it with that thing and hide inside!*

Mr. Yanez: *Oh, the sheet! Aquiles, Roger dice que podrian cubrir la Tinkertoy casa con esta sabana y esconderse adentro!* (The boys start making their house.)

Explain the context of children's statements. Young children sometimes make statements that seem out of context because they often do not link one topic of conversation to the next, or because they do not frame their ideas with statements such as "Remember last week when . . .". Adults who know the children in their setting well can sometimes fill the gaps in such statements, thus helping children's conversations to continue:

These adults talk with children throughout the day. They give their full attention to each child and understand that each conversation unfolds at the child's pace.

Callie: *I'm writing letters.* (She fills the front of an envelope with letters.)

Linda: *I can write my name. L-I-N-D-A.*

Callie: (Licks and seals the envelope.) *We need a box.*

Linda: *A box?*

Callie: *For letters.*

Linda: *We don't need a box. You just write 'em.* (She continues to write.)

Callie: *You can't get letters 'til you put 'em in the box.*

Linda: *That's dumb.*

Adult: *I think Callie is talking about a mailbox, Linda.*

Linda: *Oh, you mean with stamps!*

Callie: *A box for letters and stamps and stuff.*

Acknowledge conflicting viewpoints. Children's conversations can fall apart when they disagree. Sometimes, adults can assist the conversation by acknowledging each child's point of view, as illustrated in the following conversation, which occurred as Troy and Erin stacked inch-cubes at small-group time:

Erin: *I made a family.*

Troy: *Me, too.*

Erin: *Just people. No dogs.*

Troy: *No dogs and no pets.*

Erin: *See.* (Points to the tallest stack of cubes.) *The mom's the biggest.*

Troy: *No. That's the daddy. The daddy's the biggest.*

Erin: *NO! THE MOM'S THE BIGGEST!*

Troy: *Teacher, isn't the daddy the biggest?*

Adult: *In some families the mom is the biggest, and in some families the daddy is the biggest.*

Troy: *My dad's the biggest. I know.*

Erin: *My mom's the biggest 'cause she's 28!*

▶ **Converse with *all* children.**

"Substantive talk is not a frill," stresses educator Elfrieda Hiebert (1990, p. 503). "It is a primary means for becoming literate." Since having personally meaningful conversations is extremely important for young learners, it is imperative that adults converse with *all* the children in their care. The following strategies will help you reach out conversationally to all the children you work with.

Make time to talk with children. Conversations with young children take time to unfold. They suffer when held on demand or when children or adults feel hurried. In a setting with large numbers of children and the framework of a daily schedule, this means giving your full attention to the child you are talking with for the duration of the conversation. It also calls for leaving enough "breathing space" during each part of the day for conversations to occur. Remember, enabling children to converse is a major part of the active learning approach; it is not a waste of time or a distraction from something more important.

Look for comfortable opportunities for dialogue. Conversations between children and adults are most likely to occur in cozy, intimate settings, such as reading a story with a child, sitting in a rocking chair together, having a snack outside under a tree, walking hand-in-hand. It is important for adults to seek out comfortable places and opportunities for engaging in conver-

sations with children. Educator Jerome Bruner (1980) reminds us that "perhaps the best inspiration to prolonged and connected conversation is a teacher joining a small group of children as a *participant in the play*" (p. 188).

Be aware of your personal preferences. Every adult finds some children easier to talk with than others. Our job as early childhood educators, however, is to talk with *all* children in our care, regardless of our personal preferences. An excellent way to track your conversations is to record them to see with which children you are having meaningful conversations and which children you may be overlooking. Also, you can examine your anecdotal records. Few or no entries under **language, literacy, and communication** for a particular child may mean that this is a child you need to converse with.

Key Developmental Indicator
Describing Objects, Events, and Relations

"I'm pumping my legs!" Brianna says as she swings.

∾

"If you want to be a dragon, you need fire," Brian tells Alana.

∾

"I'm slithering in the water," Kacey calls to Julia from under the slide.

∾

"It's a machine that twists and gives you candy flavors," Trey says, showing Douglas what he is making. *"I'm making an exercise machine that strongs up your legs,"* Douglas replies.

∾

"She couldn't breathe and her heart stopped and we had to push on her stomach and take an x-ray," says Amanda at recall time, describing her work-time role play.

∾

Douglas tells Beth how he hits the ball. *"I just hold it in my hand and whack!"* Then he hits the ball to demonstrate.

∾

Hannah tells Betsy how she made her picture. "I took the shiny side and scribbled with the crayon around and around. Then I drew on the top with the marker."

∾

"It uses sharp things sticking out of the wheels to climb up steep things that go straight up," Douglas says, showing Nathan his monster truck.

∾

"You shake it and it turns to bubbles," Alana says to Brian at the water table.

∾

"It's a special tool," Jonah tells Colin about the garlic press he is using with Play-Doh. *"Close it and push it. Then it comes out like this."*

∾

"Julia's just a little shy," Sarah says to Becki in the "beauty parlor." *"She doesn't want her hair done."*

∾

"I'm taking my paper out," this child says, describing her actions as she works with paper and paint. When she unfolds her paper, the print she finds and shows to her teacher speaks for itself!

This indicator often occurs with another one: *talking with others about personally meaningful experiences.* As children talk about their experiences, they often *describe objects, events, and relations.* In their own time and in their own way, children express what they know in words and attempt to construct a coherent understanding of things that capture their interest or puzzle them. Listening to young children as they struggle to describe things will alert adults to what children are thinking about and how they perceive what they are doing.

When children are *describing objects, events, and relations* they are using familiar words and also adding new words to their vocabulary.

Adults can help them largely through their attentive listening and alertness to situations children are particularly interested in describing. The strategies that follow are ways adults can encourage children to think about and describe their experiences.

Suggestions for Adults

▶ **Provide children with interesting materials and experiences.**

At small-group time, Timmy and Joey bend over a photograph of their field trip to the pumpkin patch and carry on the following conversation:

Timmy: *There's me!*

Joey: *There's me, too!*

Timmy: *Look at Ricky. He's bald-headed!*

Joey: *Who that?*

Timmy: *My daddy.*

Joey: *What's that thing he's wearing?*

Timmy: *That's . . . let me see . . . That's his hat!*

Joey: *That ain't no hat.*

Timmy: *That's a fishin' hat. See* (pointing to hat) *. . . here's where . . . where he sticks things.*

Joey: *That hurt?*

Timmy: *No, you stick it in . . . in the . . . that thing that goes around. Like a pocket.*

Joey: *A hat pocket?*

Timmy: *Yeah, a hat pocket . . . it's long.*

In settings where children are free to talk, providing them with interesting materials and situations gives them something to talk about. To begin, think about the children in your care. What does Timmy like to do? What does Joanie like to play with? One team, for example, noticed that one child, Tracy, was much more likely to talk when he was outdoors because there he could engage in two of his favorite activities: climbing, and looking for bugs under rocks and logs. Building on these interests, the adults took pictures of Tracy on the climber at outside time, used the photos at small-group time, and then added them to the book area. They also provided materials indoors for Tracy to make a bug cage so he could watch some of these creatures more closely. Gradually, surrounded by things he was comfortable with, Tracy began to talk more while he was inside.

Another approach to providing materials that stimulate children's language is to use the ideas for preparing the setting presented in Chapter 5. Skim the lists of materials, noting items to add to your setting that might be particularly appealing to your children. Focus on materials that will involve children closely with their peers (see p. 326).

Finally, whenever you add new materials to your setting, involve the children in labeling them and deciding where to store them. This kind of discussion necessarily involves talking about the new material and how it relates to other, similar items.

► **Listen as children describe things in their own way.**

One of the most effective ways to encourage young children to talk and describe things is to *listen* to them. The more adults *talk*, the fewer opportunities children have to speak; but the more adults *listen,* the more children talk.

Accept children's descriptions. As you listen to children you will find that what children see and describe will not always match what you see and might expect them to describe. In a discussion about mustaches, for example, Troy said that his mom had a mustache. "Oh?" said his teacher. "It's up here . . . by her eyes," Troy said, tracing the line of his eyebrows. In another preschool setting, Brian waved good-by to his dad and said to his teacher, "I'm my father's son." A few minutes later he confided, "My dad is my son." While neither Brian nor Troy were correct from an adult point of view, they were calling upon and using the best descriptive capacities they had. They were communicating everything they knew about mustaches and family relationships. Troy's and Brian's teachers accepted the children's descriptions because they understood that the children's *descriptive processes* were more important to focus on than whether or not their statements were correct by adult standards. They also understood that as Troy and Brian have more experiences, their descriptions of

Thoughtful play conversations are a natural outcome when spaces are well organized and stocked with engaging materials.

mustaches and father-son relationships will become more complete and accurate.

► **Encourage children to talk about their plans.**

As children become involved in the planning and recall process, their capacity to include details in their plans and to recall narratives increases. They also become increasingly able to talk about abstract events, a skill that lays the groundwork for subsequent reading comprehension (Snow 1991). For specific strategies that support children's descriptive detail as they plan and recall, see the sections titled **Adults**

converse with routine and elaborate planners (pp. 188–190) and **Adults converse with children about their work-time experiences (pp. 234–240)** in Chapter 7. You can also listen for and support children's descriptions of their plans and play at other times of the day—for example, during outside time, small-group time, and large-group time.

► **Let children be the leaders in "describing" games.**

Adapting games to include opportunities for describing things and then having the children be the leader-describers is one way to build *describing objects and events* into games children enjoy. Here are some examples:

• "Simon Says"—Instead of having Simon say "Do this," have a child think of and describe the action: "Put your legs far, far apart." "Slap your hands on the floor."

• "Little Foxes"—Have a child think of and describe a place for all the foxes to run to: "Run to the stone steps." "Hop to the log."

• "Let's Be . . ."—Each child takes a turn describing something for everyone else to pretend to be. "Let's be . . . a man paintin'." "Let's be . . . a dog licking his feet."

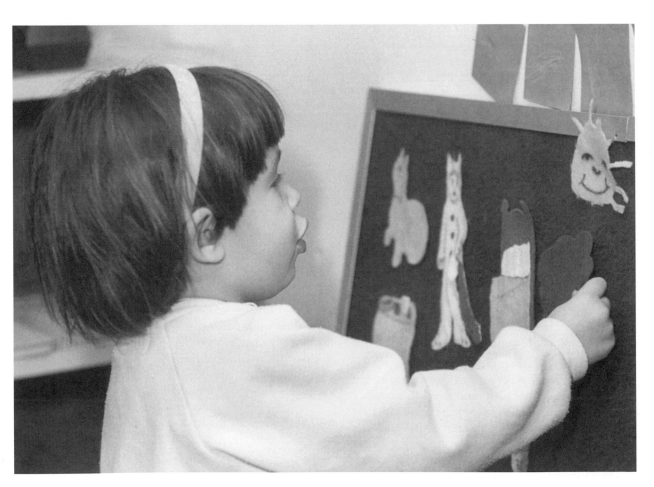

This child enjoys making up her own story and illustrating it with flannel-board figures.

Key Developmental Indicator
Having Fun With Language: Listening to Stories and Poems, Making Up Stories and Rhymes

Kenneth is playing with a tub of ground coffee beans. He says to Beth, an adult who is nearby, "I made a coffee cake. Get it? A coffee cake. Isn't that funny!"

~

Jessa looks at Corrin's cut-up name symbol and says, "It got lawn-mowered!"

~

Andrew is talking about a boy named Randy. "Candy could be his sister and Andy could be his brother!"

~

"Beth," Jessa says to her teacher as everyone gets ready for outside time, "you're standing on my mitten." Beth moves her foot. Jessa holds her mitten up and says, "Squished to death by teacher Beth!" She and Beth laugh.

~

"Knock, knock," says Colin to Nicholas at lunch.
"Who's there?"
"Orange peel."
"Orange peel who?"
"Orange peel tree!" Both boys laugh.

~

When Douglas comes to greeting circle he says to Julie, an adult, "See you later, alligator!"
"See you at the rug, Doug!" she replies.
"See you at the snowball, Towball,"
says Douglas.

"See you at the jam, Sam."
"See you at the jelly, Belly."
"See you at the hall, Paul."
"See you at the door, Snore."
"See you at the bridge, Midge."
"See you at the rocket, Socket."

"I jumped up and down, and you know what I said?" Jonah asks Betsy, his teacher. "Bang-a-wang!"

Colin tells a story to Jarrod to set up a pretend-play scene: "Pretend I'm lost and some ants trapped me. First, I'm going to get a cape, and then I'm going to go away from home. Then I'm going to get lost. Some ants are going to trap me. They use some sting, some hard sting. I will crash out. I will fly home."

For most young children, playing with language is a spontaneous activity they have been enjoying since infancy. Preschoolers have fun with language when they converse in their own fashion with family members and friends; listen to people tell and read stories; make up their own words, stories, and rhymes; and try out and repeat new words and expressions, even when they do not know what they mean. Three-year-old Sarina, for example, entertained herself by repeating, "Silence goes by, silence goes by" and trying out other words she had heard and liked the sound of, such as "convertible" and "carburetor." In the garden, Brian's dad and grandpa discussed the tomatoes that needed watering. "Yes," Brian stated, to be part of the conversation, "the tomatoes need a lot of water," even though, when it was time to water them, Brian had no idea what or where the tomatoes were.

Research on language development suggests that young children enjoy playing with language because it makes them feel in control (Fromberg 1987); research also indicates that children's "play with the structures, sounds, and meanings of language is related to language acquisition" (Sponseller 1982, p. 232). When children listen to stories, they are experiencing the connection between writing and reading. When they create a story or nonsense rhyme, they are learning that they can tell their own stories and put words together in a satisfying way. *Having fun with language and listening to and making up stories and rhymes* extend children's understanding of the use and effectiveness of language as a means of communication. Following are ways adults can support children's language play.

Suggestions for Adults

▶ **Listen to children throughout the day.**

Be alert for children's word play. One of the best ways to understand and support children's interest in language is to listen attentively to them as they work and play. Sometimes young children, especially 3-year-olds, talk to themselves as they play, telling a story about what they are doing. Listening to and recording these stories can help you capture and understand children's command of language as they wrestle with concepts and ideas. Educator Linda Gibson (1989, p. 50) recorded the story 3-year-old Tomo told as he rolled Play-Doh into an increasingly larger circle:

Friendly monster . . . I'm the same friendly monster . . . I'm still a baby . . . good-by . . . I'm going to be much better . . . OK . . . yes . . . he's going to be bigger-bigger-bigger now . . .

(rolls out the dough with a wooden roller—the action distorts the face and makes it bigger) . . . he's going to be 4 years old . . . the friendly monster is ready to come out . . . he's going to be his own self now, not his mother or his daddy . . . "Now I am 4 years old! Now I am 4 years old! Now I am 4 years old! I am big now. I am big now. I can jump up! Hello! I'm the same monster. Good-by! Good-by!" . . . [To Laura as he rolls out the Play-Doh even further] He was much bigger, right? He's going to get bigger, bigger than you . . . Then he's going to be daddy . . . He does grow up . . . See?

Also, be ready to listen to children who have stories they particularly want to relate to you. Children often approach adults when they first arrive in the morning or at odd times during the day with stories they want to share about something that happened at home or something they are considering. For example, Penny, a 4-year-old in England, was concerned about whether Father Christmas would have a "dancellina" (her word for ballerina outfit) in her size and how he would know that she wanted one. Jason, another preschooler, told what happened during his visit to a beach:

I was coming back from the beach with Papa. And my hands were behind my back and there was a towel on me. And all of a sudden, Papa heard me crying. He turned around and guess what happened? I bonked my face on the ground and my hands were still behind my back!

Although these stories take time to tell and listen to, it is very important that adults give them their full attention since children's spontaneous use of language as a means of communication is at the heart of the learning process.

As this adult reads the story these children have requested, he pauses from time to time for their comments and observations.

▶ **Read to children individually and in small, intimate groups.**

In one preschool setting, one team member greets children and parents while the other adult sits in the book area reading to children who gather around her. Some children huddle close to her as she reads; others select their own books and "read" to each other. Parents and grandparents who have a few extra minutes also join in reading to the children, their younger siblings, and other children who join them. Several stories are going at once and children cluster on, next to, and over the shoulders of accommodating adults. These groups of parents, teachers, and children reading first thing in the morning set the tone for the children's enjoyment of reading throughout the day.

Perhaps no single activity is more important to children's emerging literacy than

being read to by familiar adults and friends. After examining reading in 15 countries, linguist Robert Thorndike (1973) found that children who had been read aloud to from an early age became the best readers. Following 32 children from age 12 months to 11 years, British linguist Gordon Wells concluded that the more stories young children had heard, the better readers they later became. "The children who obtained relatively high scores on the knowledge-of-literacy test," Wells reported, "were likely to have parents who read more and owned more books; they were also likely to read more often to their

Perhaps no single activity is more important to children's emerging literacy than being read to by familiar adults. Nestling close to the reader, children associate stories and reading with the satisfaction of warm human relationships.

children" (1986b, p. 144). These findings are supported by psychologist Nathan Caplan's and associates' (1992) work with Indochinese refugee children in the United States. In their study, high school students who had been read to regularly as young children by parents or siblings in either English or their native language achieved higher grade point averages than children who had not been read to.

Being read to by parents, family members, and other significant adults creates a close physical and personal bond, so children associate the satisfaction of warm human relationships with stories and reading. As the process is repeated over and over again, children also begin to make connections between the written and spoken word and to gain a sense of how to use language to tell stories.

Reading to children in an early childhood setting is different from reading to children at home, simply because there are more children involved. Nevertheless, there are particular strategies adults can adopt to make reading in preschool as intimate and homelike as possible:

• As a general practice, read with small groups of children rather than one large group.

• Sit on the floor when you read so children can cluster around you as close to you as possible. Sitting on a couch also works well with a small number of children.

• Maintain a balance between introducing new stories and enabling children to select familiar stories they wish to hear.

• Re-read children's favorite stories at their request or at your own initiative. As parents understand, children love to hear their favorite stories again and again, both during the same sitting and over a period of weeks and months.

• Read interactively and with pleasure. Pause for children's comments and questions. Enjoy the story yourself as well as the children's responses to it.

• Make story-reading a regular part of your daily routine so children can count on being read to at least once or twice a day. For example, you might read every day at greeting circle, during snack time, at the end of small-group time, or just before nap time.

• Read at work time and other times of the day at the children's request.

► **Tell stories, recite poems and rhymes.**

Telling stories rather than reading from a book is a way to have fun with language, inflections, and gestures. Tell any story you enjoy telling—folk tales, myths and legends, fairy tales, tall tales, stories you were told as a child, stories about things you did as a child, stories you invent about the children in your setting. Here are some storytelling strategies to consider for small- and large-group times:

• Pass around a basket of props or puppets for children to use as you tell a story or as they make up a story themselves.

• Tell some stories without props so children can rely on their imaginations to picture situations and details. Have them act out the actions and make up the sounds the story calls for.

• Ask children for a story starter and build a story from there. They might suggest an opening line ("Once upon a time there were two monsters who lived under the bed . . .") or a particular subject ("Tell a story about a spaceship").

• Accept and build children's comments into the stories you tell. As educator and storyteller Ann Trousdale (1990) points out, this makes storytelling an *interactive* process in which children can have some control over the direction and outcome of the story.

Recite poems and verses you know by heart. Hearing and identifying rhymes attunes children to sounds in words, an awareness of which helps them when they begin to associate the smallest units of spoken sound (phonemes) with written letters (phonics). One adult always

These children listen to a "scary" story their teacher tells them on their "camping trip" inside a real tent set up on the playground.

recited "Up in the air we go so high, up in the air so blue. Oh, I don't know of a pleasanter thing, ever a child could do!" whenever she pushed a child on the swing; another chanted "Thumbs in the thumb hole, fingers all together, this is the song we sing in mitten weather!" as she and the children put on their mittens.

▶ **Make up stories, chants, and rhymes.**

As they play, some children make up their own chants and rhymes:

"Big dig. Big dig."

"Mouse in the house!"

"Up and down to get the crown."

Listen for children's chants and rhymes, and join in to let children know you enjoy their word play.

Make up rhymes with children. At one preschool, for example, as the children were making sandwiches, the adult started saying "Spread the bread, spread the bread" to which the children added, "Go to bed." "Hands on head." "Nobody said." "I like lead." This was the beginning of a book of child-created rhymes. One favorite rhyme originated from a field trip when a child saw a man crossing the street and said, "There goes Popper Noodle." From this developed

"There goes Popper Noodle.
He likes apple strudel.
When he eats with a spoon
He goes to the moon.
Mister Popper Noodle."

As children play with rhymes in this manner, they strengthen their awareness of sounds at the ends of words that are the same and initial phonemes.

Key Developmental Indicator
Writing in Various Ways: Drawing, Scribbling, and Using Letterlike Forms, Invented Spelling, and Conventional Forms

Douglas draws a faucet and writes the letter T on it. "Hot," he says, looking at his picture.

❧

Brianna scribbles on a clipboard at work time. "I made a list. I wrote your name," she says to Jalessa.

❧

Bryant writes his name on the camera sign-up sheet, BRY~~~

❧

Corrin writes her name on a picture, ⌐Orrn

❧

"Look," says Alana, writing the letter B. "I made a B."

❧

Abby writes lots of A's on an envelope. "A is my favorite letter," she says.

❧

At recall time, Andrew writes I PLAYED ✚ *(I played with Douglas.)*

❧

Alana writes PETR on the computer. "That's my teacher, Peter," she says.

❧

Bryant writes MOM on his painting. "That says Evie [his mom's name]," he says.

❧

Deola makes Sarah an invitation to her birthday party. On it she writes BFD A IM HB. "It says, Birthday. I'm having a party," she tells Sarah.

❧

Andrew writes FRIS when Audie orders French fries at the fast-food restaurant he and Chrysten have set up in the house area.

❧

Douglas dips wooden letters in paint and prints SAD and DOG.

❧

Chrysten writes DOUGLAS by copying the letters from the sign over Douglas's coathook.

❧

Corrin makes two signs for her block house: YES CORRIN and NO CORRIN. "Yes is for girls," she says. "No is for boys."

❧

Another day, Jalessa makes a sign for her block house: GO-A-WAY-DOUGLAS.

Preschoolers have some knowledge about the graphic features of print before they receive formal instruction in reading and writing and even before they can name letters and recognize words (Schickedanz 1982). Through their own encounters with print and people who read it, preschoolers have come to expect print to have meaning. Therefore, they are highly motivated to figure out how written language works so they can use it themselves. To this end, they experiment with drawing and making printlike marks to construct their own systems of writing. Over time, children's efforts become increasingly conventional as they strive to make sense of the relationships between written symbols and the sounds of oral language.

Children's writing ability develops gradually in concert with their oral language development, and we should value and support this emerging skill in all its forms. To do this, we must recognize and accept children's early writing efforts as significant attempts to use writing as a tool for communication. We must also understand that to expect young children to produce conventional written forms before they have gone through the preliminary steps of the writing process is to prevent them from fully understanding the process and making it their own. Following are appropriate ways adults can support young writers' emerging skills and abilities as they *write in various ways*.

Suggestions for Adults

▶ **Provide a variety of writing and drawing materials.**

A well-equipped art area offers children all kinds of writing materials throughout the day—paper in various sizes and colors, paints, brushes, marking pens, crayons, and colored pencils. (See the art area materials list in Chapter 5, p. 135.) Also, provide boxes of colored chalk for children to use during outside time for sidewalk writing experiences.

In addition to supplying the art area with writing materials, some teaching teams set up a writing or office area that includes such materials as pads, notebooks, blank books, folders, envelopes, stickers, stamps, ink pads, and coupons. (See the book and writing area materials list in Chapter 5, p. 139.)

In a comfortable spot on the stairs, this preschooler writes the names of two significant family members.

Computers equipped with age-appropriate software also offer satisfying, child-friendly writing tools. While many software programs use letters and numbers incidentally, preschool word-processing programs allow children to produce enlarged print, and in some cases, to actually hear what they have written. Children's drawing programs also support children's emergent writing by allowing them to use the mouse to draw and make scribbles and marks to accompany their drawings. Many drawing programs also enable children to add conventional print to their drawings by selecting letters with the mouse or keyboard. (See the monthly magazine *Children's Technology Review* [www.childrenssoftware.com] for examples of such programs.) In fact, because computers enable children to produce text without having to hold and guide a pencil, they make it easy for adults to see the capacity of young children to express themselves in writing. Three preschoolers—Ben, Kenneth, and Andrew—were very excited one day when they typed out SAM IS POP on the computer, and the computer read it back to them. As they continued to work, they delighted themselves, and everyone else in the room, with the following variations: SAM IS POP. SAM IS PEP. SAM IS PEPI. SAM IS PUPY. BETH IS PUPEE, and so forth. Because the computer gave them immediate feedback, children were inspired to write as many outrageous statements as they could formulate. Throughout this process, their teachers were impressed by their understanding of the writing process.

▶ **Anticipate various emergent forms of writing.**

Temple et al. (1988) observe that "rather than learning to write by mastering first the parts (letters) and then building up to the whole (written lines), it appears that children first attend to the

Linda uses a variety of emergent writing forms to "write" her plan. At the upper left, she draws a train track; below this drawing she writes the first two letters of her name, L and i, followed by some letterlike forms; below this line she writes more letterlike forms; and in the lower left corner she writes in scribbles. "Play with the train tracks," she says, "reading" her plan to her teacher.

whole and only much later to the parts" (p. 19). In other words, while children's early writing may resemble print in direction and appearance, it may consist of lines of scribbles, not recognizable letters. It may also include drawings as part of the text as well as recurring marks and symbols. When children do begin to use letters, they combine them in ways that make sense to them based on letter sounds—for example, writing B 4, for BEFORE, and OPN for OPEN. Following are the kinds of writing preschoolers typically produce.

Drawing. While most preschoolers can distinguish between pictures and writing, it is not yet clear to them that adults actually read the *print* in a storybook, not the *pictures.* Probably because they themselves derive meaning from storybook illustrations, children's early writing is composed mainly of pictures. In this form of writing, children create picture stories using the same techniques our ancestors used when they drew scenes of hunting and communal life on cave walls. While most preschoolers write about everyday happenings, viewing their drawings as a form of written communication expands our appreciation of their ability to express their ideas. For example, one child wrote a story by drawing four people of various sizes. "This is about my family," she read.

Scribbling. Young children who scribble-write will generate several lines of writing that are wavy or letterlike in appearance. As they scribble, they are conscious of writing something for others to read. While the dictionary defines scribbling as hurried, careless, meaningless marks, for young children scribbling is a meaningful form of communication.

"This is the best spaghetti I've had in a long time. Could you give me the recipe?" asked Becki, an adult, as she finished her last bit of pretend spaghetti. Callie, the spaghetti maker, went to the art area for paper and pencil. When she returned, she wrote down the recipe in several scribbled lines. "Thank you," said Becki as she studied Callie's writing. "Would you read this to me, Callie, so I'm sure I've got it right?" "Sauce . . . noodles . . . cheese . . . salt . . . milk," she read, pointing to each line.

Letterlike forms. As they explore writing and create stories, children invent forms that have many of the characteristics of letters but are not themselves conventional letters. They may also incorporate some familiar symbols—perhaps a circle bisected by a line or a dollar sign. Children often use such symbols as part of their dramatic play. For example, when several children were driving small yellow school buses around the room, the children in the block area made a sign that consisted of a drawing of a school bus with a slash through it surrounded by a circle. They taped the sign to the floor by the entrance to the block area. When the bus drivers drove up to the sign, they stopped, turned around, and headed for more "open" territory.

Actual letters. As they become familiar with the letters in their name and other important letters, children will begin to use them in their writing. At first, preschool children will often write a string of unrelated letters. Eventually, however, they will begin to isolate a sound or two in a word and use letters and numbers to signify the sounds. One spring, for example, when the teaching team added some tunnels to the block area, Ben made his own label for them that included the word TNLS. When Anna made a picture for Sam, she labeled it 4 SAM. Another day, Callie spent a long time setting up a restaurant outside. When she finally had everything in order, she wrote a sign, OPN, to let people know she was ready for business.

This is a story Trey "wrote" at work time. Note that Trey's "writing" includes drawings, letters, words, and numbers.

Conventional forms. Most preschoolers are not highly involved in conventional spelling, a process that in the United States takes most of (and sometimes more than) the elementary years to develop. They *are* interested, however, in the correct spelling of their own first names. Petey, for example, was using a preschool word-processing computer program. He called Ben over and asked him how to spell BEN. Together they found B-E-N on the keyboard and typed it out. Another day, Scott built a large truck out of blocks. He decided to make a sign for his truck so people would know what type of truck it was. Using markers and paper from the art area he printed out a sign that said MONSTER TRUCK and taped it on the side of the toy.

► **Encourage children to write in their own way.**

Children whose writing is supported at every step tend to have lots to communicate, and they become enthusiastic writers. Children who must master letter formation, spelling, and grammar, however, *before* they are allowed to write their own compositions, often view the writing process as tedious and unrewarding. Since we would rather support than discourage children's writing, it is important that we understand how writing evolves from drawing and scribbling to letterlike forms, actual letters, and, finally, conventional forms. It is also up to us to encourage young children to progress from wherever they are on the writing continuum. Here are some ways to do this.

Ask children to write stories. You can make a simple request at planning time, recall time, or small-group time to "See if you can write a story about your plan," or "How about writing a story about what you did at work time," or simply, "Let's write stories." Such a request can spur children to write when they might not have thought of writing as an option. Assure children of success by saying something similar to what Sulzby and Barnhart (1990)

suggest: "It doesn't have to be like grown-up writing. Just write your own way. Then you can read your story when you are finished" (p. 202). Acknowledge children's efforts as *writing* in whatever form they take. Douglas, for example, wrote a recall story that consisted of a drawing of a faucet with two handles and the letter T over one of the handles. When he read his story he said, "I used hot water!"

Encourage children to write to one another. This builds on the idea of using written language to make things happen. Trina had planned on playing with her friend Christina, but Christina was home with the flu. When Trina was unable to think of anything else she wanted to do, her teacher suggested that she write to Christina. Trina then decided to spend work time "writing a card to get better."

Anna, a 4-year-old, had made a house out of cardboard blocks. When Callie and Corrin built a wooden house right next to hers, they kept brushing against her house, knocking the walls down. Finally, an upset Anna told Beth, her teacher, what was happening. "Have you talked with Callie and Corrin?" Beth asked. Anna shook her head, then went to the art area for paper and pencil. She wrote MOVO RO S ANNA on a piece of paper and hung this sign on her house. When Callie and Corrin asked her what it said, she read, "Move your house. Anna." Duly impressed, Callie and Corrin carried out Anna's request. (See Anna's sign on p. 340.)

Accept children's additions to your writing. In High/Scope programs, as teaching teams interact with children throughout the day, they pause from time to time to jot down what they see children doing and hear them saying, and they share this information later at adult daily team planning time. One team, composed of Beth and Becki, wear necklace pens and keep notecards in their pockets for this purpose. The first time 4-year-old Kenneth observed Beth writing, he

MOVO RD
S ANNA

When Callie and Corrin built their block house too close to Anna's block house, Anna wrote this sign and hung it on her house. She read it to Callie and Corrin this way: "Move your house." Taking Anna's message to heart, Callie and Corrin moved their house!

asked what she was doing. "I'm writing stories about what I see children doing," she replied. This prompted Kenneth to borrow her pen and notecards so he could write about his friend Brian. The children became so interested in their teachers' note-taking process that Becki and Beth added necklace pens and cards to the art area.

▶ **Display and send home samples of children's writing.**

Since writing is a means of communication, sharing what one has written is a significant part of the writing process. Like other writers, young children enjoy reading their writing, especially when they read it to people who mean a lot to them. Therefore, it is important to post children's stories for others to see and to send children's stories home so they can read them to their families. We want parents to take pleasure in their children's writing process and understand its link to conventional writing. Saying something to each parent (at the door or in a parent meeting) about the value of children's emergent writing may encourage parents to respond enthusiastically to their children's work.

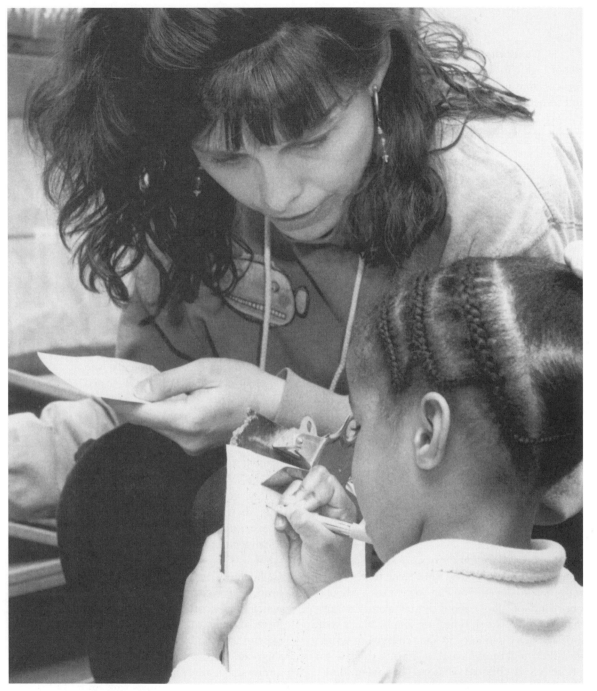

This child is so interested in her teacher's note-taking that she "writes" some notes for herself!

Key Developmental Indicator
Reading in Various Ways: Reading Storybooks, Signs and Symbols, One's Own Writing

Douglas scribbles a note to Callie and "reads" it. "I'll get you a water baby and California Roller Blades."

❧

Julia writes a letter in scribbles to Peter and "reads" it to him. "At dance class there is no fighting."

❧

Trey "reads" from a series of pictures he has drawn. "I'm fixing dinner with my key and that's silly!"

❧

Abby points to each letter on her slipper and says, "A-B-B-Y."

❧

Kenneth types the letters CR on the computer and exclaims, "It says Sir. It says Sir!"

❧

Using the computer program "Sticky-bear Town Builder," Chrysten says, "That says Stickybear. I can read that."

❧

Colin "reads" the book Frog and Toad *by looking at the pictures.*

❧

Aimee writes AIMEE CALLIE CARRIE and says, "Look, A-E-I. They all have A E I!"

❧

Kenneth and Chelsea look at an animal picture book together. When Chelsea identifies one animal as a lion, Kenneth says, "That's not a lion. It's a tiger. See, it's not an L. It's a T."

❧

"I taught Colby how to read!" Amanda tells Betsy. "I read him The Little Engine.*"*

❧

In an environment that supports language and literacy, young children spend time with books and print materials, constructing a personal understanding of the reading process long before they are actually able to read.

At greeting circle, Audie "reads" the whole Go Dog, Go *book by looking at the pictures and remembering the words.*

❦

At work time, Aimee stops by the picture chart of the museum field trip song and sings it all the way through by "reading" the pictures.

❦

Petey figures out when his turn for the camera is by "reading" the list of children's symbols on the camera sign-up sheet.

❦

During a work-time game of "Go Fish," Alana sorts out all the cards with A's on them.

❦

Isaac looks at his name symbol on his cubby for a while, then says, "I can spell my name backwards. C-A-A-S-I guitar!"

In the High/Scope approach, young children are involved in making sense of the reading process long before they are actually able to read. Every time an adult reads a storybook to them, children are reading the pictures, hearing the same words in the same order, gaining a sense of what a story means, and taking in the flow and cadence of written language. In the everyday world, children read stop signs, pick out their favorite cereals by reading the letters and pictures on the box, and read clothing and fast-food logos. They read their own writing, read the picture menus on computer programs, find the letters they need on the keyboard, and read their favorite storybooks based on picture cues and the words they know by heart. These are all legitimate approaches to finding meaning in the written word and are necessary experiences that prepare children to read pages of written words.

Because reading plays such a critical role in future school success, adults are understandably eager for young children to learn to read. Pressuring them to read like adults, however, is not advisable. It can discourage children's desire to read, and it ignores the fact that the initiative to read comes from the children themselves. Supporting emergent reading, on the other hand, while it takes time and patience on the part of adults, is more likely to promote children's eventual success in reading as well as their desire to read and their enjoyment of the process (Schweinhart and Hohmann 1991). This means taking cues from each child's own interest in books, writing, and reading; seeing reading as the gradual accumulation of many skills that are acquired in an interactive way; and understanding that each child's learning-to-read process is unique (Barbour 1987).

Interest, curiosity, success in mastering emerging skills, and desire to read must all be present for children to succeed in formal reading. Our goal is the development of the child's understanding of the power of the written word as a basis for communication, knowledge acquisition, and entertainment. In our view, while some 3- and 4-year-olds are able to read, a successful early childhood program promotes the ways preschoolers typically tackle reading. It *supports* and *builds* on children's interest in books, stories, and written words—in *reading in various ways*—because it is from these experiences that actual reading later emerges. Here are ways adults can support this ongoing process.

Suggestions for Adults

▶ **Provide a print-rich environment.**

Since children learn to read by trying to make sense of print they encounter in their everyday lives, adults can support their efforts by making familiar written materials available to children throughout the day and by joining with children in pointing out a variety of signs and written words during outdoor excursions.

Stock the interest areas with reading materials. While the computer area and the book and writing areas are, by nature, equipped with reading materials, here are some items with printing on them to consider adding to other interest areas:

• **Sand and water area:** plastic food containers and lids, measuring cups

• **Block area:** packing boxes, maps, photos of buildings and block structures

• **House area:** food boxes, cans, bags, grocery bags, receipts, recipe books and cards, menus, appliance instruction books and warranties, magazines, newspapers, comics, coupons, catalogs, phone books, emergency decals for phones, family photos, eye charts, plane tickets, luggage tags, travel brochures, business cards, computer keyboards, typewriters, calculators

• **Art area:** magazines, cards, junk mail

• **Toy area:** original toy containers for storage (such as a Tinkertoy box), playing cards, magnetic letters

• **Woodworking area:** tool catalogs, home repair magazines, picture reference books such as *The Way Things Work* by David Macauley

• **Music and movement area:** tapes, records, compact discs

• **Outdoor area:** colored chalk, gardening books, seed packets, insect guides, bird guides, tree guides

Thinking about their preschoolers as readers, one teaching team added a **message board** to the wall in the book area at the children's eye level. Children, staff, and parents often gathered next to the message board to read books together as children arrived. Each morning before the children arrived, the adults wrote messages about the day by drawing pictures and symbols that everyone then read together after putting away their storybooks. One day, for example, the children read the following messages (see the photo on this page):

"Becki [a teacher] will not be here today."

"Beth [a teacher] will be here today."

"Gregory [a photographer] will be taking pictures."

"There's a surprise in the water table."

"Remember the materials we added to the writing area."

On some days, the children added their own messages. For example, one day when Sam was teaching, Ben wrote "Sam is hek" which he read as "Sam is here." This same team also added a larger board on the back of an art storage shelf. The children called it the "wipe-off board" because they could write on it with water-based markers and then wipe it clean. One day, Jessa drew a person and then wrote her name, JESSA. Later on, Alana stopped by the board and remarked, "Oh, that must be Jessa's picture because that's her J." After these incidents, Becki and Beth, the teachers, included letters and words on the message board.

Another day, Corrin asked Becki to write down Corrin's last name, which Becki did. "I want to find it in the phone book," she said. With Becki's help, Corrin found the M's and finally her last name and address. "I can't believe it," she remarked. "We're in the book!"

The children in Becki's and Beth's program also liked reading the song cards Beth and Becki made by drawing a picture to characterize the song and printing the name beneath it. The children used the cards to pick out songs they wanted to sing at large-group time, often choosing several and arranging them on the floor in the order they wanted to sing them.

Look for things to read outside. On walks, many children enjoy reading stop signs, pedestrian crossing signs, handicapped parking signs, no-littering signs, and announcements posted in shop windows. They also like to look for "their" letters. Sarah found her S on a sign at the gas station, while Petey found his P on a STOP sign.

At work time, these two children return to "read" the message board for themselves. They decide to add their own messages!

Above, the children "read" the snack chart and find that it is Douglas's turn to pass out the napkins, which he acknowledges by raising his hand. At right, a child "reads" her name and personal symbol on a name card and looks for letter blocks to match the letters in her name.

Children also enjoy making their own signs for others to read. At the beginning of the year, the children in Beth's and Becki's classroom found that it was too difficult to ride bikes down the gentle hill on their playground sidewalk and stop before they came to the gate. To remind themselves not to ride bikes down the hill, children wrote a warning sign on the sidewalk at the top of the hill. They used red chalk to draw a bike with a slash through it and a circle around it. They then would ride to the top of the hill, stop and read the sign, and say, "No bikes down this hill" before traveling on.

▶ **Provide each child with a personal symbol.**

Providing each child with a personal symbol—a unique cutout shape—enables preschool children to identify their own and other children's belongings. (In the photograph

on p. 80, for example, are some of the symbols one teaching team provided for their children so each child could read his or her own name as well as the names of the other children.)

In a High/Scope setting, each child chooses a symbol on entering the program. This symbol marks the child's cubby, personal storage tub, coathook, and so forth. Children and adults also use the child's symbol to label pictures and other items the child creates. Children quickly develop the ability to identify their things as well as the creations and belongings of others.

Providing children with personal symbols that they can read puts children in control of many daily events. For example, one team used the children's symbols to make a snack chart so children could read it and find out when it was their turn to pass out the napkins, cups, and

snack basket, or to get the juice from the refrigerator. They also used the children's symbols when they wrote out the words to field-trip songs the children created. After a trip to a hands-on museum, for example, the teachers posted each child's symbol and then, at each symbol, wrote down what that child remembered about the trip.

A **letter link** is a type of personal symbol that consists of two elements: a child's nametag and a drawing of an object that starts with the same letter and letter sound as the child's name, for example, a butterfly for Bianca, a train for Trey, or a motorcycle for Manny. As with other kinds of personal symbols, letter links are used to label children's personal items. Letter links help children recognize the sounds of initial letters, both in their own names and those of their classmates, thus contributing to **alphabet knowledge,** a component of early literacy. (See photo, p. 345.)

▶ **Provide storybooks for children to read.**

A well-stocked book corner and a cozy place to read provide many pleasurable reading experiences for children and adults. Include all kinds of age-appropriate books: picture books, books relating to children's field trips, books relating to individual children's particular interests, books of poems, songbooks, books of photographs, books the children have made, nursery-rhyme books, books in all the languages spoken by the children, books in Braille if there are blind children. (See also Chapter 5, p. 139.)

As you read to children throughout the day, encourage them to read their favorite pages and to comment on the story and pictures as they wish. One day Beth, an adult, was reading *The Very Busy Spider* to Ben. They took turns saying the sounds each animal made. (This was part of the text.) When it was Beth's turn to read the sound the sheep made, she read "Baa baa," then turned the page. With a puzzled look, however, Ben turned back to the sheep page. "The sheep doesn't say baa baa," he said, pointing to the M at the beginning of "Maa." "It says maa maa." "You're right," Beth agreed. "It does say maa maa." Beth then understood that Ben was actually connecting sounds with written letters and that he had not just memorized the story.

▶ **Encourage children to read to one another.**

Even though it is very satisfying to read to children, it is equally important to put children in the driver's seat and turn storybook reading over to them. Try this out with wordless picture books as well as with storybooks that you have or have not read aloud to the children. There are several ways you might get this process started. When a child asks you to read a book, ask if he or she could

How to Make Children's Symbols

1. Choose 18 (or whatever number of children you have) different, easy-to-replicate shapes.

2. Draw or trace each shape on colored construction paper, then cut out two or three of the same shape at a time by using layers of paper.

3. On the day the children enter your program, or when you are enrolling them, have each child choose a shape and write the child's first name on his or her shape. This symbol will thereafter stand for that child.

4. Take a photograph of each child and attach it to each child's symbol.

5. Laminate or cover the symbols with clear contact paper and attach a loop of yarn to each symbol.

6. Hang the picture symbols on each child's coathook and use them as needed— as name tags, place markers, or indicators of whose turn it is to choose the large-group-time songs.

7. Use extra symbols (the ones without the photos) to label each child's tub, cubby, coathook, and so forth.

*Some children become very attached to their personal symbols, like Andrea, left, who waits until the last minute to remove her necklace symbol before going outside. At top, Lee hangs a coat on a hook labeled with his name and a picture of a lion. This is called a **letter link**, another kind of personal symbol that builds children's understanding of how word sounds relate to letters. (For more information on letter links, see DeBruin-Parecki and Hohmann 2003.)*

read it to you instead. Assure them that any way they read will be just fine. At large-group time, ask pairs of children to choose a book to read to each other. Also, encourage children to read their own drawings and writing in whatever forms they appear at planning, recall, small-group time, work time—whenever children have written a story, recipe, shopping list, and so forth.

These children "read" a favorite storybook together by looking at the pictures and picking out words they know by heart from hearing the story so many times.

Key Developmental Indicator
Dictating Stories

Jonah tapes a tag to his shirt at work time and asks Betsy, his teacher, to write on it, "I am the king of the puppies."

~

Aimee paints a picture and dictates the story that goes with it to Beth. "Aimee's wallpaper in her house."

~

At small-group time, Chrysten draws a picture and asks Peter to write, "She's my cousin. Her name is Pam. My mom has a sister. And my dad has a brother."

~

At work time, Colin tells a story to Merrilee, who writes it down for him: "Once upon a time in the woods, there were penny bears. And they started to throw them out of the woods. They throwed one penny, then another. Then all of a sudden a really magic penny plopped out of the woods, and the rainbow boy

picked it up, and then he saw a rainbow on it. And all of a sudden, something happened. There was a roaring thunderstorm, and then rainbow boy rushed inside, zoomed up like a rocket, and rushed up like a tornado, and pushed it away from the Giving Tree School. It's good to save people who are at the Giving Tree School."

In reviewing the role of *dictation* in language and literacy development Maehr (1991) notes, "Young children sometimes want to write and sometimes want someone to take their dictation. This is especially true when what children have to write is more complex and advanced than are their skills for reading it" (p. 37). While taking children's dictation is one way to help them begin to make the connection between oral and written language, it is probably most wisely used at the *children's* request. In general, it is more valuable for children to write and read their own writing, than to have an adult take over this process for them. With these cautions in mind, here are some suggestions for adults.

Suggestions for Adults

▶ **Write down children's personal dictations.**

Sometimes children are in too much of a hurry to write things in their own way or they may want a sample of "adult writing" either to copy or for some other reason. At work time, for example, Juan scribbled lines of text on a chalkboard and read them out loud. Then he turned to his teacher and dictated the rest of his story for her to write in an adult's way.

When you take a child's dictation, write down and read back *exactly* what the child says, without editing or correcting grammar or word

At recall time, Tommy drew this picture and described it in these words: "Paint easels. Lots of paint." When he asked his teacher to "write what I said," she wrote down his exact words.

order. This demonstrates that you value the child's work and helps children begin to connect spoken and written language. If a child dictates in a language you do not understand, try to transcribe the words phonetically or get the help of a person, perhaps a parent volunteer, who understands that language.

▶ **Write down group dictations.**

Take dictation from a large group or small group of children about a shared experience—perhaps a walk around the block, the classroom visit of a new baby brother or sister, or a special dinner preparation for parents and friends. This strategy provides an enjoyable way for children to recall significant events as well as an occasion for frequent re-reading. Give each child in the group a chance to contribute and then be sure to write down and read back each child's exact words.

▶ **Save dictations and encourage children to act out their experiences.**

As children dictate regularly, their ability to include details and more elaborate descriptions increases. Some children might want to collect their dictations and make a book. Adults might also want to keep these collections in order to watch the children's development throughout the year.

Many children enjoy acting out, on their own or as a group, the stories they have dictated. You can start the dramatic process at small-group or large-group time by asking pertinent questions: "Would you like to act out your story?" and then, "What characters do you need?" One preschooler, for example, had dictated a story that read simply, "The horses stood in the barn and went to sleep." The other children were very excited about this story because they all got to be horses. They got down on their hands and knees and closed their eyes for a while. When they were finished, they expressed great satisfaction, and thereafter, they often requested and re-enacted "the horse story."

References

Barbour, Nita. 1987. "Learning to Read." In *The Early Childhood Curriculum: A Review of Current Research*, Carol Seefeldt, ed., 107–40. New York: Teachers College Press.

Bruner, Jerome. 1980. *Under Five in Britain.* Ypsilanti, MI: High/Scope Press.

Caplan, Nathan, Marcella H. Choy, and John K. Whitmore. 1992. "Indochinese Refugee Families and Academic Achievement." *Scientific American* 266, no. 8 (February): 36–42.

DeBruin-Parecki, Andrea, and Mary Hohmann. 2003. *Letter Links: Alphabet Learning With Children's Names.* Ypsilanti, MI: High/Scope Press.

Dewey, John. 1934. *Art as Experience.* Reprint. New York: Capricorn Books. 1958.

Dickinson, David, and Miriam Smith. 1994. "Long-Term Effects of Preschool Teachers' Book Readings on Low-Income Children's Vocabulary and Story Comprehension." *Reading Research Quarterly* 29, no. 2: 104–22.

Fromberg, Doris P. 1987. "Play." In *The Early Childhood Curriculum: A Review of Current Research*, Carol Seefeldt, ed., 35–74. New York: Teachers College Press.

Gibson, Linda. 1989. *Literacy Learning in the Early Years: Through Children's Eyes.* New York: Teachers College Press.

Goodman, Kenneth S. 1996. *On Reading: A Commonsense Look at the Nature of Language and the Science of Reading.* Portsmouth, NH: Heinemann Educational Books.

Goodman, Kenneth. 1986. *What's Whole in Whole Language?* Portsmouth, NH: Heinemann Educational Books.

Halliday, Michael. 1973. *Explorations in the Functions of Language.* London: Edward Arnold.

Hiebert, Elfrieda H. 1990. "Research Directions: Starting With Oral Language." *Language Arts* 67, no. 5: 502–6.

Kagan, Sharon L., Evelyn Moore, and Sue Bredekamp, eds. 1995 (June). *Reconsidering Children's Early Development and Learning: Toward Common Views and Vocabulary.* (Goal 1 Technical Planning Group Report 95–03). Washington, DC: National Education Goals Panel.

Maehr, Jane. 1991. *The High/Scope K–3 Curriculum Series: Language and Literacy.* Ypsilanti, MI: High/Scope Press.

National Reading Panel. 2000. *Teaching Children to Read: An Evidence-Based Assessment of the Scientific Research Literature on Reading and Its Implications for Reading Instruction.* Washington, DC: National Institute of Child Health and Human Development, National Institutes of Health.

Neuman, Susan B., and Kathleen Roskos. 1997. "Literacy Knowledge in Practice: Contexts of Participation for Young Writers and Readers." *Reading Research Quarterly* 32, no. 1: 10–32.

Pflaum, Susanna W. 1986. *The Development of Language and Literacy in Young Children.* Columbus, OH: Merrill.

Schickedanz, Judith A. 1982. "The Acquisition of Written Language in Young Children." In *Handbook of Research in Early Childhood Education,* Bernard Spodek, ed., 242–63. New York: The Free Press.

Schweinhart, Lawrence, and Charles Hohmann. 1991. "Bringing Active Learning to Schools: A K–3 Strategy That Works." *High/Scope ReSource* 10, no. 2 (Spring–Summer): 1, 8–14.

Snow, Catherine. 1991. "The Theoretical Basis for Relationships Between Language and Literacy in Development." *Journal of Research in Childhood Education* 6: 5–10.

Snow, Catherine E., Susan Burns, and Peg Griffin (eds). 1998. *Preventing Reading Difficulties in Young Children.* Washington DC: National Academy Press.

Sponseller, Doris. 1982. "Play and Early Education." In *Handbook of Research in Early Childhood Education,* Bernard Spodek, ed., 215–41. New York: The Free Press.

Strickland, Dorothy, and Timothy Shanahan. 2004. "Laying the Groundwork for Literacy." *Educational Leadership* 6, no. 6: 74–77.

Sulzby, Elizabeth. 1985. "Children's Emergent Reading of Favorite Storybooks: A Developmental Study." *Reading Research Quarterly* 20, no. 4: 458–81.

Sulzby, Elizabeth. 1995. *Emergent Writing and Reading in 5–6 Year Olds: A Longitudinal Study.* Norwood, NJ: Ablex.

Sulzby, Elizabeth, and June Barnhart. 1990. "The Developing Kindergartner: All Our Children Emerge as Readers and Writers." In *The Developing Kindergarten: Programs, Children and Teachers,* Judith S. McKee, ed., 201–24. Ann Arbor: MiAEYC.

Temple, Charles, Ruth Nathan, Nancy Burris, and Frances Temple. 1988. *The Beginnings of Writing.* Boston: Allyn and Bacon, Inc.

Thorndike, Robert L. 1973. *Reading Comprehension, Education in Fifteen Countries: An Empirical Study.* New York: John Wiley.

Tizard, Barbara, and Martin Hughes. 1984. *Young Children and Learning: Talking and Thinking at Home and at School.* Cambridge: Harvard University Press.

Tough, Joan. 1977. *The Development of Meaning: A Study of Children's Use of Language.* New York: John Wiley.

Trousdale, Ann M. 1990. "Interactive Storytelling: Scaffolding Children's Early Narratives." *Language Arts* 67, no. 2 (February): 164–73.

Weikart, David P. 1974. "Devices of Art or Strategies for Change?" In *The High/Scope Report, 1973,* C. Silverman, ed., 2–5. Ypsilanti, MI: High/Scope Press.

Wells, Gordon. 1986a. "The Language Experience of Five-Year-Old Children at Home and at School." In *The Social Construction of Literacy,* Jenny Cook-Gumperz, ed., 69–93. Cambridge: Cambridge University Press.

Wells, Gordon. 1986b. *The Meaning Makers: Children Learning Language and Using Language to Learn.* Portsmouth, NH: Heinemann Educational Books.

Related Reading

Adams, Marilyn Jager. 1990. *Beginning to Read: Thinking and Learning About Print.* Cambridge, MA: MIT Press.

Bruner, Jerome. 1983. *Child's Talk: Learning to Use Language.* Cambridge: Cambridge University Press.

Bruner, Jerome. 1989. *Interaction in Human Development.* Hillsdale, NJ: L. Erlbaum Associates.

Campbell, Robin, ed. 1998. *Facilitating Preschool Literacy.* Newark, DE: International Reading Association.

Cummins, Jim, and Merrill Swain. 1986. *Bilingualism in Education: Aspects of Theory, Research, and Practice.* New York: Longman.

Epstein, Ann S. 2007. "What Is the High/Scope Curriculum in Language, Literacy, and Communication?" Chap. 11 in *Essentials of Active Learning in Preschool: Getting to Know the High/Scope Curriculum,* 109–24. Ypsilanti, MI: High/Scope Press.

Garcia, Eugene E. 1982. "Language Acquisition: Phenomenon, Theory, and Research." In *Handbook of Research in Early Childhood Education,* Bernard Spodek, ed., 47–64. New York: The Free Press.

Genishi, Celia. 1987. "Acquiring Oral Language and Communicative Competence." In *The Early Childhood Curriculum: A Review of Current Research,* Carol Seefeldt, ed., 75–106. New York: Teachers College Press.

Harris, Margaret. 1992. *Language Experience and Early Language Development: From Input to Uptake.* Hillsdale, NJ: L. Erlbaum Associates.

Hiebert, Elfrieda H. 1988. "The Role of Literacy Experiences in Early Childhood Programs." *The Elementary School Journal* 89, no. 2: 161–71.

High/Scope Educational Research Foundation. 2004. *Early Literacy Skills Assessment (ELSA).* Ypsilanti, MI: High/Scope Press.

High/Scope Educational Research Foundation. 2005. *Growing Readers Early Literacy Curriculum (GRC).* Ypsilanti, MI: High/Scope Press.

High/Scope Educational Research Foundation. 2003. *Preschool Child Observation Record (COR),* 2nd ed. Ypsilanti, MI: High/Scope Press.

High/Scope Position Papers on Reading and Writing: Infant-Toddler, Preschool, and K–3 Programs. 2001. Ypsilanti, MI: High/Scope Press.

Hohmann, Charles. 1998. "Reading Research: New Findings." *High/Scope Extensions* (March/April): 5.

Hohmann, Mary. 2002. *Fee, Fie, Phonemic Awareness: 130 Prereading Activities for Preschoolers.* Ypsilanti, MI: High/Scope Press.

Hohmann, Mary, and Joanne Tangorra, eds. 2007. *Let's Talk Literacy: Practical Readings for Preschool Teachers.* Ypsilanti, MI: High/Scope Press.

Kennedy, David. 1992. "Young Children's Discourse and the Origins of the World." In *When We Talk: Essays on Classroom Conversations,* Ronald F. Reed, ed., 19–62. Fort Worth, TX: Analytic Teaching Press.

McLane, Joan Brooks, and Gillian Dowley McNamee. 1990. *Early Literacy.* Cambridge: Harvard University Press.

Morrison, Kathy, and Tina Dittrich. 2000. *Literature-Based Workshops for Language Arts: Ideas for Active Learning, Grades K–2.* Ypsilanti, MI: High/Scope Press.

Morrow, Lesley M., and Muriel K. Rand. 1991. "Promoting Literacy During Play by Designing Early Childhood Classroom Environments." *The Reading Teacher* 44, no. 6 (February): 396–402.

Neuman, Susan B., Carol Copple, and Sue Bredekamp. 2000. *Learning to Read and Write: Developmentally Appropriate Practices for Young Children.* Washington DC: NAEYC.

Paley, Vivian Gussin. 1981. *Wally's Stories: Conversations in the Kindergarten.* Cambridge: Harvard University Press.

Piaget, Jean. 1926. *The Language and Thought of the Child.* New York: Harcourt Brace.

Ranweiler, Linda Weikel. 2004. *Preschool Readers and Writers: Early Literacy Strategies for Teachers.* Ypsilanti, MI: High/Scope Press.

Schickedanz, Judith A. 1999. *Much More Than the ABCs: The Early Stages of Reading and Writing.* Washington, DC: NAEYC.

Strickland, Dorothy S., and Lesley M. Morrow, eds. 2000. *Beginning Reading and Writing.* Newark, DE: International Reading Association.

Teale, William H., and Elizabeth Sulzby, eds. 1986. *Emergent Literacy: Writing and Reading.* Norwood: Ablex.

Wells, Gordon, and Jan Wells. 1984. "Learning to Talk and Talking to Learn." *Theory Into Practice* 23, no. 3: 190–97.

Wood, David, Linnet McMahon, and Yvonne Cranstoun. 1980. *Working With Under Fives.* Ypsilanti, MI: High/Scope Press.

Related Media

The following materials are available from the High/Scope Press, 600 N. River St., Ypsilanti, MI 48198-2898; to order, visit *www.highscope.org*, or call 1-800-40-PRESS.

Language and Literacy (Preschool). 2000. Color videotape or DVD, 60 min. Ypsilanti, MI: High/Scope Press.

Language, Literacy, and Communication Strategies: A Summary

Talking with others about personally meaningful experiences

___ Establish a climate in which children feel free to talk.

___ Be available for conversation throughout the day:
___ Place yourself at the children's physical level.
___ Listen carefully to what children are saying.
___ Give children control of conversations.
___ Accept children's hesitations and nonverbal utterances.
___ Learn and remember each child's particular interests.

___ Encourage children to talk with one another throughout the day:
___ Provide opportunities for cooperative projects and play.
___ Support children who wish to plan and recall together.
___ Refer one child's questions and problems to another child.
___ Interpret and deliver messages.
___ Explain the context of children's statements.
___ Acknowledge conflicting viewpoints.

___ Converse with *all* children:
___ Make time to talk with children.
___ Look for comfortable opportunities for dialogue.
___ Be aware of your personal preferences.

Describing objects, events, and relations

___ Provide children with interesting materials and experiences.
___ Listen as children describe things in their own way.
___ Encourage children to talk about their plans.
___ Let children be the leaders in "describing" games.

Having fun with language: Listening to stories and poems, making up stories and rhymes

___ Listen to children throughout the day.
___ Read to children individually and in small, intimate groups.

___ Tell stories, recite poems and rhymes.
___ Make up stories, chants, and rhymes.

Writing in various ways: Drawing, scribbling, and using letterlike forms, invented spelling, and conventional forms

___ Provide a variety of writing and drawing materials.
___ Anticipate various emergent forms of writing:
___ Drawing
___ Scribbling
___ Letterlike forms
___ Actual letters
___ Conventional forms

___ Encourage children to write in their own way:
___ Ask children to write stories.
___ Encourage children to write to one another.
___ Accept children's additions to your writing.

___ Display and send home samples of children's writing.

Reading in various ways: Reading storybooks, signs and symbols, one's own writing

___ Provide a print-rich environment:
___ Stock the interest areas with reading materials.
___ Look for things to read outside.
___ Provide each child with a personal symbol.
___ Provide storybooks for children to read.
___ Encourage children to read to one another.

Dictating stories

___ Write down children's personal dictations.
___ Write down group dictations.
___ Save dictations and encourage children to act out their experiences.

Using her finger as a guide, the adult reads this child's dictation word for word without changing his grammar or word order.

Preschoolers are increasingly able to form relationships with peers, show consideration for others, and solve problems cooperatively—abilities that reflect their growing capacities for complex social interaction.

Social-emotional development has always been a major concern of early childhood education. Today's practitioners face special challenges as they strive to support children confronted at ever younger ages by changing family dynamics, unsafe neighborhoods, war, natural disasters, and academic pressures. In addition to learning social norms at home and school, young children in the twenty-first century are increasingly exposed to influences from the media and technology, where they face evolving and often contradictory expectations for individual and interpersonal behavior.

For these reasons, the importance of paying attention to social as well as intellectual development is receiving renewed attention among educators and the public at large. The National Education Goals Panel (NEGP; Kagan et al. 1995) sees social development as a critical area of readiness because so much early learning takes place in a group setting.

Social and emotional development begins at birth and continues into high school and beyond. Depending on the security of their attachments with parents and other caregivers, children may learn from their earliest experiences to view the world as a welcoming and exciting place, a place to approach with caution, or one that is empty of love and stimulation—perhaps even fraught with peril. A safe environment invites exploration, while an untrustworthy one may lead to confusion, anger, or hopelessness.

The way children are treated affects how they view and feel about themselves. Their early self-image in turn determines how they approach learning and human relationships throughout their school years and, indeed, throughout their lives. In other words, their inner emotional well-being affects their outward-directed social selves.

As noted early childhood researchers Lilian Katz and Diane McClellan say, "Socially competent young children are those who engage in satisfying interactions and activities with adults and peers and through such interactions further improve their own competence" (1997, p. 1).

Characteristics of Preschoolers' Social Relationships

Preschoolers' social relationships benefit from their growing ability to talk about their ideas and represent them in play. Using words they know, they can begin to recognize and name their own emotions: "I'm happy. My daddy's coming home today!" They can also begin to recognize and name the emotions they see in others: "Betty looks happy. She'll be fun to play with." "Sammy's crying. He's sad because he wants his mom, but she has to go to work today." This emerging ability to identify their own and others' moods and emotions helps young children decide with some success when and how to approach their peers.

12
Social and Emotional Development

We are beginning to see the end of people relating to each other through force, dictatorship, obedience, and stereotypical categories. We are beginning to relate through cooperation, choice, empowering leadership, and a real understanding of being more fully human.

—Virginia Satir, 1988

Along with language, preschoolers' developing social ability is marked by a desire for **friendship** and a struggle to resolve the **conflict between** "me" and "we."

Desire for friendship. Young children's growing capacity to initiate and carry on friendly relationships with peers is helped along by their ability to express themselves in language and to engage in increasingly complex play that draws the interest and support of other children. In establishing close associations and friendships, young children seem to seek a degree of reciprocity and equality based on shared interests. However, disagreements are often a part of these friendships. In fact, developmental psychologist Shirley Moore (1982) notes, "Observations indicate that children are more likely to fight with their friends than with others in their group. Yet, they also do their share in encouraging their companions to be friendly rather than aggressive" (p. 76). Thus, young children seem to seek friends with whom they can freely share the ups and downs of their everyday experiences.

"Me" versus "we." In their dealings with others, young children can find themselves caught between their desire for friendship and belonging and their desire for autonomy and independence. "I want the car James has" can be in conflict with "I want to play with James." Steven Asher and his associates (1982), researchers in children's social development, report that "an important issue for children is to maintain the tension that sometimes exists between the need to have influence and the need to be included and receive affection" (p. 152). Sorting out these conflicting desires is not an easy task at any age. It is one, nevertheless, that young children are beginning to negotiate with varying degrees of success.

Supporting Children's Social and Emotional Development

The **five High/Scope key developmental indicators (KDIs) in social and emotional development** provide a clear picture of the ways young children are finding out about themselves and others:

- **Taking care of one's own needs**

- **Expressing feelings in words**

- **Building relationships with children and adults**

- **Creating and experiencing collaborative play**

- **Dealing with social conflict**

Adults can best support social-emotional development by establishing a safe, caring learning community. Whatever the setting—preschool classroom or child care home or center—adults exhibit kindness, encourage children's initiatives, focus on children's strengths, relate to children authentically, and take a problem-solving approach to conflict. At the same time, adults avoid punishment and domination and also avoid establishing an atmosphere of competition.

The sections that follow on each indicator include specific suggestions adults can use to affirm children's emerging awareness of themselves and others, helping them to develop emotionally and socially.

Later in the book (Chapter 19) we discuss a related but distinct content area, **social studies.** Whereas social-emotional development deals with

children's ability to regulate their feelings and behaviors and to interact with peers and adults, social studies refers more broadly to children's ability to understand communal rules and be good citizens.

In a supportive social setting, children form peer relationships around mutual interests. These two children, for example, pause for a moment to talk about a painting.

Key Developmental Indicator
Taking Care of One's Own Needs

When Alex arrives, he unzips and hangs up his coat. At outside time he gets his coat, puts his head in the hood, puts his arms in the arm holes, zips it up, puts on his mittens, and goes out to the playground.

∾

Wendy staples together pages for her book about horses.

∾

Andrew turns on the computer, selects mask features, and prints out a mask he has designed.

∾

Isaac comes to his teacher, Betsy, with tears in his eyes. "I need you to hold me," he says, and she does.

∾

Abby makes a marble chute and rolls marbles down it. "I can do this all by myself," she says.

∾

Isaac works for a long time to untie a knot in his shoelace. "I don't need any help," he says. When he gets the lace untied, he works for a while longer to tie a bow. With the bow firmly in place, he returns to his play.

∾

"Do you need some Play-Doh?" Erin asks Margo. Margo nods, and Erin hands the Play-Doh container to her.

∾

Jason gets wet playing at the water table. He changes his clothes, puts his wet things in the bag in which he carries his change of clothes, and puts the bag in his cubby to take home.

Preschool children enjoy doing things for themselves and, in doing so, grow in ability and self-confidence. As their language and representation capacities develop, preschoolers are able to express their needs and act on them. Taking care of their own needs is another way young children take the initiative. By feeding, dressing, and washing; cutting, mixing, and pouring; singing, rocking, and talking, children learn to help themselves, take some control over their own lives, and use their skills to assist others. In a sense, taking care of themselves empowers young children to relate to others in a caring manner.

Following are ways adults can support children's growing independence, desire to help themselves, and ability to help others.

Suggestions for Adults

▶ **Provide children with time to do things for themselves.**

Jackie, a home-child-care provider, took her children to music classes at a local college and made the following observation of 3-year-old Abby: "Abby insisted on going down to the snack-machine area in the basement to recycle her pop can when I just wanted to throw it out because it would have been easier at the moment. When we finally got there, she discovered that she couldn't reach the bin and got me to lift her up. She often asks if something can be recycled." This trip to the basement took extra time, but it was well worth the effort because Jackie

enabled Abby to do things for herself. At the same time, she was also able to support Abby's developing sense of responsibility to the larger community.

Other important self-help skills children should have time to practice include toileting, hand washing, toothbrushing, dressing, buttoning, zipping, and putting on shoes, boots, and outerwear. At snack and mealtimes, encourage children to pass, pour, mix, stir, cut, spread, peel, and wipe up crumbs and spills, even though you could accomplish these tasks more efficiently than preschoolers.

▶ **Encourage children to use common tools.**

Children also enjoy learning to use many common tools on their own. To help children master these skills, consider planning small-group times around using various tools: scissors, staplers, hole punches, hammers, saws, hand drills, screwdrivers, brooms, shovels, wheelbarrows, and rakes. Washing dishes, doll clothes, table tops, tricycles, and paintbrushes can be a chore for adults, but children enjoy such tasks because they involve water play and provide a great sense of accomplishment and independence. Children respond enthusiastically to small-group times based around any of these "chores."

In one center, a favorite large-group project was washing all the preschool bikes, scooters, and wagons outside, using a hose and buckets of soapy water. Children also take pride in carrying and stacking firewood, shaking out rugs, matching and folding laundry, and sorting and recycling paper, glass, and plastic—tasks that are a natural part of some settings. The sense of "I-can-do-it" that results from the mastery of these ordinary tasks enhances children's feelings of worth and altruistic spirit.

▶ **Support children's attempts to take care of their emotional needs.**

In addition to their ability to take care of their own physical needs and to use tools and equipment on their own, preschoolers are also able to take care of some of their emotional needs. These attempts at self-help give young children a sense of competence and self-control. For example, some young children comfort themselves at naptime by hugging a favorite stuffed animal or toy from home, or by looking at a favorite picture book. When Jonah needed comfort, he chewed on the corner of his nap blanket until it was reduced to shreds. Then, with his teacher's support, he substituted a special triangle-shaped teether for the blanket. Sucking and chewing on his "rocketship" (his name for his teether) helped Jonah through difficult times. Other children seek out a favorite adult's lap, or a familiar adult's leg to hold or hand to grasp when they need a little extra contact for reassurance and renewal. It is important to realize that these children are not simply reverting to the ways of toddlerhood or looking for ways to be annoying. Rather, they are recalling comforting experiences and putting them to use in times of emotional need.

Keep in mind, too, that children express and meet their emotional needs in personally creative ways. For example, when Ruth, a teacher, was away for a week, Becki (Ruth's co-teacher), along with the substitute teacher, blew up one balloon for each school day until Ruth would return. At greeting circle each day, the children took turns popping a balloon and counting the ones remaining until they would see Ruth again. One day, 4-year-old Kenneth began digging a hole in the pea gravel outside. "You're working hard on that hole, Kenneth," Becki commented.

Working the lid off of a tennis ball container is a challenge that build's this child's self-confidence.

"I'm digging a great big hole to put Ruth in so she'll never go away again!" In his own personal way, Kenneth was taking care of his emotional needs. His digging was a concrete way of channeling his longing for his teacher's return and telling himself and others that he missed her.

Key Developmental Indicator
Expressing Feelings in Words

"Heaven is where the happy people are," Andrew tells Becki at greeting circle.

❧

"I miss my mom and dad when they go to work," Aimee says to Douglas.

❧

"It makes me sad. It hurts my feelings," Kacey tells Alana when Alana won't play with her.

❧

"I am disappointed Warren is not here," Brian says at greeting circle.

❧

"I feel very sorry. I love you," Bryant says to Carmen when he runs into her.

❧

"I hate 3-year-olds," Chelsea says. *"They take stuff."*

❧

"The person won't get scared. A real monster would get scared," Corrin tells Beth as she makes a mask.

❧

"Claire!" Jonah says. *"She hates me. Why did she give me a Valentine?"* He shakes his head.

❧

"I think when somebody cries, they get sad," Abby says, watching Jason cry.

❧

Anya tries to hug Isaac while he is gluing. "I don't want a hug," he tells her, *"I'm not sad now."*

❧

Abby, Hannah, and Emma are standing on "the jumping ledge." "I'm afraid to jump," Abby says. *"I'll show you how,"* Hannah says, and then she jumps off the ledge. *"Now you go."* (Abby doesn't move.) *"She doesn't want to go right now,"* Emma says. After a few moments, Abby jumps. *"You did it!"* exclaims Hannah.

❧

A crying Jason runs to the coat room. "What's the matter?" Jacob asks. *"Robbie hit his head and I'm worried I'll get in trouble. I'm afraid the teachers will be angry."*

Preschool children want to do things for themselves. Each time this child puts on her own boots and snow clothes, the more adept and confident she becomes.

Preschoolers have been experiencing feelings all their lives. Since infancy, they have sustained their own emotions and responded to the emotions of the adults who care for them. With the development of language and representation skills, however, preschoolers are beginning to put their feelings into words, thus shaping and focusing their emotions in a way they have not been able to before this age. In addition to crying or bouncing up and down, for example, preschoolers can begin to distinguish and talk about feeling "happy," "mad," "scared," and "sad."

Expressing feelings in words is an important step for young children because it helps them gain some control over their feelings and the actions these feelings set in motion. Children also begin to look at themselves with increased self-awareness—"I miss my mom and dad when they go to work." While preschoolers are new at this task, they are often more skilled at expressing their feelings than adults realize. Following are ways adults can support children as they make the connection between language and emotion.

Suggestions for Adults

▶ **Establish and maintain a supportive environment.**

Since children are more likely to talk about their feelings when they feel safe and secure, it is important that adults provide them with a *psychologically supportive environment*. Such an environment is characterized by a sharing of control between children and adults, a focus on children's strengths, authentic adult relationships with children, a commitment to children's play, and a problem-solving approach to social conflict. To make these elements of support part of the everyday early childhood environment, review the strategies described in Chapter 2 (pp. 52–66).

▶ **Acknowledge and accept children's feelings.**

Although they are not yet able to express all their feelings in words, preschoolers experience a wide range of often intense emotions. "Leaves! Leaves!" Brian exclaimed day after day one fall as the sumac and maple leaves turned to bright reds and yellows. The adults around him accepted his excitement as a fitting response from a preschooler to the wonder of seasonal changes.

Amanda quietly sucks her thumb and watches the children at the sand table while Lynnette moves quickly from toy shelf to toy shelf. When children leave home and come to preschool or child care for the first time, they may be either unnerved or stimulated by all the new toys, people, and events. Both Amanda's hesitancy and Lynnette's eagerness are typical ways preschoolers cope with new social settings. Such situations call for adult acknowledgment and support as the first steps in helping children become comfortable with new people, surroundings, and routines.

Sometimes adults find children's emotional responses annoying because they are so intense. They may feel the child has become either too subdued or too excited. At these times, in particular, it is important to remember that young children are experiencing many events for the first time. Until they become accustomed to seeing leaves change color, for example, or confident in their ability to move between home and center, their initial reactions to these and other new situations may seem extreme. With time, and adult patience and understanding, however, children will gain their emotional bearings and respond to everyday events with increasing composure.

▶ **Listen for the names children give to their feelings.**

When children can put a name to a specific feeling, the word helps to contain that feeling—making it more concrete and manageable. In a sense, the *word* becomes a handle by which children can grasp, look at, and have some control over the *feeling*. Listening for the names children give to their feelings requires adult patience and attentiveness, such as Rosemary displays on a trip with Timmy to a fire station:

Timmy is crying outside the fire station. He doesn't go in with the rest of the children. "What is it, Timmy?" Rosemary asks him.

"I don't want to go in there," Timmy replies. Although Rosemary knows Timmy was excited about coming to the fire station, she sees that now he is unsure.

"You don't want to go in there," Rosemary responds. After a pause, she continues, "Well, I can see some of the firetrucks right from here."

"I don't like the sirens . . . I'm scared. They might go off." Timmy starts to cry again.

"I see. You don't like the sirens. You're scared they might go off when we're in the fire station," Rosemary says. Timmy nods in agreement through his tears. "The sirens do make a scary noise," Rosemary states, and pauses while Timmy wipes his eyes. She makes another observation: "The sirens are quiet now because there is no fire." Timmy takes Rosemary's hand.

"Come on, let's go in," he says, tugging gently on her hand. "But if they go off . . ." He stops uncertainly.

"If they go off, we'll come back outside."

"Okay." Timmy agrees. He holds Rosemary's hand the whole time. The sirens do not go off.

Having the opportunity to link the words "I'm scared" to a specific fear—that the sirens might go off—helped Timmy overcome his reluctance to enter the fire station. Rosemary, the adult, was helpful. She was patient with Timmy. Moreover, she accepted his explanation rather than imposing her interpretation of his feelings. She did not shame or contradict him. When he said he was scared of the sirens, she repeated *his specific words*: "You don't like the sirens. You're scared they might go off." Rosemary's comment that the sirens were silent at the time seemed to spark Timmy's initiative, and together they devised a plan for what they would do if the sirens did go off while they were in the fire station.

Helping children identify their feelings in a specific situation is not simply a matter of supplying the words yourself—"Shelly, you look angry." Rather, it entails listening to children and conversing with them about their immediate

Children express their feelings in settings where they feel safe and secure.

concerns and observations. In the course of these conversations, children have the opportunity to relate such words as "scared," "happy," and "sad" to the sensations and situations they are experiencing and then decide on appropriate next steps.

▶ **Talk with children about their concerns.**

Sometimes children come to preschool or child care with concerns about things that are happening elsewhere in their lives. A family pet is hit by a car. A hospital stay approaches. Parents separate, families break apart. Daddies and mommies lose their jobs. Children witness violence. Grandma is "broke in all the money." A flood, tornado, or earthquake sweeps through a community. Children shuttle between households. Mommy has a baby. These are the stresses children may face in our present-day society.

Psychologist Victoria Dimidjian (1986) stresses that when children bring their concerns to the preschool or child care setting, the adult serves as "mediator, information-provider, buffer, provider of coping strategies, referral source, and role model of empowerment. . . . The stable adult functions as a *buffer* of stress, helping the child to recognize and understand feelings rather

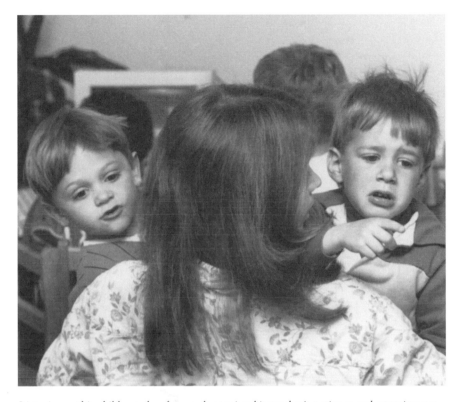

Listening as this child searches for words requires his teacher's patience and attentiveness.

than to simply act them out. Additionally, the caring adult may work to filter stimuli which might trigger emotional upset so the child's adaptive coping capacities will not be overwhelmed" (pp. 120, 124). While adults cannot automatically "make everything all better," they can provide a comforting lap, an attentive ear, and a sympathetic conversational partnership, enabling children to talk about and thus gain some dominion over the feelings and situations that may otherwise sap their energy and self-confidence.

One day, Kacey sat in Beth's lap at work time. Beth put her arms around her. "I want my daddy. I wish he was coming home today," Kacey said. Beth responded, "Sometimes when I miss people, I write them a letter. It makes me feel like

"I Want My Mommy!" A Cry for All Ages

When 3-year-old Chris and his grandfather arrive at preschool, his feet are dancing as his grandfather helps him with his coat and sweatshirt. He hangs up his outerwear, puts the cord of his tree-sign on over his head, and dashes to the bookrack to find the "choo choo" story for the reading circle. Several months later, when his grandfather is away on a trip and cannot take him to school, Chris does not want to go to preschool and spends a few days at home with his mom and little brother. When his grandfather returns, Chris comes back to preschool with some initial hesitation and then with his usual enthusiasm.

Christina, also 3 years old, arrives at preschool with tears in her eyes. Clutching a small doll, she throws her arms around her mother's knees and hugs tightly without a glance at her teacher, who is kneeling on the floor to greet her. When her mom leaves, her teacher gives Christina a hug, and, hand-in-hand, they walk to the bookrack to locate Christina's favorite book. After a month or so, when she has become accustomed to her new routine, Christina gets out of the car before her mom and hurries into preschool to greet her friends and find a book. "Bye, Mom," she says, as she waves from the greeting circle.

Young children's anxiety about separating from their parents or guardians has many of the same characteristics as homesickness in older children. In both cases, time, support, acceptance, and identification of the feelings involved enable the child or young person to develop a sense of control and purpose in the new setting. In the previous examples, Chris needed to reassure himself that he could still stay at home, and he received support for doing so. After a few days, when he was ready, he came back to preschool. Christina needed time to learn that while she missed her mom, her mom was always there at the end of the day, and that in the meantime, preschool was quite an interesting place.

I'm talking to them." Kacey was quiet for a while and then said, "I could write my daddy a letter. I could tell him to come home!" Kacey spent the rest of work time "writing" a letter to her dad.

▶ **Encourage children to tell stories.**

Another way children express their feelings in words is by telling stories (or dictating them for an adult to record). While children often make up characters, their stories generally reflect emotions they themselves have experienced. Below are three stories told by children:

- "Abby was the mother and I was the big sister, and I ran away because the mother always paid attention to the little sister."

- "The whale was in a trap and he was a humpback whale. He wanted to go home but he was lost and he was sad. He was sad because he missed his mom and dad whales a lot. Some people were after him and he was in a lot of trouble. His name is Humphrey the whale. The parents found Humphrey the whale, but the people were still after him. The people were after the parents. Another whale was going to the deep water to save Humphrey and his mom and dad."

- "The little boy pulled his wagon to the barn. It was full of rocks. He helped his daddy put down hay. The cows were happy. Spring Moon is the baby cow. The little boy gave Spring Moon milk from a bottle. He butted his head, but the little boy had very strong arms."

Key Developmental Indicator
Building Relationships With Children and Adults

Brian makes a mask and gives it to Petey saying "I made a mask for you."

⌒

Kacey shows some children the ribbons she has brought. "You pick one," she offers.

⌒

When Mikey sees Ben and Brian arguing over the snap blocks, he gives one of his blocks to Ben.

⌒

"I like you, Corrin," says Aimee as they play together.

⌒

"Want to play with me, Becki?" Petey asks his teacher.

⌒

"Hold on," Alana tells Beth, an adult swinging on the swing, "or you'll fall and get a bleed!"

⌒

"I can do that, Brian," Callie says. "Want me to help you?"

⌒

During recall, Corrin reports that she played the xylophone with "my friend Ben."

⌒

Kenneth takes Petey by both hands and says, "You're my best friend."

⌒

While no adult can automatically "make everything better," this teacher provides comfort and conversation, enabling the child on her lap to gain some control over an upsetting situation.

"Sam is silly. He can understand us!" Corrin *says about one of her teachers.*

~

"I really missed you," Bryant *tells his teacher when she returns from a trip.*

~

"I can help Anna with the hole punch," says Douglas.

~

"Do you want to come to my house sometime?" Jonah *whispers to Evan. Jonah runs over to his teacher, Betsy.* "He said YES!" *he tells her.*

~

"Do you want to come to the playhouse?" Isaac *asks Shannon at work time.* "No," *says Shannon, continuing her drawing.* "Then I'll draw with you," *Isaac says, getting paper and markers and sitting next to Shannon.*

~

Colin squeezes Isaac till he cries and runs away. "I just wanted to play with him," *Colin says to his teacher.* "Sorry."

Bolstered by the family bonds they have experienced in their earliest years, and by their growing sense of trust, autonomy, and initiative, preschool children seek and value relationships with peers and adults outside their families. According to Hartup (1986), preschoolers are motivated to initiate and maintain "social relations with other children (a special challenge of this period), as well as effective, nondependent interactions with preschool teachers (another special challenge of the period)" (p. 15).

The relationships preschoolers form with their peers provide substantial benefits: emotional support in unfamiliar settings, the opportunity to play with a partner, and experiences in leading, following, making suggestions, trying out ideas, negotiating, and compromising. As Hartup and Moore (1990) state, "Considerable evidence suggests that peer relations contribute positively to mental health, both in childhood and later on. The elements in child-child relations believed to be responsible for these contributions are the developmental equivalence of children and their companions and the egalitarian nature of their interaction" (p. 2).

Clearly, children's desire for companionship is well worth our support. The relationships children form with teachers and caregivers can

Peer relationships provide preschoolers with emotional support, play partners, and opportunities for leading and following.

contribute positively to children's sense of competence and well-being, as long as the adults involved understand and support the children's levels of development, permit children to function as active learners, and share control with children rather than try to dominate or ignore them. Following are appropriate ways adults can support children's growing relationships with people outside their families.

Suggestions for Adults

▶ **Establish supportive relations with children.**

The authentic, reciprocal relations adults establish with young children can continue to affect children's relationships throughout life. According to psychologists Alan Sroufe and June Fleeson (1986), "Early relations forge one's expectations concerning relationships. Expectations are the carriers of relationships" (p. 68). When you treat children with warmth and respect, they assume other adults will do the same, and very often these expectations have the force of self-fulfilling prophecy.

In Chapter 2 we presented numerous ways to establish positive relationships with children. Understanding and implementing the strategies described on pages 52–66 form the basis for the supportive adult-child relationships that are essential to the teaching-learning process in early childhood. In addition, it is important to treat children with kindness and to converse with them in a genuine manner.

Treat children with kindness. Daily kindness to children has a profound effect on classroom life. Children learn that at preschool they are safe, teachers and other children enjoy their company, and they can play and try new things without fear of ridicule or punishment. According to psychologists Susan Holloway and Marina Reichhart-Erickson (1988), "Children are more likely to become socially competent when a teacher interacts with them in a friendly, courteous, and responsive manner and when discipline strategies are not abusive or humiliating" (p. 41). Since children learn about the dynamics of social interaction from the adults they interact with, and since we want children to be respectful, engaging, responsive, curious, and affectionate, it makes sense for us to embed these qualities in our own interactions with children throughout the day.

Responsive, affectionate adults model attitudes and behaviors that children try out with their peers.

To do this, make a habit of using kind words with children. Start the day with a warm greeting for each child and parent. "Hi, Aaron! I'm glad to see you today! Good morning, Mrs. Smith. How nice to see you!" Respond kindly to children's desires, frustrations, and accomplishments: "Of course you can sit on my lap!" "What can I do to help?" "You did it! You made the paper stand by folding it." Acknowledge children's acts of kindness: "You held the door for Kamari so she could pull the wagon through it. That was helpful." "You wiped the juice up off the floor so now it won't be sticky where we walk. That was thoughtful."

Being kind to children, notes educator Becky Bailey (2000), begins with each adult's personal integrity and composure: "Some of us

have sensitive alarm systems or possibly difficult temperaments ourselves. We must train our brains to 'see' situations differently" (p. 52). Self-understanding and a positive belief in ourselves helps us to bring these qualities to life in our interactions with children.

Have genuine conversations with children. Conversations that are honest and sincere rather than didactic and contrived help children build trusting relationships with adults:

Child: *That tower has a light!*

Adult: *I see. I wonder why it's on.*

Child: *It's a little bit sprinkling.*

In such conversations adults do not tease, instruct, or ridicule children but attend to children's contributions with respect and interest in a way that invites the conversation to continue:

Adult: *It's on because it's sprinkling.*

Child: *It's sprinkling . . . It's wet.*

Adult: *Oh, the light is on when it's wet.*

Child: *(Makes rainlike motions with his fingers.)*

Genuine conversations are most likely to occur when adults place themselves at the children's physical level, listen carefully to what children are saying, give children control of conversations, accept children's pauses and nonverbal utterances, and learn and remember each child's particular interests. (See Chapter 11, pp. 322–329, for a full discussion and examples of these strategies.) They are also aided when adults respond attentively to children's interests, give children specific feedback, ask honest questions, and respond to children's questions honestly. (See Chapter 2, pp. 57–59 for a full discussion and examples of these strategies.)

▶ **Maintain a stable group of children and adults.**

Building relationships takes time. Friendships and close associations grow slowly through daily interactions and experiences with the same people. In an examination of peer relationships, developmental psychologist Robert Hinde and his associates spent time "in a preschool where arrangements were only moderately conducive to friendship formation. While the facilities were excellent, many children attended for only 2–3 mornings a week, meeting only some of the same individuals on each visit. In a preliminary study we obtained a picture of very few firm friendships, many passing liaisons, and a large number of temporary associations" (Hinde et al. 1985, p. 234).

To build relationships outside their families, young children need a stable community of peers and adults. In concrete terms, this means maintaining a stable teaching team. While student interns, staff-in-training, and volunteers may come and go, the core adult team needs to meet with children on a daily basis. Practices such as rotating team members from room to room or center to center, for example, are highly detrimental to the climate of trust that children depend on to venture forth into new relationships and learning. Supporting children's emerging relationships also argues for enrolling all children for the same days each week and the same core hours each day.

▶ **Look for relationships between children.**

One way to support the relations children are building is to be aware of the peer rela-

tions that exist or are emerging in your setting. Which children seem to seek each other out for comfort, conversation, play? Among the behaviors you might observe are sharing objects, talking with each other, sitting together, engaging in pretend play, working on the same activities, and planning together. Here are some examples:

- **Sharing objects —**
  Callie sees Chelsea crying, so she offers Chelsea the tricycle she is riding.

- **Talking with each other —**

Joey: *See my new shoes.*

Markie: *They got stripes.*

Joey: *Racing stripes . . . go fast.*

Markie: *Yeah!*

- **Sitting together —**
  Pattie and Tanya read a book together in the beanbag chair.

- **Engaging in pretend play —**

Alex: *Let's pretend the blue is water!*

Peter: *And there's snakes down there . . . and sea monsters.*

Alex: *So we have to stay here or they bite us!*

- **Working on the same activities —**
  Karen and Rochelle are at the art table rolling clay and singing.

- **Planning together —**
  "Me and Douglas are gonna make cartoons . . . like the ones we made that other day."

At the same time, it is important to realize that young children do not spend all their time interacting with others. As Hartup (1983) stresses, "Preschool children spend considerable amounts of time by themselves or in noninterac-

Making the Case for Stability

Carolee Howes (1987, 1988), an educational researcher who has conducted an extensive study of children's early social relations, makes a strong case for the role of stable communities in enabling children to build the relationships that help them develop social competence. Consider the following statements she has made on the subject:

> Children who form secure attachments to their caregivers would, all else being equal, be expected to be more socially competent with their peers . . . . The child who experiences a series of unstable caregivers may lose interest in and motivation to engage in the social world. Since social interest in the peer partner represents an early task in the development of social competency with peers, the child who experiences caregiver instability may be at risk for poor peer relationships (Howes 1987, p. 157).

> The stability of the peer group increases in importance as children develop specific friendships. Particular relationships with peer partners are based on the continued presence of the partner (Howes 1987, p. 159).

> The preschool children in this study received higher sociometric ratings if they had more experience with particular peers. This suggests that experience with particular peers also may contribute to the development of social skills in preschool children (Howes 1988, p. 57).

> The stability of the friendships in this sample suggests that children who have sustained intimate experiences with the same peers may receive emotional support from them. Children who have maintained a large proportion of their friendships appeared to be more socially competent than children who lost their friends through separation (Howes 1988, p. 67).

Peer relationships thrive in stable settings where children have time each day to talk and play together with the same group of children.

tive contact with other children" (p. 173). Adults need not be concerned when children choose to play alone or simply near other children. In fact, children need time to do things by themselves, especially in a full-day program when the continual stimulation of other people can be overwhelming.

► **Refer one child to another.**

Encouraging children to turn to their peers for assistance in solving problems helps build trusting relationships:

• The large plastic hair curlers Athi was playing with had a strap that buttoned to hold the rolled hair in place. Although he had tried very hard to undo the strap, he could not hold the curler and, at the same time, pull the strap sideways to release it. "Bonnie," he said to his teacher, "I can't pull this thing." "Well," she responded, "I saw Ilana opening the curlers yesterday. I bet she could help you." Athi found Ilana, and she showed Athi how to do it.

• "Teacher," Randy announced one morning, "my fish had guppies!" "That's excit-

ing," she acknowledged. "Have you told Tyrell? He has guppies, too." "Tyrell, guess what . . ."

Adults can refer children to one another throughout the day. For example, when one child makes a plan to play with another, you can suggest that they plan together and then tell you what they have decided to do. Encourage children to add to one another's recall narratives, seek assistance from one another at work time, and answer one another's questions any time. When adults refer children to their peers for help and conversation, children begin to build relationships based on mutual interests and a respect for one another's skills.

Key Developmental Indicator
Creating and Experiencing Collaborative Play

At work time, Brian marches around the room, playing the drum. Kenneth falls in behind him, shaking a kettle full of uncooked noodles, and Bryant falls in behind Kenneth, holding a maraca in each hand. "Look, Beth," says Brian as they pass her, "I'm leading the band!" As the three boys continue their band, changing leaders from time to time, other children grab a pot to bang or some bells to jingle, march a few rounds with the band, then return to their original play.

At outside time, Anna and Jessa are rolling some tires and decide to roll them down the slide. Anna goes up the ladder first, holding the railing with one hand and the tire with the other. Jessa pushes the tire from behind and calls out encouragement. "We're getting it . . . It's almost up!" Once they get both tires in position at the top of the slide, they call to the children below. "Stay back so the tire won't hit you!" When the way is clear, they let the tires roll down the slide.

Matthew and Emily plan to "work at the office." They take phone calls, type on keyboards, and put papers in envelopes. When other children and adults try to join their play, they say, "There are no more jobs here."

All during work time, Peter and Jason play together, pretending to be sharks, building with Lego blocks, drawing sharks, and pretending to be scuba divers.

Amanda "drives" Colin, Ashley, and Nicholas on the "bus" to the "church wedding." "Pick me up at 1:10," Colin tells her. Then she picks up her "dad," Isaac. After driving for a while, they go back to "the church wedding," knock, and join the ceremony.

Emma and Maria tie the wagon to a tricycle, then Emma gets on the tricycle and gives Maria a ride in the wagon.

Ashley and Isaac slide down the slide holding on to each other. "Isn't this fun!" Isaac says.

Eli, Evan, Jason, Peter, and Isaac construct a marble runway together and send marbles down it.

Sometimes, the relationships children build with peers lead to **collaborative play—making or doing something together that requires the skill, ideas, and contributions of each person.** To form a band, for example, get tires up a ladder, or work in an office, children need the support of at least one like-minded partner. But forming and sustaining play partnerships is not a simple task. It depends on young children's emerging social competence, intentionality, desire for friendship, and ability to sustain the idea of "we" over "me." In their study of 4- to 6-year-olds, developmental psychologists Rina Das and Thomas Berndt found that young children seek playmates based on positive social criteria, including "(a) lack of aggressive behavior ('He's never mean to me'), (b) similarity ('We both like dinosaurs'), (c) sociability ('He plays with me'), (d) perceptions of being liked by the peer ('She likes me'), and (e) prior association ('I have known him for four years')" (Das and Berndt 1992, p. 224). Even when all these conditions are met, however, collaborative play has its ups and downs as children grapple with conflicting viewpoints, desires, and experiences.

In spite of the conflicts that arise, or perhaps because of them, collaborative play stretches children's perceptions of themselves and others. "Such egalitarian relationships," observe psychologists Kenneth Rubin and Barbara Everett (1982), "give children opportunities to assert themselves, to present their own views of the world, and to argue freely with peers concerning different social-cognitive viewpoints. Such conflicts and interactions may ultimately help children to understand that others may have different thoughts, feelings, and perspectives than their own" (p. 106). Further, playing together tends to increase the complexity of children's play. (For examples, see the anecdotes at the beginning of this section as well as the example of the barbershop play described in Chapter 21, pp. 512–517.)

Playing together in preschool, then, is a significant social experience. The memory of such play experiences, or lack thereof, can shape children's approaches to future collaborations. Following are ways adults can support children as they grow in their ability to play collaboratively.

Suggestions for Adults

▶ **Provide materials that encourage collaborative play.**

Throughout this book, we note the importance of providing materials for active learners and list various materials to consider. In

These three children built a "sea wall" to keep their "babies" safe from the "sea monster," a play scenario they created together.

terms of supplying materials to support collaborative play, the lists in Chapter 5 are well worth reviewing. In addition, there are two other ideas about materials to keep in mind—**personal interest** and **size**.

First, provide materials that are personally interesting to individual children in your setting. Such materials encourage collaborative play because one child's interest and enthusiasm will draw in other children. Brian, for example, was interested in musical instruments, and because his teachers knew this and made them available, he was able to start a band with Kenneth and Bryant. Kerry developed an interest in birdhouses. When adults added soft pine scraps to the woodworking area, Lynette joined Kerry and together they sawed and hammered together birdhouses, and later, bird feeders.

Second, provide large materials that invite or require more than one child at a time to use them. This includes items such as rocking boats, rowboats, climbers, parachutes, tents, medicine balls, railroad ties, wagons, large hol-

low blocks, large cardboard boxes, and long jump ropes. One child in a rocking boat, for example, attracts another child (or two or three) to join. A wagon begs for riders and pullers, loaders and pushers.

▶ **Provide space for collaborative play.**

Collaborative play takes place throughout the active learning setting—"mommies," "daddies," and "babies" get ready for a "party" in the house area; robot-makers and honey-cake-makers are found throughout the art area; several children cluster around a computer to make a mask; in the block area there are "police" and some "alligators" in a "swamp"; three children re-enact scenes from *Caps for Sale* in the booknook; and a group of children fill containers and chat around the water table. As you arrange your active learning space and set up the interest areas, make sure to provide enough space for children to work together and spread out in their play experiences.

▶ **Watch for children playing together.**

One basic way to support collaborative play is to look for and acknowledge emerging and ongoing **play**

partnerships. Here are some examples of the kinds of collaborative preschool play you might see at work time and outside time:

• Anna and Jessa gather the materials they need and then set about making "honey cakes."

• Tommy and Randy dig a big hole in the sandbox, fill it with water using the garden hose, and sail the boats they made at the workbench.

• Hillary works at climbing a tree. "That's it. You almost got it. Just try, try, try!" says Hannah.

• Max and Athi are riding a "bus" in the block area. "Hit the brakes," Max says.

Using blocks and heavy cardboard rings from the art-area collage box, these play partners have invented their own version of the ring-toss game.

"We're gonna crash!" Athi replies. "Get the map. We need to find the station." "Then we can go to Atlanta," Max answers.

• Caroline and Ilana are talking over their pretend-play plans. "I'm Tiger Lily," Caroline says. "I'll be Dandelion," Ilana responds. "We need hats and stuff," says Caroline. (The two girls put on skirts, scarves, necklaces, high heels, hats, and gloves. Each one carries a purse.) "Let's pretend we're in the forest," says Ilana. "But we have a little house, okay?" asks Caroline.

• Callie, Aimee, Corrin, and Chelsea sit together on the tire swing, then call Beth, an adult, to give them a push to get started. "Just one push," they caution her, " 'cause we can do it ourselves."

• Corcy and Jeff are playing a game with beanbags and hollow blocks. "First, I throw all mine in and then you throw all yours in—okay, Jeff?"

Over time, as you watch children's collaborative play and discuss it during daily team planning, you begin to get a picture of which children seek each other out, how long they are able to sustain their play, how they deal with conflict, and the particular interests and content their play encompasses. Based on these observations, you can begin to devise strategies to support the play of particular partnerships. (For examples of strategies for supporting children's role play, see Chapter 21, pp. 510–517.)

▶ **Encourage children who play together to plan and recall together.**

Once you are aware of pairs of children who tend to play together at work time, you can

support their play by putting them in the same planning and recall groups (if they are not already together) or by simply asking them to plan with the people they intend to play with. At the same time, it is important to understand that even if play pairs plan together, their plans will continue to evolve as they play—unforeseen problems will arise, they will have new ideas, they will be inspired by what they see other children doing. Nevertheless, encouraging children to **plan together** acknowledges the importance of their collaboration; and having them **recall together** adds richness and dimension to their recall narratives and also helps them to see storytelling as a collaborative venture.

With this strategy in mind, one teacher put pairs of mittens in a bag at planning time. The children each "grabbed" a mitten from the bag, then told their plans to the child with the matching mitten. As it turned out, several of these "mitten pairs" also planned to play together.

▶ **Allow time for collaborative play to evolve.**

As with many of the skills preschoolers are developing, learning how to become a collaborative player takes time. Therefore, one of the best ways adults can support play partners is to watch and enjoy their progress without hurrying or distracting them. In a supportive, unpressured environment, children's collaborative play generally becomes increasingly complex and often expands to include other children.

Here, for example, is how one play partnership began and evolved over a three-month period:

Anna, a skilled block-builder, made elaborate block structures using large blocks for the base and small blocks for details. Douglas, who was also an able builder, joined Anna and

First, these children built a "road for lots of cars." Now they add a train track "so the train can rescue the cars that drived off the road" (and are trapped under the tunnel). While the "roadbuilder man" (by the shelf) gets more track pieces, the other builders assign their teacher to setting up railway signs.

together each day they continued to create block structures that became more detailed and delicately balanced. Now, Bryant was a friend of Douglas but he had never played with blocks before. He often watched Anna and Douglas and finally one

the scarves. They could be the roof." Gradually, Bryant began to have ideas, too, and took a more active role in building. The three continued to make big structures together that eventually turned into houses or cars they could actually enter. Later, when Anna became involved in building beehives, Bryant and Douglas continued building cars, while Jessa joined Anna as her steady partner in "bee" play.

▶ **Form partnerships with emerging players.**

Sometimes you will observe children who want to become play partners but have not quite figured out how to do so. In such cases, it may be appropriate for adults to become partners with children, so the children have the opportunity to develop the skills needed to participate with their peers. Here is an example of this strategy:

one day, but his entry technique—growling and swiping at things—only made the others tell him to go away.

After observing Mikey's unsuccessful attempt to join the play, Beth, an adult, thought of a way she might help. The next morning, when the players were gathering and assigning roles, she asked if she could be the baby (one of the least desirable roles because everybody else could boss "the baby" around). On this day, even the sitter went to the movies, leaving "baby" Beth all by herself. Seeing Mikey lingering nearby she said to him, "Mikey, would you like to be my doggy?" This suited Mikey because growling was a legitimate dog behavior. When the "family" and "babysitter" returned, the first thing they asked was "What's Mikey doing here?" Beth explained, "He's my doggy. He's very obedient, and he likes to eat dog food."

When the others had taken this information in and tested the "doggy's" ability to obey and to eat dog food, they accepted Mikey into their play. Seeing that Mikey was accepted into the role of doggy, Beth withdrew, leaving Mikey on his own with the group. Over time, Mikey graduated to the baby role, and several months later, when the role players turned to a new theme (barbershop play), Mikey was one of the first "customers" and even gave a few haircuts himself.

There are several things Beth did that enabled Mikey to be successful member of the role-play group:

• Beth viewed Mikey's intentions in a positive manner. She assumed from the outset that Mikey wanted to join the play, even though his initial actions had a negative impact on the other children.

day he said, "Hey, Douglas, I want to play with you." Douglas assented as did Anna, so Bryant joined the group—initially as a block supplier. Anna or Douglas would say, "Bryant, go get some more red blocks for the walls" or "Bryant, get

Chelsea, Callie, Corrin, Alana, Ben, Douglas, and Petey liked to play "moms," "dads," and "sisters" who went "dancing" and to the "movies," leaving the "baby" home with the "babysitter." Mikey tried to join this play

• Beth understood the structure of the ongoing play and asked for the least powerful role for herself. This gave her a legitimate inside position from which she could be a partner with Mikey without disrupting the play or displacing another player.

• Beth invited Mikey in during a natural break in the play. Rather than imposing her intentions on the other players at the height of their play, she chose a moment when they were occupied elsewhere and she and Mikey could try out their partnership at their own pace.

• Beth took advantage of Mikey's ability to growl by offering him the role of a dog, thus giving him a chance to use his growling strategy in an appropriate context and to good effect.

• Beth withdrew from the play as soon as it looked as if Mikey could be partners with some of the other players on his own.

While each child and each play situation is unique, these are the kinds of strategies adults can use to help young children join others in play.

▶ **Provide opportunities for collaborative play at small-group time.**

At daily team planning, as you consider what to do at small-group time, include experiences in which children have opportunities to work together. Consider these suggestions:

• Provide pairs of children with balls and ask them how they could roll (toss, bounce) them to each other.

• As a group, act out stories children tell.

• Wash something big together, such as everyone's cubbies, the sand toys, all the chairs, a staff member's car.

• Empty the sandbox and fill it with new sand. This requires shovellers and bucket carriers.

• Give children the choice between building on small, one-person Lego bases and large, two-person Lego bases. Many children will choose to work in pairs and then will negotiate such things as whether to build a house for dogs or people or both, and whether there can be a diving board in the living room.

Key Developmental Indicator
Dealing With Social Conflict*

Jonah pushes Owen very hard against the block shelf. "What's going on here?" Betsy, their teacher, asks. "The invisible friends gave me a magic potion," Jonah tells her.

~

Colin and Nicholas are arguing over a book. "I think I know how we can solve this problem," says Jason, who is sitting next to them. "Nicholas can finish reading it and then give it to Colin." Colin turns to Nicholas and says, "Will you, Nicholas?" "Yes," Nicholas agrees.

~

Alice and Sam are dressing up in the playhouse. At the same moment, they reach for the only colorful scarf. They tug back and forth, yelling, "I got it first! Give it to me!"

~

---

*This section was written by High/Scope certified trainer Betsy Evans. It first appeared in a slightly different version in the High/Scope Extensions *curriculum newsletter, May/June 1992. See also her book* You Can't Come to My Birthday Party: Conflict Resolution With Young Children *(2002).*

Emma and Joe are building a dinosaur house together. When Joe accidentally knocks part of it down, Emma pushes him saying, "Get out!"

Social conflicts like these can create feelings of frustration, confusion, and failure for both children and adults. Many times it may not be clear how a conflict started, who is responsible, or how the problem can be resolved. Yet, these situations provide important occasions for active learning.

In settling disputes with their peers, children begin to understand how to respect the needs of others while meeting their own needs. They also begin to see that there is often more than one "right" side in a dispute, that the feelings of others are important, and that it is possible to solve conflicts in such a way that both parties are satisfied with the result. Following are ways adults can help children deal successfully with social conflicts.

Suggestions for Adults

▶ **Keep children's developmental characteristics in mind.**

To assist young children effectively in their efforts to resolve conflicts and disputes, it is important for adults to remember the characteristics of preschoolers and how they think. Keep in mind that preschoolers are still quite self-centered; they are struggling for independence and control, and they think in very concrete terms. Since these characteristics influence the way children approach conflicts, adults can be most helpful by recognizing and talking about children's feelings, making problem solving an active process, and providing children with appropriate information when they need it.

Acknowledge and talk about what each child is feeling. Young children's self-centeredness often makes it difficult for them to understand the needs of others. They are not being "bad" or selfish when they ignore another child's rights or needs—it is simply difficult in times of conflict for preschoolers to look beyond themselves. Since a child who is having a dispute with another child often is not aware of the other child's point of view, it is important for adults to talk about what each child is feeling: "You worked a long time on this building, Hugo. I see that you're upset that it fell down." When children are upset, helping them recognize their own feelings and those of others in the situation can contribute to their sense of being in control and their understanding that all feelings need to be considered.

Engage children as active participants in the problem-solving process (rather than solve problems for them). This meets the children's need for independence and gives them a sense of control as they begin to develop relationships outside their families and to explore the world as independent persons. By acknowledging children's feelings and engaging them as active problem-solvers, adults encourage children's initiative and desire to do things for themselves. Statements such as "Let's try to solve this problem together" encourage each child involved in a dispute to take an active role in resolving it.

Give children specific information. Their tendency to think concretely also affects young children's ability to resolve conflicts. We know that preschoolers learn best when the information provided is concrete and specific. So, in helping to resolve a conflict between children, *avoid general statements* such as "You must learn to share." Instead, *give children specific information* that

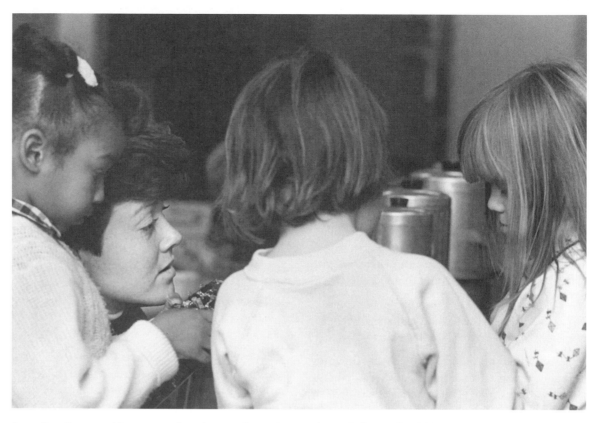

In settling disputes with peers—such as this one about who can play with the toy the child on the left is holding—children begin to distinguish between their own needs and the needs of others. (See accompanying photo on page 61.)

will help them work out the details of sharing: "Jason, you want the yellow truck because it fits in your garage, and George, you want the yellow school truck because it has a dumper."

Here is how one adult applied these strategies when Alice and Sam were fighting over the scarf they both wanted. In a calm, matter-of-fact tone she said, "Alice and Sam, I can see that you both really want to use the scarf. It's too bad that there are not enough scarves for both of you. Let's think of some ways we can solve this prob-

lem." This kind of approach helps to calm all the parties in a conflict and makes shared problem solving possible. *Note that the adult started by recognizing the feelings of both Alice and Sam in specific terms.* She then gave a clear message that they could work together to solve the problem. Then, in moving toward a solution, the adult was again careful to be specific: "Sam, Alice says she would like to wear the scarf for five minutes. Would you like to use the sand timer so you will know when her five minutes are over?"

▶ **Maintain a supportive environment to keep conflicts at a minimum.**

In the example of Alice and Sam, an adult intervened skillfully in the children's dispute. This incident might have been prevented, however, if more than one colorful scarf had been available. In fact, providing multiple sets of similar materials in each interest area is one way to decrease disputes over materials. There are several other general principles to follow that will also help keep conflicts and disputes to a minimum:

• **Maintain limits and expectations for behavior that are *developmentally appropriate.*** Respect and plan for children's differing abilities, interests, and paces. (For extensive examples of appropriate expectations, see pp. 102–103.)

• **Provide many choices for play.** Materials should be plentiful, and it should be easy for children to find them and put them away.

• **Establish and follow a consistent daily routine.** Explain it clearly to the children, using pictures or drawings to make the segments concrete.

• **Model respectful ways of interacting with others and using materials.** The behaviors you model are the easiest ones for children to learn.

• **Plan for transitions.** Keep transitions short and make them playful.

These types of strategies give children a sense of control and security. When they are implemented, children tend to be more focused and purposeful in their play and, consequently, fewer disputes and conflicts arise. Nevertheless, while conflicts may be reduced, they will not disappear.

▶ **Help children resolve conflicts when they arise.**

When conflicts do arise, there are several steps adults can take to help children settle them. These steps have been adapted for young children from the conflict-resolution literature (Crary 1984; Hopkins and Winters 1990; Prutzman, Stern, Burger, and Bodenhamer 1988; Wichert 1989), incorporating the child development principles described earlier. To illustrate each step, we will refer again to the earlier example of Emma and Joe (p. 367).

Step 1. Approach the situation calmly. Observe what is happening and prepare yourself for a *positive* outcome. Keep your voice at a conversational level, sit or kneel on the floor, and gently reach out to children who are upset or angry with a welcoming gesture or a hand on the shoulder. Stop any hurtful actions.

Step 2. Acknowledge children's feelings. Describe the feelings you observe and the details of what you see.

Adult: *Emma, you sound angry with Joe. And Joe, you look sad. (She sits between Emma and Joe, an arm around each one.) I can see that part of the dinosaur house has fallen down. Let's try to solve this problem together.*

Step 3. Gather information. Ask open-ended questions, directing your questions to one child, then another.

Adult: *Tell me, what happened, Joe?*

Listen carefully to what children say. Small details can create major conflicts!

Step 4. Restate the problem. Based on what the children say, clarify the problem and check your statement with the children.

Adult: *Joe, you feel that Emma is being mean, and Emma, you don't want Joe to build because he is knocking the house down. Is that right? (They nod their heads.) Do you both want to keep building here? (Nod their heads again.)*

Step 5. Ask for ideas for solutions and choose one together. Encourage children to talk to each other. Frequently, simple misunderstandings can be cleared up when children describe the problem to each other. If this does not work, be prepared to give suggestions:

Adult: *If you both want to continue building, what do you think we should do now? How can we work this out?*

Emma: *I want to build this part by myself. Joe can build over there.*

Joe: *Hey, I can build the dinosaurs a swimming pool!"*

Emma: *Yeah!*

When children arrive at a solution, restate it and check with them to make sure they are in agreement.

Adult: *Emma and Joe, it seems that you both want to play here, and that you each want to build different things for the dinosaurs. Is that right? (Emma and Joe nod their heads yes and turn back to the blocks. Emma rebuilds the dinosaur house while Joe starts building the swimming pool.)*

Comment on the children's efforts and the problem-solving process they have used:

Adult: *Emma and Joe, you solved the problem! You both talked about ideas for solving your problem together. And you listened to each other*

1. Evan goes to the playhouse and takes the spoon that Collin and Trevor have been using. They find Evan at the puppet stage and ask for it back. He refuses to give the spoon to them. They then ask Betsy, a teacher, for help, and they all go to talk to Evan. Evan, and then Collin and Trevor, explain why they want the spoon. Another child steps in the middle and says, "I think they should share."

Betsy: *How do you think they can do that?*

Trevor: *I know. We'll use it for a minute, then bring it right back.*

Evan: *No.*

Collin: *But we were using it to make applesauce.*

Betsy: *Evan, it seems that there are two ways we can solve this. Trevor and Collin can take the spoon for a minute and bring it back, as Trevor suggested, or you can use it for a minute and bring it to them.*

Evan: *No, I think they should bring their stuff for applesauce here and make it.*

Collin: *Yeah!*

Trevor: *Let's do that!* (They quickly go to get their applesauce-making things.)

Betsy: (To Evan) *You thought of a way to solve the problem for everyone!* (Evan smiles.)

～

2. Sara and Mei Mei complain to Betsy, the teacher, "Josh and Shakeel are bothering us through the window in the playhouse. Josh squeezed my arm and Shakeel hit Mei Mei."

Betsy: *What did you do?*

Sara: *We told them to stop, but they didn't.*

Betsy: *Did they hurt you again?*

Sara: *No . . . but they kept peeking!*

Betsy: *Did you ask them to stop peeking?*

Sara doesn't answer. She and Mei Mei go back and tell the two boys to stop peeking. Josh and Shakeel look up from their building and listen. They go back to building and do not bother the girls again.

When a conflict arises, this adult encourages the children to talk about the problem and generate ideas for a solution.

carefully. I'd like to see the dinosaur house when it is finished.

Step 6. Be prepared to give follow-up support. Sometimes solutions need clarifying as the children begin to play again: The adult stations herself nearby as Joe and Emma start to play. Soon, however, they are arguing over the building space. After the three have another discussion, they decide to place a line of tape across the block corner to clarify each child's space.

As with any new set of skills, it takes time and practice to learn to use these problem-solving steps. To see preschool children resolving conflicts with the help of adults using these six steps, see the High/Scope video or DVD *Supporting Children in Resolving Conflicts* (1998).

As you apply any of the strategies in this chapter, keep in mind, again, that children's social development cannot be hurried. They need time over weeks and months to make choices and decisions, and to experience the consequences. When we grant children time for repetition and mastery, children do change and grow. On the playground, for example, Brian sees Mikey on the tricycle Brian prefers. He walks toward Mikey. For several months Brian has tried to take the tricycle from any child riding it and has needed his teacher to step in to help him sort things out. Today, however, Brian pauses and says to himself, "After Mikey's finished, I'll use it." He then goes to the sandbox and begins to dig. Over time, after many experiences with his peers and teachers negotiating over the tricycle, Brian has learned for himself that Mikey will eventually be finished riding and that he, Brian, can decide on something else to do while he waits for this to occur.

Levels of Mediation

It is not always necessary for adults to mediate conflicts directly. Some children are able to solve problems more independently than others. Following are three different **levels of support** adults can offer to children who are resolving conflicts.

• **Level 1:** Work directly with all the children who are involved in a dispute, mediating in a way that is developmentally appropriate and supportive of all children involved. (See the first example in Effective Mediation, facing page.)

• **Level 2:** Listen to one child describe a conflict with another child. Ask questions and offer suggestions that support the child in solving the problem independently. (See the second example in Effective Mediation.)

• **Level 3:** Position yourself near a conflict, but allow children to settle the dispute without your intervention. Your presence alone may provide enough support for an amicable settlement.

Social and Emotional Development Strategies: A Summary

Taking care of one's own needs
___ Provide children with time to do things for themselves.
___ Encourage children to use common tools.
___ Support children's attempts to take care of their emotional needs.

Expressing feelings in words
___ Establish and maintain a supportive environment.
___ Acknowledge and accept children's feelings.
___ Listen for the names children give to their feelings.
___ Talk with children about their concerns.
___ Encourage children to tell stories.

Building relationships with children and adults
___ Establish supportive relations with children:
   ___ Treat children with kindness.
   ___ Have genuine conversations with children.
___ Maintain a stable group of children and adults.
___ Look for relationships between children.
___ Refer one child to another.

Creating and experiencing collaborative play
___ Provide materials that encourage collaborative play.
___ Provide space for collaborative play.
___ Watch for children playing together.
___ Encourage children who play together to plan and recall together.
___ Allow time for collaborative play to evolve.
___ Form partnerships with emerging players.
___ Provide opportunities for collaborative play at small-group time.

Dealing with social conflict
___ Keep children's developmental characteristics in mind:
   ___ Acknowledge and talk about what each child is feeling.
   ___ Engage children as active participants in the problem-solving process (rather than solve problems for them).
   ___ Give children specific information.
___ Maintain a supportive environment to keep conflicts at a minimum:
   ___ Maintain limits and expectations for behavior that are *developmentally appropriate*.
   ___ Provide many choices for play.
   ___ Establish and follow a consistent daily routine.
   ___ Model respectful ways of interacting with others and using materials.
   ___ Plan for transitions.
___ Help children resolve conflicts when they arise:
   ___ *Step 1:* Approach calmly.
   Step 2: Acknowledge children's feelings.
   ___ *Step 3:* Gather information.
   ___ *Step 4:* Restate the problem.
   ___ *Step 5:* Ask for ideas for solutions and choose one together.
   ___ *Step 6:* Be prepared to give follow-up support.

References

Asher, Steven R., Peter D. Renshaw, and Shelley Hymel. 1982. "Peer Relations and the Development of Social Skills." In *The Young Child: Reviews of Research*, Vol. 3, Shirley Moore and Catherine Cooper, eds., 137–58. Washington, DC: NAEYC.

Bailey, Becky A. 2000. *Conscious Discipline: 7 Basic Skills for Brain Smart Classroom Managment.* Oviedo, FL: Loving Guidance.

Crary, Elizabeth. 1984. *Kids Can Cooperate.* Seattle: Parenting Press.

Das, Rina, and Thomas J. Berndt. 1992. "Relations of Preschoolers' Social Acceptance to Peer Ratings and Self-Perceptions." *Early Education and Development* 3, no. 3 (July): 221–31.

Dimidjian, Victoria Jean. 1986. "Helping Children in Times of Trouble and Crisis." In *The Feeling Child: Affective Development Reconsidered*, Nancy E. Curry, ed., 113–28. New York: The Haworth Press.

Evans, Betsy. 1992. "Helping Children Resolve Disputes and Conflicts." *High/Scope Extensions* (May/June).

Evans, Betsy. 2002. *You Can't Come to My Birthday Party: Conflict Resolution With Young Children.* Ypsilanti, MI: High/Scope Press.

Hartup, Willard W. 1986. "On Relationships and Development." In *Relationships and Development*, Willard W. Hartup and Zick Rubin, eds., 1–26. Hillsdale, NJ: Erlbaum.

Hartup, Willard W. 1983. "Peer Relations." In *Socialization, Personality, and Social Development, Handbook of Child Psychology*, Vol. 4, E. Mavis Heatherington, ed., Paul H. Mussen, series ed., 103–96. New York: Wiley.

Hartup, Willard W., and Shirley G. Moore. 1990. "Early Peer Relations: Developmental Significance and Prognostic Implications." *Early Childhood Research Quarterly* 5 no. 1 (March): 1–17.

Hinde, Robert A., Graham Titmus, Douglas Easton, and Alison Tamplin. 1985. "Incidence of 'Friendship' and Behavior Toward Strong Associates Versus Nonassociates in Preschoolers." *Child Development* 56, no. 1 (February): 234–45.

Holloway, Susan D., and Marina Reichhart-Erickson. 1988. "The Relationship of Day Care Quality to Children's Free-Play Behavior and Social Problem-Solving Skills." *Early Childhood Research Quarterly* 3, no. 1 (March): 39–53.

Hopkins, Susan, and Jeffry Winters, eds. 1990. *Discover the World: Empowering Children to Value Themselves, Others, and the Earth.* Philadelphia: New Society Publishers.

Howes, Carolee. 1988. "Peer Interaction of Young Children." *Monographs of the Society for Research in Child Development*, Serial No. 217, Vol. 53, no. 1.

Howes, Carolee. 1987. "Social Competency With Peers: Contribution From Child Care." *Early Childhood Research Quarterly* 2, no. 2 (June): 155–67.

Kagan, Sharon L., Evelyn Moore, and Sue Bredekamp, eds. 1995. *Reconsidering Children's Early Development and Learning: Toward Common Views and Vocabulary.* (Goal 1 Technical Planning Group Report 95–03). Washington, DC: National Education Goals Panel.

Katz, Lilian, and Diane McClellan. 1997. *Fostering Children's Social Competence: The Teacher's Role.* Washington, DC: National Association for the Education of Young Children.

Moore, Shirley. 1982. "Prosocial Behavior in the Early Years: Parent and Peer Influences." In *Handbook of Research in Early Childhood Education*, Bernard Spodek, ed., 65–81. New York: The Free Press.

Prutzman, Priscilla, Lee Stern, M. Leonard Burger, and Gretchen Bodenhamer. 1988. *The Friendly Classroom for a Small Planet: A Handbook on Creative Approaches to Living and Problem Solving for Children.* Philadelphia: New Society Publishers.

Rubin, Kenneth H., and Barbara Everett. 1982. "Social Perspective-Taking in Young Children." In *The Young Child: Reviews of Research*, Vol. 3, Shirley Moore and Catherine Cooper, eds., 97–113. Washington, DC: NAEYC.

Satir, Virginia. 1988. *The New Peoplemaking.* Mountain View, CA: Science and Behavior Books, Inc.

Sroufe, L. Alan, and June Fleeson. 1986. "Attachment and the Construction of Relationships." In *Relationships and Development*, Willard W. Hartup and Zick Rubin, eds., 51–71. Hillsdale, NJ: Erlbaum.

Wichert, Susanne. 1989. *Keeping the Peace.* Philadelphia: New Society Publishers.

Wood, David, Linnet McMahon, and Yvonne Cranstoun. 1980. *Working With Under Fives.* Ypsilanti, MI: High/Scope Press.

Related Reading

Bretherton, Inge, Janet Fritz, Carolyn Zahn-Waxler, and Doreen Ridgeway. 1986. "Learning to Talk About Emotions: A Functionalist Perspective." *Child Development* 57, no. 3 (June): 529–48.

Crago, Hugh. 1986. "The Place of Story in Affective Development: Implications for Educators and Clinicians." In *The Feeling Child: Affective Development Reconsidered*, Nancy E. Curry, ed., 129–42. New York: The Haworth Press.

Curry, Nancy E. 1986. "Where Have All the Players Gone?" In *The Feeling Child: Affective Development Reconsidered*, Nancy E. Curry, ed., 93–111. New York: The Haworth Press.

Curry, Nancy E., and Carl N. Johnson. 1990. *Beyond Self-Esteem: Developing a Genuine Sense of Human Value.* Washington, DC: NAEYC.

Denham, Susanne A. 1986. "Social Cognition, Prosocial Behavior, and Emotion in Preschoolers: Contextual Validation." *Child Development* 57, no. 1 (February): 194–201.

Epstein, Ann S. 2007. "What Is the High/Scope Curriculum in Social and Emotional Development?" Chap. 12 in *Essentials of Active Learning in Preschool: Getting to Know the High/Scope Curriculum*, 125–36. Ypsilanti, MI: High/Scope Press.

Evans, Betsy. 1996. "Helping Children Resolve Disputes and Conflicts." "Watch Your Language!" "Punishment: What Does It Teach?" "Language That Sets Limits." "From Superheroes to Problem Solving." "Super Strategies for Superheroes." In *Supporting Young Learners 2*, Nancy A. Brickman, ed., 27–65. Ypsilanti, MI: High/Scope Press.

Fein, Greta, and Shirley S. Schwartz. 1986. "The Social Coordination of Pretense in Preschool Children." In *The Young Child at Play: Reviews of Research,* Vol. 4, Greta Fein and Mary Rivkin, eds., 95–111. Washington, DC: NAEYC.

Fischer, Kurt, Helen Hand, Malcolm Watson, Martha Van Parys, and James Tucker. 1984. "Putting the Child Into Socialization: The Development of Social Categories in Preschool Children." In *Current Topics in Early Childhood Education*, Vol. 5, 27–72. Norwood, NJ: Ablex.

Gardner, Howard. 1983. "The Personal Intelligences." Chap. 10 in *Frames of Mind: The Theory of Multiple Intelligences,* 237–76. New York: Basic Books.

Gottman, John M. 1983. "How Children Become Friends." *Monographs of the Society for Research in Child Development,* Serial No. 201, Vol. 48, no. 3.

Harris, Paul L., Kara Donnelly, Gabrielle R. Guz, and Rosemary Pitt-Watson. 1986. "Children's Understanding of the Distinction Between Real and Apparent Emotion." *Child Development 57,* no. 4 (August): 895–909.

High/Scope Educational Research Foundation. 2003. *Preschool Child Observation Record (COR),* 2nd ed. Ypsilanti, MI: High/Scope Press.

Hinde, Robert A., and Joan Stevenson-Hinde. 1986. "Relating Childhood Relationships to Individual Characteristics." In *Relationships and Development,* Willard W. Hartup and Zick Rubin, eds., 27–50. Hillsdale, NJ: Erlbaum.

Huttenlocher, Janellen, and Patricia Smiley. 1990. "Emerging Notions of Persons." In *Psychological and Biological Approaches to Emotion,* Nancy L. Stein, Bennett Leventhal, and Tom Trabasso, eds. Hillsdale, NJ: Erlbaum.

Hyson, Marion C. 1994. *The Emotional Development of Young Children: Building an Emotion-Centered Curriculum.* New York: Teachers College Press.

Katz, Lilian, and Diane McClellan. 1997. *Fostering Children's Social Competence: The Teacher's Role.* Washington DC: NAEYC.

Kemple, Kristen M. 1991. "Preschool Children's Peer Acceptance and Social Interaction." *Young Children* 46, no. 5 (March): 47–54.

Koplow, Lesley. 1996. *Unsmiling Faces: How Preschools Can Heal.* New York: Teachers College Press.

Krasnor, Linda Rose, and Kenneth H. Rubin. 1983. "Preschool Social Problem Solving: Attempts and Outcomes in Naturalistic Interaction." *Child Development* 54, no. 6 (December): 1545–58.

Oden, Sherri. 1988. "Alternative Perspectives on Children's Peer Relations." In *Integrative Processes and Socialization: Early to Middle Childhood,* T. D. Yawkey and J. E. Johnson, eds., 139–66. Hillsdale: Erlbaum.

Oden, Sherri. 1986. "Developing Social Skills Instruction for Peer Interaction and Relationships." In *Teaching Social Skills to Children,* 2nd ed., E. Cartledge and J. Milburn, eds., 246–69. New York: Pergamon Press.

Oden, Sherri. 1993. "Implementing Research on Children's Social Competence: What Do Teachers and Researchers Need to Learn?" *Exceptionality Education Canada* 3 nos. 1 & 2: 209–32.

Paley, Vivian Gussin. 1992. *You Can't Say You Can't Play.* Cambridge, MA: Harvard University Press.

Piers, Maria W., and Nancy E. Curry. 1986. "A Developmental Perspective on Children's Affects." In *The Feeling Child: Affective Development Reconsidered,* Nancy E. Curry, ed., 23–36. New York: The Haworth Press.

Ramsey, Patricia G. 1991. *Making Friends in School: Promoting Peer Relationships in Early Childhood.* New York: Teachers College Press.

Rogers, Dwight L., and Dorene D. Ross. 1986. "Encouraging Positive Social Interaction Among Young Children." *Young Children* 41, no. 3 (March): 12–17.

Rubin, Kenneth H., and Nina Howe. 1986. "Social Play and Perspective-Taking." In *The Young Child at Play: Reviews of Research,* Vol. 4, Greta Fein and Mary Rivkin, eds., 113–25. Washington, DC: NAEYC.

Related Media

The following materials are available from the High/Scope Press, 600 N. River St., Ypsilanti, MI 48198-2898; to order, visit *www.highscope.org*, or call 1-800-40-PRESS.

Initiative and Social Relations. 2001. Color videotape or DVD, 60 min. Ypsilanti, MI: High/Scope Press.

It's Mine! Responding to Problems and Conflicts (The Tender Care Infant-Toddler Series). 2002. Color videotape or DVD, 40 min. Ypsilanti, MI: High/Scope Press.

Supporting Children in Resolving Conflicts. 1998. Color videotape or DVD, 24 min. Ypsilanti, MI: High/Scope Press.

As they play alone and with others in an active learning environment, children gain a sense of pleasure and self-confidence through daily opportunities for physical development.

13

Physical Development, Health, and Well-Being

Since movement is one of the child's earliest modes of communication, adults need to support this natural means of expression in the preschool years.

—Ruth Strubank, 1991

In the High/Scope Curriculum, the content area of **physical development, health, and well-being** emphasizes **movement** because the young child's neuromuscular system plays a central role in early development. Psychologist Howard Gardner (1983, p. 206) defines movement as *a person's capacity to control bodily motions and handle objects skillfully.* Movement experiences are not only essential to children's physical development but also are one of the primary ways young children learn about the world.

Freedom to Move, Freedom to Learn

Infants and toddlers experience the world primarily through their senses, and they engage in fairly simple ways of moving. Infants, for example, interact with the world by reaching, smiling, kicking, tasting, and so forth. They express what they know and understand through movement. When 4-month-old Jack sees and hears his dad coming to pick him up at the child care center, he comes alive with wiggles, squirms, and smiles. Jack's whole body says "Hi, daddy," as well as any words could.

By the time they reach preschool age, children move with increasing skill, and they exhibit a newfound ability to tailor the way they move to suit their play and intentions: "I'm the mama bunny and I'm jumping to the store . . . ." Yet young children still construct an understanding of the physical and social world through the direct actions and experiences they have with their bodies and senses.

For example, to understand the characteristics of a dog, preschoolers need to pat, hold, and curl up next to the family dog. And because they can keep their experiences in mind, they can use their bodies very skillfully to move like dogs themselves—to act out what they know about dogs and other animals. For young children, **action**—*movement*—is a key to understanding and acquiring knowledge.

In an active learning environment, children have repeated opportunities for movement as they play alone, with their peers, and with adults. They run, climb, throw, dance, jump, hop, gallop, skip, pretend and role play, bounce balls, make up games with scarves, and play traditional games such as "Tag" and "Red Rover." In the process, they not only learn about themselves and their world but also develop coordination and basic timing skills, improve their physical conditioning, and gain a sense of pleasure and self-confidence about their physical abilities.

Supporting Physical Development

High/Scope's **eight key developmental indicators (KDIs) in physical development, health, and well-being**, developed by High/Scope movement consultant Phyllis S. Weikart (1987), describe and draw attention to the ways in which children develop physically. Four KDIs focus on *experiencing movement:*

- **Moving in nonlocomotor ways** (anchored movement: bending, twisting, rocking, swinging one's arms)

- Moving in locomotor ways (nonanchored movement: running, jumping, hopping, skipping, marching, climbing)

- Moving with objects

- Expressing creativity in movement

Two indicators focus on *observing and describing movement*:

- Describing movement

- Acting upon movement directions

And two indicators focus on *basic timing*:

- Feeling and expressing steady beat

- Moving in sequences to a common beat

KDIs in Physical Development, Health, and Well-Being

- Moving in nonlocomotor ways (anchored movement: bending, twisting, rocking, swinging one's arms)

- Moving in locomotor ways (nonanchored movement: running, jumping, hopping, skipping, marching, climbing)

- Moving with objects

- Expressing creativity in movement

- Describing movement

- Acting upon movement directions

- Feeling and expressing steady beat

- Moving in sequences to a common beat

Adults who support physical development have a great respect for and commitment to children's play and its educational value. They recognize the pleasure children take in physical activity has health and well-being benefits. They enter into the spirit of children's play—for example, joining them on the slide, in a game of catch, or in a parade around the playground. Adults understand that to develop basic movement abilities, children need to try out things for themselves, experiment with various ways of moving, have space and time for active physical play, interact with peers, and imitate others.

The discussions that follow on each of the indicators include specific strategies adults can use to support children's movement activities within the context of an active learning setting.

Key Developmental Indicator
Moving in Nonlocomotor Ways (Anchored Movement: Bending, Twisting, Rocking, Swinging One's Arms)

Aimee bends her arms and flaps her elbows against her sides. Petey watches Aimee, then tries the same motions with his elbows.

❧

A group of children are moving to "Yankee Doodle," and Kenneth (kneeling on the floor) is moving his arms up and down.

❧

Amanda and Roxanne turn their arms around and around as they sing the "Hokey Pokey" song.

Moving in nonlocomotor ways is one of the first ways infants move. Though remaining in one place, infants are often in motion: they lie on their backs and wave their arms, study the motions of their fingers and hands, kick their legs, and turn their heads from side to side. They also lie on their stomachs and push themselves up with their arms, lift and turn their heads, and make swimming motions with their legs. Although preschoolers have long since achieved mobility, they continue to gain balance, control, and an awareness of movement as they assume a variety of positions—lying down, sitting, kneeling, squatting, curling into a ball, standing. They also engage in a variety of motions from these positions—bending, swinging, twisting, rocking, and moving their arms, legs, trunk, or head in various ways. This process of acquiring experienced-based knowledge provides children with an understanding of what their bodies can do, and it also strengthens children's capacities to isolate and use the motions they want and need in games, role play, problem solving, and self-expression.

Following are ways adults can support children as they move in nonlocomotor ways.

Suggestions for Adults

▶ **Encourage children to explore a wide variety of positions.**

Children enjoy assuming various physical positions in the course of their play or as they participate in group games. At work time, for example, you may see children curling up in a box under the table, pretending to be "sleeping bees," or during a large-group game you may observe children standing on one foot and using their arms for balance.

Watch for and acknowledge the positions that children assume as they play. One day during work time, Kenneth made a plan for the block area. He placed a number of carpet squares on the floor so he would "be protected from the hot lava." After moving from square to square, he selected one square for his "house" and for the rest of work time he remained standing on his "house" square to avoid getting "burnt up." In the meantime, from his stationary position, he solicited the help of his friends: "I'm hungry. Can you get me some food?" he asked another block player, who obligingly tossed him a beanbag. "Thanks for the hamburger," Kenneth responded, as he reached out from his "house" to catch the beanbag. In the course of his play that morning, Kenneth reached, twisted, bent over, squatted, curled up, and stretched to avoid the "hot lava." At recall time, Kenneth and Beth, his teacher, talked together about all the ways he had moved his body. As he talked, he often paused to demonstrate what he had done.

Play position-games with children. At small-group time, large-group time, and outside time, adults can play "position-games" with children. Children enjoy playing "Statues"—twirling themselves around, freezing at a given signal, and examining and commenting on the unusual positions they have assumed. They may end up sitting with their legs and arms in different positions, kneeling with their arms held out for balance, curled into a ball, or standing on one foot. As children search to find words to describe their positions, they build body awareness and control.

"Angels" is another game children can play while lying on their backs in the snow, sand, or grass and moving their arms up and down, and their legs apart and together. They can also see what happens when they repeat the same motions on their sides or stomachs, or while sitting, as well as what other kinds of motions they can make in these positions with their arms, legs, and heads. An adult participating with the children can comment on children's observations about what they are doing as well as support their further experimentation.

▶ **Look for opportunities to swing, bend, rock, and twist with children.**

Experiencing whole-body movement helps children develop control of themselves and a sense of physical coordination. For example, at work time watch for children pretending to move like animals such as cats, dogs, or baby lions. Imitate their actions and comment on how they are twisting and bending like real cats and dogs. When children rock their doll babies, join them in rocking or hold a doll baby yourself and rock from side to side. Play music as children gather for large-group time and stretch, bend, twist, and rock to it. See how children modify these motions and encourage them to try out their twisting and bending ideas.

▶ **Play games that focus on one movement at a time.**

There are many stories, rhymes, and chants such as "Hokey Pokey" that include specific actions children can do. In the action-chant "Going on a Lion Hunt," for example, children use their hands to "part the grass," "swim across a river," "beat on the ground," and so forth.

During work time, this child (pretending to be a "kitty") curls up into a ball in her "kitty house."

You can also make up your own rhymes and chants. One adult made up this action-packed version of "Wee Willie Winkie":

Wee Willie Winkie shakes his head.
Wee Willie Winkie pushes blankets off his bed.
Tapping at the window, pounding at the lock,
He slides into his nightshirt
And winds up the clock.

When you are making up stories, rhymes, and chants, include action words such as touch, thump, pound, shake, rise, punch, press, wring, push, fall, flick, float, slide, dab, cut, turn, and pull. Once children understand the idea, they also enjoy making up their own action stories and rhymes to share with the group.

Another more open-ended game is to select or ask the children to suggest an action word, such as "shake," and then to encourage the children to find all the parts of their bodies they can shake.

▶ **Attend to the direction, size, level, intensity, shape, and timing of children's nonlocomotor movement.**

Direction. As children move their limbs, they move them closer to and farther from their bodies, up and down, around, apart, and together. While watching a child make a snow angel, for example, one adult commented, "You're making your feet go apart and together, Sandi."

Size. Children make small stretches and big ones, small waves and big waves. As you comment on the extent of the motions you see them making, give children time to formulate their own comments and observations. Thinking about these types of movement experiences, one adult made up an action story about mice and included a mouse who knocked with a small knock and a mouse who knocked with a big knock. These same two mice

also curled themselves into small balls to fit into their "mouse dens" and spread themselves out to take up a big space when they slept "outside."

Level. Children can move close to the ground or "up high." One group of preschoolers and adults made up a game of "ants and birds." It started at a large-group time after the children had been squatting down and lying in the grass watching some ants on the playground. "Let's get down low and pretend we're watching ants," an adult suggested. The children assumed various low, ant-watching positions. "I know! Let's wave to the ants!" Michael suggested. After that, everyone had different movement ideas to share with the ants. Several days later, one of the adults suggested a variation, "standing tall" and watching birds. Eventually the game evolved so someone would simply say "ants" and everyone would get down low, followed by "birds," which was the signal to repeat the action at a higher level.

Intensity. Children can make strong and weak movements. At outside time, for example, several children were lying on their stomachs "swimming" in the grass. One of their teachers joined them, saying "You are making strong swimming movements with your legs. I hope I can be a strong swimmer like you." After a period of strong "swimming," one of the "swimmers" observed, "I'm too tired to be strong. My legs are taking a rest."

Shape. As they play position games such as "Statues," children often discover that they have

At the end of the day's opening activity, with many parents still present, children transition to the next activity with a nonlocomotor movement game in which they twist their bodies into "statues" and freeze in place until the teacher releases them with a pat on the head.

inadvertently made shapes with their bodies. In one such game, after the "statues" had "frozen," an adult said, "Look around. What do you see?" It was quiet as the children looked at themselves and one another. Then one child announced, "I'm an O, a big fat O!"

Timing. In general, preschoolers prefer to move fast—they like to wave, shake, and twist using fast motions. From their point of view, "slow" more often means "not-quite-as-fast-as-fast." Nevertheless, one group of children became very interested in dropping scarves from the climber and were quite amazed at how *slowly* they drifted to the ground. "It takes a long time for them to go down," one child noted. This observation led the children to try out being "slow scarves" during a large-group time in which they exhibited an understanding of and tolerance for moving slowly, a capacity they had not shown before.

Key Developmental Indicator
Moving in Locomotor Ways (Nonanchored Movement: Running, Jumping, Hopping, Skipping, Marching, Climbing)

At the end of greeting circle, Kenneth has the idea of moving "like snakes," so all the children and their teachers, Becki and Beth, lie on their stomachs and slither like snakes to their planning tables.

ॱ

At recall, Mikey jumps to all the places he played during work time.

ॱ

Corrin climbs hands-first to the middle of the inverted-U-shaped climber, stops in the middle, turns around, and climbs feet-first down the other side.

ॱ

On the playground, a group of girls, boys, and adults play a fast game of soccer with lots of kicking and running after the ball.

ॱ

Anna and Jessa walk all the way around the playground "looking for bees."

Preschoolers in active learning environments, such as the children above, are generally full of energy and zest. They want to run, jump, leap, slide, climb, and gallop. As infants and toddlers they moved from place to place by scooting and crawling, then by toddling with short, awkward steps, and finally, by walking with increased steadiness and speed. As preschoolers, children

continue to explore their environment and add to their movement repertoire. Their developing strength, balance, and coordination allows them to try out and master various motions, such as jumping, hopping, galloping, sliding, climbing, and skipping. In their eagerness to communicate their experiences to others, young children also begin to talk about the ways they are moving:

On a trip to the local railway depot, this child leaps from the steps of a stationary caboose to the sidewalk.

"Look what a big . . . what a big jump I jumped, Corey!"

Following are ways adults can support and encourage preschoolers' expanding capacities and desires to run, jump, hop, skip, march, and climb.

Suggestions for Adults

▶ **Provide space and time for children to move.**

In their efforts to move from place to place in all the ways they can, children need lots of space. They need **open space**, both indoors and outdoors, where they can move about freely without endangering themselves or others. They also need **"psychological" space,** that is, a supportive atmosphere in which adults encourage children to experiment with various ways of moving and anticipate their vigor and robustness rather than expect them to sit quietly and follow directions. Finally, children need time each day to **practice, repeat, and experiment with movement at their own pace** until they are satisfied. (For specific ways to set up supportive active learning environments, see Chapter 2 and Chapter 5.)

▶ **Encourage children to move about in a variety of ways.**

Walking, running, rolling, climbing, marching, jumping, hopping in place and from one place to another, galloping, and skipping— these are ways of moving that preschoolers imitate, experiment with, and practice. They are motions adults in active learning settings anticipate and plan for throughout the preschool day.

Look for and acknowledge all the ways children move about. As children play indoors and outdoors, they move about spontaneously as part of their play. At these times, it is important for adults to watch for and support children's movements in the spirit of their play and to comment on what they see without disrupting children's play or concentration. Consider these two illustrative examples:

• At outside time, Corrin and Anna climbed on the new cargo net that was anchored between the ground and the tree house. Beth, their teacher, noticed their excitement and persistence, but because they were so busy with their climbing, she just watched until they summoned her. "Look at us, Beth!" they called. "I see!" she responded, coming over to them. "It moves a little bit," Corrin told her. "But you just got to hold on hard," Anna added. "You found a way to climb up the wiggly net," Beth commented. "And we can climb down," Corrin added, and then showed Beth how she did it.

• In the block area, Christopher and Athi were jumping from block to block. "Don't step in the water," Christopher warned, "or the alligators'll get you!" "They bite your foot off," Athi added. Ruth, an adult, looked up from another part of the block area. "Will the alligators get me?" she asked. "Yeah, get on that one," Christopher told her, pointing to a block near her. When Ruth was safely on her block, Christopher continued, "Now, when I tell you, jump!" "Like this?" Ruth jumped straight up and landed on the same block. "No! You got to jump over there to that other block!" "Okay," said Ruth, "I'll jump to another block."

Play games that call for running, jumping, and other types of locomotor movement. Adults can plan activities in which children move from place to place for small-group time, large-group time, and transition times. They can also look for opportunities to incorporate jumping, hopping, leaping, and galloping motions into children's outside play. Here are some examples:

• "I wonder," Ann said to the children in her small group, "if we could build some walking paths with blocks." The children in her group headed for the block area and built one path with large hollow blocks and another with unit blocks. As they tried out their paths, Ann and the children talked about what they were doing: "This one's harder to walk on." "Walk on the walk, don't fall off! Walk on the walk, don't fall off! Walk on the walk . . ." "Let's push 'em together so we can walk on both!" "This is a funny way to walk!"

Running games like racing a ball down a ramp develop locomotor movement skills.

• During an outdoor large-group time, Beth and Sam introduced a game of galloping horses. The object was to gallop to a tree when an adult or child said, "Galloping horses!" As Sam and Beth galloped to trees along with the children, they noticed that some children knew how to gallop, some children ran, and some children stopped to ask the others, "How do you do that?" As the children continued to play this game, more and more children learned to gallop. By spring, several children had progressed to skipping as well as galloping. The children also introduced variations in their play. One day Deola said, "Look, I'm galloping a different way!" "Yes, you are," Beth replied. "You're galloping sidewards. You're sliding. We can be sliding horses." From that time on, children called for galloping horses or sliding horses, and eventually, with observation and practice, many children gained considerable skill with sliding.

• At the transition time between greeting circle and planning time, Becki and Beth asked their children how they would like to move to their planning tables. Each day, children came up with different movement ideas, including slithering like a snake, hopping on one foot, crawling, walking on their heels, galloping, walking bent over, and walking on their knees.

• At outside time, several children were drawing with chalk on the pavement. They made a row of connected squares for "hopscotch" and began hopping from square to square. "Wait, you need numbers," Andrew told the players, and he began writing numbers in the boxes. Other children joined, adding boxes with numbers and hopping and jumping from box to box. After this play had continued for several days, Beth, an adult, drew some boxes that were not connected. "These are leaping boxes," she remarked to Kenneth, who was watching her, "because the boxes are so far away you have to leap to them." She and Kenneth tried them out and soon other children joined. At the end of the day Kenneth told his mom, "Guess what! Now we play 'Hopscotch' and 'Leapscotch'!"

► **Attend to the direction, size, level, pathway, intensity, and timing of children's locomotor movement.**

As children move from place to place, the ways they move can change. They may, for example, walk "high on their toes" while stretching their arms in the air, or they may walk "down low" with their arms and legs bent—moving close to the ground. They may hop with a "floppy" body or with a "strong" body. Adults can comment on the types of movement they observe and suggest additional ways to move. Here are some examples:

• **Direction**—"Tanya, I noticed that you walked around Ivan's tower on your way to recall."

• **Size**—"I'm taking little jumps, 'cause I'm just a little baby bunny," Sara told Ruth, her teacher. "Well, I'm a sister bunny," Ruth replied, "what kind of jumps should I take?" "Are you a big sister?" Sara wanted to know. "Yes." "Well, then, you can take big jumps, like this."

• **Level**—"I have an idea," Mrs. Greene said at large-group time. "Let's walk on our tip-toes." After the children had tried this movement for awhile, Maya suggested, "Let's try walking with our bodies down low."

• **Pathway**—During a game of galloping, Bryant told Beth he was going to be a "crooked horse." When Beth asked him what he meant by this statement, Bryant began to gallop in a zigzag path. "See," Bryant said, "I went crooked." "You

In the course of her work-time "circus" play, this child leaps over a stack of cushions.

At cleanup time children lift fairly heavy objects and move with them.

galloped in a crooked path to the tree," Beth agreed. "I'm going to try galloping in a crooked path." And she did. After several days of crooked-path galloping, Beth said, "I wonder what other kinds of paths we could gallop in." After some thought, Corrin suggested "circles," and they then proceeded to gallop in a series of curves.

• **Intensity**—At large-group time, everyone had a hoop. "I know," Joey said, "Let's have one foot in and one foot out." After everyone had

tried walking around his or her hoop with one foot in and one foot out, Linda, their teacher, suggested, "Let's try that again, but this time we could be *very strong* and stamp our feet as we walk!"

• **Timing**—The children in one preschool enjoyed this transition-time movement activity: "Quickly, quickly go like a mouse; go to your planning-table house."

Key Developmental Indicator
Moving With Objects

Bryant walks around the room balancing a plastic circle from the shape sorter game on his head.

∾

Outside, Aimee and Callie tie colorful streamers to their arms and watch them flutter as they run. "Look, our arms are flying!"

∾

Petey bounces a big rubber ball on the pavement and against the wall.

∾

Eighteen Norwegian preschoolers and their teachers strap on their cross-country skis and ski across the playground to the park.

∾

Kerry and Jeff load their arms with rubber balls to see how many they can toss into the "bat cave" they are building.

Moving with objects is a familiar activity for preschoolers who have been doing it since they first learned to bang a spoon on their highchair tray. However, as 3- and 4-year-olds move with

objects, their intentions are more complex ("I want to wear a cape and run so it flies out behind me like Batman"). Due to their improved balance and coordination, preschoolers can move with objects in increasingly challenging ways. For example, they imitate games they see people playing in real life and on television (playing basketball; kicking, hitting, bouncing, and throwing balls). They also want to try new things such as walking in daddy's big shoes, "skating" with boxes secured to their feet, and "flying like a bee" with a block for a "stinger" and scarves for "wings."

With easy-to-manipulate materials, time for practice, and patient support from adults, preschoolers can enjoy the sense of confidence that accompanies moving successfully with objects. This self-confidence encourages them as they continue to develop more complex movement skills. Following are ways adults can support young children as they move with objects.

Suggestions for Adults

▶ **Provide children with time and space to move with objects.**

As with any kind of movement, children need space indoors and outdoors to move with objects. They also need time. Just as children like to put the same puzzle together over and over again, hear the same story every day for several days, and sing the same songs, they need time each day and over the course of several days to play and practice with scarves, beanbags, and balls at their own pace and comfort level. As they play and practice, they need adult encouragement and support for their original intentions rather than an adult's instructions on how to improve their aim and so on.

► **Provide a wide variety of easy-to-manipulate materials.**

An active learning environment is equipped with accessible, appealing materials that children are eager to use and manipulate—balls, beanbags, sticks, hoops, scarves, streamers, musical instruments, and so on. (See Chapter 5 for detailed information on arranging and equipping the classroom or center.) For example, in his active learning preschool, Douglas made a fishing pole from foam

and yarn and spent the rest of work time "fly casting" into the toy area. In the block area, several children made an "up-and-down" road with big hollow-block ramps over which they drove three school buses. This required moving themselves and the school buses up and down along the ramps.

In terms of movement, however, several types of materials can enhance children's awareness of how they move and can add to children's comfort and skill in moving with objects.

Add light, floating materials that are easily set in motion as children move. Scarves, streamers, and ribbons float and move as children move. Preschoolers enjoy wearing big scarves as capes and tying smaller scarves on their arms and legs to see how they move as the children run or "fly." Streamers and ribbons work in the same way. Ribbons tied onto bracelets enable children to move freely with lots of ribbons. One group of children covered their arms with ribbon bracelets and developed

what they called "fringed-arm dancing." During their fringe dancing they became very aware of the shape and pathway of the ribbons' movements: "Look! Mine are going around." "See, it's smooth . . . now it's wiggly!" "Look how far out they go when you twirl . . . let's see if ours can touch!" Children also use scarves, streamers, and ribbons as low boundaries for jumping over, as harnesses for "galloping horses," and as blindfolds for "feeling walks."

Add novel objects to hold and move with. For many children, holding on to something when moving increases their comfort level. It also gives them something clearly in their control to focus on and watch. Holding on to a pinwheel, a milk jug of water, rhythm sticks, chopsticks, or paper fans increases children's awareness of how their arms are moving and how they can move to create certain effects—running fast to make the pinwheel turn fast and slowing down to make it turn slowly, moving so the water in the jug stays smooth and moving so it ripples.

Sticks and paper fans inspire children to attempt fanning, thrusting, patting, and striking motions. When Ben's uncle visited Ben's preschool, some of the children noticed that he had splints on his wrists and hands. The day after his visit they made their own splints from popsicle sticks and kept them on their hands while they tried to work at the computer and play with Legos. "These make my fingers stiff!" Ben noted.

Add foot-focused materials. When children add objects to their feet, they become more aware of how their feet move. As they walk

On the playground, these children kick and throw the grocery bags they stuffed with newspaper and sealed with tape at small-group time.

and slide around on paper plates or inside box "shoes," hollow-block "shoes," adult-sized shoes, or tin-can stilts, children become quite eager to share their discoveries: "I'm walking tall." "I can't jump in these shoes!" "But wait! I'm gonna make some straps!" Children are especially intrigued by standing on paper plates since this is such a unique experience! In snowy climates, young children enjoy gliding on short skis strapped securely to their boots.

Add balls and other materials for tossing, throwing, kicking, striking, and catching. Children of all ages play with balls, and preschoolers are no exception. Not all preschoolers, however, are comfortable with the speed and resilience of rubber balls, so it makes sense to provide lightweight items that do not bounce or roll easily as they land, such as pompoms, beanbags, stocking or yarn balls, and very lightweight foam balls. It is also important to provide objects that move slowly through the air and thus are easy to catch, such as scarves and netting. When children have regular access to such materials, they enjoy tossing them into convenient boxes and baskets; throwing them at large, easy-to-hit targets; tossing them up and catching them; and using them to play catch with another person.

Large and small rubber balls, tennis balls, plastic Wiffle balls, beach balls, and soccer balls provide children with a variety of opportunities to roll, throw, catch, and kick. Also, providing light, child-sized plastic bats gives children a chance to practice striking a ball and coordinating all the motions this act requires. Given a ready supply of balls and the chance to play with their personal favorites, the ball games young children make up to play on their own or with others are endless. Alana, for example, was very excited when she discovered she could bounce-pass a big rubber ball to Becki, her teacher, and then catch the ball when Becki bounced it back to her.

Add big things for pushing and pulling. This includes wagons, wheelbarrows, buggies, tires, and large boxes. Pushing and pulling each other in wagons, walking and rolling tires, and rolling themselves up inside boxes require children to use strength, balance, and coordination to move. For example, a group of preschoolers regularly rolled tires across the playground. One day, they discovered they could put a ball inside a tire and it would roll for a while with the tire. This discovery led to a game of rolling the tires with balls in them at different speeds and along varying pathways, and guessing at what point the balls would "pop out" of the tires.

Key Developmental Indicator
Expressing Creativity in Movement

Brian and his dad see an owl flying near Brian's house. The next day at preschool, Brian moves his arms up and down to show Sam how the owl flew.

&

Christy jumps rope, runs with the rope, and winds it around her body "like a twister."

&

Andrew stands on the tire swing by himself and swings, then he tries bouncing and swinging. "Look, Beth, I'm jiggling!" he says. When Beth comes over to watch, Andrew tells her, "You have to bend your knees a lot of times."

&

Mercedes is lying on the floor wiggling her arms and legs in the air above her. "I'm a spider who fell down the spout!" she exclaims.

In active learning environments, adults support young children's innate desire to move and to express themselves through movement. Confident that adults will not criticize or ridicule their experimentation with movement, preschoolers invent and try out new ways to move in the course of their play and at the suggestion of adults during small- and large-group activities. Because they are now able to **represent,** that is, hold images of their past actions in mind, move-

"I-am-a-ro-bot. Give-me-some-food!" says the child on the right, speaking in a choppy voice and moving her arms and legs in jerky motions to create the impression of a mechanized being.

ment becomes another "language" preschoolers use deliberately and imaginatively along with speaking, drawing, modeling, and role play. Having many opportunities to express their feelings, experiences, and ideas in their own way through movement builds children's confidence in their ability to move and communicate with their bodies. This sense of bodily comfort and creativity in movement spills over into other areas of endeavor and strengthens children's belief in themselves as capable, imaginative people.

Following are ways adults in active learning settings can support and encourage children as they express themselves creatively in movement.

Suggestions for Adults

▶ **Watch for and acknowledge children's creative use of movement.**

In an active learning setting where children freely move in place, from place to place, and with objects, adults who understand the learning value of such movements and are attuned to children's interests and abilities will observe many examples each day of children expressing creativity in movement. Earlier in this chapter, we described Kenneth moving his arms and confining his motions to a carpet square to avoid the "hot lava." Other children in our examples fly like bees, curl up like sleeping bees, wave to ants, figure out how to move like slowly falling scarves, gallop in different ways by zigzagging and looping, walk "one foot in and one foot out," make up "fringed-arm" dances, and so on.

As adults observe such creative movement experiences, one way they can support children is to comment briefly on what they see. Mikey, for example, played with beanbags throughout work

time. At cleanup time, he carefully balanced some of the beanbags around the rim of their storage basket and some of the beanbags on his head and shoulders. As he carried the basket to the toy shelf, he walked very slowly with small steps so the beanbags would not fall. Becki, his teacher, had never seen Mikey move so carefully. "Mikey," she said, as he placed the basket of beanbags on the shelf, "you found a different way to walk." (Mikey smiled.) "You walked slowly with little steps so the beanbags would balance." (Mikey nodded and joined his buddies for recall time.)

▶ **Encourage children to solve movement problems at small-group, large-group, and transition times.**

While children generate and solve their own movement problems as they play, they also enjoy solving movement problems adults set for them. This is one way adults can introduce new movement ideas that children may later incorporate into their own play and movement vocabulary. Here are four examples:

• "How could we move to planning time," Peter asked all the children in the greeting circle, "without our feet touching the floor?"

• One day, when the children's enthusiasm for cleanup time was lagging, Beth offered this movement challenge: "I saw Julia picking up blocks with her elbows. I wonder if we could put away all the blocks just using our elbows."

• Caroline took her children outside to the railroad ties for small-group time. "Let's see how many different ways we can walk on these railroad ties," she challenged.

• At large-group time Julie sat down on the floor with the children and put a beanbag on her head. "You put the beanbag on your

head!" the children exclaimed. "Where else do you think I could put it?" Julie asked. "On your knee," Brianna suggested. Julie replied, "Well, I'm going to give you each a beanbag. See if you can put it on your knee." After balancing their beanbags on their knees and heads, the children experimented with creative ways to balance beanbags on their elbows, shoulders, backs, cheeks, toes, and so forth.

▶ **Talk with children about how they are moving.**

When children find creative ways to move, one way to help them become more conscious of their motions is to encourage them to talk about what they are doing. At large-group time, for example, Julie is playing the guitar and stopping. As she plays, the children move their arms to the music. When she stops playing, they stop moving. When she plays again, the children move their arms in a different way. During the "stop" time she comments, "You moved your arms in all kinds of ways!" The children offer a variety of responses: "Mine goed around." "I bounced mine like you played the guitar." "I bended mine like this . . . like a train." "I made mine go faster than anything!"

▶ **Encourage children to represent their experiences through movement.**

Because preschoolers are able to represent, they can move according to mental images that reflect their personal experiences. In fact, in an active learning setting, recall time is a natural time for children to use movement to represent their experiences. Just as children talk, draw, or sing about what they have done, they can use movement to describe their past actions. At one small-group time, for example, Beth asked the

As large-group time begins, these children and their teacher move creatively to re-enact their favorite parts of a story about fish. Some children move like fish, while others pretend to catch fish. "I'm pulling in a big one!" says one child.

children to demonstrate what they had done by just using their hands or their bodies. Mikey moved his fingers to show how he had worked at the computer. Ben made painting and cutting motions. Callie and Aimee lay on the floor and showed how they covered themselves up with a blanket. Anna and Jessa flew and buzzed like bees. Kenneth made small movements with his hands to show how he put together Legos, and Corrin pounded the table as she had pounded clay.

Children also enjoy representing field trips through movement. One group of children in New England, for example, went to the town square for a local harvest celebration. When they came back to their classroom and were recalling their trip at large-group time, it quickly became apparent to their teachers that what the children were most interested in was the bus trip. "How could we show what it was like on the bus just using our bodies?" one adult asked. After some thought and discussion, the children sat down in pairs and groups of threes and fours, and swayed from side to side while the "driver" steered around one sharp

corner after another. They managed to capture the highlight of their trip in these simple movements.

During transition times, children like to make up ways to move like objects or animals they know. Depending on what they are familiar with, try asking them to go to the playground, the lunchroom, or naptime while moving as if they were trees in the wind, a dog, a ball, or a blinking neon sign.

Key Developmental Indicator
Describing Movement

"Go down [the slide] like this, one [leg] down and one up," Petey challenges his buddies at outside time.

☙

During large-group time, Callie adds a new movement to a favorite song based on what she saw the neighborhood kitty doing earlier in the morning: "Let's wave our arms like the kitty's tail!"

☙

Mikey finds a spring in the parts box at the workbench and says, "Boing, boing," as he jumps up and down, imitating the movement of the spring.

☙

"I cut it in half," Aimee says, demonstrating the action with her fingers at recall time.

☙

"Put your arms out and step, step, step on here," Brian says to Beth, as he climbs the spiral climber.

☙

"Look!" says Callie as she jumps off the climber. "I bend my knees and it's easy."

As preschoolers such as Petey, Callie, Mikey, Aimee, and Brian move in the course of their play, they often take on the challenge of describing their movement experiences to others. Because they have lots of choices, interesting things to do, and people who both set relevant tasks and listen to them, preschoolers in active learning settings want to talk about all kinds of experiences, including movement experiences. Because their command of language is growing, they are able to go beyond economical toddler descriptions ("Me go down!") to more complex statements ("Watch me! I'm slidin' down the slide with my arms out in front!").

Preschoolers' growing ability to describe their actions increases their awareness of what they are doing, gives them more control over their movements, and builds feelings of confidence and success. "Look, Beth, I can jump over two blocks!"

Following are ways adults can support children as they describe movement experiences that are meaningful to them.

Suggestions for Adults

▶ **Listen as children describe movement in their own way.**

As children talk with you and with one another throughout the day, listen for their movement descriptions, accept their language, and build their descriptions into your own speech. Here are two examples from outside time:

Brian: *Look, Beth, I'm standing up!*

Adult: *Yes, I see. First you were sitting and now you are standing up on the swing.*

☙

at the top of the image:

808 Kayla

Me running to preschool

"Me running to preschool" is the way Kayla describes the movement she experiences each weekday morning and captures in her drawing.

Christy: _It went up . . . behind me!_

Adult: _The ball went up and came down behind you!_

Christy: _It went backward!_

Adult: _It went backward when you hit it._

▶ **Find opportunities to comment on how children are moving.**

One way to draw children's attention to their physical movements and encourage them to describe what their bodies are doing is to comment briefly on how you see children moving. This strategy is most effective when you can comment in a natural, interested way, without disrupting children's play or stopping the movement they are engaged in. Here are some examples:

- "Michael, you had to bend way over to get that block on the bottom shelf."

- "You threw the ball overhand, right to me, L. J.!"

- "You're wiggling your feet, Jalessa." "And I can wiggle my whole legs. Watch, I can wiggle 'em fast!" Jalessa responds.

- Sliding down a snowy slope on a plastic sled, Vince and Winnie rolled off when they got to the bottom. "You both rolled off when the sled stopped," commented their teacher. "Me and Vince leaned back and we rolled off in the snow!" Winnie explained.

▶ **Encourage children to plan, do, and recall movement.**

When children plan movement, they naturally have to talk about it. Therefore it makes sense to provide opportunities throughout the day for children to plan and describe the way they want to move from place to place or how they will move as part of an ongoing activity. Here are two examples:

- _At transition time:_ "Think of a way you would like to move from here to the playground."

"I'm gonna jump."

"Hold hands with Tara."

"I'm taking b. . .i . . .g steps like this. . ."

- _At snack time:_ "Prya, it's your turn to pass out the napkins. What's a different way you can move when you do that?" Prya thinks for a minute then says, "I'm going backwards," and she proceeds to walk backwards around the snack table, giving a napkin to each child as she passes.

Recalling movement also calls for describing it. At recall time or during an appropriate pause in the day's activities, ask children to recall their movements. Here are some examples:

- "At work time today, I saw lots of people moving in different ways. Some people were crawling. Some were curled up on the block shelf. Tell me how you moved during work time."

- "How did you get that tire to the top of the slide, Chelsea?"

- "I saw you pretending to be a bee today, Anna. How did you make your body move like that?"

▶ **Plan large group experiences in which children use a single word to describe a single movement.**

This is an enjoyable way to do and describe a common movement together as a group. For example, you might begin such an activity by tapping your head with both hands. When the children have joined in and are tapping their heads, add the chant "Tap, tap, tap, tap." When all the children have joined in the tapping and chanting, move your hands to some other part of your body, such as your knees, and continue tapping and chanting, "Tap, tap, tap, tap." Once they are comfortable with the idea of tapping and chanting simultaneously, ask children for their ideas of other motions to repeat and describe. They will probably come up with simple motions such as "nod," "wave," "jiggle," "bounce," "shake," "pound," "twist," and so forth. They may also come up with movements that take time for them to describe. Mikey, for example, demonstrated turning his arms. When Beth, his teacher, asked him what to call what he was doing, he just smiled and kept doing it. "I know," volunteered Andrew. "We could say 'up' when your hands are up and 'down' when your hands are down." "Up, down, up, down, up, down, up, down," the children chanted as they rotated their arms.

Key Developmental Indicator
Acting Upon Movement Directions

Aimee asks her friend Chelsea to show her how to tie. "Okay," Chelsea responds. "First, go like this." (She grasps a lace in each hand and waits for Aimee to do the same.) "Then turn this one around this one and pull. (She pauses while Aimee imitates her movements.) Then bend it . . . and go around . . . push this one through for the other loop . . . pull . . . and there!"

∽

"When the music stops, stand on a carpet square," Peter tells the children at large-group time. When the music does stop, some children go to the nearest carpet square while others search for "their" carpet square (the one they started out on).

∽

"Follow me! I'm the leader of the band," says Kenneth. Other children wave their arms, following Kenneth's lead.

∽

Standing in the circle between his parents, 4-year-old Brian participates in a simple folk dance. "Step, step, step, lift. Step, step, step,

kick," says the leader. Watching closely, Brian follows the leader at his own pace. Although he is several steps behind the adults, he is learning the dance along with the rest of the group.

Like the children in the examples above, preschool children who have many opportunities to move in different ways bring all these experiences to bear as they copy and interpret—that is, as they make sense of and act upon—movement directions. While toddlers are able to respond to simple movement directives such as "Go find daddy" and "Bring me the ball," preschoolers can use their own words to describe movement ("I'm jiggling!") and generate their own movement directions ("Go down like this, one leg down and one up"). They can also begin to comprehend and reconstruct simple adult- or peer-generated movement sequences, as Brian did when he folk-danced with his parents.

Adults who are aware of preschool children's movement capacities, and who give

"I pushed it flat," this child says at recall time, describing and demonstrating the movement she used at work time to make "pancakes." Her teacher and several children imitate her hand motions.

children time to move and respond to movement at their own pace, can support children's interest in acting upon movement directions. Following are some strategies to support young movers.

Suggestions for Adults

▶ **Listen for the movement directions children generate as they play.**

Adults who are with children throughout the day may be surprised at the movement directions children generate and interpret during the course of their play.

- "Walk on that part. It doesn't wobble."

- "You're the dog, Mikey. You push your dish with your nose when you're eating."

- "I'll hold the paper for you while you cut, okay, Trey?"

- "You gotta put both feet in the wagon, Alana."

At large-group time, this adult demonstrates a movement for children to try.

- "Move the mouse over to the paint bucket, Nathan. Then you'll get color!" (*Andrew to Nathan about a computer drawing program.*)

- "Wanna know how I pump? Put both feet out hard and then pull 'em back. It makes you go back."

- "My dad knows how to do underdog! He goes under while I'm on the swing!"

One way you can acknowledge and support children when you hear them giving movement directions is to follow the directions yourself if you are in a position to do so without disrupting their play.

▶ **During group games, give or demonstrate simple movement directions.**

Four-year-old Brian could participate comfortably in an adult folk-dance session because the leader provided simple movement directions. Because young children can focus most readily on one thing at a time, it makes sense to give them either verbal directions or visual demonstrations rather than both at the same time.

Provide verbal directions. Try using simple directions to get movement started. At the beginning of large-group time, for example, you might say the following (without demonstrating with your hands):

"Tap both hands on the floor." (Pause to give time for each child to consider and interpret the words.) "Tap both hands on your head." (Pause and watch to see how children interpret your verbal directions.) "Where else can you tap

your hands?" (Pause and watch to see the original responses children generate.)

At planning time you might try giving simple movement directions such as "Jump to a toy you plan to play with today."

Give children visual movement demonstrations. At large-group time and transition times, show children how you would like them to move without using any words. For example, while waiting for the bus with children, you might begin a brief movement activity by saying, "Watch and move the way I move." Without saying anything, put both arms out in front of you and hold them there while the children interpret and copy your visual movement demonstration. Next, put both hands on your shoulders, hold them there, and watch to see what the children do. Once the children get the idea of this game, give children turns being the leader, that is, the person demonstrating the visual movement directions.

Key Developmental Indicator
Feeling and Expressing Steady Beat

Kenneth drives by on the scooter, pushing steadily with his "ground" foot. "Push, push, push, push," he says.

〰

"Rock, rock, rock, rock," Joanie says softly to her baby doll, as she rocks her back and forth in the rocking chair while listening to music.

〰

L. J. pumps his legs on the swing to the beat of "Old McDonald," which he sings as he pumps.

〰

Sarah sits on a big hollow block and sings, "Row, row, row your boat" while she sways back and forth in time to her singing.

~

At outside time, Ruth, an adult, and Athi walk around together with Athi standing on Ruth's feet. To keep their balance in this position, they sway from side to side as they walk, and they add a rhyme they both know to keep the beat.

~

It's large-group time. Children are moving to "Yankee Doodle," a musical selection that plays on the CD player. "Look, Beth! We're having a parade!" says Kenneth. He, Douglas, and Ted are marching around the big carpet to the steady beat of the music. "Our feets are going together!" "They sure are!" Beth replies.

Many children first experience a steady, repetitive beat or pulse when they are rocked and sung to as infants. As they are swayed from side to side, or rocked back and forth, they feel the motion with their whole bodies. Infants and toddlers who ride in front- or backpacks feel the steady beat of their parents' walking motions especially if their parents sing as they walk. Infants who are able to pull themselves up by holding on to the sides of their cribs or a piece of furniture often bounce to their own internal beat or to music they hear playing. When toddlers are able to rock themselves on rocking chairs or rocking horses, they find satisfaction in generating and feeling their own steady beat. In addition to all these experiences, which they still seek and enjoy, preschoolers can generate and feel their own beat as they swing, pedal, and jump. With adult support or imitation they can express their awareness of the beat or pulse they feel with words such as

"pat, pat, pat, pat" or "step, step, step, step," or "voom . . . voom . . . voom . . . voom." They can also keep a steady beat as they sing songs and chant rhymes.

Feeling and expressing beat is an enjoyable experience for young children, one that helps them organize the way they move as well as coordinate movement with others. Choirs, crew teams, ballroom-dance partners, orchestras, and marching bands all rely on a common beat or common timing to accomplish their performances. While preschoolers are involved in less complex endeavors, their experiences with feeling and expressing steady beat, while important and satisfying in their own right, are also laying the groundwork for future movement activities. Following are ways adults can support young children's desire to feel and express steady beat.

Suggestions for Adults

▶ **Provide equipment on which children can rock, swing, and pedal.**

Rocking chairs and rocking horses provide safe and satisfying opportunities for children to generate and feel a steady beat. Many preschoolers still enjoy being rocked, especially when they are cranky. The steady, predictable motion of rocking soothes young children and helps them "gather themselves back together." Swings, scooters, and other pedal toys also provide preschool children with satisfying ways of setting and feeling their own steady beat.

▶ **Build rocking to the beat and patting the beat into music and language experiences.**

Feeling and expressing steady beat begins with simple motions such as rocking to music, or

patting your knees to the beat of a song, chant, verse, or nursery rhyme. Preschool children can gain beat awareness through rocking, swinging, and marching as well as through many opportunities to pat the beat.

Distinguish **beat** *from* **rhythm.** To build children's awareness of beat, it is important to distinguish beat from rhythm. **Beat is a steady sequence of pulses in which each pulse is of equal duration. Rhythm is the variation within beats.** For example, there are two or four steady beats in the phrase "Mary had a little lamb," but there are seven rhythmical pulses:

Beat: Mary <u>had</u> a little <u>lamb</u>
       1   2   3   4
              1 or   2
Rhythm: Ma-ry had a lit-tle lamb
         1 2 3 4 5 6 7

Because it is steady, consistent, organized, and predictable, **beat** is what we want to emphasize with young children.

Rock, sway, or pat a steady beat while singing and chanting. As you sing with children or recite chants and nursery rhymes together, pat the beat on your knees, shoulders, or head. First, set up a steady beat by patting your knees, and have the children do the same; then add the song or chant to the steady beat. Once children become familiar with this practice, they can set the beat and add the songs or rhymes of their choosing. For example, one day at large-group time, Trey said, "I have a song." He started by tapping his pointer finger on his other palm. When he had established his beat, he added his own words to "Twinkle, Twinkle Little Star."

If you are rocking a tired or upset child, you can sing or recite a rhyme and pat the beat gently on the child's back or legs. This serves as a source of comfort and solace and also provides a natural opportunity to strengthen a child's awareness of beat.

Pat a steady beat when children are playing musical instruments. One day at work time, Brian marched around the room beating a drum. To acknowledge and support the steady beat that he had established for himself, Becki, his teacher, walked behind him, all the while gently patting the same beat on his shoulders. Douglas looked up and, thinking there was a parade, joined the line, also patting the beat on Becki's back.

▶ **Provide opportunities for children to walk to a steady beat.**

This strategy works well for musical activities. Put on some music (see p. 149 for information on High/Scope's *Rhythmically Moving* CDs) during small-group or large-group time and try the following with the children:

• Walk or "march" around the room to the beat.

• Jump to the beat.

• Walk like a stiff-legged robot to the beat.

• "March" on a carpet square to the beat.

• Walk to the coatrack to the beat.

Watch what children do and encourage individual children to invent motions and lead the group.

▶ **Look for and acknowledge children's movement to a steady beat as they play.**

Once you begin to think about this **movement** indicator, you will probably become

Swinging on the swing provides this child with an enjoyable opportunity to feel a steady beat.

more aware of times when children move to a common beat during their play. Here is what one adult team saw over several days:

• Two "policemen" swaying back and forth to the same beat as their "patrol car" swerved around corners.

• A small group of children working with clay and pounding with the same steady beat to "make it flat."

• Several children beating drums together and "having a parade."

When it is possible to join such play without disrupting it, adults can support the steady beat children have established themselves. One teaching team member, for example, sat down with the group of children pounding clay (mentioned above); the teacher got her own piece of clay and proceeded to pound it and chant "Pound, pound, pound, pound" to match the children's beat. The children readily joined in her chant.

▶ **Play group games with a steady beat.**

One teaching team made up a simple action game and found that many children were able to move to the same steady beat. It went like this:

Stamp, stamp, stamp your foot,
Stamp, stamp, stamp your foot,
Stamp, stamp, stamp your foot,
Stamp, stamp, stamp and stop.

Eventually, the children changed the action to "pat your knees" and "hit the floor." Because the motions were simple, repetitive, and had a defined endpoint, such as hitting the floor or patting a body part, the children enjoyed this game.

At large-group time, these children and their teacher walk around the circle to the steady beat of a recorded musical selection.

Key Developmental Indicator
Moving in Sequences to a Common Beat

At large-group time, Rodney demonstrates his idea for jumping to the beat of the music playing on the CD player. He jumps first with his feet apart and then with his feet together, repeating this sequence several times. When his teacher, Beth, asks him to describe what he did with his feet he says "open and shut . . . like scissors." When Beth starts the music again, she and the children say "open," "shut" as they try out Rodney's way of jumping.

Moving in sequences to a common beat may be somewhat difficult for preschoolers, who are most likely to focus on one motion at a time.

Yet trying out simple movement sequences, while challenging, can be very enjoyable for children, especially for those who begin to "feel" the beat, enjoy choosing the motions and the sequence, and wish to share their experiences with others.

This KDI can occur as children play together. In addition, adults may introduce this type of activity at small-group time or large-group time. Following are ways adults can support young children as they move in sequences to the beat.

Suggestions for Adults

▶ **Encourage children to name the actions they are doing in a movement sequence.**

One day, at recall time, Rafe was showing what he had done at work time. As he pretended to paint, he made his arm go up and down to re-enact the strokes he had made with his brush. After the children guessed that he had "painted a *big* picture," Sam, his teacher, asked "What did your arm do when you painted?" Rafe thought for a moment then said, "Up" making the up-stroke, and "Down" making the down-stroke. "let's all try moving our arms up and down to paint like Rafe," said Sam. Sam chanted the words "up" and "down" in a steady beat as he "painted" and many of the children joined in, some doing the motions and others doing the motions and saying the words.

At outside time with lots of "swing time," many preschoolers learn to pump. For those who are trying out pumping but have not yet mastered it, providing them with words like "out" and "back" can help them to organize the two-part leg movement sequence pumping requires and coordinate it with the forward and backward motion of the swing.

▶ **Include two-part movement sequences in action songs.**

Julie's preschool children liked to sing "Row, Row, Row Your Boat" and often requested it at large-group time. Thinking about moving in sequences to a common beat, Julie asked the children one day what they could do with their arms that would be like rowing. The children decided to put both arms out in front of them and then draw them back to their bodies by bending their elbows. They decided to call these motions "straight" and "bend." Now they had a new way to sing and move to the song. Instead of the traditional words, they sang "straight, bend" to the tune of the song while doing the motions they named. For other ideas, see *Movement Plus Rhymes, Songs, & Singing Games* (referenced on page 395).

The "cars" in this "train" enjoy locomotor movement as they march down the steps and around the room.

Physical Development, Health, and Well-Being Strategies: A Summary

Moving in nonlocomotor ways (anchored movement: bending, twisting, rocking, swinging one's arms)

___ Encourage children to explore a wide variety of positions:
  ___ Watch for and acknowledge positions children assume as they play.
  ___ Play position-games with children.
___ Look for opportunities to swing, bend, rock, and twist with children.
___ Play games that focus on one movement at a time.
___ Attend to the direction, size, level, intensity, shape, and timing of children's nonlocomotor movement.

Moving in locomotor ways (nonanchored movement: running, jumping, hopping, skipping, marching, climbing)

___ Provide space and time for children to move.
___ Encourage children to move about in a variety of ways:
  ___ Look for and acknowledge all the ways children move about.
  ___ Play games that call for nonanchored movement.
___ Attend to the direction, size, level, pathway, intensity, and timing of children's nonanchored movement.

Moving with objects

___ Provide children with time and space to move with objects.
___ Provide a wide variety of easy-to-manipulate materials:
  ___ Add light, floating materials that are easily set in motion by children's movement.

___ Add novel objects to hold and move with.
___ Add foot-focused materials.
___ Add balls and other materials for tossing, throwing, kicking, striking, and catching.
___ Add big things for pushing and pulling.

Expressing creativity in movement

___ Watch for and acknowledge children's creative use of movement.
___ Encourage children to solve movement problems at small-group, large-group, and transition times.
___ Talk with children about how they are moving.
___ Encourage children to represent their experiences through movement.

Describing movement

___ Listen as children describe movement in their own way.
___ Find opportunities to comment on how children are moving.
___ Encourage children to plan, do, and recall movement.
___ Plan large-group experiences in which children use a single word to describe a single movement.

Acting upon movement directions

___ Listen for the movement directions children generate as they play.
___ During group games, give or demonstrate simple movement directions:
  ___ Provide verbal directions.
  ___ Give children visual movement demonstrations.

Feeling and expressing steady beat

___ Provide equipment on which children can rock, swing, and pedal.
___ Build rocking to the beat and patting the beat into music and language experiences:
  ___ Distinguish *beat* from *rhythm*.

___ Rock, sway, and pat a steady beat while singing and chanting.
___ Pat a steady beat when children are playing musical instruments.
___ Provide opportunities for children to walk to a steady beat.
___ Look for and acknowledge children's movement to a steady beat as they play.
___ Play group games with a steady beat.

Moving in sequences to a common beat

___ Encourage children to name the actions they are doing in a movement sequence.
___ Include two-part movement sequences in action songs.

Climbing is an important form of locomotor movement for preschoolers.

References

Gardner, Howard. 1983. *Frames of Mind: The Theory of Multiple Intelligences.* New York: Basic Books.

Rhythmically Moving 1–9. 1982–1988. Series of musical recordings, available on CDs (Phyllis S. Weikart, creative director). Ypsilanti, MI: High/Scope Press.

Strubank, Ruth. 1991. "Music and Movement Throughout the Daily Routine." In *Supporting Young Learners,* Nancy A. Brickman and Lynn S. Taylor, eds., 104–11. Ypsilanti, MI: High/Scope Press.

Weikart, Phyllis S. 1997. *Movement Plus Rhymes, Songs, & Singing Games,* 2nd ed. Ypsilanti, MI: High/Scope Press.

Weikart, Phyllis S. 2000. *Round the Circle: Key Experiences in Movement for Children,* 2nd ed. Ypsilanti, MI: High/Scope Press.

Related Reading

Boisvert, Christine, and Suzanne Gainsley. 2006. *Teacher's Idea Book: 50 Large-Group Activities for Active Learners.* Ypsilanti, MI: High/Scope Press.

Epstein, Ann S. 2007. "What Is the High/Scope Curriculum in Physical Development, Health, and Well-Being?" Chap. 13 in *Essentials of Active Learning in Preschool: Getting to Know the High/Scope Curriculum,* 137–48. Ypsilanti, MI: High/Scope Press.

Haraksin-Probst, Lizabeth, Janet Hutson-Brandhagen, and Phyllis S. Weikart. 2008. *Making Connections: Movement, Music, & Literacy.* Ypsilanti, MI: High/Scope Press.

High/Scope Educational Research Foundation. 2003. *Preschool Child Observation Record (COR),* 2nd ed. Ypsilanti, MI: High/Scope Press.

Weikart, Phyllis S. 1991. "Movement Experiences: Needed But Neglected." In *Supporting Young Learners,* Nancy A. Brickman and Lynn S. Taylor, eds., 96–103. Ypsilanti, MI: High/Scope Press.

Weikart, Phyllis S. 2003. *Movement in Steady Beat,* 2nd ed. Ypsilanti, MI: High/Scope Press.

Weikart, Phyllis S. 2004. *Movement Plus Music: Activities for Children Ages 3 to 7,* 3rd ed. Ypsilanti, MI: High/Scope Press.

Weikart, Phyllis S. 2001. "Moving With Purpose: Rhymes, Action Songs, and Singing Games." In *Supporting Young Learners 3: Ideas for Child Care Providers and Teachers,* Nancy A. Brickman, ed., 209–15. Ypsilanti, MI: High/Scope Press.

Weikart, Phyllis S. 2006. *Teaching Movement & Dance: A Sequential Approach to Rhythmic Movement,* 6th ed. Ypsilanti, MI: High/Scope Press.

Weikart, Phyllis S., Lawrence Schweinhart, and Mary Larner. 1987. "Movement Curriculum Improves Children's Rhythmic Competence, Study Shows." *High/Scope ReSource* 6, no. 1 (Winter): 8–10.

Related Media

The following materials are available from the High/Scope Press, 600 N. River St., Ypsilanti, MI 48198-2898; to order, visit *www.highscope.org,* or call 1-800-40-PRESS.

Movement and Music. 2004. Color videotape or DVD, 79 min.

In a High/Scope program, children move throughout the day. These children, for example, run at large-group time and shoot baskets at outside time.

When children arrange materials in a graduated series or create simple patterns, they are using seriation, a building block for mathematics.

Young children enjoy and are capable of mathematical investigation and reasoning. For example, when Herbert Ginsburg and his colleagues observed children's free play, they were amazed not only by how much the children used mathematical ideas but also by how advanced their thinking was (Ginsburg et al. 1999). Professor Arthur Baroody (2000) says preschoolers actively construct basic mathematical concepts and use them to solve problems.

The **mathematics** section of this book is divided into three components: **seriation** (this chapter), **number** (Chapter 15), and **space** (Chapter 16). Child development researchers refer to these as **logical operations** because they underlie the development of logical thought and problem-solving abilities. These curriculum components parallel three of the categories listed by the National Council of Teachers of Mathematics (NCTM; 2000) in its early childhood standards—namely, algebra, number and operations, and geometry. The other two NCTM standards—measurement and data analysis—involve not only mathematics but also science, and they are described in the **science and technology** chapters (Chapters 17 and 18).

Preschoolers are just beginning to use the process of seriation, that is, ordering objects based on differences and gradual variations in their qualities. Seriation, like the related process of classification (discussed in Chapter 17), builds on children's awareness of attributes (qualities or properties of materials) and is another way children learn about

their world. In classification, children group objects by their common attributes (all the crayons in one basket, all the markers in another). In seriation, children assign a logical order to a series of objects based on *gradual variations in a single attribute* (toy fire engines arranged from largest to smallest) or on a *sequence of attributes that repeats* (red sequin, blue sequin, blue sequin, red sequin, blue sequin, blue sequin). Sometimes, older preschoolers may *match one ordered series to another* (placing the small, medium, and large cups on the small, medium, and large saucers), a more advanced form of seriation.

Finding order in difference is how educational psychologist Charles Hohmann (1991) defines seriation:

Differences may be the basis for ordering objects in a collection, for example, for ordering by size, weight, smoothness, or intensity of color. Unlike such color differences as blue versus green, the differences used for ordering are usually differences in degree. They imply a progression, such as from large to small, from heavy to light, from rough to smooth. Thus, any difference that may be graduated—size, weight, intensity of color, temperature, loudness, resistance to bending—can serve as the basis for ordering a collection of objects (p. 55).

14

Seriation

*From early experiences with objects, the child is able to construct relations among them; the **relations of difference** among objects, which form the basis for seriation, are also the basis for the child's understanding of number.*

— Charles Hohmann, 1975

Children's Creation of Order and Patterns

Children's awareness of differences begins in infancy as they distinguish between the formula they prefer and the "other brand," or as they refuse food that is not prepared at the preferred temperature. More mobile as toddlers, children begin to discover gross differences, such as bigger and smaller, through their own trial-and-error explorations. After numerous attempts at stacking, for example, they discover that putting the bigger blocks on the bottom and the smaller ones on top produces a sturdy structure. In their extensive studies of the development of seriation in young children, Barbel Inhelder and Jean Piaget (1964) found that "seriation exists at the sensori-motor level even if the relevant behavior is unsystematic. A necessary condition appears to be that the difference between the elements of the series must be fairly sizeable" (p. 248).

With their newfound ability to hold mental images in mind and their growing capaci-ty to express their thoughts and experiences in words, preschoolers can identify and describe variations among similar things—"I've got way big mittens because my hands are almost bigger like my daddy's!" They can also make decisions based on these variations—"I want the biggest one."

Preschoolers also find it satisfying to arrange things in series or patterns to make something they particularly want or need, such as a string of beads in alternating colors, or a row of blocks ordered by size to make stairs. As children create such patterns, they discover new combinations, and since they are not particularly bound by rules—even their own rules—their patterns often change after one or two repetitions. Preschoolers also enjoy the puzzlelike challenge of matching one pattern or ordered set to another.

Working with differences and gradual variations, and creating patterns and order among them, is an important way that young children organize and make sense of the world.

Supporting Children in Using Seriation Skills

Three key developmental indicators (KDIs) in seriation describe the way young children create order based on differences. The first indicator focuses on *gross differences*:

- Comparing attributes (longer/shorter, bigger/smaller)

In the art area, this child discovers that she can stretch her elastic so it is longer than her teacher's!

The last two indicators involve the ability to *explore finer distinctions and to create patterns*:

- Arranging several things one after another in a series or pattern and describing their relationships (big/bigger/biggest, red/blue/red/blue)

- Fitting one ordered set of objects to another through trial and error (small cup and small saucer/medium cup and medium saucer/big cup and big saucer)

Adults can help children develop seri-ation skills by understanding that in an active learning setting such experiences arise and flourish within the context of children's play. The logic of order and patterns emerges over time as children manipulate materials and devise ways to order objects to suit their own particular needs and plans. Following are ways adults can support young creators of order and patterns.

KDIs in Seriation

- Comparing attributes (longer/shorter, bigger/smaller)

- Arranging several things one after another in a series or pattern and describing their relation-ships (big/bigger/biggest, red/blue/red/blue)

- Fitting one ordered set of objects to another through trial and error (small cup and small saucer/medium cup and medium saucer/big cup and big saucer)

Key Developmental Indicator
Comparing Attributes (Longer/Shorter, Bigger/Smaller)

"It's getting longer and longer!" Jacob says as he rolls a piece of Play-Doh.

❖

"It's bigger than you!" Jalessa tells Peter about her tower.

❖

"You have a longer tail," Brian says to Alana, who is also pretending to be a rat.

❖

"The [rhythm] sticks were shorter at my other school," Corrin tells Anna as they select instruments for a parade.

❖

"My arm's too short for this shirt," Kenneth tells Beth, showing her how his hand is hidden in his sleeve. "I think the laundry did it!"

❖

"Yours are the biggest," Anna tells Becki, her teacher, as they look at boot prints they have made in the snow.

❖

"I'm measuring to see which one is thick," says Jason, as he staples sticks. "This one is the thickest!"

❖

"I'm bigger than Donald," Julia tells Sam as she arrives with her younger brother.

❖

Mikey and L. J. are building Lego towers. "Let's see how tall yours is compared to mine," L. J. suggests.

❖

"My house is getting bigger and bigger," Kacey observes, as she builds with snap-together blocks.

As they play and work with materials, young children observe differences and compare attributes that are personally meaningful to them. Often they are struck by the relative size of things: "We have a bigger house." "The brown can is the biggest." Occasionally they observe and compare other attributes such as color: "Brown and green make lighter brown." Following are ways adults can support children's explorations and observations about the comparative attributes of things.

Suggestions for Adults

▶ **Provide materials whose attributes children can easily compare.**

Sets of materials in two sizes. Since the relative size of things makes a significant impact on young children, it makes sense to provide sets of materials in two sizes. (See Materials for Comparing Sizes, alongside, for examples.)

Materials children can shape and change. Provide materials that children can use to make their own large and small creations. Include pliable materials, such as clay, dough, Play-Doh, modeling beeswax, and damp sand; blocks and other building materials such as wire, pipe cleaners, boxes, and glue; and various painting and drawing materials.

Materials with other contrasting attributes. While young children seem especially attuned to size comparisons, they also notice other obvious distinctions. Consider stocking

pairs of materials that have contrasting attributes, such as wet and dry sand, rough and smooth stones, curly and straight macaroni, and dark- and light-colored crayons. Also provide a variety of musical instruments that children can play in contrasting ways (fast and slow; loud and soft).

▶ **Store and label materials in a way that encourages children to compare attributes.**

Again, think about labels and storage containers that focus on children's interest in relative sizes. For example, store large nails in one clear container and small nails in another, large dinosaurs in one basket, small dinosaurs in another, and so forth.

▶ **Listen for and support the comparisons children make as they play and solve problems.**

As children carry out their plans and intentions, they make observations that give attentive adults a glimpse into their thinking about comparisons:

• "The worms [tent caterpillars] in this bush," Abby said at outside time one day, "are a lot smarter than the worms in that bush, 'cause these worms know not to hang low enough to get into my hair." "Yes, I suppose that does make them smarter," Jackie, her teacher, agreed.

Materials for Comparing Sizes

Sets of large and small:
dinosaurs
farm animals
trucks and cars
buttons
nails
shells
Tinkertoys
blocks
boxes
dolls
blankets
cookie cutters
paintbrushes
sponges
balls
buckets
cymbals
drums

• Chelsea was washing her hands when Beth, an adult, joined her at the next sink, turning her faucet on "full blast." "I have mine running slower," Chelsea told her. Following Chelsea's lead, Beth adjusted her faucet to decrease the flow. "Now yours is running slower, too," Chelsea observed.

Sometimes children make comparisons of attributes to solve problems they encounter in play. For example, Juanita and Paula were building a block tower that had gotten so high they could not reach the top. Paula tried standing on a block, but it was not high enough, so she and Juanita enlisted the help of Isobel, a nearby adult. "You tried standing on a block, but that didn't make you high enough," Isobel said, acknowledging their progress so far. "We need something higher," said Paula. She looked around, then got a sturdy wooden chair. When Juanita saw that Paula could now reach the top, Juanita got a sturdy chair for herself. Standing on chairs with Isobel holding them steady, the two girls completed their tower.

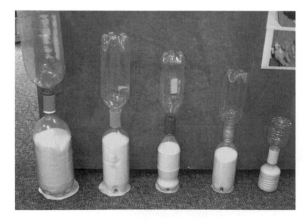

This set of sand timers provides opportunities to order by size.

Key Developmental Indicator
Arranging Several Things One After Another in a Series or Pattern and Describing Their Relationships (Big/Bigger/Biggest, Red/Blue/Red/Blue)

"This is the little one, this is the middle-sized one, this is the big one," says Corrin, sorting out pieces of graph paper with different-sized squares.

ᴥ

Trey uses connecting pegs to make three "trumpets" that he refers to as "the short one, the longer, the longest."

ᴥ

Chrysten arranges paper strips and buttons in an alternating pattern—paper strip, button, paper strip, button— all the way around the edge of her collage.

ᴥ

Mikey fits all the nesting blocks together and puts them away at cleanup time.

ᴥ

As she draws, Alana observes, "The pearl is big. Now it's very big. Now it's very bigger!"

ᴥ

At small-group time, Athi makes a "train" of alternating rods and circles.

ᴥ

Deola makes four Play-Doh stars and arranges them in order by size: "The mama, the papa, the sister, the baby."

ᴥ

Jonah draws a spiral that starts out large and gets smaller and smaller. Several children become very interested: "How did you do that, Jonah?" they ask. He then proceeds to show them how to "start big and then go small and smaller."

ᴥ

At cleanup, Corrin sorts the markers into three piles: "Good" [works well], "bad" [dry but still makes a mark], and "not at all" [makes no mark].

ᴥ

Jason pauses to look at his paper airplanes: "This one is the biggest. This is the next biggest. Then this, and then I'm going to make one even littler."

As preschoolers play, they sometimes order things into series or patterns. These series often reflect size differences that are referred to in terms of family roles: "The daddy one, the mommy one, and the baby one." (As physically smaller family members, children are particularly aware of size and status relationships.)

While preschoolers create series that include three or four elements ("big, very big, very bigger"), their patterns generally consist of two alternating elements, such as rods and circles, stones and shells, or red and blue beads. Following are ways adults can support young children as they arrange things in order to make series and patterns.

Suggestions for Adults

▶ **Provide collections and sets of materials.**

Sets of materials in three or four sizes. Preschoolers are inclined to attend to size differences, so it makes sense to provide materials that

Pressing a seriated set of four star-shaped cookie cutters into Play-Doh, this child creates a series of star outlines with the smallest star in the center, followed by the two next-largest stars, and ending with the largest star on the outside surrounding them all.

Materials to Gather or Make in Three or Four Sizes

boxes	tossing rings	tires
boards	shells	beanbags
paper	buttons	
pillows	tree rounds	

are the same or similar except for size. Some common sets of materials that come in graduated sizes include nesting blocks, stacking rings, Cuisenaire rods, measuring cups, measuring spoons, funnels, mixing bowls, and canisters. (For suggestions of related sets of materials, see the materials list at upper right.)

Materials that children can use to make their own series and patterns. When provided with appropriate materials, preschoolers are often inspired to create their own series and patterns, such as families of people in different sizes or necklaces in simple patterns. The following materials are particularly appropriate: blocks, clay, and collage materials (for making towers, clay models, and constructions in various sizes); paper, paints, crayons, markers, and pencils (for painting and drawing families, spirals, monsters, and so forth, in three or four sizes); and beads, counting cubes, rods, and collage materials (for making "necklaces" and "trains" with patterns).

Computer programs that feature series and patterns. If you have computers, obtain software for preschoolers in which they can create their own series and patterns. For listings of such programs, see the monthly magazine *Children's Technology Review* (*www.childrenssoftware.com*).

▶ **Watch and listen for the series and patterns children make.**

Children often signal their awareness of series and patterns as they talk about what they are doing:

• "This is the dad, the mom, and the baby kitty," Anna says about a cat-family drawing.

• "Put the measuring cups inside each other to make noise," Andrew advises another music-maker.

• "I need an *E*," Hannah says, after arranging the letter blocks *A*, *B*, *C*, and *D* in order.

At other times, children may make series or patterns without describing them:

• At recall, Leah showed her rainbow painting with "two rainbows," which were actu-ally two sequences or patterns of color that were exactly the same. "Look," her teacher commented, "this rainbow has green, red, purple, yellow, and so does this one—green, red, purple, yellow." "One's in California for my dad," Leah added, "and one's here for me and my mom."

• One day at small-group time, the children made shadows behind a backlit sheet that Beth, their teacher, had hung in the doorway. As they looked at one another's shadows, Matthew was struck by T. P.'s crew cut: "His hair is small!" As the children looked more closely they decided that Carmen, with her many ponytails, had "the biggest hair"; Afret, with short curly hair, had "the next biggest hair"; Chad, with short, straight hair, had "small hair"; and crew-cut T. P. had "the smallest hair." They lined these four children up behind the sheet to look at their "hair shadows" and then asked Beth, their teacher, to take a picture, which she did.

▶ **Ask children to draw or make families, necklaces, and trains.**

At small-group time, provide children with paper and markers and ask them to draw their families, or give them clay or Play-Doh and ask them to make their families. While some children may choose to draw or make something else, others will become involved in creating family members in a variety of sizes to correspond to their perceived age or importance.

Notice the pattern this child has created in the "cherry tree" at right: line/perpendicular line/dot, line/perpendicular line/dot, and so forth, all the way around the tree.

Another way to observe children as they create patterns is to give them beads and strings at small-group time and suggest that they make necklaces. Or give each child small blocks or inch-cubes and little people or animals and suggest that they make trains. While some children will string beads or line up blocks randomly, others may create a pattern. You might also give children pegs and pegboards and watch to see if some children make patterns.

► **Read stories and encourage children to represent stories in which size relationships play an important role.**

Traditional children's stories in which size relationships play an important role, such as

The Three Billy Goats Gruff and *The Three Bears,* offer opportunities for children to place things in order.

After the children have heard these stories a number of times, plan some small-group times around them. Here are some activities, for example, to consider after reading *The Three Bears:*

• Provide materials so the children can make pictures to tell the story of *The Three Bears.* See if any of the children order the bears, bowls, chairs, or beds by size in their pictures.

• Provide a variety of materials—Play-Doh, buttons, blocks, pipe cleaners—and encourage the children to make their own bears, beds, chairs, and bowls. See which children decide to make things in three sizes.

• Ask the children to re-enact the story. Watch to see if and how they make themselves big for the papa bear, medium-sized for the mama bear, and small for the baby bear. Encourage them to find or make different-sized bowls, chairs, and beds.

• For a re-enactment involving music, have the children choose the kind of bear they want to be and what sound the mama, papa, and

baby bears make as they look for food, eat, sleep, and so forth. For example, the children might decide to have the mamas make a medium-pitched sound; the babies, a high-pitched sound; and the papas, a low-pitched sound.

Key Developmental Indicator
Fitting One Ordered Set of Objects to Another Through Trial and Error (Small Cup and Small Saucer/Medium Cup and Medium Saucer/Big Cup and Big Saucer)

At cleanup time, Alana matches three measuring cups of different sizes to their outlines and hangs them up.

❧

Jon draws a large face on a large piece of paper, a medium face on a medium-sized paper, and a small face on a small piece of paper.

❧

Hannah is playing with plastic animals that come in three sizes. She covers the small animals with a small cloth, the medium animals with a medium cloth, and the large animals with a large cloth.

❧

Kenneth sets the table using a big cup for "the dad," a smaller cup for "the mom," and the smallest cup for "the baby sister."

❧

Jonah builds a nesting-block tower with the blocks arranged from largest to smallest. Then he makes a series of balls out of modeling wax and puts the largest ball inside the largest block,

At cleanup time, this child puts the bear family away by matching the daddy bear to the daddy bear picture, the mommy bear to the mommy bear picture, and the baby bear to the baby bear picture.

the next largest ball in the next largest block, and so on, until each block holds a ball of corresponding size.

～

As she plays at the magnet board, Hannah lines up all the squares in order from smallest to largest. Beneath her series of squares she lines up all the circles in the same manner—from smallest to largest.

Sometimes preschoolers take the opportunity to fit one ordered set of objects to another because doing so serves their purpose in play or solves an immediate problem they have encountered. They want to find the lid that fits the shaker-can they are making, or they need the

Ordered Sets of Materials That Go Together

Three or four sizes of the following items:

    flower pots and saucers
    mixing bowls and lids
    coffee cans and lids
    cups and saucers
    canisters and lids
    squeeze bottles and tops
    muffin papers and muffin tins
    envelopes and cards
    boxes and covers
    nuts and bolts
    dolls and doll clothes
    doll beds and covers
    Lego blocks and Lego people

chairs that fit their dollhouse people. In addition, they enjoy the puzzlelike challenge of fitting and matching ordered sets or the feeling of control that comes with deciding who gets the biggest cup, cover, or ball of wax. Following are ways adults can support children's attempts to fit together, or match and create, ordered sets of things.

Suggestions for Adults

▶ **Provide ordered sets of materials that go together.**

Children are most likely to become involved with ordered sets of materials that go together when these materials are related to their interests and play. During their beauty shop play, for example, Joanie and Lynnette were very intent on sorting and matching the three sizes of rollers and roller clips for the "sets" and "perms" they were doing. (For suggestions of related materials, see the materials list above.)

▶ **Label some materials so children can match ordered sets to ordered labels.**

To create ordered sets of labels, trace around ordered sets of materials. For example, trace around a small, a medium-sized, and a large measuring spoon and attach these labels to a pegboard. Then, whenever children put away the measuring spoons they can match the spoons to their outlines. You might also have the children make these labels at small-group time.

▶ **Watch to see how children put ordered sets together.**

Once you provide ordered sets of materials, watch to see how children put them together or how they generate their own matched sets of things. Here is how one child created ordered sets and put them together:

One day, Oscar used clay to make three model cars in different sizes. Next he decided to make "speed-jump ramps," that is, flattened strips of clay anchored at each end to the table with a hump or "jump" in the middle. Oscar worked quite a while fashioning ramps proportioned to fit each car. Just before cleanup, Manuel, one of his teachers, helped him move the ramps and cars from the table to a piece of cardboard so he could take his cars and ramps to recall time. Since most of the children had attended a local car race the previous weekend, everyone had lots to say. The next day at small-group time, the adults gave clay to all the children to represent something they had seen at the race. The adults also wanted to see if some children might create their own ordered sets of things. The children made cars, fences, bleachers, and flags, and one child even made a family with "the baby on the daddy's shoulders so she can see."

Seriation Strategies: A Summary

Comparing attributes (longer/shorter, bigger/smaller)

___ Provide materials whose attributes children can easily compare.

    ___ Sets of materials in two sizes

    ___ Materials children can shape and change

    ___ Materials with other contrasting attributes

___ Store and label materials in a way that encourages children to compare attributes.

___ Listen for and support the comparisons children make as they play and solve problems.

Arranging several things one after another in a series or pattern and describing their relationships (big/bigger/biggest, red/blue/red/blue)

___ Provide collections and sets of materials.

    ___ Sets of materials in three or four sizes

    ___ Materials that children can use to make their own series and patterns

    ___ Computer programs that feature series and patterns

___ Watch and listen for the series and patterns children make.

___ Ask children to draw or make families, necklaces, and trains.

___ Read stories and encourage children to represent stories in which size relationships play an important role.

Fitting one ordered set of objects to another through trial and error (small cup and small saucer/medium cup and medium saucer/big cup and big saucer)

___ Provide ordered sets of materials that go together.

___ Label some materials so children match ordered sets to ordered labels.

___ Watch to see how children put ordered sets together.

This child creates a pattern as she strings beads—big beads followed by little beads.

References

Baroody, Arthur J. 2000. "Does Mathematics Instruction for Three- to Five-Year Olds Really Make Sense?" *Young Children* 55, no. 4: 61–67.

Ginsburg, H. P., N. Inoue, and K-H. Seo. 1999. "Young Children Doing Mathematics: Observations of Everyday Activities." In *Mathematics in the Early Years*, J. V. Copley, ed., 88–99. Reston, VA: National Council of Teachers of Mathematics and National Association for the Education of Young Children.

Hohmann, Charles. 1975. "Finding Order in Difference: Seriation in Elementary Curricula." In *The High/Scope Report, 1974–75*, C. Silverman, ed., 14–16. Ypsilanti, MI: High/Scope Press.

Hohmann, Charles. 1991. *The High/Scope K–3 Curriculum Series: Mathematics.* Ypsilanti, MI: High/Scope Press.

Inhelder, Barbel, and Jean Piaget. 1964. *The Early Growth of Logic in the Child: Classification and Seriation.* New York: Norton.

National Council of Teachers of Mathematics. 2000. *Principles and Standards for School Mathematics.* Reston, VA: Author.

Helena has drawn her family in a pattern: little person, big person, little person, big person.

Related Reading

Flavell, John H. 1963. "Quantity, Logic, Number, Time, Movement, and Velocity." Chap. 9 in *The Developmental Psychology of Jean Piaget*, 298–326. Princeton, NJ: Van Nostrand.

Epstein, Ann S. 2007. "What Is the High/Scope Curriculum in Mathematics?" Chap. 14 in *Essentials of Active Learning in Preschool: Getting to Know the High/Scope Curriculum*, 149–58. Ypsilanti, MI: High/Scope Press.

Epstein, Ann S., and Suzanne Gainsley. 2005. "Seriation." In *Teacher's Idea Book: "I'm Older Than You. I'm Five!" Math in the Preschool Classroom*, 49–77. Ypsilanti, MI: High/Scope Press.

Ginsburg, Herbert, and Sylvia Opper. 1969. "Classification." In *Piaget's Theory of Intellectual Development: An Introduction*, 119–52. Englewood Cliffs, NJ: Prentice-Hall, Inc.

Graves, Michelle. 2005. "Young Children and Math." "Motivated Mathematicians." In *Supporting Young Learners 4: Ideas for Child Care Providers and Teachers*, Nancy A. Brickman, Holly Barton, and Jennifer Burd, eds., 119–32. Ypsilanti, MI: High/Scope Press.

High/Scope Educational Research Foundation. 2003. *Preschool Child Observation Record (COR)*, 2nd ed. Ypsilanti, MI: High/Scope Press.

Hohmann, Mary, Bernard Banet, and David P. Weikart. 1979. "Seriation." Chap. 9 in *Young Children in Action*, 217–27. Ypsilanti, MI: High/Scope Press.

Hunt, J. McVicker. 1961. *Intelligence and Experience.* New York: The Ronald Press Company.

Piaget, Jean, and Barbel Inhelder. 1969. *The Psychology of the Child.* New York: Basic Books.

Related Media

The following materials are available from the High/Scope Press, 600 N. River St., Ypsilanti, MI 48198-2898; to order, visit *www.highscope.org*, or call 1-800-40-PRESS.

Classification, Seriation, and Number (Early Math). 2003. Color videotape or DVD, 52 min.

Preschool children are very interested in numbers and enjoy counting the number of things in their play.

Number

Through their interactions with people and materials, preschoolers are beginning to construct what mathematicians call **number sense** (Baroody 2000). That is, they develop a basic understanding of what numbers are and how they work. Numbers become "real" things that can be manipulated and transformed, not just abstractions to which we apply mechanical rules. In the view of developmental psychologist John Flavell (1963), preschoolers are developing an understanding of the "essential and fundamental properties of the number system, the underlying assumptions about the nature and behavior of numbers" (p. 310).

The Development of Number Concepts

Preschoolers build their emerging notions of number on the concept of **object permanence**, which they developed as infants and toddlers. Through their sensorimotor explorations, infants and toddlers discover that objects exist apart from their own and others' actions on them. They learn that if a toy car rolls out of sight under the sofa, they can find it, carry it in a bucket, set it down, and find it the next day. The separate existence of objects means that the objects are available for manipulation, sorting, ordering, and quantifying. Because objects exist (rather than appear and disappear arbitrarily), young children correctly conclude that it is safe and natural to assess them in terms of how many there are: "More cookie!" "Two trucks!"

Preschoolers' concept of number emerges as they sort similar materials into groups and collections. At some point, for example, they begin to understand that counting four toy cars involves focusing on the cars' similarities; even though the cars may not be the same size, for example, they all belong to the same set of four objects and can be counted as equals. Preschoolers' understanding of number thus relates to and develops along with their understanding of **classification** (grouping things together based on common attributes; see Chapter 17).

At the same time, preschoolers begin to understand that although the four cars in the set have similarities, each car is different because it is a discrete part of an series ordered from the smallest to the largest (or vice versa). In this respect, preschoolers' understanding of number relates to and develops along with their understanding of another mathematical concept, **seriation** (finding order in difference, discussed in Chapter 14).

Preschoolers' understanding of number also involves their emerging understanding of the concept of **one-to-one correspondence** as the basis for numerical equivalence. By physically matching a set of four toy cars with a set of four toy people, for example, preschoolers begin to see that the number of cars and the number of people are the same. They begin to understand that when two sets

The preschooler does have a concept of number— a concept that contains many of the seeds from which modern arithmetic has grown.

—Rochel Gelman and C. R. Gallistel, 1986

Adults in High/Scope programs understand that young children learn about number by working with interesting manipulative materials. This child, for example, counts the number of clay pieces she has cut with a popsicle stick.

such an understanding, they need to be able to exercise their current numerical capacities, however simple and apparently erroneous their conclusions about numbers may be. As young children make observations and draw conclusions based on their emerging concept of number, they are building a base for logical thinking and also learning about relationships: "Whew!" Abby remarked on her fifth birthday, "now I'm finally the oldest [in my class]!" Through many experiences in ordering, comparing, one-to-one matching, and counting collections of things, children build the knowledge they will need to begin to understand and use arithmetic in later years.

Supporting Children's Understanding of Number

Three number KDIs focus on the ways preschool children are developing an understanding of the nature and uses of numbers. In the first KDI, preschool children are often influenced by *appearances:*

- **Comparing the number of things in two sets to determine "more," "fewer," "same number"**

In the second two KDIs, young children often resort to more *logical strategies* to arrive at conclusions about the numbers of things:

- **Arranging two sets of objects in one-to-one correspondence**
- **Counting objects**

Adults help develop number sense in children by creating active learning settings that provide opportunities for these KDIs as children

of objects can be matched one-to-one—one car to one person—with nothing left over, there are the same number of things in each set.

Finally, preschoolers' understanding of number is shaped by their developing sense of **conservation**, that is, their emerging understanding of the idea that a quantity of things remains the same regardless of the shape or spatial arrangement of the things to be counted. Preschoolers are only beginning to become aware that a pile of four toy cars and a line of four toy people have the same number of objects even though they take up different amounts of space. Preschoolers are often torn between the truth of appearances (if the set of people takes up a

lot of space and looks like more than the set of cars, it is more) and the truth of counting and matching (if you count the cars and then the people, or match them one-to-one, you come up with the same number in each set). When preschoolers are working with large quantities of things, appearances generally win out over matching and counting. When preschoolers are working with small quantities, however, counting and matching often carry more weight than appearances (see Counting on Appearances and Counting, next page).

Forming a basic understanding of the assumptions that underlie the use of numbers is an important task for young children. To develop follow their initiatives and interests and discuss what they are doing with adults and peers. They understand that young children learn about number by working with manipulatives, such as blocks, balls, and art materials. As children explore, pretend, build, gather and put away toys, and solve problems, adults support the many occasions for number exploration that arise. Following are specific ways adults can support young children as they use their understanding of numbers to compare, match, and count sets of things.

Key Developmental Indicator
Comparing the Number of Things in Two Sets to Determine "More," "Fewer," "Same Number"

Corey is building with rods at small-group time. "I need some more!" he tells Sam, his teacher. "How many more?" Sam asks. "Lots more!" says Corey.

~

Jonah counts six sticks on his collage and seven pieces of foam. "There are more of those," he says, pointing to the foam pieces.

~

KDIs in Number

- Comparing the number of things in two sets to determine "more," "fewer," "same number"
- Arranging two sets of objects in one-to-one correspondence
- Counting objects

"Jeanette's my cousin," Chrysten tells Sarah. "She's ten." She holds up ten fingers. "That's way more than me."

~

On a day when several children are absent, Andrew looks around the greeting circle and says, "There are not much kids here."

~

Brianna and Becki are picking up paper clips with magnets. Looking at the paper clips on both magnets Brianna says, "I have more." "How can you tell?" Becki asks. "Well, you just have two and I have a whole bunch!" Brianna replies.

~

Douglas and Kenneth are making a "see-saw" out of unit blocks. "There's more weight on that side," Douglas tells Kenneth. "That's why it's balancing."

~

"Doctor" Andrew looks at his teacher Beth's "hurt" foot and tells her, "It's ten percent bad and ninety percent good!" "Well, what exactly does that mean?" Beth asks. "It will be all better in ten days," the "doctor" tells her.

Comparing numbers of things around them is one way young children begin to construct an understanding of quantity. Talking about the tomatoes in her garden, Wendy cups her hands together and explains, "First we had this many." She then continues, "Now we have this many," making a big circle with her arms.

Counting on Appearances and Counting

One day at work time, Kevin made a picture of a werewolf, gluing both brown and white beans on its legs. At recall time he counted 37 white beans and 22 brown beans and concluded that he had used more brown beans than white beans.

"How do you know that?" Nick, his teacher, asked him.

"Well, look at all of them!" Kevin replied.

On another day, as Kevin got the scissors to pass out at small-group time, Nick asked him if he had enough scissors. Kevin counted six people and seven pairs of scissors. "There're more scissors than we need," he told Nick, putting the extra pair in the middle of the table "in case we have a visitor."

In addition to making such gross comparisons, preschoolers also use counting to make specific comparisons between small numbers of things: "Look," Douglas says about the "happy spider" he has painted. "He has one, two, three, four, five, six, seven, eight . . . *eight* legs, but only *two* eyes and one mouth!" Following are ways adults can support children as they compare numbers of things.

Suggestions for Adults

▶ **Provide materials for comparing numbers of things.**

If you have followed the guidelines presented in Chapter 5 for stocking your active learning setting to support the interests and needs of young children, you have already provided many sets of things they can use to compare quantities. Following, however, are specific types of materials that children often use to compare numbers of things.

Discrete materials. These include sets or collections of countable materials such as beads,

At the easel, this child compares the number of brushes she holds in one hand to the number she holds in the other. For actual four-brush painting in action, see the photo on page 25!

blocks, cars, dolls, buttons, and cans that are easy for children to line up and count. Children's own collections of rocks, shells, leaves, cards, bottle caps, and so forth are also important counting materials.

Art materials. Keeping a well-stocked art area is another way to support children's interest in comparing numbers. Just as Jonah enjoys counting the sticks and foam pieces in his collage (in the anecdote at the beginning of this section), many children enjoy comparing the numbers of things in their own works of art.

▶ **Listen for children's spontaneous number comparisons.**

As children work and play, listen for their observations and questions about number. Remember, too, to keep your own questions to a minimum. Young children are more apt to learn from the questions *they* pose than from the questions adults pose.

Comparing numbers of materials. As you watch and listen carefully to children, you will note that they often compare the numbers of materials they are playing with:

• "Plates?" Trey says to Audie, who is pretending to be a cook, "we've got tons more of them over here!"

• There is a new camera to use at work time. Since so many children want a turn to take pictures, Beth helps them make a sign-up sheet for turns (using children's personal symbols to indicate their turns). Brian currently has the camera, and Callie counts the number of symbols between Brian's symbol and hers. "One, two, three. *Three* more people—then I get a turn!" she says.

Comparing numbers of things in representations. Children also compare the numbers of things in their own pictures and drawings as well as those in books, magazines, and photographs: "I have a lot of teeth . . . more than my mom," Jonah says about the picture he is drawing of himself. "And a lot of mouths. Now I can talk a lot of times."

Comparing ages. Even though age is a fairly abstract concept, many preschoolers know how old they are and enjoy comparing their ages to those of other children. For example, Hannah, Roxanne, Jonah, and Jacob are drawing: "You know what," Jonah says to Jacob. "My sister's older than both of us. She's seven." "My cousin is eight!" Hannah says. "That's older than seven. See: one, two, three, four, five, six, seven, eight!"

▶ **Accept children's findings about number.**

Again, because preschoolers are assessing the numbers of things using their very best logic, it is important for adults to accept their conclusions, even when they are incorrect by adult standards. For example, when Abby turns 5 and remarks, "Whew, finally I'm the oldest," her teacher accepts Abby's assessment of her new status rather than explaining to Abby that no matter what her age, she has always been the oldest because she was born before the other children in her class. Abby knows that 5 is more than 4, so she reasons that turning 5 makes her older than the 4-year-olds. When she was 4, however, she reasoned that she could not be older than other children who were also 4. Her conclusions represent her understanding of the logic of whole numbers. With age and experience, she will shift her logic when she begins to construct an understanding of parts or fractions of numbers (4 years and 2 months, 4 years and 7 months, and so forth).

In her book *Wally's Stories: Conversations in the Kindergarten*, teacher and child-observer Vivian Gussin Paley (1981, p. 13) records a revealing dialogue between children about the relative size of two rugs:

Wally: *The big rug is the giant's castle. The small one is Jack's house.*

Eddie: *Both rugs are the same.*

Wally: *They can't be the same. Watch me. I'll walk around the rug. Now watch—walk, walk, walk, walk, walk, walk, walk, walk, walk—count all the walks. Okay. Now count the other rug. Walk, walk, walk, walk, walk. See? That one has more walks.*

Eddie: *No fair. You cheated. You walked faster.*

Wally: *I don't have to walk. I can just look.*

Children arrange sets of things in one-to-one correspondence in the course of their play. This child, for example, dishes up four servings of "scrambled eggs," one serving for each of the four plates with handles.

The discussion continues. Wally and Eddie recruit other children as "rug measurers" but are only content to measure using the same people each day. Even when the boys use a ruler, they are not convinced of their findings because "rulers aren't really real" like human "rug measurers." Their teacher, Paley, wisely supports their ongoing thinking and reasoning process and accepts the fact that her adult knowledge about measurement means less to them than the conclusions they draw from their own logic about the number of walks, people, or rulers it takes to specify the size of each rug.

Key Developmental Indicator
Arranging Two Sets of Objects in One-to-One Correspondence

Hannah lines up seven plastic bears and gives them each a piece of Play-Doh. "They each have a piece to eat," she tells her friend Roxanne.

Audie carries three chairs to the phone table. "Here are three chairs for three people," he says.

At planning time, Amanda says that she is making five plans. Then she draws pictures of a rug, a butterfly, a gnome, a dollhouse, and a tambourine—one picture for each plan.

Brian sets the house area table laying out one spoon, one plate, one cup, and four pegs for each "family member."

Using an ice-cube tray for a boat, Aimee puts one small bear in each "seat."

L. J. sets up a "bowling alley" with large and small cylinder blocks for "pins," standing one small "pin" next to each large "pin" so that the numbers of small and large "pins" are equal.

Corrin counts out 13 plastic circles for "beds," then places one small kitty on each "bed."

Mikey brings four cans of Play-Doh to the art table. He puts one at his place, then gives one can to each of the other three children.

Hannah lines up six circles, six squares, and six rectangles on the magnet board. "They each have the same number," she says. "See, it matches."

Douglas paints three hearts at the easel, then paints one line below each heart.

In the course of their play, preschoolers find it satisfying to put together sets of things in one-to-one correspondence—one cup for each saucer, one bear for each "seat" on the "boat," one ring for each finger, one hat for each firefighter, one brush for each jar of paint. Generally, matching two sets of things in a series of pairs serves some functional purpose in their play ("We're firefighters. We need hats!"). As they pair up sets of things, children gain physical experience with equivalences (one hat for each head means there are the same number of hats and heads), although they may not yet be thinking about what they are doing in these terms. These one-to-one matching experiences also support children's emerging understanding of counting, since counting calls for matching one number word ("one, two, three . . .") to one and only one item counted. Following are ways adults can support children's experiences with one-to-one correspondence.

Suggestions for Adults

▶ **Provide materials that fit together in one-to-one correspondence.**

Children will use almost anything at hand to create their own personally meaningful matched sets (bears and blocks, circles and kittens, big cylinder blocks and small cylinder blocks). Many of the materials listed in Chapter 5 will support children's construction of the concept of one-to-one correspondence. In particular, consider these materials: countable collections of things and sets of things that actually fit together in one-to-one correspondence—pegs and pegboards, egg cartons and plastic eggs, jars and lids, felt-tip pens and tops, a Chinese Checkers set, and so forth.

▶ **Watch for the sets of corresponding materials children generate.**

As children play and work with materials throughout the day, watch for the corresponding sets of things they create to serve their own purposes. Here are some examples of child-created one-to-one correspondence experiences you might observe:

• Outside, Corrin and Callie gather walnuts that have fallen to the ground. After filling a bucket, they round up all the tires and hide one walnut in each tire.

• At small-group time, Jonah lines up and counts 12 blocks, then places one small bear on each block.

• Anna, Martin, and Ben build a block house with several "bedrooms." In each bed-

In this drawing, Susanna creates her own corresponding sets—one wagon for each person.

room they place one toy farm animal, one "bed," and one "couch."

• Martin lines up the teacups and puts one piece of plastic fruit in each one. "Want some apple juice?" he asks Beth, his teacher. "Sure," she says. Martin hands her the cup with the plastic apple. "One cup, one apple—apple juice!" Beth acknowledges.

▶ **Encourage children to share and talk about their one-to-one arrangements at recall time.**

Generally, when children are engrossed in their play or a project, they will be reluctant to stop what they are doing to talk about a one-to-one correspondence you have just seen them make. At recall time, however, children may be more receptive to the idea of thinking back over this aspect of their work-time endeavors. In fact, with some encouragement, children may be willing to show how they put two sets of things together and to talk about the correspondences they made.

▶ **Encourage children to gather and distribute materials.**

"Kevin," said Nick, an adult, "please bring enough scissors so each person at our table has one." Having children gather and distribute needed materials is a natural, functional way of involving children with one-to-one correspondence experiences.

At snack and meal times. Set up a turn-taking chart so each child has the opportunity to gather and distribute enough cups, napkins, spoons, plates, and so forth for each person at the table.

At small- and large-group times. When there are materials such as musical instruments, carpet squares, or glue bottles to gather and distribute, turn this job over to a child.

During card games. Playing simple card games with children—such as "Go Fish," "Memory," and child-created card games—provides another opportunity for experience with one-to-one correspondence since the "dealer" must figure out a way to give each player an equal number of cards. In such games, it is important for adults to refrain from taking over or correcting the dealing process. For children, dealing cards so each player has the same number is a significant problem to solve.

Key Developmental Indicator
Counting Objects

Alana counts the 12 beads she has strung on her necklace. Later, carrying out another plan, she counts 9 letter Rs on the computer screen.

∽

Audie is pounding a pile of snow and counting as he pounds. "It takes forty-five pounds!" he announces.

∽

Julia makes a Play-Doh birthday cake, puts on the "candles," and counts them to 12. "This is for your twelve years' birthday," she tells Sam.

∽

As Brian plays with the train, he counts 12 holes "for the train to fit together."

∽

On the playground, Chrysten counts eight tires she and Jalessa are stacking.

∽

Douglas makes a pair of handcuffs, then breaks them apart. "Look, Peter," he says. "I have two halves!"

∽

Kacey counts the Play-Doh cookies she is making. "I have four cookies," she concludes.

∽

One day at work time, this child was inspired to count wood scraps and "write numbers" in the "number book" she was making.

*Trey makes a mask on the computer and counts, "One, two, three, four . . . **four** pieces of scary guy."*

❧

At lunch, Amanda counts 12 people at her table.

❧

Isaac counts the 12 blocks he is using, then says, "I have fourteen blocks."

❧

Chelsea counts ten wheels at small-group time and gives them to Callie.

❧

Kenneth makes a tower of snap-together blocks and counts them. "Wow! I used thirty-four blocks!"

❧

At cleanup time, Abby counts and tosses 16 small plastic bears into the "bear bowl."

❧

Douglas rolls a ball off the deck over and over again. Each time, he counts the number of steps the ball hits on its way to ground level. "All four steps!" . . . "Two steps!" . . . "No steps!"

❧

As she swings, Jalessa counts to 15.

❧

Jeff makes five Play-Doh airplanes. "These three have three lights because they fly at night and these two have two lights because they only fly in the day," he explains.

Children see it, and they count it. Anecdotes of preschool children's counting experiences, such as the ones just presented, are easy to gather because young children love to count. In describing children who are around 4 years of age, psychologist Howard Gardner (1991) observes, "Often with surprising speed and ferocity, preschoolers see the world as an arena for counting. Children want to count everything—facial features in a drawing, beads, blocks, 'pounds,' candles, holes, tires, letters, lights" (pp. 75–76).

Young children's delight in counting has also captured the attention of developmental psychologist Rochel Gelman. Gelman has spent the last several decades working with young children and preschool teachers and studying the relationship of counting to children's understanding of number. In children 3 years and older, Gelman has found that the child's ability to count is governed by a set of counting principles that arise spontaneously to both guide and motivate his or her developing proficiency at counting. Following are the counting principles Gelman and her colleague C. R. Gallistel (1986) describe:

• **The one-to-one principle.** Using one and only one number name (such as "one, two, three" or "A, B, C") for each item counted.

• **The stable-order principle.** Using the number names in a stable order, such as "one, two, three," even though the order may be unconventional, such as "six, eleven, fifteen."

• **The cardinal principle.** Using the last number name spoken to describe the number of objects in the set, "One, two, three . . . Three snakes!"

• **The abstraction principle.** Counting part of a mixed set of items, for example, count-

ing the red blocks in a building made of multi-colored blocks.

• **The order-irrelevance principle.** Recognizing that the order in which objects are counted is irrelevant. Six balls are always six balls no matter which one you count first.

Generally, preschoolers employ the first two principles when they count—one number name for each item counted and a stable number-name order. Many preschoolers also employ the cardinal-order principle: "I made one, two, three, four, five . . . **five** balls, and one, two, three, four. . . **four** snakes." It is not as common to see 3- and 4-year-olds using the last two principles, although these capacities are also developing at this time. Further, preschoolers generally count the things they are using or making simply for the love of counting rather than to compare sets to determine equivalence (although they may do so if asked). Following are ways adults can support young children's natural love of counting.

Suggestions for Adults

▶ **Provide sets of countable objects.**

A well-stocked active learning setting is filled with sets of interesting countable materials. For example, in the anecdotes at the beginning of this section, children counted beads, "pounds" of snow, pegs ("candles"), holes in a train, tires, handcuff parts, Play-Doh cookies, parts of a computer-generated mask, persons at the lunch table, blocks, wheels, snap-together blocks, plastic bears, the bounces of the ball, swinging motions, and lights on a Play-Doh airplane. As you assess your active learning setting for countable items, consider the following:

• **Blocks.** Blocks are smooth, pleasurable, durable objects to handle and count. Children find blocks satisfying to stack, build with, and incorporate into their pretend play. They will use and count as many sets of unit blocks, hollow blocks, multicolored blocks, inch-cubes, and snap-together blocks as you can make room for.

• **Collections of small things.** Collections of items that children can hold in their hands are natural targets for counting. These may include collections of beads, bottle caps, pebbles, small shells, poker chips, chestnuts, and buttons, as well as snack foods such as popcorn, raisins, cereal, and fish crackers.

• **Messy things.** Many children are moved to count and play with materials that make them wet and dirty. For example, children like to count worms they find in the garden after a rain, bugs under a log, the number of buckets of water it takes to fill the baby's bath or the water table, the number of towels it takes to clean up a spill, handprints they can make on one piece of paper, and the rocks it takes to make a jar of water overflow.

• **Computer software.** Children often invite their friends to count with them at the computer. For age-appropriate software programs that call for counting, refer to the monthly magazine *Children's Technology Review* (*www.childrenssoftware.com*).

• **Materials with numerals.** Once they begin to count, some preschoolers become interested in making their own numbers. For these children, number writing evolves spontaneously when the numbers they want to reproduce are close at hand. Therefore, it makes sense to provide materials with numerals, such as an adding machine, a calculator, a typewriter, computers, playing cards, play money, number stamps (and ink pads), and number stickers.

• **Board games.** Simple board games that include dice or spinners and pieces to move around the board prompt children to count spaces as they move their game pieces. Remember, however, that rules are not particularly important to children at this age. They make up their own rules, which are generally based on moving around the board and counting rather than on arriving at a particular point.

▶ **Listen for children's counting throughout the day.**

As children play and work with materials, be alert to the opportunities they take to count. The anecdotes that open this section are typical of the kinds of spontaneous counting you can expect to observe.

▶ **Accept children's numerical ordering.**

As Gelman and Gallistel (1986) point out, "Children can count without using the conventional count words or the conventional count

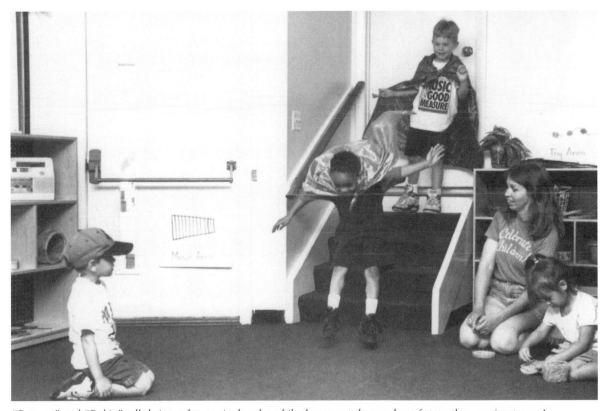

"Batman" and "Robin" tell their teacher to sit close by while they count the number of steps they can jump over!

This child's teacher holds him up so he can count the balloons that represent the number of days until the other regular teacher returns to the classroom.

sequence" (p. 244). Here are two examples of what this statement means:

• One day, Jonah was stringing beads. He counted them in the conventional sequence up to 25, then counted the remaining beads, "twenty-seven, twenty-nine, fifty, sixty, sixty-six." His teacher was impressed with how high he could count and agreed with him that he had strung 66 beads. She was not concerned about the mixed-up order of Jonah's numbers because she knew that Jonah would develop the skill of counting in the correct order at some future time when he understood the logic of counting large sets. In the meantime, she saw that he had used the first three counting principles (one-to-one, stable-order, and cardinal). The process of counting and the delight children take in it are far more important at this point than their using conventional counting words in the proper order. In fact, correcting preschool children as they count actually may discourage them from counting.

• One day, Julia counted all the stacking pegs she was using, ending her count with "fourteen, nineteen, sixteen, twenty. Twenty pegs!" Then, as if a new idea had just occurred

These children use "telephone numbers" at planning time. "Eight rings! That's your turn to plan!"

This is the cartoon Trey made at work time. He numbered each box to indicate the order in which to read the story.

to her, she added, "And look, I have one, two, three, *four* towers. Twenty pegs in four towers!"

Although Julia's counting order was unconventional it did not prevent her from recognizing that she had arranged "twenty" things into four different groups. This insight indicated that she was forming an understanding of the concept that numbers can be divided into parts.

▶ **Listen for children's number talk.**

As children are "bitten by the counting bug," references to numbers and quantities also begin to creep into their discourse. Here are some samples of the kinds of statements you may hear:

• As Chrysten plays with a "baby" dinosaur, she tells Sarah, "She's only eight years old."

• "It will cost three hundred dollars to get Chrysten out of jail," Douglas tells Becki.

• "If your car crashes you get one hundred twenty points. If it crashes again, you get two hundred twenty points!"

• "What comes after five more minutes?" Becki asks, alerting children about the end of work time and the beginning of cleanup time. "Four more minutes!" Petey replies.

Occasionally, preschool children use their understanding of number to solve problems they encounter in the course of their play. When Beth and the children made a sign-up sheet to help children take turns to use a new camera, several children put a number of lines after their names to indicate how many turns they wanted:

Kenneth \/ /

Callie | L | |

Another day at work time, Chelsea, Callie, Corrin, and Aimee discussed an upcoming trip to the movies. They knew that five people were going (the four girls and Chelsea's dad) and that Chelsea's dad drove a pickup truck. Here is a portion of their conversation:

Number Strategies: A Summary

Comparing the numbers of things in two sets to determine "more," "fewer," "same number"

___ Provide materials for comparing numbers of things.
   ___ Discrete materials
   ___ Art materials
___ Listen for children's spontaneous number comparisons.
   ___ Comparing numbers of materials
   ___ Comparing numbers of things in representations
   ___ Comparing ages
___ Accept children's findings about number.

Arranging two sets of objects in one-to-one correspondence

___ Provide materials that fit together in one-to-one correspondence.
___ Watch for the sets of corresponding materials children generate.
___ Encourage children to share and talk about their one-to-one arrangements at recall time.

___ Encourage children to gather and distribute materials.
   ___ At snack and meal times
   ___ At small- and large-group times
   ___ During card games

Counting objects

___ Provide sets of countable objects.
   ___ Blocks
   ___ Collections of small things
   ___ Messy things
   ___ Computer software
   ___ Materials with numerals
   ___ Board games
___ Listen for children's counting throughout the day.
___ Accept children's numerical ordering.
___ Listen for children's number talk.
___ Watch for children's recognition of written numbers.
___ Support children who are interested in writing numbers.

▶ **Watch for children's recognition of written numbers.**

As they count and become aware of numbers around them (in books, on signs, on the computer screen) some preschool children learn to recognize some written numbers:

• Looking at the computer screen one day, Brianna pointed to and named the numbers 3, 4, 5, and 9. When she saw an 11 she said, "Two number ones!"

• Looking through a picture book, Kacey noticed the number 3. "I'm three," she commented.

▶ **Support children who are interested in writing numbers.**

Occasionally, some preschool children begin making and writing numbers for themselves. Here are samples of the kinds of _child-initiated_ number-making situations you might observe:

• As he worked with Play-Doh and paper tubes, Douglas turned to his friend Kenneth and said, "Look, I made a nine!" Indeed, he had.

• Bryant was building with blocks and saw that he had made a familiar-looking structure. "That's almost the letter eight," he said, then added a final block to make the "letter" complete.

• At home, Trey watched his brothers make cartoons. The next day he made a cartoon at work time (see page 417). He divided his paper into six boxes, drew a picture in each one, then numbered each box in the order he had drawn the pictures. He explained each picture to Beth and had her write down what he said.

Corrin: _He can't fit five people in there._

Callie: _There are four kids, so how are we going to fit your dad in the truck?_

Aimee: _A kid has to drive the truck!_

Corrin: _If one was out, your dad could fit in._

Chelsea: _We're taking Mom's car. I have to sit in the dumb seat._

Callie: _The back?_

Chelsea: _We have to sit in the back. Corrin and Callie are sitting in back with me, and you have to sit in front, okay, Aimee? 'Cause only three people fit in back. (Aimee does not look too pleased about this arrangement.) But you can sit in the back with me when we go to the movies._

Corrin: _There's no more room in the back._

Chelsea: _Wait. We can find some more room in back. Me and Aimee can share one seat and you and Callie can share one seat in the back._

References

Baroody, Arthur J. 2000. "Does Mathematics Instruction for Three- to Five-Year Olds Really Make Sense?" *Young Children* 55, no. 4: 61–67.

Flavell, John H. 1963. *The Developmental Psychology of Jean Piaget.* New York: D. Van Nostrand.

Gardner, Howard. 1991. *The Unschooled Mind: How Children Think and How Schools Should Teach.* New York: Basic Books.

Gelman, Rochel, and C. R. Gallistel. 1986. *The Child's Understanding of Number,* 2nd ed. Cambridge: Harvard University Press.

Paley, Vivian Gussin. 1981. *Wally's Stories: Conversations in the Kindergarten.* Cambridge: Harvard University Press.

Related Reading

Butterworth, Brian. 1999. *What Counts: How Every Brain Is Hardwired for Math.* New York: The Free Press.

Castaneda, Alberta M. 1987. "Early Mathematics Education." In *The Early Childhood Curriculum: A Review of Current Research,* Carol Seefeldt, ed., 165–81. New York: Teachers College Press.

Copley, Juanita. 1999. *Mathematics in the Early Years.* Reston, VA: National Council of Teachers of Mathematics.

DeVries, Rheta, and Lawrence Kohlberg. 1987. "Number and Arithmetic." Chap. 7 in *Programs of Early Childhood Education: The Constructivist View,* 186–222. New York: Longman.

Epstein, Ann S. 2007. "What Is the High/Scope Curriculum in Mathematics?" Chap. 14 in *Essentials of Active Learning in Preschool: Getting to Know the High/Scope Curriculum,* 149–58. Ypsilanti, MI: High/Scope Press.

Epstein, Ann S., and Suzanne Gainsley. 2005. "Number." In *Teacher's Idea Book: "I'm Older Than You. I'm Five!" Math in the Preschool Classroom,* 79–108. Ypsilanti, MI: High/Scope Press.

Fuson, Karen C., Walter Secada, and James Hall. 1983. "Matching, Counting, and Conservation of Numerical Equivalence." *Child Development* 54, no. 1: 91–97.

Gardner, Howard. 1983. *Frames of Mind: The Theory of Multiple Intelligences.* New York: Basic Books.

Graves, Michelle. 2005. "Young Children and Math." "Motivated Mathematicians." In *Supporting Young Learners 4: Ideas for Child Care Providers and Teachers,* Nancy A. Brickman, Holly Barton, and Jennifer Burd, eds., 119–32. Ypsilanti, MI: High/Scope Press.

Halford, Graeme S., and Frances Boyle. 1985. "Do Young Children Understand Conservation of Number?" *Child Development* 56, no. 1: 165–76.

High/Scope Educational Research Foundation. 2003. *Preschool Child Observation Record (COR),* 2nd ed. Ypsilanti, MI: High/Scope Press.

Kamii, Constance. 1982. *Number in Preschool and Kindergarten: Educational Implications of Piaget's Theory.* Washington, DC: NAEYC.

National Council of Teachers of Mathematics. 2000. *Principles and Standards for School Mathematics.* Reston, VA: National Council of Teachers of Mathematics.

Piaget, Jean. 1965. *The Child's Conception of Number.* New York: Norton.

Piaget, Jean. 1969. *The Early Growth of Logic in the Child: Classification and Seriation.* New York: Norton.

Piaget, Jean. 1953. "How Children Form Mathematical Concepts." *Scientific American* (November).

"One . . . two . . . ," at small-group time, this child counts the number of blocks he used in his tower.

Related Media

The following materials are available from the High/Scope Press, 600 N. River St., Ypsilanti, MI 48198-2898; to order, visit *www.highscope.org,* or call 1-800-40-PRESS.

Classification, Seriation, and Number (Early Math). 2003. Color videotape or DVD, 52 min.

Preschoolers take pleasure in moving through space, fitting things together and taking them apart, arranging materials, and drawing people and objects in various locations. Through these kinds of actions children construct knowledge about spatial relationships that enables them to act confidently in the physical world.

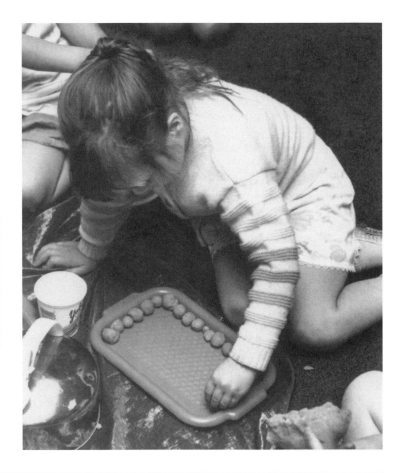

Early mathematics is more than just **numeracy** (reciting numerals or rote counting). It also includes investigations into patterns, size, and quantity (as discussed in Chapters 14 and 15), and **spatial relations** (the position and movement of people and objects in space relative to one another).

Anna fills her paper with layers of paint; Corey makes two stacks of blocks and places a long block across the stacks, forming a bridge. Young children like Anna and Corey want to find out for themselves how to solve such physical problems as filling up a surface with paint or creating a continuous surface with blocks. Through such actions and reflections, children construct a basic understanding of spatial relationships. According to Jean Piaget (1956) the key spatial relationships preschoolers are becoming aware of are "correspondences involving concepts like proximity and separation, order, and enclosure" (p. viii).

What did Piaget mean by proximity and separation, order, and enclosure? *Proximity* and *separation* are terms for "nearness" and "apartness." Preschoolers love to fill and empty and to cut and paste. These kinds of experiences satisfy their desire to create proximity or nearness (putting shells together in a bucket, pasting pieces of paper on top of one another) and to create separation (emptying the shells out of the bucket and cutting paper into fringes and pieces). *Order* involves physically locating or positioning objects one after another. Preschoolers like to roll balls as well as stack and line up blocks, because in doing so they create spatial order—ordering the locations

and positions of balls and blocks in space. *Enclosure* involves surrounding or containing things. Young children enjoy getting inside boxes and wrapping themselves in scarves. Getting inside of things helps children create a sense of enclosure as they envelope or surround themselves with a continuous surface, in this case, a box or scarf.

Building a Basic Understanding of Space

Children's experience with and understanding of spatial relationships begins in infancy as they visually track the paths of people and objects. Once they become mobile, they learn to move through space as they creep, crawl, and toddle to caregivers or to interesting objects—finding their way from one location to another. They become skilled at finding toys they have watched roll out of sight or have seen someone hide. Toddlers enjoy carrying favorite toys from place to place and spending time putting things inside other things, taking them out, and repeating the process.

Preschoolers move through space in more daring ways than infants and toddlers—climbing up a ladder, sliding down a slide, pedaling a tricycle, sledding down a hill. They find their way along familiar

Space

Spatial intelligence arises from the child's action upon the world.
—Howard Gardner, 1983

Children experience a variety of spatial positions in their play and then represent their experiences in their drawings. (See child's drawing on p. 420.)

routes to places in their neighborhoods. They take pleasure in fitting together and taking apart puzzles and Tinkertoys and arranging blocks in stacks, lines, and enclosures. With language increasingly at their command, they talk about some of their most striking spatial experiences:

- "I crumpled it all up so it can fit in my cubby!"

- "Look, I painted the inside and the outside."

- "We live next to each other . . . smooshed together!"

Their growing ability to represent means they can form mental images of things in space ("I know where my mom is—at home"), plan where they want to go ("I'm going to the art area to get some scissors"), and make drawings of themselves in various locations—inside a car, on swings, and so forth.

As preschoolers work with people and materials and solve spatial problems—"It couldn't fit so we biggered the door"—they gain an awareness of the **spatial relationships** in their immediate surroundings. This knowledge enables them to move and act with confidence in the physical world. Moreover, preschoolers are forming the foundation for a more complex understanding of space, an understanding that psychologist Howard Gardner (1983) states involves children's "ability to recog-nize instances of the same element; the ability to recognize a transformation of one element into another; and the capacity to produce a graphic likeness of spatial information" (p. 176).

Supporting Children's Understanding of Space

The **six space KDIs** present a composite picture of things preschoolers do that enable them to construct an understanding of simple spatial relationships. The first three indicators involve *action on objects*:

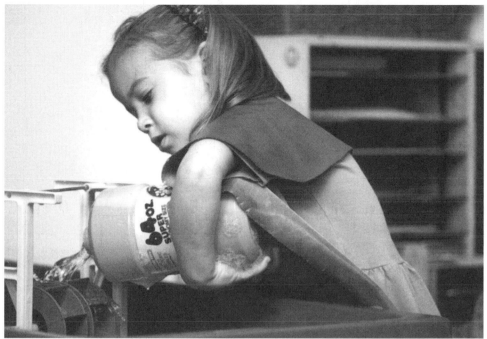

The simple act of filling and emptying is an absorbing activity for this preschooler.

- Filling and emptying
- Fitting things together and taking them apart
- Changing the shape and arrangement of objects (wrapping, twisting, stretching, stacking, enclosing)

The remaining three indicators involve not only *actions* but also *observations and interpretations of spatial relations:*

- Observing people, places, and things from different spatial viewpoints
- Experiencing and describing positions, directions, and distances in the play space, building, and neighborhood
- Interpreting spatial relations in drawings, pictures, and photographs

Adults appreciate the importance of **setting** and **materials** in developing children's understanding of spatial relations. They understand that children learn about *proximity* because there are people and things they want to be near and can be near. Children learn about *order* because there are blocks to stack, beads to string, and balls to roll. Children learn about *enclosure* because there are small spaces they can huddle within and materials and time to build their own enclosures. Young children learn about *space* by moving about freely and carrying out their intentions using objects that interest them. Following are ways adults can support young children in their development of logical thought about the relations of things in space.

Key Developmental Indicator
Filling and Emptying

At the house-area sink, Brian fills a mixing bowl with small plastic bears, empties the bears into the sink, and puts them back into the bowl.

∾

Vanessa uses her hand to scoop sand into a baby bottle, pours out the sand, then fills the bottle again—this time scooping the sand into the bottle with a spoon.

∾

Audie tosses beanbags into a cardboard box, empties the box, then tosses all the beanbags into the box again. As he continues this process, he moves farther away from the box for each round of tosses.

∾

Alana experiments with the turkey baster at the water table by figuring out how to fill it with water for "a long squeeze."

∽

Outside, Colin and Athi fill a wagon with walnuts, pull it to "the dump," and dump the walnuts out. When they run out of walnuts, they fill their wagon with tires for "the dump."

∽

Caroline fills a small purse with poker chips, takes it over to her friend Mychael in the block area, gives her all the chips, and returns to the house-area canister for more.

The simple act of filling and emptying is a satisfying activity for preschoolers. Many find comfort in the actions of filling, pouring, and

Children find pouring, filling, and emptying to be engaging and satisfying, whether they are playing alone or comparing results with friends.

dumping because they can use familiar materials and actions while keeping a close watch on what is happening in the rest of the setting. At the same time, they gain experience with putting objects together (filling) and separating them (emptying), actions that eventually help them "see objects as together or separated in space" (Flavell 1963, p. 328). Here are ways adults can support children's filling, pouring, and emptying experiences.

Suggestions for Adults

▶ **Provide materials for filling and emptying.**

Continuous materials for pouring. Include materials such as sand, water, salt, and flour that can be poured from one container to another and molded or packed into containers of various shapes. A sand and water table provides indoor filling and pouring opportunities. Outdoors, a sandbox close to a water spigot or pump can accommodate larger containers and messier pouring experiments.

Discrete materials. These include small collections of things children can easily scoop up in their hands, such as sets of small plastic animals, beads, poker chips, nuts, shells, stones, pea gravel, buttons, inch-cubes, and bottle caps.

A variety of containers and scoops. Children enjoy filling and emptying cups, bowls, food storage containers, milk cartons and jugs, boxes, bottles, funnels, pails, buckets, crates, wagons, wheelbarrows, purses, suitcases, lunch boxes, bags, and envelopes. While they often scoop things up with their hands, they also use spoons of all sizes, plastic scoops, trowels, and shovels (large and small). In water play, children enjoy figuring out the mechanics of various squeeze containers, such as turkey basters and plastic ketchup and mustard bottles.

Computer software. If you have computers or other technology devices in your preschool setting, include drawing and coloring programs or games in which children fill and empty the screen or parts of the screen with vivid colors they select. The monthly magazine *Children's Technology Review* (*www.childrenssoftware.com*) contains many more suggestions.

▶ **Watch for children's filling and emptying play.**

There are certain locations in which filling and emptying play tends to occur: around the sand and water table; in the sandbox; at the sink as children wash dishes, dolls, and paintbrushes; in the house area; and in the small-toy area. Children also enjoy emptying containers of toys and even entire toy shelves.

▶ **Imitate children's actions.**

To join children's filling and emptying play, move to the child's level, find your own container and filling materials, and do what the child is doing. Watch for and imitate subtle variations to gain an appreciation of what often is a deceptively simple task. Once children see that you are taking your cues from them, they often initiate conversations about what they

In the block area, this child carefully fits long blocks into her block enclosure.

are doing or about an unrelated topic. Thus, imitating children can lead to conversation and an exchange of ideas.

▶ **Anticipate repetition.**

While children begin filling and emptying things as infants and toddlers (filling cups with Cheerios and emptying out the ground-level cupboards) they never really outgrow their enjoyment of this activity. Therefore, it is important to support this type of play whenever it occurs. Many children return again and again to filling and emptying experiences, with many personal variations, as a way of exploring and creating, socializing around a satisfying task, and seeking comfort or respite during a busy day.

Key Developmental Indicator
Fitting Things Together and Taking Them Apart

Jason cuts a long strip of paper, cuts a slit in it, and fits another paper strip into the slit.

∾

Amanda and Isaac put together a 20-piece puzzle with occasional help from Betsy, their teacher. Then they take all the pieces out and put them together again all by themselves.

∾

Andrew builds a hollow block enclosure, then lays a "floor" of unit blocks that fit tightly into the space.

∾

Jalessa puts her five-finger gloves on all by herself, carefully working each finger into the proper pocket.

∾

This child fits together pieces of plastic tubing to make a "hose" that will stretch from the sink to the water tub on the table.

Kenneth and Douglas are lowering plastic tubing over the edge of the tree house: "That black tube would fit in that hole," Kenneth says to Douglas, pointing to a hole in the climbing net.

❧

Chrysten figures out how to unpin one safety pin from another and then sticks the pin through the paper on which she is drawing.

❧

Johnny cuts off the top of his pumpkin, scrapes off the seeds, then works to put the top back on so it fits exactly.

❧

Julia nests the right-angle blocks. "Look, they fit!"

❧

At the computer, Trey can't get his mouse to work. Mikey sees that it has come unplugged and plugs it back in for Trey.

❧

When the pan hook falls off the pegboard, Christy works to fit it back on. "There!" she says at last and hangs up a pan.

❧

Joey takes apart the insides of the coffeepot, lays them carefully on the table, then, piece by piece, re-assembles them inside the pot and puts on the lid.

❧

Deola draws a heart, cuts it out, then fits it back into the paper from which she cut it. "Look," she says, "a puzzle!"

❧

During a role-play episode, Max twists the top off a plastic soft drink bottle, pours some "pop" into several glasses, and screws the top back on "so the bubbles won't get out."

Fitting things together and taking them apart provides preschool children with both spatial challenges and a sense of accomplishment. Through trial and error, persistence, and repetition, children gain firsthand experience with putting things together, taking them apart, and twisting and turning them. These types of experiences help children with *spatial problem solving*, as preschoolers ask and explore answers to questions such as, "How can I fit my toothbrush into its slot? Will this part of the zipper go into this other part? Will the Tinkertoys fit together to make a space shovel?" Following are ways adults can support children as they take things apart and fit them together.

Suggestions for Adults

▶ **Provide materials that fit together and come apart.**

Commercial materials. As you buy and order materials, look for things that children can easily take apart and put together, such as trucks and cars with removable parts, Tinkertoys, Lincoln Logs, interlocking blocks, snap-together trains and train tracks, pegs and pegboards, puzzles, slotted squares, parquetry blocks, beads and strings, Connecto-Straws, geoboards, dolls and doll clothes, markers and tops, staples and a stapler, a drill and drill bits.

Common household materials. Children also enjoy fitting together and taking apart everyday materials, including all kinds of boxes; vacuum cleaner attachments; jars and lids; pots and lids; coffee percolators; plastic bottles and tops; screws and nuts; jewelry that clasps or snaps; keys on a key ring; and dress-up clothing that buckles, buttons, zips, and ties.

▶ **Provide materials children can use to make things that fit together and come apart.**

In the anecdotes at the beginning of this section, Deola cut out a heart and fit it back into the space it left in the paper, while Jason fit together paper strips he had slotted. As children gain skill with taking things apart and fitting things together, they also enjoy making their own things that come apart and go back together. Therefore, it is important to provide them with a broad range of art and woodworking materials. (See the art and woodworking materials lists in Chapter 5.)

▶ **Provide time for children to work with materials on their own.**

Since fitting together and taking apart often begins with trial and error, children need time on their own to experiment with materials that fit together and come apart. They need time to make their own discoveries without adults hovering over them instructing on "how to do it right."

If you wish to join a child working with materials that fit together and come apart, gather similar materials and imitate the child's actions. Try to match the child's pace to get an idea of what the child is experiencing. A conversation may emerge during a natural pause if the child makes a comment about what he or she is doing or observing:

Trey: *This is a robot arm.*

Adult: *I see!*

Trey: *Watch, he can pick up stuff.* (Demonstrates.)

Adult: *He picked up a straw.*

Trey: *See, 'cause it fits in his holder.* (Turns around to sort out more robot-making materials.)

▶ **Support children as they solve fit problems.**

Many of the problems children encounter during play involve *fit*—getting into a favorite costume, cutting a string the right length to keep a mask on. With persistence, preschoolers often solve these problems on their own, but sometimes their patience wears thin. Adult support at this point can help children overcome frustration and follow through on their intentions. In the following situation, Susan, the adult, provides an immediate suggestion from her own experience. This gives Traci a new strategy to try independently:

Traci: *THIS WON'T COME OFF!*

Susan: *Sometimes, when my wheel won't come off, I try twisting it.*

Traci: (Twists the stuck wheel.) *There, it's off!*

▶ **At recall time, encourage children to talk about things they put together and took apart.**

When you observe children putting things together and taking them apart, encourage them to talk about their experiences at recall time. Here are some sample openers:

- "Today I saw Traci put together Tinkertoys with lots of wheels."

- "I saw Joanie take apart her bead necklace."

- "I noticed at cleanup time that Kenneth and Douglas had to take apart their Legos to put them away."

- "Amanda and Isaac had to put together their puzzle to put it away."

- "Jason, you made something with long paper strips that fit together. How did you figure out that way of keeping them together?"

▶ **Include fit-together, take-apart materials at small-group time.**

Providing each child with a set of take-apart, put-together materials at small-group time gives children the opportunity to experiment with how things fit in ways that are personally meaningful. One day, Helena and Sara filled a shoebox for each child with nuts, long screws, and strips of wood in which they had drilled holes. When the children opened their "surprise boxes" they got right to work. Some spent all of small-group time fitting their long screws into the holes and twisting on the nuts. Other children discovered that they could screw wood pieces together, and this procedure fully occupied their attention. And some children saw that they could build something—a house, a window—by screwing their wood pieces together in a particular configuration they had pictured in their minds. While every child was involved in the process of fitting wood strips together with screws and taking them apart, each child's approach and outcome were unique.

Key Developmental Indicator
Changing the Shape and Arrangement of Objects (Wrapping, Twisting, Stretching, Stacking, Enclosing)

Jason puts two hollow ramp blocks together, walks up one side and down the other. Then he separates the ramps, puts two blocks between them, and drives cars along his extended ramp.

❧

Brianna takes the diaper off her doll baby, folds it, gets a "clean" diaper, unfolds it, and puts it on her baby.

❧

Jacob sings "Roll, roll, roll your boat" as he rolls Play-Doh into long strands and then uses scissors to snip the strands into short pieces.

❧

Jalessa twists herself around and around on the swing and then lets the chain unwind. "I'm going twisty!"

❧

Jonah and Jason tie jump ropes to chairs, then climb up the climber holding the free ends of their ropes and begin pulling to hoist the chairs onto the climber.

❧

After small-group time, Oscarina gets the broom and sweeps the paper scraps into a pile and then into the dustpan.

❧

Markie holds his bread dough in both hands above the table and watches it stretch. "It's oozing," says his friend Corey, who has stopped to watch.

❧

Rachel covers her whole paper with paint, moves the clips that hold the paper to the easel to one side, and paints over the unpainted space where they had been.

❧

Douglas builds a "rat house," then adds another room for more "rats."

❧

At small-group time, Abby stacks inch-cubes until they topple, then stacks them again.

Changing the shape and arrangement of things by wrapping, twisting, stretching, stacking, and enclosing comes naturally to preschoolers in active learning settings as they explore and use a variety of materials. Through such manipulations, preschoolers learn firsthand that many materials can be reshaped and rearranged yet still remain essentially the same. While to most preschoolers a Play-Doh ball rolled into a long strand looks larger than it did when shaped as a ball, they know that both the ball and the strand are still made of Play-Doh. As they reshape and rearrange materials, preschoolers discover that they can make enclosures and make things closer together or farther apart by bending, twisting, stretching, and squeezing. Following are ways adults can support young children as they construct spatial understanding by changing the shape and arrangement of materials.

Cutting and taping are two common activities that involve children in rearranging and reshaping tape and paper.

Suggestions for Adults

▶ **Provide materials to shape and arrange.**

Most of the materials you normally provide for children in an active learning setting are ones that children can arrange and shape. The lists presented in Chapter 5 document these types of materials. Since certain materials are particularly useful in relation to this particular KDI, they are discussed here as well. As you think about small-group times that provide children with arranging and shaping experiences, these are materials you might consider using.

Blocks. Unit blocks, large hollow blocks, cardboard brick blocks, small multi-colored blocks, inch-cubes, snap-together blocks, sandstone building blocks—blocks of all sorts and varieties are natural candidates for arranging and rearranging. As children carry, stack, and line up blocks, and make bridges and houses, they learn about proximity, order, and enclosure.

Paper and cloth. All kinds of paper and envelopes along with fabric scraps, scarves, cloth napkins, towels, doll blankets, table-cloths, doll clothes, and dress-up clothes afford children opportunities to enclose things as they play.

Clay and dough. These pliable materials allow children to shape and reshape materials through stretching, molding, and modeling.

Rubber bands and elastic. Using these stretchable materials, children experiment with stretching and twisting, making things close together and far apart.

Thread, string, yarn, ribbon, rope, wire, and pipe cleaners. Flexible materials like these allow children to deal with the spatial complexities of twisting, looping, tying, and threading.

▶ **Support children as they rearrange things to solve problems.**

In the examples presented here, we see how adults support two children who are trying to solve problems—in the first case, by ob-serving Colin's determined efforts to gather his out-of-reach dinosaurs, and in Erica's case, to join her in finding a way to put a roof on her house:

• During work time, Colin was playing with the dinosaurs. Some of the ones he needed, however, were on top of the block shelf beyond his reach, so he got three large hollow blocks, arranged them into a stair formation, climbed the stairs, and gathered the rest of the dinosaurs. Colin did this on his own. The adults who saw him do so recognized his ability to solve a spatial problem of *separation* by building his own stairs to bring himself close to the dinosaurs that had been too far away for him to reach.

• Erica was putting a roof on her house. She got a board and placed it on one wall of the house but it fell into the middle because it did not quite reach to the opposite wall. So, she moved the board to the opposite wall, but the same thing happened again, because now the board did not reach to the first wall. Erica tried the board at different parts of each wall. "What's happening?" asked Linda, her teacher, who had been observing Erica's play. "It keeps falling," Erica answered. Linda, not wanting to interfere with Erica's

At work time, this child rearranges and reshapes (twists and turns) her teacher's hair!

efforts to solve the problem, replied to Erica's statement with a simple "Hmmm" and paused. Then Erica said, "You hold it." Following Erica's directions, Linda held up the end of the board Erica had rested on the wall of her house, while Erica got more blocks. Erica stacked these blocks under the other end of the board Linda was holding. With Linda as the "holder," Erica repeated this process of building an interior wall until she completed the roof to her satisfaction. At the end of the day, Linda said to her team member, "I really wanted to tell Erica to go get a longer board, but I didn't, and Erica came up with her own solution. I never would have thought of building a whole new wall!"

▶ **Listen for children's awareness of how they are shaping and arranging things.**

As children shape and arrange materials, they sometimes indicate an awareness of the changes they are making by commenting on them:

• One day, Jason arranged a set of wooden letters in the order that spelled his name. Then he had the idea of rearranging "his letters" into new orders like *NASJO* and *OJSNA*. "What does this say?" he asked Betsy, his teacher, after each rearrangement of the letters. Jason was beginning to realize that the *spatial order* of the letters in his name was significant.

• Kacey had colored her nose with green marker, then decided to wash it off. "Look," she said to Becki, holding up her washcloth. "My green nose disappeared. It's on the washcloth now!"

• Callie was writing letters to send to people. "This is for you, Ann," she said to her teacher. "I made a lot of folds to get it in [the envelope]."

▶ **Take cues from children to comment on changes they have made.**

Often, children will bring you things or call you over to see things they have shaped and arranged. You can provide support and encouragement by commenting on what you see and the changes children have made:

Trey: Look at my pictures!

Adult: You cut sticky pieces and put them all over.

Trey: This one is a face.

Adult : Oh, yes, I see.

Trey: This one has big pieces and tiny ones. They were hard to get off.

Adult: I saw you working to get the backing off that really tiny piece.

Trey: They're for my dad. (Puts pictures in his cubby.)

Key Developmental Indicator
Observing People, Places, and Things From Different Spatial Viewpoints

"My feet are up. My head is upside-down. I'm on the tallest trapeze," says Abby.

❧

At small-group time, Jacob hides toy animals under a cup. "Where are they?" he asks Isaac. Isaac lifts up the cup. They laugh.

❧

Anna and Jessa stand under the slide. "That's funny. It's not wet under here. The slide blocked the rain," says Anna.

❧

Douglas leans over to look through his legs. "The car is going right through my legs," he observes.

❧

"Uh-oh, Merilee," says Abby from her perch on the climber. "I can't see the babies in the playhouse."

❧

Ian walks two dinosaurs up the climber slide. "Uh, oh," says Abby, "the dinosaurs are back again!"

❧

Nathan and Brianna make "telescopes" out of paper-towel tubes and walk around looking at people through them.

Preschoolers, mobile and dexterous, can get themselves into all kinds of new and unusual positions. They may hang upside-down from climbers, climb to the top of hills and block piles, and crawl around things they have made to make sure they have painted every spot. Moving easily from one location to another, preschoolers begin to notice that as they change positions, things they are used to viewing in a certain way look somewhat different in a new position. "You look different, Peter! I can see your curly hair tops!" Following are ways adults can support children's desire to assume and see things from many physical vantage points.

Suggestions for Adults

▶ **Provide sturdy play equipment.**

Outside. Provide sturdy equipment that allows children to climb and change position, such as swings, climbers, climbing nets, tree stumps, merry-go-rounds, ladders, hills, bridges, slides, tree houses, tunnels, seesaws, wheel toys, tricycles, scooters, a sand pile, a small trampoline, and large inner-tubes.

Inside. Include large sturdy blocks, cardboard boxes, stools, a small stepladder, a rocking boat, and a hammock. If you have a gym or large-motor room, include as many outdoor and indoor pieces of play equipment as possible.

▶ **Encourage children to crawl, roll, bounce, lie on their backs.**

During transitions, small-group time, large-group time, and outside time, encourage children to move in many different ways so they have the opportunity to notice how things look from different physical levels:

• When Sam, L. J.'s teacher, was giving L. J. a piggyback ride to the slide, L. J. said, "Sam, I can see in your pocket!"

• "Swing me around again," Laura said to her teacher, Joanna. "I want to see everything blurry!"

• For small-group time, one teaching team covered the underside of their small-group meeting tables with butcher paper and covered the floor under the table with pillows. The children then lay on their backs on the pillows and drew with markers on the paper above them.

• A group of children were very interested in the cocoons they had found. One day at large-group time, the adult provided large scarves and encouraged children to roll themselves into their own "scarf cocoons."

▶ **Join children in a variety of positions.**

Assume a variety of positions yourself as you play and converse with children. Go down the slide, climb the climber, hang from your hands or knees, roll down the hill, crawl through the tunnel, lie on your back to look up at the sky or ceiling, stand on a tree stump or a bench. Joining children's play in this manner gives you an opportunity to see things from their point of view and provides natural conversational opportunities. In the following exchange, Becki, an adult, and Brianna have climbed to the top of a tire structure:

Brianna: *There're handles up here!*

Becki: *When you climb up here you can see them.*

Brianna: *I see the top of the shed.*

Becki: *Yep, there's the top of our bike shed.*

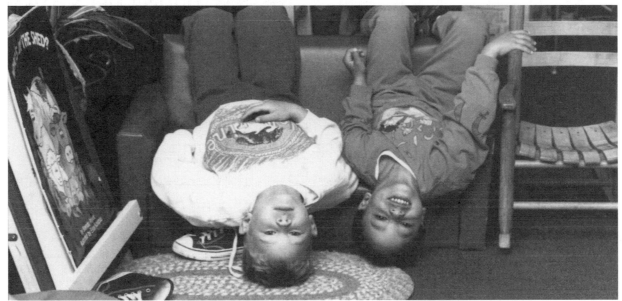

These children take a moment to observe their world by hanging upside down over the edge of the sofa and by looking out from the top of the slide.

Brianna: *Don't ride a bike up there. You'll fall.*

Becki: *That's why we ride bikes on the ground.*

Brianna: *My brother fell off his big bike and he had to have two Band-Aids!*

Becki: *Two Band-Aids! It's a hard job learning to ride a big bike.*

Brianna: *Look at me, Sarah! I'm up here.*

▶ **Take walks with children.**

A neighborhood walk at small-group, large-group, or outside time can provide children with many opportunities for looking at things from different spatial viewpoints. One day, neighbors invited Susan and Joanna to bring their preschoolers to pick grapes from their grape arbor. As they sat in the yard eating grapes, two of the children made these observations:

First Child: *I can still see our school except not the door.*

Second Child: *But we can see it when it's time to go in.*

At small-group time, children observed their classroom from a different point of view.

First Child: We can see it in our yard but not here.

Second Child: I know. 'Cause this place doesn't go to our school.

On a walk around the block at small-group time, Michelle and her children stopped to look at a new house going up. "Look," said Nathaniel, "that man's coming out the window!"

Key Developmental Indicator
Experiencing and Describing Positions, Directions, and Distances in the Play Space, Building, and Neighborhood

"I made you a wacky water present for your birthday," Audie says to Julia. "If you stick it on top it will burst, but if you stick it in the middle it will not burst." (Position)

∽

Abby tells Jackie about her visit to the dentist. "The film goes in my mouth to take a picture of my teeth. It goes in my mouth instead of in the camera." (Position)

∽

"I made a cake with blueberries on top and strawberries on the bottom," says Colin at small-group time, pointing to a stack of poker chips. (Position)

∽

"Look," says Kacey at outside time, "the squirrels are chasing each other behind the bushes." (Position)

∽

At recall time, Jason displays the steamroller he made. "I attached the rollers to the front and back. The smokestack sits in here. The exhaust goes through here." (Position and direction)

∽

Amanda shows Rachel how to tape her box. "Put it [the tape] like this . . . Across and over. Now you try." (Direction)

∽

Jacob shows Eli how to prime the old-fashioned hand pump in their preschool playground. "I'll show you how to get the water in there. You get some water and dump it in, and go like this [pumps handle]. Up and down, and water will come out." (Position and direction)

∽

After coming down the tire tree, Brianna says, "I'm going up again!" (Direction)

∽

"Hey, Julie," Brian says to his teacher. "They came over to ask me the way to the church and I said 'Left to right.'" (Direction)

∽

Outside, Amanda watches a hoop she has rolled. "It's going forward toward the sandbox . . . toward the bench. I'll throw the hoop farther . . . more farther." (Direction)

∽

Douglas and Audie are making paper airplanes. "My plane is heavier," Douglas tells Audie, "so mine will fly farther." (Distance)

∽

"My grandma's is closer to the airport [than is my house]. It's in Boston," Amanda says at snack time. (Distance)

∽

"I'm going to move this closer," says Kenneth, moving his ramp, "so this [a tube] will roll farther." (Distance)

∽

On a walk back from the farmer's market, Callie observes, "We're behind Depot Town!" (Position)

As preschoolers explore and play in familiar environments, they experience and begin to describe *positions, directions,* and *distances* in ways that make sense to them. They are generally more likely to talk about the positions of significant things ("I hammered over the nail") and people ("Sam is in jail under the table") than about directions and distances, which are more abstract.

In an active learning setting children feel free to try out spatial language without fear of correction or ridicule. For example, Colin and Nicholas are sitting next to each other but around the corner at the snack table. "I think you're between," Colin says to Nicholas. "Me, too," agrees Nicholas. "And this is in between of me and you," he says, patting the table corner.

Adults must recognize that children's understanding of spatial terms comes from their own actions and experiences. Children need many ongoing personal experiences with "betweenness" (being between people on the block train, putting butter between slices of bread) before they begin to experiment with the word "between" in their own conversations. Following are ways adults can support young children as they try out and talk about various positions, directions, and distances of familiar people and things.

Suggestions for Adults

▶ **Provide materials children can set in motion.**

Children can arrange and position most of the materials mentioned in this book. In addition, consider materials and pieces of equipment that are specifically designed to be *set in motion.* Keep in mind that small-group time is a good time to introduce such materials. These materials include things with wheels, such as toy vehicles and ride-on toys; things that roll, such as balls,

"Mine's coming into the round house!" As these children play with trains, they experience and describe the positions of their train cars and move them in a variety of directions.

Children experience different positions and directions when using materials and equipment they can set in motion. These children enjoy standing and sitting on the tire swing and pushing it so they go "round and round."

spools, beads, tubes, dowels, marbles, rings, hoops; things that spin, such as tops, pinwheels, board-game spinners; things that drip, such as water, paints, glue; and outdoor equipment that can be moved in a predictable path, such as swings, a merry-go-round, and a seesaw. Such materials and equipment can help children experience and gain an awareness of direction and distance.

▶ **Provide lots of opportunities for children to move.**

Throughout the daily routine, active learners experience positions, directions, and distances with their own bodies and through their actions on objects. In fact, one way a teaching team can evaluate their active learning setting is to look at the *freedom of movement* each part of the daily routine provides for children. If children are required to remain still for any length of time, it may be time to make a change in that part of the routine.

▶ **Converse with children about positions, directions, and distances.**

As you observe and play with children throughout the day, *listen* for cues that may reveal their thoughts about the positions, directions, and distances of things:

Abby: (Holding onto the trapeze with her hands and spinning) *I'm going round and round!*

Abby's spontaneous statement indicates both an interest in spinning and an understanding of what "going around" means. A supportive adult's *comment* at this point can also build on Abby's interest and understanding of "going around" and perhaps sustain a conversation about this child-initiated subject:

Abby: *I'm going round and round!*

Adult: *You're going round and round on the trapeze.*

Abby: (Stops spinning.) *I twisted it. But I can go the other way.* (She twists the trapeze so it will spin in the opposite direction.)

Adult: *Oh. You're twisting it the other way so you can go around the other way.*

Abby: *Watch!* (She spins.) *I'm going round and round!*

Adult: *You're going around the other way!*

Abby: *Whoa, that makes me dizzy! Here I go again!* (She twists the trapeze, lifts her feet off the ground, and spins again.)

Rather than giving directions to children, whenever possible *take directions* from them about positions, directions, and distances. This allows children to put their thoughts into their own words.

Abby: *Now you do it.*

Adult: *Okay.* (Holds onto the trapeze and lifts her feet off the ground.)

Abby: *No.* (Laughs) *You have to twist it first. Twist it tight and then lift your feet up!*

Adult: (Follows Abby's directions.)

Abby: *Now **you're** going round and round!*

▶ **Support children as they encounter and solve position problems.**

Throughout the day, children encounter position problems they must solve using their emerging understanding of spatial relationships. Adults can help children clarify their ideas, as illustrated in the following example:

It is cleanup time. Brian and Deola have put all the long unit blocks on the shelf except for the last one. Brian puts the last one directly on top of the block label (a tracing of a block attached to the shelf where the blocks go). Deola moves the block to the top of the block stack. Brian puts it back on the label.

Deola: *No. It goes here.* (Puts it on the stack.)

Brian: *No. It goes here.* (Puts it on the label.)

(Both children hold on to the block and push each other.)

Adult: *It looks like there's a problem with this block.*

Brian: *It goes on the label.*

Deola: *No, it goes up here with the other blocks.*

Brian: *It goes here.*

Deola: *It goes up here.*

Adult: *So you're saying there are two places for the block. It can go on the stack and it can go on the label.*

(Brian and Deola still hang on to the block.)

Adult: *What do you think?*

(Nobody says anything for a while. Then Brian speaks up.)

Brian: *Sometimes we could put it on the stack.*

Deola: *Sometimes, on the label.*

(The tension dissolves. The children put the block on the stack. When Deola leaves, Brian takes it off the stack, puts it on the label, moves it back up to the stack, and turns to another cleanup task.)

▶ **Encourage children to explore their immediate environment.**

The more children explore and feel at home in their active learning setting, the more likely they are to experience and talk about the *positions*, *directions*, and *distances* that strike them. Here are some ways to encourage such exploration:

Implement the plan-work-recall sequence. During this sequence, as children carry out their own initiatives, it is natural for them to become involved with *positions* ("I want to play at the computers on the one next to Andrew"), *directions* ("Let's pretend you're stuck up here and we climb up the net to save you"), and *distances* ("Let's go to the bridge—it's closer than the trees").

A Caution About Traditional Games With Rules

Many traditional children's games, such as "Follow the Leader," "A Tisket, a Tasket," "Duck, Duck, Goose," "London Bridge," and "Simon Says," by their very nature, involve children in working with *positions, directions,* and *distances.* However, 3- and 4-year-olds are not particularly bound by the rules that guide early elementary children. Playing such games with preschoolers works best in small, intimate groups when children are free to be the leader, if a leader is called for, and to make up their own directions, movements, and variations. One group of preschoolers, for example, played "Duck, Duck, Goose" with half of the children as ducks and half as geese, so everyone was active each round. After several rounds, the "ducks" and "geese" traded roles.

Value cleanup time. Even though cleanup time sometimes seems to take forever, remember that as they return toys to their shelves, children deal in a natural, functional way with the position and location of items.

Go on walks with children. At small-group, large-group, or outside time, take walks around the inside and outside of the building, around the block, to the park, to see the neighbors' flowers, to watch the workers at a nearby construction site. As children become familiar with these walks, and the sights along the way, they often incorporate them in their everyday play and conversations: "Let's make big stairs like the ones that go up and up at the big house." "Let's pretend we go under the pear tree like we did over at Mrs. Ross's house."

Key Developmental Indicator
Interpreting Spatial Relations in Drawings, Pictures, and Photographs

Jonah is making a picture about a trip to the zoo. "I saw ducks. See," he says, pointing to ducks in his drawing, "there are a lot in the pool."

∽

"Look," Amanda says about her painting, "I took off my skin. Then you take off your blood and your pipes and then you're at your bones."

∽

"You know why you can't see his other arm?" Trey says to Peter as they look at Trey's drawing, "because they're together like this." Trey puts his arms together to demonstrate.

∽

Alana looks at a photograph of planning time. "I was sitting right over here," she says, pointing to a spot just outside the photo.

⌐◦⌐

"It's a mess up," Jason says, looking at his drawing. "The neck's curved so the body should be over there."

⌐◦⌐

Kenneth looks at a photograph of greeting circle. "There's the clock," he says, "so that wall was behind me."

Most preschoolers like to look at pictures and photographs of familiar things and places and often spontaneously identify things that strike them: "There are the monkeys with the caps!" However, they are just beginning to notice and comment on *where things are* in drawings and photographs. In many children, the capacity to discuss positions in pictures emerges soon after they begin to make their own representational pictures. When they see or have created a picture that is personally meaningful to them, children sometimes stop to ponder a spatial detail that catches their attention: "The exhaust goes out through here," Jason says, pointing out the tailpipe on the car he has drawn. Following are ways adults can support children who are beginning to examine and comment on spatial relations they notice in drawings, paintings, and photographs.

Suggestions for Adults

▶ **Provide a wide variety of pictorial materials.**

Children respond with interest to materials with pictures related to their experiences at home, in preschool, and in the community. As they browse through picture books, magazines, catalogs, and photo albums; use computer software programs; and look at drawings, paintings, and books they have made, children sometimes comment on the location of whatever they are viewing.

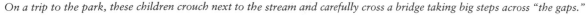
On a trip to the park, these children crouch next to the stream and carefully cross a bridge taking big steps across "the gaps."

► **Provide materials for children to make their own pictures.**

An art area that is accessible and well stocked (see art area materials list in Chapter 5) enables children to make their own drawings and paintings at work time as well as find the materials they may need for picture-making at recall and small-group time.

► **Provide opportunities for children to draw at recall time.**

When children draw at recall time, after outside time, or following a field trip, they will sometimes include and comment on significant spatial details:

• In the drawing at right that Trent created during one recall time, he notes that some of the bears are on the plane and some of them are off the plane.

• One day, Jonah brought four drawings he had made to recall time. "This one isn't a picture," he told his recall group. "It's a map." This was the beginning of a conversation involving Jonah, Betsy (the teacher), and the other children in the group concerning Jonah's map as well as other maps the children had seen. The next day, the teaching team added some maps to the house area, and several other children, along with Jonah, became involved in map-making. Over the next several months, the conversations about maps, places, and directions continued as children made and played with maps and brought maps to recall.

► **Display photos and drawings of block structures.**

Occasionally, children will see a photograph or a picture of a block structure and decide to build one "just like the picture." Once children

As he described his drawing, Trent noted the position of the bears in relation to the airplane. His teacher wrote down what he said.

set this task for themselves, they automatically become involved in interpreting the spatial relations in the drawing or photo they are working from. "Let's see. I need a big block on the bottom . . . and a long one across here." Some children may view these photos and pictures and decide to add their own details and variations, rather than following the "blueprint" exactly.

► **Look at picture books with children.**

As you look at a book with a child and listen to his or her comments about the pictures, you can discover what attracts the child's attention, and you can listen for references to spatial relations: "Those monkeys up in the tree. They don't want to throw down their caps!"

► **Take photographs of children in action.**

Keep a camera handy. This allows you to take pictures of children throughout the day. If you take photographs on a regular basis, children become used to the camera and continue their play rather than stop to pose.

Take photographs of the shaping and arranging process. As young children shape and arrange materials, they generally focus on the present state of the materials they are using. Taking a series of photographs of children engaged in shaping and arranging things gives them a chance to see and perhaps comment on the changes they made along the way. "These [pipe cleaners] are straight . . . Here's twisted ones . . . I stuck loops in the Play-Doh!"

Take photographs from different spatial viewpoints. At outside time, take photographs from the top of and underneath the climber, from the swing and the slide, inside the tunnel, lying in the grass or on a blanket on the blacktop. Inside, take photographs from under the table, while sitting on a sturdy block tower, or looking across the water table. Take photographs of classroom objects and of things the children have made from a variety of viewpoints.

Make photographs available to children. Pass the photographs out at greeting circle or small-group time. Listen to and support children's comments and observations about what they see: "This is funny. There's just grass and the bottoms of shoes!" At the end of small-group time, have children put their photos in an album and put the album in the book area so children can look at the photos whenever they want.

The teacher began small-group time by reading a picture book about snow. Here, a child talks with the teacher about how she arranged the "snow" on her glue picture.

Space Strategies: A Summary

Filling and emptying
___ Provide materials for filling and emptying.
   ___ Continuous materials for pouring
   ___ Discrete materials
   ___ A variety of containers and scoops
   ___ Computer software
___ Watch for children's filling and emptying play.
___ Imitate children's actions.
___ Anticipate repetition.

Fitting things together and taking them apart
___ Provide materials that fit together and come apart.
   ___ Commercial materials
   ___ Common household materials
___ Provide materials children can use to make things that fit together and come apart.
___ Provide time for children to work with materials on their own.
___ Support children as they solve fit problems.
___ At recall time, encourage children to talk about things they put together and took apart.
___ Include fit-together, take-apart materials at small-group time.

Changing the shape and arrangement of objects (wrapping, twisting, stretching, stacking, enclosing)
___ Provide materials to shape and arrange.
   ___ Blocks
   ___ Paper and cloth
   ___ Clay and dough
   ___ Rubber bands and elastic
   ___ Thread, string, yarn, ribbon, rope, wire, and pipe cleaners
___ Support children as they rearrange things to solve problems.
___ Listen for children's awareness of how they are shaping and arranging things.

Having a picnic calls for unfolding and spreading out the picnic blanket.

___ Take cues from children to comment on changes they have made.

Observing people, places, and things from different spatial viewpoints
___ Provide sturdy play equipment.
   ___ Outside
   ___ Inside

___ Encourage children to crawl, roll, bounce, lie on their backs.
___ Join children in a variety of positions.
___ Take walks with children.

Experiencing and describing positions, directions, and distances in the play space, building, and neighborhood
___ Provide materials children can set in motion.
___ Provide lots of opportunities for children to move.
___ Converse with children about positions, directions, and distances.
   ___ Listen.
   ___ Comment.
   ___ Take directions from children.
___ Support children as they encounter and solve position problems.
___ Encourage children to explore their immediate environment.
   ___ Implement the plan-work-recall sequence.
   ___ Value cleanup time.
   ___ Go on walks with children.

Interpreting spatial relations in drawings, pictures, and photographs
___ Provide a wide variety of pictorial materials.
___ Provide materials children can use to make their own pictures.
___ Provide opportunities for children to draw at recall time.
___ Display photos and drawings of block structures.
___ Look at picture books with children.
___ Take photographs of children in action.
   ___ Keep a camera handy.
   ___ Take photographs of the shaping and arranging process.
   ___ Take photographs from different spatial viewpoints.
   ___ Make photographs available to children.

References

Flavell, John H. 1963. *The Developmental Psychology of Jean Piaget.* Princeton: Van Nostrand.

Furth, Hans G. 1969. *Piaget and Knowledge: Theoretical Foundations.* Englewood Cliffs, NJ: Prentice-Hall, Inc.

Gardner, Howard. 1983. "Spatial Intelligence." Chap. 8 in *Frames of Mind: The Theory of Multiple Intelligences,* 170–204. New York: Basic Books.

Piaget, Jean. 1956. *The Child's Conception of Space.* London: Routledge and Kegan Paul.

Related Reading

Epstein, Ann S. 2007. "What Is the High/Scope Curriculum in Mathematics?" Chap. 14 in *Essentials of Active Learning in Preschool: Getting to Know the High/Scope Curriculum,* 149–58. Ypsilanti, MI: High/Scope Press.

Epstein, Ann S., and Suzanne Gainsley. 2005. "Space." In *Teacher's Idea Book: "I'm Older Than You. I'm Five!" Math in the Preschool Classroom,* 109–37. Ypsilanti, MI: High/Scope Press.

Gardner, Howard. 1991. *The Unschooled Mind: How Children Think and How Schools Should Teach.* New York: Basic Books.

Graves, Michelle. 2005. "Young Children and Math." "Motivated Mathematicians." In *Supporting Young Learners 4: Ideas for Child Care Providers and Teachers,* Nancy A. Brickman, Holly Barton, and Jennifer Burd, eds., 119–32. Ypsilanti, MI: High/Scope Press.

Herman, James F., Jon Shiraki, and Beth Miller. 1985. "Young Children's Ability to Infer Spatial Relationships: Evidence from a Large, Familiar Environment." *Child Development* 56, no. 5: 1195–1203.

High/Scope Educational Research Foundation. 2003. *Preschool Child Observation Record (COR),* 2nd ed. Ypsilanti, MI: High/Scope Press.

Hirsch, Elisabeth S., ed. 1984. *The Block Book,* rev. ed. Washington, DC: NAEYC.

Hohmann, Mary, Bernard Banet, and David P. Weikart. 1979. "Spatial Relations." Chap. 11 in *Young Children in Action,* 238–65. Ypsilanti, MI: High/Scope Press.

Keating, M. B., B. E. McKenzie, and R. H. Day. 1986. "Spatial Localization in Infancy: Position Constancy in a Square and Circular Room With and Without a Landmark." *Child Development* 57, no. 1: 115–24.

Liben, Lynn S., Marta Moore, and Susan Golbeck. 1982. "Preschoolers' Knowledge of Their Classroom Environment: Evidence From Small-Scale and Life-Size Spatial Tasks." *Child Development* 53, no. 5: 1275–84.

Newcombe, Nora S., and Janellen Huttenlocher. 2000. *Making Space: The Development of Spatial Representation and Reasoning.* Cambridge, MA: MIT Press.

During work time, these children play with a wooden take-apart-and-put-together vehicle.

A train, train tracks, and a tunnel provide opportunities for fitting things together and taking them apart, changing the shape and arrangement of things, and experiencing and describing positions, directions, and distances.

Piaget, Jean, and Barbel Inhelder. 1960. *The Psychology of the Child*. New York: Basic Books.

Pontius, Anneliese A. 1983. "Links Between Literacy Skills and Accurate Spatial Relations in Representations of the Face: Comparisons of Preschoolers, School Children, Dyslexics and Mentally Retarded." *Perceptual and Motor Skills* 57, no. 2 (October): 659–66.

Somerville, Susan C., and P. E. Bryant. 1985. "Young Children's Use of Spatial Coordinates." *Child Development* 56, no. 3: 604–13.

Steiner, Gerhard. 1987. "Spatial Reasoning in Small-Size and Large-Size Environments: In Search of Early Prefigurations of Spatial Cognition in Small-Size Environments." In *Piaget Today*, Barbel Inhelder et al., eds., 203–16. London: Lawrence Erlbaum Associates.

Tompkins, Mark. 1996. "Spatial Learning: Beyond Circles, Squares, and Triangles." In *Supporting Young Learners 2: Ideas for Child Care Providers and Teachers,* Nancy A. Brickman, ed., 215–22. Ypsilanti, MI: High/Scope Press.

Related Media

The following materials are available from the High/Scope Press, 600 N. River St., Ypsilanti, MI 48198-2898; to order, visit *www.highscope.org*, or call 1-800-40-PRESS.

Space and Time (Early Math). 2004. Color videotape or DVD, 44 min.

Children discover knowledge about the physical world using all their senses. Organizing and classifying are science skills that begin to develop as children notice similarities and differences in objects and begin to group them accordingly.

Children are naturally curious; they pose questions about how the world works, they make observations, and they then use the information they collect to answer their questions. In this way, they **construct knowledge** about the principles and systems that govern daily life and the universe at large. We can encourage young children to engage in this ongoing process of investigation and discovery. Specifically we can guide them as they discover two important building blocks of **science and technology.**

Classification, the process of grouping things together based on common attributes and properties, is covered in this chapter, and **time** is the subject of Chapter 18. Many of the key developmental indicators in these two chapters parallel the National Council of Teachers of Mathematics (NCTM) early childhood standards for measurement and data analysis (NCTM 2000).

Why Early Science and Technology Development Is Important

Early science is more than memorizing information about the biological and physical world. Curriculum developers and researchers Rochel Gelman and Kimberly

> "The operations of classification originate essentially in active behavior."
> —*Inhelder (1969, p. 36)*

Brenneman point out that "to do science is to predict, test, measure, count, record, date one's work, collaborate and communicate" (2004, p. 156). In other words, science is as much about the investigative process as it is about knowing facts and formulas. And science also uses math, literacy, and social skills.

Educators are increasingly recognizing the appropriateness of introducing science as a distinct content area in the early childhood curriculum. Israeli professors Haim Eshach and Michael Fried (2005) argue that young children should be exposed to science for many reasons, and first among these is that children naturally enjoy observing and thinking about nature.

A hundred or more years ago, science was primarily the study and classification of nature. As chemistry and physics took their place alongside biology, science became increasingly concerned with how things change when acted upon in different ways, a process sometimes called **transformation.** Children too, are interested in observing and sorting objects and in understanding what happens to them.

Learning About the Attributes of Things— A Child's View

In order to classify objects children must first learn about their attributes, a process that begins in infancy. Infants explore with their mouths and discover that some things

Classification

Classification is said to exist when two or more distinguishable objects are treated equivalently.
— Susan Sugarman, 1981

are pleasant to suck on; they notice and respond to familiar voices; as they explore with their hands and feet, they discover different touch sensations and movement qualities.

After a period of sensorimotor explorations, young children discover the capacity for what Jean Piaget (1962/1951, 1965/1941) describes as *intuitive thought*; that is, preschool-aged children have the ability to form conclusions and plan actions based on immediate physical impressions.

Sorting, a basic classification activity, often occurs in children's play as a means to an end: they may sort out all the metal cars to play with, or all the red beads to string. They may find it satisfying to group identical things together. At cleanup time, they may enjoy putting all the small blocks on on shelf and all the triangle blocks on another.

Exploring attributes of things, and *sorting and matching* are ways young children construct their understanding of the physical and social world. Young children's ways of organizing and communicating their observations are largely intuitive and, hence, unique: "We just need the long squares." "Only little kids sleep in boxes." "I only get married when it's dark." Nevertheless, these early experiences in classification are essential to their development of logical thought.

Supporting Children's Classification Experiences and Discoveries

Eight classification key developmental indicators (KDIs) provide a picture of the way young children sort out and organize their observations. The first five can usually be observed in preschoolers' play:

- Recognizing objects by sight, sound, touch, taste, and smell

- Exploring and describing similarities, differences, and the attributes of things

- Distinguishing and describing shapes

- Sorting and matching

- Using and describing something in several ways

The three remaining indicators involve a more rigorous logic that is most likely just emerging in older preschool-aged children:

- Holding more than one attribute in mind at a time

- Distinguishing between "some" and "all"

- Describing characteristics something does not possess or the class it does not belong to

Adults can begin to introduce children to science and technology by providing play experiences that involve classification. As adults observe and join children whose play includes classification experiences, they seek to understand each child's particular intuitive logic rather than impose their own logic on children. As professional educators, adults are responsible for establishing a psychologically safe, and hence logical, environment for children. At the same time, however, they also understand the importance of valuing and accepting children's intuitive explanations, even if these explanations are inaccurate by adult standards. The sections that follow on each classification KDI

give adults ideas about how to support children's developing logic in appropriate ways.

Key Developmental Indicator
Recognizing Objects by Sight, Sound, Touch, Taste, and Smell

On the playground, Mikey hears a siren. "A policeman is coming!" he tells Sam.

Julia takes a sip of juice at snack time. "This has pineapple in it," she says.

Without looking up from her block play, Chelsea hears Beth reading a story on the sofa. "I know who's reading," Chelsea says to Corrin. "Beth." "Yep, she is," Corrin confirms.

Petey sees the head of a pig on the computer screen and says, "The pig is coming up!"

∽

"Look," says Kacey to Sarah at the art table. "I made footprints with my fingers!"

∽

"Who's playing the recorder?" Brian asks, looking around the room. "Oh, it's Julie."

Classification begins as children develop internal rules for treating things the same or differently; they begin to sort and organize. In order to develop these rules, they first learn to recognize objects, especially to recognize them from their indices or sensory clues—the way things sound, feel, taste, smell, and look when partially hidden. For example, the sight of a handle protruding from sand may trigger images in the child's mind of a shovel; a loud roar overhead, an airplane; a spicy aroma, time for lunch; a wet foot, a puddle; a bandage, yesterday's fall; a shadow, the sun.

To interpret a sensory cue, a child must have experience with the object or event in question. A child who hears a tambourine but has never encountered one may imagine that bells are producing the jingling sound. A child in a basement room may not notice how light and shadow are affected by weather and time of day. The more direct experiences children have with objects and events, the more confident they become as "readers" of tell-tale sensory cues. A bootprint in the snow means somebody's been out walking. A brown jacket on Tommy's hook signals that he is here today.

Adults can help children develop their classification skill by looking for everyday opportunities for children to enjoy and talk about sights, sounds, tastes, textures, and smells they encounter.

Eating foods with a variety of tastes may cause a child to pause and wonder, "What kind of juice is this?"

Suggestions for Adults

▶ **Provide materials with distinctive sensory features.**

In your early childhood setting, take stock of the materials you currently provide for children. Examine the interest areas for materials with distinctive visual features as well as for things with noticeable textures, sounds, smells, and tastes. Here are some examples:

• **Parts of things.** Steering wheels, hubcaps; feathers from local birds; doorknobs, faucet handles; book jackets; empty food containers, bottle caps; buttons, shoelaces; leaves, branches, sticks, and nuts from neighborhood trees

• **Things that create light and shadow.** Flashlights and covers of different color and density; shapes and colored cellophane taped to windows; movable lamps; curtains and blinds that can be opened and closed

• **Covers and things to cover up.** Sand (straw, snow, pea gravel) and things to bury in sand (shells, stones, rubber animals and people, small toy vehicles, shovels, buckets, containers), blankets, large scarves and dolls, stuffed animals

• **Things with distinctive textures.** Bark, logs, stones, straw, grass, gourds, plants; sandpaper, bricks; dress-up clothes in a variety of fabrics; cotton balls, natural wool, twine, leather

• **Aromatic things.** Plants, flowers, animals; cooking equipment and spices; modeling beeswax; windows that let in outdoor smells

• **Things that make noise.** Musical instruments (see the list on p. 141), voice recorder; timers that tick and ring; computers with appropriate software; workbench and tools; noisy things to pour and fill with, such as pea gravel, stones, beads, bottle caps; running water, hoses, tubs, or a water table; bird feeder

• **Foods with a variety of tastes.** Fresh fruits and vegetables; a variety of seeds and grains both raw and baked in breads and muffins; a variety of dairy products; and a variety of condiments

▶ **Provide opportunities for children to notice sensory cues.**

Provide and take advantage of opportunities throughout the day for children to **notice and identify sounds, partially hidden objects, smells, and textures.** Consider these strategies:

• At snack or mealtime, cover the basket of fruit (muffins, nuts, crackers) with a napkin so the pieces of fruit are partially hidden. As a child passes the basket around, converse with children about what they think is in the basket.

• As you cook with children, encourage them to smell and taste the ingredients. Listen to and comment on their observations.

• As sounds occur throughout the day—birds chirping, dogs barking, block towers toppling, doors opening and closing, water running, balls bouncing—comment on them to the children near you and listen for children's comments.

• At the end of work time, when children are returning things to the shelves, suggest that they look for the blocks, for example, that are "hiding" under the table.

• Record children's voices and other sounds at work time, and play and discuss the recoding at recall time. Listen to children's comments and talk with them about their observations.

• Have children bring materials to recall time that they used at work time. After children

have had a chance to talk about and examine everyone's materials, cover all the materials with a blanket. Have all the children reach under the blanket at the same time (so no one has to wait) and figure out what they are feeling. Anticipate that some children will be able to do this without looking, while others will need to "peek" under the blanket.

• Provide memory-game software for children to use.

• Outside, encourage children to observe how sunlight affects colors and shadows, to notice what happens when the sun goes behind a cloud, how shadows and tree branches move when it's windy, how the presence or absence of foliage affects what we see. Listen to and comment on their observations.

▶ **Notice and make imprints and rubbings with children.**

Imprints and rubbings are special forms of sensory cues because they can only be made by using the objects themselves. It takes a foot to make a footprint, for example, and a leaf to make a leaf rubbing.

Imprints. Look for opportunities at work time and outside time to join children as they play with sand, clay, Play-Doh, plaster, fingerpaints, snow, leaves, mud. If they have made imprints, comment briefly about what you see ("You made a print with the potato masher, Delila") and try making a similar imprint yourself. Imitating and commenting on the child's actions may lead to a conversation about prints that fits in with, rather than disrupts, the child's play.

Plan small-group times around materials children can use to make prints. For example, meet at the sand table or outside in the sandbox; provide water for each child to moisten his or her

patch of sand and ask children how they might make prints in the sand. Watch, imitate, and comment on each child's work. Try the same procedure, starting with different materials such as clay, fingerpaints, or snow.

Rubbings. Plan small-group times around materials children can use to make rubbings. For example, meet outside and provide the children with paper, chalk, and something to put under their paper, such as a leaf. After children have made their first rubbings, ask them what else they could put under their paper and then chalk over. Listen to children as they work, make some rubbings yourself, comment on what you see them doing, and be ready to follow their conversations wherever they lead. Children may also decide to carry their paper and chalk around the playground to make rubbings of trees, the side of the building, the slide steps, and so forth.

Key Developmental Indicator
Exploring and Describing Similarities, Differences, and the Attributes of Things

Jonah has filled a cup with paper and cloth pieces and has taped it closed. He shakes the cup: "It doesn't make a sound. It has only quiet things in it!"

∾

"Oh, it's so soft!" Kacey says, feeling the shaving cream on her hands.

∾

"You can use half my tray," Jacob says to Jared, as he draws a line on the tray with his finger. "This side is yours and this whole wide, wide part is mine."

∾

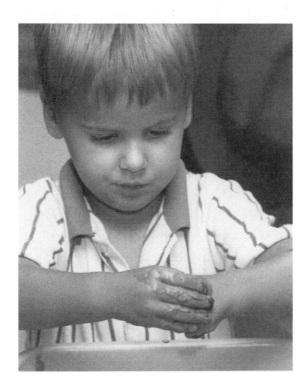

This child explores the way tempera paint feels when he rubs it on his hands as if it were soap.

"Mice have little teeth and little hands,"
Jalessa tells Peter after singing "Three Blind Mice."
∽

Brian and Alana are flattening Play-Doh to make hand prints. "Do it on the smooth side," Brian advises.
∽

"That's the same as our dinosaur puppet," Alana observes, looking at pictures of puppets in a toy catalog.
∽

"You and Sam both have glasses," L. J. tells Peter at snack time.
∽

"Your hair is dark black today," Erica says to her teacher, who had dyed her hair the night before.
∽

"I look different," says Kenneth, looking in the mirror. "I colored my nose!"

Preschoolers are seasoned explorers as well as emerging conversationalists. They sometimes stop to reflect on their actions and comment on significant attributes of things they are playing with. A particular texture, sound, movement, or design becomes personally useful or meaningful to preschoolers, and they begin to understand in their own way the similarities and differences that exist between things: "You can't see green [marker] on green [paper]!" "Something is different. You moved the block shelf!" Following are ways adults can support and encourage children's thinking as they explore and describe the attributes, similarities, and differences they encounter as they play.

Suggestions for Adults

▶ **Provide interesting materials.**

Preschool children investigate and talk about materials they find personally intriguing. Therefore, to encourage children to explore attributes, provide materials that will interest them. These might include *household and natural materials with attractive characteristics* (shaving cream, baby oil, foil, sandpaper, wrapping paper, crêpe paper, stones, nuts, shells), *materials with moving parts* (tools, kitchen utensils, musical instruments, cameras), and *materials that change* (clay, Play-Doh, computer drawing programs, sand, water, animals, insects). (Chapter 5 contains lists of all kinds of materials that are attractive to preschoolers.)

It is also important to consider *materials specifically related to children's immediate purposes*, such as boxes for building forts, telephone books for playing office, or nails for pounding. In this regard, one teaching team made these observations about Ric, one of their preschoolers:

Ric is intrigued with objects he can control, operate, and change so he can see the results immediately—water and a sponge, a flashlight, a metronome, anything in squeeze bottles, a wind-up clock, balloons, balls, and screw-together toys. These are the kinds of things we could use at small-group time and add to the interest areas.

▶ **Support children as they collect things.**

Preschoolers are natural collectors of things that appeal to them. Supporting this inclination is a way to understand what attributes attract children's attention.

Make time for collecting. Outside on the playground, on walks around the block, and on field trips, allow time for children to examine and collect things that attract their attention. For example, on a walk up a local hill to see the view, one teaching team was struck by the children's desire to stop, examine, and collect things along the way, such as ants, discarded papers and cans, bits of charred wood "you can draw with," pebbles, and sticks. Arriving at the top of the hill to see the view was not nearly as interesting to the children as stopping to look at all the things along the way.

Listen for children's comments and descriptions. No matter how ordinary the things children notice and collect may appear to adults, these "treasures" are the things children are very apt to talk about and describe: "This is a humongous rock," says Audie, using both hands to pick it up. Alana finds some magic markers on the sidewalk: "Look what happened! They have no tops. They're gonna dry out!" Other children are fascinated by the living things they encounter:

At small-group time, these children explore and describe the way shells look and feel.

"This bug's waving his legs . . . he's trying to turn over." "Hey, this bush smells like a Christmas tree, and it's not even snowing!"

▶ **Accept the descriptive names children use for objects.**

Children's own names for things give adults an idea of what attributes they are noticing. At outside time, for example, Abby found a worm and put it in a cottage-cheese container to take home. "But," she told Jackie, her teacher, "I have to put some oil-dirt on it." "Oh," said Jackie, "oil-dirt. What's that?" "You know," Abby told her, "dirt that has its own water."

In Beth's and Becki's program, children often used Styrofoam packing bits in their artwork and pretend play. Some children referred to them as "popcorns," focusing on the material's structural resemblance to popped corn, while other children called the material "white squishes," apparently focusing on their color and texture.

▶ **Encourage children to make labels for new materials.**

Throughout the year, children find and collect things they want to add to the classroom, and adults also introduce new materials. Asking children to make the labels for these new materials provides a natural opportunity for them to focus on specific attributes. In one program, a child labeled a bucket of chestnuts she had collected by taping a piece of the chestnut casing to the outside of the bucket. In another setting, a child made a label for the basket of new multicolored beads by making dots with colored magic markers.

▶ **As children solve problems, listen for their references to attributes, similarities, and differences.**

Listening to and supporting children's problem solving will often provide another perspective on their understanding of the attributes of the things they are using. Here are some examples:

• Kacey and Trey were both playing with the plastic dinosaurs. Kacey wanted the large triceratops Trey was playing with. "Trey," she said, "I need that one with the three horns because I have the baby one [with the three horns] and it needs its mommy." Trey paused to consider Kacey's request. Kacey continued, "If you give me the mommy, you can have all the yellow ones." "Okay," Trey agreed, handing over the triceratops and gathering up all the yellow dinosaurs.

• Corrin and Anna were playing "bees." Some other children joined them in the block area and began to build a house. But when the house builders started using two particular kinds of blocks, Corrin exclaimed, "Wait! We need to use the cylinder blocks for honey cakes and the long triangle blocks for stingers!"

• Douglas was showing some other children how to make "fliers" [kites]. As he showed them where to tie the string, he also advised them, "Get the yarn with the three colors in it. It's less fuzzy than the other yarn."

- "I want the scoop," Jason tells Tara. "I'm using it," she replies. "But I need it for digging," responds Jason. Tara replies, "You can have it when I'm done." Jason answers, "But I need it to dig now 'cause the sand is falling in." Ann, a nearby adult, joins the children's conversation. "What can you do about this scoop problem?" she asks. Both children are quiet for a moment. "He could dig with something else 'til I'm done," Tara suggests. Jason looks around. "I can use a spoon . . . but then I want the scoop, 'cause it's big."

Key Developmental Indicator
Distinguishing and Describing Shapes

"Find the long squares!" Trey advises Brianna as they play a shape-sorting game on the computer.

☙

Lying on her back at nap time, Abby counts the corners of the room. "Hmmm," she muses, "four corners. It must be a square." "How many corners does a circle have?" her friend Robert whispers. Abby answers, "One, right in the middle." "Right in the middle," Robert agrees.

☙

Kenneth walks around a circle he has made on the floor using wooden spools. "Hey," he says, "we could listen to 'Wheels on the Bus' 'cause they go round and round!"

☙

"Want a sandwich?" Anna asks, offering "sandwiches" made from matched pairs of square, triangular, and circular attribute blocks.

☙

Jacob paints a square. "Look," he announces. "I made a block!"

☙

"It looks a little bit like a triangle," Rachel observes, as she studies her block structure.

Shape is one of many physical attributes of interest to preschoolers as they play. Children enjoy using regularly shaped blocks because these blocks make satisfying building materials that can be stacked and balanced. Preschoolers are also struck by the regular shapes they generate as they paint, glue, shape, and arrange things: "I made a circle!" They also notice irregular shapes: "It's kind of like a triangle but it's a little bit round!" Following are ways adults can support children's interest in shapes.

Suggestions for Adults

▶ **Provide a variety of regularly shaped materials.**

Consider providing these and similar regularly shaped materials: blocks, boxes, carpet pieces, plates, lids, food containers, cookie cutters, blankets, scarves, towels, rings, bracelets, buttons, beads, bottle caps, cards, books, dominoes, Tinkertoys, shape-sorter shapes, attribute blocks, Cuisenaire rods, pieces of wood, tambourines, triangles, and wood blocks.

Many teaching teams provide a collection of regularly shaped collage materials in the art area: pieces of paper, cloth, sandpaper, card-board, ribbon, netting, Styrofoam, balsa wood, foam rubber—all cut into circles, triangles, rectangles, and squares for children's everyday use.

▶ **Use regularly shaped materials at small-group time.**

At small-group time, watch to see how children use regularly shaped materials—for example, collage materials, attribute blocks, or buttons and food containers. Listen for their comments and observations about shapes.

▶ **Watch for shape-making play.**

In certain types of play, children often generate their own shapes—during movement and dance games, when drawing and painting, when making a collage, when playing with clay and Play-Doh, when coloring with chalk on outdoor blacktop surfaces, when working with wood at a workbench, and when playing with sand. Observing children closely during these kinds of activities will often tell you something about their understanding of and interest in shapes. Consider this episode as an example:

One day, Pookie and Angie needed a "round dancing stage," so they got the masking tape and began to lay out their stage on the floor. Pookie led the way with the tape and Angie followed, walking on the tape "to make it stick." When the girls finally got back to their starting place, they stopped to look at their stage. They saw that it was "too crooked" to be a round stage but decided they could still use it for dancing.

▶ **Listen for shape talk.**

As children make collections of favorite materials, play with regularly shaped objects, and make their own shapes, listen for what they have

In the art area, this child decides to make a circle by gluing pompoms to a sheet of paper.

to say about shapes. Keep in mind that children's thought processes and willingness to share their discoveries are much more important at this age than the accuracy of their conclusions, which will improve with time and experience.

- "That will be fifty cents . . . . Some of the round [money] and some of the square."

- "I need a triangle, two—no three—triangles for my crown."

- "I almost made a circle track but it [a marble] stopped at the corner."

Key Developmental Indicator
Sorting and Matching

Tracy fills a pegboard with red pegs on one half of the board and yellow ones on the other. "Birthday cake," he says to Linda. "Candles. Blow!" And they do.

ↄ

Kacey sorts through all the streamers until she finds the green one that matches her green shirt.

ↄ

Douglas goes around the room gathering metal things "for the magnet to stick to."

ↄ

Julia is playing doctor. Looking over the "patients" in her "waiting room," she tells them, "Class A means you're better. Class B means you're still sick."

ↄ

Isaac puts all the design cubes back in their box so all the pink sides are facing up.

ↄ

Alana builds a block house with two rooms. She puts the "girl people" in one room and the "boy people" in the other.

ↄ

Noah sorts out the red and blue snap-together blocks, then builds a house with the blue blocks on one side and the red ones on the other.

ↄ

Aimee puts small plastic bears into an ice-cube tray—first a pair of red bears, then a pair of blue bears, then a pair of green bears, and finally, a pair of yellow bears.

ↄ

Trey matches the M on the computer screen to the M on the keyboard, then types a whole row of M's.

ↄ

Kristan builds two block towers that are exactly the same.

ↄ

At small-group time, Jason selects all the rectangle blocks and lines them up along the edge of the rug.

As they play, preschoolers sort and match materials to fulfill their own purposes. They create their own ways of grouping things as they sort through pegs, blocks, bears, or dollhouse people to find just the ones they want. Because they can form mental images, they can hold one attribute in mind, such as "red" or "*M*-shaped" or "metal," to organize the red pegs, the *M*'s, or the "things that stick to magnets." Following are ways adults can support children as they sort and match within the context of their play.

Suggestions for Adults

▶ **Provide materials for sorting and matching.**

If you have set up an active learning environment following the guidelines for appropriate materials presented in Chapter 5, you have provided abundant materials to sort and match in each of your interest areas: sets of toys such as blocks, Tinkertoys, cars, trucks, toy animals, and dollhouse people; and collections of nuts, stones, shells, pine cones, buttons, marbles, bottle caps, beads, pegs, collage materials, crayons, markers, food containers, silverware, dishes, scarves, ties, hats, gloves, cards, tools, musical instruments, and balls. Encourage children to bring in collections of things they find outside, at home, or on field trips to the grocery store, market, farm, hardware store, lumber yard, or greenhouse. Also, provide art and building materials children can use to make similar things (for example, clay balls, paper "tickets," and pipe-cleaner bracelets) that they can group into collections and sort and match. If you have computers, provide appropriate software programs that call for sorting and matching. For a listing of such programs, see the monthly magazine *Children's Technology Review* (*www.childrenssoftware.com*).

► **Consider times for choosing and storing toys as ongoing opportunities for children to sort and match materials.**

The way the space is divided and the materials are stored in an active learning setting presents children with daily opportunities to sort and match. As they carry out their plans, children collect the materials they need, use them according to their own purposes, and then return them to their storage places so they will be able to find them the next time they need them. Storing similar materials in well-organized spaces so children can easily find and return them means that children are involved in sorting and matching every time they gather or put away the materials they need.

Keep in mind that the containers and shelving you choose will encourage specific kinds of sorting. Divided storage containers such as silverware trays involve children in sorting such items as forks, knives, and spoons or green, yellow, and blue pegs. Baskets and undivided containers mean separating things into larger groups—all the crayons together in one basket, all the markers together in another. An open shelf labeled with

a catalog picture of dollhouse furniture encourages children to sort and arrange the furniture as they desire and also to change their arrangements from day to day. Labeling materials in a variety of ways also involves children in a variety of sorting and matching experiences. Labels such as a tracing of a block or a photograph of a basket of puppets encourage children to match the blocks to the tracing or the basket of puppets to the photograph.

Allowing children to decide where to store new materials provides another opportunity for them to think about and make sorting and matching decisions based on similarities and differences.

► **Watch for and acknowledge children's spontaneous sorting and matching.**

In an active learning setting, children sort and match materials as a natural part of their play. The anecdotes at the beginning of this section (p. 450) are real-life examples of sorting and matching that alert and interested adults observed as children worked and played. When children finish what they are doing or pause to look at their work in progress, it is often possible for adults to converse with them about the sorting and matching decisions they are making. Consider the following example:

As they make up a story using flannel-board cutouts, these children group the flowers together, the leaf clusters together, and the rocks together.

After a trip to the hardware store, Chris looked through the fliers and brochures she had collected, then cut out and pasted pictures of doorbells onto a sheet of yellow paper. As Chris examined her doorbell collage, Linda, her teacher, joined her.

"This is the one I'd like for my door," Linda said, pointing to a star-shaped fixture.

"I like this one because it's on my daddy's [Air Force] uniform," Chris replied.

"It looks like wings."

"It is wings on his uniform!"

Next Chris found two series of doorbell pictures, many of which were identical. After she added them to her collage, she caught Linda's eye and Linda joined her again.

"You've added some more doorbells, Chris!" Linda said.

Chris nodded and pointed to two that were the same. "These could be for the same door . . . in case one got broken!"

"They could be for the same door. Let's see . . . maybe these two flowered ones could be for another door," Linda suggested, pointing to another identical pair.

"I know!" said Chris, proceeding to connect all the doorbell pairs with different-colored lines.

▶ **Ask children to make things that are the same.**

When you see children making things that are similar or identical, you might try this idea to encourage similar experiences at small-group time. Provide each child with a set of art or building materials, such as blocks, clay, pipe cleaners and wire, or collage materials. Ask children to make some things that are the same, then watch closely to see what they do. Though some children will choose to do something else with the materials, others will become involved in making identical or similar creations. Joey, for example,

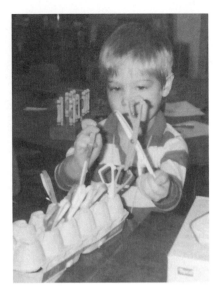

Cleanup time provides a natural opportunity for children to sort and match!

made two quite similar figures out of pipe cleaners and wire. "I made two boys," Joey said. "But this one's a little bit sad 'cause his leg is hurt. . . see where it's bended."

Key Developmental Indicator
Using and Describing Something in Several Ways

"Brrum, brrum, round and round. Brrum, brrum, round and round," Corey chants as he drives his dump truck. A few days later he uses the same truck to haul blocks. "Down dumper," he says, as he pushes the "dumper" down and all the blocks spill out. "Up dumper," he says, as he reverses the process.

～

Darla plays with some plastic interlocking building squares, experimenting with how they fit together. "Slots . . . punch the slots together . . . hmmm, it looks green through these . . . ," she says to herself. Another day, Darla uses the same squares as windows in a house she is building.

～

Lisa stands on a large hollow block so she can reach the easel more easily. Later, at recall time, Lisa brings the block to her group and shows how she stood on it. Then she turns it on end and uses it for her chair for the rest of recall. "You found two ways to use that big block," Linda, her teacher, comments.

～

At small-group time, Lainie and Athi talk about the pine cones they are using: "Look, my pine cone rolls!" says Lainie. "Mine stands up!" answers Athi.

～

At snack time, Douglas and Sarah vigorously stir their pudding with their spoons. The next day at work time, Douglas shows Sarah how to build a catapult using a spoon, a triangle block, and a plastic apple.

As children play and carry out their plans in an active learning setting, they discover through their own actions and observations that they can use most materials in a variety of ways.

This realization strengthens their understanding of the various attributes of objects and enables them to be flexible and creative in using materials to solve everyday problems. Here are some ways adults can support children's growing ability to use and describe things in several different ways.

Suggestions for Adults

▶ **Be aware of the various ways children use materials.**

In an active learning setting, children are free to explore materials and discover their many uses. They find that blocks are not just for building. They also make great chairs, telephones, and weights for propping doors open. Scarves, another versatile material, are used by children for capes, wings, baby blankets, roofs, dog leashes, and bandages for "broken arms."

Observe children's use of materials. Sometimes children work with the same materials for days or weeks at a time. This provides a natural opportunity for adults to watch for all the different uses children find for the materials. When Anna and Jessa played "bees" one winter, they used blocks to build the walls of their "hive" and also to represent "stingers" and "honey cakes." They sat on blocks, slept on blocks, jumped off blocks, and built block tables. They used block ramps to roll the "honey cakes" out of the "hive." They balanced blocks on their "wings." They taped bee messages to blocks. They taped blocks to their feet so they wouldn't get "stuck to the honey."

Acknowledge children's uses of materials. "Look at us, Beth! We've got bee shoes!" Anna calls out, pointing to the blocks taped to her feet. "You taped blocks to your feet for bee shoes!"

Beth acknowledges, taking a close look at Anna's and Jessa's uniquely secured shoes.

Refer one child to another. Whenever possible, refer one child to another for observations about materials:

• Deola makes a pair of paper shoes at the computer, cuts them out, and then cannot figure out a way to keep them on her feet. "Maybe you could talk to Anna and Jessa about how they kept their bee shoes on their feet," Beth suggests.

• At the computers, where several children are working, Peter, an adult, comments to Andrew, "It looks like Trey used thick lines."

• As children finish working with found materials at small-group time, Beth, their teacher, comments, "Mikey put his white squishes in a bag, Sarah pasted hers, and Alana stuck hers together with toothpicks!"

▶ **Support children's use of materials in problem solving.**

Sometimes children solve problems they encounter in play by finding alternative uses for materials. Supporting children at these times not only strengthens their sense of initiative and efficacy but also their understanding of attributes and how things work. In the situations that follow, Kacey finds a new use for gloves, while Audie discovers he can use boxes in place of blocks:

• "Kacey," Andrew says, bringing her the stuffed bunny he is playing with, "will you fix my bunny's ankle?" Kacey looks around for a moment, then takes off one of her long white gloves and ties it around the bunny's leg.

This child discovers another use for socks—"sock mittens!"

• Audie is building a rat house but needs more wooden blocks. "Becki," he says to his teacher, "I need more blocks!" "You sure do," she agrees. "But," Audie says, "everybody's using 'em!" "Well, that's true," Becki agrees. "I wonder if there is something else you could use instead." Audie looks around and spots cardboard boxes he and his friends had used earlier in the week to make a "ride-in" train. He chooses two of the boxes to complete his rat house.

Key Developmental Indicator
Holding More Than One Attribute in Mind at a Time

"I'll push you higher and faster," Callie says to Andrew, who is on the tire swing. After a few pushes Andrew says, "I am going higher and faster!"

∾

"Puppies are little dogs," Deola tells Sam during a snack-time conversation about pets.

∾

*"You have to have pink **and** purple in your mittens if you want to push the tire swing with me and Corrin," Kenneth tells Brian.*

∾

After soaking up some water with a sponge, Douglas looks at his sponge and says, "It's wet and heavy."

∾

"I knew that piece fit," Hannah explains to Betsy after completing the dog puzzle, "because it had the same color on it and the same shape."

∾

"Pumpkins are large and scary," Trey tells Peter at greeting circle one fall morning.

∾

Hannah sorts a group of colored magnetic shapes of various sizes on the magnet board. She makes one grouping and says, "These are all the biggest shapes and they're all blue!"

There are times when preschoolers focus simultaneously and briefly on two attributes of a personally meaningful object or experience. For the moment, they are moved to stretch their usual "either/or" thinking to "both/and" considerations. During the same day, however, they may vacillate between both kinds of thinking. For example, several children were noticing and talking about their skin colors, and Troy said that his skin was brown. However, later in the day at snack time, one of the children said to Troy, "You're brown," and Troy replied, "No I'm not. I'm African-American." Following are ways adults can support young children as they begin to hold in mind more than one attribute at a time.

Suggestions for Adults

▶ **Listen for children's references to more than one attribute at a time.**

As children use materials, listen for comments and observations they make about more than one attribute at a time. Since this is an emerging capacity in most preschoolers, do not be surprised if a child mentions two characteristics but then attends to just one:

In the block area one day, Amanda points out a block she has used for a "special" chair. *"It's square and it's blue," she tells Rose, one of her teachers. "It is square and blue," Rose agrees. When Amanda adds some other "special chair" blocks, some are blue but not square, some are square but not blue, and some are blue and square. Amanda's only comment upon lining up her new "chairs" and arranging the rest of the people on them is, "These special chairs are just a little bit special."*

▶ **Try using labels that encourage children to sort a set of materials according to two attributes.**

Keep in mind that this strategy may not work; on the other hand, it may be worth trying just to see what children do. Here is what happened in one center: Because their children were so interested in dinosaurs, one teaching team added a set of plastic dinosaurs to the toy area. The dinosaurs came in two sizes (the children called them "mommies" and "babies") and four colors (blue, yellow, green, and purple). At first, the team stored all the dinosaurs in one basket, but after observing that children often referred to the dinosaurs' size and color, they made a new storage box. It had four *large* storage cubicles on one side and four *small* storage cubicles on the other. The inside of each of the large and small cubicles was either blue, yellow, green, or purple. The teachers put the big blue dinosaurs in the big blue cubicle, the small blue dinosaurs in the small blue cubicle, and so forth.

On the first day of using the new storage system, one of the children said, "Look, the dinosaurs have beds!" The new storage box was well received. Over time, as they watched children clean up the dinosaurs, the teaching team observed that some children sorted the dinosaurs according to both size and color. Other children sorted either by size or color but not both; of these children,

Some children enjoy the challenge of labels that encourage them to sort according to two attributes. This child, for example, puts away a dress-up shoe that has "low heels" and "laces."

some figured out how to fit the big dinosaurs into the little "beds" by standing them on their heads.

▶ **Appreciate the complexity of children's guessing games.**

As they grow older, some preschoolers become interested in guessing games and riddles. Since these guessing games require them to hold a number of mental images and meanings of words in mind at once, they can be quite a challenge. Following are one teacher's observations during a guessing game with Becky, Lisa, and Trina:

Becky began a guessing game using the lotto cards. She'd hold one against her so I couldn't see the picture and say "Guess what this is." Lisa and Trina joined in once they understood the game.

When I asked questions such as, "Is it an animal? A plant? Something you wear? Something you ride on?" Becky generally answered appropriately. Once, when I asked, "Is it a fish?" she answered, "No," because she knew that the specific fish on her lotto card was a shark. When she had a picture of an ear of corn and I asked if it was a plant, she said no, but when I asked her if it was something you could eat, she said yes. "Oh, it's corn," I said as she showed me the picture, "a plant you can eat." "No," she said, "you can't eat plants. Plants are green things in the ground!"

Becky also provided clues to her pictures: "It flies." "It goes in the water." "Something you can roll on" [roller skates]. "Something you are and something else" [a person and a dog].

When I held a lotto card for her to guess, Becky asked questions such as, "Is it an animal?" I gave her a clue, "It's something you ride on." "Car, truck, bus," she guessed. "It doesn't have wheels," I told her. When she finally looked at my picture and saw a sailboat, she said, "Boats

In the course of their play, these children discuss several attributes of cylinder blocks: "You can roll it on your head but do it gently 'cause it's hard." "You can hold it under your chin and it smells like . . . sand!"

Once she saw her picture, her main goal was to tell us what it was as soon as possible.

Trina could answer questions about her pictures as long as she knew what they were. She might be more successful using real objects rather than lotto-card pictures. I think I'll make some lotto-like cards with real objects attached to them (such as a key, leaf, stone, nail) and look for an opportunity to play this game with her again. She and Becky might also become interested in making their own guessing cards.

Key Developmental Indicator
Distinguishing Between "Some" and "All"

On the tire swing, Chelsea has an idea: "All the kids with sandals, stand up! All the kids with tennis shoes sit down!"

⌒

"I don't want all your Legos," Ben tells Petey, so Petey gives some of the Legos to Ben and puts the rest away.

⌒

At recall time, Hannah talks about a Lincoln Log house she made with Claire: "I didn't put on all the pieces. Claire put on some."

⌒

"Some went in but not all," Andy observes, after pouring marbles into a small shoebox.

⌒

"Let's make a whole big airplane and use *all* of them [blocks] and that could be for recall!" Kristan says to Sarah.

⌒

have wheels—you just can't see them 'cause they're on the bottom of the sea."

Lisa was so focused on her picture that she had little patience with the guessing part of the game. When I asked her for a clue about her picture she told me what it was and showed me the picture. One time I asked her, "Is it an animal?" "No," she replied, "it has stripes. It's a zebra!"

Trina had a picture of a hat and coat from a band uniform. When I asked her if it was something to wear, she said no. She finally showed us the picture, saying "I don't know what this is." Becky

decided it was "a drummer's coat." When Trina had a picture of a watermelon, and I asked if it was something you could eat, she said, "Yes, it is."

As I look back on this game, I see that my sailboat clues for Becky were too obscure. Better ones would have been these: "Something you sail on" or "Something that goes on the water." I was also fascinated by her belief that boats have long legs with wheels that ride along the ocean floor keeping them on top of the water! Lisa, the youngest player, really enjoyed being with her friends and being part of the game.

Jonah plays with bears and Play-Doh at work time: "Some bears are here and some bears are under [the Play-Doh]. I can't fit all the bears under!"

Preschoolers are beginning to see the relationship between parts of a set (some of the blocks) and the whole set (all of the blocks) and are beginning to use the terms "some" and "all" appropriately. Their understanding is based on their experiences with sets of materials such as blocks, marbles, and crayons, and their judgments about "some" and "all" are based on appearances. For preschoolers, the set of "all the blocks," for example, generally includes all blocks in the can or on the shelf rather than all the blocks in the building, the toy store, or the world. "All" generally stands for "all [the crayons] I can see" while "some" generally indicates "The ones I want or need." Following are ways adults can support children's emerging and still very personal understanding of parts (some) and wholes (all).

Suggestions for Adults

▶ **Store similar materials together.**

Storing similar materials together in the interest areas encourages children to think about "some" and "all" each time they choose and return the toys and things they need for play. A child who plans to make a drawing looks at the entire collection of magic markers and decides whether to use all of the colors or just some of them. A block builder wonders, "Do I need all the cardboard blocks for my house or some of the cardboard blocks and

some of the wooden blocks?" Upon returning materials, a child must decide, "Do all the scissors go back in this can or do some scissors go in this can and some in the other can?" "Did I get all the chestnuts back in the canister or have I missed some?"

▶ **Listen for children's use of the words "some" and "all."**

As children find, use, and return materials during their play both indoors and outside, listen for their use of "some" and "all." For example, one adult heard this conversation at work time as children gathered around the sandbox:

Abby: *Shh! The bears are asleep.*

Hannah: *Not all the bears are asleep. Just a few.*

Abby: *Let's cover the sleeping bears, then the other ones can get up, okay?*

When this child showed her creation at recall time, she reported, "I used some of the bottle caps."

Hannah: *Okay, and when these guys wake up, let's pretend they all go swimming!*

Abby: *Yeah, but what if they get drowned?*

Hannah: *Well some of them know how to swim and they have a boat . . .*

Later on at recall time, Rose, their teacher, said to Hannah and Abby, "I heard that all your bears were going swimming." "Well," Hannah reported, "it snowed, so they went sliding instead." "And ice fishing," Abby added.

Key Developmental Indicator
Describing Characteristics Something Does Not Possess or the Class It Does Not Belong To

"I don't want that truck. It doesn't have any wheels," Corey says.

∾

"Look!" Jeff holds up the two halves of the apple he has just cut apart. "This part has seeds and this part has no seeds."

∾

Looking at Anna's picture, Becki comments, "You used all the colors." "Not brown!" replies Anna.

∾

"I live in Northfield," Jacob tells Betsy. "It's the brown house, not the yellow one."

∾

Chelsea says to the children using the tire swing, "All the kids with hoods stand up! All the kids with no hoods sit down!"

∾

Outside, Martin has made a collection of small stones. He spits on each one and examines it carefully. He puts the stones that change color when they are wet into one bucket and the stones that do not change color when they are wet into another bucket.

∽

Deola finds a wooden inch-cube among the wooden beads and says, "It doesn't have a hole. It doesn't belong here!"

Dealing with absent attributes or characteristics ("does not have wheels," "no hoods") calls upon two developing capacities in young children—forming mental images and thinking about two things at once. These are complex thought processes for preschoolers. Corey's statement shows that he has pictured a truck with wheels in his mind and compared it to the truck whose wheels are missing. To sort children into the "no-hoods" group, Chelsea has to pick out an attribute that some children's clothing has—"hoods"—and then mentally place all the remaining children in the group without hoods. Following are ways adults can support children in describing characteristics something does not possess ("does not have seeds") and the class it does not belong to (the "no-hoods" group).

Suggestions for Adults

► **Encourage children to use the symbol for the "no" concept.**

The ∅ is the international symbol for "No . . . ." Many children have seen this symbol used on "No Smoking," "No Dogs," or "No Left Turn" signs. Once children have experience with this symbol, they enjoy "reading" it and using it on their own. Therefore, teachers Beth and Becki started using the ∅ on their message board. For example, when Beth was away for the day, Becki drew Beth's face (with medium-length hair and glasses) with the ∅ over it on the message board. The children quickly figured out that this meant, "No Beth today."

Later on in the year, when the children in this class discovered that the hill on their bike path was too steep for the red bikes, Andrew got some red chalk and drew a bike with a ∅ over it on the blacktop at the top of the hill. The children found it very satisfying to ride the red bikes to the top of the hill, stop, read "No red bikes on this hill," turn around, and ride off in another direction. In another instance, when Douglas got tired of being "stung" by "bees" during Jessa and Anna's bee play, he drew a bee with

a ∅ over it and taped it to the entrance of the toy area where he was playing. The "bees" read his sign and flew off to more receptive parts of the room.

▶ **Watch and listen for children's everyday use of "not."**

As children work and play, listen for moments when they are struck by an attribute something does not possess or by a group to which it does not belong:

• Corrin decided to bathe the baby dolls, but she realized that some dolls were not suitable for getting wet. So, she put all the "washing babies" on the table and all the "not-for-washing babies" in the bed.

• One day Kenneth wrote   B e t h
                               K e n n e t h
on a piece of paper and said to Beth, "We both have E-T-H, but I don't have a B and you don't have K and N."

• When Mikey arrived one morning, he looked at all the coathooks and noticed that some children had worn coats and some children had not. Then he found the symbols of all the children who came without coats and showed them to Becki. "Corrin didn't wear a coat. Petey didn't wear a coat. Alana didn't wear a coat," he said, "reading" the symbols in his hand. "You found all the no-coat kids!" Becki commented.

Classification Strategies: A Summary

Recognizing objects by sight, sound, touch, taste, and smell

___ Provide materials with distinctive sensory features:
- ___ Parts of things
- ___ Things that create light and shadow
- ___ Covers and things to cover up
- ___ Things with distinctive textures
- ___ Aromatic things
- ___ Things that make noise
- ___ Foods with a variety of tastes

___ Provide opportunities for children to notice sensory cues.

___ Notice and make imprints and rubbings with children.

Exploring and describing similarities, differences, and the attributes of things

___ Provide interesting materials.

___ Support children as they collect things.
- ___ Make time for collecting.
- ___ Listen for children's comments and descriptions.

___ Accept the descriptive names children use for objects.

___ Encourage children to make labels for new materials.

___ As children solve problems, listen for their references to attributes, similarities, and differences.

Distinguishing and describing shapes

___ Provide a variety of regularly shaped materials.

___ Use regularly shaped materials at small-group time.

___ Watch for shape-making play.

___ Listen for shape talk.

Sorting and matching

___ Provide materials for sorting and matching.

___ Consider times for choosing and storing toys as ongoing opportunities for children to sort and match materials.

___ Watch for and acknowledge children's spontaneous sorting and matching.

___ Ask children to make things that are the same.

Using and describing something in several ways

___ Be aware of the various ways children use materials.
- ___ Observe children's use of materials.
- ___ Acknowledge children's uses of materials.
- ___ Refer one child to another.

___ Support children's use of materials in problem solving.

Holding more than one attribute in mind at a time

___ Listen for children's references to more than one attribute at a time.

___ Try using labels that encourage children to sort a set of materials according to two attributes.

___ Appreciate the complexity of children's guessing games.

Distinguishing between "some" and "all"

___ Store similar materials together.

___ Listen for children's use of the words "some" and "all."

Describing characteristics something does not possess or the class it does not belong to

___ Encourage children to use the symbol for the "No" concept (∅).

___ Watch and listen for children's everyday use of "not."

Observant adults find examples of sorting and matching in children's play. These children, for example, sort and match flannel-board flowers as they create a story together.

References

Eshach, Haim, and Michael N. Fried. 2005. "Should Science Be Taught in Early Childhood?" *Journal of Science Education and Technology* 14, no. 3: 315–36.

Gelman, Rochel, and Kimberly Brenneman. 2004. "Science Learning Pathways for Young Children." *Early Childhood Research Quarterly,* no. 1: 150–58.

Inhelder, Barbel. 1969. "Some Aspects of Piaget's Genetic Approach to Cognition." Reading I in Hans G. Furth, *Piaget and Knowledge: Theoretical Foundations,* pp. 22–40. Englewood Cliffs, NJ: Prentice-Hall, Inc.

Inhelder, Barbel, and Jean Piaget. 1964. *The Early Growth of Logic in the Child: Classification and Seriation.* New York: W. W. Norton & Company.

National Council of Teachers of Mathematics (NCTM). 2000. *Principles and Standards for School Mathematics.* Reston, VA: Author.

Piaget, Jean. 1951. *Play, Dreams, and Imitation in Childhood.* Reprint. New York: W. W. Norton, 1962.

Piaget, Jean. 1941. *The Child's Conception of Number.* Reprint. New York: W. W. Norton, 1965.

Sugarman, Susan. 1981. "The Cognitive Basis of Classification in Very Young Children: An Analysis of Object-Ordering Trends." *Child Development* 52, no. 4: 1172–78.

Related Reading

Epstein, Ann S. 2007. "What Is the High/Scope Curriculum in Science and Technology?" Chap. 15 in *Essentials of Active Learning in Preschool: Getting to Know the High/Scope Curriculum,* 159–66. Ypsilanti, MI: High/Scope Press.

Epstein, Ann S., and Suzanne Gainsley. 2005. "Classification." In *Teacher's Idea Book: "I'm Older Than You. I'm Five!" Math in the Preschool Classroom,* 19–47. Ypsilanti, MI: High/Scope Press.

Flavell, John H. 1963. *The Developmental Psychology of Jean Piaget.* Princeton: Van Nostrand.

Gardner, Howard. 1983. *Frames of Mind: The Theory of Multiple Intelligences.* New York: Basic Books.

Ginsburg, Herbert, and Sylvia Opper. 1969. *Piaget's Theory of Intellectual Development.* Englewood Cliffs: Prentice-Hall, Inc.

Graves, Michelle. 1996. "Classification: Collecting, Sorting, and Organizing." In *Supporting Young Learners 2: Ideas for Child Care Providers and Teachers,* Nancy A. Brickman, ed., 207–14. Ypsilanti, MI: High/Scope Press.

Graves, Michelle. 2005. "Successful Science: Starting With Children's Curiosity." "All in a Day's Science." In *Supporting Young Learners 4: Ideas for Child Care Providers and Teachers,* Nancy A. Brickman, Holly Barton, and Jennifer Burd, eds., 153–66. Ypsilanti, MI: High/Scope Press.

Graves, Michelle. 2005. "Young Children and Math." "Motivated Mathematicians." In *Supporting Young Learners 4: Ideas for Child Care Providers and Teachers,* Nancy A. Brickman, Holly Barton, and Jennifer Burd, eds., 119–32. Ypsilanti, MI: High/Scope Press.

High/Scope Educational Research Foundation. 2003. *Preschool Child Observation Record (COR),* 2nd ed. Ypsilanti, MI: High/Scope Press.

Hohmann, Mary, Bernard Banet, and David P. Weikart. 1979. "Classification." Chap. 8 in *Young Children in Action,* 191–216. Ypsilanti, MI: High/Scope Press.

Kofsky, Ellin. 1968. "A Scalogram Study of Classificatory Development." In *Logical Thinking in Children,* Irving Seigel and F. H. Hooper, eds., 210–24. New York: Holt.

McCabe, Ann, Linda Siegel, Ian Spence, and Alex Wilkinson. 1982. "Class-Inclusion Reasoning: Patterns of Performance From Three to Eight Years." *Child Development* 53, no. 3: 780–85.

Piaget, Jean, and Barbel Inhelder. 1969. *The Psychology of the Child.* New York: Basic Books.

Post, Jacylyn. 1996. "Science: Here, There, and Everywhere." In *Supporting Young Learners 2: Ideas for Child Care Providers and Teachers,* Nancy A. Brickman, ed., 193–200. Ypsilanti, MI: High/Scope Press.

At the workbench, this child selects "only nails" to use on his airplane wing.

Related Media

The following materials are available from the High/Scope Press, 600 N. River St., Ypsilanti, MI 48198-2898; to order, visit *www.highscope.org,* or call 1-800-40-PRESS.

Classification, Seriation, and Number (Early Math). 2003. Color videotape or DVD, 52 min.

Preschoolers experience time very concretely as they anticipate and recall sequences of events, such as peeling bananas, mixing them in the blender, and drinking "banana smoothies"; and as they experiment with stop-and-start activities and making objects move at different speeds.

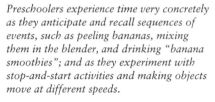

18

Time

Grasping time is tantamount to freeing oneself from the present.

—Jean Piaget, 1927

T he concept of **time** is so important to understanding science and technology and to understanding the physical universe that it needs a chapter of its own.

Although time is an abstract concept (you cannot see, hear, touch, taste or smell time), preschoolers' thinking about time is grounded in concrete experiences in which they actively use all their senses:

- "Mikey's been gone for a long time," Trey says at greeting circle, missing his friend who is absent for the third day in a row.

- "I lost my milk bottle this year about three weeks ago!" Brian tells Alana, as he describes a significant event that occurred several days earlier.

Preschoolers like Trey and Brian are beginning to construct their own personal sense of time. This is quite an achievement for young children.

Adults measure time objectively, using clocks and calendars. This time measurement system is based on the movements of celestial bodies: Our days are measured by the rotation of the earth on its axis once every 24 hours, while our calendar year is based on the orbiting of the earth around the sun once every 365 days. When we consider how removed this time measurement system is from the daily experiences of most preschoolers, it comes as no surprise that they do not find clocks and calendars meaningful and that their understanding of time is based on personal experience. Time really does "stop," "fly," or "crawl" for young children, depending on what they are doing.

The Development of an Understanding of Time

A lthough it may take many years for preschoolers to understand time the way adults do, several fundamental capacities for understanding time are emerging in the preschool years. Because preschoolers are able to keep mental images in mind, they can remember and talk about things that happened in the past and anticipate things they want to do in the future. This emerging awareness of time sequences is a marked change from an infant's one-dimensional concept of time— that things exist only in the present. Psychologist John Phillips (1969) explains that for infants "time is limited to that which encompasses a single event, such as moving a hand from leg to face, feeling the nipple and beginning to suck, or hearing a sound and seeing its source" (p. 20).

Preschoolers, while still very focused on the present, can recall the past and think about the near future. In studying children's conversations relating to time, educator Lorraine Harner (1981) found that preschoolers "have mastered some of the rudiments of the ordered system of past, present, and future relations. They have a basic understanding of events as preceding or following the present moment in which they are speaking" (p. 503).

Preschoolers' participation in events such as birthdays, holidays, trips, and weekends forms the basis for their growing intuition about time sequences: "I only need one more day," Jonah says at greeting circle. "One more day after today and I get a toy. I'm going to get a ninja guy. I make 'em fight and kill all the bad guys."

Preschoolers also form their own ideas about the length of time—long times and short times—based on their experiences of both waiting and feeling rushed: "You have to wait a while for me to get it started," Jason tells Colin, as he tries to get a top to spin. As active members of families and communities, preschool children engage in experiences that encourage them to think *in their own way* about time intervals. Seconds, minutes, and hours have little meaning to preschoolers, but they live in a social world where adults also refer to time in ways that young children can interpret from their own experiences—"bed time," "cleanup time," "party time," "spring time," "time to go."

With language at their command as well as the ability to hold mental images in mind, preschoolers often express their own ideas about time:

• "The moon is up," says Trey. "That's why it's night."

• "It's almost snow time," Abby muses, "because the leaves are coming off the trees." (She pauses.) "Or maybe people are pulling them off. That's not good for the trees."

Some preschoolers make the meaning of time more concrete by bringing an object or toy from home to remind them of the people they will return to at the end of the day. They may also have to deal with such major life events as births, divorces, and deaths, which may challenge and reshape whatever notion of time they have already constructed: "We flied to my Granny's,"

Kelli tells Karen, her teacher. "Uncle James died, but he was old and sick. Children aren't that old yet." As their old routines shift and change, children may struggle to adjust to new routines and re-set their internal clocks: "Friday is my Daddy day. This is not the last day of the week yet," Abby says. "Friday is." Because of the events in her life, knowing when Friday will occur becomes personally meaningful for Abby.

Supporting Children's Understanding of Time

The **four time key developmental indicators (KDIs)** describe the ways preschool children are experiencing and are beginning to understand time. The first three KDIs deal with the *duration* of time:

• **Starting and stopping an action on signal**

• **Experiencing and describing rates of movement**

• **Experiencing and comparing time intervals**

The last one involves time *sequences*:

• **Anticipating, remembering, and describing sequences of events**

Adults who are aware of these **time** KDIs understand that preschool children experience and conceive of time in very personal ways and that children's measurement of time has little to do with the standard time units of clocks and calendars. Rather, children relate time intervals and the passage of time to familiar events, places, and feelings. Lunchtime, for example, occurs when

you are at the lunch table. Further, if something *seems* to be a long time, it *is* a long time.

Adults also understand that in an active learning setting, the daily routine is built around supporting children's intentions and is designed to give children control over what they do with their time. They realize that children are less anxious and more confident when they can work at their own pace and are not rushed or pushed to complete activities at the same time or within certain time limits. When time does run out, adults help children plan to continue their activities some other time either that day or the next day. Following are suggestions on how to support young children as they construct a basic understanding of time *duration* and *sequences*.

Key Developmental Indicator
Stopping and Starting an Action on Signal

"Stop!" says Lynnette, holding the toy stop sign in front of Markie's truck. "Okay, go," she tells him, moving the stop sign aside.

∽

Kenneth skips some pages in his book so he can finish "reading" it before the end of the book-time part of greeting circle.

∽

"When the alarm clock goes off," Sarah (the "mom") tells Jalessa (the "sister") "we have to get up. We have to do our hair."

∽

"Five times up, Jacob," says Jason. "I turned it [the sand timer] over five times so it's my turn now!"

∽

This child holds the stop sign on his head to signal the end of work time. "Stop playing," the sign announces in this case. "It's time to clean up!"

"It will shut off by itself," Abby says, holding her hands under the automatic hand dryer. "It's magic."

"You can have the bike in twenty minutes," Mikey tells Audie. He gets on, rides around the bike path for two laps, and gets off. "Now it's yours, Audie!" he says.

"We're almost done," says Alana, as she and L. J. grind cooked apples in a food mill to make applesauce. "We're done!" says L. J. a few minutes later. "No more sauce is coming out."

Brian hands Erica a cup of "cocoa." "It's hot," he warns her. "Wait till it cools down."

Stopping and starting an action on signal is one concrete way preschoolers experience *time intervals*. Sometimes in pretend play, as with Sarah and Jalessa, children incorporate stopping-and-starting experiences they have had with stoplights, kitchen timers, and alarm clocks. They also make up their own stopping-and-starting signals for taking turns—such as Mikey's two laps around the bike path. Some children also begin to notice that certain actions—for example, grinding cooked apples through a food mill to make applesauce—have a definite beginning and ending, and that some stopping-and-starting points involve such judgments as deciding when a liquid is cool enough to drink. Following are ways adults can support children's interest in stopping and starting.

Suggestions for Adults

▶ **Provide materials children can use to signal stopping and starting.**

Children enjoy exploring and playing with *timers* they see adults using at home. This includes egg timers, sand timers, mechanical kitchen timers that tick and ring, and alarm clocks. Remember that children generally spend lots of time shaking and tipping over sand timers and making mechanical timers ring before they satisfy their curiosity and begin to use these objects as timing devices.

Musical instruments and voice recorders allow children to signal stopping and starting times at will. "Joanie, when I beat on this drum, you dance, okay?" asks Joey. "I stop, you stop."

You can also provide materials so children can signal when parts of the routine begin or end. A child can hit a metal bowl with a spoon to mark the start of a meal or hold up a series of signs for a "cleanup countdown" (5, 2, and 0 minutes to go). Using each signal consistently and assigning turns for these jobs on a job chart allow children to have more control over changes in activities.

▶ **Let children know when time periods begin and end within the daily routine.**

Through the daily routine, children regularly experience time intervals that stop and start in a consistent sequence. Knowing the order of

These children play a streamer stop-and-start game they made up at work time.

the daily routine, and which events signal the beginning and end of each time segment, gives children a sense of anticipation and control. Here are some sample signals to consider:

• **Greeting time**—Begins as the first children arrive. Ends after everyone has "read" and talked about the message board when an adult asks a child to decide how to move to the planning tables.

• **Work time**—Begins as each child starts his or her plan. Ends five minutes after adults give a verbal five-minute warning and ask a child to ring the cleanup bell, sing the cleanup song, or play a cleanup musical selection.

• **Large-group time**—Begins when the first adult and child leave the snack table and sit on the floor in the block area. Ends after the story when an adult says, "Let's get dressed for outside time!"

▶ **Sing, dance, and play musical instruments together.**

Since people often sing, dance, and play instruments together, doing these things in large and small groups provides natural opportunities for starting and stopping on signal. At large-group time, for example, one group of children and teachers combined music and dancing by having children take turns playing an instrument while everyone else danced. The children agreed that they would start and stop dancing when the drummer or the bell ringer started or stopped playing. Children took turns being the instrument player and deciding how long the dancing should last. This same group made up their own version of musical chairs. While one child played an instrument, the others moved quickly around a circle of chairs. When the instrument player stopped, the children quickly sat down on the available chairs. The person who did not find a chair exchanged places with the instrument player. (The number of chairs in the circle remained constant—one less than the number of runners. No other chairs were removed. Thus, every child was always an active participant in the game.)

▶ **Watch for and support children's interest in stopping and starting.**

One place to watch for stopping and starting experiences is in children's pretend play. Often, when children build large cars and trains, they let their riders know when to "get on board" and when to "get off." In one preschool center, children were very excited about a local car race that was scheduled to occur on the weekend. Since the teachers knew one of the drivers, they invited him to visit the center, and he brought his racing car and wore his racing clothes. Then, over the weekend, many of the children attended the race with their families. The following Monday, the teachers brought in the Sunday newspaper with photographs of the cars, the track, and the crowd, which the children examined and talked about at greeting circle. Over the next several months, the children built race tracks in the block area and cut out paper flags to signal the beginning and end of their car races. At outside time they set up their own races using white, black,

and red streamers to signal "go," "stop for gas," and "the winner!" Taking note of the children's interests, the teaching team planned several small-group times around making drawings of the race and models of race cars.

Key Developmental Indicator
Experiencing and Describing Rates of Movement

"Hey," says Corey, looking at the end of his glue bottle, "this glue isn't coming out very fast!"

∾

Becki gives the five-minute warning for the end of work time. "Maybe I should make this map quick," says Jessa.

∾

Jason flies his airplane around the room, making a high-pitched engine noise when his plane flies fast and a low-pitched engine noise when his plane flies more slowly.

∾

"Mommy can get to my school faster than Daddy," says Kelli, "'cause her work is closer."

∾

Douglas is making a rapid series of dots on his paper. "I can do twenty thousand in one minute," he says.

As they move and play, preschool children begin to notice the rates at which things move: "That helicopter's going fast," says Abby, watching the propellers go around in a blur.

Preschoolers are also pleased with their own ability to move at different rates: "Let's sneak up on Beth!" "Watch how fast I can put on my coat." "We better hurry up with this puzzle 'cause it's almost cleanup time." Following are ways adults can support children's growing interest in rates of movement.

Suggestions for Adults

▶ **Provide materials children can set in motion.**

Children have the opportunity to explore their own ideas of "fast" and "slow" as they use materials they can set in motion. Such materials include objects with wheels and objects that roll, spin, and drip.

Also, rocking chairs, rocking horses, swings, seesaws, and rocking boats enable children to experience different rates of periodic movement. These experiences help them develop an awareness of basic time units. For example, the regular forward-and-backward movement of a rocking horse is similar to the regular ticking of a clock. Each movement is a way of measuring time. Children are not actually measuring time as they rock and swing, but they do have the opportunity to internalize the physical feeling of regular, equal time units. (See also the section on Feeling and Expressing Beat in Chapter 13.)

Computer drawing programs also permit children to draw and erase at whatever speed they wish. When they are exploring a new program, many children tend to work quickly. As they become familiar with the computer equipment and the possibilities of each software program, their rate of movement tends to decrease as they draw with increasing precision and control.

▶ **Provide opportunities for children to move at different rates.**

It is important that children have the opportunity to move at their own pace throughout the daily routine. Some children look at books quickly; others linger over each page. Some children dress themselves rapidly, while others take half of outside time to get into their coats, hats, scarves, boots, and mittens. During work time, some children move from one type of play to another, while others remain in one place doing one thing. For example, at the easel, one child paints with slow, deliberate strokes while another child quickly completes two paintings and is off to the block area.

Play fast and slow music. As you play music at cleanup time, transitions, and large-group time, include selections with varying tempos. Quick-tempo marches and dance music can inspire rapid cleanup. On the other hand, there are days when "nap-tempo" music helps children slow down and focus on their cleanup tasks.

Re-enact stories that incorporate different rates of movement. Such stories as "The Gingerbread Man" include movement instructions: "Run, run as fast as you can. You can't catch me, I'm the Gingerbread Man!" As another example, one group of preschoolers repeatedly requested a story one of their own members had made up about how horses stood in the barn and went to sleep. The children found the slow movements of this story very satisfying to act out.

Encourage children to pour their own juice and milk. Pouring from child-sized pitchers at snack and meal times provides a natural daily opportunity for children to gain the control to pour both *fast* and *slow*.

▶ **Listen for and support children's observations about speed.**

Children who have many opportunities to move and do things at various rates will sometimes comment on the rate they are moving if speed is an important aspect of their actions. One day, for example, Brian built a ramp and a long road with large hollow blocks. He launched his bus with a big push from the ramp at the end of the road to see how far it would travel until it "crashed" off the road:

Beth: (After a bus crash) *It looks like it went off the road again.*

Brian: *It was going real fast!*

Beth: *Hmm. I wonder how it could stay on the road and still go real fast.*

Brian: (Looks at the road and thinks) *I know. Sides!*

Brian then gets more blocks and builds "sides" along the road. He launches his bus again, and this time it goes "real fast" all the way to the end.

Key Developmental Indicator
Experiencing and Comparing Time Intervals

"I see you're doing your plan," Betsy says to Abby. *"I had to wait a long time,"* Abby replies. *"Jonah was on my favorite trapeze."*

∾

"It will be a long time before snack," Nathan says at greeting circle.

∾

"A long, long time ago, I was in Ann's group," Deola tells Brian at small-group time. *"We were at that table."*

∾

"I bought her lots and lots of weeks ago," says Brian, referring to his doll.

∾

"I said we were gonna play till eight minutes," Julia reminds her friends, *"and it's eight minutes!"*

∾

"It's waterproof," Douglas tells Sam, showing him the "wrist thing" he made. *"It can stay in the water for a hundred minutes."*

∾

"Don't worry," Callie says to Corrin. *"When it's almost out, I'll flip it [the sand timer] over and get more [time to] work."*

∾

Douglas is wrapping things at work time. "This package will take until cleanup," he tells Sam.

∾

When Amanda realizes that the piñata will take a "long time" to dry, she laughs and says to Betsy, her teacher, "You mean until I'm a teenager?!"

Preschool children have a lively, subjective perception of time. For example, to a 3- or 4-year-old, waiting five minutes for a "favorite trapeze" feels like a "long time." Something that happened last month happened "lots and lots of weeks ago" or "a long, long time ago." Taking cues from adults, they also refer to time intervals using the numbers they recognize. Thus, a wristwatch that can stay under water for "a hundred minutes" is a wristwatch that can stay under water for a "really long time." Children also gauge time intervals using parts of the daily routine as markers, just as Douglas does when he talks to Sam about his package. In an active learning setting, children also know that if they need more time, they can get it. (Just flip the sand timer over one more time!) In general, preschoolers seem more likely to comment on their experiences with longer time intervals rather than shorter ones. Following are ways adults can support young children's awareness of time intervals.

Suggestions for Adults

▶ **Establish and follow a consistent daily routine.**

A consistent daily routine enables children to experience and anticipate time intervals of varying lengths. The length of time periods varies within the day (work time is longer than recall time) and from day to day (some work times are longer than others). Children's perceptions of the length of each time period, however, are based on their subjective perceptions rather than on clock time. They may tell you that cleanup time (10 minutes) is longer than outside time (30 minutes) because to them cleanup seems to last a long time and outside time is never long enough.

▶ **Relate lengths of time to familiar actions or events.**

When children gauge time, they use familiar events as markers. Jonah is anticipating his birthday. He knows it is not today, and he knows it will be when the weather is warm, so he says, "When all the snow melts it will be my birthday." When children ask "How long until . . ." questions, or when you cannot respond to a request right away, use concrete markers (rather than abstract time terms) in your responses. Here are some examples:

• "I'll come see your picture when I finish this story with Trey."

Children take turns holding the bunny, turning the sand timer on each turn.

• "We'll be ready for outside time as soon as all the toys are back on the shelves."

• "Let's check to see if the piñata is dry after naptime."

► **Accept children's observations about time.**

"It's late for nine o'clock," Alana comments one day to her friend, who has joined the group at work time. By adult standards, this is a curious statement, but to Alana it seems to express a feeling she has about the timing of her friend's arrival.

Preschool children like Alana experience and comment on time in ways that make personal sense to them. It is important for adults to support their reasoning process rather than attempt to "correct" their emerging perceptions about time.

► **Provide sand timers for children to play with.**

When given sand timers, preschoolers at first tend to explore them rather than use them to

measure time: they enjoy shaking them, tipping them upside down, and watching the sand pour back and forth. Once they have had these exploratory experiences, however, children sometimes incorporate the timers into their play to define personally meaningful time periods. One day, for example, Markie and Joey built a house in the block area and used a sand timer to tell them when it was morning. They decided that when all the sand was at the top of the timer, it would be night, and when it all had emptied into the bottom, it would be morning: "Time to get out of bed!" Also, children sometimes use sand timers to solve turn-taking problems. "Five flips, then it's your turn, okay, Jason?"

Key Developmental Indicator
Anticipating, Remembering, and Describing Sequences of Events

At outside time, Mikey sees Douglas's dad arrive and says, "It's time to put the bike away . . . I'll ride it tomorrow."

∾

Kacey hears the cleanup music and puts the ribbons she has been playing with back on the shelf.

∾

"Tomorrow when I come here I'll make a big old tower," Erica tells her mom when she comes to pick Erica up.

∾

"I'm going to make you a surprise and put it in an envelope and give it to you," Alana says to Beth. "I'm the mail carrier."

∾

"We get candy on Hanukkah, Shabbat, and I think on Friday and Saturday," Jonah tells Amanda.

∾

"I like that day when the rabbit brings the candy," says Corrin.

∾

"Nine more days till my birthday!" Douglas announces at greeting time.

∾

"I'm getting married when I'm five," Brian tells Becki at snack time. "I'm marrying my dad."

∾

"I put Cheerios on my bracelet," recalls Brianna. "Then I tied 'em up and now I can eat them."

∾

"When I brought cupcakes, you wanted the blue one with the smiley face, didn't you?" Julia asks Kacey at snack time.

∾

"At Halloween at Pa and Grammy's we made popcorn!" says Brian.

∾

"I asked my grandmother if I could have some cookies," said Sarah, "and she said, 'After dinner!'"

∾

"My great-grandmother died," Alana tells Beth at greeting circle. "She slept and then she got dead."

∾

"I remember when mom and Meira and me went to Granny's and we counted acorns,"

says Isaac. "We ate them [nuts]," Amanda adds, "but that's when me and my mom lived in Montague."

∾

"Once I got stung by a bee," Hannah tells her friends. "My mom and dad washed my fingers, then put powder on, then put a Band-Aid on."

∾

"I had a dog named Omar at my old house," says Kacey, "but Jesus took him up to heaven and I miss him very much."

Preschool children anticipate and remember personally meaningful events. In a secure active learning setting they look forward to upcoming parts of the daily routine, birthdays, family celebrations, and even pretend play events: "Go to sleep, baby. After your nap Granny's coming for a picnic." They also remember and talk about significant past events, such as figuring out how to make a special necklace, popping popcorn with grandma and grandpa, or the death of a beloved pet or relative.

Like adults, young children's anticipation and recall are tinged with emotions that make some events or parts of events memorable. In other words, they anticipate and recall things that strike them, and this gives them a sense of personal order and control. By holding images or an event in mind and talking about what has happened and what they hope for, children begin to shape their own understanding of the events they experience. Following are ways adults can support children's growing inclination to anticipate and recall personally meaningful parts of their lives.

Suggestions for Adults

▶ **Establish and maintain a consistent routine.**

A consistent daily routine gives children a sense of control over their lives by maintaining a regular set of communal activities against which they can think about time:

• "Large-group time is next," Mikey tells a visiting child, "and then outside time, and then your mom will be here."

• "Don't bring over any more blocks," Callie says to Corrin near the end of work time. "It's almost cleanup!"

The High/Scope plan-work-recall sequence is specifically designed to help children anticipate and recall work and play on a daily basis. At planning time children decide what to do; at work time they carry out their plans; and at recall time they talk about what they have done. (For a thorough discussion of plan-work-recall and the daily routine, see Chapters 6 and 7.)

▶ **Help children learn the daily routine and anticipate what comes next.**

Once you have established a consistent daily routine, here are some ways you can help children anticipate each time period:

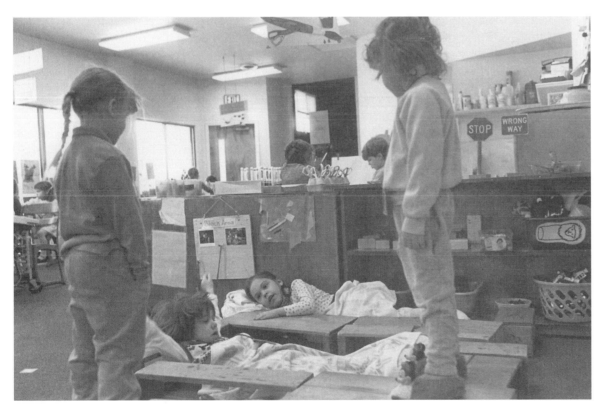

During this pretend play episode, everyone has a different idea of when it is time to wake up!

- Warn children that the end of a time period is near: "Five more minutes until cleanup time!"

- Signal the beginning and end of time periods (for example, by singing a cleanup song).

- Ask children at the end of each period what comes next. "What do we do after large-group time?"

- Give *brief* introductions to small- and large-group times so children will know what to expect. "Today at small group we're going to use watercolors."

▶ **At planning time, converse with children who are ready to make detailed plans.**

Adult: *What do you plan to do today, Jonah?*

Jonah: *Make a bow and arrow.*

Adult: *A bow and arrow. Hmm. What will you make them with?*

Jonah: *Pipe cleaners.* (He pauses.) *And maybe tape. And then a boat.*

Adult: *I see. You're going to make a bow and arrow with pipe cleaners and tape, and then you're going to make a boat.*

Jonah: *Yeah, but the boat will have sticks and paper and tape.* (He leaves to get started.)

Children's daily experience with planning and doing strengthens their capacity to envision what they want to do before they begin doing it. Some children, like Jonah, begin to make more detailed plans as they become familiar with the planning process, the materials in the interest areas, and their teachers and peers. When you become aware of these children, use the following conversational strategies to help them elaborate on their ideas:

- Converse about space and materials.

- Talk about details.

- Talk about sequence.

- Remind children about prior related work and experiences.

▶ **Encourage children to recall events.**

Recall time encourages children to recall events on a daily basis. One day Corrin was very pleased with a heart necklace she made and had a lot to tell Beth about at recall: "I traced the heart, then I drew the stripes, then I colored one circle, then the other. Then I punched the hole, and then I put the string through it and then Becki tied it." (For a full discussion of recall time, see Chapter 7.)

Children also recall meaningful events throughout the day as a conversation or situation triggers their memories. Looking at the book *Rain Makes Applesauce* reminded Amanda of one of her experiences: "I had applesauce for lunch. Gramp was making it and Mama fed it to me."

▶ **Illustrate the order of daily events with children.**

Make up charts with children that will help them see *sequence*—the parts of the daily routine, the steps in a recipe, the turns children will take for various chores. Use objects, photographs, pictures, or drawings to represent each step in the sequence. For example, a daily routine chart, showing children in action during each time of the day, records the sequence of the daily routine in a way that children can "read" for themselves.

One teaching team made a snack chart and used the children's symbols to illustrate the order of turns for passing out the snacks. Here are their observations:

At the beginning of the year it was really chaotic. The children were frustrated because they didn't know when their turn to pass things out was going to come. We developed a chart so they could actually see when their turn was. Once they could see this, they could understand and accept the order of turns. They were, of course, interested in whose turn it was going to be that day, but they were also interested in seeing the flow of turns from day to day.

Children also enjoy "reading" recipe charts for making simple foods such as popcorn, jello, pudding, sandwiches, salad, and applesauce. These charts also inspire children to create their own recipes, such as the one Andrew made using both real and pretend ingredients:

First you mix it with egg and a beater. Then boil an egg and put it in a bowl. Then take some rulers and break them apart. (Use only old rulers.) Draw a color on them and put them in a water bowl and then do more color. Stop water and then scoop with another bowl and take a spoon and eat it. It's called color soup!

▶ **Watch for children's sequenced representations.**

Sometimes children represent sequences of events in their drawings and paintings and in their role play. Several weeks after Alana's great-grandmother died, Alana held a funeral for her "pretend grandmother." Alana, Nathan, Brianna, Julia, and Erica "viewed the body" and then held a burial. Re-enacting sequences of such real events gives children a way of making sense of them.

Preschool children experience seasonal changes in ways that are directly and personally meaningful—for example, eating popsicles outside in summer and sliding down a snowy hill in winter.

▶ **Inform children about changes in the daily routine.**

In an active learning setting, knowing what will happen next in the daily routine gives children feelings of comfort and security. When changes in the routine occur, such as field trips, visitors, and special events, children can retain a sense of control when they learn about the changes at the beginning of the day.

One concrete way to keep children informed about changes in the daily routine is to include a message board as part of the morning greeting circle. The board can be any large piece of paper, chalkboard, or wipe-clean surface. The messages are simple drawings illustrating changes the children need to know about—for example, a stick figure with long hair and glasses to let them know that Ms. Jones will be joining them for the day, and a picture of an apple to remind them that at outside time they will be walking to the farmer's market. After a brief discussion of the morning's messages, children often return to the board for their own "reading" and remembering.

(For an illustration and discussion of the message board, see Chapter 8, p. 265.)

▶ **Include children in the change process.**

There are some changes in the routine that children can participate in, such as adding a new material or area to the play space. At small-group time, children can unpack and decide where the new blocks should go and make the labels for them. Or they can help move the shelves and rearrange the furniture to make room for a new workbench. Children can prepare for the new rabbit Melissa's mom is bringing tomorrow by lining the cage with cedar chips, filling the water jar, and putting the food bowl in the cage. When children take an active role in bringing about anticipated changes in the environment or routines, they retain a sense of control over what happens to them.

▶ **Include living things indoors and outdoors.**

Including plants and animals in the play space provides children with opportunities to observe growth and change. Taking photographs

periodically is a concrete way to help children keep track of these changes.

▶ **Look at seasonal change through preschoolers' eyes.**

• "It doesn't smell like it's going to rain," Jessa says at outside time.

• Callie notices something different about the windows in her preschool one warm day. "Before the plastic was on the windows. Now it's off."

• In the house area, Hannah fills containers with rice. "This is food I'm storing for winter. Winter comes after summer." Hannah and her friends have watched squirrels on the playground carrying walnuts and acorns.

As we noted earlier, preschoolers anticipate and remember personally meaningful events. At ages 3 and 4, children's experiences with seasons are just beginning, and the information they recall and anticipate about seasons tends to be concrete and observable. It makes sense, therefore, for adults to take conversational cues from children's statements so they can support children's ideas at whatever level they have reached.

▶ **Plan holiday celebrations around children's understanding of time.***

The month before. Typically, adults who are planning special-occasion activities for early childhood programs are guided by the calendar, and they begin their special classroom activities about a month before the actual event. For

---

*This section on planning holiday celebrations was written by former High/Scope consultant Susan Terdan. It first appeared in the November/December 1993 High/Scope Extensions newsletter, pp. 2–3.

This child still wraps "presents from Santa Claus" for her teacher, even though it is almost time for summer break!

children, however, anticipating an activity that is a month away—especially one that as yet has no relation to their daily experiences—may not be meaningful. Therefore, instead of planning many holiday activities, art projects, and lessons for the month before the event, an approach that makes more sense to preschoolers is to *let the special event or holiday emerge through the children's conversations and actions.* Listen to children carefully, talk with them, and observe their play. What children know and understand about a special event or holiday will reveal itself. There can be many factors—the experiences of siblings, what their parents are doing, the displays they see in stores, holiday advertising—any of which can inspire children to talk and play-act about an approaching holiday. Most likely, children will begin to show interest in an event immediately before it is to occur rather than weeks in advance. This is the time for adults to think of ways to build on children's expressed interests.

Right before and during the event. Once children express an interest in an upcoming event, it is important for adults to listen, observe, and interact with them to discover what children know and the extent of their interest. The team can then plan ways to support and extend children's ideas and interests by adding related materials to the interest areas; planning field trips and small-group times; inviting special visitors; and interacting with children as they re-enact and talk about the special occasion. You will probably note a wide variety of interest levels among children in your group. Adults need to be attuned to such differences as they support children's holiday-related activities. Adults should also recognize that, in some children's eyes, other activities may be just as important (or even more important) than the special event.

After the event. One of the most dramatic changes that can be observed in many early childhood settings is the transition that occurs on the day after Halloween. One day, the center looks like "Halloween Heaven," and the next, like "Plymouth Rock Feast." Overnight, it is as if Halloween has never been, and pilgrims, turkeys, and cornucopias fill the setting.

Once a special event is over, adults can flip the page of a calendar or cross off the day, turning their attention to the next big event on the calendar. This does not work for young children, however. You will observe children "living out" a special event or holiday long past its actual date. This is because, once an event has occurred, it becomes concrete and real to children. When an event becomes part of their actual experience, it becomes something to understand and relive. Therefore, a special occasion that is fresh in children's minds will usually lead to a variety of play activities. Some children will re-enact an event through building and art projects, and they will often build on one another's ideas as play develops and expands. Adults should keep to the children's timetable when this happens, continuing to support this play by offering appropriate materials and interacting with children.

For example, two weeks after Halloween in one center, teachers noticed that there was still much interest in Halloween-related play. So, the adults made plans to continue singing some Halloween songs at large-group time, restocked the art area with glitter and other costume-making materials, kept the big black hats in the house area, and kept the computer open to the drawing program they had been using to draw pumpkins. Of course, Halloween was just one topic on the teachers' minds as they planned; they also discussed children's strong interest in racing cars and castle-building, and made additional plans to support these interests.

Time Strategies: A Summary

Stopping and starting an action on signal
___ Provide materials children can use to signal stopping and starting.
___ Let children know when time periods begin and end within the daily routine.
___ Sing, dance, and play musical instruments together.
___ Watch for and support children's interest in stopping and starting.

Experiencing and describing rates of movement
___ Provide materials children can set in motion.
___ Provide opportunities for children to move at different rates.
   ___ Play fast and slow music.
   ___ Re-enact stories that incorporate different rates of movement.
   ___ Encourage children to pour their own juice and milk.
___ Listen for and support children's observations about speed.

Experiencing and comparing time intervals
___ Establish and follow a consistent daily routine.
___ Relate lengths of time to familiar actions and events.
___ Accept children's observations about time.
___ Provide sand timers for children to play with.

Anticipating, remembering, and describing sequences of events
___ Establish and maintain a consistent routine.
___ Help children learn the daily routine and anticipate what comes next.
___ At planning time, converse with children who are ready to make detailed plans.
___ Encourage children to recall events.
___ Illustrate the order of daily events with children.
___ Watch for children's sequenced representations.
___ Inform children about changes in the daily routine.
___ Include children in the change process.
___ Include living things indoors and outdoors.
___ Look at seasonal change through preschoolers' eyes.
___ Plan holiday celebrations around children's understanding of time.

References

Harner, Lorraine. 1981. "Children Talk About the Time and Aspect of Actions." *Child Development* 52, no. 2: 498–506.

Phillips, John L. 1969. *The Origins of Intellect: Piaget's Theory.* San Francisco: W. H. Freeman and Company.

Piaget, Jean. 1927. *The Child's Conception of Time.* Reprint. London: Routledge and Kegan Paul. 1969.

Terdan, Susan M. 1993. "Celebrating With Preschoolers." *High/Scope Extensions* (November/December): 1–3.

Related Reading

Elkind, David. 1970. "Of Time and the Child." *New York Times Magazine* (October 11): 22–24.

Epstein, Ann S. 2007. "What Is the High/Scope Curriculum in Science and Technology?" Chap. 15 in *Essentials of Active Learning in Preschool: Getting to Know the High/Scope Curriculum,* 159–66. Ypsilanti, MI: High/Scope Press.

Epstein, Ann S., and Suzanne Gainsley. 2005. "Time." In *Teacher's Idea Book: "I'm Older Than You. I'm Five!" Math in the Preschool Classroom,* 139–68. Ypsilanti, MI: High/Scope Press.

Evans, Betsy. 2007. *Teacher's Idea Book: "I Know What's Next!" Preschool Transitions Without Tears or Turmoil.* Ypsilanti, MI: High/Scope Press.

Flavell, John. 1963. "Quantity, Logic, Number, Time, Movement, and Velocity." Chap. 9 in *The Developmental Psychology of Jean Piaget,* 298–326. Princeton, NJ: Van Nostrand.

Ginsburg, Herbert, and Sylvia Opper. 1969. *Piaget's Theory of Intellectual Development.* Englewood Cliffs, NJ: Prentice-Hall, Inc.

Graves, Michelle. 2005. "Successful Science: Starting With Children's Curiosity." "All in a Day's Science." In *Supporting Young Learners 4: Ideas for Child Care Providers and Teachers,* Nancy A. Brickman, Holly Barton, and Jennifer Burd, eds., 153–66. Ypsilanti, MI: High/Scope Press.

Graves, Michelle. 2005. "Young Children and Math." "Motivated Mathematicians." In *Supporting Young Learners 4: Ideas for Child Care Providers and Teachers,* Nancy A. Brickman, Holly Barton, and Jennifer Burd, eds., 119–32. Ypsilanti, MI: High/Scope Press.

High/Scope Educational Research Foundation. 2003. *Preschool Child Observation Record (COR),* 2nd ed. Ypsilanti, MI: High/Scope Press.

Tompkins, Mark. 1993. "It's About Time!" *High/Scope Extensions* (March/April): 1–3.

Van Scoy, Irma J., and Steven H. Fairchild. 1993. "It's About Time! Helping Preschool and Primary Children Understand Time Concepts." *Young Children* 48, no. 2 (January): 21–24.

Related Media

The following materials are available from the High/Scope Press, 600 N. River St., Ypsilanti, MI 48198-2898; to order, visit *www.highscope.org,* or call 1-800-40-PRESS.

Space and Time (Early Math). 2004. Color videotape or DVD, 44 min.

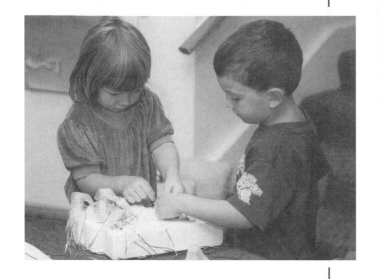

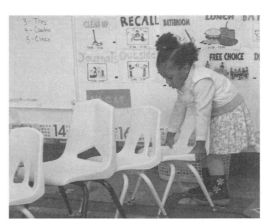

As children interact with peers and adults, they are gradually becoming more aware of the needs and feelings of others and of group expectations. As they participate in group routines that allow for individual interests, they learn how to meet their own needs while contributing to the community.

Social Studies

High/Scope views the preschool classroom as a place where children form their identities as both individuals and members of a group. They learn that one part of being themselves is being connected to a network of people who share their interests and care about their feelings.

Why Social Studies Is Important

The Standards of the National Council for the Social Studies (NCSS) says social studies is "designed to promote civic competence . . . and integrates knowledge from several disciplines including history and geography" (1994, p. 3).

History and geography are too abstract for preschoolers. However, if one focuses on the notion that the ultimate goal of social studies is to foster **civic competence,** or the ability to be a good citizen, then it is clear that early childhood programs do a great deal toward accomplishing this end.

In Chapter 12 we discussed **social and emotional development,** which refers to children's ability to regulate their feelings and behaviors and negotiate everyday interactions with adults and peers. **Social studies** refers more broadly to understanding and applying the rules and sensitivities that govern interactions among members of groups, communities, and society as a whole. Given the complexity of today's society, the field recognizes the importance of helping children develop the knowledge and skills they will need to negotiate multiple roles in a rapidly changing world.

Supporting Social Studies

High/Scope has **two key developmental indicators (KDIs) in social studies.** One focuses on children's emerging sense of community, and the other, on their ability to feel empathy and take another's perspective. These indicators, and the strategies adults use to support their development, are discussed below.

Key Developmental Indicator
Participating in Group Routines

After painting at small-group time, Isaac washes his hands, sponges off his place at the table, sees that Roxanne has completed her painting, and sponges off her place, too.

～

Megan gives each person at her table a cup for juice.

～

At work time, James puts on his smock, selects a brush, and starts a painting.

～

Deanne and Kalynn together carry the basket of balls out to the playground. "Wanna roll 'em down the hill?" Kalynn asks.

～

"I know. Let's sing 'Little Red Caboose,'" Brian suggests at large-group time.

～

"I don't hide under the climber when it's cleanup time anymore," Jason says to Betsy. "I like to clean up. I pretend I'm a cleaner dog or a steam shovel or something."

Awareness of research on children's cognitive, affective, and social development is critical [to] improve teaching and learning in early childhood social studies. Curriculum developers and teachers with [such] knowledge can design appropriate social learning experiences to enable young children to begin to think about and conceptualize their life experiences.

—N. Wyner and E. Farquhar, 1991

Preschoolers are physically independent, communicative, and able to represent and anticipate future events. They enjoy entering into group routines that make sense to them, permit them to be active learners, and involve them in interesting experiences with supportive people. Such routines support children's personal initiatives, and at the same time, involve them with other people. In other words, group routines that take children's choices and decisions into account can help children build positive social relationships and a sense of community. Here are specific ways adults can support young children's participation in group routines.

These children willingly participate in group routines that call for important jobs such as carrying chairs and getting juice for snack.

Suggestions for Adults

▶ **Establish** *consistent* **group routines.**

Consistent group routines encourage children's active participation and give them a sense of control and self-confidence. Such routines enable children to anticipate what happens next, when it will be their turn, what adults expect of them, and how to act on these expectations. Below are three kinds of group routines and expectations that encourage children's active participation.

High/Scope daily routine elements. A **daily schedule** that includes the basic elements of a High/Scope daily routine in the same sequence each day (for example, **greeting circle, planning time, work time, recall time, large-group time, small-group time, outside time**) helps children look forward to each part of the day and the kinds of activities available. It allows them to plan for and act on their particular interests. In fact, some parents of children in High/Scope programs report that their children make plans for the day at home or on the way

to preschool. This degree of active participation occurs when children have experienced and can count on a supportive, predictable, consistent daily routine. (Review Chapter 6 for specific daily routine strategies.)

Group maintenance routines. Young children like to do things they see adults do. They want to pass out the napkins, feed the gerbil, and wipe the table, and they find it difficult to understand why they cannot all do these satisfying tasks every day. Helper charts (such as the ones pictured on p. 344 and above right on p. 476) enable children to predict when they will have a turn to carry out daily jobs. For example, by "reading" the chart's pictures and symbols, Alana can see for herself that even though she does not get to pass out anything today at snack time, it will be her turn to pass out the napkins tomorrow. By establishing a public and democratic rotation of communal tasks and procedures, adults help young children participate in group routines even when it is not their turn, and children thus begin to form a notion of themselves and others as contributing group members.

Reasonable expectations. Young children are more likely to participate in group routines when there are reasonable, consistent adult expectations that children can understand and meet successfully. The exact nature of these expectations will vary from center to center. What is important, however, is that (1) adult team members have agreed on a common set of expectations, (2) these expectations remain the same from day to day and from adult to adult, and (3) the expectations are well within the realm of things that 3-, 4-, and 5-year-olds can do. Here are examples of reasonable, routine expectations:

• Each child chooses a book to read until everyone has arrived.

• At greeting circle, children look on the message board to see if there will be visitors or new toys.

• Children wash their hands with soap after they use the toilet.

• Children put on a smock when painting or working with materials that might get on their clothes.

• When a child is finished eating a snack, he or she joins large-group time.

Children find unique ways to "participate" in group routines. During this cleanup time, for example, two children wash the message board as one child watches and another relaxes in the beanbag chairs!

• Children store the things they plan to take home in their cubby.

(For more on everyday expectations, see Chapter 4, pp. 102–103.)

▶ **Make active learning a part of group routines.**

Young children participate willingly and enthusiastically in group routines that are built around their desire for active learning. Therefore, throughout each part of the daily routine, make sure children have materials to manipulate and enough time to make choices and decisions about them. In addition, make sure they have time to talk about what they are doing and observing and that they receive attentive adult support for their efforts. (Refer to Chapters 7 and 8 for ways to include active learning in each segment of the daily routine.)

It is important as well to establish **group maintenance routines** that involve children in experiences in which they can make some choices when their turn arises. For example, when Jimmy passed out napkins at snack time, he placed a napkin on each child's head. The next day, Mimi placed each child's napkin at the edge of the table. When it was Claude's turn, he sat in his chair and slid the napkins toward each child.

Another important strategy in promoting active learning in group routines is to **maintain consistent daily expectations** that provide for child action and choice. For example, each day, children are expected to put their toys away. The way children meet this expectation, however, will vary. Some children will clean up after finishing one plan and before starting another. Other children's play will be more fluid—one plan leading to another—and they will not clean up anything until work time ends. Some children will be methodical in putting toys back on the shelf, while others will need music or some sort of game to help them along. Maintaining consistent expectations and enabling active learners to fulfill them requires our time, patience, and an enduring belief that while active learning may appear inefficient at times, we know that in the long run it is worthwhile and rewarding for both children and adults.

▶ **Focus on children's interests, intentions, and strengths.**

Sometimes, no matter how patient we are or how many choices are available, some children may still be reluctant to come to large-group time, pass out the napkins, or put toys away. At these times, let the reluctant children know that they are welcome to join the activity when they have completed what they are doing, but then focus on the children who are full of ideas and energy for large-group time, who are putting toys away, or who are ready to take a turn with the napkins.

Generally, children are social creatures. They want to participate in group routines and will join an activity to see what is going on. Reluctance to participate is usually their way of telling you something about themselves or the activity. For example, their reluctance may signal that they are tired or simply in need of a quiet moment alone. At other times, it may be their way of letting you know something is bothering them and that you need to find time for a quiet one-to-one conversation. And sometimes nonparticipation is a child's way of telling you that the experience you have planned for small-group time, for example, does not interest him or her. Consider Ricky's experience. Ricky lay on the floor for a while during one small-group time that involved children in cutting pictures out of magazines. Finally, Ricky approached his teacher and said, "I don't want to cut. I want to tear." His teacher said, "Fine," and Ricky joined the small group and began tearing out pictures while the other children continued cutting their pictures with scissors.

Key Developmental Indicator
Being Sensitive to the Feelings, Interests, and Needs of Others

Callie is not feeling well but comes to preschool because she wants to play with her friends. When she vomits, Alana, Kenneth, and Aimee run to get tissues and wipe off her face.

❧

Jared is crying at small-group time. "Jared, are you sad 'cause you miss your mom?" his friend Jason asks. Jared nods "yes." "You love her so much, don't you?" Jason says. Jared nods "yes" again.

❧

Andrew notices a change in Corrin, who usually looks sad when her mom leaves. "Corrin is happy today!" he says.

❧

Jonah sees Ashley crying for her mom. He makes her some "gold" and draws a picture of her smiling.

❧

At recall time, Callie says to Deola, "I'm sorry I didn't get to play with you today." "That's okay," Deola replies. "You spent a lot of time with me yesterday."

❧

Abby is having trouble putting on her shoe. "I can help you," Isaac says, and he does.

❧

Ben is crying. Petey pats him gently on the back.

❧

Erica is upset at work time. "Don't worry," Andrew says. "I'll play with you." He hugs her.

❧

Anna's cousin is visiting for the day. "I can see you're not feeling so good," Kenneth says to her. "You're new here." He gives her a "magic hat."

Even at the ages of 3, 4, and 5, children can be sensitive to the feelings, interests, and needs of others. They can observe other children, understand their feelings, imagine what they might be wanting, and respond with supportive actions. According to psychologists Charles McCoy and John Masters (1985), "Young children can recognize emotions in other children, have common ideas about how experience influences affect, and are often motivated to intervene in others' emotional states" (p. 1214).

Preschoolers can exercise these capacities because they have the ability to **represent** and **pretend**. As psychologist Paul Harris (1989) observes, this representational ability "allows children to engage in an imaginative understanding of other people's mental states. Given their capacity for pretend play, children can imagine wanting something they do not actually want. They can also imagine believing something they do not actually believe. On the basis of such simple pretend premises, they can proceed to imagine the emotional reactions of another person who does have such a desire or belief" (p. 55). Furthermore, young children have been feeling emotions and sensing other's emotions all their lives. Most preschoolers, for example, feel anxious when their moms leave the room, go shopping, or go to work, and are quick to respond when they see that other children miss their moms, too.

Developing and using these sensitivities enables young children to interact positively with others and expands their often self-centered perspectives. Further, children who consistently recognize and respond to other children's emotions tend to establish and maintain friendly peer relationships. Following are ways adults can support children's sensitivity to others and their emerging sense of social responsibility.

Suggestions for Adults

▶ **Respond to children's feelings, interests, and needs.**

We know that young children have the capacity to respond sensitively to others. We also know that they are more apt to do so when adults treat them with care and concern. By being sensitive, warm, and responsive to children, adults create an atmosphere of trust and security. When adults respond appropriately to the feelings, interests, and needs of children, they help children feel safe and confident, and empower them, in turn, to care for others.

We offer strategies for responding to children's interests throughout this book. For example, adults respond to children's interests when they encourage children to make choices, plans, and decisions; when they include the plan-work-recall sequence in the daily routine; when they provide for children's active learning during adult-initiated activities; when they imitate children's play; when they follow children's conversational leads and listen attentively to what children have to say. Adults respond to children's feelings and needs when they create a supportive social climate in which they share control with children, focus on children's strengths, form authentic relationships, support children's play, and adopt a problem-solving approach to social conflict. (Chapter 2 contains a complete discussion of specific strategies for these topics.)

Finally, it is also important for adults to respond positively to children who express their feelings and needs in potentially annoying ways. Jessica, for example, follows her teacher like a shadow. Pete clings to his caregiver's leg. Markie pouts but does not talk, while Vera talks to her teacher all day long. These children are all seeking adult attention and reassurance; in such instances, it is our obligation to see that they receive it. Although responding to particularly expressive children takes time, ingenuity, and good humor, it is more effective than withholding attention. By providing children with the attention they need, we ultimately free them to engage in more satisfying interactions. Here is how one adult supported Pete:

Pete: (Enters room, takes off coat, finds adult, and throws his arms around her leg.)

Adult: *Good morning, Pete.* (Squats down next to him and puts her arm around him.)

Pete: (Puts his arm around her neck.)

Adult: *You can help me greet the rest of the kids and moms and dads.*

Pete: (Stays by her side.)

Adult: (Talks with each child and parent as they arrive, maintaining contact with Pete as she changes positions.)

Adult: *All the kids are here, Pete. We can go to the circle.* (They walk hand-in-hand and sit next to James, a child Pete sometimes plays with.)

Pete: (Sits in adult's lap throughout greeting circle. Goes to planning group holding adult's hand. Once there, scoots chair close to adult's chair so he can lean against her. She puts her arm around him whenever she can.)

Adult: (Plans with the other children, saving Pete's plan for last.) *What about you, Pete. What would you like to do?*

Pete: (Looks around for a while. Points to the sandbox where James is playing.) *Play over there.*

Adult: *Play over there.*

Pete: *James has a car.*

Adult: *James has a car in the sand.*

Pete: *I'm gonna get me one.* (Looks at cars on a shelf.)

Adult: *I'll come and see your car in the sand after you get started.*

Pete: *Okay. I'll get you.*

Adult: *I'll come to see your car when you get me.*

Pete: (Walks to the car shelf and then to the sandbox.)

After repeating this ritual for several weeks, Pete gradually became more independent and involved with other children. He called his teacher over when he needed her, or simply checked in with her from time to time. One day, Pete was the first person to plan. "Pete, it's really easy for you to make a plan now," his teacher said, commenting on the growth she had seen in him. "Yep," he agreed, as he made his way to the block area.

▶ **Recognize and comment on children's sensitivities.**

An effective way to support children's sensitivity to others is to comment on their efforts whenever you see them occurring:

• A group of "mothers" are playing in the house area. When one of their "babies" begins to cry, they spank her. Hearing all the commotion, 4-year-old Anna looks up from her block building and says, "I would take her in my bed if she was crying that hard." Sam, an adult who was nearby, hears this comment and responds to Anna, "Yes, that is a way to help a crying baby feel better."

• Petey and Brian are playing at the water table. Alana joins them. They all get "a little bit wet." "Uh-oh," remarks Petey, noticing that Alana isn't wearing a waterproof smock like he and Brian are. "Wait, I'll get you a smock." The play pauses while the boys help Alana put on her smock. "You helped Alana with her smock so she wouldn't get wet," Becki, their teacher, comments, as she joins them at the water table. "You helped your friend."

• "Shut up," Kacey tells Mikey. "Don't say 'Shut up' to me. I don't like those words!" Mikey responds. After a pause he adds, "You can say, 'Be quiet.'" Kacey looks at Mikey and then says, "Be quiet!" Beth, an adult who has witnessed this exchange, comments to both children, "Mikey, you told Kacey how you felt about her words, and Kacey, you listened to Mikey."

Comments on actual instances of sensitivity, like the ones Sam, Becki, and Beth offered, are more apt to strengthen children's caring capacities than just telling them to be kind and helpful to their friends.

▶ **Support children's concerns for absent group members.**

When someone in the group, a child or adult, is absent, the other children often express concern. It is important to acknowledge these concerns and converse with children about the absent person—what the person might think about the song they are singing or the plans they are making, or how they might let the absent person know they are still thinking about him or her. These conversations enable young children to care for people who are not immediately present. For example, Annette and the children in her small group are frosting cookies and thinking about Teetee, a 3-year-old in the hospital with a broken leg.

Preschoolers Care for One Another

Educator William Ayers (1989) relates this story about the experiences of 2-year-old Cameron, and two 4-year-olds, Henry and Max: "On his third day of day care, Cameron's mother felt he was comfortable enough for her to leave. After Cameron waved good-by from the window, . . . Henry took Cameron's hand, without any adult encouragement, and led him to the block area to build. As they worked, Henry said, 'They always come back.' Max added, 'Sometimes I get lonely but I know it's okay.' Cameron watched and listened. When he woke up from his nap, Henry touched him gently and said, 'Today was your first nap,' and Max added, 'And you're still here'" (p. 71).

In supportive settings, children often support each other. The child at the left, for example, helps adjust a balloon ring, while the child holding the basket waits patiently while his classmate takes as many pretzels as he needs.

Cory: *This one broke . . . like Teetee's leg!*

Annette: *I visited Teetee in the hospital yesterday.*

Markie: *Did you see his leg?*

Lynnette: *Is it still broke?*

Annette: *His leg is in a cast and the break is healing. (Children continue frosting.) I wonder what he'd think about our cookies.*

Jeff: *He likes cookies.*

Cory: *He likes frosting! . . . We could save some for him.*

Wendy: *His mom could take them. I know 'cause my mom talked to his mom.*

Social Studies Strategies: A Summary

Participating in group routines

___ Establish *consistent* group routines:
  ___ High/Scope daily routine elements
  ___ Group maintenance routines
  ___ Reasonable expectations
___ Make active learning a part of group routines.
___ Focus on children's interests, intentions, and strengths.

Being sensitive to the feelings, interests, and needs of others

___ Respond to children's feelings, interests, and needs.
___ Recognize and comment on children's sensitivities.
___ Support children's concerns for absent group members.

References

Ayers, William. 1989. *The Good Preschool Teacher: Six Teachers Reflect on Their Lives*. New York: Teachers College Press.

Harris, Paul L. 1989. *Children and Emotion: The Development of Psychological Understanding*. Oxford: Basil Blackwell.

Jantz, R. K., and Carol Seefeldt. 1999. "Early Childhood Social Studies." In *The Early Childhood Curriculum: Current Findings in Theory and Practice*, Carol Seefeldt, ed., 159–78, 3rd ed. New York: Teachers College Press.

McCoy, Charles L., and John C. Masters. 1985. "The Development of Children's Strategies for the Social Control of Emotion." *Child Development* 56, no. 5 (October): 1214–22.

National Council for the Social Studies. 1994. *Expectations of Excellence: Curriculum Standards for the Social Studies*. Washington, DC: Author.

Wyner, N., and E. Farquhar. 1991. "Cognitive, Emotional, and Social Development: Early Childhood Social Studies." In *Handbook of Research on Social Studies Teaching and Learning*, J. Shaver, ed., 101–46. New York: Macmillan.

Related Reading

Crago, Hugh. 1986. "The Place of Story in Affective Development: Implications for Educators and Clinicians." In *The Feeling Child: Affective Development Reconsidered*, Nancy E. Curry, ed., 129–42. New York: The Haworth Press.

Denham, Susanne A. 1986. "Social Cognition, Prosocial Behavior, and Emotion in Preschoolers: Contextual Validation." *Child Development* 57, no. 1 (February): 194–201.

Epstein, Ann S. 2007. "What Is the High/Scope Curriculum in Social Studies?" Chap. 16 in *Essentials of Active Learning in Preschool: Getting to Know the High/Scope Curriculum*, 167–72. Ypsilanti, MI: High/Scope Press.

Fischer, Kurt, Helen Hand, Malcolm Watson, Martha Van Parys, and James Tucker. 1984. "Putting the Child Into Socialization: The Development of Social Categories in Preschool Children." In *Current Topics in Early Childhood Education*, Vol. 5, 27–72. Norwood, NJ: Ablex.

Gardner, Howard. 1983. "The Personal Intelligences." Chap. 10 in *Frames of Mind: The Theory of Multiple Intelligences*, 237–76. New York: Basic Books.

Gottman, John M. 1983. "How Children Become Friends." *Monographs of the Society for Research in Child Development*, Serial No. 201, Vol. 48, no. 3.

Graves, Michelle. 1999. "A Child Development Approach to Rules and Limits." *High/Scope Extensions* (November/December): 1–3.

Grusec, Joan E., and Lyn Arnason. 1982. "Consideration for Others: Approaches to Enhancing Altruism." In *The Young Child: Reviews of Research*, Vol. 3., Shirley Moore and Catherine Cooper, eds., 159–74. Washington, DC: NAEYC.

Harris, Paul L., Kara Donnelly, Gabrielle R. Guz, and Rosemary Pitt-Watson. 1986. "Children's Understanding of the Distinction Between Real and Apparent Emotion." *Child Development* 57, no. 4 (August): 895–909.

High/Scope Educational Research Foundation. 2003. *Preschool Child Observation Record (COR)*, 2nd ed. Ypsilanti, MI: High/Scope Press.

Hyson, Marion C. 1994. *The Emotional Development of Young Children: Building an Emotion-Centered Curriculum*. New York: Teachers College Press.

Katz, Lilian, and Diane McClellan. 1997. *Fostering Children's Social Competence: The Teacher's Role*. Washington DC: NAEYC.

Kemple, Kristen M. 1991. "Preschool Children's Peer Acceptance and Social Interaction." *Young Children* 46, no. 5 (March): 47–54.

Oden, Sherri. 1988. "Alternative Perspectives on Children's Peer Relations." In *Integrative Processes and Socialization: Early to Middle Childhood*, T. D. Yawkey and J. E. Johnson, eds., 139–66. Hillsdale, NJ: Erlbaum.

Oden, Sherri. 1986. "Developing Social Skills Instruction for Peer Interaction and Relationships." In *Teaching Social Skills to Children*, 2nd ed., E. Cartledge and J. Milburn, eds., 246–69. New York: Pergamon Press.

Oden, Sherri. 1993. "Implementing Research on Children's Social Competence: What Do Teachers and Researchers Need to Learn?" *Exceptionality Education Canada* 3 nos. 1 & 2: 209–32.

Paley, Vivian Gussin. 1992. *You Can't Say You Can't Play*. Cambridge, MA: Harvard University Press.

Piers, Maria W., and Nancy E. Curry. 1986. "A Developmental Perspective on Children's Affects." In *The Feeling Child: Affective Development Reconsidered*, Nancy E. Curry, ed., 23–36. New York: The Haworth Press.

Ramsey, Patricia G. 1991. *Making Friends in School: Promoting Peer Relationships in Early Childhood*. New York: Teachers College Press.

Rogers, Dwight L., and Dorene D. Ross. 1986. "Encouraging Positive Social Interaction Among Young Children." *Young Children* 41, no. 3 (March): 12–17.

Rubin, Kenneth H., and Nina Howe. 1986. "Social Play and Perspective-Taking." In *The Young Child at Play: Reviews of Research*, Vol. 4, Greta Fein and Mary Rivkin, eds., 113–25. Washington, DC: NAEYC.

Stockdale, Dahlia F., Susan M. Hegland, and Thomas Chiaromonte. 1989. "Helping Behaviors: An Observational Study of Preschool Children." *Early Childhood Research Quarterly* 4, no. 4 (December): 533–43.

Related Media

The following materials are available from the High/Scope Press, 600 N. River St., Ypsilanti, MI 48198-2898; to order, visit *www.highscope.org*, or call 1-800-40-PRESS.

Initiative and Social Relations. 2001. Color videotape or DVD, 60 min. Ypsilanti, MI: High/Scope Press.

Consistent group routines, like taking your own set of materials to your small-group table, enable children to participate in a classroom community with shared expectations.

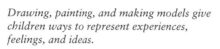

Drawing, painting, and making models give children ways to represent experiences, feelings, and ideas.

Early experiences shape how we see our artistic abilities. Adults often marvel at the wonderful pictures, dramas, dances, and songs that children create. Art is more than freestyle play: it's a language, and just like any other form of literacy, once we learn how to "speak" this language, there is no limit to our ability to create and converse. Moreover, the arts in their many forms can become a means of exploring other content areas.

We begin this three-chapter section on the arts with **visual art.** In Chapter 21, we will move on to **dramatic art,** and in Chapter 22 we will cover **music.**

Why the Arts Are Important

Art has been a standard feature of early childhood programs since their beginning. Researcher Carol Seefeldt (1999) says that even when educators are pressured to focus on other academic skills, such as reading, most continue to believe art should remain an essential component of the curriculum in preschool and the early grades. Research shows that experiences in the arts benefit children throughout their school years.

The value of artistic instruction for students is both emotional and intellectual. Art is **intrinsically rewarding,** that is, studying art is important for its own sake. We learn to value artistic expression in ourselves and others and derive inner satisfaction from appreciating its beauty or wrestling with its challenges.

Stephen Dobbs, professor of arts and humanities at San Francisco State University, says that through art education, "Students begin to see the rich mosaic of the world from many perspectives" (Dobbs 1998, p. 12). For young children in particular, art provides an inner sense of competence and control. The Task Force on Children's Learning and the Arts notes that "As they engage in the artistic process, children learn that they can observe, organize, and interpret their experiences. They can make decisions, take actions, and monitor the effect of those actions" (Arts Education Partnership 1998, p. 2).

Art is also **extrinsically valuable** in that it promotes other areas of development: for example, analyzing the spatial relationships among a group of dancers or developing the eye-hand coordination to weave a scarf. Noted art educator Rudolph Arnheim (1989) emphasizes that art is as much an intellectual activity as an intuitive one. And, as emphasized by the Arts Education Partnership, art education contributes to the development of many social and academic skills. "For all children, at all ability levels, the arts play a central role in cognitive, motor, language, and social-emotional development. The arts motivate and engage children in learning, stimulate memory and facilitate understanding, enhance symbolic communication, promote relationships, and provide an avenue for building competence" (Arts Education Partnership 1998, p. v).

Visual Art

The invention of symbols is natural and a source of great pleasure and satisfaction. Through symbols, experience is clarified and shared.

—Nancy Smith, 1982

The developmental changes that occur during the preschool years make young children especially open to enjoying and learning from the opportunities that art education presents. Preschoolers, as distinct from infants and toddlers, are able to form mental images. They convey these through various forms of **artistic representation,** such as drawing a picture of their family, pretending to be a favorite character in a book, or making up a song about the birthday party they are planning.

At the same time that young children are developing their language skills, art also opens up new avenues for expression and communication. As their expanding cognitive capacities combine with their growing physical and social abilities, preschoolers have a wide array of options for appreciating and creating art. They can make drawings and build models, imitate and pretend, sing and invent the words to songs, and do many of the things that adult artists do.

From Objects to Abstractions, From Simple Forms to Complex Images

Preschoolers feel a powerful urge to construct their own symbols as substitutes for actual objects and experiences. **Representation** is the internal process by which children construct mental symbols to stand for actual objects, people and experiences. This ability is just beginning to develop in preschoolers.

The ability to create and understand representations evolves in the preschool years, and children need time within a supportive environment to develop and grow as symbol-makers. Children's representational thought and expression arise from their active sensory experiences and first appear as simple forms that become increasingly complex, resulting in unique creations.

With that in mind, High/Scope is guided by four developmental principles in its approach to early art education.

Representation arises from children's experiences with actual objects, people, and events. A child's ability to create and understand representations develops from a solid base of active experiences with people and materials. Preschoolers are primed as symbol-makers by their years of intense sensory-motor exploration as infants and toddlers. During this critical time they grasp, taste, bang, clutch, and carry everything within their reach. They develop an awareness of an object's permanence (for example, imagining and searching for a ball that has rolled behind the couch). Also, preschoolers can identify people and objects by their indices or sensory cues (hearing mommy's voice and knowing that mommy is nearby; seeing Rover's tail in the kitchen doorway and concluding that Rover is in

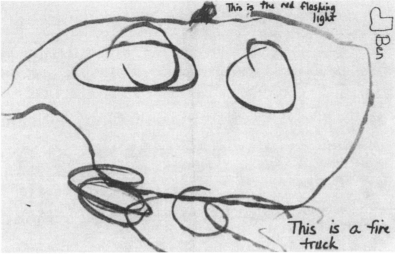

This is the red flashing light

Ben

This is a fire truck

the kitchen). In their review of Piaget's work, developmental psychologists Herbert Ginsburg and Sylvia Opper (1979) describe the value of children's sensory experiences this way: "The child looks at things, handles them, and acts like them, and in these ways incorporates a great deal of information about them. These actions of the child lay the foundation for mental symbolism" (p. 81).

To form vivid mental images, then, young children need a hands-on familiarity with objects and people. Preschoolers play "mommy" and "baby" based on their own real-life experiences with mommies and babies. They make simple clay models and drawings of people based on experiences with their own bodies and the faces, arms, and legs of family members and friends. For example, 3-year-old Margo had a dog for a pet and often played "doggy" or drew pictures of dogs at work time. When her friend Joey wanted her to play "hermit crab," however, Margo was completely stymied until she was able to feed, hold, and watch the hermit crabs in Joey's terrarium. Margo needed to see how hermit crabs moved before she could pretend to be one.

Children's early representations consist of simple forms that gradually become more complex. Whether the medium is pretend play, clay, blocks, paints, paper, or markers, children's representations evolve from simple gestures and lines to more complex interactions and differ-

This is a firefighter truck. Firefighter Bill.

entiated images. Children's early symbolic efforts reflect their "inexperience with representational media, slow discovery of forms, emphasis on action, and quick satisfaction with crude form-symbols, as well as their playfulness and willingness to simplify and economize" (Golomb 1974,

Each child's firetruck is a unique, one-of-a-kind creation reflecting his or her specific interests and observations.

A fire engine out of blocks.

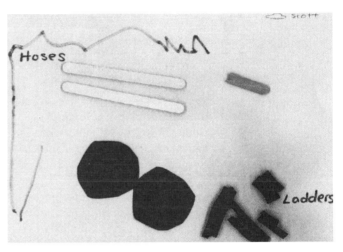

Hoses

Ladders

scott

It's just a fire truck with someone inside

KDIs in Visual Art

- Relating models, pictures, and photographs to real places and things
- Making models out of clay, blocks, and other materials
- Drawing and painting

p. 187). As children become more adept at manipulating the media, and as their representations become increasingly influenced by the visual attributes of objects, their pretend-play scenarios and constructions with various materials become less accidental, less in need of supplemental verbal explanation, and more structurally detailed, integrated, and complete.

Each child's representations are unique. Each child invents unique forms of pretend play and symbol-making at a pace and in a manner that makes sense to him or her. As preschoolers pretend, draw, write, and make models, they vary in their intensity; sense of playfulness; familiarity with the representational medium; experiences with the objects, people, and situations they are representing; and their inclination toward art or dramatic play. Consequently, their representations are one-of-a-kind reflections of their specific interests and concerns—the result of "an exuberant, noisy activity of body and mind, in which producer and product are still inseparable" (Golomb 1992, p. xviii).

Young children are capable of appreciating as well as making art. Educators often think that art appreciation is too abstract or analytical for preschoolers. But because young children are so observant and in-tune with all their senses, they are ideal candidates for appreciating the world of art. In fact, they are often eager to share their reactions to a picture, song, or story. The key, says art educator Marjorie Schiller, is that "talking about art should spring from the inter-

ests of the children and be initiated, for the most part, by them" (1995, p. 34). High/Scope therefore includes appreciating as well as making art in its curriculum, grounding both in the experiences that young children relate to and find meaningful in their own lives.

Supporting Visual Art

High/Scope has **three key developmental indicators (KDIs)** in visual art. They help children connect visual art objects and experiences with their everyday lives. Looking at a representation, such as a sculpture or drawing, and understanding that it stands for a real object or event is a precursor of reading in young children. After realizing that visual images can represent concrete things, a next step in literacy is seeing that written words can stand for spoken words. The KDIs in the visual arts are

- **Relating models, pictures, and photographs to real places and things**

- **Making models out of clay, blocks, and other materials**

- **Drawing and painting**

The sections that follow will examine how adults can help open the door to the visual arts, helping children develop this avenue for communicating their perceptions and experiences.

Key Developmental Indicator
Relating Models, Pictures, and Photographs to Real Places and Things

"This is my grandma's house," says Antoine as he walks a little rubber doll through the door of the dollhouse.

∾

Using a picture book about firefighters, Michelle "reads" her dental patient a story, interpreting the pictures to fit her ideas about tooth care. "Once upon a time, there was a firefighter . . . with cavities. He ate all that stuff."

∾

Jonah puts on a wool cap. "This is a fire cap," he tells Betsy, his teacher, then shows her a picture of a firefighter in a book wearing a similar cap.

∾

Trey sorts through a box of photographs and sets aside photos of Douglas, Andrew, Sam, and Peter. He puts them in his bristle-block camera, takes pictures of Douglas, Andrew, Peter, and Sam and then gives them the photographs he has "taken."

∾

Minna looks through some postcards with reproductions of art work. She holds up a picture of "Haystacks" by Claude Monet and says, "My grandpa has hay . . . in his barn. It's for the cows, but sometimes we can jump in it. It sticked to my pants . . . and in my hair!"

∾

Concrete objects: *Experiences with real objects enable children to form mental images of the objects. These children, for example, construct their own understanding of firetrucks by climbing on a firetruck, holding on to the hand rail, and feeling the hoses.*

Symbols: *A symbol of an object is a model, picture, or re-enactment of it. When children play firefighters, make a model firetruck, or draw a picture of a firetruck, they are creating symbols that resemble firetrucks.*

◗ kathryn   fire engine

fire fighter Bill

FIRTRK

Signs: *A sign of an object is the written or spoken word that stands for that object. Writing the word "FIRTRK" is a very abstract form of representation because the letters F-I-R-T-R-K bear no resemblance to an actual firetruck.*

Abby brings a tree book outside and turns the pages slowly, searching for a leaf that looks like the leaf she holds in her hand. "Here it is!" she says to Jackie, her teacher.

With their growing capacity to form mental images and express their understanding in increasingly complex language, preschoolers are beginning to see the relationship between toys, photographs, and pictures, and the objects they represent. In fact, relating models, photographs, and pictures to real places and things is one very important way that preschoolers "read." (See Chapter 11, Language, Literacy, and Communication, for more information on this topic.) Following are ways adults can support children's emerging awareness of the connection between models and pictures and the things they represent.

Suggestions for Adults

▶ **Provide models for children to play with.**

Throughout the interest areas it is important to provide models of objects, animals, and people that children encounter in their everyday lives. This includes things like toy cars, trucks, and little people. (See Models for Children to Play With, below, for examples to consider.) While children like to play with dollhouses, they also enjoy playing with a model of their actual preschool room or rooms. "In general," note psychologist Judy De Loache and colleagues, "the more physically similar a model is to the corresponding larger space, the more likely it is that young children will use what they know about one of them to figure out the other" (De Loache et al. 1991, p. 122).

▶ **Provide photographs and pictures for children to look at.**

Photograph the children in your program. Take pictures of children at play indoors and out, by themselves, in small and large groups, on trips, making discoveries, with their favorite tree or play structure. Display these photographs at the children's eye-level throughout the play space as well as in photograph albums or special books so children can look at them whenever they wish. One teaching team labeled and hung up a series of photographs showing children involved in each part of the daily routine. The children stopped to examine them as they passed between the block and art areas. Another teaching team always made double prints of each photo. They put one set of prints in an album for children to look at, and they posted the other set around the room. Eventually, they took these prints down (to make room for new ones) and sent them home with parents.

Provide children with a simple working camera. Encourage them to take their own pictures of their peers at work and play. This allows you to collect photographs that are truly taken from a child's point of view.

Provide illustrated storybooks and art reproductions. Children can look at and "read" books whenever they choose. Include picture books related to local family and community life as well as field trips the children have taken. Encourage children to "read" or interpret the pictures to you as you look at the books and read together. Also include prints, posters, postcards, and books that reproduce actual paintings and drawings by current and past artists and illustrators. These can be purchased from museums, bookstores, catalogs, and Web sites.

Models for Children to Play With

Model Objects
Dollhouse, dollhouse furniture
Child-sized furniture—stove, sink, refrigerator, crib
Plastic, fabric, or wooden fruits, vegetables, flowers
Toy vehicles of all kinds—trucks, cars, planes, boats, buses, tractors, trains, fire engines, bulldozers, back hoes
A model of the actual preschool room or rooms

Model Animals
Wooden, rubber, and plastic animals
Stuffed animals
Animal puppets

Model People
Dollhouse people
Sets of wooden, rubber, or plastic people, baby dolls, puppets
Wooden nesting people

Include all sorts of catalogs and picture magazines in the art area. Children can use these materials for cutting and pasting. While some children will cut and paste indiscriminately simply for the sake of cutting and pasting, others will look for pictures of animals or cars or whatever they find particularly appealing.

Use photographs of children at small-group time. Give each child several photographs and listen to what children have to say about them as they cover them with contact paper, put them into a photograph album, or paste them into books they have made.

▶ **Support and encourage children's comparisons of models and pictures to the things they represent.**

Listen to children as they look at pictures and photographs. Be available for conversation, just as Jeff's teacher was when Jeff noticed a plant on the window ledge and announced, "I know what this is called! A zebra plant!" (See How the Zebra Plant Got Its Name, p. 494.) As children cut and paste pictures, talk with them about what they see. When possible, encourage children to locate corresponding real objects or people around them doing similar things. For example, take children to observe at a nearby construction site, then read a book with them that has pictures of construction vehicles. It is important to accept a child's interpretation of what he or she sees, even if it is not the conventional view. One child looked at a picture of a crane and called it "a tractor with a long neck."

As children use models in their play, encourage them to compare the models they are using to the objects they represent, whenever this can be done in a natural, conversational way:

Charlotte: *Hey, Ms. Stewart, look at my bunny. He's hopping, hopping, hopping into his little house.*

Mrs. Stewart: *Your bunny is quite a hopper, like our real bunny.*

Charlotte: *Hop, hop, hop. (Hops her bunny to the real bunny.) Look, they're sniffing each other!*

Mrs. Stewart: *They're touching noses.*

Charlotte: *Yep. My bunny's very, very tiny. I have to hold him in my hand so he won't get hurt. He's going back to his house now. Hop, hop, hop.*

This child examines a photograph of himself that he is about to attach to his cubbie.

Key Developmental Indicator
Making Models Out of Clay, Blocks, and Other Materials

Corey molds Play-Doh into a bumpy oblong, puts a small wooden bead on top of it, and then puts two small Tinkertoy sticks on either side of the bead. Using his deepest voice to make the sound of an engine, he flies it over the table.

～

Andrew makes a rainbow with arcs of blue, green, red, yellow, and purple Play-Doh.

～

"Look at my muscles," Brianna says, holding up "barbells" she has made by attaching two Play-Doh balls to the ends of a paper-towel tube.

～

Chrysten puts a large square hollow block on top of a large rectangular hollow block and says, "It's a couch piano!"

～

Mikey builds a bus out of large hollow blocks, then makes a jack out of snap-together blocks "to jack up the bus."

❧

Using big wooden blocks and colored scarves, Anna and Jessa make a beehive big enough for them to get into.

❧

Douglas works with bobby pins. "Look," he says, "It's an eight-legged spider!"

❧

Donna hammers three pieces of wood together to make an airplane.

❧

"I'm making a drum set," says Trey, taping together three round oatmeal boxes.

❧

Alana makes "pizza with cheese and pepperoni" using cornmeal.

❧

Ben makes a "boy puppet" by stapling paper strips for arms and legs to a head/body made from a piece of cardboard with a slit in the middle.

Young children enjoy creating models of people and things from clay, blocks, wood, boxes, and practically any other materials they can find. They are able to make models because they can form mental images of people and things, and they can see resemblances between their images and a particular medium. They can see, for example, that a snake and a rolled piece of clay share certain structural and dynamic characteristics. Both are long, thin, and pliable. In fact, children's model-making often begins with the spontaneous

How the Zebra Plant Got Its Name: Comparing a Plant and a Picture

One day during work time, a preschool teacher recorded the following conversation with 4-year-old Jeff:

Jeff: (Points to zebra plant growing on a low window ledge.) *You know what this is called?*

Adult: *What?*

Jeff: *A zebra plant.*

Adult: *A zebra plant?*

Jeff: *Uh huh.*

Adult: *Why do you think they call it a zebra plant?*

Jeff: *I don't know.*

Adult: *What does a zebra look like?*

Jeff: *It looks like 'tripes!*

Adult: *Like what?*

Jeff: *'tripes!*

Adult: *Stripes!*

Jeff: *Yah, I'll show you where I know.*

Adult: *OK.*

Jeff: *I'll show you where you can find one.* (Goes to the bookrack and returns with a picture book about animals.)

Adult: *OK, a zebra?*

Relating a zebra plant to a picture of a zebra, this child tells his teacher about stripes!

Jeff: *Yep! Find one here.* (Pages through the book.) *That's what it looks like.* (Points to a picture of a zebra.)

Adult: *That's what a zebra plant looks like?*

Jeff: *Yah. See, it's just like that.*

Adult: *And this is a zebra plant.*

Jeff: *Yah.*

Adult: *How does a zebra look like a plant?*

Jeff: *Well, he has 'tripes and this has 'tripes.* (Indicating the picture of the zebra with one hand and the actual plant with the other.)

Adult: *The zebra has stripes, and the plant has stripes.*

Jeff: *Yah. That's how you know it.*

Adult: *That's why they call it a zebra plant?*

Jeff: *Yah!*

recognition of similarities—"Masking tape looks like Band-Aids!"—and gradually becomes more deliberate as children gain skill with materials. Aimee makes a Band-Aid for Kacey by cutting out a long thin rectangle of tan paper, putting a square of masking tape in the middle, and covering the rest of the Band-Aid with dots.

Model-making strengthens children's understanding of both the real things they are attempting to represent and the complexity of the symbol-making process itself. As model-makers, children are creators and problem-solvers, starting with raw materials and figuring out for themselves how to put them together to make something that resembles the original materials. A child can see a pile of snap-together blocks, for example, and through imagination, trial and error, and persistence, turn them into a one-of-a-kind airplane, walkie-talkie, kitty house, or insect catcher.

Adults who understand the inventive nature of the representation process respect the child's need to construct his or her own models rather than copying models made by adults. Here are ways adults can support the creative processes of young model-makers.

Suggestions for Adults

▶ **Provide a variety of model-making materials.**

Clay. Because clay is easy to mold and change, it is a natural choice for model-making. Working with clay is inherently satisfying to people of all ages. "A material fundamental to the human species," says educator Sydney Clemens, "clay interests and absorbs children. Play-Doh is not the same, Plasticene isn't either; both are pleasant but less basic to people histori-

cally and functionally. If you can go with children to dig out your clay from the earth, so much the better" (1991, p. 10). While clay requires hand washing, the right amount of moisture, and airtight storage, it offers a liveliness and elasticity that no other medium provides. Other pliable, clay-like materials to consider, in addition to clay, include bread and cookie dough, Play-Doh, Plasticene, modeling beeswax, and damp sand.

Blocks. Wood, like clay, is an elemental medium, and wooden blocks—from large hollow blocks, to unit blocks, to small multicolored blocks—provide a unique kind of model-making experience. Unlike clay and other moldable materials, their shape and structure are fixed. Children appreciate their durable nature, harmony, and scale as they use blocks to bring their own images to reality. Wooden blocks are satisfying to handle because of their unchanging structure, heft, smoothness, and density. Other types of blocks to consider stocking include cardboard blocks, box blocks, boards, lumber scraps, and plastic snap-together blocks.

Other materials. Young children also make models from a variety of natural and found materials, including stones, shells, wood, leaves, grass; boxes, cardboard, paper; fabric, yarn, raw wool, and cotton; wire, string, pipe cleaners, tape; industrial scraps; and household recyclables. In combination with some of these materials, they will often use tools such as scissors, staplers, glue, rubber bands, string, hole punches, hammers, and saws.

▶ **Provide time and support for children to explore and gain skill with tools and materials.**

Before young children begin to make models from clay, blocks, and other materials, they need time to explore and figure out how these materials work. Children just beginning to work with clay, for example, generally need lots of time to poke, pound, squeeze, and roll the clay before they use it to make something else. They need the same exploration time with blocks—time to stack, balance, line them up, fill a wagon or bucket with blocks, and dump them out—before they can imagine using blocks to build a house or a beehive. And finally, many young children need time to figure out how to cut fringes and strips

In High/Scope programs, children use a variety of materials to construct unique models.

with scissors, squeeze the glue bottle and watch the glue come out, pound with the hammer, and make sawdust before they are ready to use these materials and tools to make models. Therefore, if you introduce modeling materials and tools at small-group time or simply have them available at work time, anticipate that children will use them in the way that makes most sense to them. They will take as much or as little time as they need to explore them and then move on to making models at their own pace.

Educator Carol Seefeldt (1987, p. 201) reminds us that we need to nurture children's emerging representational and artistic skills over days, months, and years, thus providing

This child is using the large hollow blocks to build a child-sized model house to play in.

children with ongoing, daily opportunities for unhurried exploration and experimentation with materials:

Children continually faced with new media are never able to gain control over or develop skill in the use of any one medium. Nor are they able to discover and explore the opportunities present in any one medium. Visitors to the Far East note that very young children cut wood block prints well in advance of those cut by much older children in the United States. Asian children are introduced to block carving early in life and are allowed to continue developing skill and proficiency with the tools of this medium. Children in the United States usually only experience wood cutting in the fifth or sixth grade, as they cut wood, or some other materials, to create a block-print holiday card. Unless children have the opportunity to gain experience with a medium over time, they will find it difficult to achieve the skills required to use the medium as a means of artistic expression.

▶ **Anticipate a variety of approaches to model-making.**

As you watch children work with clay, blocks, and other materials, anticipate the following approaches:

Exploration. Children exploring clay and blocks are involved in holding, turning, banging, and carrying; rolling, flattening, standing, stacking, and lining up; and bridging, enclosing, and patterning. Basically, they use clay, blocks, and other materials for "sheer pleasure in action for action's sake" (Golomb 1974, p. 177). In other words, everything children do with clay, blocks,

and other modeling materials is not "modeling." Sometimes children simply use the materials for their own sake.

Romancing. "Romancing" (in the sense of embellishing) is a term Golomb (1974) uses to describe what children do when they form something fairly basic from clay or blocks and then use words and actions to fill in for the missing parts. For example, Jalessa hops a blob of clay across the table while saying "Boink, boink, boink. This is a jumping bean." Mikey pushes a block across the floor and makes huffing and chugging noises, pushing things out of the way with his "bulldozer."

Simple models. Children making simple models are determined to create a specific object and sustain this intention as they work. Their ability to hold an image in mind while shaping clay, building with blocks, or cutting and gluing paper is a significant achievement. For example, children planning to make a person might do the following: poke facial features into a slab of clay; make a ball of clay for a head, and poke in two Tinkertoy sticks for the legs; or, on a piece of cardboard, glue one Popsicle stick down for a body, head, and legs, and glue two other popsicle sticks on either side of the first for arms. A child planning to make a house might surround herself with large hollow blocks, leaving an opening for the door, or position pillows and cardboard pieces at an angle against the wall and crawl under them. As Golomb (1974, pp. 90–91) points out, when children make simple models "the difficulty of modeling tends to reinforce the inclination toward economy and simplicity in representation. . . . The youngster displays freedom from constraints, license to include a feature or leave it out, much as he pleases, so long as the basic structural requirements are met."

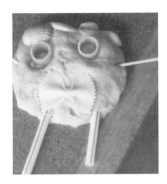

Preschool children made these clay models of people. The figures range from simple models in which the arms are attached directly to the head, to detailed models that include fingers and toes.

Detailed models. When making more detailed models, young children are apt to focus on whatever part they are working on with great intensity and enthusiasm, regardless of its overall importance to the whole piece. As Golomb (1974) watched children making clay people, she observed that "the need for a visually intelligent subdivision of the figure into distinctive parts is the main concern at this stage of modeling; aspects of realistic proportion are generally ignored. When the arms are first endowed with fingers, their size is determined by the zest of creation and need for symmetry rather than by realistic proportions. The modeled parts seem to increase in size as the child proceeds with his work" (p. 144).

When children make more detailed block models, they tend to do so by adding small blocks, small-scale figures, and furniture to larger blocks. They are also apt to work cooperatively with one or two other children on larger, more detailed models—big block towers, dinosaurs or robots made from boxes, forts built out of tree stumps and sheets, a car fashioned out of milk crates and old tires.

Children making detailed models are generally very persistent because they have a picture in mind of what they are making and what they want it to look like. Sometimes, however,

even the most determined children stop in frustration. Ben, for example, had spent almost all of work time making a mask. He had assembled the whole mask except for attaching the yarn needed to tie it to his head. Ben punched two holes in the mask and threaded the yarn through the holes, but each time he tied the string to his mask and tried it on, the strings were too short to fit around his head. Sam, an adult, had been keeping track of Ben's progress all morning. When it became apparent that Ben had done everything he could

This adult watches and listens carefully as these two children work on their "garage."

to solve the string problem on his own, Sam sat down next to him and helped him measure the string around his head before cutting it in lengths for tying. With Sam's assistance at this critical juncture, Ben was able to put on his mask in the way he had envisioned.

▶ **Find out from children what they are making.**

To show respect for children's intentions, it is important that adults listen to children to find out from them what they think they are making. This helps adults avoid making statements such as, "Oh, Jimmy, what a long boat you're making," when, in fact, Jimmy is making a school bus.

Listen to children as they plan their models. At planning time, some children plan to make models. They make statements such as these:

"I'm gonna make a birdhouse." "We're making an ambulance with all the big blocks and the steering wheel." "I'm gonna make snakes . . . clay ones . . . and snake food. It will be little bits." Plans do change, but if Kerry says she is going to make a birdhouse at the workbench, and you see her later at the workbench assembling a house-like structure, it is probably safe to make a comment such as "I see you've got a start on your birdhouse, Kerry."

Listen to children as they work on their models. Children will often comment on what they are doing in the midst of their work. Their commentaries may serve to consolidate and communicate the process of thought enacted in their model-making: "This can be the top . . . steering wheel here . . ." Also, verbalizing their thoughts may help them solve problems they encounter: "Let's see . . . How am I gonna keep this wheel on?"

Listen to children as they share their models. Children generally want to show someone what they have made. When they have finished their boats or birdhouses, they will often bring them to an adult to see and acknowledge. If what you are looking at is not perfectly clear to you, start with a descriptive comment:

Child: *Look!* (Gives adult a creation made from construction paper.) *It's for you.*

Adult: *Thank you.* (Not sure what she is receiving, she examines it carefully.) *This part opens up.*

Child: *It's a pencil holder . . . Like this.* (Demonstrates.)

Adult: *I see. This part that opens up is where the pencils go.*

Child: *Yep. It's for a lot of pencils . . . so they can't be lost. You'll know where to find 'em.*

Adult: *I will know where to find them.*

Children may also demonstrate and talk about their models at recall time.

▶ **At small-group time, ask children to make something using clay, blocks, or other materials.**

One way to observe the process of model-making up close is to provide children with clay or blocks or other model-making materials at small-group time. You might begin such a small-group time in one of several ways:

- "Here is some clay. See what you can do with it."

- "Here is some clay. I wonder if anyone can make a person with it."

- "Here is some clay. I wonder if anyone can make something we saw on our trip to the barbershop."

Regardless of how you begin, children will respond in a variety of ways—including exploring, romancing, making simple models, and making detailed models—depending on the children's experiences with the material you offer and their ability to work from their own mental images.

Key Developmental Indicator
Drawing and Painting

Abby paints by dipping a golf ball in paint and rolling it across her paper. Ursula watches her.

∽

Jonah and Rachel stand side by side at the easel. On his half of the paper, using a brush full of black, then red, then white paint, Jonah makes vertical strokes that all run together. On her side, with a brush in each hand, Rachel makes distinct green lines.

∽

Alana bends intently over her paper as she fills it with marks and squiggles in orange, green, blue, and brown magic marker.

∽

Brianna makes lots of dots on her paper. "Julie, here's a whole bunch of ants," she says.

∽

"I was thinking of making an envelope and I made it!" Through paintings and drawings such as this one, young children communicate—simply and economically—their thoughts, feelings, and experiences.

Colin draws a tiger with lots of stripes and 15 legs. Then he draws "a rock" on its back. "That makes it safe for bad guys," he says.

∽

Shannon paints four things: a large black shape, a large yellow shape, a brown circle, and a series of interconnected blue circles. When she shows her painting to her teacher, Shannon asks her to write down these words: "Don't worry about the tornado. God has matters well in hand. From Shannon to Jessica."

∽

Hannah draws "a rainbow" with lots of colors, then glues on Styrofoam "raindrops" and a ribbon on the bottom "for the ground."

∽

Using a pencil, Ben draws a person sitting on a chair at a table. Just above the table he draws an envelope. In a cartoon-like bubble above the person's head he draws another enve-

Both tables and easels make good painting surfaces. Some children find it easier to control their hand movements when painting at a table.

lope. He dictates the following caption for his drawing: "I was thinking of making an envelope and I made it."

Preschool children use paints, markers, and pencils to make marks and create their own symbols and images to stand for the mental images they have formed of the things they have seen and done. Working alone and sometimes in pairs, they easily become absorbed in painting and drawing in ways that are playful and inventive.

Through drawing and painting, children communicate, simply and economically, what they understand about their world. According to Gardner (1982), the images children create on paper are characterized by a "simplicity of forms, disregard of fine detail, and freedom in rendering spatial relations" (p. 110). As illustrated in Shannon's explanation about tornadoes and God in the preceding examples, children also attempt to create a certain amount of order in their knowl-

edge and gain some degree of control over the often confusing things that happen in their world. The page they begin with is blank, but they learn through their own experiences with paints and pencils that they can fill it in a way that makes sense to them and gives them almost magical powers to create images, stories, and outcomes.

Yet, drawing and painting are not simple processes for young children, as Golomb (1974) reminds us: "The complex coordination of intention, action on the medium, and the looks of the final product is a difficult task. The young artist must sustain his intention throughout the intricate process of creating forms and recognizing the outcome of his efforts as the figure he set out to make" (p. 14).

In their support of young artists, it is important that adults understand and respect each child's efforts to invent, transform, and communicate mental images through the media of paper, paints, pencils, and markers. Following are ways adults can support children as they paint and draw.

Suggestions for Adults

▶ **Provide materials for drawing and painting.**

Stock the art area with a wide variety of materials for painting and drawing—paints, paper, paintbrushes, markers, crayons, colored pencils. (See the art-area materials list in Chapter 5, p. 135.) Be sure these materials are available for

children to use during work time and the rest of the day—whenever they wish to paint or draw.

An *ample supply of paper* is very important for young artists. This means finding lots of sources of scrap paper, including paper remnants from offices, recycling centers, printers, and photo-copying businesses, as well as providing "clean" sheets and rolls of paper. Along with a range of papers, provide sturdy, high-quality brushes, colored pencils, crayons, and markers.

Also, think about *surfaces* for drawing and painting. Consider both conventional easels and large side-by-side easels that make painting a more communal affair. Consider also that many children find it easier to draw and paint on a table than at an easel. In one study comparing easel paintings to table-top paintings, observers concluded that "the use of tables as a painting surface facilitated the use of more advanced hand positions during painting tasks than did the use of easels" (Seefeldt 1987, p. 202).

If you have computers or other technology devices, you will want to look for appropriate open-ended computer drawing programs that enable young children to create all kinds of images by drawing with a mouse and adding colors.

Also, do not forget to consider *outdoor drawing and painting experiences*. Provide painting and drawing materials suitable for children to use outdoors such as colored chalk, water, large brushes, paints, and butcher paper for group painting.

▶ **Provide time and support for children to explore and gain skill with drawing and painting materials and procedures.**

Painting and drawing are thoughtful processes, so it is important to provide enough unhurried time at work time, small-group time, outside time, and other times for children to com-

These children have drawn themselves at their small-group table. Note that they use lines and details sparingly and that each figure is unique.

plete their pictures to their own satisfaction. Since a child may take more than one day to complete a drawing or painting, it is also important to give children daily access to paints, paintbrushes, paper, markers, crayons, and pencils.

As with model-making, many children experiment with color and technique before they begin to use paints and pencils to make images that represent or stand for things. Therefore, time for exploration is necessary. Painter and educator Nancy Smith (1982) explains that "it is essential to the creation of meaning with materials for the child to develop a deep and rich understanding of the physical and visual properties of materials. In order for this to take place, opportunities for experimentation with appropriate materials over sufficient time are necessary" (p. 302).

Early in the year, help children learn to mix their own paints so they can provide themselves with the colors they desire.

▶ **Anticipate a variety of approaches to drawing and painting.**

As you watch children draw and paint, you will probably see them making many kinds of pictures.

Marks and scribbles. Children new to drawing and painting become absorbed in using paints and drawing tools to make marks. They are fascinated with the physical process of making dots, lines, blobs, and swirls. "In the pure scribble stage," Golomb (1974) observes, "motor joy rules supreme and the child is unconcerned with the looks of the final product, though he is generally pleased that his vigorous motions leave visible marks on the paper" (p. 3). Children using paints and markers in this fashion are apt to keep painting or drawing on the same piece of paper until it is completely covered. The fact that they are drawing or painting over marks and lines they have just made does not concern them and need not concern adults either.

Shapes. When children have had plenty of time to fill up lots of paper with marks and scribbles, they eventually discover that they can make shapes. Once children find that they can make shapes, they do so quite deliberately with a great deal of concentration and care: "Drawing a single line that encloses an area and arrives back at its starting point demonstrates a remarkable visual-motor control. . . . The successful drawing of a contour illustrates a new degree of mastery and the deliberate use of lines to create a stable and meaningful shape" (Golomb 1992, p. 15).

Simple figures. Children who make simple figures and objects are beginning to use painting and drawing to represent images they have in their minds. They draw sparingly and economically using the fewest lines possible to capture the most salient features of whatever they are drawing or painting. The people they make are often what are commonly referred to as "tadpole people"—a circle with two descending lines. When the drawing itself does not tell the whole story, the child uses words to fill in the missing details. "The notion that a drawing should present a self-sufficient statement is as yet absent from the child's mind, and he adopts the easiest solution available to him, namely to *verbally* correct the imperfections" (Golomb 1992, p. 25).

More distinctive figures. Eventually, young children add more details to their drawings and paintings to distinguish people from animals, girls from boys, houses from forts, firetrucks from pickup trucks, older children from babies, and so

forth. "The early human and animal drawings are much alike, and it is this lack of differentiation that prompts the child to alter the figure, to add defining marks that distinguish between humans and animals. In the case of humans, the differentiation occurs along the vertical axis; in the case of animals, it is mostly along a horizontal axis" (Golomb 1992, p. 26).

Regardless of whether children are making simple or more detailed drawings and paintings, Golomb reminds us to focus on what the child *has* drawn rather than on what the child has *not* drawn: "We ought to be extremely cautious when interpreting missing features from the drawings of children of all ages: (a) the child may not consider them essential; (b) there may be insufficient space to accommodate the features; (c) the item may be difficult to represent so the child substitutes a verbal designation for a missing part" (Golomb 1988, p. 234).

▶ **Watch and listen to children as they draw and paint.**

Again, as with children's models, it is important that adults find out *from children* what they are drawing and painting rather than jumping to conclusions based on their own adult interpretations of children's art.

One way to do this is to sit near a child who is painting or drawing and simply watch

By giving the child control of the conversation, the adult who talked with this young artist found out what she had in mind as she drew: "The baby zebra's holding the mom's tail. She doesn't want to be lost."

and listen. Adults who have done so find that children often talk aloud to themselves about what they are drawing as they draw. Listening to and watching the work-in-progress gives adults a view of what the drawing or painting means *to the child*. As artist and educator Christine Thompson (1990) explains, "Not only does the child recognize more in the drawing than the adult is likely to detect; she may also offer a series of seemingly incompatible interpretations for the same set of marks" (p. 229).

▶ **Talk with children about their paintings and drawings.**

Often, when children finish a painting or drawing they want to show it to someone who will take the time to look at and acknowledge what they have done. When children bring you their paintings and drawings or call you over to view their creations, you have a valuable opportunity for engaging in a dialogue about their art.

By studying the child's drawing, giving the child the opportunity to make the first observation, and commenting on the elements of art you see—such as line, pattern, texture, shape, space, mass, and color—you become part of a conversation in which you begin to discover what the child is thinking about and trying to express. As Thompson (1990) puts it, "The child who receives such recognition, whose work and works are deemed worthy of respectful acceptance, grows in the certainty of her power to affect the world in concrete and meaningful ways" (p. 230):

Child: *Look!*

Adult: (Looks at child's drawing.)

Child: *That's the mom . . . and the baby.*

Adult: *I see. The mom and the baby.*

Child: *The baby's holding the mom's tail . . . she doesn't want to be lost.*

Adult: *She wants to stay by her mom.*

Child: *Yep, in case of the alligators.*

Adult: *Oh, I see . . . The mom and the baby have lines.*

Child: *That's 'cause they're zebras! They have stripes . . . like grass.*

Adult: *The zebra stripes are like the grass.*

▶ **Provide many examples of artists' paintings and drawings.**

As they draw and paint, children may become interested in how other people use the same materials. If an image, material, or technique a child is using reminds you of an existing work of art, mention it conversationally and show the child the two works side by side. Give children the opportunity to comment on the relationships they see. Hang reproductions in the art area so children can examine the styles and media different artists use.

▶ **Include drawing opportunities in planning, recall, small-group, and large-group times.**

Planning and recall times provide regular opportunities for drawing. Once a week, for example, you might ask children to draw what

Displaying children's paintings allows children to see and enjoy one another's creations.

Visual Art Strategies: A Summary

Relating models, photographs, and pictures to real places and things

___ Provide models for children to play with.
___ Provide photographs and pictures for children to look at:
    ___ Photograph the children in your program.
    ___ Provide children with a simple working camera.
    ___ Provide illustrated storybooks and art reproductions.
    ___ Include all sorts of catalogs and picture magazines in the art area.
    ___ Use photographs of children at small-group time.
___ Support and encourage children's comparisons of models and pictures to the things they represent.

Making models out of clay, blocks, and other materials

___ Provide a variety of model-making materials:
    ___ Clay
    ___ Blocks
    ___ Other materials
___ Provide time and support for children to explore and gain skill with tools and materials.
___ Anticipate a variety of approaches to model-making:
    ___ Exploration
    ___ Romancing
    ___ Simple models
    ___ Detailed models
___ Find out from children what they are making:
    ___ Listen to children as they plan their models.
    ___ Listen to children as they work on their models.
    ___ Listen to children as they share their models.
___ At small-group time, ask children to make something out of clay, blocks, or other materials.

Drawing and painting

___ Provide materials for drawing and painting.
___ Provide time and support for children to explore and gain skill with drawing and painting materials and procedures.
___ Anticipate a variety of approaches to drawing and painting:
    ___ Marks and scribbles
    ___ Shapes
    ___ Simple figures
    ___ More distinctive figures
___ Watch and listen to children as they draw and paint.
___ Talk with children about their paintings and drawings.
___ Provide many examples of artists' paintings and drawings.
___ Include drawing opportunities in planning, recall, small-group and large-group times.
___ Display and send home children's paintings and drawings.

---

they plan to do, and at recall time, to draw something they did at work time. Within the planning and recall groups you will probably see a range of drawing styles—from marks and squiggles, to shapes, to simple and detailed images.

Periodically asking children to draw at small-group time provides another opportunity for children to draw and for you to give support by watching and listening attentively. Here are some approaches to try:

• "Here are some markers and paper. Let's make some drawings."

• "Remember our trip to the barbershop yesterday? . . . I wonder if you could draw something you saw on the trip."

• "We've been doing lots of things with apples since we visited the apple orchard . . . Let's see if we can draw apples. Here are some red, green, and yellow apples and some apple-tree branches you might want to look at as you draw."

• "On our wall we have photographs of our families. I wonder if we could draw our families today."

▶ **Display and send home children's paintings and drawings.**

Displaying and sending home children's pictures allows children to see one another's paintings and drawings and to share them with family members. As part of the drawing and painting process, children can also hang their own pictures on walls and bulletin boards.

Taking photographs of children's paintings and drawings is another way to show children you value their work and also to share children's artwork with parents. Sharing a series of such photographs at a parent meeting, for example, not only displays children's work but also serves to make parents aware of and appreciative of the variety of approaches children take to drawing and painting. Thus, parents will feel assured that making marks and squiggles, shapes, and simple and detailed images are equally important efforts in the life of the young artist. At one preschool center, the teaching team helped children prepare an art gallery for their parents. Adults and children grouped children's paintings, drawings, and models throughout the room and invited parents to tour the gallery at the end of the day.

In the drawing, handwritten labels: "Douglas" at top, "Its a person. It walks." at bottom.

In this drawing, dots and circles stand for a variety of features, including eyes, ear holes, multiple elbows, and knees!

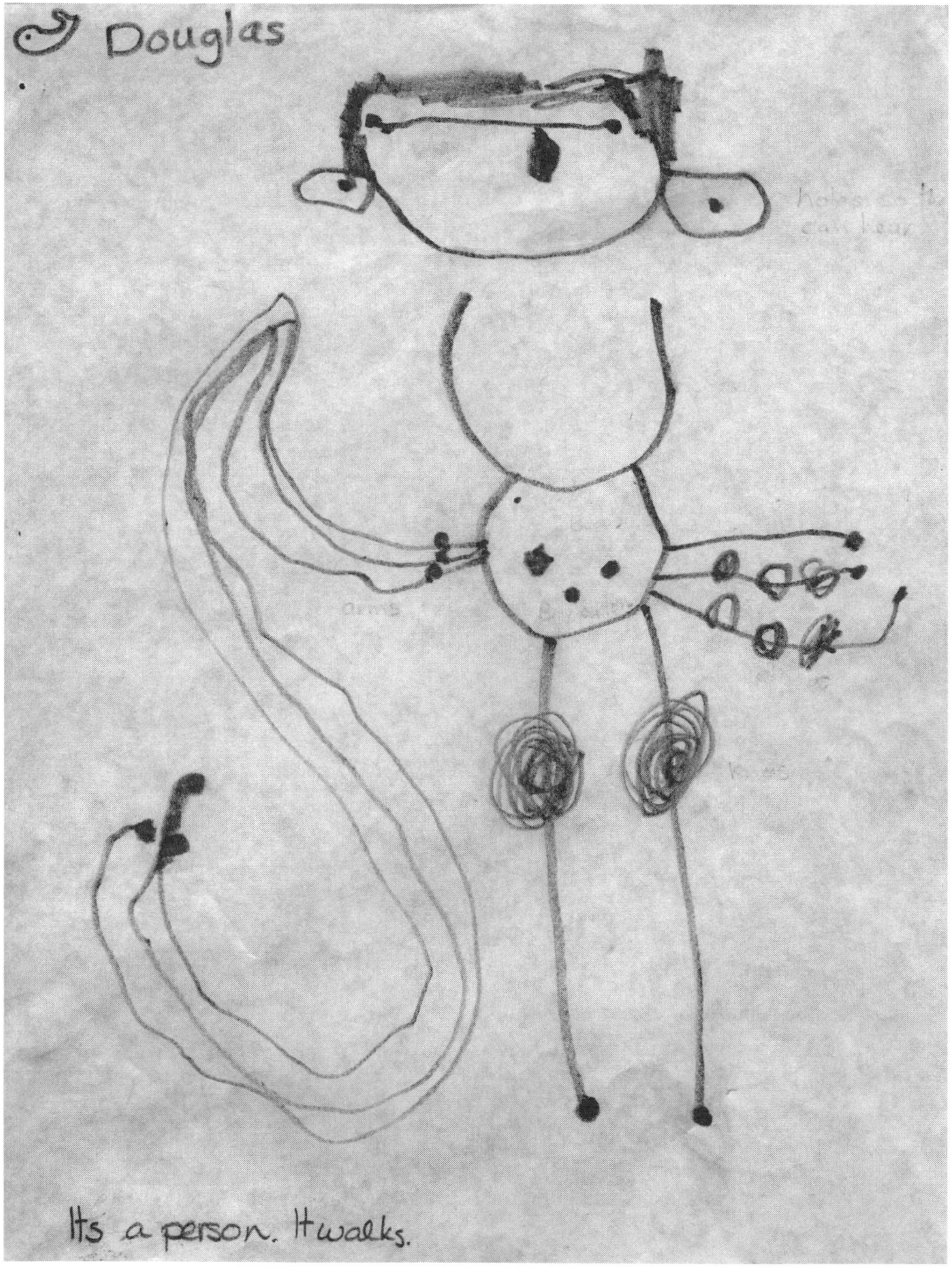

References

Arnheim, Rudolf. 1989. *Thoughts on Arts Education.* Los Angeles: The Getty Center for Education in the Arts.

Arts Education Partnership. 1998. *Young Children and the Arts: Making Creative Connection — A Report of the Task Force on Children's Learning and the Arts: Birth to Age Eight.* Washington, DC: Author.

Clemens, Sydney G. 1991. "Art in the Classroom: Making Every Day Special." *Young Children* 46, no. 2 (January): 4–10.

Dobbs, Stephen M. 1998. *Learning In and Through Art.* Los Angeles: The Getty Education Institute for the Arts.

Ginsburg, Herbert, and Sylvia Opper. 1979. *Piaget's Theory of Intellectual Development.* Englewood, NJ: Prentice-Hall.

Golomb, Claire. 1988. "Symbolic Inventions and Transformations in Child Art." In *Imagination and Education,* Kieran Egan and Dan Nadaner, eds., 222–35. New York: Teachers College Press.

Golomb, Claire. 1992. *The Child's Creation of a Pictorial World.* Berkeley, CA: University of California Press.

Golomb, Claire. 1974. *Young Children's Sculpture and Drawing: A Study in Representational Development.* Cambridge: Harvard University Press.

Schiller, Marjorie. 1995. "An Emergent Art Curriculum That Fosters Understanding." *Young Children* 50, no. 3: 33–38.

Seefeldt, Carol. 1999. "Art for Young Children." In *The Early Childhood Curriculum: Current Findings in Theory and Practice,* 3rd ed., Carol Seefeldt ed., 201–17. New York: Teachers College Press.

Seefeldt, Carol. 1987. "The Visual Arts." In *The Early Childhood Curriculum: A Review of the Current Research,* Carol Seefeldt, ed., 183–210. New York: Teachers College Press.

Smith, Nancy. 1982. "The Visual Arts in Early Childhood Education: Development and the Creation of Meaning." In *Handbook of Research in Early Childhood Education*, Bernard Spodek, ed., 295–317. New York: Macmillan.

Thompson, Christine Marmé. 1990. "'I Make a Mark': The Significance of Talk in Young Children's Artistic Development." *Early Childhood Research Quarterly* 5, no. 2: 215–32.

Related Reading

Edwards, Carolyn, Lella Gandini, and George Forman, eds. 1998. *The Hundred Languages of Children: The Reggio Emilia Approach to Early Childhood Education*, 2nd ed. Norwood: Ablex Publishing.

Eisner, Elliot W. 1990. "The Role of Art and Play in Children's Cognitive Development." In *Children's Play and Learning*, Edgar Klugman and Sara Smilansky, eds., 43–56. New York: Teachers College Press.

Epstein, Ann S. 2005. "So, You're Not Picasso? You Can Still Teach Art!" "How to Talk to Children About Art." In *Supporting Young Learners 4: Ideas for Child Care Providers and Teachers*, Nancy A. Brickman, Holly Barton, and Jennifer Burd, eds., 179–84. Ypsilanti, MI: High/Scope Press.

Epstein, Ann S. 2001. "Thinking About Art: Encouraging Art Appreciation in Early Childhood Settings." *Young Children* 53, no. 3: 38–43.

Epstein, Ann S. 2001. "Thinking About Art With Young Children." In *Supporting Young Learners 3: Ideas for Child Care Providers and Teachers*, Nancy A. Brickman, ed., 185–93. Ypsilanti, MI: High/Scope Press.

Epstein, Ann S. 2007. "What Is the High/Scope Curriculum in the Arts?" Chap. 17 in *Essentials of Active Learning in Preschool: Getting to Know the High/Scope Curriculum*, 173–90. Ypsilanti, MI: High/Scope Press.

Epstein, Ann S., Beth Marshall, Rosie Lucier, Mary Delcamp, and Suzanne Gainsley. 2001. "Walking and Talking About Art." In *Supporting Young Learners 3: Ideas for Child Care Providers and Teachers*, Nancy A. Brickman, ed., 195–97. Ypsilanti, MI: High/Scope Press.

Epstein, Ann S., and Eli Trimis. 2002. *Supporting Young Artists: The Development of the Visual Arts in Young Children*. Ypsilanti, MI: High/Scope Press.

Gardner, Howard. 1980. *Artful Scribbles: The Significance of Children's Drawings*. New York: Basic Books.

Graves, Michelle. 1996. "Field Trips: A New Definition." In *Supporting Young Learners 2*, Nancy A. Brickman, ed., 257–64. Ypsilanti, MI: High/Scope Press.

Graves, Michelle. 1996. *The Teacher's Idea Book 2: Planning Around Children's Interests*. Ypsilanti, MI: High/Scope Press.

High/Scope Educational Research Foundation. 2003. *Preschool Child Observation Record (COR)*, 2nd ed. Ypsilanti, MI: High/Scope Press.

Hohmann, Mary. 2001. "Supporting Children's Development in Drawing and Painting." In *Supporting Young Learners 3: Ideas for Child Care Providers and Teachers*, Nancy A. Brickman, ed., 175–84. Ypsilanti, MI: High/Scope Press.

Johnson, Harriet M. 1984. "The Art of Block Building." In *The Block Book*, Elisabeth S. Hirsch, ed., 15–49. Washington, DC: NAEYC.

Marshall, Beth. 2005. "Art Vocabulary Words." In *Supporting Young Learners 4: Ideas for Child Care Providers and Teachers*, Nancy A. Brickman, Holly Barton, and Jennifer Burd, eds., 185–89. Ypsilanti, MI: High/Scope Press.

Tompkins, Mark. 1996. "A Partnership With Young Artists." In *Supporting Young Learners 2*, Nancy A. Brickman, ed., 187–92. Ypsilanti, MI: High/Scope Press.

Related Media

The following materials are available from the High/Scope Press, 600 N. River St., Ypsilanti, MI 48198-2898; to order, visit *www.highscope.org*, or call 1-800-40-PRESS.

Adult-Child Interactions: Forming Partnerships With Children. 1996. Color videotape, 60 min. Ypsilanti, MI: High/Scope Press.

Creative Representation. 2000. Color videotape or DVD, 40 min. Ypsilanti, MI: High/Scope Press.

In imitation and dramatic play, children use gestures, sounds, and props to represent and tell stories about the world they know.

21
Dramatic Art

Dramatic art in young children involves both **imitation** and **imagination.** When children imitate and pretend, they use gestures, sounds, and props to represent and tell stories about the world they know. In using their imagination, preschoolers express their fantasies. They act out the "what if's" that fill their thoughts and reveal their feelings and intentions. Recreating or modifying the events in their lives also helps young children understand and feel a sense of control over their environment. For more on imitation as a form of representation, see Chapter 20.

Supporting Dramatic Art

In preschool, the purpose of dramatic art is discovery and exploration, not performance—just as High/Scope emphasizes process over product in the early development of visual art. **Pretending** and **role playing** are also inherently social activities. Children interact with one another and partnering adults; they contribute ideas and build on the ideas of others. And although High/Scope teachers do not pressure preschoolers to put on dramatic productions, they recognize that children can and do enjoy watching and discussing the performances of others. Live theater, especially productions whose length and content are created with young children's interests and developmental levels in mind, presents exciting opportunities for children to experience and reflect on theater as yet another means of artistic representation.

High/Scope has **two key developmental indicators (KDIs)** in dramatic art.

- **Initiating actions and sounds**
- **Pretending and role playing**

The first encourages children to be aware of and imitate the movements and sounds in their environment. The second focuses on pretending and role playing—a type of play that is a significant part of preschoolers' spontaneous activity. Adults can encourage and extend these natural processes in the ways suggested below.

Key Developmental Indicator
Imitating Actions and Sounds

Timmy stands in front of the mirror in the house area, his face covered with shaving cream, and uses a small spatula to shave.

∽

Kara stops building her block house, picks up the telephone, and calls Jeff.

∽

Joey walks on hands and feet. "Look! I can walk like a spider!"

∽

Alana puts a tie around her neck, then goes up to her teacher and says, "Tie it just like yours."

∽

Tracy whizzes by Maurine, turns the steering wheel sharply to avoid the corner of the shed, makes a screeching sound, and brings the wheel-toy bus to a stop.

∽

In preschool children's dramatic play we can often see almost all the qualities of drama as an art form—plot, characterization, setting and scenery, story, intensity, and themes that are a reflection of society and self.
—Ursula Ansbach, 2001

- Imitating actions and sounds
- Pretending and role playing

As Julie plays the guitar for large-group time, Andrew holds his hands in a similar position and "strums" along with her.

Jonah spins around on the trapeze and chants, "I'm going down the drain. I'm going down the drain!"

As Betsy videotapes the children at work time, Amanda walks around behind her, holding a box and making her own "videotape" with it.

Nathan plays the drum and occasionally hits a metal measuring cup for his "cymbal."

Jalessa "flies" two snap-together blocks around the room as she makes an "airplane noise."

At recall time, Mikey shows how he worked at the computer keyboard by moving his hands to simulate typing motions.

These preschoolers are imitating the actions of familiar people, animals, and things. They began this process as infants by copying adult actions such as drinking from cups, waving, and making sounds. As they grew into toddlers and preschoolers, they continued to learn through imitation, imitating increasingly complex actions—driving a car, riding a horse, dancing, and writing. Through imitation, preschoolers re-enact with their own bodies and voices what they understand about their world.

Ginsburg and Opper (1979) observe that "during the sensorimotor period, the infant develops abilities in imitative behavior. When he is proficient at imitation at a later age, he begins to imitate internally, and thereby forms the mental symbol" (p. 81). Imitation, then, lays the groundwork for mental image-making, pretending, and make-believe. Tracing the development of children's art, Golomb (1974) points out that "both sensorimotor imitation and representation reflect a desire to create a likeness of the model. In the former, however, the aim is to achieve a very close approximation, possibly identical behavior, while in the latter the aim is to create structural and dynamic equivalences" (p. 183).

Here are some ways adults can support preschool children as they continue to imitate, that is, reproduce with their own bodies, the actions and sounds they encounter.

Suggestions for Adults

► **Watch for children's spontaneous imitations.**

As children engage in active learning, be on the lookout for imitative elements in their play. For example, you might see children rocking dolls or stuffed animals, stirring pretend concoctions at the stove, talking on the phone, writing a message in scribbles, using a screwdriver to "fix things." You might also see children imitating each other: Erica makes a window tower; Billy watches her and tries the same technique. Troy develops a "limp" and so does his friend Alyce. Tuning in to children's imitations tells you something about what they understand, what is interesting to them, and what they may be imagining.

► **Imitate children's actions and sounds.**

One way adults can support young children's inclinations toward imitation is to become

These preschoolers use their bodies and voices to imitate a goose they see in the park!

imitators themselves. By imitating children's actions as they build with blocks, play with dolls, put together a puzzle, pour sand, or mold clay, adults not only convey their interest and respect but also enter the flow of the child's thought and action. Research psychologists George Forman and David Kuschner (1983) describe how imitating children affects the adult's understanding of the child:

> When the teacher begins to imitate the child, something interesting happens. The teacher, perhaps for the first time, begins to feel what it is like to be a child again. Imitating the child is an excellent way to gain insight into the child's intentions, style, and problems. As the teacher begins to make the same moves— and, consequently, the same mistakes—as the child, the actual movements influence her thinking. The teacher not only imitates the child but begins to reflect on her own movements. The child's use of repetition, difficulty with simple motor coordinations, lack of foresight, attention to action, and sensation of movement while watching—all make a greater impact on the teacher when she is imitating the child (p. 134).

Imitating children's actions can also bring about an "action dialogue." For example, a child is sitting on a block "driving a car." You sit on a block and imitate the child driving a car. After a bit, you "beep" your make-believe horn. The child "beeps" her "horn" then turns on the "radio," so you turn on your "radio." Back and forth you go in this fashion, creating a play sequence built on mutual imitation.

▶ **Build opportunities for imitation into the daily routine.**

At **recall time** you might suggest that children show what they did through pantomime—

making pudding, stacking blocks, stringing beads, painting, playing the drums, hammering—and encourage the other children to imitate them. When you read stories at **small-group time,** encourage children to imitate the actions of characters in the story. At **large-group time,** when you sing and make up new verses for songs such as "This Is the Way We Wash Our Clothes," children can imitate familiar actions like going to bed, waking up, dressing, eating, going to school. You can also modify these songs so they reflect the actions the children participated in at work time or on a field trip. And in games like "Everybody Do This," children enjoy imitating the actions and sounds of others.

Becki Perrett (1992), High/Scope teacher and consultant, recommends imitation at **cleanup time:** "Sometimes children enjoy carrying toys in unique ways. If you see Athi carrying something on his back, try imitating him as you carry a toy to its place on the shelf. This will probably catch the attention of other children who will then imitate what they see you and Athi doing" (p. 4).

After a **field trip** make up stories or songs with children. Include actions and sounds children saw and heard on the trip that they can imitate as they sing or listen. After a field trip to a farm, for example, children might come up with such ideas as mimicking a cow mooing, milking a

After watching a mom bathe her baby, this child imitates the mom's actions as she bathes her doll baby at the water table.

cow, driving a tractor, and putting bales of hay on the wagon. After a trip to a fire station, the children might imitate a firefighter putting on his boots, coat, and hat, climbing onto the firetruck, and ringing the bell.

Key Developmental Indicator
Pretending and Role Playing

Outside, Andrew pretends the climber is his rocketship.

❧

Kacey puts "magic blue" marker on her hands to "catch a rabbit."

❧

"I have some checks to mail," Erica says to Nathan. "Here's a bank house so you can get some more money," Nathan replies.

❧

"I'm Santa Claus," Douglas says to Brian and Sarah. "It's Christmas Eve. Everybody go to sleep!" Brian and Sarah lie on the floor, cover themselves with scarves, and go to sleep.

❧

Alana picks up a plastic banana, pushes some "buttons" on it, holds it between her ear and her mouth, and says, "Hello . . . I need some pizza!"

❧

Jonah and Jason, both "puppies," crawl together, then stop. "Pretend I'm sad 'cuz my parents died," Jonah says to Jason. "They were killed by a hunter."

❧

"Don't take out your ponytail," Kacey says to the kitty puppet. "Okay," she makes the puppet reply in a soft, squeaky "kitty" voice.

❧

Timmy and Ricky put on fire hats, boots, and coats and load their hollow-block firetruck with a ladder and hoses. "Brriing, brriing!" Ricky

intones, and then answers the phone. "Fire at Becky's!" he says. "Fire at Becky's!" says Timmy as they get in the firetruck and "drive" to the fire.

❧

Lisa washes dishes inside a cardboard house. "I'm home, honey!" Billy calls through the window."Okay, baby," Lisa replies. "I need some clothes," Billy says. He finds pants for himself and throws a dress to Lisa. "Here's yours, honey," he says.

Making-believe—pretending to be a mom, a baby lion, a robot, a princess—is another way young children represent what they know about people, animals, and situations. Through their play, they act out the mental images they have formed of common human events such as eating, sleeping, working, shopping, moving, and having birthdays. Pretending is an **intentional process** that involves what psychologist Otto Weininger (1988) calls "what if" thinking leading to "as if" play: "For example, the child thinks, 'What if I were a firefighter? What would I do?' The child thinks about this for a while, assembling the bits of reality known about firefighters derived from observations of real life, storybooks, the comments of adults, and television. The child first imagines what being a firefighter would be like and how it would feel to be one, and then plays it out 'as if' he or she were one" (p. 144).

In her long-term observations of children's dramatic play, psychologist Sara Smilansky (1990) sees children's pretending as an ongoing improvisational process that calls for both imitation of reality and imagination or make-believe to smooth over contradictions and inconsistencies. ("Let's pretend it's winter now and we're penguins at the zoo . . . and we can fly!") Pretend play tends to be fluid and flexible, and children often engage in complex dialogue, making up the script as they go.

Through imitation and make-believe, children sort out what they understand and gain a measure of mastery and control over events they have witnessed or taken part in—making breakfast, going to work, going to a party, visiting friends, taking care of a baby, going to the dentist, attending a wedding, putting out a fire.

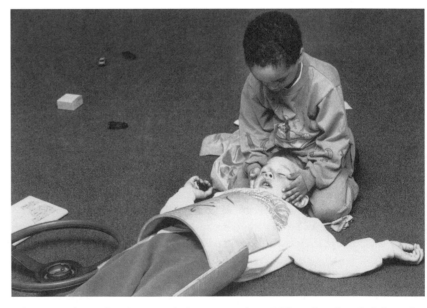

After a "smash-up" the "doctor" aids the "race car driver." Through such make-believe play, children gain mastery and control over events they have witnessed, experienced, or imagined.

"Once, a razor fell on my leg," Jason says to Betsy, his teacher. "I'm pretending this [block] is a razor." The logic and meaning of these events often escape young children, but pretend play helps them begin to make sense of their world.

Pretending and role playing tend to be highly social undertakings and seem to have a positive effect on children's social and language development. Educator Greta Fein (1981) reports on a series of studies that correlate dramatic play with cooperation, friendliness, general adjustment, and the use of language during play. Fein also finds that "children who tend to play imaginatively may also be less aggressive in their nonplay social interactions" (p. 1103).

It is important for adults to support children's pretending and role play by providing appropriate materials and props, observing and listening to pretend play, and interacting as partners with children, honoring the flow and pace the children have set for themselves. Following are suggestions for adults to use in supporting children's pretend play.

Suggestions for Adults

▶ **Provide materials and props for pretending and role play.**

A well-equipped preschool space divided into interest areas provides all kinds of materials children can use for pretending and role play and for making their own props—tickets for the play, masks, hats, a beehive, a barber's chair, and so forth. (See also the materials lists in Chapter 5, pp. 125–145.)

Remember also to provide outdoor materials and equipment for pretending and role

play. With more space and fewer boundaries, outdoor make-believe often involves robust and highly mobile play. Children will make use of anything available—wagons, tricycles, and other wheeled toys to serve as cars, buses, trains, boats; large packing boxes, boards, sheets, ropes, and tires for houses, stores, forts, and caves; sand and sand utensils for cooking, eating, and "going to work." They may also wish to bring loose materials—such as hats, scarves, baby dolls, dishes, and chalk—from inside to add to their outdoor play.

▶ **Support pretend play that moves from place to place.**

Pretend play often begins in the house area where materials such as dress-up clothes, baby dolls, and dishes are stored, or in the block area where children build pretend-play props such as houses, cars, firetrucks, and beehives. A fish restaurant may spring up at the sand and water table, and any unoccupied floor space may be turned into a stage, a clinic, or a barbershop. Further, once children begin their play, they often need additional locations, so they "go to school" near the coatrack or "go to the store" in the toy area.

Children involved in pretending also use materials from various parts of the room to support their play. For example, a child who needs some "money" to put in her purse might decide to make some in the art area, or she might go to the toy area to gather beads, shape-sorter chips, or puzzle pieces to use.

Whether they are on a search for materials or on their way to another location, it is natural and appropriate for children involved in pretend play to move about the preschool space as part of their play. Therefore, confining role players and pretenders to one area or part of the

room frustrates rather than supports their intentions and is not appropriate. When a child's use of space and materials conflicts with other children's use of space and materials, the opportunity for group problem-solving arises.

▶ **Watch and listen for the elements of pretend play.**

Pretending is a complex undertaking. To appreciate and support what children are actually doing, watch and listen for the following pretend-play elements during work time and outside time:

Pretending to be someone else. Children may pretend to be real people, animals, or fictional characters. One day, Andrew built a zoo in the block area, then got into one of the "cages" and pretended to be a monkey. Another day, Kacey, Brianna, Andrew, and Douglas pretended to be baby rats in Douglas's rat house. Linda often rocked a baby doll, as she had seen her mother do with her sister. Sara frequently pretended to be Cheetara—a favorite superheroine from television.

Using one object to stand for another. Preschoolers are able to substitute one object for another based on their ability to hold images in mind and see similarities between their mental images and the leaf or block they have in their hand. Nathan uses a wooden O for a steering wheel. Sarah feeds her baby using a cylindrical block for a baby bottle. Brian eats cereal made of small plastic bears. Alana orders pizza on a banana phone. Petey ties a doll blanket around his shoulders for a cape. Brianna strums a broom for her guitar. Julia makes spaghetti using long bead necklaces. Aimee puts her doll baby to sleep in a cradle she made from an upside-down tunnel block.

Using gestures, sounds, and words to define an object, situation, or setting. Children may do this along with their use of props, or in place of objects. Audie makes his fingers go apart and together like scissors as he "cuts" Mikey's hair. Jalessa rocks back and forth with her baby doll in her arms, saying "Shh, shh." Scott paws the ground, saying "Neigh, neigh." Sarah sits in front of Julia, holds Julia's hand, and makes painting gestures over each fingernail. Colin says, "I want to play Dawn Treader and I'm Caspian." Alana turns to Becki and hands her a sports coat, tie, and hat: "You be the daddy and I'm the mommy." Julia tells Sam about her baby, Kacey:

"Now she growed up. She can stand up and talk." Trey holds a long string of interlocking pegs to his lips and makes trumpet sounds: "I'm playing my trumpet." Another day, Trey hands some drumsticks to Nathan and says, "Let's play pool." Jason tells Betsy, "We're making something to kill all the bad guys. They stole our sister and turned the puppies into baby rabbits!"

Sharing pretend play and roles with others. In her observations of children's play, psychologist Catherine Garvey (1990) notes that "as play develops, its forms become less determined by properties of the materials in the immediate situation and come increasingly under the control of plans or ideas" (p. 79). The development of such ideas is often the basis for cooperative play. L. J. makes a car out of large hollow blocks: "Oh, no," he says to Douglas, "it ran out of gas." "We better push it to the gas station," Douglas replies, and that is what they do. Anna and Jessa build a beehive out of blocks and scarves, make honey cakes in their hive, and exchange clarifying statements: "I'm a mommy bee." "Let's pretend these are our wings." "This is my stinger, okay, and we sting people who try to get the honey."

Talking with others within the context of the role-play situation. This kind of talk differs from objective statements such as the following *about* roles, objects, and changes in the play situation: "Let's use this big box for the back seat of the bus." Instead, we are referring here to instances when children make conversation from *within* the assumed role. The following example of such talk that occurred in a "barbershop" is taken from preschool teacher Beth Marshall (1992, p. 26):

> Chelsea tied a scarf around Martin's neck. She picked up the scissors and started to "cut" his hair. After a few minutes she stopped and said, *"Wait one minute. I have to get the phone."* She went to the shelf, picked up the phone, brought it back to the "barbershop" and spoke into the receiver: *"Hello . . . Yes . . . Well, let me check . . . No, you can't come in Thursday. If you want a haircut, come in today . . . Two o'clock . . . OK, goodbye."* She hung up the phone, searched for and found a pad of paper, clipboard, and pencil, "wrote" something down, and then went back to cutting Martin's hair. When she finished she said, *"OK, Martin, that will be 52 bucks."* Martin handed her

This "doggy" uses a long-handled spoon from the house area for his "bone" and the space under the table for his "dog house."

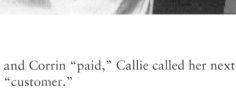

four strips of paper. *"This is 52 bucks?"* Martin handed her one more strip, and she made a notation on her pad. *"OK, who's next around here?"* Callie sat in the "barber chair" for her turn.

▶ **Participate in pretend play respectfully, taking cues from players.**

After you have watched and listened to children's pretend play, and understand as much as you can about its content and direction, you may want to join in, either because the children have invited you or because you think you can support and perhaps strengthen their play in a respectful manner. Here are some guidelines for doing this:

Follow the theme and content set by the players. According to Garvey (1990), you can expect most preschool pretend play to revolve around *domestic scenes, treating-healing,* and *averting threats.* For example, be ready to join the established situation whether the children are playing mommy and baby, dogs and baby lions, barbershop, bees, ambulance emergency, moving day, jungle rescue, pizza delivery, or monster robots.

Offer suggestions within the pretend situation. Make sure that any idea you offer fits within the ongoing pretend situation. Here is how Beth Marshall (1992, p. 28) joined a "barbershop" play situation within the context the children had established:

One day, Douglas, Martin, and Callie were setting up the "barbershop." Callie got the clippers and scissors. Douglas and Martin wanted a haircut, and so did Corrin, who had joined them. When the three potential haircut customers began struggling over the "barber chair," Beth decided to join them: "Is this barbershop open? I think I need a trim," she said.

"Well," responded Corrin, "I think it's a problem. There's only one hair-cutting place and everybody needs to get their hair cut."

"I see," said Beth. "There's only one hair-cutting place. What do you think we should do?" (The children didn't say anything but resumed their struggle for the "barber chair.")

"Douglas could have the first turn, and then Corrin, and then you, Martin, OK?" Callie suggested.

"Well, my appointment is not for a while. I wonder what I could do while I'm waiting," Beth thought out loud.

Douglas had an idea. "We could make a waiting area!"

"Yeah, like a big bench," Corrin added. Corrin, Douglas, and Callie gathered big hollow blocks from the block area and arranged them in one long line in the "barber shop."

"Sit here on the waiting bench, Beth," Douglas instructed. Martin brought some books over, handed one to Beth, and sat down next to her. Douglas gathered magazines from the art area, piled them on the bench, and selected one to "read." Corrin sat down in the "barber chair," Callie tied a scarf around her neck, and proceeded with the first haircut of the day. When she finished and Corrin "paid," Callie called her next "customer."

"Douglas, you want to be next?" He put down his magazine and took his place in the "barber chair."

Respect children's response to your ideas. Notice that in the barbershop play just described, the adult (Beth) simply joins the play by stating that she needs a trim. Corrin responds by describing the only-one-chair problem. Beth asks, "What do you think we should do?" Callie suggests taking turns. And then, in the form of the statement "I wonder what I could do while I am waiting," Beth offers the word "waiting." The children come up with the idea of a waiting room with a bench, books, and magazines.

On another day, several sets of children were playing in houses they had built in the block area. When Beth went up to one and rang the doorbell, the child who answered simply said, "Go away. We don't want any," and that's what Beth did. Later, when Beth built her own block house, one of her "neighbors" came to borrow a "cup of sugar"—an invitation into the play that Beth readily accepted.

Address the pretend person rather than the child. As a participant-player, it makes sense to address the other players according to the roles they have assumed just as you would accept a block as a telephone, a plate as a steering wheel, or Play-Doh as baby-lion food. Therefore, when Brian is a "baby lion," it is important to address him as such out of respect for the pretend situation he has created and is striving to maintain:

Brian: *Meow, meow. I'm a baby lion.*

Adult: *Hi, baby lion.*

Brian: *Meow, this is my food.* (Indicates scoops of Play-Doh in a bowl.)

Adult: *You have a lot of baby-lion food.*

Brian: *Meow.* (Pretends to eat from his bowl.)

▶ **Pretend at small- and large-group times.**

Small-group time. Small-group time can be an opportunity to introduce the idea of pretending to children who are generally engaged in other pursuits at work time. The key is working from the *children's* ideas or themes. One way to begin is with children's paintings and drawings. Have a child "read" or tell about his or her picture, then ask the children to act out the story. For example, Alana's picture read, "A fire burned

up a house." "How can we act out this story?" her teacher asked. The children made suggestions— "We could be fire!" "And the house smashing over!"—and tried them out with great enthusiasm.

Another way to begin is to ask children to tell stories, write down what they say, and then re-enact the stories. Here, for example, is Ben's story:

Once upon a time there lived a brown whale. Then came a sea monster. The brown whale was very frightened. But the sea monster just said, "Boo!" Then the sea monster goed away. Then the whale goed in the water. Then the sea monster came back, and the whale was frightened again. Then the sea monster goed away. The whale goed back into the water.

❧

The children decided to be whales or monsters and acted out the story as Ben told it again. Later, Ben turned his story into a book.

"Oh, no!" this adult "big sister" says to the "bad guy" who attempts a "hold up."

Large-group time. When the ideas come from the children, playing "Let's Pretend" can involve a large group of children in pretending to be someone else and using one object to stand for another. One team initiated such a game this way: "This morning," said one of the adults, "I saw Brian pretending to be a baby lion. Let's pretend to be baby lions." After the children acted out their ideas of baby lions, she asked the children for other ideas: "What else could we be?" One child said, "I know, a stingray! A baby stingray!"

Another way to start "Let's Pretend" is by giving each child an object such as a block and saying something such as, "At work time, I saw Julia using a block for a comb. See if you can try out your combs." Ask children for other suggestions and try them out.

You can also make up and sing action songs about people and animals that are of interest to children. Here's a song one group of children created and acted out after a trip to the fire station (sung to the tune of "This Is the Way We Wash Our Clothes"):

What do the firefighters do?
 the firefighters do?
 the firefighters do?
What do the firefighters do
At the fire station?

The firefighters slide down the pole . . .
The firefighters put on their boots . . .
The firefighters put on their hats . . .

▶ **Plan ways to support children's pretend play.**

In daily team planning meetings, think of ways to support children's pretend play. Here are some strategies to consider:

Add materials. Are there materials you could add to support children's pretend play? For example, one teaching team brought in large appliance boxes for children to use in their spaceship play.

Take field trips. Are there places you could visit that would give children more ideas for their pretend play? Adults Beth and Sam (Marshall 1992, p. 16) watched children's barbershop play for a number of days and then decided to visit a local barbershop:

After Sam and I talked about what we hoped might happen on the visit, I stopped by our local barbershop (within walking distance of our center) to talk with the barbershop staff about our goals, which were to watch one of the children get a haircut and to see what really happens in a barbershop. Although the barbershop staff were excited about our plans, they were unsure about what the children would do, other than watch. I suggested letting the children get into the barber chair, make the chair go up and down, feel the vibration of the electric clippers, feel the air from the blow dryer, look in the big mirror and the hand mirror, and try out the cash register. I also suggested that the staff talk to the children during the actual haircut. The barbershop staff agreed to try these things, and we set a date for our visit.

After the field trip, the children continued to play barbershop, adding more details to their

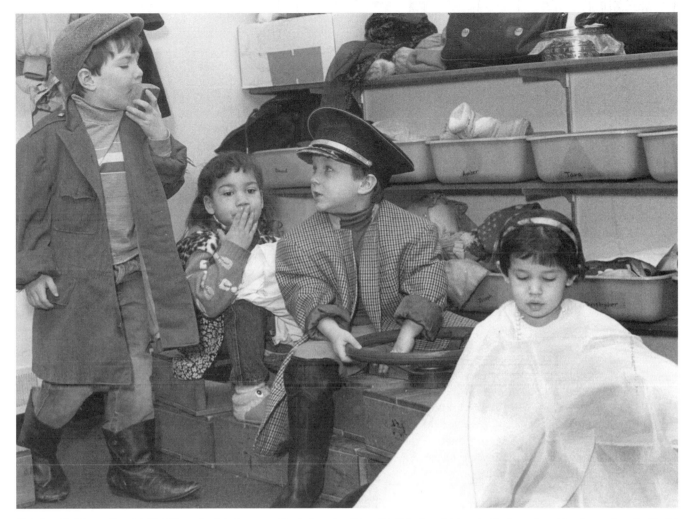

This "taxi" driver talks with his "dispatcher" (who uses a block for a "walkie-talkie") before driving the "princess" and her "mom" to the "ball."

play each day over a period of a month or so. (See also Details in Children's Barbershop Play, p. 516.)

Invite people and bring in animals to visit. Are there people or animals who could visit the children to give them more ideas for their play? After noting a lot of baby-doll play, for example, one team invited a mother and baby to visit for a day, and a father and baby to visit on another day. The children were very interested in seeing how the babies were actually fed, bathed, and dressed. Another group of children were very attentive to a friendly family dog who visited for several days. In both cases, the adults noticed a thoughtful change in the children's "baby" and "doggy" play after the visits.

Details in Children's Barbershop Play Before and After the Trip to the Barbershop*

Before the Trip	Immediately After the Trip	Two Weeks After the Trip
3 children	6 children	13 children
Chair	Chair	Chair
Scissors	Scissors	Scissors
	Scarves	Scarves
	Clippers	Clippers
	Clipping noise	Clipping noise
	Floor mirror	Floor mirror
	Baby doll	Baby doll
	Detailed cutting	Detailed cutting
	Blocks for combs	Blocks for combs
	Open and close shop	Open and close shop
		Phone
		Wash doll's hair
		Charge money
		Exchange money
		Write on pad
		Waiting area with bench, books, magazines

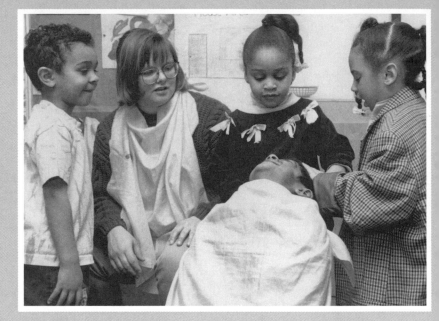

*Marshall 1992, p. 33.

Discuss unsettling pretend-play themes as a teaching team. In their pretend play, children may include situations that make you uncomfortable—using blocks or sticks for guns, pretending to get drunk or take drugs, pretending to fight or argue. Instead of ignoring such play or intervening to end it, it is important for adult team members to consider their personal views of these issues and to balance them with the need to support children's play and intentions matter-of-factly. In the process it may be helpful to remember this advice from educators Greta Fein and Shirley Schwartz (1986):

> Teachers need to be careful about interpretations of children's pretense. While there is truth in the feelings expressed, events and characterizations are not necessarily true. Children from peaceful families may play about family violence and only children may give realistic renderings of sibling rivalry. Play may have more to do with children's need to feel competent and in control than with actual events (p. 109).

For a discussion of ways to deal with unsettling play, see What About Superheroes and War Play? (p. 214).

Provide time for children's pretend play to unfold and develop.* Having enough time to explore, discover, and practice is an essential element of children's pretend play. Children may stay with a particular topic for days, weeks, or months, eventually acting out detailed scenarios like the barbershop play described throughout this section. The evolution of the barbershop play was docu-

*This section was written by High/Scope consultant and teacher Beth Marshall. It first appeared in a slightly different version in the High/Scope Extensions curriculum newsletter, October 1993.

mented in anecdotal records, video footage, and photographs as part of a study of the development of children's play (Marshall 1992). Data from the study provide insights about how preschoolers' complex role-play evolves over time and why adult patience is necessary during this process.

Using the study data, here is a week-by-week account of the development of the barbershop play:

Weeks 1 and 2: *The repetitive theme of haircutting first surfaces in children's fairly simple work-time play. In this phase, 3 children use 2 props—scissors and a chair—to enact one activity: cutting hair. Responding to the children's interest in haircutting, adults Beth and Sam plan a field trip to the local barbershop.*

Weeks 3 and 4: *Following the trip to the barbershop, the number of children playing at cutting hair doubles to 6, and the number of* play elements (props used and activities depicted) increases from 3 to 11. The children also add details to ongoing activities. The props now include scarves (used for clothing drapes), a floor mirror, clippers, and blocks (used for combs). Haircutting becomes more realistic, including both "clipping" and "cutting" motions and sounds. Children now give "haircuts" to dolls as well as to one another, and they act out the opening and closing of the shop.

Weeks 5 and 6: New effects of the field trip are still surfacing during this phase of the play, in the third and fourth weeks after the trip to the barbershop. Beth and Sam note another jump (from 6 to 13) in the number of children consistently playing barbershop. The complexity of their play also continues to increase, with children incorporating several new activities and accompanying props. They begin charging for the haircuts, using paper strips and poker chips to represent money, and they take appointments with the help of the phone they have added. They also wash as well as cut their dolls' hair, and they construct a "waiting bench" complete with books, magazines, and numbers for those waiting. It appears, then, that for some children the observations they made on the field trip need to "percolate" for several weeks before they can re-enact them.

⌀

This documentation of the unfolding of a richly detailed play scenario suggests both the potential complexity of young children's long-term play and the need for adults to pace themselves to the young child's slower timetable. Adults who wish to support complex play may want to ask themselves, "Are we allowing enough time for children's play to blossom and develop?"

Dramatic Art Strategies: A Summary

Imitating actions and sounds
___ Watch for children's spontaneous imitations.
___ Imitate children's actions and sounds.
___ Build opportunities for imitation into the daily routine.

Pretending and role playing
___ Provide materials and props for pretending and role play.
___ Support pretend play that moves from place to place.
___ Watch and listen for the elements of pretend play:
   ___ Pretending to be someone else.
   ___ Using one object to stand for another.
   ___ Using gestures, sounds, and words to define an object, situation, or setting.
   ___ Sharing pretend play and roles with others.
   ___ Talking with others within the context of the role-play situation.

___ Participate in pretend play respectfully, taking cues from players:
   ___ Follow the theme and content set by the players.
   ___ Offer suggestions from within the pretend situation.
   ___ Respect children's responses to your ideas.
   ___ Address the pretend person rather than the child.
___ Pretend at small- and large-group times.
___ Plan ways to support children's pretend play:
   ___ Add materials.
   ___ Take field trips.
   ___ Invite people and bring in animals to visit.
   ___ Discuss unsettling pretend-play themes as a teaching team.
___ Provide time for children's pretend play to unfold and develop.

Playing "barbershop" enables these children to consolidate their understanding of a real-life process they have experienced.

References

Ansbach, Ursula. 2001. "Master Pretenders: Dramatic Arts in the Preschool Classroom." In *Supporting Young Learners 3: Ideas for Child Care Providers and Teachers,* Nancy A. Brickman, ed., 199–208. Ypsilanti, MI: High/Scope Press.

Fein, Greta G. 1981. "Pretend Play in Childhood: An Integrative Review." *Child Development 52,* no. 4 (December): 1095–1118.

Fein, Greta G., and Shirley S. Schwartz. 1986. "The Social Coordination of Pretense in Children." In *The Young Child at Play: Reviews of Research,* Vol. 4, Greta Fein and Mary Rivkin, eds., 95–111. Washington, DC: NAEYC.

Forman, George E., and David S. Kuschner. 1983. *The Child's Construction of Knowledge: Piaget for Teaching Children.* Washington, DC: NAEYC.

Garvey, Catherine. 1990. *Play.* Cambridge, MA: Harvard University Press.

Ginsburg, Herbert, and Sylvia Opper. 1979. *Piaget's Theory of Intellectual Development.* Englewood, NJ: Prentice-Hall.

Golomb, Claire. 1992. *The Child's Creation of a Pictorial World.* Berkeley, CA: University of California Press.

Golomb, Claire. 1974. *Young Children's Sculpture and Drawing: A Study in Representational Development.* Cambridge, MA: Harvard University Press.

Marshall, Beth. 1992. *"Want Your Hair Cut?": Strategies for Increasing Children's Representational Play.* Unpublished masters' thesis, Rochester, MI: Oakland University.

Marshall, Beth. 1993. "Lights, Camera, Action! Spotlight on Pretend Play." *High/Scope Extensions* (October): 1–3, 8.

Perrett, Becki. 1992. "Shifting Gears Smoothly: Making the Most of Transition Times." *High/Scope Extensions* (October): 1–3.

Smilansky, Sara. 1990. "Sociodramatic Play: Its Relevance to Behavior and Achievement in School." In *Children's Play and Learning,* Edgar Klugman and Sara Smilansky, eds., 18–42. New York: Teachers College Press.

Weininger, Otto. 1988. "What If and As If: Imagination and Pretend Play in Early Childhood." In *Imagination and Education,* Kieran Egan and Dan Nadaner, eds., 141–49. New York: Teachers College Press.

Related Reading

Brown, Victoria, and Sarah Playdell. 1999. *Dramatic Difference: Drama in the Preschool and Kindergarten Classroom.* Portsmouth, NH: Heinemann.

Cuffaro, Harriet M. 1984. "Dramatic Play—The Experience of Block Building." In *The Block Book,* Elisabeth S. Hirsch, ed., 121–51. Washington, DC: NAEYC.

Edwards, Carolyn, Lella Gandini, and George Forman, eds. 1998. *The Hundred Languages of Children: The Reggio Emilia Approach to Early Childhood Education,* 2nd ed. Norwood: Ablex Publishing.

Eisner, Elliot W. 1990. "The Role of Art and Play in Children's Cognitive Development." In *Children's Play and Learning,* Edgar Klugman and Sara Smilansky, eds., 43–56. New York: Teachers College Press.

Epstein, Ann S. 2007. "What Is the High/Scope Curriculum in the Arts?" Chap. 17 in *Essentials of Active Learning in Preschool: Getting to Know the High/Scope Curriculum,* 173–90. Ypsilanti, MI: High/Scope Press.

Graves, Michelle. 1996. "Field Trips: A New Definition." In *Supporting Young Learners 2,* Nancy A. Brickman, ed., 257–64. Ypsilanti, MI: High/Scope Press.

Graves, Michelle. 1996. *The Teacher's Idea Book 2: Planning Around Children's Interests.* Ypsilanti, MI: High/Scope Press.

High/Scope Educational Research Foundation. 2003. *Preschool Child Observation Record (COR),* 2nd ed. Ypsilanti, MI: High/Scope Press.

Marshall, Beth. 2001. "Ban It, Ignore It, or Join It? What to Do About Superhero Play." In *Supporting Young Learners 3: Ideas for Child Care Providers and Teachers,* Nancy A. Brickman, ed., 43–52. Ypsilanti, MI: High/Scope Press.

Marshall, Beth. 2005. "TRUST in Children's Play." "Overcoming Roadblocks to Playing With Children." In *Supporting Young Learners 4: Ideas for Child Care Providers and Teachers,* Nancy A. Brickman, Holly Barton, and Jennifer Burd, eds., 287–98. Ypsilanti, MI: High/Scope Press.

Paley, Vivian G. 1990. *The Boy Who Would Be a Helicopter.* Cambridge: Harvard University Press.

Saltz, Rosalyn, and Eli Saltz. 1986. "Pretend Play and Its Outcomes." In *The Young Child at Play: Reviews of Research* 4, Greta Fein and Mary Rivkin, eds., 155–73. Washington, DC: NAEYC.

Smilansky, Sara, and Leah Shefatya. 1990. *Facilitating Play: A Medium for Promoting Cognitive, Socio-Emotional, and Academic Development in Young Children.* Gaithersburg, MD: Psychosocial & Educational Publications.

Spolin, Viola. 1986. *Theater Games for the Classroom.* Evanston, IL: Northwestern University Press.

Related Media

The following materials are available from the High/Scope Press, 600 N. River St., Ypsilanti, MI 48198-2898; to order, visit *www.highscope.org,* or call 1-800-40-PRESS.

Adult-Child Interactions: Forming Partnerships With Children. 1996. Color videotape, 60 min. Ypsilanti, MI: High/Scope Press.

Creative Representation. 2000. Color videotape or DVD, 40 min. Ypsilanti, MI: High/Scope Press.

Making things (constructive play) and pretending are two types of play that often happen together.

Listening to, moving to, and making music are vital artistic experiences that allow children to express themselves and participate in the rituals of their communities.

Music accompanies us throughout our lives, marking occasions from birth to death. Like the other arts, it is way of sharing and communicating, and is a kind of language that can be learned. For more on why the arts are important, see Chapter 20.

Music is a series of sounds organized through rhythm, melody, and harmony to elicit an emotional response in the listener. Think of the times music makes us smile or releases our tears. In making the case for the affective core of musical intelligence, psychologist Howard Gardner (1983) turns to the writings of two twentieth-century composers, Walter Sessions and Arnold Schoenberg. Gardner quotes Sessions as follows: "Music is controlled movement of sound in time . . . . It is made by humans who want it, enjoy it, and even love it" (p. 105). Schoenberg elaborates: "Music is a succession of tones and tone combinations so organized as to have an agreeable impression on the ear, and its impression on the intelligence is comprehensible. . . . These impressions have the power to influence occult parts of our soul and our sentimental spheres" (p. 105).

Music: An Important Ingredient in Early Childhood

Even *in utero*, infants can hear music, responding to it with kicks and other motions. As newborn or older infants, children continue to be strongly affected by music.

Depending on the mood of the music, the situation, and the time of day, they may respond by making soft coos and cries, by enthusiastically waving their arms and legs, or by dropping off to sleep. Toddlers generate their own musical babbling and often sing fragments of familiar songs as well as repetitive two- or three-note songs they have created. Preschoolers, who are steadier on their feet than toddlers, can move to music and play simple musical instruments in a deliberate and organized manner. With their increased command of *language* and ability to *represent* (to hold images in mind), preschoolers can sing entire songs and even create their own songs. They also are able to associate music with familiar situations—"That sounds like parade music!" "It's scary music!"—and act accordingly—"Let's march!" "Wanna be monsters?"

Indeed, music is an important ingredient of early childhood because young children are so open to hearing, making, and moving to music. Music actually becomes another language through which young music-makers learn about themselves and others. Music draws children into their culture and communal rituals—birthday celebrations, religious observances, weddings, and festivals. Just as important, music conveys emotions, heightens experiences, and marks personal and historic occasions. As

Young children certainly relate music and body movement naturally, finding it virtually impossible to sing without engaging in some accompanying physical activity.

—Howard Gardner, 1983

literacy emerges in a language-rich environment, musicality emerges in a music-rich environment. Children's musical development and their ability to communicate through music flourish in cultures and settings where community members value and enjoy music.

Supporting Children as Music-Makers

Six key developmental indicators (KDIs) in music, developed by Elizabeth Carlton (1994), music consultant to the High/Scope Foundation, draw attention to how young children develop as music-makers. Three of these focus on *exploring music:*

- **Moving to music**
- **Exploring and identifying sounds**
- **Exploring the singing voice**

One indicator emerges as young children use a particular *element* of music:

- **Developing melody**

KDIs in Music

- Moving to music
- Exploring and identifying sounds
- Exploring the singing voice
- Developing melody
- Singing songs
- Playing simple musical instruments

And two indicators have to do with *making music:*

- **Singing songs**
- **Playing simple musical instruments**

Adults can support music literacy by making music a daily occurrence in an active learning setting. Adults also realize that music is an integral part of each child's culture. They therefore provide children with as many active musical experiences as possible so children's musical ability and understanding can develop and flourish. Adults approach music experiences with enjoyment and understand that children need to generate and shape their own musical ideas. In fact, adults act as musical *partners* with children rather than as directors, performers, or entertainers.

Following are suggestions for ways to help children develop an appreciation for music and become active music-makers.

Key Developmental Indicator
Moving to Music

Teachers Jackie and Ann, and 18 preschool children make two "rowing sandwiches." Jackie and Ann sit on the floor with their legs spread apart, each sitting feet-to-feet and holding hands with a child partner. The rest of the children scoot up, legs apart, sitting in line behind the "rowers." As Jackie and Ann sing "Row, Row, Row Your Boat," the children "row" and sing with them (rocking forward and backward) to the steady beat of the song.

~

During work time, Deola builds a stage of large hollow blocks, listens to three taped musical selections, and then chooses one that she plays and dances to on her stage.

~

Grandpa Jack, a Head Start volunteer, plays his harmonica at large-group time. "Hey, that sounds like dancing music," Zachary announces. Zachary begins to dance and the rest of the children join him.

~

When Becki puts the cleanup music on, Corrin initiates her own cleanup dance, twirling around with two blocks she has been building with. Eventually, she twirls over to the block shelf, puts the two blocks away, and twirls away for more.

Moving to music is a natural process for both children and adults. Through the ages, humans have responded to drum beats, singing, chanting, the call of the conch shell, and the bamboo flute. Music and dance have developed together as people of all ages have danced, sung, and made music to pray for rain, to ward off evil, to celebrate, and to mourn. While these communal rituals may be less common today, people still tap their toes to march music, pat their steering wheels in time to music coming from their car stereos, and dance at weddings and other events. And young children still respond intuitively to music with their whole bodies. Following are ways adults can support children's natural inclination to move to music.

Suggestions for Adults

▶ **Play a wide variety of music for children.**

Playing a wide variety of recorded and live music for preschool children provides them with opportunities to hear and move to many different kinds of tunes. When you are stocking your

During work time, this child chooses a recorded musical selection, plays it on the CD player, and makes up a vigorous "jumping dance."

music area and selecting music to use at large-group and cleanup times, consider the following kinds of music:

- Folk music from around the world (for example, the musical selections on the High/Scope *Rhythmically Moving* recording series)
- Classical music
- Jazz and modern music
- March and circus music
- Waltzes, tangos, ballets

Provide live music for children to move to at small- and large-group times. Perhaps you or your team members can play a musical instrument or you know of parents or community members who can play instruments. Remember, no instrument is too humble or too complex to engage children's interest and inspire their movement.

They enjoy hearing, watching, and moving to music from live drums, harmonicas, guitars, autoharps, dulcimers, xylophones, as well as pianos, flutes, violins, trumpets, sitars, banjos, steel bands, gamelans, and so forth. Seeing people make music before their very eyes and moving to live sounds add new dimensions to children's understanding of music and to their perceptions of themselves as music-makers.

▶ **Encourage children to create their own ways of moving to music.**

Whenever you play live or recorded music for children, they will want to move to it. Encourage them to do so. As you play a musical selection for the first time, watch to see how children respond and then imitate their responses. One day, for example, Ruth, an adult, played a Sousa march at large-group time. Hearing the music, Danny, who was sitting on the floor, bent his arms at the elbow, formed two fists, and began to swing his arms back and forth in time to the march. Ruth swung her arms in the same way, and soon the other children joined in. When Ruth stopped the music, other children eagerly suggested different ways to move: "Let's pound our feet." "Let's march." "We could jump!" And one by one they tried out these movement ideas.

Another day, Ruth played a very different kind of music, a quiet selection called "Oh How Lovely" (a musical selection on the High/Scope *Rhythmically Moving 1* recording). The children responded by "floating" their arms, swaying and bending, and "skating" (sliding their feet along the floor).

▶ **Create simple movement sequences to music with children.**

Some pieces of music, such as "Yankee Doodle," have two distinct parts, a chorus and a verse. When the children are familiar with such a selection, you might say something like this at small- or large-group time: "'Yankee Doodle' has two parts." Play the music, indicating where each part begins. Together with the children come up with two different motions, one to do with the first part, and another to do with the second part. After listening to and talking about the "Yankee Doodle" selection, one group of children decided to "twist" at the waist to the first part and "punch" their arms during the second part.

Key Developmental Indicator
Exploring and Identifying Sounds

Steven, a toddler, listens to a robin singing near his house. In the background, another bird calls "whowoo-who-who-who." Steven's 4-year-old brother says, "Pa, there's a mourning dove, too!"

∼

It's a warm spring day and the windows are open. After a vigorous outdoor time, adults Ruth and Isobel sit with their preschoolers at large-group time. After closing their eyes, everyone listens to the older children, who are still playing outside. "That's Oscar calling to George!" "I hear feet . . . running feet." "The door. That's the door." "I hear bells!"

∼

*Abby has tied a shoelace to a flexible plastic "spider web" and is twirling it over her head. "Listen," she says. "Do you hear that sound? . . . It's the wind, but not the **real** wind because that's outdoors."*

∼

Andrew is listening to a CD during work time. "Hey," he says, "that's a guitar!" He glances at his teacher's guitar on the shelf, as if to confirm his discovery.

Children are surrounded by sounds—the sound of rain drumming on the roof; water running; birds chirping; motors humming and roaring; people talking, nailing, walking, sawing, opening and closing doors; clocks ticking; bells ringing; dogs barking; horns tooting; sirens wailing; music coming from an ice-cream truck. Because of their newfound ability to represent, preschoolers enjoy listening to and identifying the sounds they hear and then matching the sounds to their own mental images. Following are ways adults can support this **music** ability.

Suggestions for Adults

▶ **Assess your environment for sound.**

Many unalterable factors affect the kinds of sounds children hear in an active learning setting: location, climate, building construction. Wherever you are, however, there are several strategies you can adopt to provide interesting sounds and make the most of naturally occurring sounds.

Provide simple musical instruments.
Make a wide variety of simple musical instruments available to children at work time and throughout the day, including drums, tambourines, bells, rattles, triangles, xylophones, and so forth. (See the section on the music area in Chapter 5, p. 141.) Children enjoy playing these instruments as well as hearing other children play them.

Provide other sound-generating materials.
These might include electronic equipment, such as voice recorders, computers, digital audio players

On a walk in the park, these children and adults pause on the bridge to listen to the sound of water in the stream below.

(for example, MP3 players), CD players, and CDs containing a wide variety of music. Also consider simple household and recycled materials such as spoons, chopsticks, boxes, and food containers that children can use to make their own drums, shakers, ringers, and other rhythm instruments.

Provide quiet moments for listening.
There are many noisy times in an active learning setting—at these times, children are too involved with what they are doing to notice the sound level. Therefore, it helps to provide or attend to the occasional moments of quiet that arise throughout the day, as did adults Ruth and Isobel after outside time in an earlier example. Snack and meal times are other times when quiet often descends and children can hear and identify footsteps on the stairs, the sound of tree branches against the window, or the singing of the children next door. One teaching team took their children

on a "quiet walk to collect sounds." After the walk, they talked about what they had heard.

▶ **Be aware of sounds that attract children.**

Watch for children's responses to sounds: As the blocks fall down with a crash, Nigel looks startled, smiles, and resumes activity. At outside time, three firetrucks race by on the way to a fire, and Emma and Stan run along by the fence, imitating the siren in loud voices. Daniel taps on the side of the water table, listening to the water-deadened "thunk" that his tapping produces. Alana hears Peter singing the cleanup song and hums the first three notes of it to herself, over and over.

You can acknowledge children's responses to sounds in several ways: making a brief factual comment ("Your blocks made a crash when they fell"), joining the children in their sound imitation (make a fire-engine sound with Emma and Stan, hum along with Alana), or joining the child's sound explorations (tap the side of the water table along with Daniel).

▶ **Play "sound" guessing-games with children.**

Playing sound guessing-games at small- and large-group times is another way to capitalize on children's interest in the sounds around them. Here are some games to consider:

• Once children are familiar with the instruments in the music area, place the instruments in a large box. Have one child pick an instrument and play it inside the box for the other children to identify by sound alone. Pass the box around so each child gets a turn to choose and play an instrument. If the box is too small to hide the instrument while the child plays it, drape a doll blanket over the opening, leaving room for the player's hands.

• Give each child a bag or box and ask the children to find and put something in it that makes a sound. Have children take turns making their sounds while the others guess what made the sound.

• Throughout work time or outside time, record environmental and instrumental sounds. At the beginning of small-group time, play one or two of the sounds you recorded and listen to what children say about what they hear.

▶ **Encourage children to describe the sounds they hear.**

Throughout the day as you join children in listening to sounds, acknowledging the sounds they hear, and playing sound guessing-games, encourage children to talk about these experiences. These conversations may arise spontaneously, but if not, you might attempt to initiate them by making a brief comment on what *you* hear

("I hear your rope making a thumping sound") or by occasionally asking an open-ended question ("How does the wind sound today?").

Key Developmental Indicator
Exploring the Singing Voice

At work time, three "dogs" crawl back and forth between the house and block areas chanting "ow" (crawl-crawl), "ow" (crawl-crawl), "ow" (crawl-crawl).

∾

"Oo-oo-oooo, Oo-oo-oooo" two train drivers intone, using a high note, a slightly lower note, and then returning to the first note with each "Oo-oo-oooo."

∾

Andrew pokes sticks in mud puddles at outside time and sings, "Mud, mud, I love mud. Mud, mud. I love mud!"

∾

"Wooooow!" Julia exclaims, her voice starting out high and becoming lower. "It does fly!"

∾

Steven sings "Ooooo" as he slides, starting with a high note that becomes lower as he goes down the slide.

∾

Jason pretends to be a puppy. "My voice is light and sweet," he says. Later in the same play episode he says, "My voice is getting lower and I'm getting older."

In the course of their play, young children use their voices expressively to create pretend characters, heighten dramatic situations, and

"Choooooo," intones the "train driver." "Mmmmmmm," hums the "caboose driver" as these children drive their train to "New Mexico and Massachusetts" during work time.

exclaim over their discoveries. It is important for adults to recognize that as children make these kinds of sounds they are not only adding to their play but also exploring the expressive qualities of their voices—discoveries that lend richness and range to their singing. Following are ways adults can support children's vocal explorations.

Suggestions for Adults

▶ **Listen for and acknowledge children's creative vocalizations.**

Listen for the ways children use their voices in play. Acknowledge the singsong sounds they make by commenting on what you hear and incorporating children's vocalizations into your own play and conversations. For example, Mikey would often greet his teachers by singing "Ding-dong!" so they would return his greeting with "Ding-dong! Good morning, Mikey!"

▶ **Encourage children to explore the range of their voices.**

During small-group times, large-group times, and transitions, encourage children to explore the range of their singing voices. Here are some examples:

• At recall time, Rosa said to the children in her group, "Today I listened for sounds people were singing. I heard someone singing 'Boo-hoo, where's my shoe?'"

• "I heard something!" A preschool child, Kelly, sang "Whoo-ooo" to explain a memorable event: "That's when the fire truck went by."

• As Paul, an adult, told a story during large-group time, he stopped from time to time to ask children to make up and supply appropriate musical sounds—the sound of a bird singing, a baby cooing, a cat drinking milk, the wind blowing, a mother singing to her children.

• At the end of the day, as the last few children waited for their parents, they played a singing-and-movement game with their teachers. One child sang "Twist, twist, twist, twist," and

the others made up a movement to accompany the singing. One by one, each person took a turn at singing a word for everyone to try out and move to.

• After encouraging children to play with their voices in a variety of ways, one preschool teaching team made sound cards—simple line drawings to stand for each of the sounds their children made (for example, a train for the "Oo-oo-ooo" sound). The children enjoyed "reading" these sound cards and started illustrating their own cards to add to the pile. In fact, the team planned a small-group time around this interest and the sound-card pile grew.

• At large-group time, Ruth, Isobel, and their children made up high-voice/low-voice stories featuring a mouse who sang in a high squeaky voice and a bear who sang in a low deep voice.

Key Developmental Indicator
Developing Melody

"We all live in a yellow submarine. We all live in a yellow submarine . . ." Deola and Corrin sing over and over again as they work at the art table.

～

"Vanessa," sings Karl, her teacher, "I am here. I came when you called me." Vanessa laughs and points to a stack of blocks. "You built a stack of blocks," Karl sings in acknowledgment.

～

"Hi, little baby. Hi, little baby," this "mom" sings as she waves her baby's hand.

"Who me? . . . Who me? . . . Who me? . . ." Brian sings to Alana, teaching her the phrase he likes from "The Cookie Jar" song.

～

"We've got to get away. We've got to get away. We've got to get away. We've got to get away . . ." sing several children at snack time, jutting out their chins each time they repeat the phrase.

～

At work time, Jonah carries marbles in a bag and sings, "Toys for sale. Toys for sale."

～

"That's an interesting tune," Becki comments to Brian as he hums at work time. "It's 'Peter and the Wolf,'" Brian tells her, as he continues putting together a track for his train.

Young children derive great satisfaction in singing and humming parts of songs over and over again. When they hear the same songs repeatedly, some phrase catches their attention and they enjoy making that phrase their own—singing or humming it as they engage in repetitive work or play, sharing it with friends, and singing it to themselves. It is by putting these bits and pieces of songs together that children develop a sense of melody. Following are ways adults can support emerging singers.

Suggestions for Adults

▶ **Listen for and acknowledge children's use of pitch and melody.**

As you observe, play, and converse with children throughout the day, listen for the song fragments and phrases that children sing to themselves and with others. One morning, for example, adults Beth and Jackie observed the following: A group of children in the rocking boat singing "We will, we will, rock you . . . We will, we will, rock you . . ."; a child "reading" *The Gunny Wolf* to herself and singing "Kum kwa ke wa . . . Kum kwa ke wa . . ."; and a child humming the E-I-E-I-O part of "Old MacDonald." Here are the ways Beth and Jackie acknowledged these melody-developing experiences:

• Jackie sat down with the boat rockers and sang, "We will, we will, rock you . . ." along with them for several minutes. Her voice helped them stabilize their pitch.

• As her children were gathering for recall, Beth sang, "Kum kwa ke wa," using the same pitches she had heard at work time. The children in her recall group joined in singing this phrase until everyone had gathered.

• Beth and Jackie began large-group time by singing "Old MacDonald" as Jackie accompanied them on the Autoharp.

▶ **Play pitch-matching games with children.**

Children who are singing and humming song fragments are beginning to be aware that melodies are made up of a series of specific pitches. As you listen to children, notice the range of pitches they seem to be most comfortable with; then, for brief periods during transitions, play pitch-matching games with children to help them stabilize their sense of pitch and melody. Here are some examples to try as you go to the playground or lunch room:

• Sing or play (on a harmonica, recorder, or pitchpipe) two notes well within the children's singing range (usually between middle C and the A above it). Listen for how closely any of the children sing back these same notes. Repeat this process at another time using three notes.

• Sing or play the first three notes of "This Old Man." Listen to the children who join you. Try the same thing with the first few notes of "Do You Know the Muffin Man?"

• Sing or play the first several notes of a song you have heard the children humming or singing fragments of, such as the first four notes of "Old MacDonald." Listen for notes sung by the children who join you.

It is not important for the children to match your pitches exactly. Over time, and with experience, they will begin to hear and sing pitches more clearly.

▶ **Sing your comments to children.**

As you play and converse with children, take the opportunity to sing your usual verbal comments and acknowledgments. This is a way of supporting children's interest in short song fragments, showing them that they can make up their own phrases, and putting music in a personal, playful context. For example, you might sing phrases such as these: "I see you!" "I'm coming, Melissa." "Thank you for the pine-cone soup." "What is your plan for work time today?" "I see some blocks under the table." "I think I'll try that with my finger-paints." "George is putting on his coat . . . Trina is zipping her jacket . . . Ivan is buckling his boots." If you sing your comments well within the children's singing range, which may be higher than your usual singing range, children will find it easier to sing back to you.

▶ **Play "Guess This Tune" with children.**

Listen to the song fragments and tunes children are singing and build "tune-guessing" games around them. Here is how this game developed in one preschool program: One day Beth, the adult, hummed "Old MacDonald" to the children at snack time, and they identified the song right away. At the children's urging, Beth hummed another song. This time she hummed "Row, Row, Row Your Boat," which the children also identified immediately. Then Julia hummed "Twinkle, Twinkle Little Star," which Audie guessed, and then Audie hummed "Hail to the Victors" (the University of Michigan fight song), which everyone guessed. After the children had played this game over several days, Jalessa added a new twist. She put tape over her mouth and hummed "Mary Had a Little Lamb," and then everyone else wanted to "tape hum."

Key Developmental Indicator
Singing Songs

Jalessa, Chrysten, Alana, and Sarah sing "Twinkle, Twinkle Little Star," "Mary Had a Little Lamb," and "Baa, Baa Black Sheep" as they play together in the block area.

∾

On the tire swing, Andrew and Julia sing "The Froggy Song" and then sing it again with their own words.

∾

Kacey stands in front of the mirror singing "Five Enormous Dinosaurs."

∾

Max and Wendy sing quietly at small-group time as they work with bottle caps and other found materials.

∾

*As he works at the computer, Trey sees the letter **K** on the keyboard and sings "We Three Kings of Orient Are."*

∾

All the children in Devkumari's preschool in Soweto, South Africa, stand together in an outside meeting space. Devkumari's teacher gives them a starting note and the children begin singing a song in Zulu. As they sing both melody and harmony, they dance their way into school.

Preschoolers take particular pleasure in being able to sing entire songs. Singing connects them with the "grown-up" world of older siblings and family members who sing along to music on the radio, at church and school, at birthday parties, in the car, at bedtime, or just to pass the time. Knowing the words and melody to "Happy Birthday," for example, enables young children to participate in birthday celebrations for everyone from baby brother to Grandma. Because of their growing language and recall skills, 3- and 4-year-olds can remember the words and melodies of songs they have heard many times and have had a chance to practice on their own and in groups, at their own pace, and in their own manner. In active learning settings, young children sing with their friends and by themselves for pleasure, comfort, and their own satisfaction. Following are ways adults can support young singers.

Suggestions for Adults

▶ **Sing songs with children.**

Preschoolers enjoy singing nursery rhymes, traditional children's songs, simple folk songs, and songs associated with celebrations and holidays. The way they learn to sing them is by hearing them sung, joining in, and singing them over and over again until the songs are their own.

Consider the following core repertoire a preschool teaching team set for themselves and their children in the fall. By late spring, all the children could recognize these songs, most could sing them all the way through with the group, and many could sing them on their own or with friends:

- *Nursery rhymes*

  "Rain, Rain Go Away"

  "Twinkle, Twinkle Little Star"

  "Mary Had a Little Lamb"

  "Baa, Baa Black Sheep"

  "Do You Know the Muffin Man?"

These preschoolers concentrate on singing the words to a new song they are learning. Over a several-week period, they ask to sing it again and again until they know it by heart.

  "Jack and Jill Went Up the Hill"

  "Ring Around the Rosey"

- *Traditional children's songs*

  "Old MacDonald Had a Farm"

  "The Farmer in the Dell"

  "The Bear Went Over the Mountain"

  "This Old Man"

  "If You're Happy and You Know It"

  "Hokey Pokey"

  "Eensy Weensy Spider"

  "The Wheels on the Bus"

- *Simple folk songs*

  "Are You Sleeping?"

  "Row, Row, Row Your Boat"

  "She'll Be Comin' Round the Mountain"

At large-group time, these children sing the words and do the motions to a favorite song, "In a Cabin in the Woods." One of their favorite variations is to sing the "bear" verse in a low voice and the "rabbit" verse in a high voice.

- *Special occasion songs*

  "Happy Birthday"

  "Jingle Bells"

Sing at large-group time. Because everyone is involved, large-group time is an enjoyable time to sing old favorites and introduce new songs. Less experienced singers are carried along by the enthusiasm of more experienced singers. Guitar or Autoharp accompaniment helps keep everyone on pitch, but singing without instruments is also quite satisfying.

To introduce a new song, begin by establishing a steady beat, patting it on your legs or on the floor, and encouraging the children to pat the beat along with you. Then, sing the whole song through once so children can hear the melody and the words. Start on a pitch within the children's voice range, usually a little higher than you would normally sing. (This is necessary because children's vocal chords are short and thus able to produce the higher pitches with ease.) Continue to sing the whole song again several more times. Each time you will notice that children join in singing more of the melody and words as they become familiar with them. Eventually, over time and with many repetitions, the children will learn the entire song. Sing a new song for several days in a row until you see that most children are comfortable singing it.

Sing at work time. Singing often fits into children's ongoing play. If you are rocking a "baby" you might sing "Rock-a-Bye Baby" or "Are You Sleeping." If you are riding a "bus" or a "boat," you might sing "The Wheels on the Bus" or "Row, Row, Row Your Boat." If you join a group of block builders you might change the words of "Jingle Bells" to "Build with blocks, build with blocks, build with blocks today. Build with blocks, build with blocks, build with blocks today."

Including books in the book area that are actually illustrated songs, such as *Down in the Meadow, The Fox Went Out One Chilly Night, Frog Went A Courtin',* and *Old MacDonald*, provides you with a natural opportunity to sing to one or two children at work time. You can also include illustrated songbook collections in the book areas and sing the songs children request.

Sing at small-group time. Children enjoy singing into a voice recorder and listening to themselves: "I hear Kenneth!" "That's me!" They also enjoy illustrating the songs they sing.

Sing at outside time. Children often sing to themselves as they swing. Or they sing together with their friends on a tire swing or on individual swings if they are close together. You can join them in singing, or if no one is singing, try initiating a song as you push or swing yourself.

Sing during parent meetings. Singing at the beginning or end of a meeting attended by parents helps draw the group together and introduces parents to the songs you are singing; parents can then sing these songs at home with their children. You can also ask parents about favorite family songs that you can add to your preschool repertoire.

▶ **Begin with motions.**

It is easier for children to focus either on motions or on words, rather than both at the same time. When teaching a song, it often makes sense to begin with the motions and add the words after the children have learned the motions.

With traditional movement songs and fingerplays, such as "Eensy Weensy Spider" and "The Wheels on the Bus," begin with the motions, then say or sing the words, and finally, try both together.

▶ **Encourage children to create their own songs.**

Children who are used to singing enjoy making up their own songs either by changing the words of an existing song or by making up their own words and melodies. You can encourage this process by doing the following:

• Listen for children's spontaneous songs as they sing them throughout the day. Acknowledge these songs by commenting on them, singing along with children, or asking children to sing them at small-group or large-group times.

• Ask children to change the words of a song they know. For example, at recall time, one adult asked her children to sing about their experiences to the tune of "Jingle Bells." Another adult encouraged her group of children to add other things that Old MacDonald had on his farm as they sang the familiar song. Then they changed "Old MacDonald" to "Mrs. Leonard" and the "farm" to a "store," in honor of a local shop owner and grocery they often visited.

• At large-group time, simply ask children if they have a song they would like to present. When Peter, a teacher, asked this question of members of his group, one child, Trey, said that he had a song. First Trey established a steady beat by patting his hands on his knees. Since he was composing the song on the spot, he sang a line at a time. Then, while he paused to make up the next song line, everyone else sang the line he had just sung. This line-by-line process continued for several minutes until the song ended. While Trey's song had a fairly random tune and his words

seemed to follow his own thoughts, altogether his song seemed to tie together some ideas about a baby bird he had seen, and everyone was happy to sing it in this fashion.

Key Developmental Indicator
Playing Simple Musical Instruments

Sarah figures out how to play "Hot Cross Buns" on the xylophone, then plays it over and over.

❧

Audie, Douglas, Jalessa, and Sarah play their tambourines as they march around the room singing "Jingle Bells."

❧

These children play several instruments at once in their "fireman band."

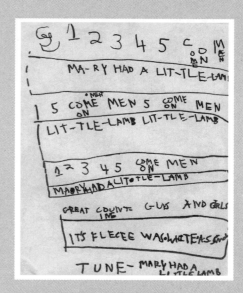

Here are the words Andrew wrote to the tune of "Mary Had a Little Lamb." The mark in the upper left corner next to the number "1" is Andrew's version of a clef sign.

Andrew's Song

Andrew already knew the melody and words to "Mary Had a Little Lamb" since this was a favorite large-group-time song. He had also been reading and writing on his own since before he entered preschool.

First, Andrew wrote the four lines of "Mary Had a Little Lamb" in four boxes, which he spaced at intervals down the page. He also wrote each word in syllables because as the song is sung, each syllable has its own note. Then, above each line, he wrote his own words:

1 2 3 4 5 Come on men,
5 Come on men, 5 Come on men.
1 2 3 4 5 Come on men.
Great counting guys and girls!

Alana hums the "Kitty Cat" song on a "recorder" she has made out of pegs. Mikey makes his own peg "recorder" and "plays" (hums) "Old MacDonald" on it.

∾

Brianna strums the Autoharp and hums her own song as she plays.

∾

Nathan and Trey play the xylophones, drums, and chimes. "We have a band, don't we, Trey?" says Nathan. Trey nods his head and keeps playing.

∾

Jalessa plays the xylophone and sings a song about her home, mom, and grandma.

∾

At small-group time, Lanie and Louie tape together small twigs and branches to make their own "flutes."

Preschool children like to play simple musical instruments by themselves and with their friends. While they like to make noise, they are also beginning to organize the sounds they make into steady beats, particular rhythms, and simple musical phrases. Through trial and error, some children can learn to play some familiar songs on pitched instruments such as the xylophone or a small keyboard. They also enjoy using musical instruments to create bands, parades, and dance music. Following are ways adults can support young instrumentalists.

Suggestions for Adults

▶ **Set up a music area.**

Include a wide range of musical instruments—wood blocks, drums, xylophones, tambourines, triangles, bells, spoons, maracas, a washboard, old pots, wooden spoons for drumsticks, heavy glass soda bottles "tuned" with water, homemade noise makers, and so forth. (For more information, refer to the section on setting up a music area in Chapter 5, p. 141.)

▶ **Provide opportunities for children to play musical instruments on their own.**

While it makes sense to introduce and include musical instruments at small-group and large-group times, children also need time to explore and play these instruments on their own. By establishing a music area and making instruments easily accessible, children have the option on a daily basis to play musical instruments at work time. If your indoor space is limited and you do not have room for a music area inside, provide musical instruments for children to play at outside time.

▶ **Play musical instruments at small-group and large-group times.**

While many adults introduce musical instruments at small-group or large-group times and then have children play them as they sing

After making instruments at small-group time, these children play them in a parade at outside time.

"Cleanup time, cleanup time," this child sings as he rings the bells to signal the end of work time.

Dancing. Provide instruments for half the children and encourage the other half to dance to the music the instrumentalists make. After one selection, change roles so the dancers become players and the players take their turn as dancers. Try this idea both indoors and outdoors to see where your children seem most comfortable playing and dancing.

Storytelling. As you tell or read a story to children, such as "The Three Billy Goats Gruff" or "The Three Little Pigs," ask the children what kinds of instrumental sounds could accompany the story at various points to emphasize specific situations or feelings. Then have them try out their ideas as you talk or read.

Stop-and-start games. Children like to devise their own stop-and-start games with musical instruments. Julia, for example, made up a game in which she and three other children beat the drums while the rest of the children danced. Then, when the drums stopped, the dancing stopped. Another group of children played a modified version of musical chairs. Part of the group played the game while the rest accompanied them on simple musical instruments. As the musicians played, the "chair people" moved quickly around the chairs. When the musicians stopped playing, the

"chair people" sat down. (No chairs were removed, so the emphasis was simply on stopping and starting, and no one was ever "out.") After a while, the musicians and the "chair people" traded roles.

▶ **Use musical instruments to signal transition times.**

Children enjoy playing musical instruments to signal transitions from work time to cleanup time, from outside time to inside time, and so forth. In one program, parents had built a small stage, and several children announced transitions by getting on stage and playing for the rest of the group. In another program, one child played the triangle to signal transitions, while in a third program, it was one child's task each day to turn a stuffed chicken upside down so it went "Cock-a-doodle-doo" at the ending of each time period.

This is "The Basketball Song" that Trey wrote on the "bus" and gave to Barbara, the music passenger, to sing and play on the guiro.

Trey's Basketball Song

One day at work time, Trey said he was "the music passenger" on the "bus," and he sang and played "The Basketball Song" on the guiro. "We will, we will rock you!" he sang. After a while, he decided to be the bus driver and he asked Barbara, his teacher, to be "the music passenger." To make sure she sang the right song, he wrote out the notes for her to sing. He also told her how to play the guiro. "You have to scrape it and knock it, too," he said.

songs they know, there are several other ways to use instruments with children at these times.

Parades. Have one child be the leader and establish a steady beat on his or her instrument. Then ask the children to match that beat on their instruments as they march around the room or playground behind the leader. Have children take turns setting the beat and leading the parade.

One teaching team, whose children were used to parading in this manner, took a phrase they had heard some children singing at work time—"We like rats and we like mice. We like rats and we like mice."—and used the phrase to set the beat. First they had everyone chant the phrase; then, as they chanted, children and adults played their instruments, and finally, everyone chanted, played, and marched. The next day, several children made rat and mouse masks and had their own parade at work time.

References

Carlton, Elizabeth B., and Phyllis S. Weikart. 1994. *Foundations in Elementary Education: Music.* Ypsilanti, MI: High/Scope Press.

Gardner, Howard. 1983. *Frames of Mind: The Theory of Multiple Intelligences.* New York: Basic Books.

Rhythmically Moving 1–9. 1982–1988. Series of musical recordings, available on CDs (Phyllis S. Weikart, creative director). Ypsilanti, MI: High/Scope Press.

Related Reading

Epstein, Ann S. 2007. "What Is the High/Scope Curriculum in the Arts?" Chap. 17 in *Essentials of Active Learning in Preschool: Getting to Know the High/Scope Curriculum,* 173–90. Ypsilanti, MI: High/Scope Press.

Haraksin-Probst, Lizabeth, Janet Hutson-Brandhagen, and Phyllis S. Weikart. 2008. *Making Connections: Movement, Music, & Literacy.* Ypsilanti, MI: High/Scope Press.

High/Scope Educational Research Foundation. 2003. *Preschool Child Observation Record (COR),* 2nd ed. Ypsilanti, MI: High/Scope Press.

Weikart, Phyllis S. 2003. *Movement in Steady Beat: Activities for Children Ages 3 to 7,* 2nd ed. Ypsilanti, MI: High/Scope Press.

Weikart, Phyllis S. 2004. *Movement Plus Music: Activities for Children Ages 3 to 7,* 3rd ed. Ypsilanti, MI: High/Scope Press.

Weikart, Phyllis S. 1997. *Movement Plus Rhymes, Songs, & Singing Games: Activities for Children Ages 3 to 7,* 2nd ed. Ypsilanti, MI: High/Scope Press.

Weikart, Phyllis S. 2000. *Round the Circle: Key Experiences in Movement for Children,* 2nd ed. Ypsilanti, MI: High/Scope Press.

Related Media

The following materials are available from the High/Scope Press, 600 N. River St., Ypsilanti, MI 48198-2898; to order, visit *www.highscope.org,* or call 1-800-40-PRESS.

Movement and Music. 2004. Color videotape or DVD, 79 min.

Music Strategies: A Summary*

Moving to music
___ Play a wide variety of music for children.
___ Encourage children to create their own ways of moving to music.
___ Create simple movement sequences to music with children.

Exploring and identifying sounds
___ Assess your environment for sound:
   ___ Provide simple musical instruments.
   ___ Provide other sound generating materials.
   ___ Provide quiet moments for listening.
___ Be aware of sounds that attract children.
___ Play "sound" guessing-games with children.
___ Encourage children to describe the sounds they hear.

Exploring the singing voice
___ Listen for and acknowledge children's creative vocalizations.
___ Encourage children to play with their voices.

Developing melody
___ Listen for and acknowledge children's use of pitch and melody.
___ Play pitch-matching games with children.
___ Sing your comments to children.
___ Play "Guess This Tune" with children.

Singing songs
___ Sing songs with children:
   ___ Sing at large-group time.
   ___ Sing at work time.
   ___ Sing at small-group time.
   ___ Sing at outside time.
   ___ Sing during parent meetings.
___ Begin with motions.
___ Encourage children to create their own songs.

Playing simple musical instruments
___ Set up a music area.
___ Provide opportunities for children to play musical instruments on their own.
___ Play musical instruments at small- and large-group times:
   ___ Encourage children to create *parades* with musical instruments.
   ___ Encourage children to play musical instruments as other children *dance.*
   ___ Encourage children to use musical instruments to create sound effects to accompany *storytelling.*
   ___ Play musical *stop-and-start games* with some children playing the game and others providing the musical accompaniment.
___ Use musical instruments to signal transition times.

*See also *Feeling and expressing steady beat strategies,* p. 394.

At large-group time, these children and adults take turns suggesting different ways to move to music.

INDEX